## Theatre in Europe: a documentary history

This is the second volume to be published in the series Theatre in Europe: a documentary history. This book chronicles the emergence of a national feeling in the theatres of Northern and Eastern Europe from the mid-eighteenth to the late nineteenth centuries. During this period, acting and playwriting, management and staging often reflected nationalistic aspirations and cultural agendas. Using original documents and sources, including architects' plans, royal edicts, censors' reports, contemporary journalism, directors' blocking notes, memoirs and letters, this volume provides a chronological exploration of theatrical trends in eight countries. The documents reveal that in Denmark, Sweden and Norway the gradual development from royal patent houses and municipal theatres led to a genuinely public and Scandinavian institution. In Poland, Hungary, Bohemia and Rumania, theatrical records reveal the evolution of distinctly national repertoires and organizations removed from foreign influences. Similar sources demonstrate that Russia pursued native concepts of acting and playwriting after the retreat of Napoleon that culminated in the foundation of the Moscow Art Theatre. The result is a unique and fascinating picture of theatrical cultures, little known in the West, taking shape under the pressure of the political and socio-economic ideas that were creating modern Europe. The volume contains numerous illustrations, the source location for each document and a substantial bibliography.

**Theatre in Europe: a documentary history**

---

*General editors:*

Glynne Wickham
John Northam
John Gould
W.D. Howarth

This series will present a comprehensive collection of primary source materials for teachers and students and will serve as a major reference work for studies in theatrical and dramatic literature. The volumes will focus individually on specific periods and geographical areas, encompassing English and European theatrical history. Each volume will present primary source documents in English, or in English translation, relating to actors and acting, dramatic theory and criticism, theatre architecture, stage censorship, settings, costumes, and audiences. These sources include such documents as statutes, proclamations, inscriptions, contracts and playbills. Additional documentation from contemporary sources is provided through correspondence, reports, and eyewitness accounts. The volumes will also provide not only the exact source and location of the original documents, but also complementary lists of similar documents. Each volume contains an Introduction, narrative linking passages, notes on the documents, a substantial bibliography and an index offering detailed access to the primary material.

*Published*

*Restoration and Georgian England, 1660–1788*, compiled & introduced by David Thomas and Arnold Hare, edited by David Thomas

Theatre in Europe: a documentary history

# National theatre in Northern and Eastern Europe, 1746–1900

Edited by
LAURENCE SENELICK
*Fletcher Professor of Drama and Oratory*
*Tufts University*

Associate editors:
PETER BILTON, GEORGE BISZTRAY,
BARBARA DAY, BOGDAN MISCHIU,
KARYNA WIERZBICKA-MICHALSKA

The right of the
University of Cambridge
to print and sell
all manner of books
was granted by
Henry VIII in 1534.
The University has printed
and published continuously
since 1584.

CAMBRIDGE UNIVERSITY PRESS

Cambridge
New York Port Chester
Melbourne Sydney

Published by the Press of the University of Cambridge
The Pitt Building, Trumpington Street, Cambridge CB2 1RP
40 West 20th Street, New York, NY 10011, USA
10 Stamford Road, Oakleigh, Melbourne 3166, Australia



First published 1991

Printed in Great Britain at the University Press, Cambridge

*British Library cataloguing in publication data*

National theatre in Northern and Eastern Europe. – (Theatre in Europe: a documentary history).
1. Europe. Theatre, history
I. Senelick, Laurence II. Series
792.094

*Library of Congress cataloguing in publication data*

National theatre in northern and eastern Europe, 1746–1900/edited by Laurence Senelick: associate editors, Peter Bilton, . . . [*et al.*].
p. cm. – (Theatre in Europe)
Includes bibliographical references.
ISBN 0-521-24446-3
1. Theater – Europe – History – 18th century – Sources. 2. Theater – Europe – History – 19th century – Sources. I. Series.
PN2570.N38 1990
792'.094'09034 – dc20 90-1651 CIP

ISBN 0 521 24446 3

SE

# *Contents*

# *List of documents*

SWEDEN, 1765–1900

*I The Gustavian period, 1765–90*



*II The Royal monopoly, 1790–1810*



*III Management and acting at the Royal Theatres, 1796–1841*

NORWAY, 1825–1909

*I Strömberg's theatre in Christiania, 1825–32*



*II The new theatre in Christiania, 1835–40*



*III The first Bergen venture 1849–63*

*VI Managing and enlarging the Christiania Theatre, 1874–87*



POLAND, 1765–1830

*I The First National Theatre, 1765–74*



*II The repertoire expands, 1778–1808*

## Czech lands (Bohemia and Moravia), 1784–1881

HUNGARY, 1810–1838

*I Canvassing for a National Theatre, 1810–27*



*II Building and managing a National Theatre, 1832–38*



RUMANIA, 1818–1852

*I Early Rumanian-language performances in Bucharest, 1818–19*

# General editors' preface

In appointing appropriately qualified editors for each of the sixteen volumes of this documentary history it has been our aim to provide a comprehensive collection of primary source materials for teachers and students on which their own critical appraisal of theatrical history and dramatic literature may safely be grounded.

Each volume presents primary source documents in English, or in English translation, relating to actors and acting, dramatic theory and criticism, theatre architecture, stage censorship, settings, costumes and audiences. Editors have, in general, confined their selection to documentary material in the strict sense (statutes, proclamations, inscriptions, contracts, working-drawings, playbills, prints, account books, etc.), but exceptions have been made in instances where prologues, epilogues, excerpts from play texts and private correspondence provide additional contemporary documentation based on author's authority or that of eye witnesses to particular performances and significant theatrical events.

Unfamiliar documents have been preferred to familiar ones, short ones to long ones; and among long ones recourse has been taken to excerpting for inclusion all passages which either oblige quotation by right of their own intrinsic importance or lead directly to a clearer understanding of other documents. In every instance, however, we have aimed to provide readers not only with the exact source and location of the original document, but with complementary lists of similar documents and of secondary sources offering previously printed transcripts.

Each volume is equipped with an introductory essay, and in some cases introductory sections to each chapter, designed to provide readers with the appropriate social background – religious, political, economic and aesthetic – as context for the documents selected; it also contains briefer linking commentaries on particular groups of documents and concludes with an extensive bibliography.

Within this general presentational framework, individual volumes will vary considerably in their format – greater emphasis having to be placed, for example, on documents of control in one volume than in another, or with dramatic theory and criticism figuring less prominently in some volumes than in others – if each volume is to be an accurate reflection of the widely divergent interests and concerns of different European countries at different stages of their historical development, and the equally sharp differences in the nature and quality of the surviving documents volume by volume.

The editors would like to thank Michael Black and Sarah Stanton at Cambridge University Press for their unwavering interest, encouragement and practical support in bringing this enterprise forward from thoughts and wishes expressed at a Conference in 1979 to publication of the first volume to reach maturity a decade later.

Glynne Wickham (Chairman)
Bristol University, 1988

# *Editor's preface*

The national theatres in many of these countries were branches of the government run from official chancelleries, and recent regimes have considered the theatrical heritage an important facet of the nation's life: the result is that extant documentation is substantial. The difficulty of choice was immediately apparent, but in this collaborative effort each editor has been free to determine matters of selection, emphasis and format for each given nation. It could be (and has been) argued that each of these cultures deserves a separate volume to itself, but within our spatial limitations we have tried to be representative, not comprehensive. The arrangement is largely chronological, with sub-divisions used to demarcate specific areas of interest. Except for certain Scandinavian and Polish manuscripts, all the documents we have culled have previously been published in their original languages, and the bibliographic citation is usually made to their appearance in print, not to the actual physical location of an item.

The translations in each section have been made by the given editor, with two exceptions. New translations from the Czech are by Jitka Martin; but, in both the Czech and Russian sections, wherever an adequate translation already existed, it was preferred to a new version. I have revised the translations throughout for consistency of spelling and terminology. The system of transliteration used from the Cyrillic to the Roman alphabet is given on pages xxix-xxx.

In an enterprise of this scope, a great many persons must take a hand if it is to succeed. My thanks go first to the far-flung associate editors themselves, who have been remarkably thorough, industrious and efficient. Next I must express my gratitude to the General Editors of the series and the editorial staff at Cambridge University Press, who have been seraphically patient during a long gestation period, in particular Sarah Stanton, Kevin Taylor and Victoria L. Cooper. This work has benefited from the much-appreciated advice of a number of individuals, including Stanley Hochman, Stanley Buchholz Kimball, Barbara Kròl-Kaczorowska, Ludwick Krzyzanowski, Anthony Pearson, Claude Schumacher, František Svejkovský, Boleslaw Taborski, Paul I. Trensky and Gordon M. Wickstrom; whether I took their advice or not, any errors must light on my head. A good deal of the preliminary labour on this volume was begun while I was a Fellow at the

Wissenschaftskolleg zu Berlin (Institute for Advanced Studies) in 1985–6, and I wish to express my thanks to its staff, especially the librarian Frau Gesine Bottomley, and to my colleagues in the drama cadre, Peter Jelavich, Herta Schmid, Jurij Striedter and Andrzej Wirth, for support and suggestions. Thanks also go to Dr Jeanne Newlin of the Harvard Theatre Collection for permission to use illustrations in that archive. My research and secretarial assistants at Tufts University, Thomas Connolly and Joseph Keller, have earned my thanks for a good deal of last-minute checking and compilation, as has Michael McDowell for help with the photography of the illustrations.

The associate editors have their own thanks to offer. Peter Bilton wishes to acknowledge the assistance rendered by Trine Næss, librarian of the Theatre Collection of the Oslo University Library, and Kari Gardner Losnedahl, librarian of the Bergen Theatre Museum. Barbara Day would like to thank her translator Jitka Martin and Dr James Naughton of Oxford University for advice and suggestions. George Bisztray is grateful to his colleague at the University of Toronto, Professor Scott Eddie of the Department of Economics, for providing currency equivalents.

# *Cyrillic 〉 Roman transliteration*

| Cyrillic | Roman |
|---|---|
| А | A |
| Б | B |
| В | V |
| Г | G |
| Д | D |
| Е | E |
| Ж | ZH |
| З | Z |
| И | I |
| Й | Y |
| К | K |
| Л | L |
| М | M |
| Н | N |
| О | O |
| П | P |
| Р | R |
| С | S |
| Т | T |
| У | U |
| Ф | F |
| Х | KH |
| Ц | TS |
| Ч | CH |
| Ш | SH |
| Щ | SHCH |
| Э | È |
| Ю | YU |
| Я | YA |

| | |
|---|---|
| **Ы** | Y |
| **ЫЙ** (final) | Y |
| **ИЙ** | Y |
| **Ь** | ' |
| **Ъ** | .. |
| **Е** (pronounced *yo*) | Ë |

# General introduction

## I

'Nationalism', to the Victorian English mind, was a dirty word. The earliest usage traced by the *OED*, to *Fraser's Magazine* in 1844, was pejorative: '"Nationalism" is another word for egotism.' The term was no substitute for such an accepted if more abstract concept as 'patriotism', and its later association with the Irish independence movement kept it at a remove from respectability. On the eve of the First World War, whose outcome would make nationhood a crucial issue in Europe, the eleventh edition of the *Encyclopædia Britannica*, that compendium of all that the nineteenth century believed it knew, failed to bestow an entry on 'Nationalism' but defined 'Nationality' as:

> a somewhat vague term, used strictly in international law [. . .] and in a more extended sense in political discussion to denote an aggregation of persons claiming to represent a racial, territorial or some other bond of unity, though not necessarily recognized as an independent entity. In this latter sense the word has often been applied to such people as the Irish, the Armenians and the Czech [. . .]

The arm's-length aloofness of this definition suggests a reluctance to admit the lesser breeds without the law into the exclusive precincts of nationhood. Longer-established nations like Great Britain, France, Austria, Russia and the United States tended to regard aspirants to that status as mere ethnic groups, linked by a cultural bond but without justifiable claim to political sovereignty. Newer nations, Germany and Italy, were more sympathetic to nationalist claims, so long as these did not infringe their own freshly drawn boundaries.

This attitude *de haut en bas* recurs whenever cultures which lack political autonomy attempt to gain acceptance as being distinct and equal to cultures of the old-established firms. However, in the wake of the French Revolution and the dissemination of democratic ideas throughout Europe, the 'principle of nationalities', the notion that each ethnicity is entitled to statehood, had gained currency. It was assumed that, once given a voice, no people would choose to be ruled by strangers or imposed on by alien values. 'As a result of these developments,' writes

Benjamin Akzin, 'consciousness of one's nationality assumed in the Western world the character of a permanent and mass phenomenon rather than of a sporadic and isolated one, and was increasingly linked with the attribution of a positive value to the preservation of that nationality both in the cultural and in the political spheres.'[1]

Throughout the nineteenth century, the struggle of various European tribes, ethnic groups, principalities and enclaves to become independent nations was commonly bound up with the promotion of the arts, literature, music, folklore and other cultural manifestations peculiar to the struggling minority. Literacy, higher education and improved technology were regarded as tools to build autonomy. Keenly aware of their ethnological and linguistic community, these cultures chafed under alien domination, and frequently insisted that they were more progressive than the state which held them in thrall. This was, for instance, very much the case that Poland argued against the Russian Empire.

Since the principle of nationalities required that each individual in an ethnic group contribute to self-government, the logical conclusion was that nationhood would provide the optimal chance for self-expression and promotion of the group's values. Moreover, nationhood was strongly endorsed by a burgeoning bourgeoisie, which substituted 'the nation, the culture, and traditions of the fatherland' for the unattainable high culture of the aristocracy. Sprung from the folk, yet devotees of the ideals of enlightenment and high culture, the ambitious middle classes were anxious to establish traditions of which they themselves would be the guardians.[2] Since the bulk of the populace was illiterate, the best way to educate it to new nationalistic ideals until such time as it learned to read was by spectacle and sound: hence the crucial importance of the theatre to nationalistic movements.

These theatrical johnnies-come-lately were at a serious disadvantage, for the major European powers had stolen a long march on them. France, Italy and England, with their well-established dramatic and musical traditions, along with those later theatres of Germany and Austria, presented a double obstacle. The emerging theatres were attracted to the models presented, and could not help but try to emulate Shakespeare, Molière, the *commedia dell'arte*, the Englische Komödianten and the Comédie française as paradigms of what a developed stage was like; at the same time, they were anxious to avoid being overwhelmed by foreign example and to preserve what was unique and idiosyncratic in their own traditions. The tension between these poles of attraction and repulsion was particularly keen wherever a dominant or occupying power imposed another language or taste from above, or where a new national audience, inchoate and inexperienced, was attracted to already established if outlandish modes.

Throughout the documents published in this volume, the same notes are sounded again and again. There are the initial manifestos which proclaim the need for a national theatre in order to fortify the language, improve manners and morals, educate the people and, ultimately, validate the credentials of the nation, putting it on a par with its European fellows. To this end, Schiller's famous essay on the moral benefits of the theatre is quoted, adapted and referred to frequently. Crawling out from under foreign repertoire is thought a step in the right direction, so heated debates are held on whether it is preferable to foster native talent, whatever its quality, or to preserve those outside models which may be beneficial to local progress: the 'Buy Czech (or Norwegian, or whatever)' approach vs. the 'Don't throw out the brilliant baby with the bathwater' approach. The new genres of melodrama and vaudeville, imported from France and Germany, proved attractive to untried audiences and, not infrequently, to playwrights; but how were they to be adapted to local circumstances and character?

These early stages (in both senses) are usually thwarted or aborted by two obstacles: governmental and financial. The powers-that-be, King, Viceroy or bureaucracy, have their own agendas to pursue, and wish to keep the theatre under firm control. Therefore the emerging national drama finds itself hampered by official regulations, censorship, fines, and a weighty influence that insists on the plays and players that suit its taste. In many cases, the rise of a national theatre is concurrent with the formation of a national administration, and the latter has considerable say in the former. Our documents trace running battles between officialdom and the interests of artists.

Internal upheavals and theatre fires occur with aggravating regularity. Less predictable but equally destructive are events which cross national borders and affect whole sectors of European life. The Napoleonic invasions, aiming to force a new foreign rule on European nationalities, stirred native patriotism both in opposition to the French and to previous rulers, a patriotism which suffered a setback following the retrograde Congress of Vienna. The cholera epidemic of 1829–30 closed many theatres by emptying audiences and killing off promising performers. The revolutionary movements of 1848 and the Dano-Prussian, Crimean and Russo-Turkish wars also interrupted the normal course of events leading towards cultural autonomy.

Within the artistic sphere, concern is shown to nurture a national acting style, which often turns out to be a natural acting style, opposed to the declamatory or artificially stylized conventions imported from abroad. To foster this, schools are proposed and established. Over the course of the century, the intendant or administrator of the theatre is replaced by the stage director. Power that was once invested in a bureaucrat is now wielded by an 'artist', whose control over productions leads to a more unified effect. It would seem that the control over their own political destinies gained by the emerging nations of Northern and Eastern

Europe was paralleled in the theatre by this rise of the *metteur en scène* or *Regisseur*. The improved literacy and taste of audiences over time also enables a refinement of technique and a move to experiment in new 'isms' as they spread from Paris and Berlin.

It is also interesting to observe the same foreign works surfacing as evidence for the progress made in these theatres, suggesting a homogeneity in the European dramatic scene not unlike the ecumenism of medieval Christendom, an internationalism of taste. The opera and ballet of *Cora and Alonzo* are among the earliest experiments in those genres in Sweden and Poland. The ability to stage Shakespeare, particularly *Hamlet*, is made a touchstone of a theatre's maturity. Hungary and Rumania both commence their dramatic activity with Voltaire's *Mahomet*, challenging with Enlightenment principles the Islamic invader who had once threatened their independent existences. Later on, melodramas with a broad emotional appeal like Birch-Pfeiffer's *Die Grille* become showcases for skilled actresses as different as Johanne Dybwad and Mariya Ermolova. But for all the recurrences, it is the divergences among the new national theatres and their careers which arrest the imagination.

## 2

The Scandinavian nations differ from other emerging nationalities because they were not under imperial domination, but had been independently ruled by Danish kings since the late Middle Ages. Denmark, Sweden and Norway each preserved a sense of separate nationality, but had to cleave together until the nineteenth century for mutual protection against stronger powers. Sweden managed to draw independence from the victories of Gustav Adolf during the Thirty Years' War, whereas Norway did not achieve an autonomous government until 1905. Reinhold Niebuhr has remarked,

> Their languages, being dialects of the same tongue, prove both the force of affinity and of separateness in the building of nations. Geographic factors have also contributed to their collective, as well as separate independence. Their collective independence was due to their remoteness from the main currents of imperial politics, and their separate independence was due to the water barrier between Denmark and the two northern countries and to the mountain barrier between Sweden and Norway, and, of course, also the increasing economic strength of Sweden in the nineteenth century.[3]

Of these three countries, Denmark enjoyed the oldest theatrical tradition, tracing its mystery plays to the Middle Ages and the Reformation. School drama and court theatre flourished, but a genuine 'public' did not develop before the nineteenth century. The modern Danish theatre paradoxically owes its origins to a French restaurateur, Etienne Capion, who obtained a patent in 1718 to give public performances; these were presented in French and German and, after 1722, Danish, thus commingling middle-class spectators with an aristocratic audience. It was thanks to this mixed audience that Ludvig Holberg could successfully found a Danish repertoire, which enriched all the Nordic cultures. The primacy of Holberg means the primacy of comedy, which may explain why, in the nineteenth century, Denmark developed a characteristic school of vaudeville writing. In other emerging theatres, such as Russia's, reformers deplored vaudevilles as unworthy (though Russia itself also bred a rich national school of vaudeville writers). J. L. Heiberg, again under French influence, adapted the genre to Danish manners, played up the role of music and stressed the moral. Denmark also enjoyed a greater freedom of the press than any other monarchy in Europe, although under Russian pressure limited censorship was imposed in 1799.

Sweden had the benefit of a king in the person of Gustaf III who was a connoisseur and a patriot. When A.J. von Höpken had tentatively offered a national repertoire at the Konglig svensk Skådeplats (Royal Swedish Stage) in 1737, he had had a hard time finding worthy plays in Swedish, for Swedish playwriting and production at this period followed French and Italian models rather closely. Von Höpken's efforts were effaced by a mediocre French troupe summoned by Queen Louisa in 1753, but it was dismissed by Gustaf on his accession to the throne. A dramatist who wrote the opera which opened the National Theatre in 1773, a savant who founded the Swedish Academy in 1786, Gustaf was an ideal patron of the arts. Unfortunately, it took him two *coups d'état* to consolidate his power, and he continued to be despised by a Russophile aristocracy which eventually had him assassinated. Not until the liberally inclined and anti-German Oscar I ascended the throne in the mid-nineteenth century did the monarchy take an interest in the theatre again.

Norway is the odd-man-out here, for during its period as a Danish dominion there was no aristocracy to serve as patron to the drama. The first glimmers of a Norwegian theatre flicker in the amateur dramatic societies or *Dramatiske Selskaber* of the 1780s, essentially social clubs in the larger towns. The theatre as an institution run by groups of citizens would become the norm; although the dramatic societies would eventually be effaced by a developing dramatic profession, the committee approach to theatrical management was a long time dying.

Denmark had fought on the wrong side during the Napoleonic Wars, and so in 1814, as punishment, it was forced to cede Norway to Sweden. An Act of Union established Norway as 'a free, indivisible kingdom, united with Sweden under one king', but very soon a cultural-separatist movement arose, the Young Norway party led by Henrik Wergeland. Battles raged long and loud over whether the theatre should be *norsk–norsk* or whether it should retain the best of the Danish legacy. The development of the theatre was not, unfortunately, assisted by the absence of a foreign governing power interfering in artistic affairs, since internal dissensions and an unsympathetic parliament provided their own disruptions. Representatives of peasant districts had begun to enter the Storting in 1833, and their often ludicrous zeal in pursuing economy at the expense of the arts became notorious. It was not until the Bergen playhouse was opened in 1850 that a theatre could be called programmatically Norwegian. Ibsen himself tended to be international in his tastes; Bjørnson, though not a radical, voted with the separatists and was a prime mover in the establishment of an exclusively Norwegian theatre. The Declaration of Independence from Sweden in 1905 set the political seal on what had long been a *fait accompli* in the cultural sphere.

Finland was wrested from Sweden by Peter the Great, but by the end of the eighteenth century it was a semi-independent grand duchy with a Diet to supervise domestic matters while foreign affairs were dictated from St Petersburg. As a result, the structure of Finnish officialdom was Russian but the official language, replacing Latin, was Swedish. Finland's actors, directors and repertoire were also Swedish – when they were not German – even though the subject matters of many plays dealt directly with Finnish life. Yet there were permanent stone theatres in towns like Turku and Viipuri before Helsinki received the New Theatre in 1860; typically, when its interior burned out three years later, the replacement was designed by a Russian architect and its name changed in 1887 to the Swedish Theatre. By that time, however, Swedish-speakers were under attack by Finnish champions.

The signal-gun for this attack was an 1864 pamphlet by a post-office employee named Matthias Weckström, *Notes on the Theatre in Finland* (the title is, of course, in Swedish: *Anteckningar rörande teatern i Finland*), which deplored the paucity of plays in Finnish. The cause was taken up by Karl Bergbom, a young playwright who changed his Christian name to Kaarlo and dedicated himself to promoting theatre in Finnish, a language in which he was barely proficient. He sponsored a Finnish drama festival in May 1870, and the enthusiasm it generated led to a Finnish theatre two years later, represented by a touring company and, from 1875 to 1902, a permanent playhouse in the ramshackle Arcadia Playhouse in Helsinki. The subsidies it received from the government were equal to and eventually larger than those made to the Swedish Theatre, whose repertoire came to be seen as more trivial than that of its Finnish rival.

During the 1880s and the repressive regime of Alexander III, Slavophile policy from Petersburg sought to russify the country. This merely intensified the nationalist spirit, which was manifested in an intense rivalry, played out in every sphere of public life, between the 'Fennoman' or Finnish camp and the previously dominant 'Svecoman' or Swedish camp. In 1902, the Finnish company moved to the impressive National Theatre (Suomen Kansallisteatteri), designed by Onni Alcides Törnqvist-Tarjanne, a move which symbolized its supremacy over the Swedish faction. Still, for years to come, hostilities between the Swedish and Finnish companies kept up the foundation of more theatres by both camps. A typical bone of contention was whether actors in the Swedish troupes should speak standard Swedish or Finno-Swedish, an issue kept alive even through the civil war of 1918.

It would be inaccurate to speak of a Latvian theatre, since the notion of an independent Latvia was barely a gleam in a patriot's eye. Nevertheless, its principal city, Riga, a major intersection between Western Europe and the Slavic East, long held the germs of a Lettish culture. Lett had alternated with German and Latin in early church spectacles, but by the eighteenth century German was paramount as the language of theatre. A comic actor named Sigismundo obtained a licence to perform in 1742, with the proviso that he offer public spectacles in the city. However, there was no building to serve as playhouse, and in 1760 a Russian troupe had to perform in a barn. The requisite building was finally erected in 1768 to house Hilverding's German company; rebuilt, it would be the theatre where Wagner conducted from 1837 to 1839, while he composed *Rienzi*. With more rebuilding and refurbishment, this German-language opera- and playhouse was to remain one of the leading cultural centres in Eastern Europe until the end of the First World War. A Russian theatre opened in Riga in 1886.

The first national Lett-language theatre may be considered that of the Rīgas Latvīešu Biedrība (RLB) or Riga Latvian Society, which opened on 27 September 1870, and gave twenty-five performances a year. Its history falls naturally into three phases. The first, the administration of the dramatist and director Adol'f Alunans, 1870–85, was primarily concerned with developing a repertoire and training young actors. The nationalist cause was set back in the second phase, the administration of the German Rode Ebeling, 1885–93, who invested his interest in elaborate scenic effects and translated plays of the naturalist school. The third phase, the administration of Peteris Ozolinš and Jekab Duburs, 1893–1908, which reverted to nationalism and public education, ended with the destruction of the theatre building by fire. Meanwhile, the city saw considerable activity among private and amateur enterprises before 1918, when Latvia was made an independent nation with Riga as its capital.[4]

German cultural hegemony prevailed in Estonia for almost seven centuries, the native Finnish-speaking inhabitants in virtual serfdom to German landowners even after the territory was ceded to Russia in 1721. This dominance was patent in the German playhouse in Revel (now Talinn) directed by August von Kotzebue from 1795 to 1798; supported by shareholders, the elegant and spacious playhouse constituted a club where they dined, played billiards and gave balls.

Censorship was comparatively liberal: at a time when Schiller was bowdlerized and emasculated for the Petersburg stage, his plays were performed intact in Revel. This theatre later received a governmental subsidy which was revoked after the First World War when it went private again; its pan-German character was reinstated during the Second World War under Nazi supervision.

One beneficial effect of the German influence in nineteenth-century Estonia was that it boasted better educational standards and a higher literacy rate than most of the Russian Empire. The official date for the start of the Estonian national theatre is Midsummer Day 1870, which marked the sixth aniversary of the Wanemuine Association of Music and Song. On that occasion, Theodor Körner's farce *Der Vetter von Bremen* (a German forerunner of *Charley's Aunt*) was recited in an Estonian version by the poet Lydia Koidula. This initiated a series of regular performances, and very soon a large number of music societies in many towns followed suit. They survived the repressive russification programmes of the 1880s and, in 1906, the Wanemuine Association went professional. In 1916 a group of actors founded the Draamateater, which lasted until 1924. By the time it gained political autonomy in 1918, this country of one million persons possessed four professional companies.

The fate of the Polish national theatre cannot be divorced from the fate of Poland itself. Poland had a long-standing theatrical tradition, but each form of its activity appealed to a different public: mystery plays for the laity, school drama in Latin for the clerisy and courtly entertainments such as Italian opera for the elite. In the absence of an influential middle-class, which all but disappeared during the interminable warfare of the seventeenth century, a national theatre was unlikely to emerge. As usual, the impulse towards that goal was Francophile, as enlightened noblemen joined with Jesuits in providing a fund of Polish plays on classic models with the aim of educating the people.

The catalyst for change was the election to the throne of Stanislas Augustus Poniatowski, who founded both the royal Warsaw opera and the National Theatre, which opened on 19 November 1765 with a Polish-language adaptation of Molière's *Les Fâcheux*. It is noteworthy that, like its earlier Danish counterpart, the Polish theatre had an affinity for the comedy of manners and, later, bourgeois tragedy, but did not go in for high tragedy until the Romantic movement made its voice heard.

Like Gustaf III, Stanislas Augustus, for all his success as a Maecenas, was continually at loggerheads with the nobility, and his attempts to reform the *sejm* or Diet met with defeat, owing largely to the machinations of Russia which had supported his election but did not care to see an independent Poland. The three partitions of Poland (1772, 1793, 1796) among Russia, Austria and Prussia quelled any serious efforts at national unity.

A recurrent feature of early national theatres is that they are often animated by a single energetic and gifted virtuoso – Holberg in Denmark, Gustaf III in Sweden, Sweden, Ole Bull in Norway, J.K. Tyl in Bohemia, and in Poland Wojciech Bogusławski, who not only managed the Warsaw theatre from 1783, but inspired similar projects in Lublin, Lvov, Cracow, Poznań and Vilna. (On the principle that it is harder to hit a moving target, Bogusławski shifted his troupe from city to city whenever the situation in Warsaw became too difficult.) He was adept at surviving no matter which occupying force was in power, and his success brought about the almost unthinkable bankruptcy of the Italian opera in 1803.

Between 1807 and 1815, Central Poland recovered a sort of independence as a Grand Duchy; but this perished with Napoleon's ambitions. The Congress of Vienna created 'the kingdom of Poland', a Russian province with a new constitution. Sustained by a new university-trained audience, Bogusławski hoped to realize his dream of a National Theatre maintained and subsidized by the State, but this stability was not of long duration: a military revolt in 1830 prompted severe repression by Russia. Tsar Nicholas I was determined to stamp out Polish national culture and aspirations; so although the Warsaw stage continued to offer performances in Polish, it was under the heavy thumb of Russian censors. Even so, before that time, Bogusławski and his theatre had managed to nurture the movement of Polish romanticism, which carried on in exile.

From the thirteenth century Lithuania comprised a grand duchy, whose native language was one of the most ancient of the living Indo-European tongues. In 1569 it was united as a Commonwealth with Poland with which it would share a rich tradition of Jesuit theatre and aristocratic spectacles; but no ethnic Lithuanian theatre existed, owing to the country's largely agricultural nature and its shifting fortunes as the map of Europe altered. The court of the Grand Duke of Lithuania was entertained by Italian, English, French and German ballets and operas, while the commercial class that might have supported an ethnic theatre was composed mainly of Germans, Jews and Poles. The first public performances took place in Vilna in 1785 when Bogusławski's troupe appeared there; in 1796, Dominik Morawski founded a company which throve. When Russia annexed Lithuania in 1802, Morawski's widow managed to secure a patent, but could hardly count on permanence. Napoleon invaded the province in 1811; a revolt, simultaneous with that in Central Poland, occurred a generation later, but was put down by the Russians. For a while, the city played host to both a German and a Russian theatre, and a 'Young Lithuanian' movement tried to efface German influence, but after 1863 everything was russified. The Lithuanian language was prohibited as a medium of public expression. Mass emigration to America, to avoid military service, ensued, and there immigrant theatre, both Lithuanian- and Yiddish-speaking, flourished. The homeland itself was not to hear its first public performances in Lithuanian until 1904, and the nation of Lithuania was not proclaimed until 1918.

Those national groups which were under the control of the Habsburg Empire suffered what Niebuhr calls 'ethnic confusion': not only were German, Slav and Magyar elements held in a loose colloidal suspension, but individual groups were widely scattered over a vast geographical expanse, complicating the formation into nations.

The struggle for a Czech national theatre in Bohemia and Moravia deserves an extended look, because of its exemplary nature. (Czech and Bohemian are synonymous; Moravian refers specifically to the Slavs of Moravia.) A Slavonic people dominated by a Germanic civilization, the Czechs used theatre in their own tongue as a potent tool to achieve nationalistic goals. Indeed, in old Czech, *jazyk* means both nation and language. It is noteworthy that the Czechs should have been cited by the *Encyclopædia Britannica* as a prime example of a 'nationality' unrecognized as a political entity but held together by a bond of unity; in their case the bonds were cultural and territorial as well as linguistic, for the Czechs looked back to the ancient kingdom of Bohemia as a model.

The first so-called Czech theatre, the 'Stavovské divadlo' or Theatre of the Estates, built by Count Nostitz-Rieneck in 1789, was allowed to play only on Sunday afternoons and holidays. During this period, Bohemia's autonomy was severely limited, but greater freedom of the press opened the way for newspapers in the national language. After 1815, with the shadow of Metternich darkening the land, long-suppressed national aspirations found their sole outlet in literature. It was then, the era of J.K. Tyl and J.J. Kolár, that the Czech theatre had animators energetic and talented enough to give it strength. When the insurrections of 1848 occurred, the theatre became a forum for patriotic dramas; but this was soon ended by the bombardment of Prague. The ensuing reaction from Vienna imposed stronger censorship and bureaucratic centralization; the German language was made exclusive in schools and offices, and all Bohemian newspapers were suppressed. Tyl was forced to vegetate in the provinces with a touring company. It was not until the proclamation of the 1861 Constitution that an independent Czech theatre could be countenanced, but German influence did not evaporate all at once, and it would be another twenty years before the long-awaited National Theatre was actually built, with this inscription over its portals: 'The People, to Itself'.

The situation in Slovakia, the homeland of the Slavs of West Hungary, was even more retrogressive. During the Hungarian domination, the Slovaks were treated as an inferior race; the aristocracy was Magyarized and the peasants took no interest in the arts. After 1830, amateur dramatic troupes fostered a national consciousness, and a number of Slovakian playwrights evolved. In the *annus mirabilis* 1848, when the Hungarians rose against the Austrians, the Slovaks rose against the Hungarians, but with equivalent lack of success. In the wake of this mutiny, suppression of Slovakian culture became even more virulent as Slovakia was made a separate and independent crownland. Although the Slovaks continued their active sympathy with Czech home-rule, their numbers were decimated by a mass migration to America. When a municipal theatre building was at last erected in the capital, Bratislava, in 1886, its stage was occupied by German and Hungarian companies. It was not until the formation and recognition of Czechoslovakia in 1918 that a professional Slovakian theatre could be born.

Hungary had appealed to the Habsburgs to save it from Islamic incursions, only to find itself subjugated beneath the Teutonic power. The growth of the Hungarian theatre in some degree resembles the Czech, not least in the struggle to emancipate its native tongue. It was a desire to give pre-eminence to Hungarian over the two official languages, German and Latin, a desire sparked by Enlightenment *philosophes*, which led to the canvassing for a theatre. Although the first play in Hungarian, György Bessenyei's *Agis* (1772), was based on a tragedy by Gottsched, the Hungarian public was enthralled merely to hear its language publicly exercised: hence the success of the amateur performances given in Buda in 1784, the same year that a Language Edict made German the official tongue. The public was not sufficiently cultivated, however, to support the first professional theatre, László Kelemen's troupe, 1790–5; Kelemen's experience would be replicated again and again. The tale of the Hungarian national theatre in the early nineteenth century is one of various individuals trying to sell their visions to a divided Diet, a dubious Viceroy and a recalcitrant public. No one wanted to support a theatre financially, no one could agree on where such a theatre should be built. Before the National Theatre was opened on 22 August 1837, actors roamed the countryside offering mostly German plays refashioned into chronicles of Hungarian history in a style imitated from the German theatres of Pest. After the opening of the National Theatre, its management had to feature operas, conjurers and trained animals in order to combat the competition of the more professional German theatre. Only very gradually, as the audience grew more refined from exposure to it, was the neoclassic French repertoire eased out and supplanted by German sentimental drama, French romantic melodrama and the new Hungarian genre of historical comedy. The gradual refinement of taste was abetted by a school of demanding critics; but playwrights still felt obliged to preach nationalism and independence from the stage, particularly in view of the worsening political situation.

Magyar became the official language in 1839, but this ended after the independence movement of 1848 was defeated by an Austro-Russian alliance. Martial law prevailed until 1860, when the infamous 'Bach system', named for the Austrian Minister of the Interior, was imposed. All constituent states were to be subsumed under the individual state of Austro-Hungary, and German was reinstated as the official tongue. Only after Austria had been weakened in its war with Prussia in 1866 and Hungary gained free and independent status with a new constitution were Hungarian playwrights no longer under the moral obligation to infuse their works with militant patriotism.

The Rumanian principalities, like their neighbours, had centuries-old traditions of church drama, folk drama, processionals, magical dance rites, puppets including the ubiquitous Karagheuz, all of which exuded an authentic popular flavour, whatever their individual origins. Still, owing to the area's precarious political position, now under Turkish suzerainty, now under Russian 'protection' (from 1711), so-called *Rumanian* national art could not be promoted, not least because of the internecine and factional disputes among the voivodes of Wallachia, Moldavia, Transylvania, Bukovina and Bessarabia. Under hospodars chosen by the Sublime Porte from among wealthy Greeks, anything Rumanian was discounted. Suddenly, in the nineteenth century, influenced by French concepts of *nationalité*, Rumania strove for unification. Again, the theatre was boosted as a critical factor in that process: the earliest to be founded, the Societatea Filarmonica (Philharmonic Society, Bucharest, 1833) and the Conservatorul Filarmonic-Dramatic (Philharmonic-Dramatic Conservatory, Jassy, 1836) were conceived as militant tribunes of civic virtue, what Gheorghe Asachi called a 'veritable school of morality and the source of innocent merriment'. Significantly, these moves coincided with the Organic Law of 1834 which upheld the feudal privileges of the boyars and permitted a greater involvement of the Russians in Rumanian politics.

A secret society of French-educated boyars with a libertarian programme was nurtured in the Bucharest Philharmonic, to teach the actors to skirt censorship by improvising inflammatory remarks into their parts. After the collapse of the 1848 uprisings, the Russians had the actors arrested, forbade the performances, kept close watch over the repertoire and exiled the incendiary supporters of the theatre. The Great Theatre of Bucharest, opened in 1852, would not bear the name National Theatre until 1877 when the independence of a united Wallachia and Moldavia was proclaimed.

One cannot speak of a Yugoslavian theatre before 1918, for most of the reasons pertaining to Czechoslovakia and Rumania. In the sixteenth century, Marin Držić of Dubrovnik had founded a number of theatre companies to play his comedies in the open air, and Dubrovnik would remain the centre of trans-Balkan theatre life. Otherwise, it was the same old story: despite a growing Pan-Slavic movement, the development of a native tradition was arrested by separatism and foreign domination: Upper Croatia under the sway of Hungary; Dalmatia under Venice; Slovenia under Austria; Serbia, Bosnia and Herzegovina, Montenegro, Macedonia and the rest of Croatia under Turkey.

As a result, the development of theatre differed from region to region. In Dalmatia and Dubrovnik, which managed to retain a modicum of political and artistic independence and even to extend its influence, the audience came from a good cross-section of the population. The tradition of *al fresco* performances, which by the eighteenth century included loose adaptations of Molière, was preserved. In Slovenia, a native playwright, Anton Tomaž Linhart, had emerged, but practically from the time of his death in 1795 until 1848, Austria forbade Slovenian plays to be staged. The first dramatic society, Dramatično Družtvo, was founded in 1867 by France Levstik, a realist writer, whose audience was drawn almost entirely from the educated class. In Vojvodina, North Serbia, the audience was made up of a developing commercial bourgeoisie, congenial to nascent nationalism. A theatre established there in 1834 housed the earliest professional acting troupe of Southern Slavs. In Upper Croatia, whose Jesuit schools in Zagreb had bred a Kajkavian dialect theatre, the audience was composed of university students and clerics; no women were allowed on this stage until about 1840. The Croatian nobility, on the other hand, invited third-rate German or Italian touring companies, whose influence was greater than their talent owing to the Germanizing policies of the Emperor Joseph II.

In the wake of Napoleon's short-lived union of Slovenia and Croatia as 'Illyria', a union of Slovenes, Croats and Serbs, the so-called Illyrian Slavs, became a desideratum. Theatre was seen not only as a means of promoting Southern unity but of forging closer bonds among all Slavs. In the face of further encroachment by the Turks and a Hungarian attempt to impose Magyar as the official language in Croatia, the Yugoslav theatre took on a more deliberately nationalistic tinge. In 1840, a travelling troupe from Novi Sad (Vojvodina) began a twenty-year struggle with a German troupe to win over the Zagreb audience. A permanent theatre opened in Zagreb in 1860, followed by the Serbian National Theatre (Srpsko Narodno Pozorište) at Novi Sad the next year, and a National Theatre (Narodno Pozorište) in Belgrade in 1869, soon to be joined by a permanent playhouse in Ljubljana. Their repertoires emphasized plays drawn from medieval history, in an attempt to teach the people about their shared past.

Macedonia, whose territory is mostly present-day Bulgaria, saw its first plays staged in the 1850s by a schoolteacher, Jordan Hadži Konstantinov-Džinov, didactic dramas with clear nationalist coloration. Development was complicated by the Berlin treaty of 1878 which insisted on political representation for each ethnic group and thus further divided the country. The resulting rivalries bred the secret revolutionary societies that fomented Balkan unrest and detonated a world-wide catastrophe in Sarajevo in 1914.

Russia would, at first blush, seem an exception to these rules. Independent, boasting its own language, religion and monarchy, it would appear to be more a cultural aggressor in such lands as Poland, Lithuania and Finland than an aspirant for its own national expression. With Russia, the situation is subtler, but the nationalist urge equally strong. The hegemonies to be overthrown were those of French and German literary and artistic styles and, more important, the yoke of a bureaucracy infested with Baltic Germans, which sat heavily on the arts' collective neck. Of all the theatres under examination here, the Russian was most subject to the red tape and interference of governmental agencies imposed *from within*; and, because alien culture was officially sponsored not by a foreign oppressor but by the Russian authorities themselves, it was that much more difficult to agitate for native culture. Such agitation was most often regarded by the Establishment as political activism and revolt, and harshly suppressed.

The Russian mind consequently was torn between a sense of inferiority and a sense of pride in national identity, a schism exemplified by the on-going debate between the Westerners and the Slavophiles throughout the nineteenth century. The Westerners wanted to turn their backs on what was ugly and regressive in Russian life and look to Europe for a pattern of modern progress; the Slavophiles insisted on distilling the unique and distinct in Russian life, in order to set their country apart and above its neighbours. Boths schools of thought agreed that the theatre was a prime medium of public enlightenment, and fought bitterly for control of its soul.

What happens in the Russian theatre is closely associated with the characteristics of the administration in power. The eighteenth-century empresses, Anna, Elizabeth and Catherine, had favoured foreign players, although Catherine was willing to sponsor Russian drama, so long as it was untainted by revolutionary principles. Rare individuals like the actor and playwright Pëtr Pavilshchikov argued for a national drama, which would treat of Russian life in a Russian manner. Gallomania was regularly assailed in satiric comedy, but for the aristocracy, French modes remained the paragon, even after the Napoleonic invasion. Napoleon's depredations fostered an upsurge of Russian patriotism at the same time it destroyed the estates that kept indigenous serf theatres: the dispersal of serf troupes led both to the rise of professional provincial theatres and to greater governmental control in the capital cities. The reign of Nicholas I, begun with the thwarted Decembrist revolt, grew progressively more dictatorial: this proved to be a restraint on the national repertoire which came to comprise chiefly witty vaudevilles and irreproachably chauvinist dramas. Acting flourished, however, even though the actors had to hone their craft on unworthy material and often longed for Russian themes and characters.

The reign of Alexander II promised a thaw, and the first years of reform, including the emancipation of the serfs, were accompanied by the introduction of a more realistic school of playwriting and a more naturalistic style of performance. The reform atmosphere was short-lived, but it did not dissipate before a taste for more serious theatre had been instilled in the intelligentsia. Non-commercial private theatres, organized as clubs or societies, sprang up. Along with the populist or *narodnik* movements of the 1870s, efforts were made to bring theatre to the common people, since the playgoing audience comprised an infinitesimal proportion of the Russian populace. These outreach programmes were stifled when Alexander III came to the throne; outraged by the assassination of his father, he instituted a harsh repression of anything that sounded like political protest throughout the Empire and drove a juggernaut of Russian-style Pan-Slavism over his dominions. An already powerful censorship was abetted by the scrutiny of the Holy Synod, whose medievally-minded, rabidly Slavophile Procurator Pobedonostsev would be the tutor of the next tsar. In contrast to the activist seventies, the eighties became known as a period of torpor and passivity. For the theatre, it meant more emphasis on technique and less on content, a move towards spectacle and polish; when the Imperial monopoly was revoked in 1882, the few commercial managements found themselves compelled to feature sensation drama, *féeries* and operettas, although new plays of quality would be sneaked in at special matinees.

With the accession of Nicholas II, the long-suppressed desires for political representation burst forth in an intense campaign for a Duma, a Constitution and other major reforms. The Tsar's policies wobbled between faint concession and blind reaction, but it was now too late for the throne to control its subjects. An important new ingredient in the ferment was the wealth held by industrialists and bankers, often of peasant or plebeian origins, who took a serious interest in the arts. Suvorin's theatre in St Petersburg had one of the most advanced repertoires in the country, since its proprietor was a magnate and influential newspaper editor with close ties to the government. The millionaire Savva Mamontov founded a private opera theatre which rivalled, some would say surpassed, the glories of the Imperial stages both in brilliance of performance and lavishness of design. Such was the money and the interest which made the Moscow Art Theatre possible. The Art Theatre was a culmination of a century-long quest for realism in acting, devotion to ideals of enlightenment and serious work, and the pre-eminence of director and ensemble over the star system.

The artistic movements in these Northern and Eastern European theatres towards greater naturalism or symbolism or stylization resulted in rich creativity and will be traced in a later volume. However, such creativity could become possible only after these countries had achieved a strong sense of national identity.

1 Benjamin Akzin, *State and Nation* (London, 1964), p. 51.
2 See Orlando Patterson, *Ethnic chauvinism: the reactionary impulse* (New York, 1977), p. 78.

[3] Reinhold Niebuhr, *The structure of nations and empires* (New York, 1959), p. 165.

[4] Estonia, Latvia and Lithuania were first recognized as independent, sovereign nations by the Versailles conference in 1919. As a result of the German–Soviet non-aggression pact, in 1940 they were absorbed into the USSR as constituent republics; a considerable portion of their populations was deported to Siberia.

# *Denmark, 1746–1889*

Edited by PETER BILTON

## INTRODUCTION

Ludvig Holberg (1684–1754) hit not only the Danish funny bone, but also a deep sense of national character and identity. Comedy is the mainstream of Danish drama, the mirror Danes have preferred to see held up to their own nature. Classical satire has often been tempered by lyricism and romance, in blends which survived the Kotzebue dominance of one period and the Scribe dominance of another: a tradition and taste which proved resistant at various times even to Shakespeare and Ibsen. Oehlenschläger's tragedies were the main exception to prove the rule, appealing perhaps as much to a feeling for the Nordic past as to a hunger for tragic dimensions; and they had to wait for the right performers, whereas the company was steeped in comedy lore handed down from Holberg's contemporaries. The main force for continuity, not to say survival, in the Royal Theatre has been the excellence of its acting company – often despite the lack of theatrical insight of officials appointed from other spheres to manage the theatre's affairs. The origins of the latter in the Establishment, and the pressure on them to keep deficits down, also tended to keep the mainstream flowing.

Some of the theatre company's most serious competition came from the allied arts performed within its own walls. The Royal Theatre's history covers periods in which opera was at least as highly favoured as drama, and others when it could take great pride in its ballet. The selection of documents below does next to nothing to reflect the importance of these two arts. Music is also, however, a vital ingredient in Danish drama, with musical plays (*syngespill*) and vaudeville emerging as virtually native genres and sources of renewed theatrical vigour. Members of the acting company had to be able not only to make up the numbers in the operatic chorus or in the *corps de ballet*, but also to sustain main parts in plays where they were called upon to sing and dance.

In view of the relative dominance of an unabashed taste for entertainment (despite the theatre's slogan *Ej blot til lyst* – 'not for pleasure alone'), one turns for two major historical landmarks literally to the theatre itself: the buildings of 1748 and 1874, the second replacing the first. The interim is rich in stories of maintenance, extensions, and the technical developments which permitted changes in acting styles. A third landmark is the constitutional change which in the revolutionary mid-nineteenth century moved the theatre from royal will to party-political whim and from privy purse to ministerial budgets. Keeping the Royal Theatre going throughout has been a strong urge to express pride in things Danish and maintain a national theatre tradition.

## I LEGISLATION AND ADMINISTRATION, 1746–70

*Thielo wins a Royal privilege*

When King Frederik V (1723–66) ascended the throne with his English queen Louise (1724–51) on 6 August 1746, he lost little time in bringing to an end the theatrical drought ordained under his pietistic father. The Queen, a daughter of George II, was popular and a booster of the theatre. Holberg rejoiced in the new regime and his occasional visits to Court were not unconnected with the welfare of the Danish theatre. Carl August Thielo (1707–63), composer, theatre entrepreneur, music teacher, organist, born in Saxony, came to Copenhagen in the 1720s; he obtained his privilege expressly to perform comedies partly on Holberg's recommendation.

### 1 Frederik V grants C.A. Thielo a privilege to perform comedies, 30 December 1746

Thomas Overskou: *Den danske skueplads* [*The Danish Theatre*], vol. 2 (Copenhagen: Thiele, 1856?–76), pp. 28–9.

Know all men by these presents: That upon most humble application and petition we have most graciously licensed and permitted and do hereby license and permit Carl August Thielo of our royal seat of Copenhagen, when mourning for our dearly beloved father of sacred and blessed memory has been observed, to present Danish plays in the same place, in accordance with the plan previously laid before us by our well-beloved Ludvig Holberg, etc., for which purpose he shall employ such qualified persons as can for reasonable payment please all and sundry with their comedies; which comedies shall not, however, deal with such matters as relate to religion or Holy Scripture or are contrary to decency, accepted custom and good order, or can in any way be offensive to the public, if he is not to infringe this our most gracious license.

*The actors assume Thielo's privilege*

When the troupe went on strike against Thielo [see 3], Holberg was again active behind the scenes; the upshot was that the Privilege was in principle transferred to the troupe. The first three sections are given below for what they tell us about the site, the building plans and, incidentally, the company's monopoly.

### 2 The privilege is reassigned to the actors, 29 December 1747

Overskou, vol. 2 (1856?–76), pp. 51–2.

1

Whereas the foremost requirement in the interest of the plays is a sizeable theatre and a practical building equipped with the necessary boxes and various means of ascent and descent, in the construction of which the necessary precautions according to the fire regulations shall be observed and the building otherwise provided with the most essential fire equipment, and whereas Carl August Thielo, in whose name the aforesaid privilege was made out, lacks the resources to pay for the same; the entire troupe, as it is now or shall hereafter become, shall accordingly have a share in the privileges and immunities of this house, which, however, shall attach permanently to the building now being fitted out for plays, that the same may be further security for the mortgagees for the capital which must be borrowed for its erection. In exchange for which the aforesaid Thielo shall, in accordance with the association entered into by him with the present actors, content himself with what he receives – the same as an actor of the first class – from the income from the plays, without acquiring any special sole rights under this privilege before the other members of the troupe.

2

The site and the old building located at the end of our foundry by Holmens Canal which, on the most humble petition of the Danish actors, we have most graciously given and bestowed for the construction of a theatre shall hereafter have and enjoy immunity from billeting, ground rent, and all other burdens and fees of whatever name.

3

In this building alone and nowhere else in Copenhagen aforesaid shall the performance of any kind of play in whatever language be permitted, on pain of a substantial penalty to be awarded to the theatre by the police court whenever anyone is found to have acted to the contrary.

### *A new theatre is built*

This pioneering theatre in the reputable district of Lille Grønnegade has left virtually no physical trace. The company which began performances again in 1747 put them on in hired or provisional premises: from 14 April to 15 December in a concert hall known as Bergs Hus in Læderstræde; then from 18 December 1747 to 7 June 1748 in a naval storehouse, Tjærehuset, which stood on the site granted by the King; and, finally, while Tjærehuset was being pulled down and the new theatre built, in a rented building.

The design by the architect and builder Nicolai Eigtved (1701–54) received royal approval on 7 June 1748, and the building was completed on 11 December. The gala opening, in celebration of Queen Louise's twenty-fourth birthday, was on 18 December 1748. The theatre was built to accommodate 782 spectators, affording a maximum box-office take of 300 rigsdaler. With numerous repairs, extensions, etc., it was to remain in use until 1874.

Extensive repairs and reconstruction were found to be necessary in 1772. Not until 1821 did an extension provide for an actors' foyer or greenroom. In 1855 there were very substantial alterations, providing seating for 1,370 spectators, and in 1857 the stage was rebuilt; but from the outside the result was, so many said, misshapen.

*The new management is empowered*

When King Frederik V thrust his Trojan horse of a debt-ridden Theatre on the City of Copenhagen, this privilege replaced the earlier ones [see **1** and **2**]. Section 5 is given here as an example of the many attempts, varying from enlightened despotism or government by committee to virtual *laissez-faire*, to devise a viable theatre administration. It also shows the King retaining his influence on the management of the Theatre.

## 3 Frederik V's Royal privilege to theatre managers, 11 September 1750

Overskou, vol. 2 (1856?–96), pp. 111–12.

5

The Board responsible for the Danish theatre's finances and troupe shall consist of a Senior Director, whom we shall most graciously appoint ourselves, and three Directors whom the Senior Director shall request to serve voluntarily and without remuneration. Among which Directors one shall be chosen by the Senior Director aforesaid to manage the theatre's income and expenditure and to submit an annual account of them to the city hall to be audited by the Councillors like the city's other public accounts; similarly the theatre's cash shall be deposited with the city treasury insofar as it is not required by the Director aforesaid for the payment of current expenses. No step shall moreover be taken in respect of the finances, the troupe, or anything else relating to the plays except after previous consideration and deliberation among the Directors, and as divergent opinions may arise on occasional matters, they shall in every case be resolved or decided by the Senior Director, as likewise no innovation or anything of importance relating to the finances or the troupe shall be implemented, although all three Directors are of the same opinion, without the Senior Director's previous or subsequent consent, in which connection the Board shall keep Minutes of its deliberations;

everything otherwise relating to the finances and similar specific measures shall be on the authority of the Senior Director and Directors themselves, and shall not require our most gracious approval or confirmation.

*Holberg's 'hands-off' management*

In the autumn of 1752 Holberg did in fact 'stand in' as Director of the company, advising on the selection of plays and the recruitment of actors, but not staging productions.

## 4 Holberg refrains from directing plays, 1750

*Epistle* 447 (1750) in Ludvig Holberg: *Epistler* [*Epistles*] (edited by F.J. Billeskov Jansen), vol. 5 (Copenhagen: H. Hagerup, 1944–54), p. 20.

Since I have adopted such a principle [of steering clear of business worries and assemblies], some have wondered at my having undertaken in recent years to be a kind of caretaker for the Danish theatre. That, however, was something from which I was unable to excuse myself; having been one of the founders of the theatre in this country and having contributed so many plays myself, I have had to see to it that they were reasonably well executed. I have, however, never undertaken any directing, being well aware that it is harder to keep order in a troupe of actors than in an army made up of several nations; and the conflicts that have arisen in connection with the drama prove that it was not unwise of me to refrain from all directing.

*Holberg on censorship*

Censorship of Royal Theatre productions and play texts was self-censorship; beyond compliance with the terms of its various privileges, the Theatre faced the permanent dilemmas of artistic standards versus box-office success and of tradition versus new trends: directors and readers were kept busy. In Holberg's own day, his works were not beyond the reach of Danish Bowdlers.

## 5 Holberg discusses liberal language and changing tastes in drama, 1750

*Epistle* 249 (1750) in Holberg, vol. 3 (1944–54), p. 229.

As for the liberal expressions which have given certain delicate souls occasion to malign our comedies, the plays have all been corrected to forestall such opinions, however unfounded. Several of them have in consequence lost much of their ingenuousness. But it was deemed needful to bow to the taste of the time, which is as changeable in this as in costume. The very same plays which were performed twenty years ago without any indignation either at Court or in the city are now more than some people can bear to hear. What rings harsh now may well sound harmonious again in twenty years' time. In Axel Thorsen's day it was the fashion for a matron or maiden to faint if she heard a young fellow's name mentioned. The clichés then were 'By your leave my corset', 'My stockings saving your grace'. But what was then thought decent has since been ridiculed as unreasonable affectation. It now seems that we are returning to the times of Axel Thorsen and Fair Valborg:[1] for affected niceness has now gone so far that one dare name nothing by its right name. Such affectation is no more proof of chastity than folded hands and a bowed head are proof of piety. [. . .]

Do not imagine, Sir, that this is a plea for indecent or improper speech, which I hate: I am simply pleading for our plays, which contain none and have never previously been described as containing any. What I would maintain is that overmuch correction can spoil plays, making them akin to the current and fashionable Parisian comedies, which consist of dry and stilted dialogue, serving no purpose but to lull the spectators to sleep. With regard finally to plays which please the eyes more than the ears, I note that the taste of the nation differs in this respect, too, from what it was twenty years ago, when hardly any comedies could succeed on our stage except Molière's, which are performed alternately with our original works, whereas today the most unreasonable plays, such as *La Coupe enchantée, La Baguette de Vulcain, L'Oracle* and others of the same kind do best:[2] from which I conclude that Molière's *Misanthrope* would scarce gain applause these days, since it contains nothing for the eyes . . . Yet I do not entirely reject plays which are entirely for the eyes, provided they are at least coherent: For comedies have two objects, both to entertain and to instruct, and I have therefore often wished that as much were done by way of action, movement and presentation for my comedies as for the translated French plays, which is not the case: for more is often spent on a single French play than on all my comedies. However, this is also the reason why many think all the better of our originals, since they have held their own against the French plays without expense, measured strides and comic gestures, maintaining their place thanks to their inherent value. [. . .]

[1] Axel and Valborg are the excessively virtuous hero and heroine of a medieval Danish ballad set against a (vaguely) Norwegian historical background; the ballad has a reputation for 'sensibility' and the protagonists for their 'honour'. Oehlenschläger wrote a tragedy about them.

[2] La Fontaine's *La Coupe enchantée*, Saint-Foix's *L'Oracle* and Regnard and Dufresny's *La Baguette de Vulcain* were all published in Danish translations in 1748 following productions in the 1747–8 season.

## 6 The Board's instructions for the troupe at the Danish Theatre, Copenhagen, 28 December 1754

Overskou, vol. 2 (1856?–76), pp. 160–6.

1 They shall in their acting on the stage always endeavour to observe decency, carefully study the characters of the persons they are representing, and attempt to express their affections and passions according to the intention and purpose of the play, the class and condition of the characters, and the varying circumstances in which they find themselves, without overdoing their acting beyond what is natural, reasonable and decent, or by low and unsuitable actions and gestures rendering the acting offensive to the spectators.

2 If at the rehearsal of a play, whether new or old, original or translated, it should appear to them to contain anything contrary to the above, or expressions offensive to modesty and good manners, they should make this known to the Director in charge of the plays, in order to have it changed or corrected in time, if possible, or the entire play abandoned; for Danish plays are not only to be performed for the innocent amusement of the spectators but also (if possible) rather to correct errors than to corrupt good manners.

3 Their theatre costumes shall be judiciously chosen to accord with the nature of each play and (as far as possible) with the customs of the country where the scene is laid, as with the age, class and rank of the characters, with special consideration for whether the part is serious and reasonable or ridiculous and unreasonable, since even clothing should serve to proclaim the nature of the characters in the play, for nothing should be neglected or disregarded which can serve to make the play pleasing to the audience. Should the members of the troupe be unable to agree among themselves on this or other such matters, they should in good time lay the matter before the Director in charge of plays rather than hazard anything on their own initiative which might prove unsuitable, desecrate the play and displease judicious spectators.

4 To learn a five-act play in verse or prose they shall be allowed a period of six weeks; a three-act play four to five weeks according to its difficulty, and for an afterpiece three weeks counting from the day when they have all been given their parts; and in order that they shall not need to burden their memories unnecessarily by learning what is not in their parts, the person who writes out the parts should not include in them more than the last few words of the character who is to be addressed or answered, but otherwise note the acts and scenes in their order. Rehearsals of the plays must be completed by the time appointed, and every actor and actress must have learned his or her part so as to be able to present the piece in the theatre without delay. If anyone owing to negligence is found unable to do so after such a length of time, and the play for that reason cannot be performed at the

appointed time, the person responsible shall forfeit one quarter of a week's wages.
5 All members of the troupe shall unquestioningly accept and play the parts assigned them by the Director in charge of plays, and in the unlikely event that any actor or actress refuses and another for that reason has to be employed instead, the same unwilling actor or actress shall have forfeited his or her wages for each time the aforesaid play is subsequently performed, of which half shall be paid to whoever took the unwilling one's place in addition to his or her own pay, and the other half shall be forfeited to the theatre's funds, and it shall not be a mitigating circumstance that the unwilling person is given another part in the same play.

[. . .]

7 To prevent the irritation of the spectators at excessive delays, of which there have been numerous complaints, plays should begin promptly at 5 p.m. sharp and there should be no unprofitable pauses between the acts or between the main play and the afterpiece. If anyone is found when dressing or during costume changes or in other connections to be drawing out the time unnecessarily and to no purpose, the same shall be noted by the two actors who shall hereafter be appointed to see to such matters, and the offender or offenders shall forfeit $\frac{1}{2}$ rigsdaler if they are in the first class and 2 marks in the second and third class for each time they so offend.
8 Every play whether new or old shall be industriously rehearsed and sufficiently often for them all to be ready to proceed with it at the appointed time and to do justice to their parts; and all shall attend rehearsals whether they have parts in the play or not at the exact time appointed for the next assembly by the two actors who are that month's supervisors, no interim allowed. Anyone absent and unable to speak or reply on cue, or present but needing to be fetched and called in, shall be regarded as under section 7 above.
9 But if they are absent for an hour beyond the time, this shall be regarded as complete absence, in which case the forfeiture shall be doubled. Should anyone come to rehearsal drunk or pick quarrels or be a burden to the others through any kind of ill-mannered or indecent behaviour, the fine shall be redoubled, and the rehearsal should nevertheless be completed by the others present; but should such an event occur during an evening performance before an audience, and it becomes evident that the person is unable to do justice to his part or that his improper behaviour confuses the others and outrages the spectators, the offender shall have forfeited a whole week's wages, and the Board of Directors reserves the right to punish both this and other offences not specifically mentioned here even more severely according to the nature of the offence and the circumstances.
10 The dancing master is recommended to instruct new actresses in French dances at least once a month, the which is to be done at the Theatre and

nowhere else. [. . .] If any member of the troupe who has a good voice and a disposition for vocal music feels a need for instruction and training therein, it is thought reasonable that Mr Thielo, who is being paid a pension by the Theatre, should find himself willing to assist in this at least once a week before or after rehearsals, the conditions mentioned above in this section applying.

11 Two of the actors, that is one of the oldest and one of the youngest, shall each month supervise and be responsible for compliance with these instructions; one of them shall record any offences that may be committed, and the other shall countersign the written report which shall be submitted weekly to the Director in charge of plays, on whose advice fines shall be deducted by the Director in charge of the funds and accounts. Should those to whom supervision is entrusted wink at offences and fail to carry it out, they shall be liable to the same fines as the offenders, who shall nevertheless also pay according to the instructions. These two actors shall be relieved at the end of each month by one of the next oldest and youngest until they have all taken a turn, whereupon the roster shall begin again, for the permanent maintenance of good manners and order in the troupe. Fines received in this respect will be disposed of by the Director in the best interests of the enterprise. [. . .]

*The King takes over again*

One king having thrust the increasingly debt-laden enterprise on a reluctant city within a couple of seasons of its opening, his successor in 1770 re-assumed Royal control. King Christian VII (1749–1808; crowned 1766) undertook to pay off the debts and leased the Theatre for ten years to Giuseppe Sarti. Sarti (1729–1802), composer, conductor, organist, active in Copenhagen from 1755 to 1775, when he introduced 'syngespill', was able to keep the creditors at bay for only two seasons.

## 7a Christian VII's rescript assuming control of the theatre, 27 April 1770

MS in the Royal Library, Copenhagen

The Magistracy of Copenhagen shall on behalf of the City be paid the sum of 30,000 Rd[1] to meet the theatre's debt, so that 3,000 thereof shall be paid by 11 June and subsequently 3,000 annually every 11 of June, as well as the interest on the remaining capital, until the sum aforesaid has been paid. The above-mentioned Musical Director Sarti shall accordingly also be obliged to honour the contracts entered into by the former Directors of the Danish Theatres; with which you all have most humbly to comply, commending yourselves to God [. . .]

[1] riksdaler = 6 marks and 1 mark = 16 skillings. The riksdaler was roughly equivalent to two English shillings, the mark to four pence.

## 7b Professor Harsdorff's[1] plans for the reconstruction of the Danish Royal Theatre, 1772

National Museum; reproduced in Frederick Marker, *Hans Christian Andersen and the romantic theatre* (University of Toronto Press, 1971), p. 4.

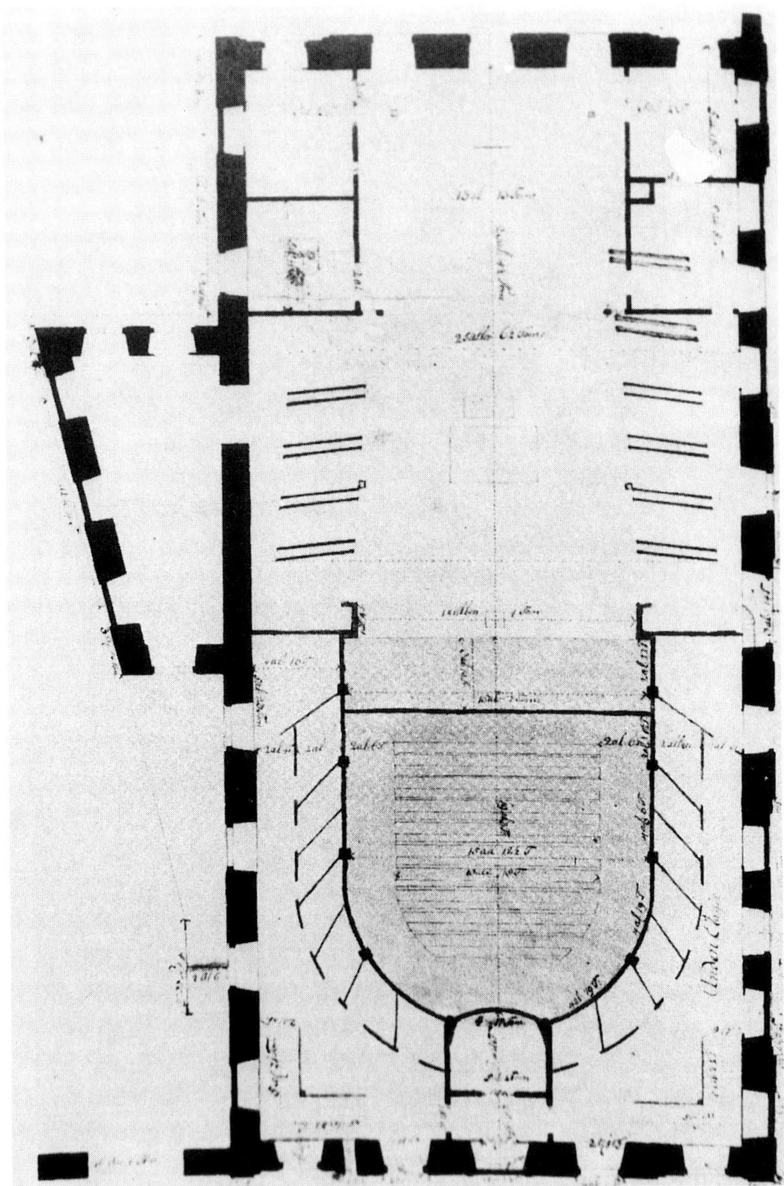

[1] Caspar Frederik Harsdorff (1735–99?), the architect who rebuilt the theatre in 1772, enlarging the stage and improving the machinery.

## 7c The theatre façade after the reconstruction of 1774

Reproduced in Peter Hansen, *Den danske skueplads: illustreret theaterhistorie* [*The Danish theatre: illustrated theatre history*], vol. 1 (Copenhagen: Ernst Bojesens Kuntsforlag, 1889–96), p. 314.

Theatret efter Ombygningen 1774.

## 7d The theatre with the pavilion added in 1792

Reproduced in Hansen, vol. 1 (1889–96), p. 335.

### II THE AUDIENCE IN 1771

Denmark's earliest systematic theatre reviewing appeared in *Den Dramatiske Journal*, written and published in 1771 and 1772 by the youthful law student Peder Rosenstand-Goiske (1752–1803), later to become a 'Dramaturg', influenced by Lessing, a 'Censor' or reader from 1780, and member of the Theatre Board from 1786 to 1792. His very first review, 7 October 1771, was an outspoken attack on *Tronfølgen i Sidon* by the Norwegian-born Niels Krog Bredal (1733–78), who contributed to the establishment in Denmark of the 'syngespill' or musical play (a genre disapproved of by Goiske). Audience tumults, occasioned by Rosenstand-Goiske's criticism and the subsequent staging of Bredal's riposte in an afterpiece, *Den Dramatiske Journal*, drew the attention of the police. (Police chiefs would be issuing similar warnings over a century later.)

The same incidents also caught the eye of the great poet and playwright Johannes Ewald (1743–81), who in *The Brutal Claque* satirized those – especially military persons – whose main purpose in going to the theatre apparently was to uphold authority and if necessary literally beat down any criticism.

## 8 Police notice forbidding audience tumults, 30 November 1771

Reproduced in Hansen, vol. 1 (1889–96), p. 301.

NOTICE

Since it has been brought to my attention that on Monday 25 and Thursday 28 inst. a number of spectators at the Royal Danish Theatre did behave themselves rowdily, and partly by whistling, threats and abuse, and partly by tramping and unmannerly shouting did disturb those spectators who were looking to take peaceful pleasure in the performance of the play, I do by virtue of my office and at the request of the Directors of the aforesaid theatre hereby seriously warn all citizens of this city of all classes to abstain from this date from such and other unseemly behaviour, and strictly to comply with His Majesty's most gracious order, which was proclaimed by notice of 24 September 1753 and the contents of which are here repreated, to wit:

> That in order to prevent all insolence at the Danish playhouse, the Board has been most graciously authorized to have the Police observe, arrest and prosecute any person or persons who cause and initiate any kind of disturbance in the playhouse while the Danish plays are being performed, whether by whistling or other unseemly behaviour.

The which all will know hereafter to comply with and beware of infringing.

Copenhagen Police Station 30 November 1771.
His Majesty's duly appointed General and Police Chief for Copenhagen
W. Bornemann

## 9 Ewald's satire on rude spectators, 1771

Johannes Ewald, *De brutale klappere* [*The brutal claque*] (Copenhagen, 1771), p. 31.

*Bister* . . . first tell me, youthful sir,
Wherefore we and others haunt parterre?
Why should one go to comedies so oft?
Merely to record that they are soft?
*Erast* Far be't from me to think so bold a thought!
*Bister* For poets' sakes alone are tickets bought,
And actors' honour, to encourage them.
*Erast* To what?
*Bister* To what? Haha! – Gottz Blitz – ahem!
*Erast* Oh noble traits! for who so well defends
And heartens for such great unselfish ends
As he who knows not with what aim or why,

Who sets himself no slightest goal thereby?
*Bister* None, 'pon my soul!
*Erast* No doubt. But if you will
Excuse me: one can clap both good and ill,
Loudly, or softly –
*Bister* We clap as public should.
*Erast* Might not attentiveness be thought as good?
*Bister* Enough's enough! What more can they demand
Than to be honoured by a rousing hand?
*Erast* Glory indeed! Might we not then employ
At every bench a clapping-mill? What joy!

## III ACTING AND STAGE MANAGEMENT, 1773–1843

### *Stage managerial records*

Regular records were kept at the Royal Theatre relating to the various aspects of stage management, costumes, props and the machinery, and have survived from an early date. Torben Krogh's richly annotated edition of the MSS retains the varying spelling and takes account of changes and additions, but expands shorthand and abbreviations; it omits the casting, available elsewhere.

## 10 Costumes and properties for Holberg's *The Political Tinker*, 1773–84

Torben Krogh: *Holberg i det kongelige teaters ældste regieprotokoller* [*Holberg in the Royal Theatre's oldest stage-managerial records*] (Copenhagen: Gyldendal, 1943), pp. 19–22, 25.

(a) From the stage manager's records ('Regieprotokoll') for 1773–6: the costumes and properties for Holberg's *The Political Tinker* (*Den politiske kandestøber*, 1722).

*Herman von Bremenfeldt* Speckled linen casaquin, brown worsted apron, blue lined cap. Later a speckled blue tailcoat with enamelled buttons, black waistcoat, round wig.
*Geeske* Old red taffeta jacket, flowered calamanco skirt, blue check apron, cap with earflaps and linen NB which she provides herself, vinaigrette, dog.
*Engelke* Green laced moiré dress.
*Antonius* A comb, a brush, neckerchief, yardstick, grey suit, round wig. Later as Geert, old red tailcoat and waistcoat, round wig, old hat, cane.
*Henrik* Bread and butter, fur, leather apron, shaggy wig. Later an old grey frock coat with paper braid.
*Anneke* Blue taffeta jacket and skirt.
*2 Boys* (in scene 5). Each an old sleeved waistcoat, shaggy wigs and old hats.

*Collegium Politicum*:

*Host* Purple cloth frock coat, waistcoat, round or Mirleton wig, hat and cane.
*Sivert Snooper* Dark grey cloth suit (Richard's in Henry 4),[1] hat and cane
*Richard Brushmaker*, Old green frock coat and waistcoat, wig, hat and stick.
*Geert Furrier*. NB. See Antonius.

*2 Councillors* Both suits with braid, full-bottomed wigs, chapeaux bras, red damask robes.
*2 Lackeys* Both red liveries with gold braid and braided hats. (NB these two enter again with the councillors' wives.)
*A Maid* Rose-coloured taffeta jacket ditto rose-coloured skirt.
*2 Councillors' Wives* 1 Blue silk dress with silver.
2 Red ditto with ditto.
*Another Councillor's Wife* Straw-coloured brocade ditto.
*Arianke Blacksmith's* Old wife's costume.
*2 Lawyers* Both black gowns, full-bottomed wigs, chapeaux bras.
*A man with a watch* Blue suit with narrow gold braid, hat with ditto, sword, watch.
*Servant to a foreign Resident Minister* Blue livery with red undergarments and silver braid, braided hat.
*Two Aldermen*
The hatters'. Old suit, Mirleton wig, hat, cane, a complaint written on four sheets of paper.
The stocking weavers'. Ditto suit plus wig, hat and cane.
*Old wife* in Act V. Old wife's costume.
*Peiter* An extra as tinsmith's boy, who drives the old wife off. Old fur, leather apron, shaggy wig.

(b) From the stage-manager's records for 1777–84; settings and properties for the same play.

SET

The scene is Herman v. Bremen[feldt]'s house, i.e. a bourgeois front room. Act II scene 1 a large table, a mug of beer, six tobacco pipes, a tin of tobacco, a bottle of spirits (white wine), a couple of glasses, one wooden jug of beer.

NOTES

The Danish theatre opened with this play.[2] Act II scene 1 A large table and six chairs for Collegium politicum. A mug of beer, some tobacco pipes and a tin or

packet of tobacco. A bottle of spirits and a couple of glasses. Act IV scene 4 Geeske with a big dog on her arm. Henrich carries on a coffee table with three pairs of ordinary cups and a pot of coffee. A teacup containing syrup. Act V scene 3 Henrich brings on a large packet of papers. An 8vo book in a white binding, which is torn to pieces. Act V scene 6 A rope. NB In the last two acts there is frequent knocking, and in Act V scene 3 noise is heard in the entrance.
ad Notam: Besides the mug a large wooden jug of beer. White wine instead of spirits. A dozen tobacco pipes, the tobacco on a pewter plate. A paper spill to light pipes with. The syrup in a drinking glass. Some wooden teacups which will not break.

1 *La Partie de chasse de Henri IV* (1764) by Charles Collé (1709–83), performed in Danish in 1770, was itself an adaptation of Richard Dodsley's *The King and the Miller of Mansfield*.

2 This must allude to the first performance in the company's hired theatre, Bergs Hus, on 14 April 1747.

### STAGE HANDS' RECORDS

Sometimes the stage mechanics also recorded their observations and second thoughts, as here after a production of Holberg's *The Lying-in Chamber* (*Barselstuen*, 1723, first produced 1731). Evidently there was also a performance at Court.

## 11 Scenes and machines for a Holberg comedy, 1777?

Krogh (1943), pp. 38–9.

The first two scenes were played in the town [backdrop] with the mansion in the middle and then change to the plain room [the interior of the lying-in room], where they completed the first Act. Then the garden curtain was lowered. Act II began in Fabris's[1] old front room with the fireplace in the middle and the mirror painted on either side, for there must be no door on it, and a bedside table towards G.[2] with its accessories where the midwife sits, and some gilt leather chairs and a screen towards M. by nr. 3[3] is set up, behind which is the cradle. And at the end of Act III the front curtain is lowered and then the fireplace set piece is removed* and a door put in its place and a table towards G., which they drink at, and some chairs, but on the table at which they drink there is no cloth, and here the two remaining acts are played.
*NB A door on either side, and mirror off, but the fireplace was left on. Last time Act V was played in the plain room, which is correct. And between Act II and Act III the front curtain is not lowered, for there is no change. On the bedside table pancakes and a bottle of tincture.
Court theatre. Hung the town backdrop between nr. 3 and 4 for the first two scenes and the front room backdrop behind in its proper place. Act I and Act II

were in the plain room backdrop [which was] where it belonged, i.e. in front of the front room backdrop, with eight wings.

[1] Jacopo Fabris (1689–1761), the Theatre's first stage designer, scene painter and technician, already an authority when he settled in Copenhagen in 1747. Evidence is plentiful that he designed the 'staple' sets for the new Copenhagen theatre. Scenery had to serve as long as possible, but fell into disrepair because the low roof meant that it had to be rolled or folded up when hoisted into the flies.

[2] G. and M. were local jargon denoting the Theatre's two neighbours, the cannon foundry (Giethuset) and the market-place (Markedet), stage right and stage left respectively.

[3] A reference to the wings ranged on either side behind each other in pairs, ready to be wheeled on along guideways in the stage floor by means of wheeled trucks below stage. The guideways were numbered from downstage to upstage.

### *Michael Rosing's acting*

The Norwegian Michael Rosing (1756–1818) made his debut in 1777 and became one of the giants despite being prevented from performing much of the classical tragic repertoire. Early in his career, however, he did not seem to find much favour with this young critic.

## 12 Goiske describes Rosing's strutting and bellowing, 1778–80

Peder Rosenstand-Goiske: *Kritiske efterretninger om den kongelige danske skueplads . . .* [*Critical accounts of the Royal Danish Theatre . . .*] (edited by C. Molbech) (Copenhagen, 1839), pp. 64–5.

In my opinion, Mr Rosing will have to make it his main concern to study his art in the book of nature, without which no amount of study of books by the foremost aesthetic judges can help the actor one iota; let him moreover beware of becoming tumid and affected; and let him finally beware of what I may call false beauty in tragedy, in which the least exaggeration so easily approaches parody. – He will excuse my adding a few more remarks, especially since he may well consider and make use of them. My advice, therefore, is: let him entirely abandon his convulsive movements; let him simplify his attitudes, which smack far too much of the dancing master, or resemble ballet positions; let him desist from using his left arm instead of his right; let him similarly rid himself of his continual swaying from side to side; let him endeavour to render his figure or his bearing both more genuinely noble and free than they are; let him not be so stiff-necked, or throw his head back so far that the spectators scarcely see his face other than foreshortened; and let him not hunch his shoulders as much as he is wont – all which make his figure unhandsome, especially in profile. Finally I would recommend him not to kick so much in his stride, an error which is the more offensive in tragedy as being in itself the closest to parody.

### *Stage managerial chronicles*

The earliest stage manager's register [*Regiebog*] covers the period from November 1781 to December 1787, and was kept by Niels Hansen, who held the post from 1776 to 1799. To Hansen's records were added the comments of W. (Warnstedt, the Theatre's Director), S. (Schwarz, director of musical plays and operas) and R. (Rose, director of plays).[1]

[1] Hans Wilhelm Warnstedt (1743–1817), officer and enlightened theatre administrator 1778–92.
Frederik Schwarz (1753–1838) made a strong impact on acting styles through his own example and through his teaching and direction, with a call for ensemble playing; he served the theatre for fifty years from his entry as a ballet pupil in 1766 and is a major source of theatre history for Overskou.
Christopher Pauli Rose (1723–84), actor and stage director, joined the Theatre from its start in 1747, played on opening night in 1748, and stayed with it until his death.

## 13 A stage manager's journal for 1781

Torben Krogh: *Det kgl. teaters ældste regiejournal* [*The Royal Theater's oldest stage-managerial journal*] (Copenhagen: Kongelige teater og kapel, 1927), pp. 11ff.

### 1781

In the year 1781 on the 1st of November this Journal was begun in accordance with the above order. And on that day at 11 a.m. a rehearsal was held at the Court Theatre of *The Political Tinker*.

Mr Thessen was absent from the rehearsal as Sivert in Act II. At 11¾ I sent the messenger to fetch him to rehearse the lawyer's part in Act V. At 12¼ the messenger returned the excuse that his wife had been taken ill without the gates, where she was attending a wedding, for which reason he was unable to come. [W.]: Mr Thessen is fined according to the Regulations for absence from a whole rehearsal.

[R.]: Correct as stated above; otherwise the rehearsal went fairly well, if I overlook in some a lack of enthusiasm or lukewarmness in the performance of their parts.

On the evening of the same day the aforesaid play was performed at the Court Theatre in the presence of Their Majesties,[1] who this evening for the first time after their return from the country honoured the theatre with their noble presence. In which no errors of importance occurred, except that Saabye[2] in Act V scene 3 made his entry to announce the Foreign Resident one speech too early, whereby Mr Arends[3] was deprived of the opportunity to crawl under the table. [W.]: Saabye shall be excused this time.

[R.]: Mr Thessen as Sivert was very uncertain in his part. [W.]: Because Mr

Thessen was uncertain in the part of Sivert, he shall be reproved by Mr Rose in my name, but in the presence of the stage manager.

*2 November. Aglaë.*[4]

[S.] The performance went smoothly and well, Mrs Preisler[5] especially distinguished herself by her good acting and singing in the part of Aglaë.

[W.]: Mrs Preisler acted and sang decently, but ought to have done better.

*3 November*

At 11½ the whole theatre company: actors and dancers were assembled, to whom on the spoken order of the Director both the graciously approved Regulations and the proclamation issued on 1 November by the Director of the company were read; with the added admonition: 'that no one may bring unauthorized persons with them to their rooms on performance evenings, or have food and drink brought there'.

[1] In 1781 His Majesty was Christian VII, but by then both his marriages had been dissolved and he was well into insanity. So it is unclear which members of the Royal family were at the theatre.

[2] Peter Rasmussen Saabye (1762–1810); acting debut in 1781, stayed with the company till his death; went with Preisler and Rosing on the continental tour in 1788 as recorded in their diaries.

[3] Jacob Arends (1743–1801), acting debut 1775, went on till his death.

[4] *Aglaë* by Sarti.

[5] Marie Catherine Preisler (1761–97), singing pupil 1776, acting debut 1778, a lively and beautiful soprano; married Joachim Daniel Preisler (1755–1809), whom she attracted from theological studies into acting. They were divorced in 1795 after he ran off with someone else, and the moral of the story is that they both died in abject circumstances. His travel diary, especially from pre-revolutionary Paris, is worth reading.

### *The Frydendahls go to jail*

Members of the Royal Theatre company were not infrequently sentenced to periods in 'Blaataarn' (The Blue Tower) for breaches of theatre discipline, from not knowing their parts to insubordination. This episode originated in Mrs Frydendahl's (1760–1831) failure to attend a rehearsal under the noted composer and singing-master H.O.C. Zinck (1746–1832), and grew into verbal and written exchanges with the Board and the Director, General Walterstorff (1775–1820, Director 1798–1801). On 11 December 1800 the King sentenced the couple to four weeks' imprisonment, but ordered their release on 22 December.

## 14 Imprisoned actors plead for clemency to the Crown Prince, 21 December 1800

Robert Neiiendam: *Breve fra danske skuespillere og skuespillerinder* [*Letters from Danish actors and actresses*], vol. 1 (Copenhagen: J.L. Lybecker, 1911–12), pp. 78–9.

The most painful emotion we have experienced in our prison is having reason to fear that the unfortunate event which brought us here could possibly be interpreted as obstinacy on our part.

Convinced by our heart's warmest sentiments that nothing could be further from our intention than such foolish rashness, we beg leave to assure you, most gracious Lord, that our most eager efforts have always been aimed at devoting our weak skills to the most gracious pleasure of the Royal Family which, like all honest and good subjects, we highly honour and love, and that we desire nothing more heartily than to be able still to provide testimony of this our most humble and faithful devotion.

In accordance with these sentiments, we most humbly beg Your Royal Highness to consign what has passed to oblivion . . .

Blaae-Taarns Arrest-Hus [Blue Tower Prison]

### *Tragedy on the Danish stage*

There had been earlier tragedies on Nordic themes, notably Johannes Ewald's *Balders død* (*The Death of Balder*, first performed in 1778), but Oehlenschläger's *Hakon Jarl* (*Earl Hakon*) marked a major breakthrough for him and for the genre. Oehlenschläger's letter to K.L. Rahbek's[1] wife Kamma Rahbek (1775–1829) is evidence to support the suggestion that without the great Norwegian-born actor Michael Rosing, it might not have come about. It is also a comment on the dearth of tragedy on the Danish stage: Rosing did not live to perform Shakespearean heroes. Other Oehlenschläger heroes found their embodiment in Ryge [see **16** and **19**], and the blonde heroines theirs in Anna Nielsen (1803–56),[2] who was held by some in as high esteem as Mrs Heiberg would be.

[1] Knud Lyhne Rahbek (1760–1830), would-be actor, dramatist, reviewer, journalist and editor (*Minerva*, *Den danske Tilskuer* [*The Danish Spectator*]), professor of aesthetics and literary history; helped to found the Royal Theatre's drama school, for which he taught classes and wrote historical plays 1805–16, publishing *Om Skuespilkunsten* (*On the art of acting*) in 1809; served as Censor and member of the Theatre Board from 1809. His wife, Kamma (Karen Margarete) helped make their home a literary centre. She was a brilliant conversationalist and letter-writer and appears to have been a thoroughly admirable person.

[2] Anna Nielsen had been recruited for her singing voice, when she made her debut in 1821 in O.J. Samsøe's *Dyveke*. She went on to play thirty Oehlenschläger parts, in addition to a great deal else, and married the romantic leading man N.P. Nielsen.

## 15 Oehlenschläger discusses Rosing, *Hakon Jarl* and tragedy, 1806

*Breve fra og til Adam Oehlenschläger, Januar 1798–November 1809* [*Letters from and to Adam Oehlenschläger*] (edited by H.A. Paludan *et al.*) (Copenhagen: Gyldendal, 1945), pp. 275–6.

Berlin, 19 March 1806

How unutterably your joy at my Hakon Jarl delighted me you cannot – I do not exaggerate – imagine. It would also be excessive pride on my part if I thought the play alone was the cause of your enthusiasm and joy. Friendship, hidden behind Melpomene's kirtle-tail, added fuel to the flames, and absence stood in a far corner blowing with all his might [. . .]

How could you doubt for a moment that it was inexpressibly pleasing to me that my friend Rosing read the play to you, that Hakon Jarl spoke in his own name? Without Rosing Hakon Jarl would probably not have come into existence; [Rosing's] whole dramatic-poetic figure, put together from innumerable scattered memories, in fact makes up the limbs of which this airy being consists. Only after seeing many different theatres does one learn to appreciate Rosing's irreplaceable value. That he sometimes with feigned and sometimes with genuine enthusiasm fills his mouth with Kotzebuean street rubbish counts for nothing. An actor is no poet: he presents what one gives him, as well as he can; why is nothing better given him? What we possess in him would only make itself properly heard in Shakespeare's, Goethe's, and Schiller's plays.

*Costumes as health hazards*

Dr Johan C. Ryge (1780–1842) [see **19**] looms large historically, physically and temperamentally, as a leading actor and in time as a despotic director. He also interested himself in costume design. His name is associated, like Michael Rosing's [see **15**], with the success of Oehlenschläger's tragedies, although he himself did not originally regard them as congenial. Before becoming an actor, he had qualified and practised as a physician, which lends him authority in this letter.

## 16 Dr Ryge animadverts on unhygienic costumes, 2 November 1814

R. Neiiendam, vol. 2 (1911–12), pp. 126–7

It has been known to me for some time that the Royal Theatre wardrobe has occasionally been lent to dramatic societies, masquerades and other entertainments. I regarded such loans as an abuse, however, as had already been made known through the proper channels, and one which the Board would certainly seek by wise measures to restrict; but having learned by chance and to my considerable surprise yesterday that all the Correggio[1] costumes were to be lent to a dramatic society, and that – according to persons who must be assumed to know – on high authority, I feel impelled both as an actor and a physician to draw the Board's attention to the fact that such loans not only render the actors' art more difficult, but also endanger their health. [. . .]

Any reasonably educated person knows that vermin, scabies, herpetic and other rashes, yes, even the disease more commonly found within cashmere than within homespun breeches, can be transmitted as readily from one person to another through shared clothing as through contactum immediatum; and any physician knows that even rheumatism is similarly contagious, sweat being the vehicle of rheumatic matter and perspiration openings (*pori*) being conducive to infection. I surely need say no more to the Board to convince it that loans of the Royal Theatre wardrobe can have consequences harmful to all the actors' health, a gem which the Board cannot replace and which should therefore not be held in contempt.

[1] Oehlenschläger's romantic drama *Correggio*, a panegyric of artistic creativity first written in German in 1808, was produced in Danish in 1811.

*The introduction of vaudevilles*

When one or two of his early 'vaudevilles' received hostile reviews and drew small audiences, Johan Ludvig Heiberg (1791–1860), who was to become Denmark's leading playwright of the period, wrote a lengthy essay in defence of the genre – which seemed to do the trick.

## 17 J.L. Heiberg promotes vaudevilles, 1826

J.L. Heiberg, *Om vaudevillen, som dramatisk digtart, og om dens betydning paa den danske skueplads* [*On vaudevilles as dramatic poetry and their significance for the Danish stage*] (Copenhagen: Schultz, 1826), pp. 38–40, 48–9.

The difference between *opéra comique* or (as they are generally known) musical plays and vaudevilles can provisionally be defined in terms of the different relationships between the two elements of which both consist. The musical play (*syngespillet*) is closer to opera than to drama; a vaudeville is closer to drama than to opera. In the former, everything must therefore aim at musical characters and situations, and dialogue must be no more than simply a means of leading up to them; in the latter, on the other hand, the characters and situations must be solely dramatic, for the dialogue is of prime importance, and the musical items must only be put in where the life and interest of the dialogue have reached their highest points. In musical plays, dialogue occurs in place of music; in vaudevilles, music occurs in the place of dialogue, and this is why in the latter many familiar and easy melodies are used, for the attention of the spectators is not to be captivated by the musical element, but wholly devoted to the dialogue, which is enhanced and clarified by familiar melodies, the recollection of which puts the spectators in the mood which the author requires in each particular instance. [. . .]

The artistic criteria which can be applied to vaudevilles are consequently first the observation of the necessary limitations, i.e. the presentation of interesting situations with loosely sketched characters; next the perfection of the dialogue, and especially its enhancement by means of music, which includes the consideration that in vaudevilles more than in any other art form, music and text must correspond so closely that they seem to have grown together into a unit and to be inseparable. It is this criterion in particular which gives vaudevilles high artistic status. [. . .] The artistic criteria for vaudevilles also include the simplicity, already noted, of the musical element. To such simplicity a third requirement is connected, which is the simplicity of the whole; i.e. the achievement of its effect by modest and simple means; for the greater the fuss, the more the spectators feel entitled to expect, and they might easily be misled into expecting things of which the vaudeville is not capable without destroying itself. A vaudeville should therefore not be grand, or require theatrical pomp and circumstance. I have accordingly written all mine in one act, and without scene changes, although I would not claim that that was the only way of observing the necessary limitations in size and theatrical apparatus.

*The talent of the future Fru Heiberg*

Heiberg wrote his vaudeville [see 17] *April Fools* [*Aprilsnarrene*] in a few weeks after first seeing the child actress Johanne Luise Pätges (1812–90), and went on writing *ingénue* roles in vaudevilles for her. But he also boosted her in other ways, eventually marrying her; this is from his review '*Macbeth* on the Danish stage', written in 1827, when she was fourteen.

## 18 J.L. Heiberg praises the acting of Johanne Pätges, 1827

J.L. Heiberg: *Prosaiske skrifter* [*Prose writings*], vol. 7 (Copenhagen: J.H. Schubothe, 1861–2), pp. 12–13.

[. . .] I am also justified in drawing attention to the correct diction and poetic expression with which Miss Pätges says the few words the author has given to the vision of the bloody child. If our theatre knew as well what was good for it as many a foreign theatre does, this young actress would already be a gold-mine.

*Ryge's acting style*

The distanced acting technique described here seems appropriate to someone capable of including himself in one of the pairs of actors whose work he compares and contrasts.

## 19 Ryge praises his own acting, 1832

J.C. Ryge: *Critisk sammenligning imellem nogle af det Kongelige theaters skuespillere og skuespillerinder* [*Critical comparison of some of the Royal Theatre's actors and actresses*] (Copenhagen, 1832), p. 29.

But his stage performances in the comic vein also prove [him to be in possession of great fantasy], for they are unmistakably the realized reflections of original fantasy images. When individualizing these, he often, perhaps too often, uses a special method. For he does not blend the character's personality with his own, but rather places the latter behind the former, and, letting his own individuality merely shine faintly through the fantasy image, he lends the image stage life, more or less like a puppeteer animating his puppet.

## 20a The green room of the Royal Danish Theatre, after 1821

Nordisk pressfoto.

*Phister's scanty theatrical wardrobe*

J.L. Phister (1807–96) [see **32**] served the theatre from 1819, when he was recruited from the dancing school to play a boy's part, and by the age of 21 had 119 parts to his credit. He was the mainstay of Royal Theatre comedy and musical comedy for a quarter of a century – and notorious as chronically short of money. Here he appeals to Director Collin [see **23**].

## 20b J.L. Phister complains of nothing to wear on stage, 11 November 1839

R. Neiiendam, vol. 2 (1911–12), p. 91.

Pray do not take offence, Councillor, at my importuning you with these lines; following a missive I received this evening from Mr Lassen, I have no choice but to write. For Mr Lassen writes that I may not take the clothes I need for my part in *The Comrades*[1] from the wardrobe, because the regulations state that actors are to provide their own plain clothes. God knows it is my dearest wish to get new clothes, of which I am in great need; but I have no money. What can I resort to, to provide myself with clothes for Thursday? I do not know. For my first costume, a coat, waistcoat and trousers with gaiters are essential, and later a tailcoat, waistcoat and trousers. For me to provide these myself is quite impossible, for I cannot even afford a winter overcoat, but am constantly obliged to shiver in my only coat, under which I cannot wear tails. I possess only one suit of tails, but it is old and blue, and too tight for my normal activity and even less use when I seek to be more active. Trousers have I none, that is to say which can serve on this occasion. I do have some odds and ends of waistcoats and one splendid one with gold embroidery which together with a tailcoat I had made at my own charge for Lindgreen's[2] jubilee on 1 January 1838. I cannot use the waistcoat in this play, and the tailcoat has since seen constant service with Master Hammer and Link the sexton.[3] It has now given its all, for this evening a younger and more popular one had to take its place, and the ungrateful public never noticed, or even missed the undeserving and worn-out coat. Forgive me, I jest. But, in Figaro's words – I force myself to laugh at everything, in order not to weep at everything.

1 *La Camaraderie, ou La Courte Echelle* (1837) by Scribe.

2 Ferdinand Ludvig Vilhelm Lindgreen (1770–1842), comic actor, superb in Holberg, especially as Jeppe; a teacher at the dramatic school from 1817, he instructed Phister.

3 In Heiberg's popular vaudeville *No* (*Nej*), Phister created an immortal character in Sexton Link. Hammer appears in Heiberg's *The Danes in Paris* (*Danskerne i Paris*).

*Ticket-scalping*

In the 1830s and 1840s, a subscription system encouraged a black market in theatre boxes. It was accepted that if the hucksters found tickets going at a loss, they could cram as many spectators as possible into their boxes. The satirical magazine *Corsaren* saw in the hucksters' boxes the most perfect embodiment of the ideals of liberty and equality.

## 21a Black market in theatre boxes, 1840

*Corsaren* [*The Corsair*] (1840), reprinted in Hansen, vol. 2 (1889–96), pp. 282–3.

Liberty – because here one constitutes a republic, under the rule of natural law. Each fills the space to which nature gives him title, regardless of whether or not his neighbour is thereby crushed to a pulp. Equality – because there are burdens in common. The view may be best from the front row, but in return one is obliged to support all the rest of the box, and one may see little from the back bench, but for this one has the compensation of leaning on the back, shoulders, etc. in front of one. From the middle bench one has a poorer view than from the front, but better than from behind, one carries the back bench but rests against the front bench: here is the very culminating-point of the republic.

## 21b A huckster's box packed to bursting

From a sketch by E. Westphal; reproduced in Hansen, vol. 2 (1889–96), p. 283.

*Bournonville is hissed*

On 14 March 1841, a hissing demonstration was arranged against the great ballet-master, choreographer and dancer August Bournonville (1805–79), by spectators who believed he had slighted their favourite prima ballerina. He had heard of the plot in advance. Here is part of his own emotionally charged account.

## 22 August Bournonville complains of the demonstration against him in the King's presence, 1841

Hansen, vol. 2 (1889–96), pp. 595–6.

One minute before my entrance, the Royal family entered their box, and I imagined that the unseemly performance that had been planned would be prevented out of respect for His Majesty.[1] So I mounted my triumphal litter, was carried on, and waved my cap as usual; but as I passed the lights, I was greeted by strong hissing, mixed with the noise of a whistle or two. This did not strike me at once sufficiently to disturb me in the performance of my part, but – that a gathering 1,100 strong could calmly listen to the attack of a score of ill-willed individuals on an aggrieved private person in his public calling, that no immediate shout of indignation called the hidden traducers to order and convinced me that I had friends among my countrymen – that filled my soul with rancour which despite the best will in the world I have never been able to overcome. The bitterness I felt on that occasion is beyond description; it was not the deed of the wicked that crushed me, but the indifference of the good that stabbed me to the heart. I leaped down from the litter, advanced towards the Royal box, and in a loud voice asked the King 'What does Your Majesty command me to do?' This act has since been interpreted as lacking in respect for His Majesty, but the answer I received showed that at that moment I was correctly understood. 'Carry on', were the King's words, and I obeyed as a faithful humble servant [. . .]

[1] The King in question was Christian VIII (1786–1848), crowned 1839. He was not best pleased at Bournonville's direct approach, and the following day sent him off on six months' unpaid leave, having first ordained house arrest. Or – the alternate version – Bournonville wanted to quit, but was persuaded to take six months' leave instead. Two leading ladies found Bournonville difficult to work with: first, Lucile Grahn, who left in 1838, and won European fame; then her successor Augusta Nielsen, who danced with Bournonville in his ballet *The Toreador* on the occasion in question; it was probably her supporters who made the uproar.

*The management of Jonas Collin*

By – literally – all accounts, Councillor Jonas Collin (1776–1861) was an extraordinarily fine man and a paragon among public servants. Among the many functions he was called upon to undertake was theatre administration, and when he was appointed Senior Director in 1843 this was little more than official recognition of what had for two decades been the real state of affairs.

## 23 Jonas Collin lauded as a paragon of administrators, 1843

*Fædrelandet* [*The Fatherland*] (1843), quoted in Hansen, vol. 2 (1889–96), p. 276.

In our opinion, one can safely dismiss the rumour [that Collin was planning to resign from the Board] as unreliable, for it would be a sign of almost incredible self-confidence if Mr v. Levetzau[1] were to consider himself, on the basis of the experiment so far, fitted to manage the Theatre; and it would be out of keeping with His Majesty's interest in the arts and national spirit to place a foreigner, a German, who barely understands Danish and is only able to make himself understood to his subordinates in that well-known language double Dutch, who knows neither Danish literature nor the particular sensibilities and tastes of the Danish public, at the head of the Danish National Theatre, merely on the grounds that Senior Directors have always been courtiers. What is much more probable is that the real management of the Theatre will remain in the hands of Councillor Collin, whether he continues in his capacity as second or third Director while Mr v. Levetzau retains the title of Senior Director or, as seems to us in view of the above much the best solution, Mr v. Levetzau resigns together with Councillor Adler,[2] whose influence on the Theatre has left virtually no trace, and Mr Collin is appointed Theatre Manager or sole Director with a subordinate financial director, and Professor Heiberg [see 17], who has up to now been adviser to the Board, as the Theatre's official reader replaces the aesthetic tyranny of Councillor Molbech.[3]

[1] Joachim Godsche Levetzau (1782–1859), Lord Steward under Christian VIII (1786–1848, crowned 1839), Theatre Director 1839–49.

[2] Johan Gunder Adler (1784–1852), member of the Theatre Board 1839–49. Close liaison in a variety of capacities with King Christian VIII, he had played an important part in negotiations concerning Norway's possible independence in 1814 and in the drafting of the Norwegian Constitution.

[3] Christian Molbech (1783–1857), historian, lexicographer, librarian, philologist, author, editor, professor; Theatre Censor from 1830.

*Kierkegaard on Fru Heiberg*

Fru[1] Heiberg's multitude of admirers included Søren Kierkegaard (1813–55). In January 1847 she returned after some twenty years to Juliet, a part she had played at sixteen. Inspired by her performance, Kierkegaard in 1848 anonymously published an essay called 'Crisis and a crisis in the life of an actress' (*Fædrelandet*, 1848, nos. 188–91). In 1851 he sent her a copy. In her memoirs she quotes from and comments on it.

[1] She had royal permission to be billed as 'Fru' (Mrs) rather than as the customary 'Madame'.

## 24a Kierkegaard analyses fear and freedom in Fru Heiberg's acting, 1848

Johanne Luise Heiberg: *Et liv genoplevet i erindringen* [*A life relived in memory*] (5th revised edn, edited by Niels Birger Wamberg), vol. 2 (Copenhagen: Gyldendal, 1973–4), pp. 174–6.

He writes: 'Her indefinable self-possession shows, in sum, that she has acquired the proper attitude towards stage tension. Any tension can have – a double effect; it can reveal effort, but can also do the opposite, conceal effort, and not only conceal it, but constantly trade it for, transform and transfigure it into, lightness. The lightness thus derives imperceptibly from the strain of tension, but the tension is not seen or even sensed, only the lightness is revealed. [. . .]

'But stage illusion and the burden of all eyes is a monstrous load to lay on a person; where this happy relationship is lacking, therefore, no routine, however great, can disguise the weight of the burden, but where the happy rapport is present, the weight of the burden is constantly transformed into lightness. Thus it is with the young actress; in stage tension she is in her element, there precisely she is as light as a bird, the very weight produces her lightness and the pressure produces the high flights. There is no trace of fear; backstage she may be afraid, but on stage she is happy and light as a bird which has been given its freedom, for it is only now, under the pressure, that she is free and has earned her freedom. What at home in her study or backstage seems to be fear is not impotence but its very opposite, an elasticity which frightens her precisely because she feels weightless; in theatrical tension this fear is transfigured wholly positively into intensity. It is far too narrowminded to insist that an artist of either sex must not be afraid; above all, lack of fear is a poor sign in a great artist. The greater his powers, the greater his fear, so long as he stands outside the tension which is exactly commensurate to his powers. If one were to imagine a personification of the natural force which sustains the heavenly bodies, while it is divorced from its function and waiting to assume it, it would be in a state of mortal fear. Only at the moment when the burden was laid on it would it be carefree and light. One of the worst pains for a human being therefore is to possess elasticity disproportionate to the tensions of the little world he inhabits; such an unfortunate will, for want of sufficient weight, never feel completely free. The truth is that the impact of fear is absolutely right, and for the stage artist it always exists off the stage, never on stage, though the latter is the normal case with anyone who is not afraid offstage.'

These statements by a non-actor were what amazed me. They are absolutely right, and many times I have felt just what he describes here. The whole weight of fear backstage, but light as a bird on entering and performing . . . How little an audience knows of all this is best revealed by the fact that it is always moved by and sympathetic towards those who show their fear on the stage; for they do not realise that this visible fear is the surest indication of an actor's failure to enter wholly into the performance in such a way as to become someone else and to cease being the person one is in private life.

## 24b Fru Heiberg as Lucretia in Holberg's *The Weathercock* (*Den Vægelsindede*), between the comic servants Pernille and Henrik[1]

Lithograph from a drawing by A. Hartung; reproduced in Hansen, vol. 3 (1889–96), p. 80.

[1] *The Weathercock* had never been a success and had last been attempted in 1817. Its revival was Fru Heiberg's own initiative and the production which opened on 17 February 1850 in her husband's first season, gave her her greatest success in a Holberg part, which she continued to act till her retirement in 1864. As she relates in her autobiography, she filled out what had been considered a sketchy and fragmentary role with mime and comic gesture, lending the character motivation for her shifting moods.

## IV UNDER THE MINISTRY OF CULTURE 1849–89

### *Heiberg as Theatre Director*

Proclamations of 30 May and 25 June 1849 placed the Theatre and orchestra under the Government and more specifically under the Ministry of Culture. On 23 July a Royal Decree from Frederik VII dissolved the current Board and appointed J.L. Heiberg Director, a natural choice following his long and close association with the Theatre as dramatist, critic, adviser and theorist. There was the difficulty that his wife was the Theatre's leading lady, but he accepted the post and held it for seven years. Having himself pioneered the new dramatic venture, vaudeville [see 17], he found himself as adviser and then as Director holding out for 'idealism' and resisting the trend towards realism. In a recommendation appended to the Royal Decree, the responsibilities of the new post were defined.

## 25 The Ministry of Culture defines the functions of a Director, 1849

Hansen, vol. 3 (1889–96), pp. 8–9.

In order that he should enjoy the necessary respect, the Director would presumably have to be given extensive authority to manage the employment of the Theatre's human and material resources in the service of art, while the Ministry, beyond the general control vested in it over the Theatre as its subordinate institution, will in practice have only real questions of principle to decide; the Director would moreover have to obtain the Ministry's approval for any major measures of a general nature, and submit to it his proposals concerning the appointment, dismissal and payment of the personnel, and furthermore annually submit to the Ministry at the beginning of the season a general plan for the Theatre's activity that season and a survey of work undertaken, as well as a report at the end of the season, and likewise submit to the Ministry the Theatre's budget proposals. On the other hand, the practical and specific management and care for the proper and appropriate running of the Theatre's own affairs would be left to the Director, who would thus, in addition to assessing the works submitted for performance, specifically determine the repertory and with the means available to him ensure its satisfactory performance on the stage.

### *Høedt's influence on acting and on Michael Wiehe*

The first thoroughgoing champion and passionate advocate of theatrical realism is widely held to have been F.L. Høedt (1820–85), not only in his own acting practice and influence on other actors, but during his six years as artistic director. He refused to play Hamlet in the production under rehearsal, which shows the clash between Høedt's demands for realistic drama and natural acting [see **27** and **33**] and the traditional taste defended by J.L. Heiberg.

It was, by Mrs Heiberg's account, during the performances of *Romeo and Juliet* which inspired Kierkegaard [see **24**] that she first felt the effect on her great partner Michael Wiehe (1820–64) of the influence of Høedt [see **26** and **33**]. Wiehe had been the theatre's romantic lead (and Mrs Heiberg's favourite leading man) until the new trend represented by Høedt resulted in breaches of theatre discipline and Wiehe's move for a season to the Court Theatre. In the spring of 1856, Wiehe for his part looked back with satisfaction on that hotly debated season.

## 26 Thomas Overskou[1] reports on an interrupted rehearsal of *Hamlet*, 1855

Hansen, vol. 3 (1889–96), pp. 23–4

The properly announced rehearsal of *Hamlet* began on the 19th inst. at 11:15. When the few speeches preceding Mr Wiehe's entry as Horatio had been properly spoken by the actors, Mr Wiehe interrupted the rehearsal by not entering but from the front of the wings loudly and emotionally asking 'Are we going through this farce again today?', to which I replied, 'A rehearsal has begun, and I must ask that it be continued in good order.' Mr Wiehe repeated, just as loudly and still more passionately, 'I asked whether we were going through this farce again today. All it boils down to is for us to rehearse until Hamlet enters, when the rehearsal will be stopped; and we all know that Hamlet isn't coming.' I said, 'It is not my job to interpret the Director's intentions with the rehearsal; it is being held on his orders, and must be properly conducted.' Then the previous speeches were repeated, and Mr Wiehe staggered on, completely out of character, waving his arms, and spoke his line 'Friends to this ground' in a laughing and babbling tone. A third time I enjoined Mr Wiehe to rehearse properly and not play the fool, to which he retorted 'You are making fools of us; expect nothing but foolery from me.' I went on, 'I must maintain that the rehearsal must be properly and seriously conducted.' To this fourth reminder, Mr Wiehe replied, 'Expect nothing but foolery from me, I tell you.' To those present I then said, 'Well, in view of Mr Wiehe's statement, I must hereby suspend the rehearsal; a rehearsal on those terms must not take place at the Royal Theatre.'

[1] Thomas Overskou (1798–1873), a prolific dramatist and pioneering theatre historian, acted from 1818 to 1841, and served as instructor at the Royal Theatre 1849–58; he had been appointed artistic director under Heiberg.

## 27 Realism at the Court Theatre, 1856

R. Neiiendam, vol. 2 (1911–12), pp. 163–4.

A theatre season will soon be coming to an end, the impact of which both on dramatic art and on the individual artists has been variously judged. The most general opinion appears to have been that it was harmful to both; in fact, however, there is reason to hope that it was beneficial to both. But to develop this in detail is not my object. All I wish to say is that for me personally it has been a healthy year. Such remarks about me as that I was out of my element at the Court Theatre, or that I must miss the many wonderful lyrical and tragic parts in which I had formerly delighted the audience, stem in my opinion from a somewhat short-sighted view, not only of the present theatre conditions and of me as an actor, but of the art of drama altogether. As we know, its purpose is to present people. In the lyrical drama which made up such a large part of the Royal Theatre repertoire, and for the sake of which in particular my return was agitated for and to which it was believed that I must long to return, the actor is given no opportunity for the real presentation of people, or in other words for the genuine art of acting. Perhaps I might express myself more correctly if I said that it offers him no encouragement; for the more real acting he seeks to do in such a work, the more he kills it as lyrical drama. Although it may, rightly and regrettably, be said of me that I have shown a particular talent for lyrical drama, I nevertheless hope that it must also be admitted that even in the lyrical drama my endeavour has been to the contrary, an endeavour in the direction of individualization amounting to a declaration of faith. However, this can be achieved only to a certain extent; one has to adapt oneself to a requirement which bears no relation to the absolute demands of the art of acting; the latter is, in short, inhibited and not stimulated by that kind of play.

For an actor who has been on that kind of diet for a long time, I can imagine nothing more pleasant or indeed beneficial than to work for a time with a repertoire which obliges him to speak the way we speak every day; pleasant in that it feels like emerging from fog into fresh air, beneficial because it is emerging into fresh air from fog, which is healthy. That was precisely my case. I found such a sanctuary at the Court Theatre, the privilege of which enjoined us exclusively to perform plays in which we spoke like people, and I believe that the fresh air I enjoyed there will make me better able to undertake the more nourishing atmosphere which is to be hoped for in future than I should have been had I remained where I was.

The man to whom I am indebted for such a healthy and agreeable year is my present Director, Mr Lange,[1] who granted us asylum.

[1] Hans Wilhelm Lange (1815–73), actor, theatre director of the Casino Theatre 1848–55, Court Theatre 1855–6, and Folketheateret 1857–73.

*Royalties for dramatists*

As theatre director under Sarti [see **7a**], Bredal [see section II] had tried in 1771 to attract Danish writers by offering the third evening's take, but the first regular scale of fees for original works and translations did not appear until 1791. For a full evening's (at least two and a half hours) comedy or tragedy it stipulated either 400 Rd. or the third evening's takings, which was generous seeing that a full house took in only 460 Rd. A more notorious scale introduced in 1832 became known as the 'minute scale' because of the way it measured dramatic writing. The authors themselves were actually consulted on the new scale drafted by Collin in 1842, and by the time of the Regulations approved on 23 July 1856 they were given a say in the casting of their plays, as well as being guaranteed fixed payments on acceptance and after a twenty-sixth performance and, in the case of works filling the whole or most of an evening, shares of the takings. Part of Clause 12, relating to full-scale works, is given below. Among other things, the Regulations also prevented dramatists from publishing their plays prior to performance (a fight which Administrator Fallesen was to lose in 1888 over Ibsen's *The Lady from the Sea*), and from having them performed at other theatres in or near Copenhagen.

## 28 Clause 12 of regulations on dramatists' fees, 1856

*Regulativ angaaende de til opførelse paa det Kongelige Theater indsendte og antagne stykker.* [*Regulations concerning plays submitted and accepted for performance at the Royal Theatre*] (Copenhagen, 1856).

Of the evening's income the author and, if the work is an opera or a musical play, the composer, is entitled to:

| | | | | | |
|---|---|---|---|---|---|
| from the 2nd to the 6th performance | | | | | $\frac{1}{6}$ |
| " | 7 | " | 11 | " | $\frac{1}{4}$ |
| " | 12 | " | 16 | " | $\frac{1}{3}$ |
| " | 17 | " | 21 | " | $\frac{1}{5}$ |
| " | 22 | " | 26 | " | $\frac{1}{7}$ |

and after the 26th performance 150 Rd

*An Ibsen play is rejected*

Between writing for the Theatre and becoming its Director, Heiberg functioned as its reader. However well they may have served the Theatre by refusing rubbish, most of the holders of that thankless office, such as K.L. Rahbek, the Molbechs father and son, or Erik Bøgh, are inevitably remembered for their 'rejection slips'.

## 29 Heiberg rejects Ibsen's *Vikings at Helgeland*, February 1858

J.L. Heiberg, vol. 7 (1861–2), pp. 401–2.

[. . .] I received the play *Vikings at Helgeland* by Mr Ibsen, Christiania. Like several recent Norwegian attempts to produce a characteristic national drama, this play is based on Icelandic saga literature, but the whole venture down this road is in my opinion a misunderstanding, and the road merely a dead end. Icelandic sagas are so distinctly epic in nature that they can only be spoiled by presentation in dramatic form. The wildness and savagery they describe is softened in their original form by the epic presentation, the literary and historical interest of the Icelanders being a civilizing element in their national character alongside the sheer physical power which they depict. But the moment it is dramatized, only the raw material remains, and the moderating element is lost because it is linked to the original presentation, and cannot be compensated for by any nuances which a present-day author, in the midst of our civilization, might offer in their place. It must be admitted that these authors make no such attempt, but treat their material so objectively that one can virtually be bruised by it, for in a drama everything hard becomes even harder than in an epic narrative. What is worthy of notice in this and similar experiments is the effort to promote illusion by imitating the characteristic concise style of the sagas. This gives rise to certain striking constructions, but they decline into types and in the long run seem mannered and affected. A Norwegian drama will hardly emerge from the laboratory for these experiments; the Danish fortunately has no need of them.

*The need for a new theatre*

On 5 October 1868 a Theatre Commission submitted a comprehensive report on the theatre, including a draft Bill in forty sections which was not adopted. The extract given here is from the reason for §29, showing why the Commission (like everyone else) thought a new building was needed. The law which was finally passed in 1870 appears below as **31a**. This piece of compromise legislation enabled a new theatre building to be erected and, more questionably, fitted out.

## 30 Theatre Commission's recommendations for a new playhouse, 5 October 1868

*Betænkning afgiven af den i Henhold til skrivelse fra Kirke – og Underviisningsministeriet af 7de Juni 1867 sammentraadte Theatercommission* [*Report made by the Theatre Commission convened on 7 June 1867 by the Ministry of Religion and Education*] (Copenhagen, 1868), pp. 55–6.[1]

That it must be regarded as highly desirable to have the present theatre replaced by a new one appears to have been acknowledged on practically all sides; it can therefore hardly be necessary to give an exhaustive explanation. Not only is the present building very far from satisfying the demands that can justifiably be made of a building whose chief object is the promotion of the arts, whether in its own appearance or in the relationship to abutting streets and squares which have developed as a result of the changes in the neighbourhood in recent years, but significant flaws and deficiencies also attach to many aspects of its inner workings, which in various ways have a detrimental effect, and not least on the theatre's finances. So as not to go into too much detail here, we shall in this connection merely point out that the theatre's lobby and corridors are much too small and narrow, that proper public cloak rooms are non-existent, that in parts of the house the space for the spectators is too cramped, that the space between the scenery and the outer walls is too narrow, that the dressing-rooms are too small and in some cases without light or air, that the theatre wardrobe is located in premises which are much too small as well as being difficult of access and a fire hazard [see **20a**], that several other facilities are inconveniently placed in relation to each other, and, to conclude, that there is no space at all in the theatre building itself for the sets for the current repertory, which greatly encumbers the whole daily routine. A final consideration is that a certain increase in the number of seats might be desirable, although a substantial increase on the other hand would for a number of reasons be unsuitable.

[1] Kultusministeriet and Kirke- og Underviisningsministeriet appear to have been interchangeable terms. When there was a switch from royal to public financing and administration in 1849, Minister of Church and Education Mading was replaced by Minister of Culture Bang – the same office in the same ministry.

## 31a Royal act relating to the erection of a new playhouse, 18 June 1870

*Love og Anordninger samt andre offentlige kundgjørelser Danmarks Lovgivning vedkommende for aaret 1870* [*Laws and statutes and other public proclamations relating to Denmark's legislation for the year 1870*], Part xv (Copenhagen: Gyldendal, 1871), pp. 208–11.

We Christian the Ninth, by God's grace King of Denmark, etc. etc., do hereby make known: the Rigsdag has adopted and We by our assent have confirmed the following Act:

§1. Provided the Municipality of Copenhagen allocates a sum of at least 250,000 Rd in equal amounts over five years reckoned from 1 April 1870, no conditions being imposed relating to the future status of the theatre or commitments on the part of the Treasury, and provided the Municipality cedes a site of up to 4,000 square alen [16,000 square feet, 1 alen = 2 feet] from Kongens Nytorv opposite the former military academy and permits the adjoining section of Heibergsgaden to be built over or altered, the Government is authorized to use, either as an allocation or as a loan as the legislature shall decide, up to 220,000 Rd of Sorø Academy's funds in equal amounts over five years reckoned from 1 April 1870, for the erection and fitting out of a new theatre building and the expenses related thereto (cf. §2), and may for that purpose also dispose of two corner sites on Gammelholm, located between title numbers 289 and 330 on Østre Qvarteer and Heibergsgaden, and of the site of the former military academy. Provided the new theatre is so far completed that it can be used from 1 September 1874, the present theatre building shall be pulled down at the end of the 1873–4 season, its materials and fittings sold insofar as they cannot be used in the new building, and its site made over to the Municipality of Copenhagen, subject to any adjustments that may be required for the new theatre building and on condition that it is not built on. The newly-erected building and its site shall be the exclusive property of the State.

§2. The new theatre building with all the equipment and rooms necessary for its own use and the comfort of its spectators should not occupy an area greater than about 12,000 square alen, and the total cost of its erection, equipment, furnishings and decoration must not exceed the sum stipulated in §1, plus whatever the old building's materials and equipment fetch. The auditorium shall, in addition to the boxes reserved for the Royal Family and the Court, be capable of accommodating 1,700 spectators, standing room included.[1]

[1] The remaining four Sections relate to an architects' competition for the new building, its artistic decoration, reports to be submitted to the Rigsdag on the theatre's financial status, and the terms of the debt to Sorø Academy. A curiosity worth noting is the justification for the Government's appropriation of Sorø Academy funds for theatre purposes: simply that Holberg had bequeathed the Academy a large endowment. The winning project in the competition for the design and building of the new theatre, was submitted in June 1871 by architect Vilhelm Dahlerup (1836–1907) and surveyor Ove Petersen (1830–92).

## 31b Evening of the last performance at the old Royal Theatre, 1874

Contemporary engraving; reproduced by Nordisk pressfoto.

## 31c The new Royal Theatre, 1874

Photograph, reproduced in Hansen, vol. 3 (1889–96), p. 270.

## 31d Auditorium and stage of the new Royal Theatre, 1874

Contemporary engraving, reproduced by Nordisk pressefoto.

*Phister in his greatest Holberg role*

Joachim Ludvig Phister (1807–96) [see **19**] became a ballet pupil at ten, played his first big Holberg part in 1825 and went on until 1873, notching up 649 parts in all. He was a major link in an unbroken tradition of acting Holberg, having been taught by Ferdinand Lindgreen and himself teaching Olaf Poulsen.

This description comes from Denmark's greatest critic Georg Morris Cohen Brandes (1842–1927), a leading aesthetician, literary historian and reviewer, whose lectures on 'Hovedstrømninger' (Main Trends in Nineteenth-Century European Literature), begun 1871, exercised considerable influence on contemporary (especially Norwegian) drama and 'problem plays'.

## 32 Georg Brandes describes Phister as Holberg's Jeppe, 1870

Georg Brandes: 'Holberg: Jeppe paa Berget' ['Holberg: Jeppe of the Hill'] (1870), reprinted in *Kritiker og portræter*, [*Critiques and portraits*] (2nd revised edn) (Copenhagen: no pub., 1885), pp. 94–112.

But Phister's performance is more than an accompaniment; he is not content to sustain the given theme; how deeply he has immersed himself in the part can best be felt at those points where he takes further what Holberg gives him, adding motivations, adjustments, new creation. Consider for instance a speech like 'If only I had her (Nille) here, you'd see how I'd bastinado her. Another glass, Jacob!' When Jeppe utters this rodomontade, he is not yet completely drunk, and accordingly, Phister decides, still rather frightened. So he turns around and looks back at the door as if afraid someone may have heard his rash words, and then exclaims as if seeking more courage, 'Another glass!' Or consider Phister's mime while the Doctors tell their long stories. When they arrive, Jeppe is still trembling with fear, overwhelmed, impressed; only a few moments earlier he was on his knees, begging the valet to spare his life. When they leave, he is calm, confident, secure, exulting, and ends the Act with his words of command. What brings about the transformation? One might reply 'The Doctors' soothing stories', but Phister sees it differently: 'The boredom the Doctors induce' is his answer. There is no better medicine for awe than boredom. Once a situation, impressive and confusing when new, begins to bore, it soon ceases to confuse and impress. A situation which commits the enormity of being boring is easy to master. Phister's silent acting first expresses fear, which is dispelled by the music; for a moment he looks down in embarrassment, when the story is told of the person who was so utterly confounded by 'strong drink'; then he pays attention and indeed shows pleasure at understanding the narrative; but gradually attention is replaced by honest-to-goodness boredom, which has become almost a sleep-like trance when he is suddenly aroused at the point in the story where the question occurs 'Aren't you going to eat soon?' The word 'eat' electrifies him, he sits up with a jerk thinking the question is directed at him. This shows how completely Phister is at one with Jeppe's whole nature and being. He constantly bears his entire personality and even more, his consciousness, in mind, and that alone is what he has recourse to whenever Jeppe needs a new idea or a new expression.

### *Høedt leaves the Theatre*

As far back as Holberg [see **5**] and his critical champion Rosenstand-Goiske [see **12**], one can find demands for natural performance rather than stylized declamation or artificial posturing. Frederik Schwarz [see introduction to **13**] in the late eighteenth and early nineteenth century, and then F.L. Høedt [see **26**] marked important stages in this progress. Heiberg's reluctance or refusal to put on *Richard III*, in which Høedt wanted to act, prompted a letter of resignation to the Ministry of Church and Education, dated 4 March 1853. Høedt was persuaded to stay until 1857. Another champion of realism, the scholar, critic, and dramatist Edvard Brandes,[1] later described the effect of Høedt's departure. His essay criticizes Heiberg's theatre direction and suggests that things have gone from bad to worse.

[1] Carl Edvard Cohen Brandes (1847–1931), brother of Georg, was also a scholar in classical and Eastern languages, and as a politician spoke for many liberal theatrical policies [see 37]. He served as Folketing representative 1880–94 for the Venstre (Left, liberal) party, in the Landsting (upper chamber) from 1906, and as Minister of Finance 1909–10 and 1913–20.

## 33 Edvard Brandes describes the effect of Høedt's departure, 1875

Edvard Brandes: 'Et vendepunkt i dansk theaterhistorie' ['A turning-point in Danish theatre history'], *Det 19. Aarhundrede [The Nineteenth Century]* (1875), p. 95.

From that time we can date the period of the theatre's absolute decline, not that there have not been fresh and talented recruits as the great have departed, but that the understanding of the art of acting possessed by its practitioners on our stage is too limited and narrow for any true artistic life to be built on it. There is no lack of ability, but the insight is wanting to exploit it; the material is there, but not the principles. No new dramatic literature has been able to compensate for the theatre's artistic poverty. In serious drama, declamation is spreading fast, and in comedy coarse caricature rules almost without exception. If anything of significance is to be rescued from the ruins of our sinking art of the theatre, the Board placed in charge of the theatre must have a definite dramaturgical principle to put into practice.

*Playreaders' reports remain confidential*

The censor was expected to be vigilant in preventing *lèse-majesté*, blasphemy and obscenity; and the post was also and, in time, more exclusively, that of play reader. Readers' reports were of course internal and confidential. In the late 1870s the Minister of Culture began insisting that dramatists should be sent the reasons for refusals in writing. The reader Christian K.F. Molbech[1] wrote a long and convincingly reasoned reply justifying the current practice, with which the Director, Fallesen, was in agreement.

## 34 Molbech justifies the censor's confidentiality, 21 December 1877

Robert Neiiendam: *Det Kgl. teaters historie 1874–1922, [History of the Royal Theatre]* vol. 2 (Copenhagen: V. Pio, 1921–30), p. 180.

As Your Honour will know from last season's experience, the majority of the works submitted to the Theatre belong in that mediocre category which in art is the saddest of all because it neither performs nor promises anything. In all other areas, even that of science, industry without talent can be of importance and bear fruit – but not in art. Consequently, most works will not serve and are refused. That this as a rule gives rise to the dissatisfaction or even anger of the party concerned is beyond question, and something the effects of which I have personally experienced both directly and indirectly. But just as this is hardly to be avoided under such circumstances, so experience has also taught me that dramatic authors in this respect are the hardest of all to convince, and that no argument, however detailed, is capable of shaking their faith in the quality, or even the excellence, of their works. The reason for this is not just the general frailty of authors, but also the particular circumstance that dramatists can always point to the absence of that supreme court judgement which can only follow from *performance.*

[1] Christian Knud Frederik Molbech (1821–88), son of C.M. Molbech; author, literary scholar, Censor 1871–81; translated Dante's *Divine Comedy* into Danish verse; wrote successful historical play *Ambrosius* (1877, first Royal Theatre performance 1878).

### *The Theatre's daily workings under Fallesen*

Colonel M.E. Fallesen (1817–94) was a surprising choice for Director in 1876, but in many respects a successful one. His political and rhetorical skills served the Theatre well in many parliamentary and press battles, and he was also close to the King; he implemented practical and beneficial reforms; he gave free seats to members of parliament, the press, and the Theatre's own pensioners; he appointed William Bloch [see **36**] as artistic and Johan Svendsen[1] as musical director; he overrode the more narrow-minded decisions of his readers, first Molbech *fils* [see **34**] and then Bøgh;[2] and, though quite the disciplinarian, he was also something of a diplomat in his personnel management. Early in the 1887–8 season he kept a diary. It illustrates his dictum that a Director must not keep aloof from all the little everyday matters. There are references to an address signed by many of the actors demanding a different policy with regard to the repertoire, which Fallesen regarded as virtual insubordination, and to his refusal to accept partial absence owing to indisposition.

[1] Johan Severin Svendsen (1840–1911), Norwegian composer and conductor, attached to the Royal Theatre 1883–1908.
[2] Erik Nicolai Bøgh (1822–99), author, dramatist, journalist, editor, Censor from 1881.

## 35 Director Fallesen's diary for August 1887

R. Neiiendam, vol. 5 (1921–30), pp. 84–5.

2 August. Mr E. Poulsen[1] declares himself unable to play Leander in *Masquerades* [*Mascarade*, 1724], because it is too much of a strain for him to wear pumps and silk stockings for a whole evening. In a part in which he was motivated by excitement, he might be able to, but not in *Masquerades*, where the part is less active. I replied that since he maintained quite firmly that his state of health would not allow him to play the part, he was free to relinquish it.

10 August. Complaint from Mrs Eckhardt[2] about being left out of the

repertoire. Why not *Ninon*[3] with Mr Zangenberg[4] as the Chevalier? Also complains that Miss Orlamundt was not permitted to stay on at the school of acting. I explained to her that that was on the unanimous recommendation of the instructors. Mrs E. did not sign the address. Told her we would put on *Ninon* if possible.

Mr Zangenberg, who has not been scheduled for rehearsals the first few days, requests permission to stay in the country a little longer. 'No. Every member of the company must be at the Theatre's disposal from the 15th. Everyone is receiving the same answer.'

16 August. Mr Bartholdy is sad to see *Loreley*[5] falling into other hands than originally decided.

Mr Bechgaard[6] asks me to help him to have *The Last Lamia* arranged as an opera libretto, preferably with the assistance of Mr Iver Iversen.[7]

Mr Ludvigsen[8] shows various lamps for the auditorium. I select one for trial.

17 August. Mr Simonsen[9] asks to be excused rehearsal, because he is going shooting. 'By all means, provided the conductor has no objection to re-scheduling the rehearsal.' To that man S. refuses to be indebted in any way. 'Yes, you must apply to your superior.' 'I won't, I'll miss the rehearsal without permission.' 'That could prove quite expensive to you.' 'Well, then I shall attend the rehearsal, and notify the King that you refused me permission to come shooting.' 'By all means.' He left, in a temper. But an hour later he asked the conductor to re-schedule the rehearsal. That was done.

19 August. Miss Regina Nielsen[10] thanks me for her engagement. I give her a brief course on 'contact on the stage'.

20 August. Miss Antonsen[11] asks for second-class Feu.[12] I tell her that in signing the address, she showed lack of gratitude, manners and discipline.

22 August. Mr Simonsen tells me that a deputation of companions-at-arms want him for their leader. He requests my opinion. 'This is a private matter, in which you may do as you like. But it does occur to me that, not being a soldier, you may easily be made to look ridiculous if you accept a place where you don't belong.' So he thanked me and left.

23 August. Mrs Hennings[13] would like to stay at Klampenborg, because she is not feeling very well. She will be unable to act much at the beginning of the season, or to rehearse. Reply 'that on the part of the Theatre, every consideration is given to her health when plays and rehearsals are scheduled. If she is unable to perform despite these considerations, she should take sick leave in order to make a complete recovery.' The Chamberlain must not regard the leading actors, the stars, as soldiers. Where the younger ones are concerned, that's another matter. Reply 'that it is not treating anyone like a soldier, to offer as much consideration as in her case. The artistic director could confirm this. I must maintain the rule about partial sick leave and cannot make any exception.'

[1] Christian Emil Poulsen (1842–1911), actor, debut 1867 together with brother Olaf (1849–1923); both thought of as among Denmark's greatest performers, Emil especially in great Ibsen interpretations, Olaf in Holberg and character comedy. Emil was also appointed stage director in 1874.

[2] Josephine Eckhardt (1839–1906), retired 1901 after forty years with the Theatre.

[3] *Ninon*, a play by Henrik Hertz (1797–1870), a leading contributor with Heiberg and Hostrup to a Danish 'golden age' of drama with about forty plays to his credit, of which several were very popular hits. First performed 1848.

[4] Emil Christian Zangenberg (1853–1914), debut 1873, Royal Theatre 1881.

[5] Conrad Johan Bartholdy (1853–1904), composer, teacher, choirmaster.
*Loreley*, an opera, performed at Royal Theatre in 1887, with Bartholdy's score and libretto.

[6] Julius Andreas Bechgaard (1843–1917), composer of symphonies and operas.

[7] Iver Iversen (1862–92), author and physician.

[8] Possibly Hans Valdemar Ludvigsen (1861–1939), who built up a dry-cell industry with a partner named Hellesen.

[9] Niels Juel Simonsen (1846–1906), a versatile and successful baritone opera singer, who made his debut in 1874.

[10] Regina Nielsen (1864–1933), an operatic soprano who made her debut in 1885.

[11] Ane Grethe Antonsen (1855–1930), a Royal Theatre actress from 1880 to 1910.

[12] From its foundation, Royal Theatre actors were paid according to a sliding scale. 'Feu' denotes the complex system introduced in 1842 whereby the members of the acting company were paid according to a scale which combined their artistic standing with the number of their performances and the size of the parts. It proved enduring, despite the many abuses it could lead to.

[13] Betty Hennings (1850–1939) was quite right to consider herself a star. She was the world's first Nora in *A Doll's House* (1879); and played the Princess in Holger Drachmann's *Once upon a Time* (*Der var engang*, 1887) in 182 performances.

### *Naturalistic blocking for a fantasy play*

The person who finally placed 'modern' directing on a permanent footing at the Royal Theatre was William Bloch (1845–1926), who served as director from 1881 to 1893 and again from 1899 to 1907. The following is from his prompt-book for Holger Drachmann's[1] hugely successful folk- and fairy-tale play *Once upon a Time*. It shows changes in Drachmann's rhyming couplets (not rhymed in this translation), and how they were broken up to allow for movement and business.

[1] Holger Drachmann (1846–1908), author, poet, radical, who later broke with modernism and became a late nineteenth-century romantic. One of Denmark's greatest lyric poets as well as the author of enduring stage hits.

## 36 William Bloch's promptbook for a fairy-tale play, 1887

Jytte Wiingaard: *William Bloch og Holberg* [*William Bloch and Holberg*] (Copenhagen: Gad, 1966), pp. 356–7.

He is not here. (*Fetches the barrow in, places it between the litter and the stove.*) What weather! (*Crosses to the b[ack]g[round] door to close it, stands there looking out.*) Now the red glow is fading behind the woods, the dark trees look so threatening. (*Comes down right from the background. Lights the lamp, crosses to put it on the table.*) I fear his arrival, fear his rebuke, yet long for nothing so much as . . . (*Stops and listens.*) Did anyone call? (*Crosses to stage left. Picks up a broken clay dish from the barrow, muses over it.*) (*S.L.*) (*Over to the barrow*[1] *the cello solo.*) His voice can be so harsh and rough – then something so mild comes over him. (*Sits.*)

[1] Wiingaard's quotation gives no punctuation here; presumably there is none in Bloch's pencilled notes.

*The Royal monopoly ends*

Following a long and energetic campaign in the media and in the Danish parliament (Folketing), notably by Edvard Brandes, the Act below was adopted as a political compromise, terminating the Royal Theatre's sole right to dramatic works,[1] as the liberals wished, but granting ten years of grace during which the Theatre could secure its repertoire by performing it, thus partly placating conservative opinion.[2]

[1] 'Dramatic works' had been a matter of definition: private theatres had long been free to perform varieties of the species regarded as beneath the dignity of the Royal Theatre.

[2] Brandes's major speech in favour of the Act is recorded in the parliamentary proceedings (Folketingsforhandlinger) for 24 January 1889, and is summarized in Neiiendam, vol. 5 (1921–30), pp. 171–2.

## 37 Act ending the Royal Theatre monopoly on plays, 12 April 1889

R. Neiiendam, vol. 5 (1921–30), pp. 176–7.

§1

The sole right of the Royal Theatre according to its privilege of 11 September 1750 to perform plays in Copenhagen is suspended, with the exception that, in the period from 1 October to 30 April, no plays or operas in foreign languages (among which, however, Norwegian and Swedish are not reckoned) or ballet by any foreign company may be performed without the permission of the Minister of Church and Education.

§2

Nevertheless, no private theatres shall perform any work from the repertoire of the Royal Theatre unless the Royal Theatre has not performed the work in the course of ten consecutive years following the issuance of this Act.

The Board of the Royal Theatre can shorten this time limit in respect of works which it does not intend to have performed. [. . .]

§3

Licences to perform plays in Copenhagen are issued by the Minister of Justice.

Prior to 1 October 1899, no new licences shall be issued extending to 1 April 1900, and current licences shall be renewed only for the same period.

§4

On pain of forfeiting their licences, licensees shall not acquire the dramatic works of foreign (not including Norwegian and Swedish) authors or composers, thereby restricting the right of the Royal Theatre to perform them.

Licences shall on the other hand impose no restrictions with regard to art forms, and in respect of the repertoire of the Royal Theatre only such restrictions as are authorised in §2 of the present Act. Current licences shall be extended accordingly, on condition that the above-mentioned ban on the acquisition of foreign dramatic works be included in the licences.

# *Sweden, 1765–1900*

Edited by PETER BILTON

## INTRODUCTION

Gustaf III's successful efforts to establish and maintain Royal theatres in Stockholm began a process which this selection of documents follows for over a century. The 'Royal' impact on that process can be seen in the enduring influence of the traditions established in his day: the classical Francophile culture combining with his wish to promote things Swedish; the sense of dignity and mission which it was not always easy (or financially rewarding) to live up to, but which endured to affect attitudes to such disparate issues as the choice of repertoire and the style of a new opera building.

Succeeding kings also made their various marks in theatre history. Gustav IV Adolf established a Royal Theatre monopoly in Stockholm. Nya teatern was bought in Carl XV's name. Oscar II transferred responsibility for theatrical affairs to the Ministry of Finance. Kings moreover appointed Theatre Directors from among their court officials. Even if they proved successful, as did Gustaf Lagerbjelke (Director 1823–7), they seldom held the post long enough to establish artistic policies, or continuity and harmony in their companies.

Beneath the surface always, and erupting at frequent intervals, was the vexed question of the ownership, administration and financing of the Royal Theatres. The monarchs were in the ambivalent but powerful position of being both theatre owners and heads of government. The Theatres were both Royal property and public institutions. When in 1809 the Riksdag voted its first theatre grant, it acquired a say in theatre affairs, but with it a constant dilemma: national theatres were desirable, but helping to meet royal debts was not; yet there was always the possibility that a king weary of debts and deficits could close the theatres or lease them to entrepreneurs. Whose were the Royal Theatres? For what purpose and how should they be run? Was a Royal Theatre the same thing as a National Theatre? Questions like these bear directly or indirectly on many of the events recorded and documents included below. When a workable permanent solution was finally found, it took the form of state-run limited theatre companies, with the King represented on the Board and appointing Theatre Directors: Theatres Royal still, and still in the public domain.

Finding one's way about the first century of Swedish Royal Theatre history is complicated by the variety of names by which the theatres were known. Before grappling with more detail, scholars will be well advised to note two salient features: (1) a single opera building, in use from 1782 to 1806 and from 1812 to 1892 by one or both companies; and, (2) a single dramatic company or dramatic division of a joint company, housed in Nya Bollhuset [New Arsenal] from 1787 to 1792, then for a year in the Opera while the Arsenal was being fitted out, then in the Arsenal from 1793 until the fire in 1825, and from 1825 to 1863 in the Opera. From 1863 it had its own theatre, and moved into a new one in 1907.

Anyone venturing beyond these pages to histories and contemporary sources should note that the operatic part of the enterprise is also known as the 'Large Theatre' (Stora teatern) and often referred to as the 'Lyrical' Theatre, as opposed to the 'Smaller' (Mindre) or 'Dramatic' theatre, popularly 'Dramaten'. The Arsenal is often referred to by the names it bore before becoming an arsenal, the de la Gardie palace or the 'Makalös' palace. Authors of documents and historians alike often assume local knowledge and refer to theatres by the names of the Stockholm streets and squares where they were or are situated. Thus the theatre in Trädgårdsgatan is the theatre opened by Anders Lindeberg in 1842 with the name Nya teatern, taken over by Edvard Stjernström and renamed Mindre and bought by the King in 1863, when it became the Royal Smaller Theatre or Royal Dramatic Theatre (the names of buildings, institutions, and companies having apparently been interchangeable).

## I THE GUSTAVIAN PERIOD, 1765–90

### 38 Baron Ehrensvärd[1] laments the state of the Swedish theatre in the 1760s

F.A. Dahlgren: *Förteckning öfver svenska skådespel uppförda på Stockholms theatrar 1737–1863 och Kongl. theatrarnes personal 1773–1863* [*Catalogue of Swedish plays performed at the Stockholm theatres 1737–1863 and personnel of the Royal theatres 1773–1863*] (Stockholm: P.A. Norstedt, 1866), pp. 42–3.

The taste for French theatre became so general and seductive that people forgot there had ever been a Swedish theatre, and thought it foolish to believe there ever *could* be. [. . .] Those who first encouraged it were either dead or no longer in a position to offer encouragement. Swedish theatre, a refugee in its own country, found that if you can no longer benefit or entertain, your existence is hardly necessary. Attacked by a wasting disease, it was abandoned by the physicians and unprovided with cures. In the innermost reaches of the city, where some old gloomy houses lean closely towards each other to form a narrow alleyway, in the highest attic, where daylight hardly penetrates, where art rejects stairs so one has to clamber up a steep and shaky ladder – there lies the miserable refuge sought by Swedish theatre. There it was visited by the common herd, who met their fellows, or took a cheap opportunity to see customs like their own presented. There were fights there as at an inn, language like that of street pedlar-women, coarseness as at the vilest pubs and dens of vice. It was served by the same sorts of people. Some actors came from debtors' prisons, some out of uniform; some had been wigmakers' boys and others drunken lawyers. A nobleman, Leyonmark,[2] played one of the worst parts; but it was nothing new at that time for Swedish aristocrats to play dirty parts and worse. Actresses had been fetched from the laundries and from Barkareby,[3] costumes borrowed from second-hand clothes stalls, the music hired from pub dances. – Such was the transformation of this institution following twenty years of neglect.

[1] Baron Gustaf Johan Ehrensvärd (1746–83) was to become the Royal Theatre's first Director (1773–6).

[2] Leyonmark is the name of an aristocratic Swedish family of Finnish origin and long standing; its members appear to have been paragons of virtue, even with pietistic leanings – which is a far cry from what Ehrensvärd is suggesting.

[3] Possibly 'Barkarby', a small suburban residential area near Stockholm.

### *Gustaf III sponsors the first Swedish performances*

Sweden's Royal Theatres were very much Gustaf III's creation. He had the necessary background. Born in 1746 into the rococo milieu of the Drottningholm theatre, as a child he performed in pageants, wrote small dramatic pieces and was observed acting parts in plays on his bed before lying down to sleep. In 1762 he was rescued from a theatre fire at Drottningholm. In 1771 he succeeded to the throne. In 1792 he was shot at a masked ball in the Opera which he attended despite premonitions and cryptic warnings worthy of *Julius Caesar*. In the meantime, he kept an eye on theatre affairs even from the battlefield, founded the Swedish Academy as part of his campaign for Swedish culture and language, imposed dramatic censorship, financed the theatres and, amazingly, himself provided the leading repertoire of the time, both opera libretti and plays, with the help of Swedish versifiers.

On his father's death in 1771, Gustaf III was prompt to begin realizing his plans for a Swedish theatre: in a letter from Paris dated 3 March 1771, he dismissed the French company that had been performing at Bollhuset. Their main Swedish competitor, Petter Stenborg (1719–81) took the opportunity of submitting the following petition later the same year. The original petition bears the legend in the King's hand: 'First step towards the establishment of the Swedish opera', and was as such of historical importance. All it achieved for Stenborg was that the King consented to two performances, of which at least one was given, in 1772.

## 39 Stenborg's petition for a Swedish theatre, 1771

Johan Flodmark: *Kongl. svenska skådeplatsen i Stockholm 1737–83* [*Royal Swedish theatres in Stockholm*] (Stockholm: Central-Tryckeriet, 1887), pp. 42–3.

Most mighty and gracious King!

Since the troupe of French players who were formerly here will no longer be performing their plays, a time may have arrived when the Swedish theatre can hope for greater encouragement. A national theatre which, in the country's own language, shows its inhabitants representations of virtues to be imitated and errors to be avoided, which can find its own original material in the country's ancient and modern history and cultivate its language while cultivating its customs, such a theatre is certainly worthy of the new era which our fatherland has begun with Your Royal Majesty's reign.

[. . .] I have devoted over twenty-five years to the Swedish stage; circumstances have admittedly not been favourable, but the hope of seeing a happier future dawn for the profession to which I have given myself has hitherto sustained me. Since 1756, I have had Your Royal Majesty's most gracious privilege to perform Swedish plays, which on 23 May 1758 was most graciously extended to country districts, and on 3 March 1760 to the kingdom's royal academies. On 12 February this year Your Majesty moreover most graciously consented that I alone should have the right, to be infringed by no others, to perform Swedish comedies. Throughout this time I have done my utmost to learn and practise my chosen science; my poor condition has prevented me from paying my actors well enough and providing the theatre with decent sets, nor has any encouragement enabled me to do so.

The very location in which a theatre is established is very important to its renown; and since the Royal Bollhuset is vacant at present, I make so bold as to pray most humbly for Your Majesty's most gracious permission henceforth to perform the Swedish plays there. Should Your Royal Majesty in your most praiseworthy royal grace and mercy be pleased to favour and support me with some annual sum of money, I should be so much the more capable of investing our theatre with the reputation and dignity which our country's honour demands.

Talented persons would soon be attracted to acting when they were rewarded according to their deserts and when they saw that Swedish genius was not held in contempt. Our countrymen would have the pleasure of understanding what they heard spoken. Our language would reach a perfection which without the help of the theatre it could never achieve, heaps of native folly would be attacked and abandoned and more foreign ones would remain unknown or at least not famous and accepted, and happy geniuses would be to Sweden what Voltaire, Racine and Molière have been to their country.

## 40 Announcement of Swedish performances, 1772

*Dagligt Allehanda* [*Daily Miscellany*] (1772) in Johan Flodmark: *Stenborgska skådebanorna; bidrag til Stockholms teaterhistoria* [*Stenborg's stages: a contribution to Stockholm's theatre history*] (Stockholm: P.A. Norstedt & söner, 1893), p. 44.

With his Royal Majesty's most gracious consent, new Swedish actors will today, Wednesday 11 March, at the Royal Bollhuset, perform: 'Menaechmi or The two identical brothers', comedy in five acts, translated from the French; after which will follow: 'Everyone's friend', comedy in one act.[1] Subscription tickets will be issued by Mr Stenborg, Chancellor at the Royal Court Chancellery.[2] No old subscriptions are valid.

[1] The former play was Regnard's imitation of Plautus, the second was *L'Ami de tout le monde* by Legrand.

[2] Petter Stenborg's son, Carl (1752–1813), who drafted the petition and used his contacts at court to have it submitted to the King.

## 41 Baron Ehrensvärd notes the first Swedish production, 1772

Flodmark (1893), p. 45.

The performance of these plays exactly matched the [agonizing] rehearsals; but I never saw such a numerous gathering; they applauded every word, they seemed to take most heartfelt pleasure in seeing a Swedish production, and the public seemed thereby to ask His Majesty to give the like his protection. It was at this performance that His Majesty decided to establish a Swedish theatre.

*The Royal Opera House opens*

By 1782, higher standards had been reached, according to Olof Kexél (1748–96) who was Secretary of the Theatre Directors from 1773 to 1796. No doubt theatre almanacs were an advertising medium.

## 42 Olof Kexél describes the new Royal Opera House and its opening performance in 1782

Olaf Kexél: 'Inhemske theatre-tidningar och nyheter för 1782', *Kongl. Svenska Theaterns almanach för året 1783* [*Royal Swedish Theatre almanac for 1783*], reprinted as *Kongl. teatern 1782 och 1882* [*Royal Theatres in 1782 and 1882*] (Stockholm, 1882), pp. 25–6.

On 30 September last, the new Royal Opera House at Norrmalms Torg, for which the foundations were laid in the summer of 1775, opened for the first time. On the front towards the square are carved in marble the words: GUSTAVUS III. Patriis Musis. M.DCC.LXXXII. The design and the supervision of the construction of the whole building, as well as the fitting-out of the auditorium and the boxes, were commissioned to Senior Intendant and Commander of the Royal Order of the North Star Baron Adlercrantz [*sic*].[1] The auditorium, one of the most beautiful in Europe, contains four tiers of boxes, nineteen in each tier except the first, which has only twelve, allowing for the large Royal box in the centre. The parterre can comfortably accommodate 300 persons, and on either side there is a so-called parterre noble. The chief source of lighting in the auditorium is an impressive crystal chandelier with some forty light fittings, which is hoisted up at the beginning of the performance and lowered at the end. The stage itself, with the many machines and works of art it contains, and which in respect of both solid and artistic composition is a special credit to the insight of its originator, was built by Mr Johan Schef,[2] Swedish and regular stage mechanic to the Court entertainments. From the footlights to the very back of the stage, the stage is 40 alen [=roughly 80 ft.] deep, and the forestage is 18 wide. The side towards the Arsenal yard contains all the actors' dressing-rooms, two rehearsal rooms, and a large foyer which could, to follow foreign examples, be decorated with the busts or portraits of those who have made special contributions to the beginnings and development of the Swedish national theatre. Of the rooms facing the square itself, the entire ground floor is to be fitted out on His Majesty's separate account; the first floor will provide lodgings for the Directors of the royal entertainments.

The inauguration of this new opera theatre took place in the presence of Their Majesties and the Royal Family at a performance of the opera *Cora and Alonzo.*[3] The high officials of the realm, our foreign representatives and heads of domestic ministries, the estates of the realm, and the citizens of Stockholm were invited on this occasion. The excellent taste, both in singing and in acting, with which this work was performed by the actors, supported by a numerous and well-conducted orchestra, the richness of the costumes and splendour of the sets which, despite being intermingled with earthquakes and fire-spouting mountains, were quickly and neatly presented; in a word, the noble and beautiful unity revealed everywhere, showed the height of perfection to which our national productions have attained.

1 Carl Fredrik Adelcrantz (1716–96) had rich experience of royal theatre architecture, with the Ulriksdal and Drottningholm theatres and the fitting-out of the older Gripsholm theatre to his credit by the time he began work on the new opera house. It was generally regarded as a thing of beauty, and the strong wish many felt to let it remain a joy forever was one of the main reasons why plans for a new opera house were so slow in maturing a century later.

2 Johan Schef (1740–97) served as chief mechanic from 1779 until the year he died, and was promoted to Director in 1788. He also adapted and fitted out the Arsenal for use as the Dramatic Theatre.

3 *Cora and Alonzo* is a three-act opera with a libretto by Gudmund Göran Adlerbeth (1751–1818) to music by Johann Gottlieb Naumann, the musical director at Dresden occasionally called to Stockholm by the King.

*The inception of censorship*

## 43 Cabinet protocol concerning censorship, 12 May 1785

Cons. och Cabinetts Protocollen [Council and Cabinet protocols] for 12 May 1785, in Oscar Levertin: 'Teater och drama under Gustaf III' ['Theatre and drama under Gustaf III'] in *Samlade skrifter* [*Collected works*], vol. 17 (Stockholm: A. Bonnier, 1911) p. 197.

[The theatrical 'censors' are to see to it] that nothing is introduced which is contrary to religion, the mode of government, the King's highness, respect for the nobility, the respect due to the other estates and offices, or which might diminish these among an easily misled public, nor anything indecent, contrary to accepted custom or the good name and reputation of individual people, and that the purity of the language is promoted in every possible way.

*A censor at work*

Johan Henrik Kellgren (1751–95) was a major literary figure, poet, journalist, essayist, drama critic and general champion of ideas and enlightenment. He was appointed one of the theatre censors in 1785, and here we see him in action on a play by 'a visiting foreigner' (Dahlgren [1866], p. 139), possibly J.F. Soret, who worked as a translator at the Portuguese Embassy in Stockholm.

## 44 J.H. Kellgren's report censoring a foreign play, 30 March 1793

Gösta M. Bergman and Niklas Brunius (eds.): *Dramaten 175 år. Studier i svensk scenkonst* [*175 Years of the Dramatic Theatre. Studies in Swedish scenic art*] (Stockholm: P.A. Norstedt & söner, 1963), p. 73, note 31.

I have read through the comedy *The Betrayed Originals* and found nothing contrary to the rules in it. I cannot, however, refrain from remarking that however reconcilable with good theatrical morality it has always been for a girl to run away from a mean father whom her lover deceives, it has also always been the custom for a censor to describe such behaviour if not as reprehensible then at any rate as bold, not an example to be followed, forgivable only because of need and the blindness of passion, preceded by disrepute and followed by remorse. As far as I can recall, the present play is the first in our theatre in which those contracted show not the slightest grimace of scruple before the deed or agonies of conscience afterwards. This could easily be put right, and the innocent country girl would probably not lose by being somewhat less shameless. – I have found one or two expressions in Act II scene 1 in need of correction.

*Ristell's private theatre*

The first step towards formally establishing a dramatic theatre in addition to the Opera was taken when Adolf Fredrik Ristell (1744–1829) ventured to run a theatre as his own private enterprise. In addition to being Librarian at Drottningholm Palace, Ristell was a productive translator and adapter of plays.

## 45 Gustaf III grants a privilege to A.F. Ristell, 25 March 1787

Bergman and Brunius (1963), p. 11.

As His Royal Majesty has most graciously consented that for the cultivation of the language and the encouragement of knowledge Swedish tragedies and comedies may be performed at the Smaller Royal Theatre, on terms which offer a broad and profitable field for dramatic authors, the Directors of His Majesty's Court Music and Entertainments have given thought to the realization of such a facility, and do hereby give to Royal Librarian *Adolf Fredrik Ristell* the right, for six years reckoned from 15 April this year, to administer this theatre as entrepreneur, at his own expense and risk and for his own profit, on the following conditions: [. . .]

*Ristell goes bankrupt*

Svenska Dramatiska Teatern opened on 2 June 1787 with a Ristell adaptation, *The Visiting Hour* [*Visit-timmen*], of a comedy by Poinsinnet called *Le Cercle, ou La Soirée à la mode*. But Ristell's venture lasted barely one season. He went bankrupt. He tells some of the sad story in a document appended to his bankruptcy petition, from which this passage is taken. His petition also included a list of the costumes worn in *Visit-timmen*.

## 46 Ristell's bankruptcy petition, 24 April 1788

Bergman and Brunius (1963), pp. 14–15.

Your Excellency and the noble Magistracy will be pleased to conclude from the appended bills that almost all the debt I have incurred stems from the necessary expenses of establishing the theatre. Permit me to compare this enterprise with the equipping of a mill or factory, when one cannot expect to recoup one's expenditure in a single year. In such a short time merely to have started it working to capacity, so that it can later make the earnings calculated for it, is itself an achievement. All that was needed was better housekeeping, which to begin with was impossible. One cannot recognize talents before they have appeared; and one needs time to find out where savings can be made. It was my intention during this present month of May, when most of my contracts terminated, to dismiss all the less skilful people who had so far been a burden to me; and since I was sufficiently occupied supervising and arranging plays, I intended to assign to Mr Tellerstedt and Mr Schylander[1] the task of managing all possible economies, with which they had promised their assistance. My misfortune had already been foreshadowed in the impossibility to begin with of putting on constantly new plays, particularly because most of the actors were still engaged at the Opera and were thus unable, however industrious they might be, to give me all their time; besides, among the plays which could be provided to begin with, only very few were fortunate enough to win much applause; for which reasons I was not only without any income last summer and especially in the last winter season, but also lost on my expenditure. I had every reason to hope that this would be compensated for in the future, but when the fourth quarter's pay was due to some of the actors, and I lacked the means, they reserved the right to have their claims met in full out of the receipts. [. . .]

[1] Carl Gabriel Schylander (1748–1811) was an actor with the Royal Theatre from 1788 to his death, having attracted attention as an actor earlier, perhaps under Stenborg.
Diedrich Tellerstedt (1751–93) served as an opera singer and actor from 1773 until his death.

## 47 Ristell's costume inventory, 1788

'Acta uti Concourstvisten emellan Kongl. Bibliothekarien Adolph Friedrich Ristell och samteliga dess Borgenarer' ['Records of the correspondence between the Royal Librarian A.F. Ristell and all his creditors'] in Bergman and Brunius (1963), p. 71, note 8.

List of costumes in my store for the Swedish theatre at the Smaller Royal Theatre.

For *Mr de Broen*,[1] of fine cloth – A blue uniform coat, with mostly genuine braid, and yellow silk serge waistcoat.
*Tellerstedt*[2] – grey court suit with full-skirted coat and waistband.
*Uttini*[3] – High Court uniform, whole silk serge cloth with taffeta cloak and waistband.
*Ahlgren*[4] – High Court jacket and breeches of silk serge.
*Mrs Sundmark*[5] – English costume of gase d'Italie with blue silk kirtle.
*Mlle Thomas*[6] – Yellow shot taffeta dress.
*Mlle Hollberg*[7] – Purple silk dress.
*Mlle Ryberg*[8] – An English taffeta dress.
*Mlle Frank*[9] – Pale blue taffeta costume.

[1] Abraham Isaaksson de Broen (1758–1804), a leading actor of the time, also in opera despite a poor voice. With the Royal Theatres from 1781 to 1804. He established the Djurgårds Theatre in 1801, on a privilege granted to him and his wife and children. Being outside the Stockholm city limits, it was not subject to the royal theatre monopoly decreed in 1798, and was later to be a source of activities leading to the final breach of that monopoly.
[2] For Tellerstedt, see **46**, note 1.
[3] Carlo Casparo Simone Uttini (1753–1808), born in Italy, joined the Royal Theatre in 1773 as a dancer, acting debut 1776, with the Opera to 1779, with the Dramatic Theatre 1788–1808, was one of its 'ordningsmänn' (orderlies) 1798–1808?.
[4] Johan Samuel Ahlgren (1764–1816), with the Dramatic Theatre 1788–1815; one of its 'orderlies' with Uttini and two others, and again from 1812 to 1816.
[5] Mrs Sundmark was with the Dramatic Theatre 1788; reputed to have been a good actress.
[6] Mlle Thomas was with the Dramatic Theatre from 1788; of French origin, she may have left Sweden in the 1790s.

[7] Anna Brita Hollberg, in the Opera chorus 1784–7, with the Dramatic Theatre 1788–9? Also referred to as Holmberg.

[8] Mlle Ryberg has proven to be untraceable.

[9] Maria Christina Franck (from 1808 Mrs Ruckman) (1769–1847), with the Opera and Dramatic Theatre 1788–1818, elocution teacher at the school of acting 1819–23.

### *Ristell's actors form a royal company*

Following Ristell's bankruptcy (he did not even get what he had hoped for the costumes), some members of the acting company banded together to form an association to carry on performances at their own risk, playing for shares of any profits. They now became a royal company, organized under the Court entertainments and subject (reluctantly) to Regulations.

King Gustaf's interest in placing Swedish drama on a sound footing was part of a desire to improve Swedish culture generally and literature in Swedish in particular. The passage below taken from the 1789 regulations may have been an inducement to would-be dramatists.

## 48 Regulations for the Royal Dramatic Company, 1789

Sections 2 and 3 of chapter 5 of the 1789 Regulations, in Bergman and Brunius (1963), p. 73.

The author of the play has a right, regardless of distinctions of employment or rank among actors and actresses, to distribute the parts to whom he pleases. The right also applies to those who are to double in his play, and lasts until it has been performed nineteen times. When the parts are being read, the author may change the casting if he wishes, but not after that day except with the consent of the actors or the permission of the Directors. Should the author be anonymous, or prefer not to undertake the casting, the right belongs to the theatre Directors. For refusing a part, for whatever reason, or giving it up, the penalty is five Rd.

When copies have been made of all parts in a play, they shall promptly be handed out to the actors, who shall be summoned the following day to read the parts from the script in the presence of the author. Should any actor or actress be previously employed with other reading, the author may choose whether to let his play wait or give the same part to someone available. After the reading, the time appointed for the first rehearsal shall be noted on each part, being for larger works after half the reading time allowed for the longest part has elapsed, at which time half the play should have been learned for rehearsal. At the end of the full reading time, the whole play shall be rehearsed. Short plays will not be rehearsed until they have been learned in their entirety. The penalty for failure to learn half one's part by the first rehearsal, and one's whole part by the second, is two and four Rd respectively. These rehearsals may not for any reason be postponed more than one day.

*Clewberg's reports to the king*

A.N. Clewberg (1754–1821) was made a peer in 1789, taking the name Edelcrantz; he served as Senior Director of the Royal Theatre from 1804 to 1810. His frequent reports to the King are a major source for theatre history. Document **49** comes from his account, dated 7 August 1789, of Royal Theatre affairs in June and July, especially relating to the effect of the new Regulations. Document **50** is another of Clewberg's communications on theatre matters to the busily campaigning King which received royal marginal comments in reply.

## 49 A.N. Clewberg describes how the actors choose plays and react to the regulations, June–July 1789

Eugene Lewenhaupt: *Bref rörande teatern under Gustaf III* [*Letters concerning the theatre under Gustaf III*] (Stockholm: Akademisk boktryckeriet, 1894), pp. 80–3.

To celebrate the memory of the 17th of July last year, an entertainment was submitted by Bellman[1] which only serves to prove the witty author's unsuitability for the theatre. The only thing of note in that connection was the way in which the Dramatic Areopagus judges the value of a play. After it had been read to them in silence and listened to with all possible attention, some decided whether or not to accept it by counting odds or evens on their coat buttons, others by reckoning yea and nay on their fingers, and since they began with yea and the number of their fingers was found to be even, the work could only be found wanting. Mrs Marcadet[2] voted nay, for the good reason that the play was wicked. Mrs Haeffner[3] yea because everybody else rejected it. Debroen,[4] protector of both the author and the piece, went to all the trouble in the world to get it accepted. He might even have succeeded had it not been for a new, unforeseen and insurmountable obstacle. Wig-maker Goetz declared that since, as he had heard, a large wig was required in the new piece, and the only serviceable one had been confiscated from his journeymen by the police, he could see no way in which the play could be put on. His contribution was given due consideration, and since the wig was indeed found to be its main character, the decision to refuse the play was upheld.

The new regulations were read out at the beginning of the current quarter, and have already been observed with the utmost strictness for a month. When they had been read, Mrs Remi[5] got to her feet and said with her usual naïveté: I'll never sign that. Whereto her comrades replied: the Directors don't want us to sign it, only to obey it.

Generally they have been found quite strict, and the Theatre indeed cannot help but find a law severe and impossible to observe which obliges actors to obey and actresses to keep silent. [Clewberg goes on to describe the discontent with the new regulation concerning the so-called 'flitpenningar', literally 'industry money', i.e. pay per performance, and what he had done to cool hot heads. He then continues:]

The procedure has nevertheless proved its usefulness from the first. According to the regulations, parts which authors have not assigned must promptly be doubled, which often gives rise to quarrels between those who have undertaken to double the same parts, quarrels which cannot be settled without a vote and which come before the Directors. When the repertoire is being chosen, each and every one eagerly promotes the plays in which he performs, and in performances not even the slightest part is neglected, all thanks to performance pay. Mrs Marcadet most willingly doubles for Mlle Löv,[6] and Mlle Löv most willingly for Mlle Neumann, all out of greed for performance pay. That at least has been the initial effect of this device, which seems at once to increase the desire to work and to protect the health from minor ailments.

[1] Carl Michael Bellman (1740–95) was the leading verse- and song-writer of the age. His best-loved and still popular sets of songs are sung by, to and about characters who come so alive that they are virtually parts of Swedish mythology; though 'neo-classical', he combined feeling and down-to-earth realism, and Holberg is believed to have learned much from him.

[2] Marie Louise Marcadet, whose parents had been with the French acting company, was with the Royal Theatre from 1778 to 1795.

[3] Gertrude Elisabeth Haeffner (1771–1850) was with the opera and the dramatic theatre 1788–1810?

[4] See 47, note 1

[5] Louise Saint-Remy was the daughter of the Opera's wig-maker Louis Götz.

[6] Fredrika Löf (Jeannette Fredrique Loven) (1762–1813) was the leading female star, reputed to be somewhat amorous and slow at learning her parts, possibly because she could not read.

## 50 Clewberg's theatrical memoranda with the King's commentary, 4 September 1789

Lewenhaupt (1894), pp. 100–6.

Humble Pro memoria

I

Among the translations received by the Dramatic Theatre after the implementation of the new Regulations, some, although skilfully done, have nevertheless proved impossible to use because of an unsuitable choice of originals. The Theatre therefore ventures humbly to hope that he who graciously permitted it to make use of masterpieces in foreign languages, and to please whom is the main purpose of the Theatre's work, would be pleased himself to name and point out some of the

plays the translation and performance of which would most perfectly fulfil that purpose.
[The King's marginal comment]

With Le repertoire drammatique [*sic*] and le dictionnaire des Theatres out of reach, and with my head full of bombs, cannons, raids,[1] sloops-of-war, galleys and what is worse forage and bread, it is impossible for me to recall the plays which I thought could stand translation without detracting from the primary objective, the creation of a truly Swedish theatre. What I do remember is that [I][2] thought that what the performances most needed was one-act plays and that it was in fact for them that permission to translate had been given. If one of the 18[3] who are so involved in the fate of the theatre is considering translating some plays of that kind I shall designate which ones I find most worthy of the light of day. Note that a verse play must be translated into verse.

[. . .]

3

The Directors wish also humbly to submit to His Majesty the Theatre's request that Sundays and days of performance and rehearsal not be counted as reading time for new plays. The Directors have not ventured to reply; for although it seems reasonable to except Sundays, with three performances a week the substraction of rehearsal and performance days as well could mean that no day at all was left for reading.
[King]

where performance days are concerned this appears reasonable but no other exceptions are permitted.

4

So as not to err out of ignorance of their duties, the members of the company have requested that the Regulations be printed. If Your Majesty is most graciously pleased to consent, it should only be necessary to print a small number of copies to meet the Theatre's own needs.
[King]

I think the Regulations should be written on a board set up in their assembly room where each and everyone concerned can read them and those whom they do not concern need not meddle with them, which would certainly happen if they were printed.

[. . .]

6

Having considered the doubling of all parts in accordance with the regulation, the company has submitted to the Directors a proposal for doubling in the plays on the list which is humbly attached.
[King]

I have altered the assignment of only two parts.

7

De Broen claims that under the old regulations, which forbid translations, he had already obtained Your Majesty's special gracious leave to perform *The School for Scandal.*[4] In that connection he claims the 3rd, 9th and 19th performance for his work, which is what the same regulations allow for original work; notwithstanding that under the new ones, under which the play is to be performed, he has only the right to the 19th.

[King]

If de Broen is certain that the piece will succeed, this can be permitted although the law cannot have retroactive effect. This looks to me like selling the pelt before the bear has been shot.

8

Since Mme Alix[5] is engaged only until this coming Easter, the Directors await Your Majesty's most gracious command as to whether it should be extended or a new dancer should be engaged in her place.

[King]

If one can get a better, good, one can no doubt get a prettier; as long as we don't lose Bournonville,[5] best not to seem too eager to keep her perhaps one can keep her on better terms.

9

The Governor has demanded of the Theatre Directors a list of all persons engaged at the Royal Theatre, and of their wages, in view of the forthcoming taxation. The Directors fail to see with what right those concerned undertake to tax the wages which by Your Majesty's grace are paid out of your own privy purse; but the Directors believe that they should not without Your Majesty's express command disclose the Theatre's payroll, especially since the new Decree relating to appropriations (notwithstanding what is established in item 6 of the first paragraph of its Article 2 concerning comedians and actors) in the first item of paragraph 2 of Article 6 requires the tax men only to note such wages, pensions or support as anyone receives from the *crown*, besides which the former Board of Directors for the Theatre in a similar case refused to present such a payroll. Since this is a very weighty matter for the Theatre, because several persons would have to pay 200 Rd in income tax alone and the total for the Theatre would amount to over 4,000 Rd annually, the Directors humbly await Your Majesty's gracious command.

[King]

The Directors receive money from me and my privy purse and the answer should be that on His Majesty's gracious command no account can be made for the means which belong to His Majesty alone and even less for the sums His Majesty gives to and receives of those who are in his service alone.

10

Seeing that Mrs Marcadet herself reopened negotiations for her engagement, I have after several conversations persuaded her to limit her claims to the following conditions for a five-year period:

1 Begs to be excused all meetings, except when the repertoire is being settled.
[King] agreed.

2 As a foreigner and less capable of the Swedish language, not to be obliged to learn forty lines a day.
[King] refused.

3 To keep the wages she had before at the Opera.
[King] agreed and perform there as before.

4 To receive 1,200 Rd in a lump sum at the French and Dramatic Theatres regardless of shares. Since her wages at the French theatre are 600 and her $\frac{9}{4}$ at the Dramatic Theatre about 500 a year, the requested increase should only amount to 100 Rd, for which she

5 Promises to instruct such young members of the company as might be entrusted to her in acting, as far as her time permits.
[King]
This can be permitted only if some means should be found of not infringing the Regulations and it should not serve as a precedent for others.

The increase seems modest, especially seeing that the Directors would in effect engage her more reasonably than hitherto if the Theatre's income in calmer times should increase and her $\frac{9}{4}$ should exceed 600 Rd; but the purpose of varying wages with the variation in shares would not then be achieved.

Her husband is content to serve as leading dancer at the Opera for his former wages (1,200 Rd); but as store keeper and ballet master at the Dramatic Theatre, in which capacities he must be employed but has not been engaged, he requests some small consideration, on which the Directors hope to agree with him without any difficulty.
[King]
agree but as he will probably not be able to dance much longer it seems to me that the pay for all his services should be included in the 1,200 Rd he receives but leave the Directors free hand in this.
[. . .]

12

With reference to books and plays needed for both the Dramatic and the other Theatres, I most humbly request gracious leave, in the presence of Lifkn.[6] Bussau or some other person, to visit the Royal Library at the Palace. The Åbo Librarian guarantees most humbly that the Theatre Director will not create any confusion there.[7]

Stockholm the 4th of September 1789.

Most humbly
A.N. Edelcrantz[7]

[King]
I hope that none of Royal Secretary Edelcrantz's books have gone astray.

The Librarian of Åbo has permission to enter Stockholm's Library and is desired to send me (1) Le Repertoire dramatique (2) Oeuvres de Detouches [*sic*] 3 Oeuvre de M. foix [*sic*].

NB I have the first volume, should any books have arrived from Paris I desire such new ones as are either Historical or Dramatic but no Political and much less Gallo-Democratic ones.

Artsiö the 11th of September 1789.

Gustaf

Should any chests of such books have arrived in my absence I desire a list of them.

1 In the original, 'Dessenter', probably the King's version of *descentes*, adding a Swedish plural ending to a word from French, his first language.
2 Presumably omitted in MS and added editorially in the Swedish source.
3 Eighteen, the standard number of Academicians.
4 De Broen was notoriously a quarrelsome hothead. One of the many rows he created concerned Sheridan's play, which his wife had translated, and which was subsequently referred to among theatre people as 'my wife's play'.
5 Mme Alix de la Fay, prima ballerina 1782–98, was born Julie Bournonville. Her brother Antoine Bournonville (1760–1843) was a leading male dancer 1782–95; though he left Stockholm in 1792, he retained his Opera engagement and returned from time to time for guest performances. He was ballet-master at the Royal Theatre in Copenhagen from 1816 to 1823, and the father of the renowned Danish dancer and ballet-master August Bournonville, who was to function as Stage Director in Stockholm from 1861 to 1864.
6 Presumably 'Lifknekt', from the German *Leibknecht* or Equerry.
7 One and the same person. Clewberg had been appointed Åbo University Librarian on 15 March 1780, and took the name Edelcrantz when made a peer in 1789.

### *Original Swedish plays vs translations*

Although much of what was performed was, if not translation, then at least close imitation or 'adaptation', King Gustaf held out stubbornly in principle against dramatic imports. But this protectionist policy finally had to be abandoned.

## 51 Censor Kellgren favours translated plays, 6 June 1790

J.H. Kellgren, *Stockholms Posten* [*The Stockholm Post*] (6 June 1790) in Bergman and Brunius (1963), p. 21.

Among the measures adopted for the continuation of the Dramatic Theatre, one of the most necessary was to permit the performance of translations. The public, merely seeking maximum enjoyment, as the company seeks maximum profit; our national literature, which does not benefit from the promotion of excellence alone, but almost as much from the absence of the inadequate: all stand to gain. We shall no longer be obliged to see these immature, incoherent and styleless attempts, ignorant of the art of the theatre and with no other comedy than low buffoonery, unsuitable sallies, indecent equivocations, trivial sayings, and defamatory imitations of known people in dress and speech. Original works will be absent no longer than it takes Genius to produce them; and the latter will always be more highly honoured because it creates its own subjects. In the meantime, the pleasure of the enlightened public will not be diminished, taste will become more certain, insights will be more quickly gained, through translations of the masterpieces of foreign drama. But to obtain the best possible selection and execution of these may require greater encouragement than the modest emoluments offered for translated plays in the regulations of the Dramatic company.

## II THE ROYAL MONOPOLY, 1790–1810

### *Gustav IV Adolf imposes a new order*

Despite the lack of royal encouragement, Stenborg had managed to keep a theatrical enterprise running – and competing with the royal theatres – in various locations. But the new King, Gustav IV Adolf (1778–1837), who succeeded his father Gustaf III in 1792, was to prove even less helpful. (He was deposed in 1809).

An addition to the new King's letter of 3 November 1798 which paid off Stenborg's debt and withdrew the Royal privilege effectively closed Komiska teatern from April 1799. The importance of this addition lies in the fact that it established a royal theatre monopoly within the city limits which was to last over forty years.

## 52 Gustav IV Adolf establishes a royal monopoly, 3 November 1798

Georg Nordensvan: *Svensk teater* [*Swedish theatre*], vol. 1 (Stockholm: Albert Bonnier, 1917–18), p. 74.

His Majesty also wishes to have it hereby ordained, that henceforth no establishments for private individuals' entertainments shall exist or be permitted in Stockholm, saving only that the theatres supported out of His Majesty's privy purse and subordinate to His Majesty's Directors of Court Entertainments shall be open to the capital's general public.

*The demolition of the Royal Opera is ordered*

The King soon went further, requiring the scene of his father's murder to be demolished, but a combination of delaying tactics by the Board, the use of the building as a military hospital, and political upheaval prevented the order from being carried out. From 1809, the opera house had eight decades of constant use ahead of it.

## 53 Gustav IV Adolf dissolves the Royal Opera, 27 September 1806

Nils Personne: *Svenska teatern* [*The Swedish theatre*], vol. 2 (Stockholm: Wahlström & Widstrand, 1913–27), pp. 192–3.

With a view to considerable savings for His Majesty's privy purse, the Large opera shall be completely suspended and regarded as dissolved with immediate effect. The suspension shall not however extend to the cessation of the small so-called operettas, which have as a rule only been performed at the Smaller theatre, which can manage without choruses and ballets and several of whose performers do not really belong to or serve with the Large opera. Those members of the company whose contracts have expired shall have six months' pay; and those who under normal circumstances would be regarded as entitled to pensions must present their claims, no pensions however to exceed 333 Rd 16 sk.b:ko [skillings banko].

## 54 Hjortsberg provides a retrospective of the Gustavian period[1]

Appendix 1 to Niklas Brunius, '"Alltid Ny och Alltid Densamma": Studier i Lars Hjortsbergs Spelstil' ['"Ever New and Ever the Same": studies in Lars Hjortsberg's acting style'] in Bergman and Brunius (1963), pp. 143–4.

At the end of the year 1778 I began to serve at the Royal Opera and was from the start paid 50 [Rd banco], which was of course rather to be regarded as a gift than as wages for the service to be expected from a six-year-old child. Nevertheless, when two years later I was also employed in the French company,[2] this pay was increased to 66 [Rd and] 32 skillings (which I still receive and which according to the written contract of 1 September 1807 from the Royal Directors was retained for me on the express condition that I should serve at the operetta theatre[3] for extra pay). On these terms I continued at both theatres until Royal Librarian Ristell established his theatre in 1787, where I was engaged and was fortunate enough, at an entertainment given the same year at Kiersö on the Drottningholm road, to please King Gustaf of most blessed memory, who then promised to provide for me. My boundless respect for this never-to-be-sufficiently lamented monarch laid it upon me to make myself somehow worthy of his grace. My willingness to study, my good memory, and the excellent advice and instruction I was so lucky as to receive from Mr Monvel were reasons why I was able to make some progress in this art. In 1789 the King selected me for special service as chamber lackey or as it was then called Garçon Bleu, but since he soon found me unsuited to the role of personal servant, he entrusted to me the key to and the care of the library he had bought from Count Creutz, and appointed me to serve as lector during Mr Des Roches's illness. My service at the Dramatic and French theatres continued uninterrupted until in 1790 I was present at the battle of Swenskund, and received from the King the medal struck to commemorate that occasion. At the end of the war I returned to Sweden and resumed my former employment, until I accompanied the King in 1791 on his journey to Aachen and Spa, etc. I also attended the Riksdag in Gefle, and was constantly at the King's side. In short, I was looking forward to the happiest future, when suddenly the most dreadful murder bereft me of my most worshipped benefactor, and my rising sun vanished. I then sought to quit my fatherland but was not discharged but required to fulfil my contract which lasted until 1799. In the meantime I had married, begot several children, and could no longer think of going abroad, so I renewed my engagement under Baron Hamilton[4] for a further ten years, on condition of a pension when I left the theatre or in case some accident should befall me in the meantime. I had been treasurer since 1796 and was appointed orderly in 1799, in which capacity I served for the duration of my contract. The King's Regulations state that where pensions are concerned, those who have been theatre officials or officers may reckon twice their years of service, so that I have now served forty-four years, and have not a skilling in income other than the 66RB 32S which I do not know whether I shall be allowed to keep, the 100RB I receive in respect of my service with King Gustaf, and 55RB 26S 8r ['rundstyke', popular name for a small copper coin] which is compensation for the rooms I lived in at the Royal Palace and which were taken away from me at the King's death, and 50RB in lieu of fodder for a horse, which I do not think can count as a theatre pension; however that may be, 272RB 10S 8r is not sufficient to support a household of eleven persons.

1 Any list of Sweden's three or four very greatest actors contains the name Lars Hjortsberg (1772–1843). This document was attached to an application for a pension about 1810.

2 Jacques Marie Boutet (1745–1812), known as Monvel, a French actor and manager, was called to Stockholm with his excellent company in 1781. This is not the paradox or sign of defeat it may seem in view of the fact that one of Gustaf III's first moves had been to dismiss a French company from the court theatres; it was a deliberate and by all accounts successful step aimed at training the Swedish Royal Theatre actors, by precept and example.

3 The operetta theatre was the alternative proposed by King Gustav IV Adolf when he ordered the closing of the Opera.

4 Baron Jonne Hugo Hamilton (1752–1805) was Theatre Director from 1798 to 1804, and was probably less a failure in that capacity than many anecdotes make him out to have been.

*The Theatre Director defames his predecessors*

Bernhard von Beskow (1796–1868) was a dramatist and Academician in addition to holding government and Court posts. Having been persuaded in 1831 to take over an indebted institution for which he is said to have done his best in vain, he served as Director for only a little over a year. In his memoirs he relates anecdotes about two of his turn-of-the-century predecessors.

## 55 Unflattering portraits of the directors of the theatre in the 1790s

Bernhard von Beskow: *Lefnadsminnen* [*Memoirs of his life*] (Stockholm: Norstedt, 1870), pp. 162–3.

No auspicious star shone on the art of the stage under Gustav IV Adolf, who was no friend of pleasures in general, and least of all of the theatrical. He, too, appointed a pair of theatre directors, who were, like him, thoroughly honest and respectable men, but about as much judges of art as he was a statesman. Baron Hugo Hamilton,[1] the Lord Chamberlain, known as 'French Hamilton', had in fact himself been a good party actor in comedies, but only in French and liked nothing else. The story goes that at a rehearsal of Adlerbeth's[1] *Ingiald Illråda*, he was sitting on the stage with the author. When Ragnar gave Ingiald his mortal wound, he leaped up and shouted: 'Où est donc le mortal wound? Is that how you present something to your King? Put *le mortal wound* on a cushion, bow, and say: Ingiald! I give you the mortal wound.' – *Si non è vero, è ben trovato.* – His respect for Frenchmen and for the Fersen family,[1] who possessed French culture, led him to divide the human race into three classes, the French, the Fersens, and the mob. He confined his social life to Blasieholm where the Fersens lived. and which he called *Ile de France*. For the rest he was amiable, kind, popular and not without a certain original wit. He died of a boil he cut shaving. – The other high priest of the song-goddesses' temple was Baron Rålamb[1], Master of the King's Horse, excellent horseman, expert tournament rider, first among the charioteers at Brunnsviken, unwearying at a good table, but as utter a stranger to the game of Melpomene and Thalia as he was to politics. He decided one day to place both the Steinmüller brothers,[2] famous waldhorn players, under arrest, which incidentally was quite usual at the time for negligence in the theatre's service. When they got out, they attended on their noble director to learn why they had been sent to högvakten (the prison for anyone pertaining to the Court, which included the theatre and the orchestra). 'Because', replied the director, 'I saw you not blowing during Mrs Müller's[3] aria the other day.' 'But we had a rest then,' rejoined the waldhornists. 'The King pays you to blow, not to have rests!' exclaimed the wrathful director.

[1] The dates of the persons mentioned are: Baron Hugo Hamilton (1752–1805), Director 1798–1804. Gudmund Göran Adlerbeth (1751–1818), dramatist, Academician, Minister, whose *Ingiald Illråda* was first performed in 1799. Count Carl Reinhold von Fersen (1716–86), Director 1780–86. Baron Claes Rålamb (1750–1826), Director 1792–98.

[2] Wilhelm and Johann Steinmüller were attached to the Royal Theatre from 1784 to 1798 and 1808 respectively.

[3] Carolina Fredrika Müller, née Halle (1755–1826), opera singer 1790–1806. In 1780 she ran away from her prima donna position at Copenhagen's Royal Theatre with the German violin virtuoso C.F. Müller, who had been banished precisely because it was believed that the theatre was losing her to him. They were both appointed to the Royal Theatre in Stockholm.

## III MANAGEMENT AND ACTING AT THE ROYAL THEATRES, 1796–1841

### *Nordforss as stage director*

Carl Gustaf Nordforss (1763–1832) combined a military career with service as assistant director to the dramatic theatre 1790–9 and to the opera 1799–1818, with responsibility for much of the practical management and stage direction. Historians are indebted to him for the records he kept and letters and memoranda he wrote. Morel de Chedeville's and Grétry's opera *La Caravane du Caïre* (1783) was performed on 1 November 1796 as a gala on the occasion of Gustav IV Adolf's accession; the directions below by Nordforss for Act II scene 6, the Bazaar scene, illustrate the formalities and symmetries of the traditional staging of the time.

## 56 Nordforss's stage directions for *The Caravan*, 1796

Gösta M. Bergman: *Regi och spelstil under Gustaf Lagerbjelkes tid vid Kungl.teatern* [*Directing and acting style during Gustaf Lagerbjelke's time at the Royal Theatre*] (Stockholm: P.A. Norstedt & söner, 1946), p. 201 (with Nordforss's sketch of the movements described).

As soon as the scene has been changed, one sees the ballet in a row at the back of the bazaar; behind them the choruses. The ballet promptly begins to dance; during the dance the choruses move down either side. The Tartars furthest to the front, stage left. – The Frenchwomen and the Italian woman should be at the head of the group, march down, and take up a position on the forestage, stage left. Immediately the ballet stops the Pasha's march begins. The march emerges from the upstage wing, stage right, crosses to stage left, then downstage and back across the forestage. The janissaries form up in one row along the stage right side. Three could be downstage of the Pasha's seat, and nine upstage, or six on either side. The Pasha takes his seat, surrounded by Tamorin, Husca and his courtiers. The Negroes furthest up. This is promptly followed by the presentation of the female slaves, in the following order. [. . .]

## 57 Contract of Gabriel Åman with the Royal Theatres, 2 January 1801

Nils Personne, vol. 5 (1913–27), pp. 113–14.

The Directors of His Royal Majesty's Entertainments hereby engage Mr Gabriel Åman[1] as an actor with the Opera and the Comic Opera to play all the parts given him by the Directors, it being incumbent upon him to perform his duties industriously and willingly and to take note of the theatre's Regulations and the orders of the Directors. For which in annual salary he will be paid a sum of two hundred and fifty Rd in current coin out of the Royal Opera's fund. Mr Åman shall also be an actor with the Royal Dramatic Theatre and serve there as often as the Directors shall command. For which he will receive in annual payment a six-eighths share and performance pay in accordance with the Regulations adopted for the last-named theatre. At the Opera and the Comic Opera, the Board will provide the actor Åman with the clothes, shoes, stockings, etc. necessary for his service. At the Dramatic Theatre he shall also be provided with clothes out of that theatre's stores; but at the latter theatre he should himself provide everything in the way of accessories. The Board hereby assures the actor Åman that he will continue to enjoy rises both in the salary he receives from the Royal Opera Fund and in his shares at the Dramatic Theatre when his increasing industry and skill merit further encouragement and reward. This contract shall be effective from the date below and for five and a half years, or to 1 July 1806. If it has not been terminated within six months of the expiry date, it shall remain in force until terminated by either of the parties. For the further assurance whereof, two identically worded copies have been written and signed, which was done at Stockholm the 2nd of January 1801.

Hugo Hamilton

[1] Gabriel Åman (1772–1834) was with the Royal Theatre from 1797 to 1828.

### *Lagerbjelke as Director*

It is significant that theatre historian Gösta M. Bergman has devoted an entire book to the relatively brief reign of Count Gustaf Lagerbjelke (1777–1837) as Royal Theatre Director (1823–7). His personal and cultural attachment to the Gustavian period did not blind him to contemporary developments, and he seems to have deserved his reputation as a man of the theatre and perhaps the only real *metteur en scène* in the first half of the nineteenth century. His eye for both detail and striking overall effect is shown in his stage directions for the closing scene of de Jouy's, Esménard's and Spontini's opera *Ferdinand Cortez*, first performed in 1826 in P.A. Granberg's translation.

## 58 Lagerbjelke's stage directions for *Ferdinand Cortez*, 1826

G.M. Bergman (1946), p. 220–2, with the diagram mentioned given on p. 221.

Now the emperor appears to call the sinking sun to witness the oath of reconciliation which he and Cortez are to swear to one another (during the closing bars of the music). The three united banners are raised vertical, all swords are drawn. Amazily, a short step in front of the emperor and Cortez, falls to his knees with his arms raised towards the banners; all the women of the ballet and the choruses do the same; the emperor holds up his sceptre, Cortez his field marshal's baton, Telasco his spear, Alvar, Moralez, the Spanish officers, the choruses and the ballet their swords, the musketeers raise their muskets in their right hands, the pikemen half lower their pikes; the sailors extend their pickaxes and stoop forward; the halberdiers half lower their arquebuses; the Mexican archers raise their bows into the air and stoop forward; likewise the troops with clubs, the courtiers slightly lower their staffs; the chorus and ballet women stretch their arms towards the nearest banner; the leading male ballet dancers and their quadrilles hold their swords out horizontally; the male chorus likewise. The entire movement is in unison and instantaneous. The moment it happens, the dance music should finish, and when the emperor's sceptre and Cortez's baton are stretched out, a fanfare sounds; when it ends, the curtain falls on the same tableau. The whole picture, difficult because of the large number of persons, the space, and the need for precise coordination, can be better conveyed by the diagram below. [. . .]

## 59 Stjernström[1] evaluates Lagerbjelke's influence

Edvard Stjernström: *Några ord om teatern* [*Some remarks on the theatre*] (Stockholm, 1870), pp. 16–17.

What has harmed our Royal Theatre in particular is the constant succession of Directors without responsibility. So long as the post is regarded only as a rung on the ladder to more distinguished service, it is left when debts increase or promotion at Court is offered, although the incumbent may just have been on the point of learning the ropes, and the theatre is again abandoned to whatever gusts the next change may bring.

Of all the Royal Theatre's Directors, none has known how to fill the post as well as Count Gustaf Lagerbjelke. He was also the only one who left the theatre without also leaving a debt. He adapted and translated many valuable works himself and selected and arranged the repertoire. He personally supervised every detail in the theatre; mechanics and scene-painters received their instructions from him, he supervised rehearsals himself and was the best instructor for the actors. Before every costume play the performers, young and old alike, had to pass before him in review to receive the individual instructions and comments that were needed. Performers who knew that errors which the audience missed were always noted and commented on by the Director, were thus obliged to get a grip on themselves, which could only be in the interests of the theatre.

[1] On and off stage, Edvard Stjernström (1816–77) played important parts in over three decades of Swedish theatre history: see Section IV.

*The burning of the Theatre*

One of Lagerbjelke's most remarkable administrative achievements was the rapid transition from the ashes of the Arsenal to business as usual at the Opera. He submitted his recommendations and plans within two days. There are plenty of dramatic accounts and sober reports of the fire on 24 November 1825: how the prompter's early suspicion of smoke was mistakenly allayed; how the duty pump attendant was absent from his post; how Hjortsberg prevented a panic by calming the audience, with the smoke rising around him from below the stage; how the actor Lindman[1] almost lost his life in an heroic but vain effort to rescue two young serving-girls from the doomed dressing-rooms; how King Carl Johan led the fire-fighting; and how hindsight showed how inadequate the building and fire precautions had been. Consider instead Nils Personne's sad account of an aspect of the disaster which relates closely to the present enterprise.

[1] Johan Gustaf Lindman (1789–1833), with the Royal Theatres 1812–33.

## 60a The fire at the theatre, 24 November 1825

Nils Personne, vol. 4 (1913–27), pp. 202–3.

Of the Theatre's stores and equipment nothing was saved. The costume collection suffered an irreplaceable loss, in that over one hundred complete full dress costumes in genuine gold and silver brocade, velvet and silk with precious embroideries, many of which had belonged to royal and noble persons, including the costume Gustaf III had worn at his engagement in Denmark and which had been used only once or twice on the stage, all burned up. All the sets and scenery for *Gustaf Vasa*, which had been requisitioned from the Large Theatre for *Joan of Montfaucon*[1] and the other big dramatic plays, were lost. Court Secretary Åbergsson and Mademoiselle Sara Strömstedt[2] lost all their own complete and in part costly theatre wardrobes. Theatre history, too, suffered a sensible loss, since the whole large collection of playbills from earlier times went up in smoke, and neither the Royal Library nor any other public or private institution owns one, nor has the Theatre any complete cast lists from those days. Only the valuable music library, which was stored on the lower floor of the southwest tower, the only part of the theatre building still standing after the fire, could be saved, together with most of the Dramatic Theatre's collection of manuscripts.

[1] *Gustav Wasa* (1800) and *Johanne von Montfaucon* (1799), both plays by August von Kotzebue.

[2] Gustaf Fredrik Åbergsson (1775–1852), with the Royal Theatres 1799–1820 and 1823–28; became orderly and stage manager, at which time he was also appointed court secretary.

Sara Fredrika Strömstedt (1795–1859), with the Royal Theatres from 1812 to 1834; married O.U. Torsslow [see **65**] in 1830, and went with him to Djurgårdsteatern and Mindre Teatern.

## 60b The Arsenal Theatre on fire

Lithograph from a painting by K.S. Graffman; reproduced in Nordensvan, vol. 1 (1917–18), p. 207.

*Jenny Lind comes to public attention*

The Swedish star who climbed highest in the international firmament was Johanna (Jenny) Lind (1820–87). She made a promising start very early in life; her name first appeared on a poster on 29 November 1830, when she played Angela in Pixérécourt's *The Polish Mines*. Of her performance in Kotzebue's one-act *The Testament* in 1831 and 1832, the reviewers had this to say:

## 61a Newspaper criticism of an early appearance of Jenny Lind, 1831

Quoted in N. Personne, vol. 5 (1913–27), pp. 138, 184–5.

(1) *Dagligt Allehanda*: Little Jenny Lind performs excellently, we are tenpted to say too excellently. Such boldness and confidence in theatrical action in a child, such absolute freedom from any embarrassment in a little girl, performing before an audience of 1,200 people, is an exception to nature's normal order. We hope, however, that it will not have any harmful influence on the moral development of the mature woman. One thing is certain, that if Jenny Lind continues to develop as she has begun, there is no doubt that she will become a simply outstanding support for our stage, the pillars of which unfortunately appear to be toppling one after another, threatening the entire collapse of the whole temple.
(2) *Heimdall*: Her acting reveals a quick understanding, a passion and a feeling far beyond her years, and seems to indicate an unusual talent for the theatre. Her most remarkable musicality, and an artistic education no less rare in one of her years, have also attracted a great deal of attention in the circles which have heard her, under the guidance of her teacher Mr Berg.[1] Her memory is as reliable as her ear is sure, and her perception as rapid as it is deep. One is at the same time awestruck and moved by her song. She stands the test of the most difficult solfeggios or the most intricate movements without losing her way, whatever direction her teacher's improvisations take, and follows his impulses with the liveliest expression, as if they were her own.

[1] Isak Albert Berg (1803–86) was Jenny Lind's singing teacher from 1831 when he began as the Royal Theatre's vocal instructor and singing-master at the theatre school (as well as to the Royal family); he served until 1850 and again in 1862–9.

## 61b Jenny Lind's fans in the proscenium of the Opera House, 1847

Lithograph from a drawing by Fritz von Dardel in *Teckningar ur dagens händelser* (1847); reproduced in Nordensvan, vol. 2 (1917–18), p. 64.

*The royal monopoly under siege*

The Royal Theatre's chronic financial and administrative troubles first came to the fore during Count Karl Johan Puke's directorship (1821–31). In 1828 he attempted to introduce new regulations, notably replacing shares with salaries; fourteen actors and actresses banded together and refused to sign contracts on the new terms. Among them was Olof Torsslow [see p. 94], whom Puke had found occasion to discipline the year before. Their various attempts to set up performances independently raised the issue of the monopoly. (Despite the monopoly, De Broen had obtained a privilege for himself and his descendants to run Djurgårdsteatern outside the Stockholm city limits, which proved to be a viable and popular competitor to the Royal Theatre.) However, the actors were soon back in Royal Theatre harness – working for shares. Finances did not improve under Puke, Beskow, or Westerstrand (Director, 1832–8).

The new constitution adopted on the deposition of Gustav IV Adolf included an Article 60 forbidding royal monopolies, yet no one had thought of applying this to the theatre situation. Retired Army Captain Anders Lindeberg (1789–1849), owner and editor of *Stockholms Posten* (1821–33) opened a campaign for a theatre of his own in 1828. Constantly rebuffed in his attempt to take over the management of the Royal Theatre, in March 1834 he published a letter charging the King, or his Ministers, with breach of the constitution in running a theatre monopoly. For this *lèse majesté* he had to be sentenced to death and he refused a pardon on any terms. Crafty Lagerbjelke suggested an amnesty and Lindeberg was set free. The charge against him was based on his manuscript letter; an objection to the printed version would have infringed freedom of the press!

## 2 Anders Lindeberg attacks the royal monopoly, 1834

Anders Lindeberg: *Några upplysingar rörande kungl. theatern* [*Some information on the Royal theatre*] (Stockholm, 1834), pp. 19–21.

I applied to His Majesty for the right to establish a theatre in the capital, most recently in an application submitted on 4 June 1832, which was refused by a Royal Decree of 13 October 1832, countersigned by Georg Ulfsparre. This gave me no real cause for complaint, since our Constitution gives the King the right to issue financial laws, and I know my obligation to obey a law that is in force however unreasonable and oppressive it may be. Had the King accordingly been pleased not to permit any theatre at all in the capital, no objection could have been raised to the lawfulness of the decision, but His Majesty has not done so. On the contrary, His Majesty himself owns such a theatre, and since the King to the advantage of the same forbids other theatrical establishments, and indeed even forbids persons in dire straits to save themselves from starvation or the beggar's staff by presenting small plays in any premises whatever, it becomes a monopoly, established *for the King's profit*, which is contrary to Section 60 of the Form of Government. It seems absolutely clear to me that but for this circumstance the

King, in view of the present condition of taste, education and manners in the kingdom, would not, or at least could not, deny the capital possession of a theatre. If the King again forbade this, no one could deny that His Majesty had at least the lawful right to do so, and that the Constitution had not been infringed. But as long as no such ban has been forthcoming, I am unable to see that the King in denying to others what he allows himself is acting in accordance with the Constitution.

It is consequently the above-mentioned monopoly which is the cause of my grief, and this is the reason why I am appealing against it to the Ombudsman for Justice.

I am not aware that the King at any time explicitly established a monopoly for this theatre; had that been the case, the counter-signer and those members of the Cabinet who failed to object to the decision would be liable to impeachment. The facts of the matter are nevertheless incontrovertible, which is what I hope to prove.

*The re-imposition of censorship*

## 63 Johan Gabriel Carlén[1] deplores the reintroduction of theatre censorship in 1834

Johan Gabriel Carlén: *Theatercensuren i Sverge* [*sic*]; *redogörelse för dess uppkomst och andegång* [*Theatrical censorship in Sweden*], (Stockholm: C.M. Thimgren, 1859), pp. 1, 7–9.

Ever since 1809, when the adoption of the freedom of the press ordinance explicitly did away with all prior examination of writings for publication, the hateful word 'censorship' had been as rarely pronounced in Swedish public life as it is strange to our tongue. The concept was clearly thought to conflict with *the clear and absolute prohibition against any prior hindrance to the publication of written matter imposed by the authorities*, of which the constitution mentioned assures every citizen.

So much the greater was the amazement when, during the Riksdag session of 1834, when the establishment of separate theatres was being debated, Count Otto August Cronhjelm quite abruptly and without occasion moved, 'for the prevention of self-rule', that *censorship* be introduced of plays to be performed at such theatres. Strangely enough, this motion, like the first matter, was dealt with by the finance committee; and it is equally remarkable that the committee in its first recommendation made no comment on it at all, merely recording that the question had been raised. [. . .] [When the committee after much toing and froing got round to supporting the motion, its fate among the four estates in the Riksdag was that the clergy (without a debate), the nobility and the agricultural estate approved it, only the bourgeois estate rejecting it.]

Despite these words and others like them spoken by members of the other estates, the majority vote resulted in the following submission to the King, dated 22 December:

'Seeing that the estates of the realm, in response to a motion, have found that censorship of the plays performed at independent theatres, both in the capital and in rural districts, would be both useful and needful, since the theatre can be regarded as an instrument of moral education and it would accordingly be appropriate to prevent such abuses as might be contrary to that purpose, therefore, and since it should not present any special difficulty to find persons, even in the smaller places in the kingdom, to whom the work involved in the necessary censorship and supervision can be entrusted, the estates of the realm hereby humbly ask Your Royal Majesty to issue a gracious edict to the effect: that plays may not be performed at independent theatres without prior examination and approval by the person or authority thereto empowered.' [. . .]

It goes without saying that the desire of the estates for censorship would not be left unsatisfied in high places; and it was satisfied by the circular of 7 March 1835. But who could have believed that the censorship would be assigned to such people, and with such arbitrary power, as provided in this circular! The power of censorship was placed in the hands of the *governor* in Stockholm and of the *King's officers*, who were also entitled, in the words of the circular, to 'delegate the same examining authority, in towns other than county governors' seats, on his own responsibility to the *mayor* or some *other person* whose education and reputation qualify him for the task'. No other provisions were issued.

Theatre managers were appalled, as were dramatists: appalled to find freedom's and wit's right of examination, which *they* alone, sometimes jointly, sometimes separately, had hitherto exercised so irreproachably and without provoking the slightest comment, was now so suddenly to be taken from them and instead entrusted . . . to whom? To the higher and lower instruments of the police and the crown! [. . .][2]

1 Johan Gabriel Carlén (1814–75), author of romances of Swedish life.

2 On 15 August 1842, the government issued an addendum to the circular, setting a time limit of one month for the censorship of plays from the date of their submission. Despite Carlén's booklet and other efforts, theatre censorship was not repealed until 1872.

### *The sorry season of 1834–5*

A second actors' rebellion over salaries occurred in January 1834, resulting in the departure of Olof Torsslow [see **65a**] and his wife and the dismissal of other senior members of the company in the interests of economy. With illnesses and accidents befalling other actors, the 1834–35 season gave the Directors little to look back on with any pleasure when drafting their report to the King dated 15 July 1835, and submitted according to the new 1834 Regulations. It was signed by Per Westerstrand (1785–1857), Director 1832–40; Carl David Forsberg (1793–1868), Assistant Director 1832–4, Financial Director 1836–40; and Lars Hjortsberg, who had risen to uncongenial heights as an artistic director (1834–6).

## 64 Directors of the Royal Theatre report on the effect of the cholera, 15 July 1835

Gustaf L. Torsslow, ed.: *Handlingar rörande kongl. teatern* [*Documents concerning the Royal theatre*], vol. 2, part 3 (Stockholm: D.M. Lublin, 1834–7), pp. 38–9.

Shortly before the new theatre[1] was to be opened towards the end of August last year, the cholera plague began its depredations in the western and southern regions of the Kingdom. Among its first victims was the actor Collberg,[2] a talented young artist who had taken over from the actor Torsslow and already successfully performed several of the main roles at the dramatic theatre. This unexpected loss, which was soon followed by several others, though of less importance, from among the artistic company, caused the most damaging disruption in the preparation of the planned works, on which it has continued to have a damaging influence throughout the season. The spread of the cholera to the capital, and the danger which promptly became associated with large gatherings of people, turned the attention of the public away from the theatre's performances to the sad scenes in individual homes. Two performances put on experimentally yielded such meagre results that the day's expenses could scarcely be covered by the box office take, and it was not until the beginning of October 1834, after almost six weeks of the usual playing season had been lost, that the Royal Theatre could restart an activity which had been paralysed by the general disaster.

[1] Not a new building, but formally a new establishment following reorganization, under Royal pressure for greater economy.

[2] Anders Collberg (1802–34), actor 1831–4.

### *The acting of Emelie Högqvist*

Olof Ulrik Torsslow (1801–81) is one of the very small handful of Swedish actors to have left reputations equal to Lars Hjortsberg's. He also figures largely in theatre histories as a pioneer and a rebel, having been a driving force in breaking the Royal Theatre monopoly in Stockholm. He was a director and manager, translator of plays, and a dramatist as well. A letter to Emelie or Emilie Högqvist (1812–46) links him with one of the most popular Swedish actresses of all time, whom he had seen as Ophelia.

## 65a Torsslow praises Emelie Högqvist as Ophelia, 29 April 1837

In entirety in Frans Hedberg: *Svenska skådespelare* [*Swedish actors*] (Stockholm: C.E. Fritze, 1884), pp. 41–5.

Mademoiselle! I am, as you know, married and lame;[1] you need consequently have no fear that my letter is intended to add to the volume of tender insinuations which you have no doubt already received *ad nauseam*. [. . .] My wife, who was at your benefit, gave a description on her return home which, I admit, aroused my curiosity; I wanted to see if it was true. Last Thursday I saw the performance of *Hamlet*, and *found* that it was true. Mlle Högqvist! heaven has blessed me with few talents. I cannot be a judge, but I can hold a conviction, and according to that conviction I must ask you to accept my wife's and my own sincere thanks for the pure pleasure we received from your performance in the fourth act. Had things not been as they are,[2] I should on your last exit have rushed up to the stage to give my feelings expression while they were warmest. This present unbosoming may be of some or no value to you; but I present it, for I love the theatre and talent quite as much as I love my own life, or indeed – perhaps more. [. . .]

[. . .] Your scenes in the fourth act – no more, forgive that, too – were in my opinion such that, if you continue to progress as you have begun, not even envy itself will be able at any future time to deny you the name of great artist. But – don't stop. Always believe that you can *become better*, i.e. don't trust those who tell you you are divine. [. . .]

[. . .] don't you think the verses about Robin might be even more effective, be even more sublime and penetrate even more deeply into the soul, if they were sung in the quavering and uncertain voice of a madwoman, instead of with the effort Mlle Högqvist puts into singing them *beautifully*? – it seems to me that Ophelia was not so much *singing* as *imagining* that she was singing. You see, because you are so excellent in all the rest, I believe that nothing should be wanting, which is why I add this slight observation, the rightness or wrongness of which I leave to your own discretion.

[1] Torsslow's acting career was almost brought to an early conclusion by a coaching accident in which he severely injured a knee. His skill in overcoming the ensuing handicap served if anything to add extra lustre to his reputation.

[2] i.e. had he and the Royal Theatre not been at odds at the time.

## 65b Emelie Högqvist as Ophelia in the mad scene, 1847

Lithograph from a drawing by J.V. Wallender; reproduced in Nordensvan, vol. 1 (1917–18), p. 355.

## IV THE NYA TEATERN AND CHANGES IN THE ROYAL THEATRE, 1842–68

*The royal monopoly ends*

On leaving the Royal Theatre, the Torsslows established themselves for a number of summer seasons at Djurgårdsteatern, first in partnership with Pierre Deland (1805–62), and then with Torsslow as sole manager. Another dismissed actor, Karl Fredrik Berg (1799–1841), acting on Anders Lindeberg's behalf, had received permission to build a theatre, though the venture was postponed, and in 1840 the Riksdag explicitly came out against the monopoly, though the King went on hedging.

With this wind at his back, Torsslow made a decisive advance into the city from his Djurgården base, giving performances in the winter of 1839–40 under the auspices of a private dramatic society. In October 1841, on the strength of the Riksdag resolution, he was given permission to perform there that winter; and in the same month Lindeberg received a long-awaited reply to his string of applications. And a weird one it was: he could not have permission to run a theatre, because he did not have one; he must build a theatre, and then apply for permission. Which he did. The permit arrived just in time for opening night to be lawful.

The opening of the Nya teatern in 1842 was important, not only in that it marked the end of the monopoly (and was soon followed by other Stockholm theatres), but also in providing the Royal Theatre with the stimulus of lively competition and a bold repertoire and, in due course, in 1863, with the dramatic theatre it had sorely needed since the Arsenal fire.

## 66a The opening of Nya teatern, 1842

*Dagligt Allehanda* (1842) in Barbro Stribolt: *Stockholms 1800-talsteatrar* [*Stockholm's nineteenth-century theatres*] (Stockholms kommun, 1982), p. 22 (with a front elevation and seating plan on p. 23).

On entering the auditorium, one is pleasantly surprised by the happy and inviting impression it makes. There are three circles, which have enough space between them (considerably more than the Royal Theatre) not to appear cramped despite their modest depth. Each tier becomes deeper towards the back of the hall, so that they hold only two rows of seats nearest the stage but four at the back. The horseshoe design of the Royal Theatre which, though it may be an advantage in regard to acoustics, especially in a large theatre, nevertheless has the disadvantage that spectators in many places have to remain standing or sit in twisted and uncomfortable positions to see what is happening on the stage, has in this case been replaced by an hyperbola, which should make it possible to see more or less equally well anywhere, with the possible exception of the balcony seats nearest the stage. There are no divisions into separate boxes here, and indeed they would seem unnecessary as merely reducing the available space. The fronts of the circles are tastefully decorated in gold and white which, combined with the rich illumination from the large and elegant lamp in the ceiling gives that happy appearance which promptly and agreeably meets the eye. The floor of the auditorium comprises at the top an amphitheatre, entered from the big lobby. On either side of this amphitheatre, under the dress circle, there are as at the Royal Theatre a pit with standing room, while stalls seating extends from the amphitheatre down to the orchestra. Two boxes on either side on a level with the dress and upper circles look quite tempting, and will certainly not lack subscribers if the view from them is as attractive as the view in. Everything seems both tasteful and practical. (Some minor flaws in addition to those already mentioned are of little consequence and could be put right without any special difficulty.)[1]

[1] In fact major flaws, some owing to the rapid erection, some to the inconvenient and narrow site, were soon evident. Nevertheless, Nya teatern was to be an enduring and major force in Swedish theatrical life, first, under Lindeberg, Torsslow and Edvard Stjernström, as a dramatically pioneering rival to the Royal Theatre, and then (1863–1907) as the home, Dramaten, of its dramatic as opposed to its operatic company.

## 66b Façade of Nya teatern

From an almanac of 1850; reproduced in Nordensvan, vol. 2 (1917–18), p. 4.

## 66c Seating plan for Nya teatern

Box-office diagram; reproduced in Nordensvan, vol. 2 (1917–18) p. 5.

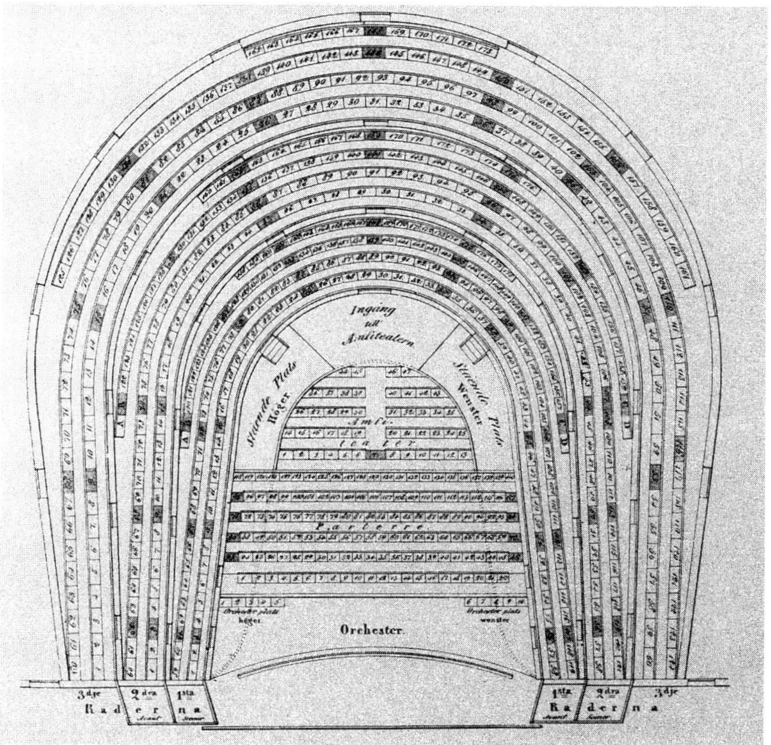


*The acting of Edvard Swartz*

Edvard Mauritz Swartz (1826–97) began his acting career as a Royal Theatre apprentice, but probably learned more from working under Torsslow at Nya teatern from 1845. He was to succeed his mentor as leading light of the Swedish theatre, and his decisive breakthrough was probably his Royal Theatre debut as Hamlet in 1853 (in a new Swedish version that was much closer to Shakespeare than earlier adaptations had been). Here is how Frans Hedberg records the event in his biographical essay.

## 67 Hedberg describes Edvard Swartz as Hamlet in 1853

F. Hedberg (1884), pp. 135–6.

The occasion was long anticipated in discussions man to man – or just as much woman to woman – of how the young actor with the beautiful pale face, the big melancholy eyes, and the slight physical frame could possibly sustain such a part, so full of different emotions from stormy passion to quiet reflection; it was thought to have been most ill-advised of the Board to entrust such a hazardous task to a debutant; and if anyone had heard that the young actor had chosen the part of Hamlet himself for his debut, the response was amazement at his lack of self-knowledge in believing himself capable of such an Herculean labour. No one realized that he had spent many years preparing himself for the bold venture he was now ready to attempt, so no wonder public expectation was as tense as a bowstring at breaking point.

It was half past six, the orchestra completed its brief overture, and the curtain rose slowly over the moonlit ramparts of Elsinore. The masterly introduction to the play, incontrovertibly the most brilliant exposition of any play yet written, casts its magic spell of secrecy over the auditorium, where even the most prosaic being felt gripped by mysterious awe as the ghost slowly stalked forth against the moonlit background. Horatio and the trembling sentries resolve to seek Prince Hamlet to tell him of the night's strange vision – and the scene is transformed into the royal hall, where the fratricide and his queen appear in a ceremonial procession, attended by their court.

The audience half listens to the king's hypocritical words, for a moment a breath as of an approaching storm fills the auditorium, followed by a deathly hush: there he is, far away upstage, the prince in black, with deep grief weighing on his form and face – a statue, eloquent in all its silence, entire as though carved by a master, at once handsome and masculine yet supple, the mild features marked by an almost childish weakness, the high, broad forehead suggesting deep thought and morbid brooding.

It is Hamlet to the life! That is how he had to look, the poor dreamer, given the horrifying task of setting right a time out of joint! He speaks! The voice is weak, almost lifeless, yet every word carries, distinct and defined and with no visible strain, to the farthest corners of the theatre. Wonderful! No one had thought of that before! That is how someone must speak who is feeling a grief so great and deep that it consumes any other emotion! How could there be resonance and steel in the voice of an unhappy brooder, who wanders about the noisy court as if by instinct, sniffing out a crime? The all-powerful mystery of the first captivating impression has silently and unnoticeably served its important purpose; all eyes are magnetically attracted to the expressive figure, the spectators hang on his lips, he has them all in his grip, and if he lets them go again before the curtain falls for the last time over the dying prince, he will have only himself to blame.

But he doesn't let them go! Conscious of his power, he holds them as if in a magic ring, from his first despairing outburst when, alone, he accuses himself in the monologue which begins with the well-known words:

> O that this too too solid flesh

through all the different moods and phases of the many faceted role, and the weak-looking man rules his audience with an iron hand.

And thus he carries them with him from scene to scene, from act to act, and when towards midnight the huge play is over, a great triumph has been achieved with noble and honest weapons, and our country has another great actor, and the name Edvard Swartz is on everybody's lips, and recorded in the honour rolls of Swedish dramatic art for ages to come and among the greatest.

### *The acting of Elise Hwasser*

Elise Hwasser (or, as Hedberg occasionally puts it, Hvasser) (1831–94) joined the Royal Theatre in 1850 and gave her farewell performance in 1888, having been Sweden's leading leading-lady for a generation. Frans Hedberg writes of her as Scribe's Queen Anne (in *A Glass of Water*), Ibsen's Nora, Lona Hessel, Dame Inger and Mrs Alving, Shakespeare's Cleopatra and Hermione, and Jane Eyre (to Swartz's renowned Rochester), among other parts more briefly mentioned. She chose Dame Inger and Queen Anne for her positively last appearance in 1860, an interpretation said to be undiminished after twenty-eight years.

## 68 Hedberg describes Elise Hwasser as Queen Anne in 1860

F. Hedberg (1884), p. 155.

Indecisive, insignificant, lazy, fickle and limited is how she appeared between the intriguing Sarah Churchill and the careless plotter Bolingbroke; she is good after her fashion, because she lacks the energy to be wicked; she is a romantic, dreaming on her throne of a cottage and a hearth, with young Lieutenant Masham of the Guards tacitly the hero of the royal pastoral, which she will hardly admit to herself. Now watch how with true brilliance Elise Hwasser grasps this perfectly ordinary character and makes so much more of it than anyone who had previously acted the part on our stage. Observe the vast indolence enfolding her whole being, so that she can hardly bear so much as to rise from her sofa; watch her fumbling for a decision at important moments, precisely as in her near-sightedness she fumbles for the book she wants to read or the document she is to sign. For she is near-sighted, extremely near-sighted, a splendid touch this on the part of the actress, the genius of whose masterly characterization appears in her being as near-sighted spiritually as she is physically. There is great, fine and true comic power in this excellent characteristic, and yet, despite all her near-sightedness in both respects, it is a queen we see before us, and when occasionally the dull eyes behind their lowered lids do blaze, we see that there are feelings and pain behind this languid calm, suffering capable of bursting out with all the violence of a destructive storm.

### The Mindre teatern

In 1844 Lindeberg had to hand the Nya teatern over to his creditors, who rented it to a company which entrusted its management to a committee including Torsslow and Stjernström (who had joined in 1842). In 1846, the theatre was auctioned to a company which renamed it Mindre (the smaller) teatern and leased it to Torsslow for ten years; he appointed Stjernström artistic director. When the latter left in 1850, Torsslow ran the theatre on his own until 1854, when Stjernström took over the lease and then in 1855 bought the theatre. In 1859 he had it thoroughly repaired and redecorated and added a storey. Under his management it flourished artistically, and on the whole financially, until the Royal Theatre, of which Stedingk was Director, bought it in 1863 (Stjernström had had medical advice to take a rest). Despite the difficulty of producing spoken drama in the Opera, both Josephson and Bournonville advised against the move; many said it was made mainly to eliminate a successful competitor.

The fact that a purchase was formally made in the name of the King (Carl XV) was to give rise to much discussion in the Riksdag and elsewhere in connection with allocations to the Royal Theatres and their transference to public ownership. Both Stjernström's essay [see 59], and Josephson's, the source of the next extract, appeared in 1870, when debate about the future of the Royal Theatres was at one of its frequent heights, the occasion being a report submitted in 1870 by a governmentally appointed theatre committee.

### The need for improvement in training actors

The name of the great director Ludvig Josephson (1832–99) is an indication of emergence from a bygone to a 'modern' period. By 1870 when this extract was first published, Josephson had spent four years directing drama, and then both drama and opera, at the 'big theatre' (which went on performing the 'grander' dramatic repertory, leaving conversation pieces, drawing-room comedy and the like to Dramaten). In 1868 he left because the Director, Edholm, refused to give him a three-year instead of the customary one-year contract – one of the truly major errors among the many committed by 'amateur' directors. Ahead of Josephson lay four years at Kristiania teater (1873–7), eight years at the new Nya teatern (1879–87), when it won the reputation of being the liveliest in Stockholm, and five years (1889–94) with the Opera again.

## 69 Acting training in the 1850s

Ludvig Josephson: *Våra teater-förhållande* [*Our theatre conditions*] (Stockholm: Samson & Wallin, 1870), pp. 169–72.

When in 1855[1] I presented myself as a would-be debutant at the Royal Theatre and gave a brief sample of my declamation before Messrs Cavallius, Torsslow, Jolin, Sundberg and Kjellberg,[2] I was advised to wait until I had for some time attended the school which Mr Cavallius had reorganized. I thought this would be the quickest way to my goal, and thanked them, if for nothing else then at least the prospect of the closer approach of the longed-for day. I went to the school – and I must admit that everything I heard and saw made me ashamed. I was not so young, had seen the world, and had taken an interest in theatres both at home and abroad; but I had never imagined that the most difficult and beautiful of all the fine arts could be communicated in such a counterfeit, uninteresting, frivolous and ugly way, by teachers apparently well-intentioned but lacking in finer insight, to a whole crowd of already affected girls and highly indifferent boys and youths who assembled on a teacher's improvised instructions to 'gather nuts' or 'pick strawberries' or manoeuvre as king or peasant, queen or maid, show their capacity for natural feeling, and develop a free conversational tone in some hastily tossed-off phrase. Others declaimed poems and fragments by Stagnelius and Runeberg[3] with accompanying gestures and gazes fixed heavenward or into the bottomless pit. I thought I should die laughing, and only wished I had Charles Dickens hidden in a corner watching and listening, preparing another of his characteristically humorous school studies. Whenever the teacher left the class, one of the girls was set in his stead, and that was when the fun really started. After a few visits to this completely anti-artistic establishment, I reported what I had seen to Mr Torsslow, who then formed a desire to take a look at a department which for good reason he seldom visited. To Mr Cavallius I said that no educated young man who loved the theatre and art could stand a week there unless he had been accustomed to such a school from childhood; and since I had no time to throw away on such childish games, I presented myself to Mr Stjernström who after testing me allowed me to make my debut. Such was the nature of the school after the grant was allocated.

[1] For various reasons I suspect that 1855 is a mistake: Josephson made his acting debut under Stjernström in 1858; Torsslow rejoined the Royal Theatre in 1856; and Hyltén-Cavallius was appointed artistic director in 1856.

[2] Gunnar Olof Hyltén-Cavallius (1818–39), Artistic Director 1856–58, Director 1858–60. Johan Jolin (1818–84), actor 1846, reader 1849–56, head of acting school 1857. Carl Gustaf Sundberg (1817–98), debut 1828, appointed actor 1839, teacher of declamation 1857–59, dramatic theatre artistic director 1863. Wilhelm Kjellberg (1810–64), assistant stage manager 1831, stage manager 1845–56.

[3] Johan Ludvig Runeberg (1804–77), Finnish poet. Erik Johan Stagnelius (1793–1823), Swedish romantic poet.

### Opéra bouffe *makes a controversial hit*

By his own account, Josephson's most amusing experience as a director was producing Offenbach – which is surprising in an idealist like him. It was in fact the Director, Stedingk, who decided on the production, from purely mercenary motives. Although previous Offenbach productions had not caused offence, in effect the box-office success *La Belle*

*Hélène* damaged theatre finances by providing hostile members of the Riksdag with moral or cultural excuses for cutting down Royal Theatre allocations (in 1868, by a majority of one vote). August Strindberg (1849–1912) described the impact of *La Belle Hélène* on his *alter ego* Johan in the autobiographical *A bondwoman's son* (1886).

## 70a Strindberg reports the impact of *La Belle Hélène* in 1865

August Strindberg: *Tjänstekvinnans son* [*A bondwoman's son*], vol. 1 (Stockholm: Albert Bonnier, 1886), ch. 8.

The youth of 1865, still trembling from his stigmatization, enervated by his struggle with flesh and the devil, his ears tortured by church-bells and hymns, entered the brightly lit theatre in the company of bold youths of good birth and position to see, from the back of the dress circle, the unfolding of those images of happy heathendom, and to hear music, original, with *Gemüt* [feeling] (for Offenbach had been Germanicized), lyrical, gay. The overture music made him laugh, and then! The temple ritual behind the curtains reminded him of communion bread being baked in the sexton's kitchen; the thunder was seen to be a sheet of unplated iron; the gods who ate the sacrifices, Carl Johan Uddman;[1] the goddesses, three beautiful actresses; the gods on high, invisible stage managers. But this too put paid to the whole of antiquity. The gods, goddesses and heroes hallowed by the textbooks were toppled; Greece and Rome, always referred to as the original sources of all culture, were exposed and brought down to our level. Our level! That was democratic, since he was now relieved of one pressure, and the fear of being unable to reach 'up' to them had been removed. This was followed by the lesson in enjoying life. Humans and gods coupled pell-mell without even asking permission, and gods helped young girls to run away from old men, weary of his own hypocrisy the priest descended from the temple and, with vine leaves encircling his moist brow, danced the cancan with the hetæræ. It was pure play! He took it in as the word of God, and had no objection or comment to make; it was precisely as it should be. Was it unwholesome? No! But he had no desire to apply it to life. It was theatre, it was unreal, and his view was still and would ever remain aesthetic. What exactly was the aesthetic, under which title so much could be smuggled in, so many allowances made? Certainly not earnest; nor jest; something very indefinable. The Decameron glorified vice, yet retained its æsthetic value. What sort of value was that? Ethically the book should be condemned, but æsthetically praised. Ethical and æsthetic! A new false-bottomed magician's box, out of which one could pull gnats or camels at one's pleasure.

Yet the piece was being performed with the authority of the Royal Theatre and by its most prominent artists, Knut Almlöf[2] himself was Menelaus. At the dress rehearsal the King and guards officers gave a lunch. The boys had that from the chamberlain's son, who gave them the tickets. It was virtually a command performance!

Meanwhile the fuss was as great as the acclaim. Nobody spoke without using some expression from *La Belle Hélène*. You could no longer read Virgil without translating Achilles as hot-headed Achilles. Johan, who got to see the show only after it had been running half a year, was even asked by his Latin master, who had used a quotation from the play which Johan failed to understand, had he not seen *La Belle Hélène*?

No!

Well, for heaven's sake, you have permission to see it, you know!

[1] Carl Johan Uddman (1821–78), singer and actor with the Royal Theatres from 1846. A stout buffo, he played Calchas the oracle-monger.

[2] Knut Almlöf (1829–99), son of the great Nils Vilhelm Almlöf (1799–1875), the first Swedish actor to be knighted (in 1858). Knut began acting at Djurgårdsteatern in 1851, learning a natural conversational style under Pierre Deland, whose actress daughter Betty (1831–82) he married. He was engaged by the Royal Theatre in 1863. Some considered him miscast as Menelaus.

## 70b Knut Almlöf as Menelaus

Photograph reproduced in Nordensvan, vol. 2 (1917–18), p. 226.

*Bjørnson appeals for dramatic copyright*

The great Norwegian dramatist (1832–1910) appealed for a copyright law which, as far as Sweden and Norway were concerned, was not enacted until 1877. The tone of this letter to King Carl XV (1826–72, reigned from 1857) suggests Bjørnson the republican. Following negotiations, *Mary Stuart in Scotland*, directed by Josephson, opened on 16 May.

## 71 Bjørnstjerne Bjørnson writes to the King about dramatic copyright, 4 March 1868

*Bjørnstjerne Bjørnsons Brevveksling med Svenske 1858–1909* [*Bjørnstjerne Bjørnson's correspondence with Swedes*], (edited by Ø. Anker, F. Bull and Ö. Lindberger), vol. 1 (Oslo and Stockholm: Gyldendal, 1960), pp. 33–4.

In July or August last year I requested payment from the Director[1] of the Royal Theatres for my play *Between the Battles* [*Mellem slagene*, 1857], which had been performed at the Royal Dramatic Theatre in Stockholm without my permission and had been a success. I argued that the former Director[1] had paid me 150 speciedollars for *The Newlyweds* [*De nygifte*, 1865]; that the Royal Danish Theatre, which could also have taken my plays without more ado, had paid me for them; that Christiania Theatre, although private, had under my management (with one exception) paid for every original work from Sweden and Denmark which is included in its repertoire. I went on to point out that Nordic dramatists, who are not protected by international laws, suffer injury without such considerations; that a linguistically small culture such as ours must agree to support its authors; that printers accordingly respect each other's publishers when this is expressly demanded in a book; that there is all the more reason for the Royal Theatres to do so, and that it is particularly incumbent on the Swedish Royal Theatre, which enjoys government support and is under the King's management, to respect the authors of its brother kingdom and not simply appropriate their works.

To this request I received no answer. After waiting in vain for two months, during which time my play went on being performed at the Dramatic Theatre, I addressed information on the matter to Your Majesty.

I received no reply to this application either. I am sending the present letter through the Norwegian-Swedish delegation in Demark, where I am at present staying. I wish thereby to be assured that my letter really reaches Your Majesty.

For I now have a further cause for complaint. During my stay in Sweden a year and a half ago, I had occasion to state that I would not give the Director permission to perform my work *Mary Stuart in Scotland* [*Maria Stuart i Skotland*, 1864] unless he agreed to give me a say in its staging. On hearing a few months later that the play had been distributed to the actors, I reminded him of my condition, and the play was accordingly withdrawn. I have now heard from a Swedish composer who is staying here that they are again thinking of performing my play and have approached him about music.

In other words, the head of the Royal Theatres is again about to make a conquest of one of my works, and no recourse thus remains for me but to seek Your Majesty's protection against this doughty warrior in Your Majesty's aesthetic service.

I am more than willing to have my plays performed by the personnel at present employed at Stockholm's Royal Theatres; but I want no play performed without a previous agreement with myself. I believe this to be a reasonable demand, with which the Swedish public will agree.

Permit me to take this opportunity to ask Your Majesty to initiate laws and treaties according to which the united kingdoms' authors (and artists) might be protected in future, and would that Denmark might be drawn into such a joint agreement! The time must be ripe for this in every respect; for the author (and artist) in the three Nordic kingdoms it is a question of welfare to be given the necessary control over their works.

[1] The Director was Edholm; *Between the Battles* was put on in 1867. The former Director was Stedingk; *The Newlyweds* was put on in February 1866.

## V NATIONALIZATION VS PRIVATE MANAGEMENT, 1870–1900

### *The new Nya teatern*

Unable to remain inactive, Stjernström rented and subsequently purchased a new 'Nya teatern' at Blasieholm, which opened in 1875 with the successful world premiere of Bjørnson's *A Bankrupt*, directed by Stjernström with Stjernström in the main part. The play was a European breakthrough for realistic and socially-committed prose drama: as the old Nya teatern had been under Torsslow and especially under Stjernström, so the new one at Blasieholm was to prove a valuable stimulating rival to the Royal Dramatic Theatre.

### *The disputed ownership of the Dramaten teater*

Although the name of Carl XV was on the Dramaten title deed following the 1863 purchase, his ownership was disputed, for instance in the Report submitted on 21 January 1870 by one of the numerous committees appointed to recommend a solution to the Royal Theatre's financial and administrative problems. The question had also exercised the Riksdag: the plea that theatre allocations were necessary to enable the Theatre to meet its growing debts was met by the question of whose those debts really were. The committee rejected both public ownership and private enterprise, but offered no detailed proposals for the continued ownership, financing and administration of that very puzzling thing, a public institution under the King to which the administration contributed funds.

In 1871 the King himself proposed that the Riksdag should grant 270,000 Rd. (the sum paid to Stjernström) and take possession of the theatre, in return for which he would settle its debts. Many speakers were not prepared to see this as the Royal favour it was made out to be, but the solution was adopted – after all, the King could have closed the Theatres if he liked. So the real estate was henceforth public property, but the institution, still receiving Riksdag allocations, remained Royal!

## 72a The façade of the Dramatic Theatre, *c.* 1863

Lithograph, reproduced in Bergman and Brunius (1963), plate 36, opp. p. 56.

## 72b Lindberg's[1] memories of the Dramatic Theatre in 1871

Johan August Lindberg: *De första teaterminnerna* [*Earliest theatre memories*] (Stockholm: A. Bonnier, 1916), pp. 197–202.

The Dramatic Theatre was Stockholm's favourite rendezvous; one went there not just to spend an evening at the theatre, but to see others and enjoy being together with persons one knew. The most delightful auditorium one could imagine had room for the right number of people, and the rows of seats divided the various classes so discreetly and unnoticeably that all distinctions seemed to have been levelled out so that each and every spectator was best pleased with his or her seat.

The orchestra pit closest to the stage, or rather the ridiculous narrow space called the orchestra, housed a few musicians, the most unassuming in the world, for they knew they played to no one, especially when the theatre was packed. It never occurred to the audience to listen; no one had ever thought of listening out of respect. As soon as the piano and the strings were heard and the double-bass began to rumble, it was if a dam had burst in the auditorium, and the general desire for conversation, which had been restrained and hushed while people assembled, found release. On the lowest benches the cadets and other young people in uniform twisted and turned to gaze at the middle section of the stalls, where the business families presided, mingled with high finance and the aristocracy, which also filled the amphitheatre and spread together with the upper bourgeoisie all over the dress circle, where singular enthusiasts and drama addicts here and there occupied flap-seats.

The regulars branched out all over the auditorium but were concentrated in the upper circle and the balcony. 'Those are our old faithfuls up there, sir' was the refrain of the old ticket-seller.

At this time the previously most comprehensive repertoire began to be thinned out, and all major drama was moved to the Opera, where one might occasionally still hear those splendid voices resounding: Dahlqvist, in *The Vikings in Constantinople* or as the Earl in *Ulfåsa*,[2] Elmlund as Lawyer Bengt, Kinmansson as the young Alba in Goethe's *Egmont*.[3] But at the Dramatic Theatre the dramatic recitations of the troubadours were falling silent, and one no longer heard a Torsslow, Kinmansson or Raa in *King René's Daughter* or other lyrical items.[4] The sun of romanticism slowly sank and finally disappeared, and no voices could be heard singing on the little stage. Everything was *spoken*, in such a natural party or everyday manner that the public was fascinated and thought it was hearing itself speak.

[1] Johan August Lindberg (1846–1916) was engaged as a Royal Theatre actor in 1866. He managed provincial tours for many years, and Gothenburg theatres from 1890 to 1893. He was artistic director for the Dramatic Theatre in the 1884–5 season and again from 1903 to 1906, returning there as an actor from 1906 to 1915. Lindberg was a pioneering producer of the new Nordic drama, with the world premiere of *Ghosts* to his credit, put on in Hälsingborg in 1883 with himself as Osvald.

[2] Carl Georg Dahlquist (1807–73) was with the Royal Theatres from 1834, from 1863 on a lifetime contract. *Väringarna i Miklagard* (1827) was by Oehlenschläger. The earl and the lawyer were parts in Hedberg's *Bröllopet på Ulfåsa* [*The Wedding in Ulfåsa*].

[3] Axel Wilhelm Julius Elmlund (1838–1901) began as a ballet pupil, but was engaged as an actor with the Dramatic theatre in 1858; he made a hit as the sculptor Thorvaldsen in Strindberg's first produced play *I Rom* (*In Rome*, 1870).

Lars Gustaf Kinmansson (1822–87) had plenty of theatre links: he was the son of Lars Kinmansson and nephew of Fredrik Gustaf Kinmansson, both Royal Theatre actors and opera singers, and he married the actress Helfrid Torsslow, daughter of Olof and Sara Torsslow. He was with the Royal Theatre 1843–7, Mindre teatern 1847–63, and Dramaten 1863–81.

[4] Georg Frithiof Andreas Raa (1840–72) moved to Nya teatern in Helsinki in 1866, after early years with Stjernström and others.
*Kong Renés datter* was by the Danish dramatist Henrik Hertz (1797–1870).

*The Opera fire*

Erik af Edholm (1817–97), Director from 1866 to 1881, when he was summarily dismissed in connection with the transfer of the Royal Theatres to government control, kept a diary from which these passages are taken. In 1888 he was appointed 'censor', with the duty of approving the association's choice of repertoire.

## 73 Erik af Edholm's diary entries on the Opera fire, 5–24 April 1877

Erik af Edholm: *Mot seklets slut* [*Towards the end of the century*] (Stockholm: P.A. Norstedt, 1948), pp. 103–4 (the third volume of Edholm's diaries, published by his son; the volumes cover the period from 1872 until Edholm's death in 1897).

1877. 5 April. A most regrettable misfortune occurred at the Opera yesterday during *Robert*,[1] when the dancer Sophie Dahl's costume caught fire from the flames of a torch and burned up, creating a dreadful sensation in the auditorium. The blaze rose several feet into the air before people rushing up managed to stifle it with their coats. The outstandingly sweet and good girl died today. Great grief and shock at the theatre. After the incipient fire at the Dramatic Theatre in February, worries among the personnel had already found expression in a request from eighteen actresses for improved safety measures in their dressing-rooms, which are backstage in the opera and have only one exit, a wooden staircase leading to the stage.

9 April. There was another accident today at the theatre, to chief stage mechanic Lindström,[2] who had designed a new safety rope and was climbing down it from the highest balcony to the stage when it broke, so that he fell and broke his arm. All these events are increasing the feeling of malaise at the theatre.

16 April. Governor af Ugglas,[3] Chief Fire Officer Captain Hollsten and I wander around for three hours in every nook and cranny of the opera, watch hoses tested and fire-proof materials ignited, etc.

24 April. Woken at half past two in the morning by a police constable saying there was a fire at the Opera, but that the danger seemed to have been averted. Went there at once, where thank God it had all been put out. Went up with Deputy Governor Bråkenhjelm[4] to the property loft, where a door and some chairs had burned up. The night watchman crawled into the thick smoke with a hose and put the fire out before the fire brigade arrived and prevented any further danger of a new outbreak from the charred roof. In the morning there was a police hearing in

the lobby, where it was found that sparks from the chorus greenroom chimney had fallen into an unused fireplace in the loft opposite the main fireplace. When it was over, the King came up to view the scene.

25 April. Mrs Strandberg,[5] who is singing Jemmy this evening at the 100th performance of *William Tell*, tells me that when she left the theatre the day before yesterday in the evening, she saw showers of sparks blowing over the theatre roof from a chimney on the other side of Arsenalsgatan, which seems a more likely explanation of how the fire began than the one the police hearing arrived at.

[1] Presumably Meyerbeer's *Robert le Diable*.

[2] P.F. Lindström made his name as a 26-year-old stage carpenter in 1867, when for Meyerbeer's opera *L'Africaine*, directed by Josephson, he created a splendidly effective moving stage and ship. Magnificent sets and costumes and the third-act shipwreck were the main reasons for the run of 143 performances.

[3] Carl Fredrik Ludvig af Ugglas (1814–80).

[4] Gustaf Anton Bråkenhjelm (1837–1920).

[5] Albertina Josefine Charlotta Strandberg (1830–1923), opera singer 1851–88; played Helen in the 1865 Offenbach production. Married to Olof Strandberg (1816–82), opera tenor 1842–65.

### *Ibsen and the playwright's new prestige*

The first of these two letters from Ibsen to the Royal Theatre Administration shows a significant change in circumstances since Bjørnson's letter [see 71]. In the second he exercises his right to have a say in the casting.

## 74 Ibsen insists on author's rights and a say in casting, 3 October 1879

Edholm (1948), p. 145.

(a) Sorrento the 3rd of October 1879.

To the Management of the Royal Theatres, Stockholm.

To the inquiry concerning my new dramatic work sent me by the Intendant Mr Oscar Wijkander,[1] which only came to hand yesterday, I have the honour of replying that a copy of the play will be addressed to the Board by the 15th of October at the latest, which is about a month before the book is to be issued for sale. Let me also take the liberty of recalling that, according to the convention recently adopted between Sweden and Norway concerning rights to literary property, no Swedish translation of a Norwegian play may be published, nor may any such play be performed at any Swedish theatre, without the author's consent. The situation is therefore quite different from what it was, and we need no longer fear competition.

With my most distinguished esteem and respect,<br>Dr Henrik Ibsen

(b) To the Management of the Royal Theatres, Stockholm
I hearby have the honour to submit to the Directors of the Royal Theatres my new dramatic work *A Doll's House*, play in three acts, and most respectfully to ask whether the Directors wish to have the play performed at the Dramatic Theatre. In case the esteemed Directors should agree, I am so bold as to request that the part of 'Nora' be given to Mrs Hwasser, to whose performance of the role I attach the highest expectations. It would in that case also be very gratifying to me if the elegance and pleasing lightness of which Mr Fredrikson[2] is master might grace the part of 'advocate Helmer,' just as the part of 'Doctor Rank' would in my opinion be in the best of hands if given to Mr Elmlund, if Mr Schwartz [*sic*] is not available.

Respectfully
Henrik Ibsen

[1] Carl Oscar Wijkander (1826–99), dramatist, literary consultant to Dramaten from 1863, often directed productions; became Court Intendant in 1876 and Royal Theatre Secretary in 1878.
[2] Johan Gustaf Fredrikson (1832–1921), Royal Theatre actor 1862–87, Director of actors' association 1888–98, and of the Dramatic Theatre as his own enterprise 1904–7.

### *The need for a new theatre*

By 1880 a new large deficit had accumulated, and a new theatre committee submitted its report in December. Among the reasons it mentioned for the financial difficulties were the unsuitable theatre premises. It proposed selling Dramaten to provide funds with which to settle the debts, and accordingly that performance be confined to the Opera building; but also pointed to the need for a new theatre building.

## 75 Theatre Committee's recommendation for a new playhouse, 1880

From a draft, not the final report, in Stribolt (1982), p. 229.

Firmly convinced that any other measures adopted for the benefit of the Royal Theatre's finances will prove insufficient, and that no lasting improvement is to be expected as long as the theatre is consigned to premises which, however excellently they may have satisfied the demands of the period which saw them built, nevertheless no longer correspond to what the public has become accustomed to expect of a theatre, and an endowed national theatre in particular, the committee had no choice but to declare the most important, indeed for the future existence of the Royal Theatre most absolute requirement to be the acquisition of a new building, worthy of its significant contribution to the art of our country. The committee has accordingly engaged an architect[1] of this city to design a rebuilding of the Royal Large Theatre.

[1] Magnus Isaeus (1841–90).

*The Royal Theatre is nationalized*

Meanwhile, however, Stjernström's widow had leased his Nya teatern to Ludvig Josephson and Viktor Holmquist (1842–95), and the new King, Oscar II (1829–1907, succeeded his brother Carl XV in 1872) was inclined to buy it; as in 1863, the motive was mainly to take over a successful competitor. The upshot of complicated and heated negotiations among the three parties, conducted partly in the press, was that the King gave up the idea. His 1881 proposal to the Riksdag was virtually a move to the opposite extreme; that the Dramaten building and such equipment as was not required by the Opera should be handed over to the King, who would settle its debts, but would be free to lease it on certain conditions and with continued Royal and Riksdag grants. There was strong conservative opposition to this proposal. Members of the first chamber (the four estates had by now become two chambers) feared the destruction of everything Gustaf III's institution had stood for. The possibility of transferring the institutions to government administration was again aired. For reasons which varied according to political views and attitudes to the monarchy as well as to the theatre, the King's proposal was rejected. The King's prompt reaction was to transfer financial responsibility for the whole theatrical enterprise to the Ministry of Finance with effect from 1 July 1881: this 'nationalization' of a Royal enterprise by the King was widely regarded as something of a coup.

Oscar II's decision to hand responsibility for the Royal Theatres over to the government is recorded in a letter written to Prime Minister Arvid Posse (served 1880–3) on the day the Riksdag rejected his proposal that he should again take over Dramaten, settle its debts and lease it.

## 76 Oscar II transfers financial responsibility for the Theatre to the government, 20 April 1881

Gunnar Richardson: *Oscarisk teaterpolitik* [*Oscar's theatre policy*] (Stockholm: Scandinavian University Books, 1966), p. 32.

I have through my Cabinet Chamberlain asked you to call a Cabinet meeting for 11 o'clock tomorrow morning. I have resolved to relinquish the *whole thing* from 1 July on, and not give one öre more than the writing off of my debt + 60,000 kr if the Royal Theatre is still open next season. I am moreover equally determined to prevent the recess of the Riksdag until all obstacles to the actual implementation of this decision have been removed, should any difficulties arise in the Cabinet, which I nevertheless hope will not be the case, remembering what we long since said concerning the possibility that the Riksdag would reject my Proposition without presenting any other acceptable proposal. I have at the same time summoned the Lord Marshal and Senior Intendant Westin, so as to have all the information available on the spot. My *advice* – but *advice* only – is to ask the

Riksdag for a letter of credit for 50,000 or 60,000, *for one year*, during which time the question can be given renewed consideration. The government will then be able, after 1 July 1882, to *more than* recoup any possible losses by selling the Dramatic Theatre. Meanwhile a decision *must* be taken at once, for I cannot leave before this matter has been settled.[1]

[1] Richardson records that the Cabinet was unable to take the decision until a week later, when it had received the necessary documents from the Riksdag. Although the state had previously taken over the theatre buildings, the transfer of financial responsibility was the real watershed.

*The Opera a fire hazard*

In 1886 a technical report on the state of the opera building described sinking foundations, cracked and leaning walls, dangers of falling masonry and an unsafe stage roof. But perhaps the strongest motivations for acquiring a new building was the fire risk. At least it appeared so after the Opéra Comique fire in Paris in May 1887.

## 77 Technical report on the state of the Opera building, 1886

Stribolt (1982), p. 264

The fire hazard within the theatre building, which is grave throughout and not diminished by the frequent use of stoves and fireplaces in the cellars and café premises and residences, is especially disturbing where the theatre audience is concerned, because there is no insulation between the stage area, where the danger is greatest, and the auditorium. Beneath the auditorium floor as well as over its ceiling there is free passage to the below-stage areas and staircase wells, where so much combustible and easily inflammable material is piled up. Smoke and flames could penetrate unhindered both above and below the spectators, for whom a rapid exit would be impossible through the narrow corridors to the cloakrooms.

*The new Opera House*

A complicating factor at the Opera, as at Dramaten, was the increasingly urgent need for theatre repairs, or better still, new premises. Finally the financier K.A. Wallenberg (1853–1938) formed a consortium for the purpose of building a new opera, the project to be financed by premium bonds. With the stipulation that, apart from the annual allocation, theatre affairs should be kept separate from government finances, under an administrative system approved by the Riksdag, this won political approval. When Adelcrantz's old opera building finally had to come down in 1891 to make way for the new one designed by Axel Anderberg (1860–1937), the government rented Nya – by now renamed Svenska – teatern for the opera company. The new Opera was inaugurated on 19 February 1899, eighteen years after the first rebuilding proposals and following a multitude of designs and counter-designs. One stumbling-block had been piety for Adelcrantz's masterpiece. Opinion was divided on the new building, but it found favour at least for its practical interior.

*The Riksdag refuses a subvention to the Theatre*

The next major milestone in Royal Theatre politics came when the Riksdag voted to refuse all allocations and to lease out the theatres. The vote not to grant any theatre funds was an invitation to political satire.

## 78 Lampoon of the Riksdag vote on subsidies, 19 May 1888

*Fäderneslandet* [*The Fatherland*] (19 May 1888) in Stribolt (1982), p. 276.

THE VANDALS

With the finer arts to blazes,
The theatres shall close perforce!
We instead have allocated
Funds to house the Royal horse.

Dramatists' and poets' sayings
Are not to our taste at all,
But how fine the proud steeds' neighing
Echoes in the gracious stall.

I, Redelius, sing hymns,
Waldenström takes up the strain;
Big and bold Liss Olof[1] dreams
No artistic dreams, that's plain.

Now that duty is done by us
Thalia is on the street,
While we with expressions pious
Silently offer prayers meet.

[1] Redelius, Waldenström and Liss Olof were members of the Swedish Riksdag which cut theatre allocations; their pietistic leanings are indicated. Liss Olof, especially, won quite a name for himself as an opponent of the theatre.

*The Actors' Association*

Faced with the 1888 decision, leading members of the Dramaten acting company did what their predecessors had done a century earlier when Ristell went bankrupt: formed an association to lease and run the theatre at their own risk. Under the actor Gustaf Fredrikson, the association prospered until the mid-1890s, when there were increasing signs that its renowned ensemble-playing was deteriorating, and complaints about the repertoire: there was no artistic director.

## 79 The formation of the Actors' Association in 1888

Gustaf Fredrikson: *Teaterminnen* [*Theatrical memoirs*] (Stockholm: Albert Bonnier, 1918), pp. 177–8.

The Riksdag no longer regarded dramatic art as such a necessary product that it was appropriate for the royal theatres to receive any grant to help their financial position, which was certainly not of the best – or that it was even necessary for the theatres to boast the epithet *royal*. So the grant, as everyone knows, was withdrawn, and the government was empowered to hire the theatres' buildings and movables out to suitable entrepreneurs.

The situation was awkward for Stockholm's theatrical life. Court musical director Nordqvist[1] lost little time in taking on the opera enterprise. What was to become of the Dramatic Theatre? The answer emerged without too much pondering: try an association. There was a model ready to hand in the Théâtre Français, which was not so distant then as it is now. Some ten or more leading members of the acting company accordingly formed the first Swedish association: their example was to be followed at the Opera in 1890.

And from Stockholm I was summoned some time in May to lead the new organization.

It was thought to begin with that the actors had ventured into a shaky business, but the opposite soon proved to be the case. A sense of artistic purpose ultimately showed itself to be a financial factor to be seriously reckoned with.

Perhaps I should recall what the association in fact was. As I just mentioned, it was the leading members of the troupe who decided to risk the outcome of the enterprise. In addition to the association members, a number of other actors were engaged at the theatre, and they had to be paid their wages. But then the association members were to be entitled to a share of the profits. A kind of communistic artistic enterprise, in other words!

[1] Johan Conrad Nordqvist (1840–1920), conductor, music teacher, composer, ran the Royal (Opera) Theatre as his own enterprise 1888–90, and with a Board to 1892.

## 80 Tor Hedberg[1] appraises the Dramaten ensemble, 1897

Tor Hedberg: 'Skådespelarkonst och regie' ['Acting and directing'] (1 October 1897), reprinted in *Ett decennium* [*A Decade*], vol. 3 (Stockholm: A. Bonnier, 1913), pp. 9–11.

As for the Dramatic Theatre in particular, it has long enjoyed a reputation for excellent ensemble-playing. That reputation is certainly beginning to fade, but still exercises its suggestive power over large sections of the audience, and it should be admitted that the traditions from the days of good ensemble-playing have not entirely disappeared from the stage either. One is occasionally reminded of it when some French conversation piece or other is put on, or better still – a worrying sign of decadence – in performances of late German imitations of the genre. For it should be noted that the famous ensemble-playing of the 1870s and early 1880s was intimately related to the genre that flourished at the time: the French intrigue and conversation plays. It was an art, by some developed to complete mastery, to maintain a drawing-room conversation or, more accurately, the stylized and pointed appearance of one, to drop one's remarks casually and lightly, to interweave with each other and together form an uninterrupted and playful dialogue, with slight, scarcely noticeable transitions from jokes to something almost like seriousness, from wit to something almost like feeling. It was unquestionably, of its kind, art, and what made it art was that the same tone pervaded all the individual performances, and that they all worked together to achieve an overall effect that governed the whole performance.

But the era of French conversation pieces is over, and modern drama has struck out in new directions. On the one hand there is the struggle to free dramatic forms from the old conventions, to inspire them with richer and more vigorously pulsating life and bring them closer to reality; on the other is the attempt to reshape drama so as to make it accord with the artistic demands being heard in other areas of literature and the fine arts, to emphasize its emotional value more strongly, its overall impact, its characteristics as a work of art. But the Dramatic Theatre is still haunted by the spirit of the conversation piece; they have been obliged, occasionally, to sacrifice to the former trend, but have almost been relieved to fail. To the latter they have sacrificed a good deal in the way of costumes, furniture, and sets, and have been glad to see the gambles generally come off. But they have not taken the trouble to try to get to grips with the new ideas seriously or to adapt their acting style accordingly. Such ensemble-playing as the Dramatic Theatre is capable of today is the feeble relict of the witty art of conversation of the 1870s, hesitant and lost in its new surroundings; and where the natural speech is concerned, to which many of the artists visibly aspire, it chiefly consists in having moved the points and accents of the old conversational tone around – and put them in the wrong places. The way they speak their lines today at our Dramatic Theatre is utterly disgusting.

[1] Tor Harald Hedberg (1862–1931), son of Frans Hedberg and a dramatist in his own right as well as an art and drama critic, was Director of Dramaten from 1910 to 1921.

### *The regime of Nils Personne and* To Damascus

The question of the out-of-date premises with their considerable fire hazard found no political solution, and the association had to make do with extensions, repairs, and electric lighting. The theatre was in fact written off by both Government and Riksdag in 1898 (at which point Fredrikson left), but the improvements were enough for it to be allowed to keep going, now under Nils Personne (1850–1928). The King had a hand in the unusually rapid decision, but the theatre, now less closely linked to the state, temporarily lost its adjective 'Royal'. During this period, thanks to the artistic director Emil Grandinson (1863–1915), it collaborated successfully with Strindberg, witness the production of *To Damascus*.

## 81 Strindberg writes to the director of *To Damascus*, 25 September 1900

Ingrid Hollinger: 'Urpremiären på *Till Damaskus I*' ['The original premiere of *To Damascus I*'] in Bergman and Brunius (1963), p. 313.

Brother Grandinson.[1]
The time is approaching, and we must consider an audience's resistance to innovations. After further thought I therefore propose no interval before the *asylum*. The spectators must be kept in their seats and in the mood that long if they are to be drawn into the situation. If we let them get out and reason and arm themselves for deliberate resistance the game may be lost. Until then, scene changes must take place in the dark; but no curtain. The moment a curtain falls, the audience moves and says no! You know the German manner: a single interval in mid-play.

If you agree, cancel the interval music which we shall not need from Hallden at once. But I do want the Overture Beethoven's Largo Maesto [*sic*].

There isn't such a favourable wind blowing towards me as last season. So I'm prepared for hostility!

If you have any counter-proposals as to the act divisions, let me know.

[1] Emil Grandinson (1863–1915), who was directing *To Damascus* at Strindberg's request, was assistant artistic director at the Dramaten in 1898, became director in 1901 and moved to the Intima teatern in 1911.

## 82a Tor Hedberg attends the first night of *To Damascus*, November 1900

T. Hedberg, vol. 3 (1913), pp. 121–4.

Yesterday's premiere at the Dramatic Theatre was remarkable in a number of respects. An attempt was made, unusually bold and consistent for our theatre, to depart from customary theatre techniques and with extremely simplified staging to create a setting in harmony with the tone and spirit of the play. Strindberg's singular conscience play, in which all the action is internalized, which consists of an individual's confrontation with himself and his past, a rough calculation and a thorough re-auditing of his profit and loss account, but in which this inner action is made visible in fantasies and visions which touch on reality, recreating it or adapting to it, does not lend itself to the usual modern staging which strives to be as realistic as possible. The constantly changing scenes alone require simpler and more easily worked machinery than our theatres are accustomed to moving with. It was probably this purely practical requirement which occasioned the stage dress in which the play here appeared before us. But as often is and always could be the case, meeting a practical requirement also served purely artistic ends.

The stage is designed with an inner proscenium between the first pair of wing-and-border pieces, presenting the half-ruined wall of an ancient theatre, pierced by a broad arch. Above the wall some sky can be seen, and a star in nocturnal scenes. Three steps lead up to the stage behind the arch, on which the play itself takes place. An advantage of this design is that props can be kept to a minimum, and that loose objects which otherwise so often clutter the stage are painted on the backdrop and the set-piece perspectives instead. Scene changes are therefore carried out almost instantaneously, with the curtain up but the stage plunged in darkness.

Another and more important benefit is that the scene is withdrawn from the spectators, and made more distant, so to speak more unreal. The constant interchange of fantasy and reality which gives Strindberg's play its special form can thus itself be mediated, although the feverish hallucination which grips one so strongly when one reads the play is made somewhat weaker and less intense by this stage design.

This is at all events a very interesting experiment, and, what is more, a step towards the realization of genuinely artistic direction. Every credit is due to the stage director behind it all, Mr Emil Grandinson, not least for the care and insight with which every detail has been worked out. It is quite some time since we last saw such a complete and unified production on the Dramatic Theatre's boards, and it would be more than gratifying if this proved more than a sporadic *tour de force* and really indicated the beginning of a new era. Together with the director, the scene painter Mr Grabow[1] should be mentioned for his sequence of beautiful and evocative sets. Both of the sea scenes, the country road, the mountain pass and at least one of the interiors are among the finest ever seen on our stages. Concerning the proscenium itself I would remark that the ancient architecture is not an entirely appropriate frame around the modern drama taking place within it; some fantasy architecture with a more modern effect would I think be more suitable.

Of the actors, Miss Bosse and Mr Hansson[2] were those who best saw how to enter into the peculiar, half real, half unreal atmosphere of the play. The former, in her appearance in particular, was excellent, whereas her speaking of the part seemed to be too exclusively aimed at illustrating her statement at one point: that she is nothing. A stronger voice, and greater variety of tone, could hardly impair the image she wishes to convey and which, to judge from some of the speeches in the play, is the one the author intended. Mr Hansson presented an excellent picture of the doctor-werewolf, not at all exaggerated yet full of a strange feeling of dread. Mr Palme[3] sustained the extremely demanding and strenuous main part with more lyrical warmth than deep and suppressed suffering, and that cannot be quite right. He never succeeds in persuading us of his inner suffering, his is a completely contrary temperament; he did best with the purely lyrical outbursts of defiance and pathos.

I wrote in detail about the play when it was published. It certainly has a stronger effect on the reader than on the theatre spectator; its sombre and fragmentary imaginings cannot always stand embodiment. But some scenes, especially towards the end, are very moving and carried away even those spectators who to begin with had been reserved and wondering. At the end there were several curtain calls for the leading actors as well as loud calls for the author who, however, was not at the theatre.

A strange but interesting performance was probably the main impression with which most of the spectators left the theatre.

[1] Carl Ludvig Grabow (1847–1927), scenic painter, with Dramaten 1890–1910. He was also to design the scenery for the first production of Strindberg's *Dream Play*.

[2] Harriet Sofie Bosse (1878–1961), Norwegian actress with Dramaten 1899–1905, 1911–18, 1922–5, 1934–43; married to Strindberg 1901–4.
Axel Mauritz Hansson (1869–1911), with Dramaten from 1899.

[3] Bror August Palme (1856–1924), with Dramaten from 1885 to 1921, played the Stranger.

## 82b *To Damascus.* On the highway I.

Rehearsal photograph with August Palme as the Stranger and Harriet Bosse as the Lady; painted backdrop by Carl Grabow. Bergman and Brunius (1963), plate 181, opp. p. 340.

## 82c *To Damascus.* By the mountain pass I.

Rehearsal photograph. Bergman and Brunius (1963), plate 182.

## 82d *To Damascus.* By the sea I.

Rehearsal photograph, reproduced in Bergman and Brunius (1963), plate 188.

*Return of two Royal Theatres*

The committee appointed in 1897 to submit a new administrative system to the Riksdag recommended selling Dramaten and buying Svenska teatern (where the opera had been housed) instead; but the Riksdag opted for a new building. (Svenska teatern was added to the rapidly growing empire of impresario Albert Ranft [1858–1938], and soon became Stockholm's leading dramatic theatre.) In 1901 another consortium offered to build a new Dramaten, financing it by means of a lottery. In his design, approved in 1902, Fredrik Lilljekvist (1863–1932) harked back to the neo-classicism of Gustaf III's day. In 1904 the association was dissolved, and Fredrikson returned to run Dramaten as his own private enterprise for its last three years, paying the state a nominal 1,000 kroner (approximately £38) in rent. The final performance at Lindberg's 65-year-old theatre was given on 14 June 1907, and the new Dramaten opened on 18 February 1908 with the latest version of Strindberg's *Master Olof.* The solution which the 1897 committee had proposed to the vexed question of ownership, administration and financing was a pioneering one, and proved enduring: a government joint-stock company was formed to run the Opera, and in 1908 a similar solution was adopted by the new Dramaten, which again became 'Royal'. As head of the Government, the King was represented on the Board, and appointed the Director; the limited company satisfied the condition that theatre finances should be kept separate from those of the Government. So Stockholm again had two Royal Theatres.

Whether Sweden has ever actually had a 'national' theatre is a question of definition and legal interpretation which the Swedes themselves have frequently debated in the course of two centuries. With the bicentenary of Dramaten celebrated in 1987, it may now be beside the point.

# *Norway, 1825–1909*

Edited by PETER BILTON

## INTRODUCTION

As Norway develops a national theatre, the emphasis is on the word 'national'. After Viking conquests and medieval power, Norway spent four centuries as more or less a Danish province. With Denmark on the losing side in the Napoleonic Wars, Norwegians saw a chance of regaining independence, and in 1814 a Constitution was adopted which still stands. But the result of great-power politics was that Norway was to be united with Sweden under one King, although in principle as an independent and equal partner except where foreign affairs were concerned. This union lasted until 1905, i.e. throughout the period with which we are concerned.

In the debate on the state of the theatre, however, one finds little attention paid to Sweden and an astonishing preoccupation with Denmark, which remained for some the embodiment of culture and the gateway to European civilization, but was for others the yoke which must be thrown off if Norway was ever to have a cultural life or theatre of her own. (Holberg, on the other hand, was to be annexed: he was, after all, a native of Bergen.)

Particular thorns in the flesh of the cultural nationalists were Danish actors and the use of Danish on the stage. This theme of getting out from under Danish influence – or of retaining it while it remained beneficial – crops up everywhere: the theatre was a burning political issue, and emerging nationhood was the context to which every theatrical question, however small or apparently innocent, was related. The underlying criterion for repertoires and reviews was often what the author or theatre director or actor stood for, which cause stood to gain, or who might take offense, rather than any merit or morality or skill – or lack of these – ostensibly invoked.

While national romanticism was at its busiest unearthing and depicting 'roots', prominent figures in cultural life were thus involved whether they liked it or not in a constant political struggle over Norwegian self-assertion. This role as controversial public figures at a time of most virulent polemics helps to explain why Bjørnstjerne Bjørnson (1832–1910) and Henrik Ibsen (1828–1906), for instance, or even the heroic Ole Bull (1810–80), periodically felt more welcome abroad than caught up at home in the cross-fire between pillars of the community and leagues of youth. Today, Ibsen's and Bjørnson's names figure with Holberg's over the entrance to the National Theatre in Oslo, and Ole Bull plays his bronze violin in the foyer of the National Stage in Bergen.

For this is also a tale of two cities (or in fact small towns). In view of the size of the population, it is surprising how many Norwegian towns did establish public theatres, but the documents selected here relate only to Oslo and Bergen. Bergen saw the first wholehearted attempt to establish a truly Norwegian national theatre, which gives Den Nationale Scene a historical claim to its name. In the capital Christiania (later called Kristiania and then Oslo, reflecting the move away from Danish and towards independence), we also have for roughly a decade a tale of two competing theatres, the older one referred to by its critics as 'Danish' but praised by its supporters for providing art, the other proudly claiming the name 'Norwegian', but often chided for pandering to vulgar taste. They were finally driven, largely by financial pressures, to amalgamate, after which the attempts began to secure the site and the money for a truly national theatre, which was finally opened in 1899. The Bergen theatre, which had to be discontinued for over a decade, moved into its present home in 1909.

Financial pressures also figured prominently in Denmark and Sweden, but the problems in Norway were even greater because the Norwegian theatres were never 'Royal'. They had to struggle to manage without grants from any privy purse, and it took the best part of the century to persuade the Storting (the legislative assembly) that a theatre should also be 'national' in the sense of receiving public funds.

## I STRÖMBERG'S THEATRE IN CHRISTIANIA, 1825–32

### *Strömberg projects a public theatre*

One of the rare occasions on which being Swedish (as against Danish) provoked opposition was when the Swedish-born dancing-master, snuff manufacturer, theatre director and impresario Johan Peter Strömberg (1773–1834) set about realizing an old plan to establish a public theatre in Christiania. Before availing himself of the Royal privilege granted on 22 November 1825, he established a dancing school which developed into a theatre school: the enterprise was intended to rely on Norwegian talents to perform in the Norwegian language. In this respect he was more far-sighted than his successors, whose neglect of training for Norwegians was not made good until the 1850s; the permission which had to be obtained within a year to employ Danish actors set a historically crucial precedent. Although some of the patricians of the amateur dramatic society (which ran its own theatre) may have had their doubts, Strömberg found enough early public support for his venture to be able to publish the announcement below. Had he been given the permission he asked for to call it the 'Royal National Theatre', this might have meant a great deal in terms of moral and possibly financial support; but the city fathers turned him down on that point.

For want of money, the theatre as planned by Henrik Grosch (1801–65) and described in Strömberg's article was not built, but a cheaper one like it was, and Strömberg opened it on 30 January 1827.

## 83 Strömberg announces a public theatre, 24 December 1825

*Christiania Intelligentssedler* [*Christiania Intelligencer*], 24 December 1825.

## Public National Theatre in Christiania

His Majesty the King has been graciously pleased to grant permission for a public theatre to be built in Christiania, and for decent and morally well-instructed persons native to this country to be engaged for the performance of operettas and dramatic productions in the country's language which, without offending propriety, combine taste with interest. In this connection it has been thought necessary to acquaint the honoured and respected public in advance with how it is believed that this institution can be established. A site has been purchased from Supreme Court Judge Motzfeldt in his field in Akers Street, 90 alen [roughly 180 feet] long and 75 alen wide, on which the intended brick-built theatre building can be quite separate from other buildings and moreover offer the convenience that one can drive right round it in a coach, so that coaches coming to plays will never meet coaches leaving, which will take the new road across the field and return to town along Pilestredet. The building will be three storeys high, and will be divided into two tiers of boxes, a gallery, an amphitheatre and stalls, and will comfortably accommodate 1,000 persons. The whole facility will cost about 27,000 Spd. including wardrobes, a library, and musical equipment, which sum, divided into 270 shares of 100 Spd. each, it is hoped that Norway's citizens in general and the generous Christiania public, with the customary willingness in which it is never lacking, in particular, will pay so that this beneficial institution may be created. To save time, it has been thought practical to issue a number of subscription lists which specify exactly and in detail both what security the institution's respected shareholders can obtain, and the manner in which the shares will be called in in due course; further, how the sum subscribed will be administered by a supervisory committee, elected by the subscribers from among their own number, and which will likewise effect payments of expenses; and finally, how the share can in time be redeemed. It is these subscription lists in particular which we are so bold as to recommend to the honoured public for signatures as soon as possible, so that Norway's capital may not long be without such an extremely beneficial and agreeable facility as a national theatre, where the natives of the country will be able to present dramatic performances in their own language. Young persons of either sex of good moral standing and habits can be engaged at this institution, which should be capable of sufficiently respectable remuneration for them to be able to live independently on an income permitting them to devote themselves to art alone, wherefore no one not in possession of the qualities mentioned above may hope to be engaged. In this connection oral or written negotiations are invited with Director Strömberg, residing in Akersgaten in Supreme Court Judge Motzfeldt's house; note that strangers from other places in Norway who seek engagement must be provided with reliable references.

## 84 The opening of Strömberg's theatre, 30 January 1827

*Morgenbladet* [*Morning Paper*], 1 February 1827.

Christiania, 31 January. Yesterday the first performance was given at Christiania's first public theatre. A large crowd streamed along Grændsen, on foot or by carriage, to partake of the event. The places, for as many as 1,000 people, were rapidly filled through four separate entrances. People seemed reasonably pleased with the auditorium, the lighting, the proscenium and the full and excellently conducted orchestra, and only longed to see what was to ensue on the stage. The curtain rose, revealing Mr Strömberg at the head of the entire theatre company, with his youngest Norwegian dancing pupils on either side, whose education both in school subjects and in theatrical skills is entirely due to his unremitting efforts. With emotion he spoke the following words:

'For the first time, I venture to present myself to a highly enlightened audience, whose judgement I hope will be mild and tolerant. [. . .] These youngsters, the firstlings of the theatre school, are all children of this city, whose natural talents may in time merit the attention of an enlightened public.

'The provisional state of readiness of both the stage and the auditorium our honoured spectators may be graciously disposed to forgive. It was needful for us all to hasten an early start, but by next year we hope that comfortably and suitably decorated boxes will beautify this residence we intend for art and taste.

'Yet again, receive, each and every one who in some way or other has contributed to this end, our most sincere heartfelt thanks! [. . .]'

After this, Miss Ely[1] sang the song below, dedicated to His Majesty King Carl Johan,[2] tastefully and to applause with all the actresses and actors repeating the refrain. [. . .] The figurants then began the dance, and were followed by Mlles Henriette Hansen and Andrine Christensen,[3] whom Mr Strömberg has received as his own children. These dancers, whose lightness and grace we may soon hope to see united with greater confidence and experience, were met with deserved applause. The ensuing performance of the play *The Housewife*[4] did nothing to impair the audience's favourable mood, since it may impartially be said that the whole play was performed with a coordination and energy, which, especially at a first performance, was a credit to all concerned. The whole, as well as certain parts, and especially that taken by Mlle Kaalstad,[5] was therefore rewarded with the audience's repeated applause. With this opening, Mr Strömberg has shown his respect for the public and his talent as a director, and justified the favourable applause and support he has received.

[1] Abigael Ely (1807–69), with the theatre only until December 1827, when she married.

[2] Carl Johan (Jean Baptiste Bernadotte, 1763–1844), King of Sweden and Norway 1818–44.

[3] Henriette Hansen (1814–92), one of Strömberg's pupils; left the stage in 1830, married H.A. Bjerregaard in 1831.

Andrine Christensen (1814–53?), also a Strömberg pupil.

[4] *Hustruen* = *Die deutsche Hausfrau* by A. von Kotzebue (1812).

[5] Erika Kolstad (1792–1830), with the theatre until her death.

*Journalists foster the new theatre*

Edited by Henrik Anker Bjerregaard (1792–1842), poet, dramatist, journalist, and Hans Lassenius Bernhoft (1793–1851), (very) minor poet, subsequently a civil servant, the Christiania *Aftenblad* provided some of Norway's early theatre reviewing. Articles in October 1827 show a critical and a more tolerant response to the pioneering efforts at Strömberg's theatre. Here are excerpts, the first by Ole Rein Holm (1795–1832), who later joined the theatre as an actor in 1831, the second by Bjerregaard, reputed to have been Norway's first theatre critic.

## 85 Newspaper reviews of Strömberg's theatre, 3 and 10 October 1827.

Christiania *Aftenblad* [*Evening Paper*], 1 (3 October 1827) and 3 (10 October 1827).

(a) [. . .] A few months ago we in fact acquired one [a public theatre]; but unfortunately it requires a complete reorganization to make it capable of entertaining an educated audience. The man behind this theatre, Mr Strömberg, showed great endurance in working towards the goal he had set himself; under unfavourable circumstances and with limited means he managed to make a start, and to bring about an establishment which is irreproachable where outward appearance is concerned. Some young children were trained for the ballet, whose first weak efforts at least gave reason to hope that they might in due course develop into something. The theatre has as yet had nothing to do with musical plays, and the samples of song which members of the company have presented have been such that it would be inadvisable to try the audience's patience with ventures of that nature; the orchestra, on the other hand, is better than all the rest. The main cause for complaint, however, is that there is little if any hope that the present acting company will be able to perform even tolerably. [. . .] Where, moreover, education is lacking and a cultivated person's ear is offended by language that appears to originate in the lower orders, criticism must fall silent, and give way to pity. [. . .] When added to this there is misunderstood pathos in the declamation, and sometimes a travestying manner, a certain standing on tip-toe in a constant fencing posture, not to mention the indescribably clumsy failures in the comic, it appears beyond doubt that the recently opened public theatre will be incapable of maintaining itself in the long run without considerable reforms of everything to do with the presentation of plays.

(b) [. . .] On the contrary, the present writer believes that anyone who has kept a steady eye on our theatre and attended its performances regularly, will have become aware, not without satisfaction, of increasingly skilful movements, signs that the establishment will be able to rise to its feet and walk quite handsomely, even if it does not march quite so elegantly as its older brother, the Copenhagen theatre. [. . .] Since the establishment had to be built up completely from scratch, the first actors could to begin with naturally only be regarded as dilettantes, performing as they were without any preparation, and without yet having had the opportunity to see anything perfect in their art which could serve as a pattern and model, apart, perhaps, from whatever chance they may have had to see something at a private theatre, which would in any case scarcely have been of much significance. It is therefore rather to be wondered at that they achieve what they do, than that they do not achieve more. That it is not always the most classical language that can be heard from the stage is unfortunately true; but this is also a fault which can be corrected with training and attention; nor is the criticism equally applicable to the whole company, since there are some at least to whose language and pronunciation little objection can be made. [. . .]

*The Union Day demonstration*

When Strömberg chose to celebrate 'Union Day', 4 November, in 1828 with a production of his own *The Peace Celebration* (*Fredsfesten*), a demonstration took place in the theatre. King Carl Johan appointed a commission, principally to investigate the extent of any anti-Swedish feeling. It took depositions from forty-nine witnesses, among them Strömberg and Henrik Wergeland (1808–45), who was already, as a 20-year-old student, on his way to becoming a nationalist figurehead, and later Norway's major poet of the period.

## 86 Wergeland testifies to the Union Day demonstration, 1828

*Undersøgelses-Commissionens forhandlinger i anledning det forefaldne i Christiania offentlige skuespilhuus den 4de November 1827* [*Investigatory Commission's proceedings on the occasion of the incident at the Christiania public playhouse on 4 November 1827*] (Christiania: Udgivne af Christiania Byes Formænd, 1828) unnumbered pp.

Question 6: The witness is all the more convinced that the object of the whistlers was only to express their dissatisfaction with Strömberg's poor piece, seeing that he, too, thought it weak, and its performance likewise.
Question 7: As far as the witness could tell, the whistlers took no special notice of particular scenes or expressions in the work, but were merely displaying their dissatisfaction with the work itself as an aesthetic failure. The witness is strengthened in his conviction by the fact that the whistling continued throughout the play, and supposes that such lulls as occurred were due only to weariness on the part of the whistlers.
Question 8: The whistling began right at the beginning of the play, when two

bandy-legged caricatures (the actors Lösch and Wang)[1] came on as Norwegian peasants, and it seemed to the witness to have been at its strongest then, and gradually to have diminished from then on. This scene, which was thus the one most loudly whistled at, took place before the actors representing Swedes appeared, and before the Norwegians and Swedes greeted each other.

[1] Hybert Lösch (1790–1847), theatrical bookbinder and rehearsal-master. Peter Munch Wang (1792–1842) was successful in comic female parts.

*Wergeland attacks the Danish element*

Henrik Wergeland attacked what he called 'the capital's Danish theatre' from many angles, appealing for Norwegian actors, Norwegian dramatists and plays, and the Norwegian language, and drawing attention to the failure since Strömberg to provide a school of acting.

## 87 Wergeland promotes Norwegian over Danish theatre, 24 January 1832

*Morgenbladet* [*Morning Paper*], 24 January 1832, reprinted in Henrik Wergeland: *Samlede skrifter, trykt og utrykt* [*Collected works, published and unpublished*] (edited by H. Jæger and D.A. Seip), vol. 3, part 1 (Oslo: Steenske forlag, 1918–40), pp. 296–7.

Almost every time the capital's Danish theatre blows its own trumpet in *Morgenbladet*, we are told that our literature affords them no plays to perform, so that the public must be pleased to accept entertainments with all manner of foreign, and especially Danish, theatre goods, or such as they themselves have translated. We hear this cried out in most decisive tones especially during those intervals in the theatre harangues when the bravura blasts are cut through by bitter bagpipe whining at the existence of some Norwegians whose eyes have been opened to the Danish abuse being practised on this country, supported merely by a peculiar prejudice which, as the offspring of dying memories, is bound to disappear, and by a tolerance to which limits can and should be set, since it springs partly from foolish indifference, and partly from a far too exalted notion of the spiritual superiority attributed to the theatre personnel's distant countrymen, indifferent to us, to whom they appeal. This institution will undeniably find firmer support, and the only secure grounds for its existence, when it can refer instead to the fulfilment of the promise to train Norwegian actors – whereupon this pen, which will otherwise never tire of attacking it in its present condition, will be laid down – and if capable and worthy Norwegians take over censorship of the repertoire. The theatre's behaviour is directly contrary to its own interests when its passionate public outcries, often affronts to national honour, truth and justice,

expose the utterly un-Norwegian spirit which still infests its personnel, and which cannot be hidden behind compliments to our public, which is certainly elevated enough for praise of its taste to be ridiculous when pronounced by such judges as our Danish actors. Among such statements are the frequent ones already mentioned concerning the utter poverty of our dramatic literature, to which we find the most apt reply and refutation in a list of plays written by Norwegians and adapted for performance, although the list, from memory, can hardly be complete.
Bjerregaard – *Mountain Adventure* [*Fjeldeventyret*, 1825], *Clara*, *Magnus Bareleg's Son* [*Magnus Barfods sønner*, 1829–30].
Bruun[1] – *Einar Thambeskjelfver*.
Falsen[2] – *The Pixie* [*Dragedukken*] and many more.
Holberg – Many.
P.A. Heiberg[3] – 2 volumes of plays.
Munch[4] – *The Priest of Hallingdal* [*Præsten i Hallingdal*].
Wessel[5] – *Love without Stockings* [*Kjærlighet uden Strømper*], and one other play, if I remember correctly.[6]
It would certainly be possible to present new original Norwegian plays each year, if there were any encouragement, if there were censorship at the theatre to which a dramatist could honourably submit his works, and provided that an author could bring himself to have his words sound no more pleasing to his Norwegian ears, than the Danish do – at least to this writer and probably to some others.

[1] Johan Nordahl Bruun (1745–1816), priest, hymn-writer, Bishop of Bergen. *Einar Thambeskjelfver* (in Wergeland's spelling) has been described as Norway's first significant historical drama.

[2] Envold Falsen (1755–1808), lawyer, judge, editor. The musical play *Dragedukken* dates from 1797.

[3] Peter Andreas Heiberg (1758–1841), Danish author and dramatist (J.L. Heiberg's father and Johanne Luise Heiberg's father-in-law).

[4] Andreas Munch (1811–84), author, editor of *Den Constitutionelle* 1841–6. His *King Sverre's Youth* [*Kong Sverres Ungdom*] won the competition for the opening production at the new theatre in 1837; a production of his *Lord William Russel* is the subject of a major critical essay by Ibsen (1857).

[5] Copenhagen attracted many bright sparks from Norway towards the end of the eighteenth century, not least as the source of university training and the civil service appointments which might follow graduation. A nucleus of leading lights formally turned their club into Det Norske Litteraire Selskab (Norwegian Literary Society) on 30 April 1774 for criticism and conviviality. The member best known to posterity thanks to his memorably witty verses is Johan Herman Wessel (1742–85). His play, *Love without Stockings*, first performed in 1772, was a parody of over-sentimental Germanic tragedy, for the group championed Voltairean classicism over the new pre-Romanticism represented by the Danish poet Ewald.

[6] Apart from Holberg's, the only plays to have survived from Wergeland's list (which looks distinctly odd as an assertion of 'Norwegianism') are Wessel's parody of neo-classical tragedy and Bjerregaard's *Mountain Adventure*.

## II THE NEW THEATRE IN CHRISTIANIA, 1835–40

### *Building the Christiania Theatre*

Strömberg's poorly-built and poorly-insured theatre was destroyed by fire in 1835. The new Christiania Theatre which replaced it was fortunate in the liaison it established with the excellently qualified Danish theatre designer and scene painter Troels Lund (1802–67), who had also on his many visits to leading continental theatres taken the trouble to learn as much as possible about stage machinery. The new theatre's architect, Christian Henrik Grosch (1801–65; previously responsible for the unrealized plans for Strömberg's theatre and for alterations to it), had studied with Lund in Copenhagen, recommended him in 1830 when the first theatre needed new sets, and sought his help from the start when designing the new theatre, which was regarded as their joint project. Lund must have undertaken to paint the sets on acceptable terms, but could not go to Christiania to do the job, so the Directors ordered their scenery by post.

## 88a Directors of the Christiania Theatre build and equip the new playhouse, 1835–6

Øyvind Anker: *Den danske teatermaleren Troels Lund og Christiania theater* [*The Danish theatre designer Troels Lund and Christiania Theatre*] (Oslo: Gyldendal, 1962) pp. 23, 26–8.

(1) Directors to Troels Lund, 29 June 1835.
1 a woodland set with six wings on each side and one backdrop with borders.
2 a street set six ditto on each side and one ditto.
3 a magnificent hall set five ditto on each side and one ditto without.
To save time and transportation, the directors request you to take the trouble to buy the necessary canvas and have it sewn, whereas they think it would be more practical to have the frames made here. Since the directors only want the hall to consist of five wings instead of the originally mentioned six, you may be good enough to paint a number of separate set pieces for the woodland set instead of the sixth wing.

You will on request receive from Messrs Prætorius & Sons the necessary sums for materials as well as your stipulated fee.

Since our theatre is urgently in need of new sets, and the directors are therefore having a number of alterations made which will make it impossible to use many of our older sets, we request you most earnestly to expedite the order quickly.

(2) Report of Supervisory Committee, 9 April 1836.
With regard to the plans for building the theatre, the committee has [. . .] engaged City Architect Grosch both to execute the necessary drawings with descriptions and estimates and, while functioning as the architect, to implement whatever plan is chosen. However, since it must be regarded as especially important that a

plan for the construction of the theatre should be prepared or at least examined by a man who combines insight into architecture in general with particular knowledge of the rules of the construction and fitting out of the theatre, the committee has, in accordance with the express wish of City Architect Grosch, also engaged scene painter Troels Lund in Copenhagen to prepare the building design and arrange and fit out the stage jointly with the City Architect.

(3) Notice in *Dansk Kunstblad* (*Danish Art Magazine*) on commencement of building, 16 July 1836.

The whole building will be 80 alen [roughly 160 ft] long and 32 alen broad and about 19 alen to the upper edge of the cornice. [. . .] The machinery has been constructed so as to permit scenery to rise vertically without being folded, and is in other respects designed to satisfy any demand that can reasonably be made of complete theatre machinery. The building is expected to be ready for use in September or October 1837, for which purpose orders have already been placed with scene painter Troels Lund for the twelve sets necessary for the opening of the playing season.[1]

[1] Lund painted many of the sets listed in the 1840 inventory [see **92**] and worked on the project in Christiania from 8 May to 7 June 1836.

## 88b Christian Henrik Grosch's painting of his Christiania Theatre on Bank Square (Bankplassen)

Theatre Collection of the Oslo University Library.

*Ebbell's urbane criticism*

In Ole Falk Ebbell (1813–71), the conservative newspaper *Den Constitutionelle* had an urbane, knowledgeable and helpful theatre critic, with an eye for costumes, sets, effects and lighting as well as for acting, and an ear for music. The first of these excerpts from 1837 concerns *La Fiancée* by Scribe and Auber. It should be noted that between the 1835 fire and the opening of the new theatre in the autumn of 1837, the company used the amateur dramatic society's theatre. This does not necessarily account, however, for the staging which Ebbell criticizes.

## 89 Ebbell criticizes the stage productions, February–April 1837

*Den Constitutionelle* [*The Constitutional*], 14 February, 3 March, 11 April 1837.

*14 February* The staging of this opera has never been more miserable and threadbare than on this occasion. Masquerades in this town are not exactly renowned for elegance, but it must be confessed by the unprejudiced that they far exceed the Spanish Legate's *redoute* in *The Bride.*[1] One sees half a score of anxious individuals tightly wrapped in shabby cloaks and gowns sneaking in from the wings; it is almost as if they had conspired to parody Holberg for having had 'This presents Troy' written on the walls of Troy; for they all carry masks in their hands, apparently declaring, with slightly greater subtlety, that 'This is to be taken for a masquerade'. Here, where there was occasion to show a little splendour, there is none; in *Parting and Meeting*,[2] on the other hand, one sees Funen masons and their journeymen with elegant slim rapiers at their sides; they would be the more likely to be going to a masquerade. At the wedding feast we saw none of the Tyroleans promised us by Saldorf. We also wondered to see one of the *modiste's* ladies wearing the same gown to the feast as she had sewn for Mrs Saldorf in the first act.
*3 March* It is praiseworthy magnificence on the part of the authority which supplies the theatre, and puts spectators in an agreeable mood, that real champagne is poured for Don Juan, so that Leporello is not obliged, as is often the case even at the larger theatres, to imitate the popping cork with his tongue. It is a mistake, on the other hand, to keep the light so bright in the last scene; the moment the Commandant knocks at the door the stage should be darkened, and even the candles on Don Juan's table should if possible go out; ghosts and spooks belong in the dark, so no one would be surprised to see the lights dim at that moment; and the effect becomes much greater if one sees the ensuing events in frightening gloom; one would not then in the Commandant's ghost recognize the chalked, painted, or flour-covered person of Mr Nielsen,[3] and the thunderbolt which destroys Don Juan would be more natural and powerful.
*11 April* [In Bayard and Vanderbruck's hit *Le Gamin*, the gamin was played by Mme Schrumpf.[4]] When she tells Elsa how she ended up in St Martin's Canal, she

must not stand holding her hand, but move about the floor. In the last act, when she has brought her sister to the General, and he orders Joseph to leave them, she must not stand still and embarrassed in the middle of the room. The Gamin has visited the General before; she already knows the place; is as good as at home there. She should therefore walk about upstage, or take a seat somewhere; by all means sit on the table or on a chair if she will, anything rather than standing still looking awkward. She can still easily keep an eye on the General and her sister. Incidentally, she looks splendid. Truly a delicious little gamin we see before us. She is even fresh from the hairdresser's, who has given her pretty curls – which, God be praised, have come to no harm in the canal.

[1] *La Fiancée* (1829) with music by Daniel François Auber (1782–1871) to a text by Scribe.
[2] *Skilles og mødes*, vaudeville by Hans Christian Andersen (1836).
[3] Peter Ludvig Nielsen (*c*. 1803–46), joined the Christiania Theatre in 1834 and was the last of the Danish actors to leave, after fifty-five years' service, 6,600 appearances, and only two absences through illness, in 1889. He lived to see the National Theatre opened in 1899.
[4] Augusta Schrumpf (1813–1900), with the Christiania Theatre 1829–60; for many years the theatre's leading tragedienne.

### *Rehearsal schedules*

From the opening of the new theatre, a record was kept of rehearsals and performances. Rehearsals of each production were few, but productions were numerous: the company and the prompter had their work cut out for them. The opening production, *King Sverre's Youth*, Andreas Munch's winning competition entry, was given on 4, 6, and 8 October with an author's benefit on the 13th. By the time Schiller's *Kabale und Liebe* opened on the 22nd, eight other works had been staged at least once. The rehearsal schedule for *Kabale und Liebe* was: 22/9 parts distributed, 7/10 reading rehearsal, 14/10 rehearsal, 15/10 rehearsal, 19/10 rehearsal, 21/10 rehearsal, 22/10 10 a.m. final rehearsal (full dress rehearsals had yet to be introduced), 6:30 p.m. premiere.

## 90 Rehearsal journal for Christiania Public Theatre, September 1837

In the Theatre Collection, University of Oslo Library.

1837
*September*

15 Distributed singing parts in *Lestocq*[1]
16 10 o'clock Reading rehearsal for male voices in *Lestocq*
Distributed parts in *Lestocq*
5 " Distributed parts and held reading rehearsal of *King Sverre's Youth*
18 10 o'clock Piano rehearsals for Mad. Schrumpf and Mr Staal[2] in *Lestocq*

| | | |
|---|---|---|
| | 12 " | Piano rehearsals for the male chorus in *Lestocq* |
| 19 | 10 " | Do. " Do. Do. |
| | 12 " | Do. for Miss Gade and Mr Jørgensen[3] in Do. |
| | | Distributed parts in *Michael Perrin, First Love* and *The Danes in Paris*[4] |
| 20 | 10 o'clock | Piano rehearsals for the male chorus in *Lestocq* |
| | 12 " | Do. for the solo voices in Do. |
| 21 | 10 o'clock | Do. for the male chorus in Do. |
| | | Messrs Bergh and Jensen[5] $\frac{1}{4}$ hour late. |
| | 12 " | Piano rehearsals for the solo voices in *Lestocq* |
| 22 | 11 o'clock | Do. " Do. " Do. |
| | | Distributed parts in *Kabale und Liebe, Jægerbruden, The Quaker and the Dancing Girl, April Fools* and *No.*[6] Notified the acting company, Messrs Schrumpf, Rasmussen and Müller[7] by circular to appear at 12 noon on the 24th in the rehearsal room. Made the repertoire for October known to the acting company. |
| 23 | 12 o'clock | Piano rehearsal for the solo voice in *Lestocq*. |
| | | Mr Jørgensen ill. Because of Mr Jørgensen's illness the rehearsal of *King Sverre's Youth* scheduled for this afternoon was cancelled. Distributed singing parts in *No.* |

1 *Lestocq, ou L'Intrigue et l'amour*, musical play by Scribe and Auber (1834).

2 Ditlev Staal (1802–59), with the Christiania Theatre 1837–59.

3 *Michel Perrin*, vaudeville by Mélesville and Duveyrier (1834); *Les Premières Amours, ou Les Souvenirs d'enfance* (1825), a one-act comedy by Scribe, translated by J.L. Heiberg; *Danskerne i Paris*, vaudeville by J.L. Heiberg.

4 Cecilie Gade (later Mrs Jørgensen, 1814–90), with the Christiania Theatre 1835–63.
Christian Ludvig Jørgensen (1812–69), actor and assistant director, with the Christiania Theatre 1831–63; played King Sverre.

5 Richard Bergh (Norwegian) with the Christiania Theatre 1837–50.
Johan Jensen, with the Christiania Theatre 1837–41?

6 *Jægerbruden* = *Der Freischütz*, musical play by Kind and Weber (1821); *Quekeren og dandserinden* = *Le Quaker et la danseuse* by Scribe and Duport (1831); *Aprilsnarrene*, vaudeville by J.L. Heiberg (1826); *Nej*, vaudeville by J.L. Heiberg (1836).

7 Adam Friedrich Schrumpf (1807–56), singing master and orchestra leader.
Poul Diderich Muth-Rasmussen (1806–55), singing master 1837–9.
Ludvig Ernst Müller (1810–39), prompter and assistant singing master 1837–9.

### *The 'Campbell battle'*

A Wergeland supporter, J.R. Krogness, published a humorous satirical account of the 'Campbell battle', at which demonstrators were defeated in their attempt to stop the second night's performance of Wergeland's *The Campbells, or The Son Returned* (*Campbellerne, eller Den hjemkomne sön*, 1837) on 28 January 1838. The play had been ranked second to Munch's *King Sverre's Youth* in the competition for a play with which to open the new theatre; the verbal and physical attacks on it were no doubt more politically than aesthetically motivated. Here Krogness is quoting.

## 91 Krogness describes the 'Campbell battle', 1838.

Johan Richard Krogness: *Tro og detailleret fremstilling av det berømte theaterslag* [*Faithful and detailed account of the famous theatre battle*] (Christiania: N.F. Axelsen, 1838), p. 14.

But when the play ended – relates this eye-witness – the armistice was over, and the third and last act of the tragicomic play on this side of the curtain was performed. People now came to blows. On which side this began is uncertain. For although the 'Constitutionals' complain that they were the only ones who were beaten, it is quite certain that some of them took opportunities to strike at isolated applauding individuals without themselves being assailed. From the rear stalls and boxes people now began to bombard the stubborn whistlers in the front stalls with improvised weapons, pages from the demonstrators' paper *Den Constitutionelle* bunched up into balls, roasted apples, bags of grapeshot, coins and the like. At this point the ring-leaders were the first to make their escape; one by one they sneaked away and sought the safety of their homes *via* long detours. The rear stalls stormed the barriers to the front and drove the remaining whistlers out. What happened to them outside I do not know. But in the theatre the whole affray ended as a triumph for the play's author, for whom the audience fought with true enthusiasm.

### *The stock of scenery*

In 1840, a thorough inventory was taken at the Christiania Theatre, and completed as of December. The list of sets and props, defined as the chief stage mechanic's area of responsibility, includes the following, omitting marginal notes on additional items, states of repair, etc. Troels Lund is thought to have been responsible for items 6 to 13 inclusive and 17, which was an innovation that reads rather like a box set.

## 92 Inventory of the Christiania Theatre, December 1840

Anker (1962), appendix.

6 A splendid hall consisting of 12 wings, 2 backdrops and 2 practicable doors plus 1 fireplace with screens and 1 set piece of a mirror without a frame.
7 A Gothic hall consisting of 8 wings and 2 backdrops and 4 doors, plus an act drop representing a secret door, which is repairable, as well as a transparent window for one of the backdrops and a gate for the same backdrop.
8 A luxurious drawing-room consisting of 8 wings, 1 backdrop, 2 practicable doors and 2 windows plus 2 fireplaces. To this also belong 4 glass windows.

9 A blue living-room consisting of 8 wings, 1 backdrop, 2 practicable doors and 2 windows, plus a secret door which is repairable.
10 A red living-room consisting of 6 wings, 1 backdrop, 2 doors and 2 windows, to which also belong 2 glass windows.
11 A yellow living-room consisting of 6 wings, 1 backdrop, 2 doors and 2 windows, to which also belongs the act drop for scene changes, consisting of a curtain, 5 doors, 1 mirror, a clock, a large painting of a knight, 1 fireplace, 4 windows, a piece of panelling, 2 doors, and 11 pieces for wings and borders.
12 A green living-room ('Holberg's living-room') consisting of 6 wings, 1 backdrop, 2 doors, 2 windows and 1 window for the backdrop.
13 A peasant's living-room consisting of 6 wings, 1 backcloth, and doors, 1 open background consisting of 2 pillars and 2 panels plus 2 borders. To this also belong 12 act-drops for scene changes.
14 A prison consisting of 8 wings, 1 backdrop, 3 borders, 1 door and 1 window.
15 A monastery hall consisting of 8 wings, 1 backdrop, 2 doors, 1 window, and in the backdrop a thin shirting curtain to cover the cloisters.
16 A monastery hall consisting of closed walls, background, and a loft. To the same set belong a small curtain with church windows painted on it and 2 painted canvases and 1 screen with which to change the aforementioned set.
17 A closed cabinet consisting of closed walls, a background with two windows and a door; a background with 2 doors and 1 fireplace plus a loft.

## III THE FIRST BERGEN VENTURE, 1849–63

### *Ole Bull proposes a Bergen theatre*

A remarkable feature of Norwegian nineteenth-century theatre is the number of great actors and actresses who were born and raised in Bergen and first trod the boards there. There was a living tradition of lively and skilful amateur theatricals, pride in the links back to Holberg and, from the turn of the century, a theatre – where also many professional touring companies performed. This rich tradition lay behind the movement in the town to establish a public Norwegian, indeed national, theatre, which found the dynamic and popular leader it needed in the famous violin virtuoso Ole Bull. Having got the project off the ground, in the process recruiting Ibsen as artistic director and resident dramatist (1851–7), Bull left its management to others.

## 93 Ole Bull advertises for a Norwegian theatre, 25 July 1849

Marie Bull:[1] *Minder fra Bergens første nationale scene* [*Reminiscences of Bergen's first national stage*] (edited by Hans Wiers-Jenssen) (Bergen: H.J. Wiers-Jenssen, 1905), p. 27.

NORWEGIAN THEATRE IN BERGEN

Ladies and gentlemen desiring to make professions of singing, instrumental music, the art of acting, or folk dancing, are invited to supply for engagements. Original dramatic and musical works will be accepted for such fees as circumstances permit. Kindly apply in writing as soon as possible to 'The Norwegian Theatre in Bergen' care of the advertising office here.

[1] Marie Midling (1827–1907) acted in the Bergen theatre's first season 1849–50 and married Ole Bull's brother, the orchestra conductor Edvard Bull, in 1851. Her recollections from the theatre's earliest days are lively and amusing.

*Winning support from the local public*

Before the first Bergen theatre could rely on enough public support to get started, it had to win the approval of an invited audience which no doubt numbered many sceptics. This is how Marie Bull recalled the occasion.

## 94a Playing Holberg to an invited audience in 1849

M. Bull (1905), pp. 78–9.

And there we were, then, in the wings, trembling in our Holbergian finery. Some from the theatre wardrobe – in the possession of our lighting man, tinsmith Feser – and some in costumes we had borrowed in the town. In those days the old families had lots of beautiful costumes hidden away from Holberg's day. I, for instance, had borrowed a magnificent silk dress from Miss v. Tangen, which had belonged to her grandmother, and which became me wonderfully – at least in my opinion.

Down there, our judges were gathering, the front curtain was fanned by the draught, and waves of sound reached us from all the talking voices.

'Well, *this* will be a comedy, and no mistake!'

I knew that the official opening performance was on 2 *January*, but I see 21 *November* as the real start, the debut for *Norway's first national theatre*, when it survived its trial by fire and won the right to live.

Ole Bull went up to the conductor's desk, we heard the applause with which he was received, and our hearts beat fit to burst our tight corsets. The overture filled the house, and the curtain rose on *Henrik and Pernille*.[1]

For a moment, the stage was empty.

And then our *Henrik* leaped on!

How clearly I see him before me this very day! In a suit of brown velvet trimmed with swansdown, a dress sword at his side, his three-cornered hat at the back of his neck. And his laugh! Johannes Brun's[2] gales of infectious laughter were the introductory music to which Norwegian dramatic art opened, – even before he got to the words, he had won the spectators over – this humour was their own flesh and blood, it had the ring of home, they could not resist!

[1] Holberg's *Henrik og Pernille* (1724).
[2] Johannes Brun (1832–90), probably Norway's greatest actor, with the Bergen theatre 1850–57, then the Christiania Theatre 1857–90, but for the 1862–63 seasons with Christiania norske theater.

## 94b Johannes Brun in his most famous comic role in Holberg, *Jeppe of the Hill*

As performed at the Christiania Theatre *c.* 1880. Photograph by Claus Knudsen in the Theatre Collection of the Oslo University Library.

## 95 Laws for rehearsals at the Bergen theatre, 1850

Tharald Høyerup Blanc: *Norges første nationale scene. (Bergen, 1850–1863); et bidrag til den norske dramatiske kunstshistorie* [*Norway's first national stage, a contribution to Norwegian dramatic art history*] (Kristiania: no pub., 1884), pp. 383–97; this extract pp. 388–9.

§1 As a rule, rehearsals are scheduled, and the repertoire fixed, each Thursday for the following week. Further details are announced on the notice board or by circular.

§2 Times are according to the theatre clock.

§3 At all rehearsals without exception there must be quiet, order and attention. Anyone causing a disturbance pays 8 skillings.

§4 At reading rehearsals, everyone concerned with the play must be present from beginning to end, on pain of a fine of 24 skillings.

§5 Everyone must be completely familiar with his or her part before a reading rehearsal. Anyone whose first attempts to learn to read a part take place there, or who in other ways tries the patience of those present, pays 24 skillings.

§6 Everyone must ensure that any mistakes in the copying of their parts are corrected at the first reading rehearsal. The stage manager or inspector shall see to it that this is done, and that foreign words and names are correctly pronounced at the first rehearsal.

§7 At all stage rehearsals, the stage manager signals the beginning of an Act by ringing his bell; all those with parts shall then muster at once, and all those not involved shall leave the stage.

§8 Anyone entering from the wrong part of the adopted set or entering too early or late on his or her cue pays 4 skillings. At the final rehearsal the fine is doubled; during performances it is 60 skillings.

§9 Anyone who does not know his or her part perfectly by heart at the final rehearsal shall be fined one quarter of a month's wages.

## 96 Ole Bull writes to his wife about preparations for the opening night, 30 November 1849 and 4 January 1850

*Ole Bulls breve i uddrag* [*A selection of Ole Bull's letters*] edited by Alexander Bull (Copenhagen: Gyldendal, 1881), pp. 373–7; translated into Norwegian from the original French.

30 November 1849

My dear Félicie!

The great day has finally arrived which is to shed its light on our national theatre! During the past week I have put on a trial performance before an audience and invited theatre representatives and some others to attend a rehearsal. The result was surprising! Even our opponents declared themselves not only astonished, but convinced that there were superior talents here whose equals had never been seen in Bergen. Oh, Félicie! – I would have given a lot to have had you here; you would have understood the satisfaction I felt at this first rehearsal. We put on a Holberg comedy, *Henrik and Pernille*, Mozart's Jupiter symphony (its first time here), a recitation (excellently done), *Sæterbesøget* (the visit to the mountain farm) with the orchestra, and a comic scene, *The Cobbler's Apprentice*, in Bergen dialect – we had to laugh.

I have taken care not to publish anything about this experiment in the liberal press; but the conservatives have seized the initiative in their paper *Bergenske blade* by stating that there were four talented persons. Our internationalists were greatly taken aback to hear the firm resolve on all sides to foster the national in theatrical matters and protect their own talents [. . .]

If you only knew how hard I have had to work to achieve this miracle in such a short time, you would be amazed at my patience; our committee now consists of sixteen members, each with allotted tasks. The orchestra was pitiful. To make it presentable, we had to have rehearsals, give the violinists lessons, have them play duets and quartets in my lodgings – some feast for the ears!!! Now the orchestra is not bad at all.

I am composing an overture, a cantata for song and orchestra, choruses, etc. I'm working with all my might to get the theatre ready. I'm having machinery constructed to heat the whole theatre; I'm having a corridor built by the forestage,[1] all so that people can go to the theatre without fear of losing their health and with a chance of hearing something good, original, new, and at the same time of supporting home-grown talent! Then everyone will go, and the theatre become a school for good taste, for national spirit, for industry, harmony and the fine arts.

Bergen 4 January 1850

My dear Félicie!

These few lines to tell you the happy outcome for the national theatre, which gave its first performance on the 2nd of January.

The choruses I composed for the occasion were very effective, and everything looks promising.

The whole performance was a marvel!

I am very busy! but I am not feeling very well, and can hardly eat. I rarely go anywhere but to the theatre. I am doing some composing at night; but a little work is no problem, if only I can arouse my countrymen.

The second performance is on Saturday, and we are giving *The Mountain Cabin*[2] on Wednesday.

I still have a sailors' chorus to write, and then everything will be absolutely ready!

[1] It is unclear from both old photographs and a scale model of the theatre whether Bull meant a covered passageway [*couloir*], a gallery or a lobby. The rows of seats stretched without a break almost from wall to wall, and were entered through doors in the side walls of the auditorium. To cross the hall, one would have to pass between all the seats in a row, or pass the first row and the orchestra pit, where there did seem to be a passageway. Could Bull have hit upon the bright idea of making this latter space available by removing the first row of seats?

[2] *Fjeldstuen*, a three-act play by Henrik Wergeland (1850).

## 97 Review of the Bergen Norwegian Theatre's first performance on 2 January 1850

*Bergens Stiftstidende* [*Bergen Diocesan Times*], 6 January 1850.

Subscriptions for ten Wednesday and ten Sunday performances have been selling briskly. Eight days before the theatre's opening, all the seats and even much of the standing room for the Wednesday performances had been sold, and there have been more subscriptions for the Sunday performances than any Danish acting company ever obtained here. The Bergen public has thus clearly shown the warm sympathy it entertains for its theatre. On the day of the performance, all the tickets, about 800, were sold out early in the day, and ticket touts were later paid more than double.

No sooner did Ole Bull appear in the orchestra pit than he was met by the cheers of the spectators, which rose to enthusiastic acclaim when he stepped up to the conductor's desk. The performance began with a dramatized prologue presenting and justifying the efforts to establish a Norwegian theatre. A man tied to the rocks addresses various conditions of people who happen to come within earshot, among whom the poet presents partly peasants and partly townspeople, who are all more or less easily moved by his complaint, but finally an artist who is not only moved to sympathy, but also sets to work and exhorts the gradually growing assembly to open the prison of the spirit. First they all kneel with him in prayer; an angel appears before the rock, at whose command the barrier falls and the people enter a magnificent hall, where a woman is seated on a raised throne. After they have expressed their joy at the reunion in a jubilant chorus, she descends among them and greets her people as their true ruler, as the one who, according to Nature's unchanging laws, must govern all the manifestations of their lives if they are to be true and valuable, since she is the fundamental law laid down in every seed to determine its growth, and accordingly also the only true guide of art. The Prologue was in other words a lively allegorical presentation of the plain truth which it has unfortunately taken us so long and cost us so much sad experience to recognize, and which we hope only a few thick skulls have yet to understand: that there can be as little reason for speaking of 'our art' when we do not freely produce it ourselves out of our own spirit, as for speaking of a flower when it is foreign, made of cloth, and tied to a sterile Norwegian stem.

The three choruses were by Ole Bull, as far as we know his first work for the stage. The introduction of the first chorus was gloomy and demonic in nature, and the theme was developed in the ensuing chorus. It was wholly composed in a completely new and, as we believe, Norwegian style, and made a gripping impression. [. . .] The final chorus created a fresh and pleasant mood and was distinctively Norwegian, the composer having used the wind instruments in a characteristic manner. [. . .]

The actors then presented *The Weathercock* [*Den Vægelsindede*], a three-act comedy by our Holberg. Rumour had had it that H. Wergeland's last work *The Mountain Cabin*, a three-act musical play, was to have been performed first, and we have heard that Ole Bull has set it to music which has already been rehearsed; but presumably it was decided to await the arrival of the country fiddler Torgeir Augundsson (Møllergutten).[1] He has arrived, and the public is all on fire to see the work staged, and all the more so since Ole Bull's music to the dramatized prologue gave a taste of what one may expect from him on that occasion also.

*The Weathercock* was given a lively performance, to the great amusement of the audience. Its execution far surpassed the expectations we had formed in view of the present circumstances. Admittedly we have not seen *The Weathercock* before on this stage; but in our opinion none of Holberg's plays – at least in the time of the Danish actors – received a better performance in this theatre than the one which graced *The Weathercock* on Wednesday. Acting like that of the title part, of Pernille, Petronius and Henrik, would disgrace no theatre, and although the other parts were less excellently acted, there was no denying that the diction was good, the language mostly pure, and the ensemble playing much better than could be reasonably expected of beginners, and equal to what we have normally been accustomed to, even from the better Danish companies which have performed here. The audience rewarded these efforts accordingly, and plentiful bravos accompanied both acts and speeches – the latter perhaps more often than many could have wished, since those who did not know the play thus missed too much of the contents.

Finally Ole Bull played his *Sæterbesøg*, that pretty Norwegian musical idyll. His soulful performance inevitably aroused general enthusiasm and rapture.

At the end of the performance, Ole Bull took the curtain calls, the public joyfully welcoming the young theatre in his person. [. . .]

[1] Torgeir Augundsson, nicknamed Møllergutten (more commonly Myllarguten, 1801–72), a renowned folk musician who performed on the Hardanger fiddle. His journey on skis from Telemark across Norway to join Ole Bull in Bergen makes quite a story; some of the other attempts by the early theatre to present Norwegian peasant culture on the stage make more of a tragi-comedy.

*Jensen serves as director*

In her recollections of the first Bergen season, Mrs Bull did justice to the first artistic director Fredrik Nicolai Jensen (1818–70). A graduate in theology who became a parson and Storting representative, he also made a name for himself as a landscape painter.

## 98 Jensen praised as artistic director in 1850

M. Bull (1905), p. 59.

At a theatre like Bergen's first, this work was harder than anyone will believe: eager and enthusiastic as the members of the company were, their talents were untried and inadequate, productions had to succeed each other rapidly, and with such a small acting company it was even more difficult to provide a repertoire.

This was the work Jensen did – patiently and with unswerving faith, even in the troughs that followed the great crest – and did everything with an unselfishness which never in any respect sought its own ends. For long periods he worked as our teacher and director for nothing, going about his tasks with no fuss or ostentation, although I believe he occasionally may have felt a little bitter at the meagre gratitude and recognition accorded to him. [. . .] To my mind, his work was so noble and great, that one could never have thanked him enough, even had his name been indissolubly linked to that of Ole Bull.

## 99 Bull applies to the Storting for funds, 2 September 1851

*Morgenbladet* [*Morning Paper*], 9 September 1851.

That the first attempt to establish a national theatre was made and succeeded in Bergen, entirely as a result of private efforts, seems to justify the assumption that the goal can be achieved there at least as well as in Christiania or any other town in the country. Nor can it reasonably be claimed that the Norwegian spirit is more widespread and prominent in any other town than in Bergen; where the art of the theatre is concerned, the town has not only demonstrated its general and very lively appreciation, which seems to promise the necessary encouragement, but has also at all times displayed the most promising talents for the stage, as far as one may judge from the performances at its private theatres, including those given at the Students' Union. It can therefore not be regarded as too bold an assumption that Bergen would be well suited to cultivating a nursery for our country's national theatre, and the attempt made there, however far it may be, like any first steps, from perfection, nevertheless appears to have succeeded and to have gained sufficient respect to have a claim to be considered first, if any grant of public support for such an enterprise is to be made. [. . .]

Finally, it should not pass unnoticed that the national theatre in Bergen aims with low prices to recruit spectators from as far down among the less fortunate or poorer classes of the people as can reasonably be expected in view of the theatre's size, and that this has already resulted in the application to this national purpose of many a copper which would otherwise have been wasted in a tavern – a circumstance which merits consideration in connection with the influence which a real Norwegian theatre may be expected to have on those classes.

*The Storting turns down Bull's plea*

*Manden*, subsequently *Andhrimner*, was an influential but short-lived satirical weekly edited by A.O. Vinje, Paul Botten-Hansen[1] and Ibsen. In its final number it jeers at the Storting for turning down Ole Bull's application, under the heading 'Fragments of the "Storting Saga"'.

[1] Aasmund Olafsen Vinje (1818–70), teacher, journalist and one of Norway's major poets and prose stylists in 'landsmål', the form of Norwegian based on country dialects and codified largely as an alternative to 'Dano-Norwegian'.
Paul Botten-Hansen (1824–69), critic, editor, librarian, reviewer.

## 100 Ridiculing the Storting's meanness, 28 September 1851

*Manden* [*The Man*], 28 September 1851

Ole Bull's cause was lost, and ironically enough Dahler[1] was the executioner. Both history and mythology afford worse cases: blind Hød killed Balder.

Parliament's 'intelligentsia', who might for certain reasons have been opposed to the cause, were naturally reluctant to fight against it; their national spirit and appreciation of higher spiritual values must have urged them to do the opposite. Dahler had no qualms about letting the matter be on his conscience. Art and nationality were no more to him than bread and butter.

So Parliament finally found a use for Dahler before dissolving!

Economists rejoice at his utility, but the patriot and national honour ask with a sigh, 'Have the last remnants of liberality fled the chamber?' Who would venture a reply?

For Jaabæk[2] to help Dahler was in order; he is a political economist and national art is beyond his province – not to mention his constituency.

But who would have believed that Aall,[3] a man of both education and taste, would apply the same economic yardstick to national art as Dahler or those western farmers who, wearing expressions of serious deliberation, judge and condemn what to them is a closed shrine? The fact is, though, that Aall has in all things identified himself with the western opposition, as being the caravan which does the most profitable trade in the land of popularity. Ah well, the goods of that country fetch far too high a price with us, and other than mercenary spirits are finding it worthwhile to haggle for them whatever the cost, even at the expense of their convictions and national sentiments.

It will be objected that 'Aall has principles and vision, he must have had underlying reasons'. Perhaps! At any rate, Parliament's and especially Aall's universal reason for opposing grants was called into service now as before: the consequences. If Parliament acceded to Bull's application, it would be snowed under by similar applications from all sides.

No, neither Aall nor any of his colleagues will see the happy day when one town, let alone several, storms Parliament with requests for support for national theatres with Ole Bull at their head! Whatever pride Norway may take in the number and reputation of her artists, let her not flatter herself with that notion.

Geniuses don't grow on trees; one can convince oneself of that by taking a look at Parliament itself.

[1] Hans Borgersen Dahler (1803–76), actually only a deputy in the Storting, but called upon to sit in 1851.

[2] Søren Jaabæk (1814–94), Storting representative and a leader of the small farmer and peasant interest; his name was associated with the strictest public economy.

[3] Hans J.C. Aall (1806–94), Storting representative, became its president (speaker).

## 101 Second season at the Bergen theatre, 1851

*Theatervennen* [*The Theatrophile*], October 1851.[1]

The Norwegian Theatre gave its second performance on Sunday the 12th to a very good house. The prologue and *Mountain Adventure* were repeated. That its music was bound to prove too difficult for our acting company was confirmed. There were clear signs that both the singing instructor and the performers had worked hard at rehearsing the songs. But who can add one cubit to his stature? The choruses went well, and the masterly overture was particularly well performed both on this and on the previous evening; certainly our orchestra is currently so well manned that we can expect to gain much pleasure from it in the course of the season, especially if the audience would pay it a little more attention than is currently the case, on Wednesday in particular. As for the performance of the play, we cannot number it among the theatre's best efforts, and are inclined to attribute this, for the women's parts at least, to the need when casting the play to let the singing weigh heavily. Madame Bruun [*sic*], for instance, would certainly have been better as Marie than Madam Hundevadt,[2] who in turn would have been a better Ragnhild than Madam Bruun, from whose speech it was not easy to guess that she had never left the district. Miss Johannesen's[3] rustic dialect was excellent; but Aagot was – a coquette; one might have been tempted to believe that this was not the first time she saw travelling students at the seter [mountain farm]. In Sheriff Østmo's character part we had really expected more of Mr Bruun; what we missed most was a certain peasant slyness, which is particularly effective in connection with Østmo's motto, 'Well, well, one has to twist and turn through life'. If he works at it steadily, Mr Prom[4] can certainly become a good lover; he has a handsome appearance and a voice which with attentive training can become beautiful, while his movements, at least for a beginner, are attractive enough. As Albek he did not entirely please us; he was too heavy and stiff. Perhaps the thought of his difficult singing part was troubling him. Mr Bucher[5] may be the member of the company who has succeeded best in mastering a conversational tone. This stood him in good stead in the part of Friberg, which he performed creditably. A little less arrogance and a little more humour in the interrogation scene might not hurt. Mr Glückstad[6] was good as Mons; the part certainly suits him well, and it was plain to see that he had studied it industriously and with pleasure. Mr H. Nielsen,[7] as the justice, conveyed a mood of good humour and dignity which was bound to please, and his contribution certainly made the interrogation scene perhaps the most successful in the whole play.

1 A 'friend of the theatre,' *Theatervennen*, timed its first numbers to coincide with the opening of the Bergen theatre's second season in October 1851.

2 Louise Gulbrandsen (1830–66) married Johannes Brun; a major actress, in Bergen 1850–7 and Christiania 1857 until her death.

Benedicte Hundevadt (1829–83), acted in Bergen 1850–4, with Christiania norske theater 1855–60 and the Christiania Theatre in 1861.

3 Miss Johanessen, the future Lucie Wolf, with the Bergen theatre 1850–3, the Christiania Theatre 1853–99, and the National Theatre 1899–1902; author of a lively autobiography [see **106**].

4 Jacob Prom (1831–65), stayed with the Bergen theatre 1851–63, moving to Trondheim when it closed.

5 Ole Johan Bucher (1828–95) joined the Bergen theatre in 1851, Christiania norske theater 1853–63, and the Christiania Theatre 1863–95; did some directing.

6 Frederik Glückstad (1812–67?) acted in Bergen 1850–2, and with Christiania norske theater 1856–7.

7 Harald Nielsen (1831–82) was with the Bergen theatre 1851–4 and 1855–61, the Christiania Theatre 1854–5, and the Trondheim theatre 1861–5.

## 102 Bull meets Ibsen, 16 October 1851[1]

*Morgenbladet*, 17 October 1851

Christiania, 16 October

The Student Union's evening entertainment for the benefit of the theatre in Bergen was given yesterday evening to an absolutely over-filled house – it was said that 1,000 tickets had been sold. The fear expressed in *Christianiaposten* that people might be restrained from attending the concert by the thought that the

Union intended it as a demonstration against the Storting in favour of the Bergen theatre was certainly without foundation; such a demonstration would be so bizarre that the idea can hardly occur to many. And this proved to be the case: many had to be turned away without tickets, because the hall, as mentioned, was over-full. Not for a long time has there been such a splendid and richly staged musical entertainment, besides which we were, after a long interval, again to be allowed to hear those tones which have delighted millions. After the overture to *A Midsummer Night's Dream*, the prologue by H. Ibsen given below was recited by Miss Svendsen,[2] who presented the beautiful poetry with life and feeling, upon which the chorus below by the same author was performed by all three musical societies to splendid and impressive music by Ole Bull. To endless cheering Bull then appeared, and played his famous and beautiful Fantasy with variations on a theme by Bellini. [. . .]

[1] This meeting probably led to Ibsen's appointment as artistic director in Bergen.

[2] Miss Svendsen, who had made her debut the year before, was the future Laura Gundersen (1832–98), one of the 'all-time greats'. Apart from the 1870–72 seasons, when she was at Møllergaten teater under Bjørnson, she acted at the Christiania Theatre from 1850 to the year of her death. Towards the end of her career, she apparently experienced some difficulty in adapting a style well suited, for instance, to the heroines of Ibsen's historical plays, to the demands of modern realism.

*Bjørnson supports the Bergen theatre*

Bjørnstjerne Bjørnson joins the autumn 1851 chorus with a long article in *Morgenbladet* entitled 'A Norwegian National Theatre'. Note in this excerpt his warm and certainly sincere praise of the Bergen venture, followed by his rejection of the very notion that any other town but the capital Christiania be the seat of a future national theatre.

## 103 Bjørnstjerne Bjørnson argues for Norwegian life on stage, 19 October 1851

*Morgenbladet*, 19 October 1851.

But on the stage a language is still to be heard which, although perhaps not foreign, we are nevertheless unable to acquire as our own, and in plays and vaudevilles a life is depicted which, while not alien, is nevertheless not the life experienced in its characteristics and singularities by the Norwegian people. When we receive an impression from the stage of the spirit of the time as it is manifested in life's conflicts, see it unfolded for us on the stage, taken from reality, we feel it is a life which is very close to us, but not our own; it is not the Norwegian bourgeois we see, or the Norwegian peasant, but a citizen of Copenhagen or a Jutland farmer. We have, admittedly, seen a few native works staged, but they have been the exception whereas the others have been the rule. The heroes of our antiquity have been depicted by that immortal bard of Denmark, but they were moulded on the plain,[1] the scattered sketches have been brought together in a painting which could not possibly have done anything but render the picture less faithful. A few of our countrymen and countrywomen have trodden the boards; but this, too, has been the exception.

If one goes on to ask why this is so, why the Norwegian nation is practically the only one in the world unable to enjoy its own language and its own poetry on its own stage, the answer is, compelling necessity. The choice was simply between having nothing and having what we did have. This being so, we naturally grasped with pleasure whatever was available, especially when the notes we heard did not sound strange to us, and the pictures we saw were not unfamiliar. A civilized people needs a theatre, and we are grateful for what our brethren offered us. But this cannot possibly last for ever. The sense of the nation is awakening, it is at last beginning to feel in itself that it has attained a level of education, an elevation, capable of guaranteeing the life of a native theatre. It is beginning to feel that independence and originality in this genre are essential if it is to join the ranks of the other nations. This feeling has recently grown to greater clarity and awareness, and the idea has indeed already found its realization in the establishment by our countrymen, the genius Ole Bull, of a national theatre in his native city, a venture which has rightly been met with general sympathy. [. . .]

[But] is it to be expected that an enduring nursery for art and poetry can be formed so far from the main seat of culture? No one, certainly, entertains this belief; it would have history and the experience of all ages against it. For one sees everywhere that the capital has been the seat of the people's national theatre; there is its natural cradle, at the centre of events, science and art; for the art of drama does not thrive in isolation, it has the closest of relations to all other art, and if separated from it becomes sapless and withers.

[1] The allusion suggests that the Danish bard Oehlenschläger could not be expected amidst Denmark's geographical flatness to create truly Norse heroes with all their 'mountainous' nature.

### *Ibsen as stage director*

'The Norwegian Theatre stage manager's register for 1852–1854' contains examples of Ibsen's detailed blocking, accompanying elaborate diagrams complete with dotted lines, letters, and numbers showing movements and positions. The theatre put on Envold Falsen's four-act musical play *The Pixie* [*Dragedukken*] (music by Kunzen) on 6 and 10 October 1852. Ibsen's diagram of the stage shows five wings, carefully numbered i to v on either side, with A between wings ii and iii and B between i and ii, stage right, being respectively 'the herbalist's house with street door and steps, and second-storey windows' and 'house with second-storey windows. a. cellar shed.' C between iii and iv stage left is 'an inn with door and stairs. Second-storey window,' and D between i and ii is 'house with windows in both storeys.' At b, c and d are lamps, upstage on the ends of wings v stage right and v stage left, and downstage on wing ii stage right. The blocking shows movements to and from the upstage area, which these no doubt helped to illuminate. To the right of the diagram is a narrow column where cues are given as marginal notes to the written description of the movements. The description gives numbers to match the blocking diagram where necessary.

## 104 Ibsen's stage-manager's register for *The Pixie*, 1852

'Det Norske Theater Regie-Bog 1852–1854' ['The Norwegian Theatre stage manager's register'] in the Bergen Theatre Museum Collection.

### First Scene

1 Jacob forward from background stage L. Cue Jacob: Well, in God's name.

1' Jacob at the door of the herbalist's shop. (The clock strikes 4) 1" Supporting himself against the cellar shed, he creeps down into it.

### Second Scene

Jacob as before. A watchman from right to left in the background. Jacob peeps out. Runden is hailed off-stage, enters from upstage right and exits downstage left.

### Third Scene

Jacob comes out, places his basket at the herbalist's door, rings and runs across to the left. Goes back to the door and rings. k: the basket.

### Fourth Scene

The herbalist enters with a lantern. Jacob tries to run but falls. Position: 2 Herbalist – 3 Jacob.

The herbalist fetches the basket and places it at Jacob's right side. The herbalist goes in. Jacob shifts his position so as to have the basket to his left.

The herbalist comes out again with another basket which he places at Jacob's right side so that he is standing between the two baskets. Position: herbalist – Jacob. Herbalist: goes in.

Fifth Scene

Jacob between the baskets. He takes them under his arm and is leaving. Three mountebanks appear on the inn steps. Jacob creeps into the cellar shed.

Sixth Scene

Enter mountebanks and host.

Position

Jacob in the shed – 1st–2nd–3rd mount. – host (a little upstage)
Cue: 3rd mountebank – well-equipped company.

Host: worse and worse

Host goes in. 1st mount. sings; meanwhile the host comes out with wine which he pours. Position as before. While 2nd mountebank sings, 1st mountebank empties his glass and passes behind the others to the host to have it filled.

Position

Jacob in the shed – 2nd and 3rd mount. – host – 1st mountebank. Exit host.

*Bjørnson takes over as artistic director*

When Ole Bull returned from his financially ruinous Oleana venture in 1857, this led to disputes over ownership of the theatre, responsibility for its debts, etc., in what was in any case a critical year, with both Ibsen and the leading actors Johannes and Louise Brun leaving for Christiania. Bull had his way, however: the Board resigned, the acting company stayed with him, and he engaged Bjørnstjerne Bjørnson as artistic director.

One of the first plays put on in Bergen under Bjørnson's directorship was the historical four-act drama *Gudbrandsdal Valley Dwellers* [*Gudbrandsdølerne*] by Chr. Monsen (1815–52). It had been performed in Christiania in 1855 and published in 1857; in Bergen it was given five performances from 14 January 1858 to 26 February 1860. Celebrating the defeat of the Scottish mercenaries under Colonel Sinclair, who were passing through the Gudbrandsdal valley in 1612 on the way to Sweden, it is packed with patriotic rodomontade and national romantic sentiment. A stage manager's register gives notes on sets, properties and cues for lighting and sound effects – which may suggest the mood.

## 105 Bjørnson's production of *Gudbrandsdal Valley Dwellers*, 1858

Stage manager's register, Bergen Theatre Museum.

*Gudbrandsdal Valley Dwellers*
Act III

| Notes | Scenery | Props | For |
|---|---|---|---|
| Set as for Act II (Midnight) | | Spirits and matches | Watchfires |
| Page 59 Sinclair Be that as it may, I shall go forward and triumph or fall. Exit | | | |
| Set changes to Forest, etc. see over Dark night | NB | | |
| Forest (2 wings deep) In the foreground right a stone monument with a rock or mound in front of it | | A loaded pistol off stage left | (Chief stage mechanic) |
| | | A rifle and some keys | Kjeld |
| | | Bengal light and flash powder | Chief stage mechanic |
| Dark night | | | |
| Page 63 Mac Donald I was once robbed of my booty; that will not happen now, I have sworn it. Die! A shot offstage left | NB | | |
| Page 65 Men singing that she belongs to Hell and the fire Red glow from the left, increases. | NB | | |
| Page 66 Berthe The enemy is falling at their hands! | | | |

| | | | |
|---|---|---|---|
| Fire put out, dark | NB | | |
| Berthe: the mighty lightning of your wrath!<br>Violent lightning and thunder | NB | | |
| Act IV | | | |
| Wild mountains. In right foreground a rock that can be climbed on (3 wings) | | A lur[1] | Gudrun |
| | | 6 to 8 loaded pistols | Off stage right |
| | | A litter of pine branches | Sinclair's body |
| Day | | | |
| Gudrun: The whole party has rounded the cliff, and they are looking up here.<br>Scottish march played offstage. right. | NB | | |
| Berthe: Now prove your courage, look out and tell me!<br>Distant shots, continue | NB | | |
| Berthe: It is too late now to hope for mercy | NB | | |
| Scene changes to an open clearing with forest to either side and high mountains in the background | | | |

[1] A five-foot long wooden trumpet.

### *Bjørnson and Ibsen compared as directors*

Lucie Wolf (1833–1902) worked under Ibsen in Bergen, where she made her debut in 1850, and under both Ibsen and Bjørnson in Kristiania where she remained from 1856 to

1899. (Later she appeared at the National Theatre.) In the chapter of her autobiography from which these excerpts on their modes of directing are taken, her tribute to Bjørnson rises to anger at the shabby treatment which drove him from the theatre to lose himself, in her view, in politics. She also laments the failure to make proper use of the great tragedienne Laura Gundersen, as when Ibsen failed to give her the part of Rebekka West in *Rosmersholm*.

## 106 Lucie Wolf evaluates Bjørnson and Ibsen as stage directors

Lucie Wolf: *Fra skuespillerinden Lucie Wolfs livserindringer* [*From the actress Lucie Wolf's memories*] (3rd edn) (Kristiania: A. Cammermeyer, 1898), pp. 195–6, 200–2.

Working with Bjørnson was a real feast. He did not show us, literally, how we should perform our parts, he just talked with us; but in such a way that it was as if he lifted a veil, so that we could see clearly and feel that his approach to the part and no other was right. He proved so clearly that such and such a character said this, that or the other in such and such a way because of the person's individual nature. Yes, he lit lights in many empty heads; he really turned stones into bread . . . His mere presence was enough to enthuse and inspire us. His burning interest in our art, his delight when one understood and did what he wanted, were so electrifying that we often found rehearsals more interesting than actual performances. If at the end of an act he joined us and was pleased with our acting, we took turns, indeed virtually fought, to be first in his embrace as he stood there beaming with his arms outstretched.

[. . .] My recollections of Henrik Ibsen's work at the theatre are neither so lively nor so interesting to me. He was for a time artistic director in Bergen. I remember him as a silent and surprisingly shy man, whom I always found at a distance from us all, one whose nature inspired no wish for private conversation, invited no confidences. He was invariably friendly and polite, but in a manner which always made me hurry my questions. There was never any direction in the Bjørnson sense of the word. [. . .] I remember him better from his time as artistic director here in Kristiania, when he was present when we rehearsed his plays. He had one big failing: he was so well pleased with whatever we did; which was often enough mediocre. It could not be because he could not judge it; presumably it was rather a kind of laziness, or better still gallantry, especially towards the ladies, whom he consistently found excellent.

### *The theatre closes in 1863*

Bjørnson's season-and-a-half as director (1857/8–59) was marked by the introduction of greater realism in stage language and acting styles, but also by hard times in Bergen. Its public had grown accustomed to a light diet and tended to refuse his more substantial offerings, while his own political activity and polemics were directed against the very parties from which the theatre otherwise drew its support. Even Bull's belated willingness to hand over ownership of the theatre (and its mortgages) to shareholders was not enough to keep it financially viable. At times, actors went without pay – until Bull could raise a little more cash by giving a concert. The last seasons up to the closure in 1863 were simply a losing struggle; in fact, the whole thirteen-year venture was a financial cliff-hanger, with banks alternately threatening to close and providing public-spirited donations, and the sales organization for alcoholic beverages always in two minds about whether to renew its annual grant. Applications for public funds were consistently turned down by the Storting, even when recommended by the Government.

## IV PRO-NORWEGIAN ACTIVITY IN CHRISTIANIA, 1847–65

### *Introduction*

Theatre life in mid-century Christiania was marked by a second wave of pro-Norwegian activity, coinciding with the emergence of Norway's major dramatists, notably with historical drama and the successful debuts in the capital of the first major Norwegian actors and actresses (Laura Gundersen in 1850, Lucie Wolf and the Bruns from Bergen in 1853 and 1857 respectively). One by one, the Danes left, the greatest loss being Anton Wilhelm Wiehe's departure in 1860.

### *Gas lighting in the theatre*

On the 28–30 March 1849, Norwegian national romanticism was celebrated on the stage with poetry, music and tableaux of some of the best-known paintings with national motifs by painters returned home from a politically troubled continent. The tableaux would not have been possible without gas lighting.

## 107 Christiania Theatre Directors weigh costs of gas lighting, 13 September 1847

Item 1933, 13 September 1847, in the Christiania Theatre Directors' Minute Book, in the Oslo University Library Theatre Collection.

Consul-General von Stahl, Groom of the Chamber, Knight, etc., Hamburg.
The Consul-General will excuse the Directors' importunity in the matter below. According to an agreement with the municipality of Christiania, Mr James Malan has undertaken to illuminate the streets of this town with gas, on which occasion he also offered to illuminate the theatre here with gas. Finding the price demanded both for the purchase and installation of the necessary pipes, etc., and for the gas to be supplied, high, but not in a position to judge its reasonableness more

accurately, the Directors, aware that the same James Malan is also illuminating the theatre in Hamburg with gas, take the liberty of respectfully requesting the Consul-General's kind assistance in obtaining information as to what he has been paid, both for supplying the equipment itself, separately itemized: gas meters, pipes per linear alen [ = 2 feet], the various cocks, etc., and for the gas supply, how many burners are used of various kinds, and roughly how much gas is used each evening and annually.

*The first Christiania staging of* Mountain Adventure

The Christiania Theatre's 'Regiebok' records the following cast, props, costumes, sets and light and sound cues for the first production, in 1850, of 'Mountain Adventure, Musical Play in 2 acts by H.A. Bjergaard [*sic*], Music by W. Thrane,'[1] a work published in 1825. A review of a Bergen production has been given in **101**.

## 108a Stage manager's register for premiere of *Mountain Adventure*, 1850

Christiania Theater *regiebok* for *Fjeldeventyret*, Oslo University Library Theatre Collection.

| Name | Persons | Props | Costume |
|---|---|---|---|
| Sheriff Østmoe | Mr Rosenkilde[2] | | *Act II*<br>In Sheriff's uniform |
| Marie | Mrs Rosenkilde[3] | *Act* I Some sewing<br>*Act* II Breakfast service | |
| Ragnhild | Miss Fjeldstad[4] | *Act* I Some sewing<br>A bottle of spirits and a brandy glass<br>Act II Breakfast dishes | |
| Mons Østmoe | Mr Hagen[5] | Act I An old sword<br>*Act* II A bag containing the Justice's register | |
| Albek | " Lund[6] | *Act* I A knapsack<br>A stick<br>A portfolio of drawings | |

| | | |
|---|---|---|
| | | *Act* II An open letter |
| Finberg | " Rasmussen[7] | *Act* I A knapsack<br>A stick |
| Hansen | " Nielsen | *Act* I A stick<br>A knapsack in which among other things a bottle of brandy and three beakers or glasses, meat, bread, smoked sausage and a couple of knives<br>A vasculum containing plants<br>A wooden bowl of punch with a ladle. |
| The Justice | " Smidth[8] | *Act* II Mons's Report *Page 83* |
| Aagot | Miss Klingenberg[9] | *Act* I A milk pail<br>A bowl of milk |
| Peasants | | *Act* I Musket, Axes, Halberds, Staffs, etc. |

| Sets | Light and Sound cues |
|---|---|
| *Act* I<br>Sheriff's living room | *Act I Scene 5*<br>Cue: Notes from a lur heard outside, and seter girls singing and calling the cattle home. |
| *scene 5*<br>Mountain scenery outside a seter cabin. Evening | |

*Act II*
The Sheriff's yard. On one side the main building, on the other a small cottage. Morning.
*Scene 9*
Sheriff's living room. In one corner a table laid with bottles of madeira and port and wine glasses. In the room a second table on which a writing set, pens and some sheets of paper, one of which has been written on *page 94*. Chairs. In the room the Sheriff's hat.

[1] Waldemar Thrane (1790–1828), violinist, composer, orchestra director under Strömberg 1827–8.
[2] Adolf Rosenkilde (1816–82), son of the great Danish actor Christen Rosenkilde, with the Christiania Theatre 1839–50.
[3] Anne Rosenkilde (1825–85), wife of the above, with the Christiania Theatre 1843–50.
[4] Louise Fjeldstad made her debut on this occasion, then moved to Bergen for the 1850–51 season, after which she disappears from view.
[5] Carl Hagen (1816–71), with the Christiania Theatre 1838–56.
[6] Anders Lund (1821–96), with the Christiania Theatre 1847–53 and 1856–65.
[7] Theodorus Rasmussen (1814–93), with the Christiania Theatre 1842–51.
[8] Anthon Smidth (1809–68), with the Christiania Theatre 1834–53.
[9] Gyda Klingenberg (1826–?) joined the Christiania Theatre in 1849; with Laura Svendsen (Gundersen) the first female Norwegian recruit of note. Despite being thought highly promising, she acted for only a few seasons.

## 108b National romanticism and costume in a similar genre play, *The Mountain Farm*:[1] portrait of Amalie Døvle[2] in a generic national costume at the Kristiania Norwegian Theatre or Christiania Theatre

Theatre Collection of Oslo University Library.

[1] *Til Sæters* (1850), a popular and enduring one-act 'idyll' with songs by Claus Pavel Riis (1826–86).

[2] Amalie Døvle (1839–93), joined the Kristiania Norwegian Theatre in 1854 and Christiania Theater in 1863. When she retired in 1879, she became its first pensioner.

*Ibsen's first produced play attacked*

Christiania Theatre put on the first-ever production of an Ibsen play, *The Warrior's Barrow* (*Kæmpehøien* by 'Brynjolf Bjarme'). The great Laura Gundersen (Miss Svendsen) was in her first season.

## 109 A damning review of Ibsen's *The Warrior's Barrow*, 28 September 1850

*Christiania-Posten* [*The Christiania Post*], 28 September 1850

Brynjolf Bjarme doubtless had any amount of material he wanted to deal with, and no lack of ideas, when he wrote *The Warrior's Barrow*. One can see signs throughout the play of his manful endeavour; but when the final execution was at hand, either patience or ability was wanting. It was thus his intention to depict the lives and customs of our forefathers on their famous Viking expeditions, and for that purpose he even carries us off to one of their most renowned stamping-grounds, Vallund; but this is very loosely and sketchily described and, what is more, the author has in his haste attributed characteristics to the old Vikings which are no credit either to us or to our ancestors: the Vikings of the sagas were by no means such inhuman barbarians that they cut down even defenceless women in their thirst for revenge; nor is it likely that Norway's seafaring heroes of old would have taken any satisfaction in burning a miserable hermit's cot because it happened to be where an insult was to be avenged; such heroic deeds are rightly reserved for the famous knight of the windmills. He has also sought to present Nordic heathendom and Christianity in conflict, and the triumph of the latter; but this, too, is no more than an outline; further development is lacking, and one is given no idea of how it comes about that Christianity is able as if by sorcery to blunt the sword of the heathen; all one registers is the author's opinion that that is how it was. Nor do the contents of the play as such appear particularly well suited to dramatic treatment.

[After re-telling the story, not without ironic comment, the reviewer continues:]

[. . .] regarded as an epic-lyric poem, *The Warrior's Barrow* is certainly a work of no little poetic value; for many details are very beautiful – almost every speech is distinguished by a lyrical swing and a wealth of poetic ideas, of which one would probably find even more by reading the play than by seeing a single performance. Besides, the whole is clad in exceptionally beautiful and harmonious verse, for which the author appears to have extraordinary talent.

[Here the reviewer refers to Ibsen's first play *Catiline* as similarly promising, and concludes with the hope that:]

[. . .] the author will in time master dramatic form.

Miss Svendsen performed the part of Blanka with warmth and feeling, a performance which perhaps was all the more winning because the part does not afford as much scope for real acting as for declamation.

*Ibsen condemns shoddy playwriting*

Ibsen did some theatre reviewing, and a handful of major reviews, mined for statements of artistic principle and the like, have already appeared in English. The early effort below shows a more humorous Ibsen than one often finds, perhaps appropriately in the short-lived satirical periodical *Manden* (sustained by its three editors, P. Botten-Hansen, A.O. Vinje and Ibsen through an expiring third quarter under the title *Andhrimner*).

## 110 Ibsen reviews a vaudeville, May 1851

*Manden* [*The Man*] (May 1851), and reprinted in Henrik Ibsen: *Samlede værker* [*Collected works*], edited by Francis Bull, Halvdan Koht and Didrik Arup Seip, vol. 15 (Oslo: Gyldendal, 1930), pp. 58–61.

### 'A Blasé Gentleman, Vaudeville in Two Acts'[1]

11 May 1851
Thus runs the title of a work with which the theatre regaled its subscribers and other spectators yesterday evening (Thursday). One can of course tell that it is French from the title alone – and it is presumably because the play is thought to speak for itself that neither author nor translator is mentioned on the posters.

If one were to set about placing this work in any particular category, one would be somewhat at a loss. Admittedly the author (or translator) calls it a vaudeville, but an author may call his product fish or fowl without its becoming either except by virtue of its contents. As one can see from the title, this is a character play; it is the state of being blasé which we are to be shown through a dramatic personality, developing, and finally leading the individual in whom it is embodied to a point at which the spectator feels that the dramatic struggle is over, and from which, looking back, he can see a rounded picture; we shall now examine to what extent the author has satisfied this requirement.

At the beginning of the play, the author invites us to visit the blasé gentleman, and naturally one sits there expecting the main element of the hero's character to reveal itself in dramatic action – but the author is of a different opinion; instead of letting the hero act, the latter begins by telling the spectators how blasé he is, how life has lost its glow, how all he beholds is endless shades of grey; although his good friends are present, it seems unlikely that this long narrative can be directed at them, for he is saying nothing but what they presumably know. We are not told how his condition has arisen – the hero assures us that he is blasé, and we must take his word for it. He has drained joy's cup to the dregs, is insensitive to any impression, is no longer susceptible to any emotion, to call one forth he would happily give 'everything beautiful life has given him'; to no avail. Finally one of his friends has an idea, – he must marry; strange, though that he hasn't conceived this not very outlandish notion himself; but this is how the author wants it, and one must accept it. The marriage project, however, grinds to a halt, bringing an end to Act I. The blasé gentleman has subsequently become acquainted with a young country girl, and before long he is head over heels in love; unfortunately, this has occurred behind the curtain, in the interval between the acts, so we have to make do with the account of events which the hero considerately provides. Some might feel doubts about the psychological justification for all this; but it is in the script, so nothing can be done about it.

The other characters in the play are of little or no interest, even the *modiste* not excepted; however interesting such ladies may be in real life, they scarcely belong on the stage. If one goes on to consider that the whole thing is heavily larded with ambiguities (which, however, are generally not *ambiguous*), fights, etc., one has a vague idea of the circumstances under which one gets to know the blasé gentleman, and the whistling by the audience must be seen as a gratifying sign that many of us can tell kernels from shells; the few who applauded must be excused; their demonstration was probably not in favour of the play, and if it was for the performance it was perfectly in order. [. . .]

The directors can hardly be blamed for agreeing to put the play on. The public complains at being served nothing but warmed-over courses, so something new has to be devised; we produce nothing ourselves, nor do the Danes, Scribe is stale, so what is left? Besides, it is healthy occasionally to see such a thorough-going demonstration of what a play should *not* be.

[1] Johann Nestroy's adaptation of *L'Homme blasé* by Duvert and Lauzanne.

### *A national drama school*

After Strömberg's failure with his early venture, the creation of a Norwegian drama school was seen by Wergeland and others to be crucial to the cause of a Norwegian theatre. Ironically, when such a school was established in Christiania in 1852, two of the three founders, the Royal gardener Martin Mortensen (1807?–67) and the actor Jens Cronborg (1803–70), were Danish-born. The third was a military engineer, J.B. Klingenberg (1817–82), whose family ran Klingenberg's Theatre in Møllergaten, where working-class amateurs were attracting large audiences to their plays. 'Christiania norske dramatiske skole' gave many popular performances and before long changed its name to 'Christiania norske theater'. (The capital's official name remained Christiania until 1925, when it was changed to Oslo, but the spelling Kristiania, thought to be more Norwegian, was adopted in some official contexts in 1877 and in others in 1897; Audhild Lund uses it in her historical account of Ibsen's relations with this theatre.)

The Norwegian theatre (and acting school) was no more successful than its rival or the

Bergen theatre in obtaining public funds. In 1854, this prompted one of its advisers, Professor Marcus Jacob Monrad (1816–97), an editor of *The Norwegian Journal of Science and Literature*, to devote a long article to the subject.

## 111 Monrad discusses nationality and a Norwegian drama school, 1854

M.J. Monrad: 'Om theater og nationalitet og om en norsk dramatisk skole' ['On theatre and nationality and a Norwegian dramatic school'], *Norsk Tidsskrift for Videnskab og Litteratur* [*Norwegian Journal of Science and Literature*] (1854–5): 1–33; excerpt from pp. 31–2.

[. . .] What is even more important is that the school is far too often obliged to perform for money. On the one hand, the need for funds makes it necessary to put on more productions and more frequent performances than is desirable from the point of view of the pupils' studies; on the other – and worse still – the choice and casting of the plays is far too dependent on what will attract the public. Admittedly the pupils of an acting school benefit from having opportunities to perform in public, for they must become accustomed to feeling at home in public; it is also quite in order for them to be regularly accountable to the public for their progress, which will likewise feed and promote public interest in the establishment. But it is self-evident that excessive public performance must disturb them in their studies and tempt them to casualness and as it were short-windedness, as well as dulling and exhausting their interest and strength. One should not force too much fruit from a young tree. What must be still more obvious, however, is that works which it might be particularly appropriate for the school to rehearse are not those which the public is most eager to see. If it is important even for an established theatre not to be too dependent on the audience in this respect, because public taste does not always run to the inherently best, how much more important must it be for a school, not only because it cannot rely on controlling audience tastes through perfection in performance, but also because its pedagogical purpose obliges it to take other than purely aesthetic considerations. [. . .] Even in mature actors, regard for audience applause is a dangerous tempter, warring with an aesthetic conscience; how much more dangerous such a collision is for unstable souls, who have yet to be guided to a standpoint and a true 'aesthetic conscience'!

[. . .] And if we have not been entirely mistaken in what we have attempted to develop above concerning the deep national significance of theatres, the necessity of a truly national theatre as a part of the self-revelation and development of nationality, its essential contribution to national feeling and especially to the formation and cultivation of the language: it would appear that the theatre school would be a most appropriate recipient of support from public funds. [. . .]

*Demonstrations in favour of Norwegian acting*

Like Henrik Wergeland a generation earlier, Bjørnstjerne Bjørnson figured prominently in theatre demonstrations. A notorious one in May 1856 was occasioned by the appearance of a new Danish actor at the Christiania Theatre. Partly because of the competition from Kristiania norske teater (note the significantly Norwegian spelling as well as the adjective), it had undertaken to employ Norwegian actors only; the appointment of Ferdinand Schmidt – on the pretext that he was coming only as a guest artist – was a breach of faith. In an article whose title can be rendered in English roughly as 'What the whistlers want', Bjørnson defended the demonstration. He appears as less extremely anti-Danish than some, but also prepared to place national interests above aesthetic.

## 112 Bjørnstjerne Bjørnson supports public demonstrations, 8 May 1856

'Pibernes program' ['What the whistlers want'], *Morgenbladet*, 8 May 1856, reprinted in Reidar A. Marum: *Teaterslag og pipekonserter* [*Theatre battles and whistling concerts*] (Oslo: Cammermeyer, 1944), pp. 54–6.

We are grateful to the artists, some of them exceptional, who have for the time being kept a foreign theatre going here. We are very far from believing that we are ready to lose them – provided art is the prime consideration, on any terms. We can go further, and say that these foreign talents no longer greatly offend our nationality, for they have become acclimatized. Since no art is so directly related to the public, so utterly dependent on it for its existence, as this one, its performers are greatly influenced and what they produce is partly our own.

But [to bring in] new foreigners, ever new foreigners, despite all our sacrifices and efforts in the name of self-help and independence – still new foreigners, is not merely to destroy what we have done and are doing, it is to scorn us. [. . .]

[Of those in charge:] We respect their care for the theatre as an artistic institution; since that demands their entire attention, we can even excuse them for momentarily forgetting their duty as the nation's providers in the important matter of keeping a rich sky over it [for people to look up to]. But that is when we have to step in and remind them of it, and that is all we have done. [. . .]

Our beloved Henrik Wergeland would have held his head high again on an evening like Tuesday's; how richly he would have enjoyed the screaming gale of whistles that tore at and shook old prejudices. He would have been in the thick of it, seeing and reading all the signs, and once more shouting his 'out of the way, aestheticians' for all the audience to hear.

*Ibsen directs the Christiania Theatre*

Ibsen became artistic director of the Kristiania Norwegian Theatre in 1857 and continued in that position to 1862. In its 1858–9 season, the Theatre produced thirty-one new plays;

but Ibsen himself was none too pleased at the level of activity, although others praised it. The passage below is taken from his report to the general meeting.

## 113 Ibsen reports on the activity of the Kristiania Norwegian Theatre, 2 July 1859

Audhild Lund: *Henrik Ibsen og det norske teater 1857–63* [*Henrik Ibsen and the Norwegian theatre*] (Oslo: Det Mallingske boktrykkeri, 1925), pp. 47–8.

*That* is not what counts; a theatre can be just as active in a year when it performs ten as in a year when it performs thirty; the question is whether one wishes to see plays more or less well rehearsed. The aesthetician will of course hear of no dispute on such an issue, but at a theatre one becomes accustomed to being practical, one gets used to admitting the force of circumstance and to temporarily relinquishing ideals when absolutely necessary. [. . .]

Unfortunately this necessity is all too often at the door in a theatre like ours, which has no other support than its daily income, and where a most extreme economy has to be practised in every conceivable direction. This is the consideration by which my directorship has been guided this year. Under the uninterrupted strain of three–four performances a week, the company has throughout almost the entire season had to rehearse a new play from one Wednesday to the next; but it is understandable that the first performance of plays forced at that rate more often satisfies the demands of the box office than those of art. A further consideration is that our theatre, as it is now, adds to the difficulty of this activity; in a large space, one can rely on overall effects – in a confined space like ours, the actor must emphasize each detail, and it is the detail which requires longer and more thorough preparation to give it the desired effect.

### *Bjørnson directs Shakespeare*

In 1863, after protracted negotiations, an amalgamation was effected between the 'Danish' theatre and the 'Norwegian' theatre. Two years later, after Ibsen, its first dramatic adviser, had left Norway, Bjørnson became the theatre's ambitious and innovative artistic director. In *Aftenbladet*, he gave an account of his interpretation and production of *A Midsummer Night's Dream*, to which reviewers had not done justice. Bjørnson's position as artistic director was under attack by the Establishment, but for political rather than artistic reasons: a squabble with the director over minor matters such as a larger office and disposal of a theatre box was to lead to his departure in 1867.

## 114 Bjørnson defends his production of *A Midsummer Night's Dream*, 28 April 1865

*Aftenbladet*, 28 April 1865.

Where then is the law in these events? The dream is the law, is their answer; but what then is the law in the dream? If it has no law, it has no aesthetic justification.

The law, dear reader, is in our midst, the play is taking place this very day, sometimes where you are and sometimes where I am.

[. . .] Between them, these dreams warn you, secure though you may feel at your beloved's side, to watch your thoughts, watch your passions; from them a flower may spring called 'love-in-idleness', which changes you unawares. A dream depicts reality reversed but capable of taking shape in unguarded moments. [. . .]

The first time it was put on in Germany, this play had the good fortune to be directed by Tieck.[1] His arrangement is still used in Germany, whence it moved to Stockholm and then here. An insignificant alteration made in Germany has been retained here, the removal of the stage division known from Shakespeare's day and used by Tieck, since it played no part in the action but rather served as an awkward reminiscence. But there is Tieck's spirit over this light and natural arrangement. The word is free at all points to make its full impact, not overloaded with elaboration or shoved aside by moveable scenery. Tieck, who knew all about stage machinery, gave it free play when, as in modern operas, there is nothing but machinery, but he let spirit be spirit. [. . .]

[*Morgenbladet's* reviewer] also complains of the lighting. To which I reply that our equipment (which costs us over 100 Spd.) is the same as was used until recently at the largest theatres. It would truly be a dreadful thing, if we were incapable of experiencing illusion created by older means, because we knew that others had something newer. The point is whether all the scenery, new or old, harmonizes, and I appeal to professionals: does not ours? If so, one must be a real pettifogger to sit and keep track of the moon while Shakespeare is speaking through Oehlenschläger and Mendelssohn[2] is adding the music. [. . .]

[. . .] this play matters to me; it is my link with the public, my appeal to it. If the public refuses to be led in this direction, I cannot lead. Anyone seeking to remove me from the theatre and its audience must attack me here: for here I am.

[1] Johann Ludwig Tieck (1773–1853) had made the standard translation of Shakespeare into German; his version retained the original metres and rhymes.

[2] For Oehlenschläger see **15**.

Felix Mendelssohn-Bartholdy's music was a usual accompaniment to the *Dream* in nineteenth-century productions.

## IV THE NATIONAL STAGE IN BERGEN 1872–1909

*The Bergen theatre is revived*

Three salient facts about the second incarnation of the Norwegian theatre in Bergen, Den Nationale Scene, which opened in 1876: that dynamic individuals breathed life into it, that dedicated actors and Bergen citizens kept it alive, and that it reached artistic heights under Gunnar Heiberg, who was its artistic director from 1884 to 1888. (The records of the first three seasons suggest that Nils Wichstrøm might have achieved great things – he succeeded with Ibsen's *Pretenders* in 1879 – but he died of appendicitis on 1 December the same year, only 31 years old.)

One of the initiators of the revival of the Norwegian theatre in Bergen was Johan Bøgh (1848–1935), a founder in 1872 of the Bergen Theatre Society, and the first chairman of the theatre's Board when it opened in 1876, after a more or less 'Danish' interregnum since 1863. Among the rallying cries was an article 'A little concerning our theatrical circumstances'.

## 115 Bøgh calls for a revival, November–December 1872

*Bergensposten* [*The Bergen Post*], 28 and 29 November, 1 December 1872.

Is it not, then, about time to make an effort to change the current state of theatrical affairs? . . . Will our public not weary soon of 'amusing itself with what there is', and find it objectionable to 'while away an evening' watching poor comedy, which is even served up in a form distant and unfamiliar to our public and our taste, and which is to be regarded more or less as a reflection of precisely that aspect of Copenhagen life which neither art nor we up here have anything to do with, and should we not, finally, with complete confidence in what is ours, soon feel a longing to hear our own language and see our national character on our stage?

The weightiest objection that has always been raised to a Norwegian theatre in Bergen is that it will simply be a training ground for recruits for the Christiania Theatre, since our best actors have previously been seen to leave for the capital as soon as they have matured. There is some truth in this, but it has not always been the case. Let me mention Prom,[1] who was perhaps in one genre the best Norwegian actor we have had – yet he stayed in Bergen; so did the richly gifted and beautiful Mrs Nielsen.[2] But even if it had been invariably true, is that to say that it will always remain so? I answer no. Much water has flowed into the sea since the days when the first Norwegian actors performed, and the little circle which then made up the Norwegian artists' colony has now been enlarged by a flock of young men and women more or less capable of standing side by side with those veterans. We have, in other words, almost reached a stage where Norwegian actors are plentiful. At that time we had no more than could be absorbed by the Christiania Theatre, but now the capital's Norwegian theatre is over-full, it cannot go on absorbing and absorbing, so now is just the time to establish a permanent theatre in our city.

[1] Jacob Prom (1831–65), debut under Ole Bull in 1850, with Bergen theatre until it closed in 1863, acted in Trondheim for the last two years of his life, one of the outstanding 'pioneers'.

[2] Fredrikke Luise Nielsen (1838–1912), with the Bergen theatre from 1853, took part in its re-opening in 1876; played many leading parts, often opposite Prom; left the theatre in 1880 to become an itinerant preacher.

*A Bergen playwright mocked*

The most sensational contribution to the revival of the Bergen theatre consisted of two highly provocative anonymous articles published in *Bergensposten* on 5 and 9 February 1873. Having created a furore, all the greater because the play in question was by M.W. Brun,[1] a native of Bergen, the author redoubled it by inviting the public to a lecture at which he would account for his motives. He proved to be Georg Fasting (1837–1914), teacher, graduate in theology, and active member of the recently-founded Theatre Society, and he lectured so persuasively that the sensation became a victory for the cause.

[1] Michael Wallem Brun (1819–91), a Bergen man and grandson of a renowned patriotic poet; dramatist and theatre director. After a quarter of a century in charge of a number of private theatres in Denmark, he was appointed artistic director of the Christiania Theatre in 1869, where he stayed for three years (i.e. almost up to the time of this document), controversially resisting 'national' pressures.

## 116 Fasting attacks the play *Swanwhite's Daughter*, February 1873.

[Ivar Siversen]: *Theaterstriden i Bergen 1873 belyst ved aktstykkerne. Udgivet som bidrag til den bergenske theatersags historie ved I. S.* [*The theatrical strife in Bergen 1873 illustrated with portions of the records. Published as a contribution to the history of the Bergen theatre cause*] (Bergen: Gyldendal, 1894), p. 6–7.

[. . .] Go, I say, and good luck go with you, and see a play like the one I saw, and inhale once and for all a strong and healthy contempt to warm you at your future work. For know, noble Sir [the editor] – see the elevation of my speech at the very idea – I saw *Swanwhite's Daughter* [*Svantevits datter*]! Yes, I have seen herself, 'Daughter of the God', in bright red make-up, medium red make-up, and white make-up, with paint beneath her eyes to make them big and shining, and with paint which allowed them to appear dull and glazed. I have seen her 'beggar costume', with greenery in her hair, as well as her other toilets, both the red dress with blue Valkyrie armour and the yellow dress with white Valkyrie armour. I have seen the woman speak and laugh, seen her smile, dilate her nostrils, walk, stand, fall, etc., and I confess that in respect of face and figure and especially clothes she was an irreproachable woman. I have seen – the King of the Danes! I saw this Erik of Pomerania and heard his royal roar, when he asks them to saddle his horse or the like, seen him knit his Pomeranian brows, seen and – envied him – his comfortable boots of untanned leather! I have watched them exiting and entering and exiting and entering for three hours at a stretch, with dances and torches and halberds. I have heard every single one of the five-and-thirty biographies which each character imparts concerning himself and his closest relatives; I have heard them all speak this, the sheerest and falsest nonsense the like of which no human being has uttered since the Creation, larded with the clichés of an entire literature, not one of which but has been chewed over and spat out a hundred times.

## 117 Costumes and sets in the 1870s and 1880s

Octavia Sperati:[1] *Theatererindringer* [*Reminiscences of the theatre*] (Kristiania, 1911), pp. 96–102.

I can certainly say that luxurious costume was not a fitting description for what the theatre was generally able to provide us with for historical plays.

In this respect, however, Holberg was an exception. An auspicious star shone on productions of his plays. For in the dramatic society's wardrobe there was a collection of costumes which dated back to Ludvig Holberg's own day.

Those strange old-fashioned costumes, handed down for generations in Bergen families, had been donated to the dramatic society, in whose possession they had remained for over 100 years and were now kept under seven seals. Mr L'Abbé was the dragon that brooded over the treasure.

At the rear of the old theatre, he lived in the historic rooms which Henrik Ibsen had occupied for all of five years during his period as director and house dramatist at the Bergen theatre.

When the Holberg costumes were to be lent, Mr L'Abbé appeared at the appointed hour, which he observed most strictly. Wearing a flowered housecoat fastened with a tasselled cord, a similarly tasselled Turkish smoking-cap, and felt slippers, and carrying a lit lantern in one hand and a big key ring in the other, he undid locks and bolts to open a vast pitch-dark clothes store where the treasures were housed. They hung down from the ceiling in rows, each item numbered and labelled. By means of a long pole with an iron hook at one end, the age-old garments were carefully lifted down. But no one left the store without signing a receipt in the register, and even then he parted with his relics only with evident reluctance.

[. . .] As for stage furniture and staging in general, we were by no means burdened with excess. The inventory was sparse and cheap. The fact that the theatre nevertheless occasionally managed surprises and variations in its staging can be attributed to the circumstances that the dining rooms, drawing rooms and best rooms of many a Bergen family with an interest in theatre stood empty as long as a particular play remained in the repertoire.

'I've had no dining room for a fortnight,' complained a young lady who had close links with the theatre, 'and I've been married only two months.' 'Well, it's our turn now,' replied her friend, the wife of a Board member. 'The removal van was at our door this morning, and the theatre messenger and his satellites emptied the best room in a twinkling, leaving nothing, not even sparing the pictures on the walls; even my sofa cushions and foot-stools were perched at the top of the load. By way of farewell, the messenger also surveyed our drawing-room, so before long I shall be admiring that, too, from my theatre seat.'

[1] Octavia Sperati (1847–1918) was a mainstay of the revived Bergen theatre, where she served for forty-two years from 1876; she evidently felt a part of a living tradition and of a resourceful theatre community.

*The world premiere of* The Wild Duck

Gunnar Heiberg (1857–1929) is a national figure, as essayist, critic, poet and principally as a dramatist (*Aunt Ulrica* [*Tante Ulrikke*], 1884; *King Midas* [*Kong Midas*], 1890; and *Love's Tragedy* [*Kjærlighedens tragedie*], 1904, are among his major plays). He served an important four years (1884–8) as artistic director at the Bergen theatre, where, among other things, he fought for the more controversial Ibsen and Bjørnson plays, including *Ghosts* [*Gjengangere*].

With Heiberg directing, the Bergen theatre put on the world premiere of *The Wild Duck* [*Vildanden*] on 9 February 1885. Heiberg later described his future wife and the Bergen theatre's leading lady, Didrikke Tollefsen (Didi Heiberg, 1863–1915), as the best Hedvig he had seen, because she was the most helpless. Octavia Sperati played Gina.

## 118 Gunnar Heiberg directs *The Wild Duck* in 1885

Octavia Sperati: *Fra det gamle komediehus* [*From the old playhouse*] (Kristiania: Gyldendal, 1916), pp. 105–6.

The last four acts of *The Wild Duck* take place in a photographer's studio, the least inviting living room imaginable.

Especially by lamplight, with gloomy shadows in every corner and the dark loft in the background, the loft that houses a strange mystical world. At the first rehearsals, these sad surroundings seemed to enervate the actors.

Speeches turned artificial, and we wandered solemnly about, as if filled with forebodings of the drama that would be played out in the 'forest' there in the loft, where the wounded wild duck lived its pitiable life. And where old Ekdal, proud hunter of yore, now went stalking among dry old Christmas trees.

Heiberg broke the spell. It was greatly to his credit that he succeeded in snapping us out of our oppressive dark mood.

Directing us, he never tired of emphasizing that the more naturally and realistically we acted, the more clearly the symbolism, the general significance, would emerge and enclose the play's action, as it does in life.

The inhabitants of the studio must be unaware of the double life lived in *The Wild Duck*. They are buried in everyday prose and up to their ears in petty worries.

## 119 Heiberg's setting for the world premiere of *The Wild Duck* in 1885

Stage manager's register in the Theatre Archives of the Bergen Theatre Museum, accompanied with a sketch.

Atelieret bestaar af Dukkehjems= Dekorationen med en Dör, som er overmalet Graa, den venstre ~~Væg~~ Væg er hel, med Undtagelse af en Dör til. Bagteppet er Skabdöre i stedet for de andre. Til Höire bruges kun förste og fjerde Del, Middelen bestaar af nyt Glastag og Væg og Skraa= stykker samt hvide Soffitter. Skraa Glastaget er bedækket med et Stykke blaat Lærred forestillende Glas, men som ombyttes i 5te Akt med et andet forestillende „Sne" det nederste Stykke er malet nogle Huse paa Lærred med Flor foran, grönne Gardiner er overtrukket over det hele i 2den Akt men er optrukket i de övrige Akter. En Hylde hænger under Skraavinduet.

The studio consists of the Doll's House set with one door painted grey, the left wall is entire except for another door. The backdrop has painted doors instead of the other kind. To the right only the first and fourth set pieces are retained, the space between consisting of a new glass ceiling and wall and sloping pieces and white borders.

The pitched glass roof is covered with a piece of blue canvas representing glass, but which is replaced in Act v by another representing 'snow'. The bottom piece is canvas with some houses painted on it with gauze in front of it, green curtains are drawn across the whole in Act II but are raised in the other acts. A shelf hangs under the sloping window.

### *The acting of Johanne Dybwad*

The *grande dame* of the Norwegian stage at the end of the nineteenth and in the first half of the twentieth century was Johanne Dybwad (née Juell, 1867–1950), who made her debut in Bergen in 1887, went to the Christiania Theatre the following year, and joined the National Theatre in 1899.

## 120 Heiberg describes the actress Johanne Dybwad in 1887

Gunnar Heiberg: *Artikler om teater og dramatikk* [*Articles on theatre and drama*] (Oslo: Aschehoug, 1972), pp. 90, 93.

I first saw Johanne Juell at a rehearsal of an amateur production in Bergen. She was a pale little girl then, with eyes ready to smile themselves sparkling, and when she was serious one could see she had a strong mouth. She was no clever amateur. She made her debut shortly afterwards, in an English play, *Gertrude*.[1] No one could doubt that she really was Johanne Reimers' [see **123b**] daughter. Her second part was Nora. It was good, but not excellent. She couldn't quite manage the lark. The bird was not distanced enough for her. And she lacked the experience for the serious scenes, when Nora undergoes her transformation, and is transformed, and so fortunately did not play them particularly well either. Fortunately, because she did not play the part according to any pattern. It was no imitation. It was no repetition. At least not where it mattered. What she put into it was that she could see that this was serious. And she had the seriousness. She played on herself and from great depth. We saw a great temperament. Then Fanchon followed, in *A Little Witch*.[2] A hit. A bull's-eye. The gipsy girl with the April spirit. Wild and tender, sensitive in every nerve, brilliantly wise – she gave it all, from inexhaustible resources. And clearly and distinctly shaped. The scene came in which she dances alone in the moonlight. Hundreds of people bent forward towards her from their seats. A great artist was born.

It was at the dress rehearsal of the first part of *Beyond Mortal Power*.[3] After the first act. I do not think I have ever been so moved in the theatre, and I did not know how to express what I felt. Finally I burst out, 'The other old boy can just pack it in now, I reckon.' By the other old boy I meant Ibsen. Well, I soon got over it. But it was Mrs Dybwad's fault that I went after strange gods, if only for a moment.

[1] A Norwegian adaptation (1861) of Augustus Harris's *A Little Treasure* (1855), itself an adaptation of *La Joie de la maison* by Anicet-Bourgeois and Decourcelle (1855).

[2] A version of Charlotte Birch-Pfeiffer's *Die Grille*, itself a dramatization of George Sand's *La Petite Fadette*. Its heroine is a country girl accused of witchcraft; the shadow dance scene was a triumph as well for Ermolova in Russia [see **247–8**] and Maggie Mitchell in the US.

[3] *Beyond Mortal Power*, part one, is Bjørnson's masterpiece *Over Ævne* I (published 1883), in which Johanne Dybwad played Klara Sang in the National Theatre's first season.

*Christian Michelsen aids the theatre to survive*

The affairs of the old Bergen theatre can be suitably wound up with this tribute to Christian Michelsen (1857–1925), lawyer, shipowner, newspaper owner, politician, parliamentarian, Cabinet Minister, and Norway's Prime Minister 1905–7, notably during the extremely delicate negotiations which resulted in the peaceful dissolution of the union with Sweden. In the midst of all his other affairs, he devoted a great deal of time to keeping the old theatre afloat, and to realizing the plans for a new building.

## 121 Joachim Grieg pays tribute to Christian Michelsen's efforts to support the theatre

From Joachim Grieg's historical survey in the special theatre number of *Bergens Tidende* [*Bergen Times*], 25 October 1926, marking the 50th anniversary of the opening in 1876 of the revived Bergen theatre.

The next event in the life of the National Stage was the erection of the new building. It had gradually become clear that the old one could no longer satisfy artistic requirements. Fund-raising for a new building was begun quite early.

It is safe to say that we owe the completion of the new building entirely to Chr. Michelsen's initiative and unwearying efforts. With all the energy that was his when he was determined to carry something out, he devoted all his power, influence and eloquence to the realization of the project.

He was a former Chairman of the Theatre Board, having entered the fray in the early years, when Bøgh was artistic director. In 1896 he returned to the post, which he held for the rest of his life. Of all the members of the Theatre Association, he is the one who, together with Johan Bøgh, has had the greatest influence on the theatre's development.

He made the cause his own, and with all the brilliant gifts at his disposal he succeeded in bringing it to a successful conclusion.

When 400,000 kroner [approximately £16,666] had been collected from private contributions, a site was requested from the city and granted free, while the Savings Bank with its customary generosity lent 100,000 kroner [approximately £4,111] indefinitely and with no interest. It should be mentioned in gratitude and recognition in this connection that over the past fifty years this institution has contributed a total of 216,500 kroner to the theatre.

By 1904, sufficient progress had been made for building to begin. On 25 July 1906, the King[1] laid the foundation stone, and in February 1909 the new building was inaugurated with three celebration performances, attended by the King. On the first evening, there was a Prologue spoken by Magda Blanc,[2] and Holberg's *Erasmus Montanus*. On the second, Bjørnson's *Beyond Mortal Power* I, and on the third, Ibsen's *Hedda Gabler*.[3]

[1] Haakon VII (1872–1957), the Danish Prince Carl who insisted on a referendum in Norway before agreeing in 1905 to become the first King of an independent Norway in modern times; reigned until his death.

[2] Magda Blanc (1879–1959), leading actress with the Bergen theatre from 1901 and throughout her long career.

[3] The dramatic society's building did sterling service for a century, until destroyed by an explosion during the Second World War.

## V MANAGING AND ENLARGING THE CHRISTIANIA THEATRE, 1874–87

### *Introduction*

During the last twenty-five years of its existence, coinciding with the last quarter of the nineteenth century, the Christiania Theatre was blessed with a number of great actors and actresses and a succession of great Norwegian plays. Although the theatre was generally on a slightly less perilous footing than before, there was no shortage of problems, including the choice of repertoire, the artistic direction, and the need for a new building.

### *The first Norwegian production of* Peer Gynt

*Peer Gynt* was published in 1867, but not staged until 1876. The premiere at the Christiania Theatre on 24 February lasted from 7 p.m. until 11:45. By 1 January 1877, thirty-seven performances had been given; a halt had to be called because of a fire at the theatre which destroyed some of the sets – although Ludvig Josephson suspected that more could have been done to overcome the problem, and that the fire provided a welcome opportunity also to put a stop to his controversial and costly opera ventures at the theatre and effectively to his tenure as artistic director. (He had been appointed in 1873.)

## 122a Ibsen writes to Ludvig Josephson to place *Peer Gynt* at the Christiania Theatre, February 1874

Tharald Høyerup Blanc: *Henrik Ibsen og Christiania theater 1850–1899: Et bidrag til den Ibsenske digtnings scenehistorie* [*Henrik Ibsen and the Christiania Theatre: a contribution to the stage history of Ibsen's writing*] (Kristiania: J. Dybwad, 1906), pp. 23–4.

In connection with a forthcoming third edition of my dramatic poem *Peer Gynt*, I have been busying myself a good deal with the work this winter, and have adapted it so that a shortened version will lend itself to stage performance. The work is being arranged as a musical drama, and the necessary music will be composed by Mr Edvard Grieg, whom I have approached in this connection. I have explained the plan I have followed in my adaptation in a letter to Mr Grieg, who will at my request inform you of it.

For it is my intention, before I apply to the Stockholm and Copenhagen theatres in this matter, to ask whether Kristiania Theatre wishes to use the piece and whether, if so, it would matter to you whether your theatre was the first to perform it.

When Mr Grieg has spoken to you about this, I shall take the liberty of expecting your preliminary answer. If this is favourable, I shall send you a corrected and shortened copy of the play. The music will be composed in the course of the summer; the theatre could at the same time make its arrangements for the sets and scenery, so that the play could be ready in time for the best period next season.

I am convinced that under your skilful direction this play will be very effective on the stage, especially if accompanied by good music. Since it is important both to Mr Grieg and to me to know which theatre we must principally have in mind, I shall take the liberty of expecting your esteemed reply as soon as you have sufficiently acquainted yourself with the matter. If the general idea appeals to you, we shall have opportunities later to agree on the details, in which case I shall be very glad to take any wish or suggestion you may put forward into account.[1]

[1] The adaptations Ibsen suggested to Grieg and some of Grieg's comments on his difficulties with the project are given in Michael Meyer, *Henrik Ibsen* (Harmondsworth: Penguin Books, 1985), pp. 404–7.

## 122b Drawing of the Hall of the Mountain King, world premiere of *Peer Gynt*, Christiania Theatre, 24 February 1876[1]

Sketch by Wilhelm Pacht in *Ny illustreret Tidende*, Theatre Collection of the Oslo University Library.

[1] Directed by Ludvig Josephson, with Johannes Brun as the Mountain King and Henrik Klausen (1844–1907) as Peer.

An ever-romanticized and prettified staging seems to have settled on the play right from the start. The very enthusiastic *Aftenposten* review (25 February 1876) lavished praise on 'the painstaking and patient rehearsals that must have been needed, simply to get the dance in the Hall of the Mountain King so smooth and precise as it was yesterday', but the reviewer also expressed concern lest 'the deeper core of the play be concealed or at least obscured by the dazzling outward display'.

### *Ibsen premieres in Christiania minus* Ghosts

Hans Schrøder (1831–1912), the theatre's first sole director, retained command through various upheavals for twenty years (1879–99), despite being seen as a representative of a fading old guard. The decision which provoked the most (radical) wrath during his long tenure came early; in 1881 he refused to produce *Ghosts*. Here are excerpts from his own retrospective account of what was to become a *cause célèbre*; it may have been written to justify his refusal when *Ghosts* was first produced at the National Theatre in 1900.

## 123a Schrøder explains why he refused to produce *Ghosts* in 1881

Carl Just: *Schrøder og Christiania theater: et bidrag til norsk teaterhistorie* [*Schrøder and the Christiania Theatre: a contribution to Norwegian theatre history*] (Oslo: Cammermeyer, 1948), pp. 169–70, 179–81; includes Schrøder's memoirs from his first few seasons as Director.

Let me not waste any words on refuting the stupid claim, among the many advanced at the time, that I was unable to appreciate the play's outstanding qualities because it did not appeal to me personally. The question was not what I personally thought of the play, but whether it could be presented to the Christiania Theatre public of those days with any hope of winning applause or even being tolerated.

And to the best of my judgement, there could be no doubt of the answer. In this case the Master had evidently written a play which, whatever its value and justification, was certainly ahead of its time where performance at the Christiania Theatre was concerned. [. . .]

One thing of which I have remained completely convinced to this day, is that if I had put on or been able to put on *Ghosts*, such a storm of indignation would have arisen that it would instantly have swept away both the play and the Director, as well as putting the theatre itself at risk by alienating that section of the audience whose support it could not do without.

[Schrøder recounts that a leading member of the Theatre's Council told him they would protest against the play's performance and dismiss him if he persevered, and that the rejection had the support of influential actors and actresses who might have been thought eager to play the plum parts; he quotes the negative opinion of his literary consultant Henrik Jæger *in extenso*, and recalls the general condemnation of the play on its publication before commenting:]

[. . .] And I therefore wish to emphasize that both the public and the press had been unanimous. Even those papers which about a year and a half later were unable to find terms strong enough to condemn my rejection of the play uttered hardly a word at the time. If any silence deserves the name eloquent, that must be it. [Schrøder also quotes the following and one more paragraph from his letter to Ibsen, dated 21 December:]

You know my admiration for the Nordic countries' most brilliant poetic genius, greatest dramatist, and most profound and serious psychologist, and will therefore understand with what reluctance I am obliged to declare that I dare not have *Ghosts* performed at the Christiania Theatre. I do not regard Christiania's theatre-going public as sufficiently mature to bring the necessary criticism to bear on the complex social issues presented to it in your play, and from what I have seen of statements in the press and know of public opinion, I am certain that its reception would be such as neither the author nor the theatre could find agreeable.[1]

[1] The storm which did arise some eighteen months later was aroused in the wake of the Scandinavian tour of *Ghosts* with August Lindberg [see **72b**] and his Swedish company, after the play had also been refused by the Royal Theatres in Copenhagen and Stockholm. In Christiania, Lindberg put it on at Møllergaten Theatre. The ensuing polemics and demonstrations – in the Christiania Theatre and outside Schrøder's home – followed familiar political dividing lines, with an increasingly vocal radical faction demanding the removal of Schrøder for not have been equally advanced.

## 123b Sketch of Norwegian premiere of *A Doll's House*, Christiania Theatre, 1880[1]

Drawing by Olaf Jørgensen in *Ny illustreret Tidende*, Theatre Collection of Oslo University Library.

[1] The tarantella scene with Johanne Juell Reimers (1848–82, mother of Johanne Dybwad) as Nora and her husband Arnoldus Reimers (1844–99) as Helmer.

## 123c Sketch of *The Wild Duck*, Christiania Theatre, 1885[1]

Drawing by Lorents Norberg in *Ny illustreret Tidende*, Theatre Collection of Oslo University Library.

[1] This production opened within a month of the world premiere in Bergen; cf. Heiberg's sketch for the Bergen set [**119b**]. The drawing shows the scene in Act v when Hedvig's body is carried off: from left to right, Lucie Wolf as Gina, Frederikke Louise Krohn (1862–1947) as Hedvig, Arnoldus Reimers as Hjalmar Ekdal, Johannes Brun as old Ekdal, and Hjalmar Hammer (1846–96) as Gregers Werle.

## 123d Sketch of world premiere of *Hedda Gabler*, Christiania Theatre, 1891[1]

From a drawing by Christian Krogh (1852–1925), a leading painter and major figure in artistic and literary circles, Theatre Collection of Oslo University Library.

[1] Constance Bruun (1863–94) as Hedda, Olaf Hansson (1856–1912) as Judge Brack.

*Bjørn Bjørnson as director*

Even allowing for the name, fame and influence of Bjørnson senior (and for junior's eagerness to *be* appointed), it was bold of Schrøder to appoint the writer's son Bjørn, at the age of 25, not only to act in but also to direct the company, with its many experienced and popular performers. However, it proved a very successful choice. Bjørn Bjørnson (1859–1942) was fresh from acting and training in Germany, notably with the Duke of Saxe-Meiningen's troupe, and full of infectious enthusiasm. He quickly established himself as a leading actor and, more importantly, as an artistic director capable of imposing his overall ideas of plays and of ensemble playing without ruffling too many feathers. He served under Schrøder until 1893 and was appointed the new National Theatre's first director in June 1898. One of his outstanding early productions for the Christiania Theatre was his first, in 1884, Shakespeare's *Richard III*, with himself in the title role.

## 124 Bjørnson rehearses *Richard III* in 1884

Bjørn Bjørnson: *Det gamle teater: kunsten og menneskene* [*The old theatre: arts and people*] (Oslo: H. Aschehoug, 1937), pp. 46–7.

Came the day – the morning – when King Richard for the first time fumbled and felt his way about the half-darkened stage. For the first time in Norway. It was the blocking rehearsal [*arrangementsprøve*], with everybody going about half reading and making notes of the positions blocked out for them by the director. And of his many explanatory introductory remarks. As always at such rehearsals. I wandered about in this whispering silence, my heart beating and my hands trembling. Nobody noticed. I knew Richard. And had no book or prompter – whispering like the others. It looked like a funeral. Somebody dying who should not be disturbed. But was meant to be something of a resurrection. A living and conscious ensemble. That is no exaggeration. That is what it became. I wandered about, among the old and the young, careful and tactful, and they all followed me as though I had always been their fully-fledged skipper on the bridge. Someone they were used to trusting. Schrøder was in the black dark stalls unseen, to get an impression of the 'historical event'.

'I couldn't hear anything,' he said. 'But I – saw that everyone was pleased. And that pleased me more than many a performance.'

Almost the whole company was in the play. At the rehearsals the ensemble rose, little by little, as when the huge orchestras in the big American cinemas slowly rise out of the orchestra pit until we see them in dazzling light, playing for all they are worth. Ensembles need their batons, just as orchestras do. The latter visible to all during performances. The former invisible to most. As they should be. In *Richard III* our ensemble rose up into the light it needed.[1]

[1] To quote Berit Erbe's account of the production, based on the prompt book and reviews, in her study *Bjørn Bjørnsons vej mod realismens teater* [*Bjørn Bjørnson's progress towards the realistic theatre*] (Oslo: Universitetsforlaget, 1976), pp. 175–6: 'It was in the blocking that the new director's influence registered most clearly. And in the pace, the pace of the whole performance. "The speed with which the whole was done was striking" (*Dagbladet*, 2 October 1884). "A speed throughout the whole performance, the like of which we have not seen before" (*Morgenbladet*, 4 October 1884). "The unusual speed of the action" (*Christiania Intelligentssedler*, 4 October 1884). Under Josephson the performance had lasted over four hours; now they were down to only three.

'The life of the extras was also generally noted as something new and unique. "Even the extras take part, so it's a treat to see," Henrik Jæger remarks (*Christiania Intelligentssedler*, 4 October 1884). In several places Jæger's review gives a detailed description of the blocking, and from that review and notes in the prompt book one can see which of the new features of stage positioning that were to characterize the Norwegian theatre revival were already apparent in this first production by Bjørn Bjørnson for the Christiania Theatre.

'In the homage scene (Act 4 scene 2), the throne was in the background. The extras playing the King's followers were in rows across the stage, from the foreground to the background, and all with their *backs* to the audience! The like had never been seen before at the Christiania Theatre.

'A further point is that the theatre had always previously observed the principle that everything should be as silent as possible both on stage and backstage while the actors were speaking. But, chiefly under the influence of the Meiningers, Bjørnson made good use of musical effects. Trumpet blasts and rolling drums outside Richmond's tent, for instance, created such an effective illusion that Henrik Jæger remarked in wonder that one simply *believes* one is in a camp and not in a theatre. [. . .]

'As actor and director, Bjørn Bjørnson enjoyed a triumph which exceeded all expectations, as well as placing great demands on his future work. "In him, the good timber in our theatre found the man capable of joining it together so it could sustain a play. The scenes were wholes, which flowed into each other, each individual part had been worked out in accordance with an understanding of the overall effect. We have never seen such precision in performance [. . .] it was a pleasure everywhere to see separate elements come together, and to feel what can be brought about when a *unified* strong will is the driving force. [. . .] Both individual parts and group scenes were given far better performances than we have been accustomed to," writes Irgens Hansen (*Dagbladet*, 2 October 1884).'

## 125 Kristiania Theater Administration's correspondence on electrifying the theatre, January–February 1886[1]

Kristiania Theater Administration journal for 1886, Oslo University Library Theatre Collection.

(a) Elektrisk Bureau to Mr Bjørn Bjørnson, 26 January 1886. We have obtained information from Berlin and Vienna concerning electric light installations for theatres and hereby offer Kristiania Theater such installations at the following prices:

| | | |
|---|---|---|
| *Apparatus of about 250 standard candlepower* | | |
| Arc lamp with reflector | kr. 150 | |
| 30 batteries | kr. 120 | |
| Wiring, etc. | kr. 30 | |
| Filling of batteries and fitting | kr. 40 | kr. 340 |
| *Apparatus of about 400 standard candlepower* | | |
| Arc lamp with reflector | kr. 180 | |
| 40 batteries | kr. 160 | |
| Wiring, etc. | kr. 30 | |
| Filling of batteries and fitting | kr. 50 | kr. 420 |

(b) Administration to Elektrisk Bureau, 8 February 1886.

[. . .] The Board wishes the theatre to obtain the equipment mentioned for the price stated. Where payment of the amount is concerned, however, it must stipulate that the theatre will pay 200 kroner in cash on the receipt of the equipment and the remaining 220 kroner by the end of the season. If these terms are acceptable, the equipment should be supplied as soon as possible.

(c) Elektrisk Bureau to the Administration 9 February 1886.

Acknowledging receipt of the Board's esteemed letter of yesterday's date ordering electric lighting equipment for the theatre, we are pleased to inform you that the order will be put into effect as quickly as possible on the terms stated by the Board.

[1] This was before the capital had been provided with electric street lighting.

*A new site for the theatre*

With the westward expansion of the capital, the Christiania Theatre's location had gradually grown less satisfactory. To this chronic condition, the fire in 1877 added a more acute urge to find a site for a new and national theatre. Solutions were found in a variety of locations and abandoned for a variety of reasons, and ten years passed before a last desperate effort succeeded. Here in Bjørn Bjørnson's blow-by-blow account of how the last obstacle was overcome, literally at the last minute. The University had 'first refusal' of the site in question.

## 126 A new location for the theatre in 1887

Bjørn Bjørnson (1937), pp. 238–41.

And it really was urgent, because the Storting would soon be dissolved, and any proposal to postpone the matter could have upset the whole applecart.

I was at the University morning, noon and night, and finally persuaded their masterships of the Senate to put the matter on their agenda. It was a Monday, as far as I remember.

I got to the Church Ministry to be greeted with the crushing news that the Government recommendation would have to be on Jakob Sverdrup's[1] desk the next morning, Tuesday. There was a young man in the Ministry. Blessed be his memory. I cannot remember his name, which is a shame, because he deserves to be remembered. He it was who was to draft the proposal and write out the fair copy. I begged him to stay there and wait for me until I came back with the University's written reply. In the good cause he might have to stay up writing all night, for the document to be ready on Minister Sverdrup's desk. The young man had just got engaged. I made him very happy at the prospect of two things: free passes for him and his beloved to our old theatre and two seats at the opening performance at the new one.

I kept both promises.

He would wait.

I dashed over to the University porter.

'Where's Professor Aschehoug?'

He was the Senate chairman.

I got his address. Next stop there: where I found only his daughter, who said her father was living up at Grefsen.

It was a matter of life and death for our cause.

I took a coach up to Grefsen and right enough, Aschehoug was there.

I don't think I've ever seen anyone more amazed than that quiet-mannered aristocratic little gentleman.

'But my good Bjørnson, my material is down in town.'

I spoke. I explained. I conjured him. I grew emotional.

If I failed to overcome his reluctance to 'act so quickly', our whole plan would fail.

I overcame it.

I piled the dear man into my coach, and we drove down to his home. I sat there and waited. And within half an hour I had the University's written statement in my hand. Then Aschehoug said, almost pityingly, but with a smile:

'Well, you must have the other gentlemen's signatures before it can be submitted to the Ministry.'

I doubt whether I stopped to say thank you.

Down to the University. I said to the porter:

'I must have all the Senate's signatures by 10 this evening. Here's 10 kroner. Half, that is.' I tore it in half, and gave him one half.

'You shall have the other half at 10 o'clock when you bring me the signatures. Take a coach at my expense.' [. . .]

The splendid porter came, with all the signatures.

I bless his memory, too.

Off again, to the waiting young man.

And the Government's proposal was ready on Jakob Sverdrup's desk in the morning.

[1] Jakob Sverdrup (1845–99), clergyman, subsequently bishop, Storting representative, Minister of Church Affairs 1885–6, 1888–9 and 1895–8 (which also entailed responsibility for educational and cultural questions).

*The new site is approved by the Government*

This cliff-hanging effort resulted in the Storting's adoption, on 25 June 1887, of a resolution, confirmed by Royal Decree, authorizing the Government to grant a 2,500 square-metre building site where the National Theatre now stands. Ten years earlier, one of the arguments against permitting that very site to be used had been that a theatre would be an inappropriate neighbour for the Royal Palace, the Storting, and the University. Permission was now granted with the following provisos.

## 127 Royal decree conferring a new national theatre, 19 July 1887

*Nationaltheatret i Kristiania: Festskrift i anledning af Nationaltheatrets aabning 1ste september 1899* [*The National Theatre in Kristiania: Celebratory volume on the occasion of the opening of the National Theatre*] (Kristiania, 1899), p. 9.[1]

1 Erection of the theatre building on the site begins before the end of 1891.
2 Any building plans and drawings are submitted to the King for approval.

3 The new theatre's limited company undertakes to implement the safety measures against fire necessary for the protection of the University's buildings, and which are required by the Ministry of Finance.

4 That the city of Kristiania takes over responsibility for the upkeep of the Students' Grove, without, however, laying out any new parks without Ministry approval.

5 That the area granted may not be sold or put to any other use than as a theatre site, and will revert to the Government immediately upon the termination of such use.

[1] This Festschrift contains an account of the events preceding and during the building of the new theatre, and detailed and illustrated descriptions of the theatre's architecture by Henrik Bull (1864–1953), and of its interior and furnishings, lighting and machinery, and foundations and contruction. Henrik Bull had come second in the architectural competition, but when the two leading prize-winners submitted revised entries, Bull's was chosen.

### *The new theatre opens*

The Storting's conditions were met, in that the first spade went into the ground on 18 November 1891. Funds remained a problem right to the end, and in 1897 the authorities had to approve plans for a premium bond lottery, some of the proceeds of which would go to the completion of the National Theatre building. The opening performance on 1 September 1899 included acts from three Holberg plays and Grieg's Holberg suite; on the next two evenings came Ibsen's *An Enemy of the People* and Bjørnstjerne Bjørnson's *Sigurd Jorsalfarer*, directed by his son and with Grieg conducting his own music.

# *Poland, 1765–1830*

Edited by KARYNA WIERZBICKA-MICHALSKA

## INTRODUCTION

The Polish national stage emerged in 1765 within the framework of the first public theatre in Poland founded by King Stanislas Augustus. The monarch was committed to a far-reaching cultural reform and assigned a special role in it to the theatre. Indeed, he expected that stage-plays would contribute to the spread of Enlightenment views and moral attitudes among Polish society.

In 1765, an Italian, Carlo Tomatis, became the State-aided entrepreneur and manager of the first public theatre in Warsaw. He took it upon himself to stage Italian, French and Polish plays. In February 1766 the national stage was given its own Polish management. Thus the Polish national theatre inaugurated its activities on 19 November 1765 by producing a comedy entitled *Natręci* (*Intruders*), based by J. Bielawski on Molière's play *Les Fâcheux*. It was only with great difficulty that the organizers of the theatre managed to bring together a company of actors. These were mostly untrained persons whose professional qualifications had to be acquired later in the course of performing. Their instructors were the playwrights themselves, as well as the managers of the Polish troupe. Of considerable help to the beginners were the instructions given them by aristocratic gentlemen very keenly interested in theatricals, the most active among them being the king's cousin, Prince Adam Kazimierz Czartoryski.

In the first two years of the theatre's existence its main dramatist was a Jesuit, Franciszek Bohomolec, who had been writing plays for school performances. He was also one of the contributors to the periodical *Monitor*, founded on the king's initiative and modelled on the London *Spectator*. He criticized in his plays, as the *Monitor* did in its articles, the typical faults of what was called 'Sarmatism', that is, the traditional ways and mentality of the Polish nobility, which included backwardness, superstition, xenophobia, and oppression of their serfs.

Comedies produced on the Warsaw stage were mostly adaptations, mainly from French. Their authors followed the instructions formulated by Czartoryski in the preface to his comedy *The Miss to be Married*. His advice, aimed at giving national expression to foreign models, very strongly influenced the leading writer of comedies of the Stanislas-Augustan period, Franciszek Zabłocki. The subjects of Zabłocki's plays are all borrowed from foreign literature, but owing to his brilliant talent some of them are artistically superior to their originals. From 1776 a new kind of play began to appear on the national stage – the *drame*, which at that time was very much in favour in all European theatres. *Drames*, by French,

English or German playwrights, translated or adapted, became a great success with the Warsaw public although they were criticized by the advocates of classicism.

In the years 1765–1831 the National Theatre in Warsaw was the major Polish stage; however, over time, other Polish theatres were emerging in other towns as well, first of all in Cracow, Lvov, Vilna, and Poznań. Plays were also produced in smaller towns, mostly by actors from major centres or by itinerant companies. Thanks to these activities, the theatre became a strong and durable element of Polish cultural life.

## I THE FIRST NATIONAL THEATRE, 1765–74

### 128 How the National Theatre was founded in 1765

Wojciech Bogusławski:[1] *Dzieje Teatru Narodowego* [*History of the National Theatre*] [1820–1] (Warsaw: Wydawnictwa Artystyczne i Filmowe, 1965), pp. 1–2.

[. . .] Stanislas Augustus,[2] the great patron of the arts, was the actual founder of the Polish national theatre. Soon after his accession to the throne, he saw to it that the training of actors be initiated and proper candidates be assembled. The selection was hasty and casual (among the would-be students only one, Świerzawski,[3] was endowed by nature with comic talent), so if the actors did not prove to be very competent, still the novelty of their acting in the native language won them the approbation of learned men anxious to see all sorts of arts flourish in this country.

The laudable intention turned into a laudable undertaking. And while other nations started by staging foreign plays, we started with a play of our own. It was *The Intruders* (*Natręci*).[4] Though patterned somewhat on Molière's *Les Fâcheux*, it presented characters who were very Polish in their demeanour and habits. Then, too, the plays of Franciszek Bohomolec,[5] not only the original ones but also those based on other playwrights, were aimed at exposing national shortcomings and comic traits [. . .]

[1] Wojciech Bogusławski (1757–1820), leading actor of the National Theatre and its long-standing manager, had been first influenced by French neo-classicism, but was responsive to the reforms of Iffland and Talma; he was the first Pole to play Hamlet, though in Schröder's adaptation (1797). A dramatist and translator, in 1820–1 he published his *History of the National Theatre* which covers the period from 1765 to 1814 and is chiefly of an autobiographical nature. See Galle, 1925; *Teatr W. Bogusławskiego*, 1954; Wierzbicka-Michalska, 1967; Got, 1971; *Słownik biograficzny teatru polskiego 1765–1965* (hereafter *SBTP*); Raszewski, 1982.

[2] Stanislas Augustus Poniatowski (1732–98), King of Poland from 1765 to his abdication in 1795. He had ascended to the throne due to Russian influence (he had been a lover of Catherine the Great) and showed himself to be an outstanding reformer, the main co-creator of the May 3rd Constitution, as well as a generous patron of the arts, a brilliant conversationalist and a splendid host.

[3] See 133.

[4] Comedy written by Jósef Bielawski (1739–1809), a courtier who was later forced by court intrigue

to emigrate to Paris; it was put on at the inauguration of the Polish national stage on 19 November 1765.

5 Franciszek Bohomolec (1720–1784), a Jesuit who ran his own theatre, staging adaptations of Molière that eliminated the love interest and many of the female characters but stressed Figlacki, a kind of Polish Harlequin; after 1766 he worked for reform in the practices of the national theatre. See Klimowicz, 1965; Wierzbicka–Michalska, 1977.

*The Polish Theatre receives an administrator*

The Polish [Comedy] Theatre, together with the Italian and French, was initially subordinate to the head manager of the Warsaw Theatre, the Italian entrepreneur Carlo Tomatis, in accordance with the contract of 3 December 1764. (See **133, note** 3) Following a royal decree it received its own administration.

## 129 Stanislas Augustus appoints a Director of the Polish Comedy Theatre, 1 February 1766

Karyna Wierzbicka: *Źródła do historii teatru warszawskiego od roku 1762 do roku 1833* [*Sources for the history of the Warsaw theatre 1762–1833*], vol. 1 (Wrocław: Zakład Narodowy im. Ossolińskich, 1951), p. 24.

By this proclamation we make known that we have decided, in imitation of theatrical productions in other realms where such spectacles are very much cherished by the citizens, to introduce such spectacles into this kingdom as well, so that they may improve manners and provide entertainment. Hence, knowing the managerial capacity and theatrical activity of Mr Józef Szubalski,[1] major in the Polish army, we have appointed him to be director of the Polish Comedy Theatre. On conferring this title of director on the nobleman Józef Szubalski we expect him to hold this post creditably and at the same time we call on all those working in the Polish Comedy Theatre to be wholly at his disposal. Major Szubalski will receive for his new services an annual salary of three hundred red zlotys.[2] In making this proclamation we inform those concerned that the nobleman Józef Szubalski is henceforth director of the Polish Comedy Theatre. So saying, we sign this appointment by our hand and seal.

1 See Klimowicz, 1965; Wierzbicka-Michalska, 1977.

2 The red zloty or ducat was officially valued at $16\frac{3}{4}$ Polish zlotys, in practice 18 Polish zlotys. At this period the Polish zloty comprised 3 grammes of pure silver; 37 zlotys equalled one pound sterling. During the period discussed in this chapter actors' salaries in Warsaw fluctuated from 126 to 432 zl. a month. A court clerk earned 100 zl. a month, a master carpenter 70 zl. a month. In 1778 1 kg. of lard or of wheat flour cost 0.5 zl., 1 kg. of sugar cost 3.3 zl., 1 metre of cloth cost 7 zl.

*The acting company and its regulations*

The regulations were laid down by Tadeusz Lipski[1] (1725–96), castellan of Łęczyca, who, as warden of the national stage, acted on the King's behalf.

[1] For Lipski, see *Polski słownik biograficzny* (henceforth *PSB*).

## 130 Lipski's rules for Polish actors, 1 August 1766

Wierzbicka, vol. 1 (1951), p. 101.

1

Anyone who comes to rehearsal without having learned his lines and does not seem eager to do so will be punished by having two red zlotys deducted from his monthly salary.

2

Anyone who seeks to pick a quarrel during a rehearsal will be punished by having four red zlotys deducted from his monthly salary.

3

Anyone who has the audacity, at rehearsal or in performance, to add his own words or gestures that have not been approved at rehearsals shall be punished by a deduction of one red zloty from his monthly salary.

4

Anyone who does not come to rehearsal at the appointed time will be punished by a deduction of eight zlotys from his monthly salary.

5

Anyone who answers back insolently or contradicts the director during the rehearsal shall be placed under arrest or lose half his monthly salary, and if it be an actress her entire monthly salary shall be forfeit.

6

Anyone who has the audacity to leave the theatre before the performance is over or refuses to wear his costume, regardless of whether the play begins early or late, or intrudes into the actresses' dressing-room, will be fined one red zloty, to be deducted from his monthly salary.

7

Anyone who has the impudence to come drunk to a rehearsal or performance will be punished by the deduction of two zlotys from his monthly salary.

8

Anyone who starts a brawl or participates in a drinking-bout in town and at 11 p.m. is still absent from the boarding-house will be punished with a fine or arrest according to the gravity of his delinquency.

9

The actor or actress who on the expiration of his or her contract would like to leave the company will not be permitted to do so if he or she has not given a quarter's notice before that very date.

10

Anyone who does not behave respectfully towards his superior at any point where it is expected of him will be punished by a deduction of half his monthly salary.

11

Anyone who strikes his fellow in a dispute will be punished by loss of his monthly salary and put under arrest for as long as it pleases his superior.

12

The money deducted from salaries will go into a bonus fund awarded to the well-behaved actors or to those who have excelled in their roles or shall be used as indemnity for injured parties.

## 131 Czartoryski describes the first actors of the National Theatre

Adam Kazimierz Czartoryski:[1] *Myśli o pismach polskich* [*Thoughts on Polish writing*], written in Vilna 1801, pub. 1810; excerpted in *Teatr Narodowy 1765–1794* [*National Theatre*] (edited by Jan Kott) (Warsaw: Panstwowy Instytut Wydawniczy, 1967), pp. 627–8.

All sorts of persons had been selected to become actors who had no idea about that art, yet the ingenuity and gumption innate in our nation was manifested on that occasion too. In an incredibly short space of time this motley crew developed into a troupe of actors of unusual promise. They included Świerzawski[2] who excelled in parts in which his figure, face, dexterity and intelligence stood him in good stead. Then there was Miss Truskolawska whose magnificent looks, charming expression, very pleasant voice, narrow waist and graceful gestures destined her for both tender and serious parts. In the next rank after them were actors (though not so talented) who through application and proper guidance would achieve perfection. One of these was Owsiński.[3] Those actors had almost no education, could speak no foreign language, least of all French (in which there are books on the rules of the actor's craft and the major dramatic works), had no models on which to base themselves, no dancing-master to teach them elegant posture, deportment, graceful movements, had only a few casual remarks to follow, and yet, relying on their own instinct and feeling, when they did appear on stage, instead of provoking laughter, aroused astonishment and recognition.

[1] Adam Kazimierz Czartoryski (1734–1823), member of one of the oldest and most powerful families in Poland, had been preferred to his cousin Stanislas as King by the king's uncles. More important than his plays, imitations of neoclassical French models, are his theoretical writings, the first dramatic criticism in Poland; he also campaigned for Diderot and Shakespeare. The remarks quoted above are a portion of his memoirs, for he himself had taken part in training the first Polish actors. See PSB; Wierzbicka-Michalska, 1977.

[2] See 133.

[3] Agnieszka Truskolawska (1755–1831) and Kazimierz Owsiński (1752–1799). See *SBTP*; Wierzbicka-Michalska, 1977; Raszewski, 1982.

## 132 Czartoryski's advice to the actors and playwrights of the National Theatre, 1771

Preface to A.K. Czartoryski, *Panna na wydaniu* [*The Miss to be Married*][1] (Warsaw, 1771); reprinted in *Teatr Narodowy 1765–1794* [*National Theatre*] (1967), pp. 142–3.

[. . .] That brief period, during which Polish shows used to be staged, proved to us all what fine actors we were going to have; indeed, such good ones, I assure you, as no other nation could ever boast as possessing in the initial phase of its theatre.

Anyone who wants to become a good actor must devote all his time to the constant improvement of his skill. He should observe nature and try to imitate her in every way. What I mean is that the actor or actress should wholly identify with the character he or she is playing, should adopt the voice, gestures, movements of that character, according to the circumstances on stage, and do it so suggestively that the spectator forgets about the actor and thinks only of the character. It is not enough, for instance, while playing an old man, to put on spectacles or for an angry man to grab a stick, etc., indeed these interpolations, when immoderately used and inappropriate to the respective characters, remind us of the antics of fairground charlatans. The actor must have the subtlety to know exactly when he may use these tricks. And to be able to see such nuances he must work, learn and train his skill [. . .]

I also wish every Polish actor or actress would apply him- or herself to study French and read books on their craft in that language. And I advise actresses to take lessons from a dancing-master who will teach them to walk gracefully and behave properly on stage. If they follow these instructions, Poland too may eventually have her Clairon[2] and her Garrick [. . .]

I should also advise those who try their hand at writing for the stage not to imitate foreign plays slavishly because alien characters will not appeal to many of our spectators; it would be better for such writers to keep the subject or perhaps the plot of such plays but introduce into them at the same time one or two characters endowed with our national traits. [. . .]

[1] Czartoryski adapted this play to Polish conditions from David Garrick's comedy *Miss in Her Teens*. His adaptations from French comedies: J.F. Regnard's *Le Joueur* (1696) as *Gracz*, *Les Ménechmes ou Les Les Jumeaux* (1706) as *Bliźnięta*, and P. Destouches's *Le Glorieux* (1732) as *Dumny*, were produced between 1774 and 1776.

[2] Clairon (Claire-Joseph Léris, 1723–1803), famous French tragedienne, renowned for her simplicity.

## 133 Bogusławski describes the comic actor Karol Świerzawski[1]

Bogusławski (1965), pp. 258–9.

The distinguished comic actor, Karol Boromeusz Świerzawski,[1] was born in Poznań [. . .] and there, having got a minor education in Jesuit schools, went to work in a law-court. Not knowing enough Latin he could not aspire to the bar and so had to be satisfied with a lesser job. His booming voice helped him to become a court crier and his mettlesome looks often stood him in good stead when he had to deliver a subpoena to an irate litigant only too ready to give him a thrashing. [. . .] Audacious and at the same time facetious, during the few years of this work he always managed to avoid such treatment by relating funny stories deriding the plaintiff on such occasions and thus winning favour with the defendant. This sense of humour and laughing disposition made him well-liked by the barristers of the contending parties whom he knew how to amuse during the breaks in court proceedings. So, although unable to rise in the justiciary, Świerzawski could have at least become well-off, had fate not compelled him to choose another job which was eventually to bring much glory on himself and his country. The reader must not inquire what kind of delinquency it was – one much more serious than that committed by Shakespeare in his youth – that cast Boromeusz into the lock-up of Poznań town-hall. His prospects were gloomy. [. . .] He managed to escape the court's severity and soon found himself in Warsaw. His comic genius could not long remain hidden in a city that was then so given to amusement and revelry. The fame of his jokes reached the royal court. Just at that time, in 1764, when the national theatre was founded, his sort of man could prove useful. Order was given to seek him out and when he was brought before the manager and asked about his qualifications his funny answers and the amusing description of his vicissitudes revealed not only his gaiety but an aptitude for acting as well. He was engaged at once and given a part in *The Intruders*[2] (*Natręci*), the leading Polish comedy which by presenting eccentric types from contemporary society gave Świerzawski a chance to imitate them. He was acclaimed as a comic actor, as indeed he was, and given a series of roles in Bohomolec's early comedies, such as *Witchcraft* (*Czary*), *Mr Staruszkiewicz (Pan Staruszkiewicz)*, *A Plucky Fellow* (*Junak*) and others. Indeed, he acted himself in all of them. When he was presenting a ribald Polish character of the day, always dressed in national costume, moving with long easy strides, he needed to be sustained by no talent or craft other than his own nature. At this point his progress had to be interrupted, because the national stage was suspended for almost ten years and all the actors dismissed.[3] [. . .] Then, in 1774,[4] came the moment when a special privilege issued for the support of national performances in the capital city enabled Świerzawski to exercise his talent once more, develop it and win the acknowledgement of the public.

Since then, Świerzawski appeared as a new artist. No longer was he satisfied with playing only Polish characters and he began to act those that required more variety and art. He could find them in the then highly regarded plays of Prince Adam Czartoryski: *The Gambler, Twins, A Miss to be Married* and others. As he knew no foreign language and was far from being well-read (a common thing then), and thus having no dramatic models to learn from he would have been unable to cope with the roles of Panfil, Menekin[5] and others, had not the illustrious translator of these plays kindly shown him the right path in that foreign maze. He pulled it off by following his teacher word for word, thereby winning his esteem as well as the applause of the public. And so his fame grew in two kinds of comic characters, those of comic fathers and valets [. . .]

Finally, convinced that he was not simply a comic actor, Świerzawski decided to surprise the Warsaw public with something much more demanding. During the absence of Owsiński and other tragic actors he thought he could add another laurel wreath to his brow. He assumed the tragic role of Pygmalion in the lyrical scene by Jean-Jacques Rousseau,[6] perhaps the most difficult role of its kind, so filled with love's ardour, passions, hope and despair, anger and madness, that even the leading tragedians could scarcely sustain such tension and violence for the full hour it takes. Having chosen this play for his benefit, he announced in the posters that 'Świerzawski is the first Polish actor to want to show the public that, like the English actor Garrick who won fame on account of both his comic and tragic parts, he too can do the same and win similar recognition.' Consequently the house was full and the public very excited to see the new Pygmalion. And there he was, dressed in a Grecian costume, but with his moustache (which he would never shave off) pomaded and powdered, wrapped up in a long cloak which covered his whole figure including his rather bandy legs, looking quite presentable. Seated at first at a small table he uttered the opening lines calmly, thus arousing the audience's expectations. The following verses were also spoken very well. And as the individual stanzas of this scene are interrupted by music, as it was being played, the first words of praise were whispered by his friends in the stalls. Then, as his lines became more forceful, a ludicrous grimace appeared on Pygmalion's face which first made the public smile; but then, when he leapt from the table and angrily cried, 'Away with you, clumsy tools, you are unworthy of my fame!', flinging the sculptor's chisel and mallet offstage, a burst of laughter shook the stalls, which so confused the new Garrick that he could not recover and proceed calmly with his role. [. . .]

[1] Karol Świerzawski (1725–1806) had been enrolled in the first Polish acting troupe in 1765 and remained on the national stage till 1806 as one of its leading actors. See *SBTP*; Wierzbicka-Michalska 1977; Raszewski 1982.

[2] See **128**, note 4.

[3] In the spring of 1767, the King abrogated the contract with the dishonest entrepreneur Tomatis, while the very difficult political situation in Poland at the time of the Radom Confederation made it impossible to reorganize the theatre. The Polish theatre suspended its work in April 1767. Theatrical performances were not resumed until 1774. See Klimowicz, 1965; Wierzbicka-Michalska, 1977.

[4] From 1774 to 1791 the Warsaw Theatre was organized on the basis of an exclusive privilege, held from 1776 by Franciszek Ryx, head butler and a favourite of Stanislas Augustus. See Wierzbicka-Michalska, 1967.

[5] Characters from Regnard's comedies translated by Czartoryski as *Gracz* and *Bliźnięta*.

[6] *Pygmalion* (1775) was Rousseau's interpretation of opera: a one-man declamation set to music, with orchestral interludes between the speeches.

## II THE REPERTOIRE EXPANDS, 1778–1808

### *Bogusławski begins his career as manager*

The first Polish public theatre had to close down after less than two years of activity, in

1767. For the next few years the political situation in the country made it impossible for that theatre to give performances in Warsaw. They were resumed only in 1774, this time with the theatre working on different organizational principles. In that year, the Diet, the Polish Parliament, passed a bill initiating a theatrical monopoly, whose proprietor, from 1776, was Franciszek Ryx, the King's trusted man. The theatrical monopoly ensured a more durable existence for the Polish stage than had the entreprise of 1765–7. Ryx's management also resulted in more durable support, both material and moral, for the national stage on the part of the king; this had a beneficial effect on its development.

The number of Polish actors began to grow steadily, trained mainly on-the-job, while learning a good deal from performances by French, German and Italian companies in Warsaw, some of the French actors giving their Polish colleagues private lessons. In 1778, Bogusławski embarked on his theatrical career; because he came of a noble country family, was well-educated and spoke good French, his presence enhanced the lowly social position of the acting profession.

One of his earliest innovative successes was to produce Polish opera. The public had taken to opera when the national theatre began to produce it in 1778, despite the fact that for a long time it was actors and not specially trained vocalists who sang in it. On 11 July 1778, the first Polish opera was staged, under the title *Nędza Uszczęśliwiona* (*Misery Made Happy*). The music contained a number of folk motives and it initiated the Polish national opera.

## 134 Bogusławski stages the opera *Misery Made Happy* in 1778

Bogusławski (1965), pp. 18–20.

The National Scene, which had already demonstrated its artists' achievement in tragic drama and almost reached perfection in comedy by modelling itself on the playing of French actors, could hardly expect that it would provoke the admiration of its audiences in singing as well. This triumph over the prejudice about the ability of Poles to produce operas was the work of a foreigner, Montbrun,[1] who knew much about music and, having trained French singers to appear in operas, wished greatly to awaken a similar talent in the Poles. He invited me one day to show me a little comedy, composed of several scenes and comprising a few songs, all of them written by Father Bohomolec[2] and entitled *Misery Made Happy*. 'If you could turn it into a two-act operetta, Mr Kamieński, who has already written very nice music to these songs, would finish the rest, and we could surprise the public with a new show.'[3] Emboldened by the public's favourable reception of my first comedy, *Lover, Author and Servant*,[4] I refashioned that play into an opera under the same title, adding arias and duets. In no time at all Mr Kamieński composed simple music, easy for beginners to learn, and very pleasant as well. He himself trained the artists and produced the first Polish opera, a wonder which aroused general admiration. [. . .] The best liked were the song of the poor mother 'Torbo kochana' ['Dear Bag'], Kasia's Polish dance, and above all Antek's rondo 'Nigdy jak dzisiaj nie czułem rozkoszy' ('I've Never Been So Happy as Today') – all of them sung everywhere and heard with pleasure. [. . .]

[1] Louis Montbrun, French singer and actor, came to Warsaw with a French troupe in 1765. From April to September 1778, he managed the prematurely terminated Warsaw theatrical enterprise. See Wierzbicka-Michalska, 1975.

[2] See **128, note 5**.

[3] Maciej Kamieński (1734–1821) is important for mining the Polish musical tradition for his operas; although derivative of French *opéra comique* and Italian arias, they were infused with national colour and sentimental moralizing. See Raszewski, 1982.

[4] An adaptation of the French comedy *Amant Auteur et Valet* (1778) by Cérou.

*Topical comedy is introduced*

The number of theatre-goers grew steadily and from 1779 they could attend performances in a big new house on Krasiński Square specially built for the public theatre. On 15 January 1791, for the first time, a political Polish comedy was staged in the theatre managed by Bogusławski; it was *Powrót Posła* (*The Return of a Member of the Diet*) by Julian Ursyn Niemcewicz (1757–1841; see *PSB*), himself a deputy, and enjoyed a huge success. The play propagated the reform policy of the Four Years' Diet and Stanislas Augustus took a keen interest in the comedy known to him in manuscript, because it endorsed tendencies he himself favoured in the promotion of a new constitution. He was eager to do away with class distinctions, to replace the royal election with a hereditary monarchy, and to abolish the *liberum veto*, which insisted on unanimity in adopting measures introduced into the Diet.

## 135a Stanislas Augustus praises the play *Return of the Member of the Diet*, 19 January 1791

Letter to Augustyn Deboli, Polish envoy to St Petersburg in *Teatr Narodowy* [*National Theatre*] (1967), p. 158.

[. . .] The other day, Niemcewicz, a member of the Diet from Livonia, staged a play of his, a Polish comedy, which ran two days to great applause by the audience and whose title is *Return of the Member of the Diet to His Father*. This colourful and merry play contains a subject that might be debated by the Diet, namely it expresses the author's favourite ideas of liberating the peasants from socage and of hereditary succession to the throne advanced against the conservative views of the old-fashioned stay-at-homes. Yesterday Suchorzewski[1] read and spoke at length on this subject and concluded by applying to the confederation marshal for the convocation of the Diet's court with a formal complaint against the police for allowing this comedy to be staged and a charge against Niemcewicz for writing such a play since it violated the *pacta conventa*[2] prohibiting any discussion of the hereditary succession to the throne. Suchorzewski's speech met with general laughter. He won no support. This infuriated him and he cursed those who had promised him that support. Anyway he eventually prevailed upon the Diet secretary to read out his motion. Then, seeing once more that it met with laughter, he said that he was putting it forward for deliberation. Yet the Diet Marshal[3] replied that he could not see how such a matter might be subject to deliberation. But once the motion has been read out by the Diet secretary and in view of Suchorzewski's well-known obstinacy, *probabiliter* [probably] it will be sustained and thus, alas, one more obstacle will appear on the road to achieving more useful things. [. . .]

[1] Jan Suchorzewski, member of the Diet from the Kalisz province.

[2] Provisos, instituted by the Diet, to be accepted by the candidate on his election to the throne of Poland.

[3] Speaker of the Diet.

## 135b One scene from Niemcewicz's comedy *Return of the Member of the Diet*

Anonymous engraving illustrating the first edition, 1791; reproduced in Wierzbicka-Michalska (1977), p. 251 and *Teatr Narodowy* (1967), plate 36.

*Ballet gains popularity*

In 1785 a ballet group began to appear on the Warsaw stage. Its members were well-trained professional Polish dancers. Thanks to them the Warsaw ballet spectacles achieved a standard equal to that of the major European theatres. Elisa von der Recke, sister of the Courlandian princess Dorothea, stayed for a while in Warsaw in 1791 where she was a frequent visitor to the court of Stanislas Augustus and attended the ballet.

## 136 Elisa von der Recke attends the ballet *Cora and Alonzo*, 18 November 1791

Elisa von der Recke: *Mein Journal. Elisas neu aufgefundene Tagebücher aus den Jahren 1791 und 1793–1795* [*My journal. Elisa's newly discovered diaries from 1791 and 1793–5*] (Leipzig: Koehler & Ameland, 1928); excerpt from the Polish translation in *Teatr Narodowy* [*National Theatre*] (1967), p. 667.

[. . .] The composition of the ballet *Cora and Alonzo*[1] is poignantly beautiful and moved me almost to tears. I have never seen a pantomimic ballet which corresponded so much to my ideal of the art of dancing.[2] Alonzo and Cora danced with a grace full of expression; Michel,[3] the much admired dancer, took the part of Alonzo. His figure is one of the most beautiful and he dances with a soulful grace, lifting himself with indescribable lightness; had his Cora been a little taller her delicately languid *pas de deux* would have been even more delightful. The dancing of the prima ballerina is also marked by adroitness, grace and expression, but she herself is rather heavy. Cora's parents, the prince, the merciless priest of the Sun who wants to sacrifice not Cora but her younger sister, the two children, and all the supers performed in a masterful manner and danced well. The ballets in Berlin were more showy but less well composed. There the dancers performed with greater skill but not so much feeling. I should have called them hoppers and those here dancers. [. . .]

1 The subject of this ballet was based on a French novel *Les Incas* by Jean François Marmontel and on Kotzebue's play *Die Spanier in Peru*.

2 The dancers in Warsaw were trained by prominent Italian and French ballet-masters in the style of Jean-Georges Noverre. See Wierzbicka-Michalska, 1967, pp. 159–215.

3 Michał Rymiński (1769–97). See Wierzbicka-Michalska, 1967; SBTP.

*How the Polish theatre appeared to a German*

Friedrich Schultz, a Livonian German, man of letters, professor of history at the ducal academy at Mitawa, capital of Poland's feudal principality Courland, stayed in Warsaw during the four-year Diet as a deputy to the Courland townsfolk.

## 137a A German traveller's impressions of the Warsaw National Theatre in 1793

Friedrich Schultz: *Reise eines Liefländers von Riga nach Warschau* [*Journey of a Livonian from Riga to Warsaw*] (Berlin, 1795–6); excerpt in Polish translation in *Teatr Narodowy* [*National Theatre*] (1967), pp. 663–5.

As I have said, Warsaw has only one theatre, which may be strange considering how much people are given to amusements here and the propensity of those who engage in them. The reason for it may be, apart from the availability of many other diversions, the difficulty of putting together a theatrical company, though there is room enough for it.

The theatre in question has been built with royal funds and that is why it does not lack for comfort, taste and beauty.[1] This applies, however, to its interior more than its exterior. I may be wrong, but it seems to me that, in contrast to their purpose, theatre buildings cannot easily be made to look magnificent, light and gay. At best the façade of the structure may display such features, whereas the rest of it, deprived of tall, attractive windows, must necessarily look like a prison. This at any rate has been my impression of most famous French and Italian theatres. [. . .] The same can be said of the Warsaw theatre. Though situated in a vast square, it is massive and compact, giving no suggestion of its interior. Surprise is all the greater at how fine the latter actually is. It is a beautiful oval with four tiers of boxes on four levels, and the whole arrangement is both simple and in very good taste. The orchestra is only half-filled with stalls. The quite spacious stage, beautifully adorned, is equipped with diverse and efficient machinery.

The Polish troupe, which played here last year, was better than any German one I have ever seen. The Poles are endowed by nature with a lightness of motion, deftness, handsome stature and good figures; they speak with greater ease and clarity than the Germans. In comedy they are close to the old French manner, though without its exaggeration of motion and language; they are also far from using the exaggerated gestures and mimicry of the Italians. In the higher kind of comedy (drama) and tragedy they are more like the Germans, but are superior to them because in passionate and violent scenes, which are played there with more austerity, here they preserve a gravity and noble expression which do not exclude fire and force, yet without dwindling into cheap Italian airs and graces of heads, hands, legs and eyes, or into French exaggeration.

A certain Bogusławski was the first director of the company and at the same time its best actor; he was a well-built man with a captivating voice and a bearing which made him look free and natural in any costume, even in the French one which usually lends some stiffness and clumsiness to even the most beautiful Polish figure, accustomed to looser attire.

I saw him as Truffaldino in *The Servant of Two Masters*,[2] *The Father*, a drama translated from Diderot,[3] *Casimir the Great* (*Kazimierz Wielki*), a national play by Niemcewicz, in three very different roles and in each of them he was perfect. In the title role of *Return of the Member of the Diet*[4] he acted superbly.

Other actors too were excellent in their roles, particularly one of them who acted with unimaginable naturalness; there was a comic who played very distinctly [for foreigners] the parts of servants, typical in this country, and an actor who, while playing jurists, pedants, lawyers, plenipotentiaries, made fun of them by imitating their conceit and sly vulgarity in handling people.

The actresses were by no means inferior to the men. The leading roles were acted by beautiful and charming ladies who had acquired the art of tasteful dressing and graceful behaviour. Even the minor parts were acted by skilled actresses.

The plays staged by the company were partly Polish, but mostly translated from French, Italian and German. Those produced during the Four-Year Diet, the Constitutional one,[5] had mainly a political purpose, as I have already said. Particularly successful among them were *Return of the Member of the Diet* and *Casimir the Great*. Their aim was to deride the ancient Polish prejudices, attachment to the free election of the king, the privileges of the nobles, abasement of the middle class, restriction of the royal prerogatives; that is, poking fun at the things the new constitution was going to abolish. The King and the partisans of the new system were usually present at these performances and the passages which referred to those changes would be received by them very warmly. During the performances of *Casimir the Great*, when the noble traits of that monarch were becoming more and more evident, the King would be the first to lean out of his box and applaud, followed by other boxes and the stalls and the entire audience would end by enthusiastically demanding encores – two or three times – of such passages. [. . .] One had the feeling that it was not so much King Casimir who was being applauded as King Stanislas, first because the former monarch was endowed by the poet with the characteristics of the present one and then because they wished to show their gratitude to Stanislas for appreciating so highly the deeds of his remote predecessor. And the leaders of the new party, proponents of revolution and their friends, tried to express by clapping their hands the feelings of those present who approved of their projects. So it was a great success and everyone gained something by it.

The farces performed by the company were mainly translations from the Italian, and the little operettas and comedies from the French. There were very few Polish ones. [. . .] The orchestra was made up of court musicians, fine artists, some of whom were of domestic make. [. . .]

1 The theatre, built in 1779 on Krasiński Square in Warsaw, had been designed by the architect Bonaventure Solari. Productions were held in it until 1833. See Król-Kaczorowska, 1971, pp. 76–7.

2 Carlo Goldoni's comedy of masks *Il Servitore di due padrone* (1746?).

3 *Le père de famille* (1758).

4 See 135.

5 The Diet or *Sejm* lasted from October 1788 to June 1792.

## 137b Painting of a ballet in progress at the National Theatre in Krasiński Square, before its reconstruction, *c.* 1791

Painting by Zygmunt Vogel, National Museum, Warsaw; reproduced in Wierzbicka-Michalska (1977), p. 236.

## 137c Exterior of the Theatre in Krasiński Square

Reproduced in Wierzbicka-Michalska (1977), p. 250.

*Cracovians and Highlanders*

After *The Return of the Member of the Diet*, several other plays of that type appeared, the most celebrated being *Krakowiacy i Górale* (*Cracovians and Highlanders*) by Bogusławski himself, first staged on 1 March 1794. The author of this account, Johann Gottfried Seume, a German poet, was secretary to Osip Igelström, Russian ambassador to Poland.

## 138a Controversy over the comedy *Cracovians and Highlanders* in 1794

J.G. Seume, *Einige Nachrichten über die Vorfälle in Polen im Jahre 1794* [*Some news about the events in Poland in 1794*] (Leipzig, 1796); excerpt in Polish translation in *Teatr Narodowy* [*National Theatre*] (1967), p. 674.

The staging in the capital of the stage play entitled *Cracovians* aroused tremendous enthusiasm. This is a play on a national subject and presents, with much talent, a dispute of peasants in the Cracow region. The Russian ambassador at first raised objections to the play being staged, but after the marshal, Count Moszyński,[1] had avouched that there would be nothing objectionable in the show, the performance took place after all.

The author, Mr Bogusławski, an expert at playing on human feelings, and at the same time as good a patriot as a playwright, showed himself a master both in the play and its production. The work very happily combines melodrama and vaudeville with ballet. Its music is thrilling and based partly on folk tunes, partly on discreetly borrowed motives from the best foreign pieces; indeed only somebody very cold-blooded could resist the audience's enthusiasm. Of the three performances, I had the luck to be at two and I must confess I have never been so ravished and moved. The political allusions of the play were rather faint and inessential, yet the patriotic character of the show was evident. Some of the actors probably belonged to the conspiracy because into the arias they made their own insertions, which soon replaced the original text and were taken up by the audience with unconcealed jubilation. The insertions were immediately circulated amongst the people, and the events near Cracow[2] turned all the inhabitants of Warsaw into opera singers. Even the Russian military bands played arias from that attractive opera. Then the Russian general learned about it all and prohibited further performances; but the play had been performed thrice and had had its effect. [. . .]

[1] Fryderyk Moszyński (1736–1817), Grand Marshal of the Crown.

[2] Reference to the Kościuszko Insurrection, a popular uprising against the Russian occupation, initiated in Cracow on 24 March 1794.

## 138b Scene from *Cracovians and Highlanders*, 1794

Watercolour sketch by Fryderyk Antoni Lohrmann; reproduced in Wierzbicka-Michalska (1977), p. 246.

*A humorous look at theatrical life*

Alojzy Żołkowski (1777–1822), of noble birth, had already become a favourite with the Warsaw public in such roles as Karl Moor and Arlecchino before joining the national theatre. Unconventional in behaviour, he was noted for his improvisations, outlandish costumes and bizarre wigs. [See *SBTP*]. He was also a playwright, translator, poet and publicist. In his *Small Theatrical Dictionary*, published in 1808, he described in a funny but critical way various elements of the theatrical life of his day.

## 139 Excerpts from Żołkowski's *Small Theatrical Dictionary*, 1808

Reprinted in *Teatr W. Bogusławskiego w latach 1799–1814* [*Bogusławski's theatre 1799–1814*], edited by E. Szwankowski (Wrocław: Zakład Narodowy im. Ossolińskich, 1954), pp. 354–66.

[. . .] BENEFIT PERFORMANCE

Benefit means advantage, in this case a profit the actor receives for his work, talent or as an encouragement to make further progress in the art of acting. Leading actors took a benefit each year, others every two years, some of them on their jubilees. The public has always shown itself very generous towards its favourite actors. Two days before his benefit the actor, having taken a number of box tickets and others, pays visits to persons of consequence and sells these tickets at a higher price than the face value. The origin of these visits with tickets came from a wish to pay respects to the theatre's patrons. In time, the growing number of benefits made them a bit importunate; nevertheless the visitor is usually received with the utmost politeness. The actor takes for himself the profit from such a performance after paying the theatre's expenses, which never amount to less than 40 ducats.

THE PRICE OF SEATS

Fixed by the Government, it may not be increased unless the production calls for extraordinary expenditures; in that case the Authorities allow the price to be raised. There are four kinds of seats: boxes, occupied mostly by the fair sex; stalls, which have the *vocem decisivam* [the decisive vote], and issue praise or criticism; gallery and the 'gods'. In addition there are the so-called chimney-sweep boxes, that is, various garrets let for a small price to the stokers. [. . .]

DRAMA

This term is given to a cross between tragedy and comedy. The Germans are particularly fond of this kind of play, especially when the author depicts in five long acts the family life of civil servants or military councillors in the smallest details; these are called 'Familien-Gemälde' [Genre Paintings]. They have also invented the chivalric drama, a regular feature of which are duels, tournaments and battles. Many of them were translated into Polish and before real battles appeared in them, very welcome were the armed encounters that made booking-clerks smile with delight in preparing the posters for a chivalric drama. [. . .]

BACKSTAGE

[. . .] For the sake of order and complete illusion it is necessary that only those who take part in the performance should be seen by the audience. For instance, the other day, during the representation of the Death of Abel in a setting not far from Paradise a few years after the world's creation, there could be seen, for half the act, a gentleman in full dress coldly watching the despair of Adam and Eve through his lorgnette. [. . .]

### SCENE-SHIFTER

As the name indicates, he shifts the scenes and runs the theatre's machinery. It is he who brings rain, wind, creates thunder, lightning, earthquakes, all this to frighten the audience with the menacing sights of nature or delight it with nature's beauty. But even though he has the machinery under his control, he should not let it be visible: so when a forest descends on the stage, the walls of a room should not remain there, and vice versa, when we see a room there should be no hunting preserve at the sides. [. . .]

### TOURING

Among the nuisances experienced by men of the theatre (and which profession is without them?) is the need to tour. It especially affects a theatre which cannot spend all year in the same town. It has to tour to other places and try to satisfy the tastes of other audiences. Because what one audience likes may not please another at all. Still, the expenses entailed by touring are usually so high that they bring the entrepreneurs scarcely any profit, but just enough to keep the business going.

In Warsaw in summer, almost nobody goes to the theatre. The lovely city parks attract the residents while the landed gentry spend summer on their estates. Therefore Warsaw actors go annually for a few weeks to Poznań and Kalisz and, although this is one of the lucky theatres that can, as we have said, stay in one place, the Poznań and Kalisz public is so nice and appreciative to the National Theatre that its actors leave them with regret. The Lithuanian and Volhynian theatres also make frequent journeys, to such an extent that there are no major civic assemblies or fairs at which a troupe of actors does not perform. [. . .]

### PROMPTER

When the poet emphasizes his devotion by saying that his affections will alter no sooner 'than when the prompter in the Polish theatre takes a breather' it means that he does not believe Polish actors will ever remember their lines. However, he must be a mean-spirited poet who seldom attends the theatres, because our actors have proved that such an opinion is unjust. [. . .] I personally wish the prompter were not indispensable to the theatre. But since the human memory can hardly hold several thousand words without a mistake at short notice, one must accept the prompter as indispensable indeed. He and his box can be tolerated only so long as his prompting is whispered and infrequent.

### CURTAIN CALLS

When an actor has played his part very well, apart from applause during the performance, the audience shows its appreciation at the end by calling him before the curtain. Actors feel very honoured by such calls. The actor who has been called expresses his gratitude with a short (and sometimes longer) address; in France bowing replaces words. The dancers, when called, show their gratitude by gestures. [. . .] Our public can appreciate the work done for the national theatre, for when the translation of a play proves very good the audience asks for the translator's name or that of the original author. It has happened that when the translator's name is stated and he is discovered among the spectators, he has been seized and lifted shoulder-high to be displayed to those present.

## III IMPROVEMENTS IN ADMINISTRATION AND ACTING, 1810–16

### *Instituting governmental control*

After the defeat of the Kosciuśzko Insurrection, Bogusławski, who had taken part in it, left with part of his company for Lvov where he ran a theatre. In 1799 he returned to Warsaw. The National Theatre, which in the meantime had lost its importance under the Prussian occupation, now began quickly to recover its status, due to Bogusławski's efforts. This became even more obvious once Poland regained, although only partially, her independence in the shape of the Duchy of Warsaw, formed in 1807. The Ducal authorities subsidized the National Theatre and also appointed a Government Management whose purpose was to control the theatrical enterprise. The Government Administration of the National Theatre was established on 14 April 1810, and began its activities in September when Julian Ursyn Niemcewicz became its chairman. Official celebrations would be held in the Theatre, and the plays it produced referred to current political events. Warsaw actors would also give performances in other towns.

In the Kingdom of Poland, a small Polish state created by the Congress of Vienna in 1815, the National Theatre in Warsaw continued to be state-subsidized with the proviso, however, that the Government interfere more and more closely with its work.

## 140 Chairman of the Government Administration of the National Theatre sets its tasks and plans, 29 September 1810

*Gazeta Warszawska* [*Warsaw Gazette*], no. 78, 29 September 1810.

[. . .] To order the necessary improvements [in the theatre] a post of director has been called into being, and the Government Administration has concluded a contract with Mr Bogusławski,[1] by which power he has been allotted funds from the public treasury to set up a school of drama, as well as funds for retired actors and funds for sending outstanding young actors abroad for further study. [. . .]

The contract also stipulates the duties the actors have towards the public, the Entrepreneur and themselves. [. . .]

There are constant complaints that the actors do not memorize their lines, that they perform casually. Although these complaints may occasionally be justifiable, the actors may also be defended by pointing out that there is usually much noise in the stalls, constant coming and going and banging of doors, likewise loud conversations in the boxes, while some bring screaming babies, occasionally even dogs – all this upsets the actors, who do not care to learn and act well since they know no one will pay them any attention. There are cases when persons come not to watch the play but to be seen and heard themselves, and by their noisy behaviour spoil the pleasure of others who have come to enjoy the performance. The management, anxious for the comfort of the audience, has placed bleachers in the pit. Those who sit on them will not be able to move around as they have done so far, and thus will be better placed to follow the play and the actors. The Management and Entrepreneur will do their best, considering the plays they have at their disposal, to stage not only works of entertainment but also those of higher quality. [. . .]

[1] The contract concluded with W. Bogusławski (18 May 1810) was to be in force until 1814. See Raszewski, 1982, p. 429.

*A dramatic school is founded*

During the reign of Stanislas Augustus, regular dramatic schooling had not been organized, despite some attempts.[1] The first school of drama, founded by Wojciech Bogusławski and opened on 4 June 1811, had to suspend its activities in 1814 because of financial difficulties. After this brief hiatus, it resumed operations and continued to operate without interruption.

[1] See Zbigniew Wilski: *Polskie szkolnictwo teatralne 1811–1944* [*Polish Theatrical Education*], Wrocław: Zakład Narodowy im. Ossolińskich, 1978], pp. 11–13.

## 141 Announcement of the opening of the drama school, 6 March 1811

*Gazeta Korespondenta Warszawskiego* [*Gazette of the Warsaw correspondent*], no. 20, 9 March 1811; reprinted in *Pamiętnik Teatralny* [*Theatre Journal*] 3/4 (1954): 348–50.

The Entrepreneur of the National Theatre notifies the illustrious Public that on May 1 of this year a School of Drama will be opened in Warsaw and will train twelve students, half of them male and half female, who will attend it under the following conditions:

First: Nobody can become a student of this School unless his parents or relations undertake to assure him food and suitable clothing for the three-year course of study and unless they are able to guarantee that the contract to be concluded between them and the Entrepreneur, representing the Government Administration, will be adhered to.

Second: Only those persons will be admitted to the School who meet such requirements as:

(a) No girl should be younger than 14 or older than 17; no boy younger than 16 or older than 19.

(b) Everyone should have a rudimentary knowledge of a foreign language and at least be able to read and write very well in Polish.

(c) Must be tall and have an unblemished body.

(d) Be of good health, have a pleasant face, strong lungs, distinct enunciation.

(e) Since half of these students will become opera singers, such candidates must have a clear, strong voice and an aptitude for carrying a tune.

(f) It is essential that each student have a good memory and a gift for learning, so that if it turns out after three months of study that there is little hope of making him proficient in drama, the Government Administration will send him away and take another candidate in his place.

(g) Finally, the student should be of good morals, well-behaved, obedient to the Instructors, and if he is not, then, after the third reprimand, he will be expelled by the Government Administration.

Those who meet these requirements will be admitted at once and become regular Students. Their three-year course at the School of Drama will be free, the expenses having been covered by the Theatre's Entrepreneur, and will include the following subjects:

First: Study of the native language and also foreign languages, that is, French, German, Italian, since it is in them that the finest plays and works on the art of drama have been written.

Second: Study of Sacred History, moral science and world history, History of the Polish Nation, History of Theatre, both ancient and modern, Mythology.

Third: Basic training in music, both in singing and various instruments.

Fourth: Study of human anatomy and costumes of various nations, which is necessary to the art of drama.

Fifth: Study of dancing since it is necessary for proper deportment.

Sixth: Finally, the study of theatre arts, divided into two parts: mimicry with various motions of the body, called movement, and declamation with various forms of elocution; a perfect knowledge of such rules and their application on the stage will conclude the three-year course of study.

The Entrepreneur who opens the school will keep at his expense, for the three years of study, teachers as well as a Monitress for the girls to keep an eye on them when they are no longer under the care of their parents or relatives; the latter are obliged to engage a person, chosen by the Monitress, to accompany the girls to and from the School. Both the teachers and the Monitress must be confirmed in their positions by the Government Administration. Once a year the latter will give a performance for the benefit of the Students, the proceeds of which will be evenly divided among them to buy the necessary aids – books, paper, ink, pens, pencils, etc.

Three years after the opening of the School on 1 May 1811 and thus after the completion of the course of study, the Entrepreneur promises to place the graduates among the actors of the Warsaw Theatre and pay them salaries according to their characters, roles and talents, with the agreement of the Government Administration.

The Entrepreneur hereby states that should he die or the Warsaw Theatrical Enterprise pass to somebody else, the State Government is bound by a contract concluded with the Entrepreneur on 1 May of last year to see to the completion of the Students' course of study and to secure them work at any theatre there may be.

The Students, for their part, will be obliged, thus paying for the expenses of their education, to stay at the Warsaw Theatrical Enterprise for six years after their graduation to serve the National Theatre with their talents, and only then will they be free to go.

During that period of three and then six years of training and work both the Parents and Guardians of these young people are supposed to take no decision concerning them without the approval of the Government Administration. [. . .]

[signed] Bogusławski

The Government Administration of the National Theatre, while confirming the above announcement, states for its part that called upon by His Excellency the Minister of the Interior to supervise the School of Drama, it will determine the order of the courses to be held at the School and will attend its performances.

The Administration is convinced that Mr Bogusławski, the Entrepreneur of the Theatre and also its leading actor, owing to his great talent and thorough knowledge of the art of drama, will add to his theatrical fame the merit of being an accomplished instructor as well; still, it feels itself obliged to follow closely the progress of the students and supervise their morals.

Finally, trusting to the support and generosity of our countrymen, the

Administration will do its utmost to send the most talented graduates abroad to enable them to see the best models of their art in other countries; they will be supported during their stay there by public funds and after their return home will, one hopes, be able to contribute even more to the graces of the art they have chosen. [. . .]

[signed] Julian Ursin Niemcewicz
Chairman

## 142 Bogusławski explains the need for three theatres in Warsaw, 1811

Bogusławski (1965), pp. 220–8.

In considering the further development of our National Stage I have been thinking of a project that might render that Stage more useful to our capital and at the same time free it from the complaints advanced by our very exacting critics, namely, that the National Theatre produces, instead of classical plays by leading writers, nothing but melodramas, German products and buffooneries! It is in vain for the Entrepreneur to justify himself by saying [. . .] that Warsaw has only one theatre and so he must cater to the cultural needs of people of various classes and education by staging a variety of shows, and that classical plays, not being well-attended, would not cover the theatre's expenses. But these remarks have gone unheeded and recur time and again.

Considering my project [. . .] to be quite feasible, I take the liberty of submitting it to the public's judgement.

### THE PROJECT

Its purpose is to organize the national performances in such a way that they satisfy all classes of people in the Capital:

Let there be three theatres in Warsaw (run either by the Government or private enterprise).

The first, called the National Theatre, will produce all original Polish tragedies and comedies of high quality, as well as foreign classical works, translated in verse; following them at each performance (as is done in the French theatre in Paris) one-act comedies will be given.

The second will be called the Polish Opera Theatre. All grand and comic operas, both by Polish and foreign composers, will be produced there, embellished by ballets.

And finally the third, called the Comedy Theatre, will entertain lower-class audiences by staging melodrama, minor comedies, comic operas and the like. On this particular stage the Schools of Drama and Ballet will be able to try out their own shows. [. . .] The present theatre building will be transformed into the Polish Opera Theatre where musical shows will also be given. [. . .]

As for the National Theatre [. . .] there is no reason for it to be housed in a great, high edifice; it could even do without the upper gallery. It should have two tiers of comfortable and ornate boxes; the stalls should comprise 300 seats and the gallery 100. This would be sufficient to satisfy all the lovers of classical plays. In 100 years' time, it will perhaps be possible to erect a larger building. The scenery room (and such plays usually need only one setting), dressing-rooms, painting-rooms, living quarters for twelve actors at most, will not take up much space. But the building's façade should be ornate and impressive, while the interior will be conceived with that agreeable Greek simplicity which shows good taste and is the sign of a perfect work of architecture. It should also be admired for the sumptuousness of its costumes, the stage sets painted by a first-rate artist and, above all, it should be well heated for the comfort of the distinguished spectators. At the same time, the prices might be a little higher.

As to the third, the Comedy Theatre, whose purpose would be to entertain those who like a good laugh, whether or not they are laughing according to the rules, would not need to be very impressive, but should instead be vast in order to seat comfortably that most numerous class of spectators. It would have, at most, two tiers of boxes, but there should be 1,000 seats in the stalls, a gallery for 500 spectators and an upper gallery for the same number.

### *Bogusławski's textbook on acting*

Bogusławski's 1811 project was not acted upon. The following year, he wrote a textbook for the drama school: *Dramaturgia, czyli nauka sztuki scenicznej . . .* [*Dramaturgy, i.e. The Teaching of Stage Art . . .*] The manuscript was lost, but a copy of the textbook's Part II, 'Mimicry', survived and was published in 1965.[1]

[1] On the influence of German and French theorists of acting on W. Bogusławski's textbook, see J. Lipiński, 'Edukacja Podstawowa' in Bogusławski: *Mimika* (1965), pp. 13–45.

## 143 Excerpts from Bogusławski's acting manual *Mimicry*, 1812

Wojciech Bogusławski: *Mimika* (1812), edited by J. Lipiński and T. Sivert (Warsaw: Państwowy Instytut Wydawniczy, 1965), pp. 63–4, 145–9, 187–9.

There are three kinds of stage mimicry: the individual, the mutual and the sympathetic [in the sense of passive].

The individual, when an actor imitates the action of the character without regard for the actions of others. The mutual, when the actor, apart from his own actions, is obliged to assume those of his partner as well. And the sympathetic, which does not reveal one's own actions nor those of one's partners, but simply reflects the feelings the spectators experience while watching a particular scene.

The last type of mimicry is different from the former in that characters who are present in a scene but are not reciting lines act out different situations. Acting the parts of knights or benevolent monarchs they should inspire the spectators with admiration; acting the parts of wretched or suffering persons, with sympathy; and acting the parts of criminals or tyrants, with fear, horror and revulsion!– that is to say, those merely present on stage should share their feelings with the spectators.

This particular type of mimicry has been neglected on our stage and this has prevented productions from being really good, especially in tragedy. We can see actors standing aside and talking to one another when somebody is dying on stage or, stricken by misfortune, is in despair.

In such scenes a mere walk across the stage draws the eye away from the performing actor; a single word, be it comic or an exaggerated grief, provokes laughter in the spectators who have noticed it and breaks the spell cast by the actors. So it is the duty of those who are merely present in the scene to behave as if they were taking an active part in what is going on. [. . .]

### ON FEAR

The sight or description of something horrible fills us with fear; true or invented, it holds one in its grip until reason and reflection dispel it.

One who believes in ghosts may be as frightened by a nightmare as one who watches a murder committed.

The feeling of fear is so strong that it affects our body and makes its movements either violent or simply numb.

Should I accidentally enter a cave and see bandits killing my closest friend, my first reaction would be a feeling of horror and though I might be unable to utter a word, my soul would be filled with such exclamations as:

'It can't be true . . . I'm trembling . . . terrified . . . unable to breathe . . . Oh, murderers! . . . my friend is dying in a welter of blood! What am I to do? Where should I go? I can't move, I'm numb with fear.'

At the first words, 'It can't be true', I should retreat a step and cover my eyes with my hands and bending backwards show on my face signs that I am taking in the situation. By knitting my brows, goggling my eyes and opening my mouth, I should express fear. At the words, 'I'm trembling', I should slowly lower my hands to my chest and at the words, 'I'm terrified' place them on my heart; and I should say the words, 'I'm unable to breathe' while keeping my hands on my heart, lowering my elbows and sinking my head to show that all my strength is leaving me. At the words, 'Oh, murderers', I should raise my head and put my trembling hands before my eyes and say the words, 'My friend is dying!'

Turning my hands and head a bit towards the object, my eyes are only half-open the whole time. At the words 'What am I to do?' I should wring my hands before my raised head as a token of despair, and the words 'where should I go?' I should say while extending my arms a bit towards Heaven and looking to either side as if seeking an exit from the cave. And at 'I can't move' I should take a step towards the exit, extending my arms, bowing my head and then stopping, and at the word 'fear' put my hands to my chest and drop them at 'I'm numb' while bending my head to my left shoulder as a sign of impotence. [. . .]

### ON COMING ON STAGE

The way an actor comes on stage should suit the age, character and rank of the personage he is acting and at the same time the feelings of the person at that moment: when sad, dissatisfied or sorrowful he should enter slowly; when filled with joy, hope, courage – quickly and buoyantly; in despair, anger and frenzy – violently.

When coming on stage one should turn one's figure halfway to the spectators, so that on entering from the right one should put one's left leg forward first and from the left, vice versa.

In order to make one's entrance look natural one should take a few steps backstage, so that the spectators will not notice how the body assumes the proper posture.

If, immediately on entering, one has to address some characters who are supposed to be offstage, one should take a few steps and speak, not with one's back to the spectators, but facing them.

When having to deliver news to those offstage or to express a feeling, one should not simply run across the stage but utter the words even when they are meant to be spoken to oneself.

The same applies to the situation when the actor is greeting his partner who enters from the opposite side – after meeting and saying their lines, they should turn together and take a step or two towards the spectators.

When the actor comes on stage from the centre he should present his whole figure to the audience even when he is being attacked; if, having to defend himself, he first shows his back, even then he should turn one side to the audience, not only because it is discourteous to turn one's back on them but also because one must not deprive them of seeing one's mimicry. [. . .]

*Osiński re-opens the dramatic school*

In 1814 Ludwik Osiński[1] (1775–1838) was appointed to the post of manager of the National Theatre; he was a highly regarded poet, translator, subsequently professor of literature at Warsaw University, and an exponent of classical aesthetics. He obtained funds for the foundation of the new drama school which opened on 4 February 1815.

[1] See Korzeniewski, 1934; Rulikowski, 1938; *PSB*.

## 144 Osiński's address at the opening of the Drama School, 4 February 1815

*Gazeta Warszawska* [*Warsaw Gazette*], no. 14, 18 February 1815; reprinted in *Recenzje teatralne towarzystwa Iksów 1815–1819* [*Theatrical reviews of the Society of X's*], edited by J. Lipiński (Wrocław: Zakład Narodowy im. Ossolińskich, 1956), pp. 574–7.

[. . .] Whatever may be said about the state of the national theatre, one thing must be stressed: given the scope of that undertaking and compared to similar ventures of other nations, no other art has developed so quickly in this country, although the rapidly occurring political changes have affected the theatre more than any other activity. It was only in the second half of the last century that Polish theatre took up residence for longer periods in the capital city. Stanislas Augustus was very generous indeed in supporting this new and noble kind of pastime and the country's most prominent personalities did not hesitate to translate foreign plays or to write their own to sustain the emerging art.

But that auspicious beginning soon met with serious obstacles. There came a time when neither the country's authorities nor the distinguished public cared for the theatre.[1] Indeed, the foreign troupes of actors brought to this town at that time managed only to divide the spectators. And the national stage could survive in such circumstances thanks only to the perseverance and efforts of its management. [. . .]

In fact one man [Wojciech Bogusławski] did it alone and to him we should now pay tribute. Over a thirty-year period he produced works of both foreign and domestic playwrights. [. . .]

Today, when the theatre enjoys so much support, when the taste of productions is more refined, when there are many outstanding talents, when the repertoire includes many fine works, in the opinion of many the standard of this institution may be raised even higher if it eliminates all the plays of dubious taste. Indeed, it is up to the public if it is to be done without any material loss.

The national theatre, wishing to emulate foreign companies, to offer its public attractive plays and so perhaps to save itself from utter decline, recently staged plays that were more striking for their brilliance than for their artistic quality.[2] It found them in a neighbouring country [Germany], whose language had for some time been the official one in this country.[3] And so the customs of that land grew less foreign here; and as its literature has become rich in all sorts of drama, it seemed to our theatre an inexhaustible source of novelty. The unexpected success of those plays, allegedly based on similar works in French, which also attracted numerous spectators in Europe's leading theatre [the Comédie Française in Paris], unfortunately caused a lowering of taste, since they took precedence over works perfect in quality. Thus the progress of our stage was halted by a craving for novelty. When the theatrical management feels itself obliged to satisfy that craving and replace at short notice one production with another, how can an actor cope with so many roles, learn the parts properly without even being able to evaluate them? [. . .]

All these remarks may lead the judicious public to the conclusion that it will take a long time for the plays of Corneille, Racine and many other distinguished authors to be resumed here; and in judging our stage it will not take as a model France's leading theatre because there, too, there are complaints that when better works are produced, boxes and stalls remain half-empty. After all, it is not up to the public to decide taste. This is the vocation of the critics, who should be servants of the arts.

[1] A reference to the period following the third partition of Poland, 1795.
[2] A reference to melodramas. On such plays on the Warsaw stage, see Korzeniewski, 1934.
[3] From 1796 to 1806 Warsaw was under Prussian rule.

### *The Society of X's*

Osiński pursued his own artistic programme, hoping to produce classical tragedies on the Warsaw stage. Between 1815 and 1819 theatrical reviews by critics who had formed the so-called Society of X's [Towarzystwo Iksów] appeared in Warsaw papers in his support. They belonged to the Warsaw high life of the period and were basically in favour of classical aesthetics, although some of them were of a more modern turn of mind and admired the plays of Shakespeare.

## 145 Review of a production of *Hamlet*,[1] 13 May 1815

*Gazeta Korespondenta Warszawskiego* [*Gazette of the Warsaw correspondent*], no. 38, 13 May 1815; reprinted in *Recenzje teatralne* [*Theatrical reviews*] (1956), pp. 4–5.

[. . .] Mad scenes seem to suit our actresses particularly well, that is, unusual states of the utmost tension of the intellectual faculties which transcend ordinary life – such are the roles they favour and at which they excel.

Pleased with the acclaim aroused by her roles of Inez, Lady Macbeth, Lanassa,[2] etc., Miss Ledóchowska[3] presented for the first time her equally famous role of Ophelia. Whatever the public's verdict in this matter, such variety should not be blamed; it gives rise to a discussion of roles and characters, enriches the art of drama by increasing the number of examples and comparisons.

If only for this reason Miss Aszpergerowa's[4] Ophelia should be considered. Having been very well received in operatic parts, Miss Aszpergerowa probably did not aim to outdo Miss Ledóchowska in a tragic role; however, she may have thought that the poignant part of Ophelia would speak for itself, and in this she was right.

This is one more proof of how easy it is to play roles in which madness justifies any raising and lowering of the tone, so that one cannot say it is not right or natural, since anything can happen in such a state of mind. True, here too, the more the actress makes us forget the theatre, the more spellbound the audience becomes, but so extraordinary is this naturalness that it is not hard to produce. Let me support this statement by recalling that in all the productions in which I have seen Ophelia, Act Five always seemed better than the four preceding ones [. . .]

Besides, this production of *Hamlet* did not escape the usual shortcomings of our stage. The actors did not know their lines well enough and while there was an extra prompter for those in the background, he was too audible! The costumes of the ghost and his sinking, etc. did not create a sufficient illusion. Such stage illusions are the chief concern of even minor German theatres; with us they are too much neglected. Likewise, the ghost's subterranean voice was badly imitated and made no impression. [. . .] It must be said, moreover, that our actors are too composed and devoid of nervous sensibility to do justice to a play of this power. For instance, the appearance of the ghost should be even more visible on Hamlet's face than on stage itself. The ghost's presence may only strengthen the impression because if the Hamlet were first-rate, it would hardly be necessary. Hamlet's wry jokes and insults should alarm the public and not amuse it; if people laugh it is proof that the role of Hamlet is badly acted. [. . .]

1 *Hamlet* was staged in the German adaptation of Friedrich Ludwig Schröder, translated into Polish by W. Bogusławski.

2 Characters in Shakespeare's *Macbeth*, J.H. Soden's *Inez de Castro* and A.M. Lemierre's *Lanassa, Widow of Malabar* (1782).

3 Józefa Ledóchowska (1781–1849), a remarkable tragedienne in Bogusławski's company. See *SBTP*; *PSB*.

4 Katarzyna Aszpergerowa (1795–1835), daughter of Andrzej Rutkowski and wife of the tenor Wojciech Aszperger, was primarily a soprano who could be heard in almost every opera produced in Warsaw, and especially in Mozart. See *SBTP*.

*Molière in Warsaw*

The classical repertoire was of little interest to the general public which was more attracted to plays written by Polish playwrights, who called them 'national tragedies', and the subjects of which would frequently give rise to patriotic demonstrations in the house. This review in favour of a classic was written by a critic belonging to the Society of X's.

## 146 Review of a production of Molière's *The Miser* [*Skąpiec*], 24 September 1816

*Gazeta Korespondenta Warszawskiego* [*Gazette of the Warsaw correspondent*], no. 77, 24 September 1816; reprinted in *Recenzje teatralne* [*Theatrical reviews*] (1965), p. 180.

[. . .] I heard some spectators criticize the acting of Mr Kudlicz.[1] They said that although he was very accurate in rendering his role he nevertheless went too far in rendering one of the quieter passions with violence bordering on madness. This seems to me an unjust criticism, because the miser he was performing had been so exaggerated by the author himself that the actor cannot moderate this character. So, in my opinion, Mr Kudlicz should stick to his interpretation of the role; but I advise him in some passages to change the acting, especially in the scene when, having inspected the hands of his servant, he orders him to show his other hands as well. That demand, so comical, so true to the miser, was greeted by no reaction from the audience. At that moment Harpagon may have thought that his servant had ten hands to rob him, so the more furious he sounded the better the acting would have been. Nor is Mr Kudlicz's walk always natural.

As for the costumes in this production, I should blame their unsuitability on the Management, whose duty it is to supervise them. The miser's costume is too ancient and thus unlike that of his son and the other characters. True, the actor in Paris wears something of the sort, but there the son wears a costume of the same rich and ancient style. This is a striking fault, especially when the miser tells the son, whom on our stage we see dressed very modestly, that he is covered with gold and that his garments alone could be invested at a high interest rate. Besides, not being historical or local, the play would make a greater impression if all the actors appeared in costumes closer to our fashion and cut; but in that case the aforementioned lines of the miser should be omitted. [. . .]

[1] Bonawentura Kudlicz (1780–1848), highly regarded by the critics of the X group for his classical style of acting; a teacher in the School of Drama. See *PSB*.

### IV THE GOVERNMENT TAKES OVER, 1821–9

In 1819 Osiński gave up his attempts to stage classical tragedies, and instead, began producing all sorts of *drames*, increasingly of the pre-Romantic type. Only occasionally were the plays of Schiller or neo-classic adaptations of Shakespeare produced. The greatest artistic achievement of these years was the presentation on the Warsaw stage of the comedies of Aleksander Fredro, the greatest Polish comedy writer, whose plays have never since left the Polish repertoire.

Meanwhile, the size and standard of the acting cadres increased considerably and, despite difficulties with censorship, the national repertoire was continually expanding. But from 1821 governmental interference took place against the background of growing reactionary repression.

### *The interior of the Warsaw Theatre*

Teresa Tyszkiewicz, née Poniatowska, inherited the building of the Warsaw Theatre after the death of her brother Prince Józef Poniatowski, who was the heir of King Stanislas Augustus Poniatowski. An inventory was made for her in connection with a project for the Government to buy the building.

## 147 Description of the house and stage of the Warsaw Theatre, 1821

Wierzbicka, vol. 2 (1955), pp. 151–2.

#### THE HOUSE

There is a large chandelier with astral lamps hanging on a brass chain; it is installed in a central opening within a rosette painted with historical figures and ornaments; the shape and arrangement of the central box harmonizes with the new decorations of the house; the pillars supporting the boxes have been straightened and new capitals and pediments added to them; there are new pilasters over the cornices which reach to the ceiling, they are gilded, set between the boxes and extend from the balustrade of the first tier of boxes to the cornice over the gallery. [. . .] The orchestra has been moved back and a double floor laid down; there is now a new division of the pit into stalls and standing-room, with an additional fifty-four seats; the benches in the upper gallery have been rearranged; the paint-work on architectural ornaments, busts and historical paintings has been touched up; and gilding has now been added to the material that covers the walls of the house; some partitions in the boxes can be installed or removed at will; there are new ceilings in the boxes; new upholstery covers the house adornments as well as the box-balustrades; the stage curtain is 18 ells wide, 12 ells high, with the sides hanging down to the stage floor.

THE STAGE

The stage-house has gained structurally by the removal of the ceiling and beams over an area of 308 square ells and by the installation of passageways and their supports all around the interior; four suspension bridges in the same part of the theatre; a huge five-storey scaffolding for storing curtains and scenery; backstage ladders; a new ladder leading to the upper passageways; new balconies on either side of the stage reaching up to the ceiling; a mechanical system of brass and iron winches to raise the house chandelier; a platform the width of the whole stage which can be safely loaded and suspended in the air by machinery; a similar platform (Gloire), somewhat smaller, at the front of the stage with a mechanism for aerial movement; smaller gears and winches, in the proper places, for moving the curtain and shifting the scenery; gears with four brass chains for shifting ceilings and raising the house curtain [. . .]

### *New governmental regulations*

The regulation of 1822 increased the interference of the Government Administration of the National Theatre in the workings of that theatre; this was the result of tightening reactionary restrictions in the Congressional 'Kingdom of Poland' and of financial difficulties experienced by the theatrical enterprise.

## 148 Theatre statutes governing repertoire, performances, rehearsals, costumes and scenery, 1822

Published in 1823.

SELECTION OF DRAMATIC WORKS

§1

Each new work shall be submitted to the approval of the Government Administration at least fifteen days before the roles are cast and shall include the original text when it is a translation.

§2

The Theatre Manager has, in addition, to obey the censorship strictly. [. . .]

THE THEATRE'S AND ACTOR'S DUTIES REGARDING THE NUMBER AND KIND OF PERFORMANCES

§3

The Theatre shall give performances in Polish at least four times a week. [. . .]

§15

The Theatre shall try to stage at least one tragedy and comedy of higher quality and one opera a week. [. . .]

§17

The number of new roles an actor is supposed to perform without complaining of overwork is based on the following reckoning of the time he has in which to learn his role:

(a) in a grand opera – 5 weeks
(b) in a lesser one – 3 weeks
(c) in a tragedy or comedy in verse – 5 weeks
(d) in a tragedy or comedy in prose – 3 weeks
(e) in plays, not operas, in fewer than four acts – 2 weeks

This time is reckoned from the first readthrough.

§18

The Manager cannot require the actor to play difficult roles day after day without a rest, with the exception of the three initial performances of a new work. [. . .]

REHEARSALS

§31

The rehearsals will take place from 10 to 12 a.m. and from 3 to 5 p.m. except on Sundays and holidays. [. . .]

§34

On the day of a performance the actors taking part in it are free from other rehearsals.

§35

Each new play will have at least one readthrough in order to get a bird's eye view of the work. [. . .]

§36

After the readthrough the next rehearsal will be carried out with the script memorized for the most part.

§37

The first public performance will be preceded by a dress rehearsal which is meant to be identical to the first performance. [. . .]

### COSTUMES AND SCENERY

§45

The director of the theatre is responsible for the historical accuracy of the costumes, for the proper scenery, stage-settings, machinery; he is answerable in the performance of these duties to the Government Theatre Administration.

§46

Before the production of each new historical play, the theatre director shall give instructions concerning costumes, their styles, materials, ornamentation and colour, which the actors must follow.

§47

All costumes, other than local ones, will be paid for by the Enterprise. [. . .]

§48

The contemporary costumes worn now in this country will be purchased by actors of both sexes themselves at their own expense.

§49

This rule excludes gala court dresses, uniforms, liveries, that is, the sort of clothing an actor does not normally wear in society. [. . .]

§51

In comic roles it is up to the actor to choose his costume.

*The Society of Artists takes over the management*

In 1825, Osiński resigned from the post of manager, and the Society of Artists was operative from 1825 to 1827. In 1827, as a result of organizational changes, Osiński resumed the management of the theatre and, jointly with Ludwik Dmuszewski, fulfilled his functions until the November Uprising of 1830 whose failure made Poland a Russian province.

## 149 Project of an agreement with the Government concerning the maintenance of the Warsaw Theatre by the Society of Artists, 1825

*Komisja Rządowa Przychodów i Skarbu* [*State Fiscal Commission*], MS no. 1792, Archiwum Glowne Akt Dawnych, Warsaw.

ARTICLE 1

All actors of the National Theatre whose monthly salary is 200 zlotys take upon themselves the care of the Warsaw theatres and in lieu of salary will have a proportionate share in the income.

ARTICLE 2

The duties heretofore performed by the theatrical entrepreneur shall henceforth be performed collectively by the Administration.

ARTICLE 3

The Administration shall consist of three members: two directors of tragedy, comedy, etc., Mr Kudlicz[1] and Mr Dmuszewski[2] and the opera director, Mr Kurpiński.[3]
The Society takes it upon itself:
to support artists who can perform in opera, tragedy, comedy, drama and comic

opera, to which end it will engage not only artists now resident in Warsaw but also new ones with the proper qualifications. The Society commits itself to support a number of dancers for the embellishment of productions. Thus, it will bring in from abroad a first-rank male dancer to instruct local dancers and dance in the ballet; likewise it will bring in a first-rank female dancer. The rest will be of local origin trained after good models. The Society commits itself to stage three new grand operas and fifteen other new plays annually, including two classical plays, either original or in translation. [. . .] All plays shall be staged with great care in regard to scenery, costumes, elegance, proper order, etc., as befits the capital city. [. . .]

[1] For Kudlicz, see **146**.
[2] Ludwik Adam Dmuszewski (1777–1847), actor, translator and playwright, was also a tenor who popularized the genre of 'komedio-opera'. See *SBTP*.
[3] Karol Kurpiński (1785–1857). See *PSB*; *SBTP*.

*Watered-down Shakespeare in Warsaw*

The announcement that Shakespeare's *Macbeth* would be produced at the National Theatre in a neo-classical adaptation by Jean-François Ducis was strongly criticized by the proponents of the Romantic school. The most violent protest came from Maurycy Mochnacki (1804–34) (see *PSB*), the leading theorist of that school.

## 150 Mochnacki criticizes *Macbeth* by Shakespeare and Ducis, 10 May 1829

*Gazeta Polska*, no. 125 (10 May 1829).

What could be the reasons the management[1] of the Warsaw Theatre is producing a play by Ducis whose title is the same as that of Shakespeare's famous tragedy? [. . .]

We had a Shakespearean *Macbeth* in a rather sloppy Polish translation, abridged and smoothed out as were other of Shakespeare's tragedies translated into Polish from early French translations. Still, they did not manage to obliterate all the beauties of the English original. The main outlines did remain, as did the general effect the work had had in every theatre [. . .]

But now, in 1829, in the ninteenth century, to announce the production of *Macbeth* in an adaptation by the Frenchman Ducis! [. . .] This is the clumsiest, most inept transformation the insolent renovators and imitators of Shakespeare have ever attempted. It has denuded the work of all its strength and beauty. Now after so many discussions, so many explications of works of art, to stage an adaptation of *Macbeth* by Ducis means that we are still prepared to look at Shakespeare through French spectacles[2] [. . .]

[1] Ludwik Osiński and Ludwik Dmuszewski. See Rulikowski, 1938, p. 15.
[2] Despite the indignation it aroused in proponents of the Romantic school, the Ducis adaptation of *Macbeth* opened on 12 May 1829, but proved to be a complete flop.

*The stage effects of a romantic fairy play*

*The Peasant as Millionaire*, an allegorical melodrama by the Austrian Raimund[1] translated into Polish, was a major success, thanks in part to its scenery which was the work of a Venetian painter and scene-shifter, Antonio Sacchetti. Sacchetti (1790–1870) opened a Gabinet Topograficzny for panoramas and dioramas in Warsaw in 1829; his productions at the National Theatre were renowned for their exquisite scenic effects, sometimes imitated from the technical innovations of Cicéri and Daguerre.[2] This production is considered the initiation of the romantic theatre in Warsaw.

[1] Ferdinand Raimund, né Jakob Raimann (1790–1836), Austrian dramatist.
[2] See Krol-Kaczorowska, 1971, p. 139.

## 151 Stage directions for the drama *The Peasant as Millionaire*, produced at the Warsaw Theatre in 1829

*Chlop milionowy czyli Dziewczyna ze świata czarownego, melodrama alegoryczna w trzech aktach z niemieckiego pana Rajmund przerobiona . . . [The Peasant as Millionaire or The Girl from Fairyland, allegorical melodrama in three acts translated from the German of Herr Raimund]* (Warsaw, 1829).

ACT II, SCENE 13

[Ludwika] falls to her knees and covers her face with her hands. Thunder. Music. Grey clouds descend and above them the huge figure of Night which covers almost the entire centre of the stage. Night's costume: a grey draped gown and a black cloak which is outspread by her arms. Her face is pale, eyes closed, a black crown on her head; in her right hand she holds a sceptre topped by a poppy-head, and her left hand enjoins silence. She sinks slowly and gravely to disappear into a trap in the stage. The clouds fade away and the former town square is now visible in the moonlight. There are myriads of twinkling stars on the horizon and the moon among them. [. . .] The Genius, a diamond star on his brow, flies across the forestage and, taking Ludwika by the hand, leads her out. [. . .] A terrible storm comes up, the moon glows red, the stars vanish, twelve night ghosts fly on stage, all of them dressed alike in grey with grey veils: pale faces, and a star on the forehead of each. They intertwine on stage, then move as a group up to Fortunatus's house; grey clouds drop on them and scores of grey ghosts are painted on the clouds. [. . .]
A huge owl with glowing eyes flies towards Fortunatus's windows, the curtain falls.

ACT II, SCENE 9

The clouds sink. Envy rides in from offstage on a green cloud and Hatred on a red one (this must be a quick change). The spirit of Envy is dressed like an ancient Roman, all in yellow, with bands of snakes, and a turban of snakes on his head. The spirit of Hatred is also dressed like a Roman, half in armour with a helmet of red scales and an alcohol flame burning on the helmet.

### *The opening of the Variety Theatre*

A growing need for theatrical entertainment, along with an increase in Warsaw's population and the by now much greater number of actors, created proper conditions for the foundation of another theatre in Warsaw, a more popular one this time; and so, in 1829, the Teatr Rozmaitości (The Variety Theatre) was opened. Not long before the outbreak of the November Uprising, a group of young Romantic writers came into their own in Warsaw's cultural life. They criticized the Theatre's repertorial policy and their demands were partly met when yet another Warsaw theatre was eventually opened.

# *Czech lands (Bohemia and Moravia), 1784–1881*

Edited by BARBARA DAY

## INTRODUCTION

The movement towards a 'national theatre' which began in the Czech lands of the Austrian Empire at the end of the eighteenth century was strongly influenced by developments in the German theatre and particularly in Vienna. As in Vienna, the Prague repertoire for much of the eighteenth century was dominated by Italian opera and by German-language comedy, pantomime and burlesque. From the 1770s the Emperor Joseph II, inspired by the model of the Hamburg *Nationaltheater*, began to reform the Viennese theatre. The principles of the *Nationaltheater*, first voiced in Hamburg in 1767 by the playwright Lessing, were marked by a more intellectual approach to the role of the theatre. Such theatres were not to be private, profit-seeking ventures, but would be committed to a responsible programme of serious drama. In Bohemia the term *Nationaltheater* as adopted by the existing theatre referred to performances in both German and Czech, and had a linguistic rather than a nationalistic meaning. (In Prague at this time – unlike in the country areas – more German was spoken than Czech.) When the National Revivalists of the late eighteenth century wanted to refer to a national theatre which would above all be in the *Czech* language, they tended (though not invariably; see, for example, **160**) to use the term *vlastenské divadlo*, i.e. 'patriotic theatre'; in German *vaterländisches Theater*. The movement both towards a repertoire of more serious drama and towards plays written in Czech was intimately linked with the revival of Czech language and literature.

There was already a long-standing and healthy tradition of vernacular Czech drama stretching back over several centuries. This native tradition included the liturgical drama of the Middle Ages which, although interrupted by the Hussite wars, served as one of the diverse sources of material for the popular or folk theatre. In the mid-sixteenth century the school drama, performed in Latin, became an important area of cultural development. The plays served an educational function, being dramatizations of Biblical stories. Some of the school dramas were translated into Czech, and incorporated elements of the older folk plays. One author who belonged to the humanist tradition was the educationalist Jan Amos Komenský (Comenius). From the early seventeenth century the school drama came almost entirely into the hands of the Jesuits and productions were highly skilled. However, until the early eighteenth century the only *professional* theatre companies were foreign touring groups: these included, for example, English companies performing Shakespeare.

In 1701 the first permanent private theatre in Prague opened in Count Sporck's palace, followed, in 1739, by the first public theatre, the Kotzen Theatre. In 1769 the new director of the Kotzen Theatre, Josef von Brunian, already influenced by the German reforms, gave it the designation *Nationaltheater* and began to stage a repertoire of serious drama which included translations of French dramatists. In 1771 the theatre ran into financial difficulties and as an experiment Brunian staged a Czech-language production of a popular German farce, *Herzog Michel*.[1] It was presumably performed by the regular actors of the company, whose first language would have been German, and who, according to contemporary accounts, had difficulty with Czech pronunciation. It appears from these reports to have been well attended, but did not mark the beginning of regular performances in Czech.

[1] *Herzog Michel* by Johann Christian Krüger (1757), translated into Czech in 1771 and published as *Kníže Honzík*.

## I THE NOSTITZ AND BOUDA THEATRES, 1784–93

### *Patriots petition for Czech performances*

The Kotzen Theatre passed into other hands, and in 1781 the company was taken over by Count Nostitz, who in 1783 transferred them to the newly built and elegant Nostitz Theatre, since famous as the playhouse where Mozart's *Don Giovanni* was premièred in 1787 before an appreciative Prague audience. Today, as the Tyl Theatre, it is one of the National Theatre houses. Count Nostitz also described his theatre as a *Nationaltheater*, but again, this referred to the nature and quality of the repertoire. There were few productions in Czech in the first years of its existence, and those there were usually took place on Sunday afternoons, when the theatre was not needed for German performances.

In 1784 a group of Czech-speaking patriots presented the following petition for a German/Czech theatre company to the Town Council. The letter, written in German, was signed by the burgher František Jiřík, but it is thought likely that the young brothers Thám, amateur theatre enthusiasts, were behind its writing. Karel Ignác Thám (1763–1816) was a linguist and a translator of Shakespeare (out of German); Václav Thám (1765–*c.* 1816) a dramatist, poet, journalist, translator and actor, who would become one of the founders of the *Bouda* theatre.

## 152 Petition to the Prague Town Council for a Czech theatre company, 10 August 1784

In the Archiv hlavního města Prahy, Sbírka listin papírových, sign. IV–2908/a: published in German and Czech in *Divadlo* [*Theatre*] no. 10 (1958), pp. 751–2; published in German by Archív hlavního města Prahy [Archive of the capital city Prague], *Documenta Pragensia* (Prague: *AHMP*, 1983), pp. 62–3.

To the most esteemed Town Council:
The undersigned asks humbly for permission to found a Czech-German theatre in the New Town of Prague and wishes to justify his petition on the following grounds:
(1) Often in the past there has been more than one theatre established in Prague, and permission to perform plays was extended to unknown foreigners. This makes the undersigned hopeful that his petition will be treated most favourably, since not only is he native to this country but also a citizen of its capital Prague, where he and his family live and provide for themselves in an honest and irreproachable manner, as can be vouched for by the municipal authorities.
(2) The undersigned chooses mostly nationalists as members of his company, people who are known not only for their professional qualities but also moral conduct because, as the undersigned believes, the one who preaches morals achieves a greater effect if he himself is seen to practise them.
(3) The Emperor Himself is favourably inclined toward the Czech language, as is apparent from His act of allowing Professorships to be set up so as to enable the teaching of Czech in Vienna; the petitioner is of the opinion that a regular presentation of plays in Czech is the best means of support and loving appreciation of our mother tongue, which has since the times of Charles IV been a recognized medium employed by educated society.
(4) Every sensible person who is also acquainted with history is aware that the art of acting has always had a great influence on a country's morals and that, in many cases, it has assisted in sharpening public awareness and education. However, a large proportion of people are deprived of the enjoyment and beneficial influence of performed plays because of their inadequate knowledge of the German language: the petitioner is therefore convinced that the regular presentation of plays in Czech to such a public will ensure that good entertainment is provided quite cheaply in place of a vulgar kind of amusement.

### *The first Czech production at the Nostitz Theatre*

In emphasizing the moral value of a Czech-language theatre as well as its educative role, the petition reflects the ambitions of the Czech intelligentsia of the period. This petition was refused, as the Town Council claimed that it had no right to give such a permission. However, in 1785, František Bulla began to stage the first Czech language productions at the Nostitz Theatre. The earliest production, in January 1785, was a German play, *Der Deserteur aus Kindesliebe* by Gottlieb Stephanie, translated into Czech by Karel Bulla in 1784 as *Odběhlec z lásky synovské*. This performance may be regarded as a significant landmark in professional Czech vernacular theatre.

## 153a Review of the first Czech language production in the Nostitz Theatre, 1785

In German in *Das Pragerblättchen* [*Prague Leaflet*] (1785), p. 145; Czech trans. in Miroslav Kačer: *Václav Thám* (Prague: Svobodné slovo, 1965), p. 118.

This is the first among regular performances in the Czech language to be given in our Prague *Nationaltheater*. The driving force behind this performance is the former director Mr František Jindřich Bulla who, out of affection for his mother tongue, had requested his brother Mr Karel Bulla[1] to translate the piece. Due to the fact that the majority of the company are themselves Czechs, the play could be prepared in a short time and shown in the *Nationaltheater*, first on 20 January 1785 and then, for a second time, on 25 January, and for a third time at the Lesser Town theatre on 6 February. The house was full each time and, amidst the general acclaim, the wish was often expressed for more Czech pieces to be seen. The actors themselves had clearly enjoyed being in this production more than in any other. The best among them were Mr Bulla as Holbek the Son, Mr Höpfler as Holbek the Father, Mr Antong as Punk, Mr Zappe as Petr and the specially invited private actor Mr Klaudius as Flink.[2] Other parts were played by the German actors and hence we must overlook occasional errors. When Mr Höpfler was thanking the audience after the play in German, as is usual, there were calls from many sides: In Czech! which he immediately acknowledged and obliged accordingly, but for the long applause was hardly able to finish the speech. During the play's second performance, between the second and third acts, Czech-printed celebratory odes had been thrown from the gallery, eagerly gathered and read by the spectators. [. . .]

[1] The brothers Karel Bulla (b. before 1750) and František Bulla (b. 1754), the former a translator, the latter a director of the Nostitz Theatre.

[2] František Jindřich Höpfler, Vincenc Karel Antong and Antonín Zappe were originally actors of the German-speaking company of the Nostitz Theatre (or Theatre of the Estates). In 1785 they led the petition to the Emperor for a Czech-language theatre, and became the founders of the *Bouda*; Antong was for a period its director.

Jan Klaudius was another actor who performed in both German and Czech.

## 153b The Nostitz Theatre

Drawn by Philippe and François Heger, engraved by Johan Berka, 1793; reproduced in *Dějiny českého divadla* [*History of the Czech theatre*], vol. 2 (Prague: Academia, 1968–77), Figure 2.

*The* Bouda *theatre opens*

After eighteen months, Czech performances on the Nostitz stage were discontinued. But in 1786 Emperor Joseph II permitted the group of Czech-speaking theatre enthusiasts to open the theatre popularly known as the *Bouda* ('Shanty') on the Horsemarket in Prague (today's Wencelas Square). The theatre gave equal weight to both Czech and German, being known as the *Vlastenské divadlo* and also the *Vaterländisches Theater*. The first play to be presented was *Gratitude and Love to the Homeland* translated by Václav Thám from a German play by A.W. Iffland.[1] The opening took place on 8 July 1786.

A number of the plays in the repertoire were originals or translations by Václav Thám, who with *Břetislav and Jitka* (*Břetislav a Jitka aneb Únos z kláštera*; the text has not survived) created the first original Czech drama of this period. An important achievement of the *Bouda* was to bring Shakespeare in the Czech language to the general public. After a short time the *Bouda* fell into difficulties and closed in June 1789. It was replaced in 1789 by another 'patriotic' theatre, the Theatre *U Hybernů* which, with a varied but Czech repertoire, survived until 1802.

[1] *Vděčnost a láska k vlasti*, adapted from August Wilhelm Iffland by the actor Vincenc Karel Antong and translated by Maximilián Štván. Iffland (1759–1814) was a German actor and playwright, whose plays, with their entertaining characterization and well-structured plots, greatly pleased the public of the day.

## 154 Opening of the *Bouda* and its Czech repertoire, July 1786

Kramerius: *Pražské noviny* [*Prague News*] (15 July 1786); quoted in J.V. Frič and J.L. Turnovský: *Almanach Matice divadelní k slavnému otevření narodního divadla* [*Commemorative volume of the theatre foundation for the solemn opening of the national theatre*] (Prague: J. Otto, 1881), pp. 41–2. Schönfeld: *Pražské noviny* (29 July 1786); quoted in Jan Vondráček: *Dějiny českého divadla, doba obrozenská 1771–1824* [*History of the Czech theatre, period of revival*] (Prague: Orbis, 1956), p. 126.

(a) Kramerius in *Pražské noviny*, (15 July 1786): We would never have believed that the patriotic love of our Czech nation could be so instantaneously revived. The opening of the Czech theatre was attended by such a multitude of people that even the spacious premises could not contain them all. The crowd also included guests of higher rank; gripped by patriotic eagerness they waited to hear the play that day performed in their own mother tongue. Those patriots of ours who presented the play to the great rejoicing of the public were accorded generous acclaim. [After that a play in German called *Wigs* was shown, followed by a new pantomimic ballet *Prague Kitchens, or Farmers on Fire* (*Pražské kuchyňky, aneb Uhořelí sedláci*), the whole spectacle being closed with noisy trumpet blowing and Italian drums drumming.]
(b) Schönfeld in *Pražské noviny* (29 July 1786): The plays written in Czech are of great benefit and the company which puts them on deserves to be highly commended. We can assure everyone that our Czech population enjoys the Czech plays enormously and comes to see them in huge numbers, and that the company has already been considering a move to larger and more convenient premises.

*Prokop Šedivý points the moral of theatre*

In 1794 an essay by the actor and playwright Prokop Šedivý (1764–*c*. 1810) of the *Bouda* theatre aroused great interest in patriotic circles with its emphasis on the moral and educational value of theatre. The essay was in fact an adaptation of Schiller's *Die Schaubühne als eine moralische Anstalt betrachtet* (1787), but it is of importance as the first publication in Czech directly to draw attention to the important role the theatre could play in the National Revival. The essay claimed that well-written drama was of immeasurable value and enlightenment for society. It looked at the effect it could have on people's ways of thinking.

## 155 Prokop Šedivý's *Short treatise on the benefit to be had from a permanent and well-ordered theatre*, 1793

Prokop Šedivý, *Krátké pojednání o užitku, který ustavičně stojící a dobře spořádané divadlo způsobiti může* (Prague, 1793); reprinted with postscript by Pavel Eisner (Prague, 1955).

The theatre is a universal source of wisdom for all well-meaning people, who spread it through the whole community. The theatre is a school where people

learn how to deliberate soundly, act consistently and open themselves to pure feelings. The theatre is the cause whereby people shed their moral depravity; superstitions pass away and the light of day is victorious over night.
[Šedivý adapted the final part of the essay in order to concentrate on the important role the theatre could play in Czech national life:]
I cannot overlook the effect which the theatre has on the particular views and inclinations of Czech patriots which differ from those of other nations. I acknowledge how necessary it is that our patrons all think alike and are at one in their inclinations. And what can achieve this better than the theatre, which permeates the whole area of human consciousness and contains all the circumstances and predicaments of human life, looking into every nook and cranny of the human heart; because the theatre unites all human states and predicaments and is at the same time the most pleasant path to reach the human heart and mind. If only such universal experiences were represented in all our plays, if only all our theatre writers agreed and practised what they agreed and chose only patriotic themes, in a word, if only we could experience the day when there would be a permanent Czech-language theatre, then we would also be one nation. What else held the Greek nation together so firmly?

### *Literary drama vs popular drama*

In practice, it was to prove difficult for playwrights and theatre workers to live up to the ideals formulated in patriotic circles. There was a recurring tension between the theatre practitioners whose main aim was to attract a broad audience to the Czech-language theatre, and those who believed that such a theatre should set the highest standards of writing and performance. Czech *littérateurs* were constantly being persuaded that Czech was a language limited in its expression; they may have felt that conversational dialogue could be expressed convincingly, but they had imposed on themselves the futile task of broadening the basis of the literary tradition to make it capable of satisfying contemporary needs. Translators of plays were still trying to find a style that would be appropriate for the plays of Shakespeare and Schiller. At the same time, the Revivalists had to recognize that, like any average audience, the Czechs preferred popular farce to Shakespeare and Schiller; whilst those among the intelligentsia who spoke both Czech and German were still accustomed to turn to the German theatre with its established traditions for more serious culture.

## II THE THEATRE OF THE ESTATES, 1814–35

### *Czech themes introduced into Czech drama*

Occasional performances in Czech continued to take place at the Nostitz Theatre (from 1797 known as the Theatre of the Estates) and in the Raymann Theatre in the Lesser Town

(1803–11). In 1809 the Czech company of actors was disbanded. In 1812 a theatre employee, Jan Nepomuk Štěpánek (1783–1844), who had begun work there as soon as he had finished his studies, succeeded in reviving Czech-language performances. He obtained permission to found the Society of Amateurs, and with this group revived Czech productions at the Theatre of the Estates. As well as being an energetic organizer, Štěpánek also wrote a large number of plays in Czech for the company. These often had an overtly Czech theme, or Czech references, such as are shown in the following quotations from *The Liberation of the Motherland* (1814).

## 156a Štěpánek's *Liberation of the Motherland* obliquely promotes Czech culture, 1814

Jan Nepomuk Štěpánek, 'Osvobození vlasti aneb Korytané v Čechách ['Liberation of the Motherland or The Carinthians in Bohemia] in *Divadlo ob J.N. Štěpánka* [*Štěpánek's Plays*] (Prague, 1822), pp. 21–2, 57–8; quoted in Vondráček vol. 1 (1956), pp. 373–4.

JAN OF STRÁŽ Can we still call ourselves Czechs? Do we still know how to avenge the pillage of our land, like those who once vanquished their enemies with courage and intrepid spirit? Oh, shame, shame upon us . . .

We have surrendered to a foreign rule which brings ruin on us and on our motherland. A tree sometimes drains the last drops of sap from its healthy tissues till, weakened, it falls and withers away. Our enemies have swarmed over our lands like poisonous vermin, can you destroy them?

HAROŠ Foreign invaders oppress and prey on our people and plunder Czech lands; Czech language and morals languish, brother fights brother, son – father, father baits son . . . the jails are filled with our Czechs; whoso dares to resist is arrested and imprisoned. . .

## 156b Act IV, scene 6 in Štěpánek's *Liberation of the Motherland*

Frontispiece by J. Berka to the printed edition (Prague, 1814); reproduced in *Dějiny českého divadla*, vol. 2 (1968–77), Figure 58, p. 168.

### *Prague petitions for a wholly Czech theatre*

In 1825 an attempt was made to found a purely Czech theatre in Prague (the *Bouda* had been half-Czech, half-German). A long but informative petition by the Prague citizen Mikuláš Müller on behalf of thirty-seven of his fellow-citizens was delivered to the Emperor

Francís in Vienna. It laid its emphasis, first, on relatively recent precedents for a Czech-language theatre and, second, on its appropriateness for the education of the Czech-speaking community. It even claimed to have their support already in securing the financial basis of the theatre. The petition was, nevertheless, refused.

## 157 Petition to the Emperor for a Czech theatre, 12 November 1821

Archiv ministerstva vnitra [Archive of the Ministry of the Interior], fond ČG, sign. Publicum 1816–25 – 59/5; Czech translation in Vondráček vol. 1 (1956), pp. 422–6.

Your Majesty [. . .]
One of the fundamental means for the revival of the Czech language, though it is given little attention, is a permanent and well-established Czech theatre, which has been neglected for a number of years. And yet an independent Czech theatre would surely soon become fertile soil for Czech literature if it were to show fine Czech plays, some of which would also deal with our patriotic past, and if these were presented by actors who, under the supervision of the watchful police, would be known to lead orderly lives and would not allow any kind of vulgarity offensive to good morals to enter the stage. Any considerate father would see fit then to provide for his sons in time of leisure the kind of entertainment that would offer an enriching opportunity to perfect much-needed, grammatically sound Czech, rather than leave them carousing in doubtful company which only destroys health and wastes money.

[. . .] May it please the Most Illustrious and Worshipful Father of the Czech lands, Patron of arts and sciences, to grant us for the love of our homeland His Gracious permission to found and build a new theatre dedicated solely to Czech plays and operettas in Prague's New Town, which will be of no detriment to the similar, already existing, enterprise, that is, the German Theatre of the Estates. Thus numerous inhabitants of the capital city of Prague, who know only the Czech language, will be given dignified entertainment in place of nightly drinking bouts which cost them considerably more than would the price of a theatre ticket. At the same time, many families will be shown how to broaden their minds, refine their social manners and come to understand their civic duties toward all other ranks of society.

Not long ago, the undersigned had submitted a similar proposal to the Provincial Board in which he petitioned for the establishment of a Czech theatre in the Prague suburb of Karlín, but the petition was refused probably on political grounds for fears that the public on leaving the theatre, placed as it would be beyond the city walls along the road leading to Prussian Silesia, might be surreptitiously joined by vagrant rabble giving a welcome opportunity for swindling, thieving and other perfidious tricks.

However, an independent Czech theatre can exist in the capital without similar fears of adverse consequences. The undersigned petitioner acts in all honesty and wishes to secure the founding and building of the theatre on a subscription basis, contributed to by Czech theatre lovers, a great number of whom have already come forward, and he hopes to set to work as soon as it pleases Your Majesty to grant him Most Gracious leave for the establishment of the theatre.

[. . .] Another circumstance which deserves careful attention, is that once a theatre dedicated to Czech plays and operettas is established, [. . .] the same conditions as were practised in the old Patriotic Theatre will be upheld, which means that all the theatre profits will remain in this country, entering its monetary circulation instead of being carried away into foreign lands. All the members of the intended theatre are to be locally born Czech persons who wish to practise their art in their own country and not in foreign German lands, in Bavaria, Saxony, Prussia, etc. In comparison, the present tenants managing the local German theatre, habitually foreigners, go abroad with all their possessions amassed in Prague, once their lease has finished. An example of this are past tenants of the local theatre such as Brunian, Bondini, Wahr and Seconda.[1]

[. . .] The heart of every Czech who cherishes his mother tongue would be filled with great pain on seeing his hopes of harmless entertainment in a Czech theatre dashed and this supplication, most humbly expounded here by the undersigned, doomed to fail in securing a happy conclusion, especially in the knowledge, supported by experience, that diverse artists arriving in Prague from foreign lands are given permission here to present their escapades, such as the owners of mechanical theatres, freaks of nature and menageries, circus-riders, dancers, funambulists, acrobats, conjurers, ventriloquists, dwarfs and giants who all compete with one another in tempting the curious inhabitants of this city to part with considerable sums of money which end up being taken abroad. If similar amusements are regarded as necessary for the human need for fun and also for the spirit, then the Czech theatre, the principle aim of which is not profiteering – on the contrary, it is to be a source of employment and income to many – should rightly be given preference over all other entertainments.

[. . .] While the undersigned begs to submit that the New Town offers itself as the most suitable location, because the majority of the Czech population lives there, he also humbly suggests that the commission directed to study the proposed building plans for the Czech theatre might take into consideration the site of the cattle market or perhaps other premises in the New Town. However, due to the fact that the erection of a new building or the conversion of a house acquired for these purposes will, according to the master-builder, take some three years, the undersigned begs for the sake of the Czech public who should not be deprived of the excitement of theatrical entertainment for too long, that a solid wooden structure be built in the meantime which, once the proper theatre is completed, can be demolished.

[. . .] The undersigned further pledges to put on every year eight different performances for the benefit of Prague charitable institutions.

[1] Pasquale Bondini, Impresario der Theatral-Spektakeln, active in Prague, Dresden and Leipzig in the late eighteenth century.

Karl Wahr, actor and impresario.

Franz Seconda, impresario and director of the Malá Strana theatre 1788–94, sometimes in partnership with Bondini.

*The re-introduction of Czech plays*

In 1824 Štěpánek was appointed as one of the triumvirate of directors at the Theatre of the Estates and professional productions in Czech were once again included in the programme. Many of these were of Štěpánek's own plays, but some of the patriots considered these farces and historical pieces to be unworthy of the revival movement. This reflects the paradox described earlier: the Czech nation had to prove itself to be worthy of an independent cultural and social existence, and therefore there was a strong desire by patriots for 'great works' to be written in the Czech language; on the other hand, for the revival to be successful it had to spread broadly among the different social classes, and therefore there was a great need for popular material. The poet and critic Josef Krasoslav Chmelenský (1800–39) expressed this second point of view.

## 158 Chmelenský sums up the state of the Czech theatre from April 1824 to the end of 1826

Josef Krasoslav Chmelenský: 'Stav divadla českého od měsíce dubna 1824 až po konec r. 1826' ['State of the Czech theatre from April 1824 to the end of 1826'] in *Časopis společenství vlastenského museum v Čechách* [*Magazine of the Fellowship of the Patriotic Museum in Bohemia*], vol. 1 (1827), pp. 127–31; quoted in Vondráček vol. 1 (1956).

All attempts by the directorship to improve Czech plays would be in vain without the public's support in attending the theatre in great numbers. What is to happen if the educated amongst the patriots, mindful of more refined amusement, cause plays which are spurned by some but enjoyed by many, not to be put on?

*Klicpera as a paragon of Czech dramatists*

In 1820 one of the leading figures in the revival movement, Josef Jungmann (1733–1847), a linguist and teacher whose Czech–German dictionary and other writings influenced a generation of Revivalists and whose programme was based on the linguistic concept of nationhood, had included a chapter on drama in his textbook *Slovesnost*, an anthology of Czech writing with a lengthy introduction on the theory of literature. Jungmann defined the genres tragedy, comedy, drama and opera, and noted the features typical to each. The passages he chose for illustration of tragedy and drama were by Václav Kliment Klicpera (1792–1859), who had as a student been a member of Štěpánek's Society of Amateurs. Klicpera, a teacher, wrote a large number of plays in different genres in the 1820s and 1830s which were only occasionally staged at the Theatre of the Estates. It was claimed that Štěpánek was jealous of Klicpera's broader knowledge and understanding of history and literature, which brought praise from revival leaders. As a Revivalist Klicpera used subjects and references oriented towards Czech nationalism. This excerpt is from the first act of the popular comedy *The Miraculous Hat* (1820).

## 159 The introduction of prosody to verse drama, 1821

Václav Kliment Klicpera, *Divotvorný klobouk* [*The Miraculous Hat*] (Prague, 1848), reprinted in *Divadlo Klicperovo* [*Klicpera's Plays*], vol. 1 (Hradec Králové, 1920).

POHOŘALSKÝ Ever since that unfortunate hour when the Czech language was milled through new mills; when Czech words, unearthed like ore from the depths of ancient times, are being forged into new shapes; since the grammarians have been keeping lookout for every deviation from their rules like a patrol lying in wait for smugglers; and, finally, since every student thinks he can poke his nose into my craft . . .

STRNAD I beg your pardon! I am a student myself, but to this day I've never composed a single phrase in Czech!

KŘEPELKA True enough. And do you know why?

POHOŘALSKÝ There hasn't been much Czech around to pick up, has there?

STRNAD There you are. Well, apart from what I've heard from my mother or in the street. But is it my fault that our schoolmasters didn't bully us about our *mother tongue* with the same zeal as they forced unpalatable Latin and other foreign tongues on us? All in all, I am as ardent a patriot as the next man!

POHOŘALSKÝ Now, to top it all, they've come up with this new thing called *prosody* – a *metre* is the word they give it, that's because you've got to check its length and breadth, tape-measure in hand – and, what's more, the lines they composed are far from soothing to one's ears because they *must* not rhyme! Just think of that, my dear friends! And if I'm to abandon my mellifluous *rhymes* – listen to this: (*he sings*)

Two roses and a lilium,
Four lilies of the vallium,

who is going to pay any attention to me?[1]

[1] Klicpera begins by making fun of the Revivalists themselves, and their pedantic insistance on 'pure' Czech. In the final speech (which he added to later editions of the play) he is referring to the neo-classical Revivalists' attempts to persuade poets to write in quantitative (vowel-lengthened) measures, rather than qualitative (stress-based) verse.

*The Theatre of the Estates re-opens*

In 1834 the director of a newly equipped Theatre of the Estates, Jan or Johann August Stöger, reappointed Štěpánek as head of Czech productions. The first production was Štěpánek's own eighteen-year-old comedy, *The Czech and the German* (*Čech a Němec*, 1816). Stöger remained director of the Theatre of the Estates until 1846.

## 160 Chmelenský's hopes at the re-opening of the Theatre of the Estates, 1834

*Česká včela* [*The Czech Bee*] (1834–5), p. 358.

We must all be grateful that Mr Stöger has put the directorship of the Czech theatre into Mr Štěpánek's hands as he is the one who knows the Czech public, the actors as well as Czech dramatic literature. Now that he is to concern himself solely with the Czech theatre, we may and must expect more, and may and must judge more severely. We are hoping therefore to see some good plays, most of all, new and *original* pieces. As it is, our public is not keen on old plays too often repeated and even considerations of profit should point to the staging of new plays, of which there is no shortage.

*Josef Tyl voices opposition to Štěpánek*

One of the part-time actors, Josef Kajetán Tyl (1808–56), editor of the Czech-language magazine *Květy*, was critical of Štěpánek's management. Tyl, as actor, writer, critic, and theatre director would become a leading member of the National Revival; the Theatre of the Estates was named after him in 1945.

## 161 Tyl criticizes Štěpánek's management of the Theatre of the Estates, 13 August 1835

*Květy* [*Blossoms*], 13 August 1835.

Some theatre directors prefer drama, others opera . . . All of them, however, have reached a point in their theatres, or rather, in trying to please the taste of the public, where they look only for a multitude of effects to entertain the eye and the ear without the mind being engaged, even though this should be the principal aim of theatre, that is, that the mind should be stimulated by what is presented on stage. Nowadays we have expensive operas and other noisy pieces with no other value but their pretty sets, showy costumes and enticing dances. It is neither our desire nor our business to wonder at the means and ends of other people's theatres, and so we turn our gaze toward our own and only theatre and ask again: what kind of plays should be staged here? Works which would reflect the life of our nation in its full diversity, which would perfect not only our mother tongue but also our love of it, as well as the love of all the other national virtues inherent in our educated people, works which would stretch the talents of our poets, challenging the taste and knowledge of our public – such plays should be seen on our Czech stage. It is quite clear that an opera is not an ideal means to achieve such goals. On the other hand, it is pleasing to the ears of our music-loving nation and testifies to the melodious quality of our tongue before foreigners who, in their turn, help the Director to fill the theatre's coffers. However, are mellifluous charms, boasting and box-office success the aims of our theatre?

## III THE CAJETÁN THEATRE AND THE THEATRE IN RŮŽOVÁ STREET, 1835–45

### *The opening of the Theatre U Kajetánů*

In his dissatisfaction, Tyl formed his own amateur theatre company, known as the Theatre *U Kajetánů* and based in the refectory of an old monastery in the Lesser Town district of Prague. Although the group was amateur and performances few – only twenty-eight in the company's three-year existence (1834–7) – it was significant in setting a new standard of production for Czech performances. The length of time between productions meant that greater attention could be given to preparation, and to details of content and language. Many of Tyl's company were also writers, and included the poet Karel Hynek Mácha (1810–36), one of the main representatives of Czech Romanticism, especially with his poem *Máj* (*May*, 1836). Another of Tyl's company, Jan Kaška-Zbraslavský (1810–69) began as a tailor and turned into a splendid comic actor who typically played jokers or dim-witted characters.

## 162a The Cajetán refectory used as a theatre

Photograph in K. Engelmüller, *Z letopisů českého divadelnictví* [*From the annals of Czech theatre life*], vol. 1 (Prague: Jos. R. Vilímek, 1946–7), Plate 8.

## 162b Kaška-Zbraslavský recalls his first performance at the Theatre *U Kajetánů* in 1835

'Zápisky starého komedianta' ['Notes of an old actor'] in *Rodinná kronika* [*Family Chronicle*] 4, 83 (1864), pp. 54–6; reprinted in Jan Kaška-Zbraslavský: *Kajetánské divadlo* [*The Cajetán theatre*] (Prague, 1937), pp. 16–22.

In the former Cajetán refectory the work on the theatre went busily ahead. [. . .] The painters Mrňák and Würbs[1] got on with the more difficult sets while Tyl painted almost all of the room interiors.

The majority of the amateur actors in the company were in the writing profession; all the contributors to Tyl's *Květy* also had to take part in the theatre.

[. . .] Our first public performance was to be the play *The Sword of Žižka* [*Žižkův meč*, 1815] by Klicpera, and I was given the part of Pohltoňský. When Tyl and his friends first conceived the idea of founding a private theatre, they agreed to put on mostly Klicpera's plays, since the Theatre of the Estates was ostracizing them. The first to be chosen was *The Sword of Žižka*. When we began rehearsals in Tyl's apartment, the part of Pohltoňský had been tried out already on other members of the company. First there had been Filípek, then Rubeš, Tupý[2] and others, but none of them seemed to satisfy Tyl's requirements. Finally he came to me. When I first read the part through I felt literally petrified: so far I had played only straight characters and having to deal with a comical part made my hair stand on end. How Tyl ever spotted a comic vein in me is a mystery to me to this day. I had been completely unaware of it myself. Feeling that I was absolutely the wrong choice for the part of Pohltoňský and being convinced that I was going to fail miserably I, nevertheless, learned the lines assiduously; after all, it was to be my last performance.

[. . .] After some six rehearsals, Sunday arrived and with it our first public performance. *The Sword of Žižka* was cast as follows: Mr Filípek as Zachariáš, Miss Magdalena Forchheimová as Marie, Mr Kaška as Pohltoňský, Mr Trojan as Birkenstein (this was originally meant to be Mácha's part, but he refused it because he did not want to be in the same play as me), Mr Tyl as Jan and Dalibor Kopecký as the Poet. Poor Mr Hajniš[3] came off worst with his part of Ivan because, a young and lean youth as he was then, he had to wrap himself in padded quilts to look as fat as his character required.

The first act went down extremely well, the full house was very enthusiastic, but as the second act drew near, when I had to make my entrance, I felt increasingly anxious. Finally, the second act began and I stood ready, rifle in hand, waiting for my cue through the scene that preceded mine, feeling like a man condemned to face a bloody battle for the first time in his life. I would gladly have exchanged my good part of Pohltoňský with the non-speaking role of the Miner who silently carries onstage a chest containing Žižka's false sword.

Ivan had already left the stage, then Zachariáš spoke a few words, and the time had arrived for my entrance. I began to speak. As I spoke my lines, I could sense a certain kind of satisfaction settling on the faces of the audience, which gradually changed into a friendly smile and I thought to myself, 'Well, perhaps you're doing it all right!' So I got on with my Pohltoňský with some gusto, and the smiles in the audience changed into loud, cheery laughter, and when I said my line referring to the Poet: 'Dear friend Zachariáš! This fellow is drunk, and thinks that all three of us are sitting on the steps!' while holding up a good-sized chicken drumstick, a thunder of laughter and applause rose up which was again repeated at the end of the act and did not finish until I came back on stage and twice thanked the public.

[1] Josef Mrňák and Jan Würbs (1807–76), painters and illustrators.

[2] Václav Filípek and František Jaromír Rubeš (1814–53), writers for *Květy*, who worked with Tyl on original plays and adaptations. Rubeš in particular followed the Klicpera tradition.

Karel Eugen Tupý (1813–81, also known as Boleslav Jablonský), writer with *Květy*, playwright and adaptor of plays, who in 1837 entered Strahov monastery.

[3] Magdalena Forchheimová (also known as Skalná, 1803–70), originally a professional comedienne and operetta singer, married Tyl and appeared with his amateur company; Tyl wrote many of his women's roles for her. Her younger sister Anna (known as Forchheimová or Rajská) was also an actress.

František Břetislav Trojan, actor.

Jan Dalíbor Kopecký, one of a number of Tyl's actors who later led provincial companies.

František Hajniš, a writer for *Květy*, playwright and adaptor of plays.

*Divergent opinions on Czech drama*

Tyl looked to the work of Klicpera for guidance and inspiration, and one of the aims of the Theatre *U Kajetánů* was to stage more of his work. Klicpera's plays, Kaška claims, were ostracized by the Theatre of the Estates; on an occasion when Štěpánek *did* stage one of the plays, the one-act comedy *Everyone for his Homeland* (*Každý něco pro vlast*, 1829), Tyl (writing in *Květy*, 18 June 1835) had little good to say of the production, although he himself was performing it. Chmelenský, on the other hand, was more generous.

## 163 Chmelenský reviews *Everyone for his Homeland*, 2 February 1835

*Česka včela* [*The Czech Bee*] (2 February 1835).

This is our first comedy written in the style known as 'conversational'. The characters in similar comedies written by the Germans usually come from the upper classes. Mr Klicpera has done the opposite; in his comedy only the lower classes are represented. The play has turned out quite well, and if it seemed a little too slow or sprawling at times, it was partly due to the fact that the action and the speaking of the parts were not executed at a faster pace. Plays like these must never lapse into even the shortest pause. However, it is surprising that the acting is as good as we saw it, since putting on two new plays in two consecutive weeks is a little too much. Where can the time be found to learn the parts and to rehearse? The performance we saw was more like a final dress rehearsal. Miss Manetínská (Minka)[1] was excellent and her progress in diction as well as acting, given such a short time, remarkable. [. . .] Mrs Šimková (the Caretaker's wife) was very good, expecially at the beginning of the play, and the same goes for Miss Forchheimová [. . .] Messrs Skalný [Tyl's stage name] and Stříbrný[2] are very skilful in the parts of the lovers; we have had no one so good since the time of Mr Svoboda. None of the others, especially the actresses, had memorized his or her part as well as one might have wished. Only the first of the scenes of the matrons' gatherings worked well. However, the theatre was quite empty and it is apparent that not everyone is for his homeland when it comes to looking after its theatre. The reasons for this may be:

(1) that only the previous day the theatre was full;

(2) that Mrs Laura Bach and her foremost wrestler and athlete, Jean Dupuis,[3] together with the German conjurer Kachne, attract the public to their circus; (3) that, as we have already pointed out elsewhere, the Czechs do not care for a modest, everyday type of play. To help them along, perhaps it would be a good idea to accompany such shorter pieces with some dancing, or a few pretty arias or duets performed by well-liked singers.

[1] Anna Manetínská, later Kolárová (1817–82), known chiefly for her tragic roles, but also a popular comedienne; praised as well for her beauty and intellect (but see the complaint in **168**).

[2] Gustav Stříbrný (also known as Silbrnägl), actor celebrated for his playing of lovers' roles.

[3] Laura de Bach (d. 1856), second wife of the Austrian circus impresario Christoph de Bach, and a renowned equestrienne.

Jean Dupuis (1791–1888), circus clown and equestrian, noted for his feats of strength.

## 164 Tyl supports original Czech plays, 9 July 1835

*Květy* [*Blossoms*] (9 July 1835).

It is certainly sad that during the whole year's season only four original Czech pieces were staged. Sad, because mere translations do not serve our aim, which can only be achieved with the help of our own national plays. It is true that the choice is not great but should it not be a duty of the Director whom we call our own, to put on those plays that already do exist? Professor Klicpera has written a vast number of plays, some good, some less so. And yet – it must be said – only a small number of these, and, it seems to me, the weaker ones, have been staged. Why don't we ever see *The Coalwoman* [*Uhlířka*, 1817], *The Liar and his Breed* [*Lhář a jeho rod*, 1823], *Hadrián* [*Hadrián z Římsů*, 1821], and why not *The Robbery* [*Loupež*, 1829], or even *Soběslav* [*Soběslav, selský kníže*, 1826]? For these, especially *The Coalwoman* and *The Robbery*, would surely become favourites with the public if they were done with care for the writing and respect for the audience.

Let us not complain that these pieces are too long with regard to the limited time allocated to our Czech plays; a capable pen will shorten a piece of two and a half hours by some half-an-hour and, to me at least, this homegrown product is dearer (especially if it turns out well) than the product from elsewhere whose only advantage is that it is shorter. What harm could it do if the Director – be it only in jest – agreed to show us a mere half or even a *third* of *original* Czech plays? There is no doubt that they would be easily found. What could not be achieved out of love for our mother tongue and for a good cause? Furthermore, the dramatic poet, who can hardly expect much reward from us, at least finds satisfaction in having his work shown. Would this not still leave enough time to stage good new translations? Just as groundless is the objection that there would be insufficient actors to stage all the plays. We used to see posters with innumerable names on them [. . .] If you spot weaknesses, cover them wisely, cast the parts with care. The weaker side of our acting ensemble is of course the women. Firstly, except for Mesdames Forchheimová and Šimková not one knows how to express herself in Czech and secondly, none of them can be considered for the part of a serious lover or heroine, nor have we had anyone like that in the past. But even this can be overcome with the help of impartiality exercised by the directorship and hard work put in by our actresses. The theatre's fame does not always depend on the excellence of the acting but on the harmonious co-existence between the care of the directorship and the diligence of the actors who, although their circumstances may be modest, support one another, creating something worthwhile out of a good drama.[1]

[1] Tyl himself wrote a number of plays on patriotic themes; one of his comedies, *Fidlovačka* (1837), included the song 'Where lies my home?' which became the Czech national anthem.

*Czech theatre as one facet of European nationalism*

The periodical *Květy* also reflected the interest of Czech nationalists in the struggle of other nations for their own theatre. In January 1837, a visitor to Lemberg (Lvov) in Poland sent his impression of the Polish theatre.

## 165 A comparison of Czech and Polish troupes, 12 January 1837

*Květy* [*Blossoms*] (12 January 1837)

Complaints of one Lemberg correspondent published in *Čechoslav* (vol. 1, p. 50) regarding the poor standard of the local theatre aroused small hope that the Slav Thalia would provide me with pleasure or elation here; however, always interested in anything leading to national edification, I took the earliest opportunity to acquaint myself with the circumstances of the local stage, and behold! to my surprise I discovered that the Polish actors surpass the excellence of all that is known so far. It is true that plays in Polish are no longer shown every other day but only twice or thrice a week and never on Sundays; more than two-thirds of evenings of the whole year have been taken up by plays in German while Polish opera scarcely exists. In spite of that, Polish heroic drama and, even more, the conversational pieces far outdo all the German plays, and the Polish company enjoys full houses. What a difference between our Czech and this Polish theatre!

*Conflicts and competitions at the theatre in Růžova Street*

In 1841 Stöger, prompted by criticism that the Theatre of the Estates was putting on unworthy Czech farces, opened a private theatre in Růžová [Rose] Street exclusively for Czech performances (*Nové divadlo v Růžové ulici*), appointing Tyl and Josef Jiři Kolár, formerly one of Tyl's actors at the Theatre *U Kajetánů*, as directors. Kolár (1812–96), also a dramatist and translator of Goethe and Shakespeare, later became the first Head of Drama at the Provisional Theatre (*Prozatímní divadlo*). Meanwhile, the two directors soon proved to be incompatible.

## 166a Stöger's New Theatre in Růžová Street

Reproduced in Engelmüller, vol. 1 (1946), Plate 10.

## 166b Plan of the boxes and stalls in the New Theatre in Růžová Street

Lithograph in the Archives of the National Museum, Prague; reproduced in *Dějiny českého divadla*, vol. 2 (1968–77), Figure 76.

## 166c Kolár registers a complaint against Tyl for assault in 1841

State Archives, quoted in Oscar Teuber: *Geschichte des Prager Theaters* [*History of the Prague Theatre*], vol. 3 (Prague: N. Haase, 1883–8), pp. 313–14. [Translated by Laurence Senelick]

Mr Kolár testifies to the honourable Royal and Imperial city constabulary that on 30 October 1841 (before the opening of the Theatre in Růžová Street) he was 'insulted by Josef Tyl, editor of the newspaper *Květy* and his colleague in the Bohemian theatrical society, in the presences of Mr Jan Nepomuk Štěpánek and other colleagues in the most outrageous and illicit manner, grossly impugning his honour and person, attacking him with the most disgraceful names and striking him violently with his fist in the area of his temples and eyes'. The reason for this curious behaviour was that Kolár had refused to play the role of the elderly intriguer Wolf in Tyl's translation of Gutzkow's *Werner*, in which he had been cast by Tyl. According to the police report, the following scene ensued:

TYL Why won't you play the role?

KOLÁR Here (in the administrative offices) is not the place to speak in such a vexed tone.

TYL You want to play boisterous heroes and leading men, which you entirely botch.

KOLÁR I will not play Wolf for the reason that Werner suits me and Wolf suits you.

TYL Oh, and just who are you?

KOLÁR That is an arrogant question!

Whereupon the catastrophe ensued. Tyl riposted to his colleague, 'Cur, I've had my eye on you for a long time, I'm going to kill you!' and hit him a powerful punch in the face, so that Kolár staggered backwards in stupefaction and warded off a second blow with his stick. Kolár dragged his opponent back to the door, where, however, Tyl sought to knock him off the stage into the remarkably deep orchestra pit. Now, when the danger was greatest, the bystanders intervened, Tyl still in his anger flung curses of all sorts at Kolár's head, e.g. 'literary murderer' and similar epithets and withdrew with the shout, 'Wait, cur, you won't escape me, I'll kill you yet!' Kolár now sought the city constabulary to order that Josef Tyl, with whom he could no longer act on the Bohemian stage and who by his behaviour had offended all of Bohemian society, 'be removed from the Bohemian theatre as violator of both police regulations and the stipulated theatre rules, that he give him (Kolár) satisfaction for the dangerous, violent slap in the face, that he similarly give him satisfaction for the humiliating insults and finally pay full restitution for a torn new black coat worth 50 f1.' Štěpánek, the theatre colleagues Mmes Manetínská, Šmillerová and Nicolajová[1] corroborate Kolár's testimony, and a postscript notes that 'Tyl has already frequently played that vulgar trick of laying violent hands on persons, e.g. the late jurist and man of letters Mácha and the graduate jurist and man of letters Jakub Malý.'[2] The grievance met with success. 'It was ascertained' what was already known unofficially, that Tyl as a reservist in the Latour infantry and as Royal and Imperial civil servant was not permitted to act on stage, and for a while he seems to have been forbidden to engage in play-acting.

[1] Manetínská was Kolár's wife. Šmillerová was probably the wife of the reliable actor Václav Šmiller, who joined the Provisional Theatre in 1845. Magdalena Nicolajová-Hynková was married to the Czech singer Wenzel, who appeared on the Czech stage under the name of Hynek.

[2] Jakub Malý, translator of Shakespeare and author of *Thoughts and memoirs of an old patriot* (*Zpominky a úvahy starého vlastence*, 1871).

## 167 Stöger announces a playwriting competition at the Theatre in Růžová Street, 1 January 1843

'Preisausschreibung für böhmische Dramen' ['Competition for Bohemian plays'] in *Bohemia* (1 Jan. 1843), trans. into Czech in Jan Vondráček: *Dějiny českého divadla, doba předbřeznová 1824–1846* [*History of the Czech theatre, period before the 1848 uprising*] (Prague: Orbis, 1957), pp. 305–7.

To the Czech community of writers.
We now have a theatre where plays in Czech can be seen more often than ever before, performed by actors specially chosen for this task. Several times a week the Czechs have the opportunity to benefit from the refined and stimulating entertainment which has always been valued as the most powerful and effective means toward a higher education of the spirit and heart.

[. . .] To incite therefore, and encourage those among us with dramatic talent, and to secure those good plays which our theatre needs for the theatre-loving Czechs to be provided with a varied choice, I have resolved to offer three prizes for the most successful original Czech plays suited for performance on the stage.

Let these plays be serious or comical, the author of the one which wins the highest recommendation from the specially invited judges will receive first prize which I have set at 20 ducats in gold; the next play will receive 15 ducats and the third most successful will receive 10 ducats, all paid out immediately after the judges have pronounced their verdict, on the sole condition that all performance rights will be passed on to my theatre. An additional award of an identical amount of prize money is promised to the best plays chosen by our jury by a certain lover of the Czech language who hesitates to reveal his name, but who wishes to obtain the rights to publish the plays. This means that the most successful writer of comedy, drama or tragedy will receive a total of 40 ducats, the second best 30 ducats and the third 20 ducats, thus ensuring that these successful authors will see their plays performed in the theatre as well as published in book form.

The judges will be men recognized as experts in the language and in this poetic genre, known for their impartiality and patriotic devotion: the renowned Mr Josef Jungmann, Principal of the Old Town Gymnasium, who will preside over the jury; Mr Václav Svoboda, Professor of Humanities at the Lesser Town Gymnasium; Mr František Palacký,[1] Historian of the Estates of the Kingdom of Bohemia; Mr J.P. Koubek, Professor of Czech Language and Literature at Prague University and Mr Erazim Vocel, the well-known scholar and poet. The works intended for the competition should be sent to the undersigned Director of the Royal Theatre of the Estates and owner of his own private theatre. Each author is to write a motto in place of his name on the first page of his work and enclose a sealed envelope marked with the identical motto and containing the author's name. The envelope will not be opened until the announcement of the results so that the prize-winner's name can be made public. All other envelopes will remain sealed, unless the authors of plays judged fit for performance wish to contact the undersigned entrepreneur, who will be willing to discuss terms with them.

We give a year as the time limit for the dramatic works to be forwarded to us and we hope that by next Christmas, that is, 1843, Czech writers will have sent us a great number of plays for which their country and countrymen, as well as the undersigned, will be most grateful. [. . .]

The Directorship of the Czech theatre will also welcome plays of quality translated or adapted from other languages, and is willing to offer a good price for them, circumstances allowing. Whoever, therefore, among our Czech writers has any such plays ready or intends to compose one, do not tarry, but add it to the expansion of the Czech theatre.

[1] František Palacký (1798–1876), historian and nationalist politician; author of the five-volume *History of the Czech nation in Bohemia and Moravia* (1836–76).

*Continued animosity between Tyl and Kolár*

The Theatre in Růžová Street closed in 1844. But Josef Tyl and Josef Jiří Kolár remained rivals in the Czech-language theatre, as this attack on Kolár and his wife in Tyl's *Květy* demonstrates.

## 168 Tyl launches a verbal attack on Mr and Mrs Kolár, 25 September 1845

*Květy* [*Blossoms*] (25 September 1845).

If the Directorship cared to take more interest in the productions, it would have to see that one actress on her own is not enough. Even the most wretched travelling company usually has three or four female members. You may well ask which women perform in our theatre. Who plays the lovers' parts? Mrs Kolárová. Who plays the heroines? Mrs Kolárová. Who the sentimental parts? Mrs Kolárová. And the youthful lovers and *ingénues*? Mrs Kolárová. Who takes care of the fashionable ladies? Mrs Kolárová. And the young mothers? Mrs Kolárová again. And who is the first lover? Mr Kolár. Who plays the heroes? Mr Kolár. And the gormless youths? Mr Kolár, etc. Good gracious, we have a veritable collarium of nothing but Kolárs. The Director no doubt thinks that so many wheelwrights[1] will secure enough speedy wheels for the Thespian chariot.

[1] Kolár had earlier changed his name from Kolář, which is Czech for wheelwright.

## IV TYL'S LEADERSHIP AND ITS OPPOSITION, 1846–50

### 169 Contract appointing Tyl to manage the Czech productions at the Royal Theatre of the Estates, 1846

J.L. Turnovský: *Život a doba J.K. Tyla* [*Tyl's life and times*] (Prague: Hynka, 1892), pp. 168–9.

[. . .] (1) Mr Josef K. Tyl, as the Dramaturge of the Czech theatre in the [Royal] theatre [of the Estates], pledges to take part in all the productions and performances put on by the Directorship during the stipulated period of this contract and to follow instructions as necessary.

(2) Mr Josef K. Tyl agrees to abide by all the existing theatre regulations as well as those that may be adopted by the Theatre of the Estates in the future – and these regulations are to be regarded as an integral part of this contract; he also pledges to contribute diligently to the honour, success and progress of this institution, and to devote all his efforts to this fine purpose.

(3) Should the Directorship grant that Mr Tyl's services are required in a different theatre during the period of this contract, Mr Tyl is entitled not only to a seat in the carriage, but also to all other privileges and expenses authorized by the Directorship to this end.

(4) In the event of the theatre's closure due to national mourning, fire, war or other causes, Mr Josef K. Tyl is not eligible for a salary for as long as the theatre remains closed; in the event of the Director's death or the cessation of the current Directorship, the Directorship or its heirs and successors will pay out to Mr J.K. Tyl the salary which is due, without entitlement to compensation.

(5) Mr Josef K. Tyl is responsible for the payment of half the charges incurred by the duty stamps and the verified copy of this contract, which is 33 silver kreutzers.

(6) The validity of this contract dates from Palm Sunday of the year 1846 and

initially covers one year. If three months prior to the expiry of the stated period neither side submits a written request to cancel the contract, it will be extended for another year, and so forth, year after year, subject to the contract's validity.
(7) Mr Josef K. Tyl undertakes that in the event of having arbitrarily contravened or discontinued the contract, he will pay a sum of 5 gulden,[1] that is five gulden in silver to the Directorship in Prague for every day of such disruption of his duties, without being exempted from these duties.
(8) The diligent observance of all the conditions stipulated in this contract entitles Mr Josef K. Tyl to a monthly salary of 33 gulden 20 kreutzers [. . .] in silver.
(9) Mr Josef K. Tyl undertakes to put on two original pieces and six plays in translation in the Czech language during every winter season.

[1] Throughout the Habsburg Empire one gulden or florin was equal to 60 kreutzer or half a thaler or one Cologne mark, an equivalency stabilized in 1773 and reaffirmed in 1818. The gulden was known in Czech as a *zlatník*; from 1811 to the First World War there were approximately ten gulden to one pound sterling. According to John Tyrrell, 'In 1847 the average weekly wage for a working man in Bohemia was 5.22 zl., somewhat less than the average of 11s. a week in England.' A clerk earned an annual salary of 1,000 zl., the chief conductor at the Provisional Theatre in 1862 600 zl., a mere chorister there 120–80 zl. (See John Tyrrell: *Czech Opera* [Cambridge University Press, 1988], p. xv.)

*A national theatre under the provisional government*

In the revolutionary year 1848 Tyl became a member of the delegation prepared to establish a provisional government for Bohemia under a federal Austria – an ambition suppressed by the absolutist government which regained power in Vienna. A leading member of that delegation was the writer Karel Havlíček Borovský (1821–56), poet, critic, editor and Nationalist politician. He opposed both compromise and what he saw as empty patriotism.

However, where policies in the theatre were concerned, Tyl and Havlíček were not in agreement. Havlíček would have preferred not to have any performances in Czech at the Theatre of the Estates, rather than those which claimed merit solely on the grounds of being written in Czech.

## 170 Havlíček Borovský's doubts concerning a Bohemian national theatre, 8 December 1849

*Národní noviny* [*National News*] (8 December 1849), quoted in Dr Z.V. Tobolka, ed., *Politické spisy* [*Political writings*], vol. 2 (Prague: J. Laichter, 1902), pp. 814–18.

It seems to us that the directorship of the national theatre overestimates original Czech plays, and that bad Czech plays are given precedence over good foreign plays. We are referring in particular to certain older Czech plays, only too well known to the public already, which we see as appropriate for being put on by amateurs for amusement but quite inappropriate for production on the stage of the Prague theatre, often frequented by people wishing to discover the latest progress of our Slavonic cause and by foreigners who, although they may not understand the Czech language, easily perceive the simple-minded and antediluvian air of such an 'original' piece, especially when helped on its way by actors and actresses who, either thanks to their natural or diligently studied plainness, mightily contribute to the vulgarization of an already vulgar and infantile play.

How rich today is the world's dramatic literature, how easily the plays can be translated and adapted, what a wonderful selection could be made for those few Czech performances!

On the other hand, it is about time that the directorship learned to recognize the abilities of its actors and particularly actresses, and also how to evaluate them in a just and impartial manner. It is also high time that our theatre had, beside Mrs Kolárová, one other actress to take the parts of a youthful lover, so that a decent man could actually fall in love a little!

We believe that we are here voicing the wishes of the whole Czech public, and we wonder whose fault it is that they have not yet been fulfilled.

### *The summer arena at Pštroska*

In the second half of the nineteenth century the lower-middle class audience was more likely to be found at the summer arenas, of which the earliest was the first completely Czech theatre, Tyl's *Aréna ve Pštrosce* (1849–61). This cheaply-built, open-air theatre opened as a branch of the Theatre of the Estates with the renewed aim of increasing the number of performances in Czech. Tyl saw this action not only in social and economic terms, but as a cautious political move, an attempt to establish the basis of an independent professional Czech theatre.

This was the first of a number of arenas, which for the next half century were a popular feature of Prague summer life. They were built in gardens in pleasant districts such as Vinohrady, at that time a suburb of Prague. Being vulnerable to the weather, they flew the nationalist red and white flag if the performance was to take place. The first arena was considered by Karel Havlíček to be yet another compromise of the Czech theatre enthusiasts with the Austrian authorities. He condemned it as a 'wooden hut'.

Nevertheless, the Prague arenas remained popular for over half a century. Few plays of intrinsic importance were shown, but audiences were delighted by comedy, spectacle and topical jokes. Actors who learned their skills in the arenas later became the nucleus of the company at the Provisional Theatre.

## 171 Havlíček Borovský protests against the opening of the Summer Arena, 18 April 1849

*Národní noviny* [*National News*] (18 April 1849); English trans. from Stanley Buchholz Kimball: *Czech nationalism: a study of the national theatre movement, 1845–83* (Urbana, Ill.: University of Illinois press, 1964), p. 32.

For a long while we have worked so that our nation would have what every cultured nation has – its own theatre. [. . .] On Sunday afternoons for a short while, when no one else wants the building anyway, miserable plays are produced for us. And even these are presented thanks only to a few enthusiastic souls. Czech actors receive nothing, while their German counterparts are well paid. Now the present Provincial Board is embarrassed by such an example of 'equality'. So Hoffmann, director of the German theatre, requests that the board vote all of 9,000 fl. to build us a summer arena. This they think is equality!

We protest in advance against such equality. If this plan were to be carried out we would end up with a wooden hut where we could only present simple plays in a poor style to a vulgar audience. I believe that if the Provincial Board can offer us nothing better, we must request that they do not concern themselves and that the matter be postponed until the sitting of the first Bohemian Diet.

## 172a The open-air theatre at Pštroska

Sketch, possibly by J. Housa, from a daguerreotype; reproduced in *Dějiny českého divadla*, vol. 2 (1969), Figure 140, opp. p. 332.

## 172b Tyl's address opening the Arena in Pštroska, Summer 1849

*Spisy Josefa Kajetána Tyla* [*The Writings of J.K. Tyl*], edited by J.L. Turnovský, vol. 13 (Prague: A. Hynka, 1888–92), p. 59.

In summer we sport on the grass
In winter we sport on the ice
The same for our theatre rites.
In summer we'll sit under heaven like Greeks,
Seeking the Muses in winter indoors
And one Czech muse there will be among them,
 no doubt.
This summer season is meant for those ladies and
 gents
Who hate watching plays in the sweat of their
 brow.
Now they can watch in the light of the day
And by a gentle zephyr refreshed
Enjoy the piece in all comfort.
Be they Czech or German speakers,
Local patrons or foreign guests
Our plays for both alike are done.

### V THE MOVE FOR A NATIONAL THEATRE, 1851–81

*The Committee to Build a National Theatre*

In 1850, when it seemed that there was no hope of any more political gains to be made from the government in Vienna, Trojan, director of the Estates Theatre, obtained permission to form a Committee to Build a National Theatre, whose chairman was the historian František Palacký (1798–1876), author of *The history of the Czech nation in Bohemia and Moravia*. In 1851, the Committee issued their declaration, *An Announcement to the True Friends of the Czech Nation*, couched in flowery phrases chosen to soothe the Austrian authorities. It was received with scepticism by Havlíček Borovský.

## 173 Havlíček Borovský attacks so-called Czech–German 'equality', 2 April 1851

*Slovan* (*The Slav*) (2 April 1851); English trans. from Kimball (1964), p. 40

After many difficulties we are finally going to organize our own National Theatre. [. . .] The government has at last given us permission to collect our own money and build ourselves a theatre in Prague. Who would say that we should not be delighted with such a favour? We Czechs have another similar job, that of paying taxes to support the German theatre. This is equality?!

Because the Czech dramatic productions in Prague are bad, the audiences are small, thus the performances are poor for there is no money to pay good actors, therefore the plays are bad, hence the audience is small, therefore – so goes the round.

[. . .] What then is the answer to our problem? All we lack is money. Give me about 400,000 fl. and in three years I will establish in Prague a Czech theatre, the equal of any in any other country, and one which even the Germans would rather attend than their own theatre. Pay our Czech artists what they can command elsewhere and see what we can create here at home.

There are doubters who will ask 'Whence comes this kind of money?' It is true that those who now acknowledge the Czech nation and nationality do not have such riches. Almost none of the nobility and none of the majority of the wealthy support our national efforts. This is true, but we Czechs each year pay 30 million fl. in taxes. If we, because of duty, can annually pay such an amount, can we not among ourselves out of love raise 1 million fl. for our country and ourselves?

### *Fund-raising for the national theatre*

An energetic programme to collect financial donations was instituted. A future Director of the National Theatre, František Adolf Šubert (1849–1915) gave a detailed account of this period in the volume he published to coincide with the opening of the National Theatre in the 1880s.

## 174 Collections for building the National Theatre

František Adolf Šubert: *Národní divadlo v Praze: dějiny jeho i stavba dokončená* [*The National Theatre in Prague: its history and the completion of construction*] (Prague: J. Otto, 1881), p. 69.

There were more substantial contributions received from Moravia. 142 gulden[1] 34 kreutzer (which included 10 gulden from Fr. Sušil), and 152 gulden from Olomouc. 180 gulden arrived from Banská Bystrica in Slovakia, besides another sum collected among Slovaks living in Vienna.

Collections diligently organized by the Doctors Plúcar and Hubert in Teschen yielded 79 gulden 58 kreutzer while Jos. Šnírch, an engineer in Sezana near Trieste, collected 149 gulden 45 kreutzer. Boleslav Jablonský sent us from Cracow 50 gulden spared from his meagre earnings, and 28 gulden were collected in Lemberg [Lvov]. The Czechs from Mürzuschlagen in Styria sent 48 gulden and the Slovenes from Graz collected 12 gulden. Mr Kazda, an engineer from Radstadt in

Salzburg, sent us 50 gulden and there were additional sums which arrived from outside Bohemia. For example, Dr A.H. Wratislaw, whose grandfather emigrated from Moravia to England, sent us 5 gulden from Cambridge.

[1] In 1856 the gulden was made equal to 100 kreutzer.

### *The Provisional Theatre opens*

In 1856 a site for the National Theatre was purchased on the banks of the Vltava and in 1862 the Provisional Theatre was opened at one end of the site. It was a controversial decision, as many patriots were afraid that the Provisional Theatre would take the impetus out of the campaign for the National Theatre. But following the fall of the absolutist Bach[1] ministry in 1860, there had been many signs of growth in Czech cultural life, including the foundation of a society for writers (*Svatobor*), of a choral society (*Hlahol*) and of an artists' union (*Umělecká beseda*).

The existence of the Provisional Theatre, with Josef Jiří Kolár in charge of the drama company, meant that for the first time professional Czech actors had their own permanent stage on which to work, and from 1864 they gave daily performances and were able to achieve higher standards. A celebration of the tercentenary of Shakespeare's birth was staged in 1864; one important aspect of this for the Czechs was to emphasize that their culture had wider international connections than those depending on German-speaking society. The festivities included a procession of Shakespeare's characters, in costumes designed by the nationalist artist Karel Purkyně.[2] The final character was Perdita from *A Winter's Tale*. In her speech, wordplay was made on the phrase *perdita ars bohemica*, to emphasize the nationalist intention of the occasion.

[1] The Austrian Minister of the Interior Baron Alexander von Bach had enunciated the 'System' of a single individual state, Austro-Hungary, which would subsume such lesser entities as Bohemia and Hungary under one homogeneous culture and language.

[2] Karel Purkyně (1834–64), an artist who studied in Paris and combined the Baroque tradition with the new wave of Realism. Best known for his creation of the Shakespeare procession, he did not live to see it staged.

## 175a Homage paid to the genius of Shakespeare before his bust during the celebration in his behalf, 1864[1]

Drawing by Č. Melka in *Rodinná kronika* 5 (1864), pp. 70–1; reproduced in *Dějiny českého divadla*, vol. 3 (1968–77), Plate 14.

[1] Down centre is Otýlie Sklenářová-Malá as Perdita about to recite Züngel's verses. The bust was by J. Čapek.

## 175b Perdita's speech in the Shakespeare Festival Procession, 1864

Jan Bartoš: *Narodní divadlo a jeho budovatelé* [*The National Theatre and its builders*] (Prague: Sbor pro zřízení druhého Národního divadla, 1933), p. 161.

I am Perdita from *A Winter's Tale*, a babe cast on a foreign shore, my father's house denied me. Do you apprehend the truth concealed in the legend? A babe banished to a foreign shore, yea, *perdita ars bohemica*, her father's land denied her, she was nursed at foreign breasts and even wandered through foreign lands in search of livelihood. *Perdita ars bohemica* is this very child, who, grown under a foreign sun, has returned to her home to find love and goodwill. Let us not, therefore, spoil this sacred moment by reviving bitter memories. Perdita, once lost, is back home; her father and all her kith and kin want to know her again. No longer will she wander through the world, dependent on foreign bread and favour!

*Laying the foundation stone of the National Theatre*

The Shakespeare Tercentenary had taken place, not in the cramped and inadequate Provisional Theatre, but in the New Town Theatre which had opened in 1859 for the presentation of plays in German and Czech. This emphasized the urgent need for the National Theatre itself to be built. In 1866 plans for the theatre were submitted and in 1867, the year that the Hungarian nation gained its autonomy from Austria, construction was begun.

The ceremonies which accompanied the laying of the foundation stone in 1868 were planned and publicized with great thoroughness. A brochure was published in advance of the event, containing a brief history of the Czech theatre, the background to the building of the theatre and details of the festivities. The writer, in his excitement, compared the process which was going to take place on the 16 May as comparable with the coronation of Ferdinand V the last crowned King of Bohemia. The foundation stone had been brought from the Bohemian mountain of Říp from which, so the legend goes, Čech, ancestor of the Czech nation, claimed the surrounding country for his people.

## 176a Preparations for laying the foundation stone of the National Theatre, 1868

*Upomínka na slavností položení základního kamene k velikému národnímu divadlu českému v Praze* [*Souvenir of the ceremony for the laying of the foundation stone of the great National Czech Theatre in Prague*] (Prague, 1868), pp. 12–13.

The committee, well aware of the fact that it would not see to all the preparations involved in such festivities on its own, has called on a great number of assiduous and devoted patriots and formed them into subcommittees concerned with invitations, accommodation, decoration and with the ceremonial procession, the regatta, choral singing, banquets and the vast national celebration in the district of Letná. [. . .] Numerous invitations have been sent out to all the outstanding men of learning, artists, dignitaries, and others whose names are famous in Bohemia, Moravia, Slovakia, Galicia, Styria, Carniola, in the Kingdom of Croatia-Slavonia-Dalmatia, in Serbia, Montenegro, Slavonic Turkey, Prussian Poland and Russia. The celebration will also be attended by representatives of the French and English nations as well as those of all the different Czech societies and fellowships abroad; even the Czechs in America have already sent their delegates. Apart from all of Prague's choirs, clubs, associations and spectators, deputies of almost every regional and district society will also be present as well as the sports clubs (Prague *Sokol* will be there on horseback), choral societies (about 4,000 singers), students, a vast equestrian formation (about 2,000 riders), workers and others from not only Bohemia but also Moravia. In order to secure adequate lodgings for all the distinguished guests to our Golden Prague, the accommodation subcommittee appealed for help to all Prague citizens who, beyond every expectation, showed their Czech sense of true hospitality; for example, the military commander of Bohemia, Prince Montenuovo, offered on loan 3,500 new blankets and 1,300 straw mattresses to 'this good cause', and the esteemed Town Council assigned local schools and officers' empty flats for accommodation; whilst the former riding-school at Rejdiště has been allocated for the horses. Countless other Prague, Karlín and Smíchov citizens have similarly manifested their devotion and good will so that the accommodation subcommittee now has a sufficient number of lodgings and stables.

In order to welcome our illustrious guests with the ancient city of Prague appropriately decked in festive garb, a special subcommittee, assisted by the esteemed Town Council and the Provincial Board, is going to adorn all the streets along the route of the ceremonial procession: namely, Penízková Street, Josef Square and Wenceslas Square, the Příkopy, Ovocná Street, Ferdinand Avenue, the National Theatre building site, and the Embankment, will be embellished in the most dignified and tasteful manner with green garlands and festoons, draperies, hangings, flags in their hundreds, diverse symbols and slogans and other such ornaments. In Příkopy, by the Powder Tower, two pyramidal structures will be erected. Following the example of Prague, the streets of Karlín will also be tastefully decorated and a triumphal arch will be built in the square. Thanks to the endeavours of another subcommittee, on 15 May a festive procession of boats will take place between Střelecký Island and the Island of Žofín, with hundreds of boats adorned with colourful Chinese lanterns and little flags which, in the glow of torches, will stand out charmingly against a background of the mighty sound of several choirs and magnificent fireworks.

## 176b The ceremonial procession accompanying the laying of the foundation stone for the National Theatre,[1] 1868

Drawing by A. Garejs, in *Květy* 3 (1868), p. 196; reproduced in *Dějiny českého divadla*, vol. 3 (1968–77), Plate 18.

Slavnost květnová v Praze: 4. Sládci v slavnostním průvodu. Kreslil A. Garejs.
Майское торжество въ Прагѣ: 4. Пивовари въ торжественномъ шествіи. Рис. А. Гарейсъ.
Slavnost květnová v Praze: 5. Typografická beseda ve slavnostním průvodu. Kreslil A. Garejs.
Майское торжество въ Прагѣ: 5. Типографическая Бесѣда въ торжественномъ шествіи. Рис. А. Гарейсъ.


[1] The top row shows the brewers', the bottom row the typesetters' floats.

*The Young Czechs and the struggle for Czech control*

Although all the Nationalists were united on this occasion, there were internal struggles amongst them. František Palacký, who had laid the foundation stone, and František Rieger (1818–1903) led the original nationalist party, which became known as the 'Old Czechs'. The 'Young Czechs', a more radical group which broke away from the original party, were led by Karel Sladkovský (1823–88). Both groups supported the projected National Theatre, at the same time blaming each other for delays. During the 1860s and 1870s, they also fought for control of the Provisional Theatre. Rieger, as Intendant, appointed his own man, Maýr,[1] as Chief Conductor at the Provisional Theatre in preference to Bedřich Smetana, who had been adopted by the Young Czechs as one of their party. In 1866 a newly-formed co-operative voted in Smetana (1824–84) as Chief Conductor. Under Smetana's guidance the opera achieved a standard comparable with other European opera houses. Nevertheless, he was bitterly attacked in Prague, particularly by Maýr's supporters, and in 1874 Rieger succeeded in reappointing Maýr to Smetana's position. Battles also took place over the control of the drama company, led first by Josef Jiří Kolár and after 1874 by his nephew František Kolár (1829–95), both of them supporters of the Young Czechs. Newspapers and writers championed the opposing sides; among the Young Czechs was the prominent journalist Jan Neruda (1834–91).

[1] Jan Nepomuk Maýr (also spelt Mayer, 1818–88), a singer and conductor, director of the Provisional Theatre 1874–6 and 1878–83.

## 177 Jan Neruda leaps to the defence of Czech drama and opera, 26 March 1874

*Národní listy* [*National Magazine*] (26 March 1874); reprinted in Jan Neruda: *Spisy* [*Writings*], vol. 17 (Prague: Československý spisovatel, 1958), pp. 310–14.

Recently [. . .] was a time full of unrest, a time full of uncertainty which hindered art and its development, artists and their enthusiasm, the theatre and its chance to steady itself; a time which allowed the public to become disgruntled. Various rumours, each worse than the last, kept circulating; apparently, Kolár Jr, head of drama for barely three months and already proving his excellent worth, was to be removed from his position, and Smetana, whose art of opera can be matched only by that of Wagner in all of affluent Germany, was to lose his position as chief conductor and head of opera.

[. . .] The drama was accused of favouring *farces* in its repertoire and siding with the *immorality* of modern times, of ignoring *original* pieces and lacking in *consistent direction*. [. . .]. Now, the fact is that, except for the striking piece *The Two Weddings of Mr Darimon*, which no one could regard as utterly useless Viennese stuff, there was not a single *evening performance of a farce during the whole of this year's winter season*. As far as the so-called modern immoral repertoire is concerned, [. . .] we will never measure the morality of the new French dramatists against the morality found in the works of Shakespeare, Goethe, Lessing and others, just as we will never agree to *everything* and anything without discrimination to be presented on our stage; but, if a modern play appears which is shown on every stage in Europe and the rest of the world, which is reported in every magazine and talked about everywhere, then, certainly, it is a *duty* of our theatre to show such a play because our public has got the *right* to demand it. Or ought we perhaps to send our public to the German theatre? [. . .] – Finally, as to the apparent lack of consistent direction, surely that depended solely on the extent of executive power granted to a *single capable* person. One thing is certain: never before has there been such consistency in the repertoire, such good acting standards and so much enthusiasm, good will and dedication generated among the company as there is now under the directorship of Kolár. All that was needed therefore was full executive power for Kolár Jr which he now *does have*. But – so the crisis would have it – Kolár was not to be fully empowered; he was merely seen as one of the directors and not as the head of drama. Mr Maýr was to be head of drama as well, a choirmaster in a Franciscan church who had *never* been interested in drama and has not been familiar with the Czech theatre these past seven years. Is there anyone who would dare to suggest Mr Maýr outright for the directorship in place of Mr Kolár? Would not Mr Maýr himself have had to submit every matter voluntarily back into Mr Kolár's hands? So where is the head or tail to Mr Maýr's story?

Now we come to the *opera*. Apparently it is *disintegrating, inactive, ignorant of original dramatic pieces*, etc. We think it best to let the Czech audiences who have been following the Czech opera for the past ten years comment on this 'disintegration' and also recall if they have ever been given a real artistic treat before the day that Smetana's spirit took charge of our opera! Many of us still remember the legacy Conductor-in-chief Maýr on his resignation bequeathed to Smetana. Miss Pisařovičová, the baritone Lev and the tenor Polák[1] were the only really valid forces left behind in our opera. Even after that, the opera seemed bedevilled with misfortunes. The prima donna Blažková died and Miss Kupková[2] had hurriedly to study all her parts, but even this prima donna did not last in the theatre beyond a year, and we were in the soup again. Of course, there were plenty of Czech sopranos in the world but none of them could sing a single part in Czech! Then the Misses Partschová and Sittová[3] arrived, both of them darlings of our public, but when they first came the only part they both knew in Czech was Marguerite. So they had to study all the parts anew, which meant that the repertoire was dependent on their progress. Now for the first time since the opera was established we have a *completely stable* company. And in case someone leaves, we now have as well our own opera school founded by Smetana, from which a replacement can be immediately found among female and male voices trained in *Czech*. We are quite sure that there are those around who would be more than willing to settle down in such ready-made, stable conditions, reaping where others have sown!

In spite of all adversities, what could not the combined efforts of Smetana and Adolf Čech,[4] for example, achieve during the year's winter season alone! The whole cast of *Don Giovanni*, with the exception of Karel Čech and Lev, was new, two thirds of the cast of *The Merry Wives* were new members and the same goes for

*William Tell, Der Freischütz,* except for Doubravský and Vávra,[5] was *completely new, Les Huguenots* was produced with Miss Partschová, and the newcomers in *Roméo et Juliette* were Čech, Kinský, Mareš[6] and Sittová. *Faust* had three new Marguerites, *Robert le diable* was produced with Miss Sittová, *The Barber of Seville* with Mr Mareš, *Lucrezia Borgia* was done completely anew, while *all the operas* had the backing of newly rehearsed choruses – and this is how the accusation of *inactivity* looks now!

Furthermore, there have been *first ever* productions of Gounod's *La Colombe*, Victor Massé's *Galathée* and *The Duel* [*Le Pré aux clercs*] by Hérold, while new *original* pieces: Smetana's *The Two Widows* [*Dvě vdovy*, 1873], Fibich's *original Bukovín*[7] and Gevaert's *Le Capitaine Henriot* are ready to be performed – thus falls the accusation that *no new* pieces are being produced! The Prague German theatre has offered one new production of *Roméo et Juliette* during a whole year, the Vienna Burgtheater put on only *Jenovefa* and is preparing *Aïda*, the Berlin theatre has so far come up with nothing new throughout the winter season.

With regard to the older *original* pieces, there have been newly cast productions of *The Hussite Bride* and *St John's Rapids*[8] and, following the repeat of *The Bartered Bride* [*Prodaná nevěsta*, 1866], *Two Widows* and *Bukovín*, we will have a new production of *The Enchanted Prince*[9] – there goes the accusation of *neglecting the repertoire of older original pieces*!

As an expression of thanks for all this, Smetana and Čech were to resign and be replaced – yet again, by Mr Maýr as director and also conductor-in-chief. We do not wish to slight Mr Maýr's artistry in the least, but we must confess in all honesty that the young, tireless conductor Čech, who has been watching over every step of the Czech century for quite a few years, is certainly a choice dearer to our hearts. And where Smetana is concerned – we do hope that Mr Maýr will willingly doff his hat to him in appreciation; after all, Mr Maýr is a courteous man who has shown some interest in music himself! [. . .]

1 Marie Pisařovičová, a soprano trained at the Prague Conservatory who first joined the Provisional Theatre in 1863.
Josef Lev (1832–98), a baritone singer greatly valued by Smetana.
Jindřich Polák, a lyric tenor, with the Provisional Theatre from the beginning.

2 Věkoslava Blažková (married name Ressová, 1841–73), trained at the Prague Conservatory, sang many parts in Smetana's operas.
Anna Kupková (married name Pštrossová, 1848–1903), trained at the Vienna Conservatory, first appeared at the Provisional Theatre in 1868. She was a popular Mařenka in Smetana's *The Bartered Bride*.

3 Olga Partschová (also spelt Paršová) made her debut with the Provisional Theatre in *Faust* in 1873, but left in 1874. She later returned to the National Theatre as a singer in the drama company.
Marie Sittová (married name Petzoldová, 1852–1907), with the Provisional Theatre from 1873 onwards, becoming a member of the National Theatre company.

4 Adolf Čech, a bass singer who was later appointed conductor.

[5] Petr Doubravský (1841–87), a baritone with the Prague company from 1865 until his death.
Karel Čech (1844–1913), brother of Adolf, a bass singer with the company from 1868.
Antonín Vávra (1847–1932), a lyric tenor who made his debut with the Provisional Theatre in 1871.

[6] František Mareš, a bass singer with the Provisional Theatre from 1873.
Rudolf Kinský, a baritone with the Provisional Theatre from 1873 to 1875.

[7] *Bukovín* (1874), the first opera by the composer Zdeněk Fibich.

[8] *Husitská nevěsta*, the third opera of Karel Šebor (1843–1903), premièred 27 September 1871.
*Svatojanské proudy*, a romantic opera by Josef Richard Rozkošný, premièred 3 October 1871.

[9] *Zakletý princ* by Vojtěch Hřimalý (1872), a fairy-tale opera based on the Arabian Nights Entertainments.

### *The maturity of the Provisional Theatre*

In spite of internal struggles, during these years the Provisional Theatre established both a drama and an opera company whose standards could be judged against other European houses. Although translations of German and Austrian plays still predominated, from the 1860s contemporary French dramatists such as Dumas *fils* and Sardou were performed; in 1865 the first performance of Gogol's *Inspector*, and in 1878 the first Ibsen in Czech, *The Pillars of Society*. Czech dramatists writing during this period included Emanuel Bozděch (1841–89) and František Věnceslav Jeřábek (1836–93). Bozděch was influenced by the French and Viennese stages; his plays include *Baron Goertz* (1868) and *The Master of the World in a Dressing-gown* (*Světa pán v županu*, 1876). Jeřábek wrote *The Servant of His Master* (*Služebník svého pána*, 1870), a play which aimed to depict the new industrial society. The first visit of the Saxe-Meiningen company in 1878 also had its influence on production. The acting strength of the Provisional Theatre company improved immensely, providing an experienced ensemble when the time came for the move to the National Theatre.

### *The costs of the National Theatre*

Work on the building of the National Theatre proceeded slowly. Of the plans submitted, the Committee had chosen the most splendid and costly, the work of the leading Czech architect Josef Zítek (1832–1909), who had designed the colonnade at Karlovy Vary (Karlsbad) and the Rudolfinum (a Prague concert hall now known as the *Dům umělců* [House of Artists]). But management was not well handled, and costs of materials and labour rose as a consequence of delays. When František Adolf Šubert prepared a commemorative volume to celebrate the opening of the theatre, he included a comparison of Zítek's estimates in 1866 with the eventual cost in 1881.

## 178a Architect's estimate, 1866, and actual cost, 1881, of the National Theatre

Šubert (1881); English trans. from Kimball (1964), p. 125.

| Item | | *Zítek's estimate* | *Actual cost* |
|---|---|---|---|
| | | IN 1866 | BY 1881 |
| 1 | Mason work | 141,700 fl. | 444,260 fl. |
| 2 | Stone work | 94,500 | 201,276 |
| 3 | Carpentry work | 12,700 | 35,768 |
| 4 | Tile work | 3,100 | 4,199 |
| 5 | Tin work | 2,000 | 26,591 |
| 6 | Joiner work | 20,000 | 110,610 |
| 7 | Locksmith work | 15,000 | 12,456 |
| 8 | Iron work | 4,700 | — |
| 9 | Water closets | 2,400 | — |
| 10 | Copper work | 16,000 | — |
| 11 | Painting | 2,500 | 5,580 |
| 12 | Glass work | 1,400 | 5,800 |
| 13 | Interior decorating | 50,000 | 220,824 |
| 14 | Paving | 2,400 | 17,187 |
| 15 | Pottery work | 1,000 | 955 |
| 16 | Water systems | 10,000 | 60,000 |
| 17 | Gas system | 15,000 | 50,000 |
| 18 | Ventilation & heating | 13,000 | — |
| 19 | Stage equipment | 65,000 | — |
| 20 | Stage machinery | — | 284,177 |
| 21 | Lead work | — | 57,466 |
| 22 | Miscellaneous | — | 20,743 |
| | *Totals* | 472,400 fl. | 1,557,892 fl. |

## 178b Caricature of the delayed work on the National Theatre, 1872

Anonymous cartoonist, *Humoristický listy* [*Comic pages*] (1872); reproduced in *Čtení o Národním divadle* (1983), p. 18

*The artistic function of the National Theatre*

Whilst the building took shape, debate continued about the theatre's purpose and programme, as in these excerpts from a *feuilleton* by Otakar Hostinský (1847–1910), a critic and writer on aesthetics and art theory.

## 179 An aesthetician points out the significance of the National Theatre as its opening is prepared, 8–9 March 1881

*Pokrok* [*Progress*] (8 and 9 March 1881); repr. in *Otakar Hostinský o divadle; sborník* (edited by Miloš Jůzl) [*O. Hostinský on theatre; anthology*] (Prague: Divadelní ústav, 1981), pp. 51–9.

The first question that arises is: What purpose is our National Theatre going to serve? To this the only answer can be the purpose of art. If we were to map out for our theatre a direction veering from the general tendency of art, it would be a mistake.

[. . .] So far the advent of the National Theatre has been regarded from two points of view. Some people have yielded completely to their enthusiasm, not devoid of a certain naïveté; others, on the contrary, regard it just as any other ordinary and everyday enterprise.

The former see it as the pinnacle of every nation's aspirations, believing that the fact of a theatre *per se* is going to achieve almost all we have been striving for. Such a view is clearly exaggerated, because a theatre can never claim such far-reaching significance. Today the theatre building is nearly completed, and already we can see that besides this theatre there are many more, even wider fields of our national work and activity awaiting us, and that once the theatre has been opened we will have to get down to accomplishing further, even more important tasks for our nation. Nevertheless, the enthusiasm which has accompanied the idea of founding the National Theatre has been in many respects justified. The National Theatre is *the first great undertaking we have attempted with all our hearts*, and also the first undertaking which has truly *succeeded*, becoming a monument to our national life.

The opposite view, which regards the theatre as a mere commercial venture whose only function is to please the public and secure for itself adequate funds, does not do much honour to those who expound it. A theatre clearly has, as I said, a different task, which is an artistic and idealistic task. It should provide entertainment, not just any entertainment, but one filled with ideals. It is often said that the theatre mirrors the world. The stage, however, does not show a mere copy, a model of the world, but depicts an ideal world. [. . .]

The motto under which our theatre has been built and completed is 'The Nation For Itself'. The nation has built this theatre for itself, which means that the National Theatre must serve solely the Czech public and the theatre management must see to it that the Czech public is shown all that is remarkable from the foreign repertoire on the stage of the National Theatre. [. . .]

The [Czech] public is not to be told: 'If you want to see a Wagner opera, go to the German theatre.' [. . .] *The Czech theatre must not allow the German theatre to supplement it but must compete with it at all times* [. . .]. The task and significance of our National Theatre is incomparably greater than that of the German theatre; the Prague German theatre is a poor relation of other German theatres and is good enough only for amusement. Our theatre, and especially our National Theatre, must become a powerful feature in all our nation's cultural life, and as such needs to be managed and directed on a different level.

### *The burning of the National Theatre*

In June 1881, two months after Hostinský's article had appeared, the theatre was provisionally opened with a performance in honour of the wedding of the Habsburg heir, Crown Prince Rudolph. The theatre was still incomplete, and in August a fire broke out. It was believed to have been caused by a careless workman. The flames spread fiercely. When Šubert's commemorative volume eventually appeared, it included an account of the fire and its aftermath.

## 180 Reactions to the destruction by fire of the National Theatre, 26 August 1881

Šubert (1881), unnumbered page between pp. 48–9.

At the time when the documents compiled about the history of our National Theatre were about to be published, the theatre building, nearly completed, fell victim to a terrible disaster. On 12 August of this year the fire, which began directly under the roof and consumed it as well as the rest of the interior, burned the whole building down virtually to its foundations.

It was a horrible blow. To start with it stupefied and devastated the whole Czech spirit, adding to the gloomy tradition of our nation's unhappy events a new, brutal calamity . . .

However, brighter than the flames enveloping the National Theatre, there shone through this misfortune the strength of our nation. The fire still burning, the smoke still rising from the scorched earth to the skies, new ruins still crashing down to join what was laid waste – and already our nation was raising itself from its first despair, hastening to donate again thousands and hundreds of thousands towards the rebuilding of its destroyed golden palace. The people's love for their sacred building burnt more fiercely than the flames which consumed the National Theatre, the nation's newly kindled enthusiasm revolted against the savage element and, it might be said, against its own darkest of destinies, with such a mighty display of defiance that almost in an instant the sum collected equalled what was needed for the reconstruction of the National Theatre. Today, on the fourteenth day after the terrible fire, the collections themselves reach half a million. A further 3,000 are to be gained from the insurance, whilst the remaining 200,000 will undoubtedly be forthcoming from the nation that wishes to see its theatre rise in even greater splendour than before.

[. . .] We have lost a lot but gained even more – we have gained so much in national consciousness and in love for the national cause that it will doubly repay our great loss. [. . .]

But now we shall continue in our work with even greater joy because, yes, it is certain that the building of the National Theatre will rise again in its former glory. As the building works proceed, we shall persevere with our 'History' so that it can be finished once the doors to the new National Theatre are opened to – we hope – a happier future. Fate has dealt it so much destruction that surely, there can be none left! –

We shall therefore continue with ever greater zeal in our task of keeping a full account of the National Theatre's history, wishing for ourselves at least part of all the love bestowed by our nation on this sacred building.

### *The rebuilding of the National Theatre*

The emotional reaction to the fire brought in funds which enabled the theatre to be rebuilt within two years. The design was in many ways improved, where criticisms had been made of the original auditorium. All the public took pride in the knowledge that their own contribution, however small, had helped toward its restoration. The decoration of the theatre was magnificent, the foyers on every level covered with frescoes by leading artists of the Nationalist movement, such as Mikoláš Aleš and J.V. Myslbek.[1] The subjects included legends from the Czech past, historical landscapes of Bohemia and allegories relating to Czech national identity. Above the proscenium arch the audience read the words '*Národ sobě*': 'The Nation for Itself.'

The theatre opened on 18 November 1883 with Smetana's opera *Libuše*, the legend of the princess who foretold the future glory of the city of Prague. '. . . It must be emphasized,' wrote Otakar Hostinský, 'that no one else in our nation was more worthy of opening the new age of Czech dramatic art than Smetana with his *Libuše*.'[2] New plays were written for the National Theatre, including Gabriela Preissová's *Her Stepdaughter* (*Její pastorkyňa*, 1890),[3] which became the basis for Janáček's opera *Jenůfa*. From 1900 the drama company was under the leadership of Jaroslav Kvapil,[4] one of the first theatre directors to see play production not only as the solving of technical problems, but also as the work of an artist. Kvapil set the foundation for much of the innovation in twentieth-century Czech theatre. Meanwhile, in reaction against what was now thought of as the 'official theatre', popular stages flourished in the form of cabarets, *šantány* (*cafés chantants*) and open-air arenas, descendants of Tyl's Arena in Pštroska [see 172]. From the foundation of the Czechoslovak state in 1918, for two decades, the Czech theatre was amongst the most original and exciting in Europe.

[1] Mikoláš Aleš (1852–1913), a painter who used traditions from Czech history and nineteenth-century literary themes to express Nationalist ideas.
Josef Václav Myslbek (1848–1922), the leading Czech sculptor of this period.

[2] This statement appears in O. Hostinský, *Bedřich Smetana a jeho boj o moderní českou hudbu* (Prague, 1901).

[3] This and Preissová's *The Farmer's Woman* (*Gazdina roba*, 1889) belong to the school known as 'village realism'.

[4] Jaroslav Kvapil (1868–1950), theatre director, dramatist, poet, critic and translator. His work was largely in the nineteenth-century realist tradition, but he also worked with the designer Josef Wenig on symbolist productions.

# *Hungary, 1810–1838*

Edited by GEORGE BISZTRAY

## INTRODUCTION

While the national theatres of the leading Western European countries emerged in the sixteenth and seventeenth centuries, once-powerful Hungary was divided into three parts: the Austrian-dominated west and north, the Turkish-occupied centre and south, and nominally independent Transylvania in the east and southeast. These regions of the country gradually acquired their own cultural identities. While the defeat of the Turks (who controlled more than half of Hungary in these years) at Vienna (1683) and Buda (1686) forced this one foreign power out of the country, for Hungarians it meant only the coming of total Austrian supremacy with effective deprivation of their language and culture, not to mention their political rights and national independence. By the late eighteenth century, Johann Gottfried Herder was prophesying the disappearance of the Hungarian language and nation within a few decades.

Herder's prediction did not come true. There was an upsurge of nationalist sentiment triggered, as elsewhere, by the complex and eventful developments of the late eighteenth and early nineteenth centuries. The Habsburgs may have ruthlessly crushed the emerging revolutionary ideas of the 1790s, but they were unable to do much against the peaceful cultural changes which characterized the first decades of the new century. A rejuvenation of the Hungarian language by the so-called 'language renewal' movement (*nyelvújítás*), led by the writer-critic Ferenc Kazinczy and his comrades, was followed by demands from many sides to institutionalize national culture. The modernized and expressive Hungarian language was spread, among other means and media, by travelling theatre groups to counter the previously abounding German and Latin idioms. The idea for a national institution to set and enforce language standards, similar to the Académie Française, had already emerged during the late eighteenth century. The three leading concepts of the age: language as a symbol of national identity, an academy to safeguard and a national theatre to spread the language, came together after 1825 when, following decades of disruptive absolutism, the Hungarian Parliament reconvened. At the 1825 session Count István Széchenyi (1791–1860), the leader of the so-called 'reform generation', offered one year's income from his sizeable estates to found the Hungarian Academy of Sciences. The question of a Hungarian National Theatre was one of lower priority and not put on the parliamentary agenda for five more years.

Another decisive circumstance was the increasing importance of the administratively independent twin cities of Buda and Pest. In 1784 the government offices moved from the site of the Parliament, Pozsony (currently Bratislava, Czechoslovakia), to the ancient Hungarian capital, Buda. In the same year, the first professional public theatre performance in the Hungarian language took place in Buda, featuring Voltaire's *Mahomet, ou Le Fanatisme*. Previously, the Hungarian language had been used only in amateur school presentations. Performances in German were, however, given regularly in both Buda and Pest, since the urban population overwhelmingly spoke German. Permanent theatre buildings were available in both cities for performances in German.

The first attempt to establish a Hungarian theatre was launched in 1790 when the actor László Kelemen gathered a group of actors to initiate regular Hungarian performances in Buda. An old Carmelite cloister transformed into a 'Palace Theatre' on the hill overlooking the Danube served as their home base, but they also played in Pest. The opening featured a Hungarian drama: Kristóf Simai's *Igazházi*. The group continually had to struggle against great odds, the lack of original Hungarian plays and the dominance of the German language being the most decisive. This theatrical experiment ended in 1796, yet the National Theatre idea had been tested. Also, it was Kelemen who first turned to Pest County[1] (or, by its full name, Pest, Pilis and Solt) for support, thereby triggering a decades-long competition between the national Parliament and the county authorities for the patronage of the National Theatre. Centralization versus decentralization, this major dilemma of Hungary's political development in the early nineteenth century, directly affected the progress of the campaign for a National Theatre.

A practical dimension to the controversy was the fact that several other regions of the country also aspired to cultural autonomy and/or domination. Most notable was the example of Kolozsvár (currently Cluj, Rumania), capital of the historic Hungarian territory called Erdély (Transylvania), which was directly governed from Vienna between 1690 and 1848. Here in 1792 a permanent Hungarian theatre was established which occupied an impressive new building after 1821 that was actually called the National Theatre but, considering Transylvania's political status as an Austrian province at that time, the success of Transylvanian Hungarians was not regarded as a cultural achievement for the Kingdom of Hungary. It was this Transylvanian theatre group that first performed Shakespeare (*Hamlet*) in a complete and adequate Hungarian translation in 1794. While occasionally hampered by year-long breaks, theatre groups did emerge in major Hungarian cities. And the travelling companies never ceased their activity during the nineteenth century.

In 1807 when the Parliament met, on exception, in Buda rather than Pozsony, the enlightened Transylvanian patriot, Baron Miklós Wesselényi, proudly presented a performance by the Kolozsvár theatre to the members of Parliament and the citizens of the Hungarian capital. This created a great deal of enthusiasm and put the issue of a permanent national theatre on the agenda. But, when it came to taking any decisive steps and responsibility, nothing happened. For a couple of years, the theatre company kept petitioning the county of Pest. The county then instructed its parliamentary delegates to petition the High Estates[2] to provide status and regular support for the company. In 1808 when the High Estates rejected the plea, Pest County assumed responsibility for the Hungarian theatre and the performances continued. A generous landlord, László Vida, became the company's managing director and financial patron: he provided an adequate location by renting a hall in the Hotel Hacker and repeatedly used his own funds to balance the company's battered budget.

[1] County (*vármegye*) a unit similar to its English counterpart but of greater significance in national politics; its chief authority was appointed by the king, his deputy by county members. With its wide and protected discretional powers, it was regarded as a safeguard against the court's efforts at centralization.

[2] Estates (*rendek*), the elective body of the nation, consisting of the nobility and some clergy. The High Estates were represented by the High Chamber, appointees of the king. The other Estates were represented by the Low Chamber, elected from the nobility and the free royal cities.

## I CANVASSING FOR A NATIONAL THEATRE, 1810–27

### *Petitioning the Viceroy for a theatre*

After 1808, it became obvious that the newly erected city theatre of Pest would in fact accommodate German performances only. In order to attract the attention of Viceroy ('Palatine') Joseph, a Habsburg crown prince who was responsible for the modernization of Pest, the county approached him with a petition.

The Viceroy's answer was as politically typical as it was pragmatic. While it was certainly not in the interest of Habsburg supremacy to support Hungarian national culture, it is hard to disregard the fact that the Hungarians themselves were not adequately supporting the cause of their own national theatre either.

## 181 Pest County petitions Viceroy Joseph, 15 March 1810

Jolán Kádár: *A Nemzeti Színház százéves története* [*The National Theatre centennial history*], vol. 2 (Budapest: Magyar Történelmi Társulat, 1938–40), pp. 3–4.

August, Hereditary Imperial and Royal Archduke, Steward Palatine of the Hungarian State, Your Excellency!

The educated world is so convinced of the utility of a well-established theatre that further argument is unnecessary. Does not virtually every European nation boast of this distinctive symbol of nationhood? How long has the Hungarian nation been striving for this? We have dreamed again and again of a national theatrical group, although we know the coarseness of our language. Yet after all endeavours this plan, overwhelmed by the opposite interest of the guests of our nation [i.e. the Austrians and Germans], is facing agonizing uncertainty. – In order to rescue the [plan of the] most beautiful patriotic institution from this fruitless instability, to make it stand bravely on its own feet, we have undertaken as our patriotic duty the establishment and maintenance of the institution of a Hungarian theatre as the most effective tool for the civilizing of morality, national character, language, sciences and arts. We have appointed a deputation to obtain what is necessary for achieving this goal.

[. . .] we venture to ask your Imperial and Royal Archduke [. . .] that the national theatre group receive just consideration, equal to that shown to foreign groups, with respect to performing in the theatre now being built in the city of Pest. This we ask especially since the theatre is being built with Hungarian funding and on Hungarian soil.

Alternatively, [we ask] that the Hungarian group may perform its spectacles by taking turns with the German group. Or, if this please the Imperial and Royal Archduke and he is agreeable to it, it would be even more to our liking if similar accommodation were built for the Hungarian group as for the German group in this spacious building under construction on the shore of the Danube. We beg for the following decree from the Imperial and Royal Archduke, that while this building is in progress the Hungarians be allowed to perform in the old German theatre upon the departure of the German performing group.

We would be fully satisfied in the latter situation if in the meantime plans for a place for the Hungarians in this new theatre, submitted to the perusal of the City Renewal Commission, be revised and approved. This being granted we would be ever grateful to Your Gracious Imperial Royal Archduke.

## 182 Viceroy Joseph replies to Pest County, 19 July 1810

Original in Latin; quoted in Kádár, vol. 2 (1940), pp. 6–7.

In order that the national theatre company can succeed as soon as possible and can strive more efficiently to achieve its salutary objective for the greater glory of the nation, not only did the royal decree of 1807 declare that the producers must pay the national theatre company one quarter of the net income after every performance, but the stipulations of the contract effected in 1808 with a producer by the name of Czibulka[1] observed the company's interests as well. The tenth clause of this contract pronounces the Hungarian theatre company and the older German company to be of equal rank, and it is stipulated that the Hungarian company would hold two performances in the playhouses of both Pest and Buda, and should not pay more than 5 forints per performance, and that only for the use of the stage and properties.

Moreover, it has also been ruled in the interest of the Hungarian theatre company that in case of unavoidable conflicts with regard to leasing, that party will have the advantage which promises to be more profitable for the revenue of the national theatre company.

Experience, however, has shown that the population of the two cities did not frequent Hungarian-language performances in such numbers as to fulfil the expectations of the aforesaid company in ensuring a proper basis for its continued existence. Hence, it seems that the Hungarian theatre company intends to cancel the performances in the playhouses of the two cities on the days benevolently reserved for them primarily because lighting and other equipment expenses swallow up a large part of the revenue, and therefore the company wishes to ensure operation in a private house which requires less costly theatrical equipment.

Therefore, it is indisputable that, considering the substantial numbers in both cities of those who favour the customary German-language productions over the national theatre company's productions, every possible advantage was due the national theatre company and was awarded to it, and in fact, over and above this, its development was dear to our hearts.

For this reason, for the time being, basic considerations go against the request submitted by the noble county. Notably, regarding the lot upon which the new theatre is being built in Pest, the city treasury intended a different type of development there. Therefore on this lot, adjacent to that of the new theatre under construction, a separate playhouse for the national theatre company cannot be built at the expense of beautifying the city, as this money has been set aside in the civic budget for another purpose. Nor can the existing theatre be rented out nearly free for the use of the national theatre company, because this would be in conflict with the intention stemming from the highest Royal provision, namely, that the above building must be assigned to the highest bidder lest Pest city's beautification budget be injured. Finally, the alternation of performances between Hungarian- and German-language productions would, as past experience has shown, not be to the best advantage of the national theatre company.

For this reason it would be best if the national theatre company would develop day by day under wise guidance and by talent and hard work win the generous support of the citizens of the national theatre.

[1] Alajos (Alois) Czibulka, co-lessee of the Pest Theatre; one source refers to him as a singer but nothing else is known of him.

### *Kultsár renovates the Rondelle and appeals for a new site*

In the meantime, Vida's means shrank and he had to return the responsibility of the theatre to the county. The solid patronage of the new theatre building of the city of Pest by the wealthy German-speaking burghers left no hope for a competing Hungarian theatre. After Vida's retirement the Hungarian group had to leave the performing hall rented at Hotel Hacker, compelled to move into the dilapidated, unattractive building called 'Rondelle' (*Rondella*) on the Pest side of the Danube, which the German company had vacated upon completion of the city theatre.

After 1813 another energetic director, the writer and newspaper editor István Kultsár (1760–1828), tried to advance the cause of Hungarian theatre. He postponed the demolition of the *Rondella* (ordered by the City Renewal Commission) by renovating it. At the same time, however, it became obvious to him that without a national campaign, and without a new, worthy location, the cause of the National Theatre was doomed. Therefore, he bought a lot for a new building and commissioned two architects to draw up plans. He also contacted each Hungarian county, asking for advice and help, even raising the possibility that the National Theatre might be built in a provincial town. While the letter to Pest County gives the impression that Kultsár had been offering his own lot for the theatre site, he did in fact finance at least part of the purchase from the county's theatre funds with the Viceroy's own permission.

## 183a Model of the Rondelle

Museum for Theatre History, Budapest; reproduced in *Magyar színháztörténet* (1962), opp. p. 65.

## 183b István Kultsár's appeal to Pest County for a theatre site, 23 June 1814

Kádár, vol. 2 (1940), pp. 8–10.

Honourable, Noble County!
The nation can feel strong only if its language is alive! We cannot, therefore, cold-bloodedly watch the impending abolition of an institution that may effectively

sustain the language. When the municipal *Rondella*, which served as the Hungarian theatre, had been sold without the county having been notified, every patriot not unreasonably became alarmed lest as a result the theatrical troupe also be dissolved, and the national language in the nation's capital, in the seat of the high courts, in the hub of Hungarian economic life, be forced into silence.

After ten months of directing the Hungarian theatre, I have brought it to such a level that apart from the personal [artistic] development of the individual members, the costumes and stage have been refurbished. I would not consider myself a true patriot if in this uncertain state I did not take care of the survival of the Hungarian national theatre, and if I did not propose the means of its preservation to the noble county.

Since I cannot hope for shared accommodation for both the Hungarian and the German theatrical troupes in the new theatre, I suggest that it would be best to erect a separate, stately building for this national institution. [. . .]

Towards the attainment of this goal I would hold two things to be most important. First, an appropriate building site would have to be found immediately. Second, in addition to the recommendation letter from the honourable and noble county, the patriots would have to be approached individually by members of the theatrical group for donations toward a new national theatre.

To accomplish the first, I am willing to give, without any profit, for the building of the Hungarian theatre that wooden-fenced, spacious corner lot of mine, which was the site of the Botanical Gardens and faces onto Hatvani Street opposite the house of the honourable Prince Grassalkovich, under the following conditions: first, that it remain my property as long as its entire value is not covered and paid for by the donations of the patriots; second, that under the supervision of the Honourable and Noble County, according to approved plans, and with the placement of a controller who would supervise all financial matters, the contruction be placed under my direction, while all the funds be placed in the treasury of the noble county. [. . .]

The refined taste for the Fine Arts was spread in every nation by the Theatre, which comprises all Arts within itself. Therefore, if we wish to preserve the dignity of our [. . .] nation, if we wish its refinement and perfection, if we do not want thoughtlessly to miss a most favourable opportunity to preserve the country, let us begin as soon as possible to work to complete this noble endeavour, by which we can certainly gain the favour of our august Lord, who, during his sojourn in Prague last year, showed his love for the Czech nation by attending a national theatrical performance.

*Kultsár's architectural proposals*

Pest county made the formal commitment in support of the theatre contingent on whether other counties would be willing to join the campaign. Kultsár continued working on the plan almost until his death in 1828. His presentation of the architectural project shows how ambitious his pursuit was.

## 184 Kultsár's project for the national playhouse, 11 November 1819

Kádár, vol. 2 (1940), pp. 15–17.

Honourable, Noble County!

When I presented the first draft for the Hungarian National Theatre as commissioned by the honourable noble county, the honourable county deigned to set down the wise order that this drawing be inspected by the appointed judicious gentlemen before it is seen by the other honourable counties or further action taken toward the building of the theatre. Upon the recommendation of the commissioned deputation and other experts in the field I have changed the draft; and so that it would be easier to send to the other noble counties, I have had it lithographed in a reduced format and had it printed, copies of which printing I am so fortunate as to present here.

Judging by these [plans], the building will be constructed so as to be: first, ornamental but not grandiose; second, sufficiently but not excessively large; third, suitable; and fourth, practical as well. The first is demonstrated by the properly designed frontal columns, the prominently beautiful forms of the two side wings of the building, and the fact that the arched ceiling of the portico is upheld by columns. The second point is evidenced by the fact that the building is so spacious that 1,500 persons can easily sit on the ground floor, in the two tiers of boxes and in the double galleries. In addition, there are dressing-rooms, storage areas for costumes, a painting and carpentry workshop, property room, a superintendant's apartment and other necessary accommodation. The spacious portico, upheld by columns, serves to achieve the third point along with easy access to all seating areas, and is arranged so that pedestrians enter from Hatvani Street while those arriving by carriage would be directed to Szép Street. Also, the staircases to the boxes and galleries are separate. Concerning the fourth point, there is an order that there be a corner coffee-house, with an apartment for the proprietor in the back, and on the other side of the façade a general store. Above the whole portico area is a large hall, which can be used not only for the theatre orchestra's rehearsals but also for concerts, recitals and banquets. These can always bring in enough revenue to cover the maintenance costs of the building.

A building designed to embrace the qualities of beauty and utility, large enough and suitable to accommodate the audience will, I dare hope, serve the national purpose.

However, in order that [the plan] which must be sponsored by public funds may also find public approval, which the nation has been eagerly awaiting since 1790, and which the current European cultural example seems to dictate may materialize, I would judge it necessary to show these printed drawings to the other noble counties as soon as possible, and to obtain their opinions and solicit their assistance.

### *Literary support for a new theatre*

Unfortunately, while working on the physical plans of the National Theatre, Kultsár neglected the Hungarian theatre group of Pest. It became impossible to pay the rent on a temporary location, and in 1815 the company moved to the town of Miskolc where the second permanent theatre building in the country designated for performances in the Hungarian language opened its doors in 1823, two years after the Kolozsvár theatre was finished. Although Kultsár's heroic struggle was unsuccessful, it made a case in favour of the National Theatre when the series of Reform Parliaments began in 1825. It was more difficult to replant stage performances in Buda and Pest; it is estimated that between 1815 and 1833 only four or five performances in the Hungarian language were given by travelling companies in the twin cities.

While the institutional attempts stalled, eminent figures of Hungarian literature, critics, playwrights and poets, took upon themselves the task of propagating the great goal. The following excerpts from the playwright József Katona and the poet and parliamentary delegate Ferenc Kölcsey reflect this shared concern with language and cultural identity. They also reflect the question, once raised by Schiller, of how the theatre contributes to the refinement and moral elevation of mankind.

József Katona (1792–1830), a rural attorney, devoted all his literary activity to playwriting and the propagation of the theatre. He wrote the first outstanding Hungarian national drama *Viceroy Bánk* (*Bánk bán*, 1815, revised 1820).

Ferenc Kölcsey (1790–1838), representative of Szatmár County in the Estates (1832–4), was the foremost poet of Hungarian classicism as well as one of the leaders of contemporary literary life as essayist and polemist. Although the posthumously published piece excerpted below was written in a rhetorical style as a pseudo-parliamentary speech, it actually comprises an aesthetic and philosophical essay.

## 185 József Katona asks why drama can't catch on in Hungary, April 1821.

József Katona: 'Mi az oka, hogy Magyarországon a játékszíni költőmesterség lábra nem tud kapni?' ['Why can't professional poetic drama catch on in the Hungarian nation?'], *Tudományos Gyűjtemeny* [*Scientific Miscellany*] (April 1821).

Drama and dramaturgy are just as unfamiliar here in concept as in practice. [. . .] We often sigh that it is only playwriting that fails to take root in our country. Outsiders reproach Hungarians for failing to take part in this form of the arts. They sometimes believe that Hungarians are unsuited to it, and that the [Hungarian] language has in fact been formed more for song than for declamation. But no one wants to face the obstacles which keep us from disproving this belief – why? If you cannot write good things, do not bother with bad! [. . .]

The first and biggest obstacle to the development of drama is the non-existence of a theatre. It is always shameful for an honest man to work on a piece which profits a dishonest one (an actor). This gave the Germans, who are more refined than we are, an idea. They established theatres in our country, and since beauty was not in demand, they gained Hungarian money by presenting foolery. At last we came to understand this aspect of the development of national refinement; but Hungarians are clever only after the battle; by that time the German has already surged ahead. To learn anything, Hungarians had to attend the German theatre. [. . .]

There are plans enough but no execution. There is the demand that each plan be executed, but who is to fund it? No one (or very few); for everyone wants to further his own project at someone else's expense and gain the glory for himself. For twenty-eight years young theatre troupes have led the poor Hungarian language from place to place and striven fruitlessly to beg a permanent home for this pilgrim. [. . .] And those who gave only their names as protection and their encouragement as nourishment made sure the pilgrim's staff stayed in the actors' hands, since a merely nominal protection provides scant comfort and commendatory encouragement puts little flesh on the bones. [. . .]

Twenty-eight years have passed, and such is the plight of the Hungarian actor! A good-for-nothing hairdresser who makes a good living out of our vanity deserves to be called an honest citizen; and he who refines and beautifies our language (the soul of our nation) has not yet been able to cleanse himself of the last vestiges of dirt. – Foolish, irrational prejudice! Only a permanent national theatre can eradicate it. The actor's way of life will be not a trade but a vocation, which anyone would be glad to attain.

## 186 Kölcsey argues for theatre in Hungary, 1827.

Ferenc Kölcsey: *Magyar játékszin* [*Theatre in Hungary*] (Pest, 1827).

Eminent, Honourable Estates! Even if theatre were not the measure of the cultural development of every refined European nation, if the theatre were not connected with any other notable consideration than language, on this single point all our attention, efforts and sacrifices would still have to be focussed. So far as all peoples are concerned, language and nation are equivalent, if they do not wish to be expelled from among the respected nations. National life without national language is unthinkable. Woe to the nation that has been driven out of its homeland! Double woe to that nation which has been deprived of its ancient tongue! Our ancestors were wanderers, but they were held together by their language, and were thereby able to win a homeland with their blood, and they Hungaricized this strange land. [. . .]

What did the great European nations lose, once they had built themselves theatres and given their excellent actors a share in their respect and a decent livelihood? And what have we gained, having left our actors to wander without shelter or support to this day, closing our eyes and ears to their performances, and denying any compassion regarding their fates? [. . .]

Only the participation of the nation can create a national theatre for us, whose distinctive symbol would be not the national coat of arms painted on a lifeless stone wall but that pride with which every Hungarian will cross its threshold; that enthusiasm which elevates the actor, who regains his self-confidence from the appreciation of the public, above everyday life; that noble patriotism by which the poet, confident in his nation, conjoins his own sentiments to those prevailing among the people of that nation, and thereby, by the only possible means, achieves a bond with his compatriots. In this way the nation will ennoble the theatre and, in turn, the theatre will ennoble the nation. If we let ourselves become enthusiastic, our national character may shine again in a new light. We shall lend the features of this character to the theatre; we shall engrave them on the soul of the poet; we shall encourage him to seek a new, glorious path and guide our theatre to this path, upon which the theatre will not copy foreign nations nor propagate foreign corruption, but will rather express the national feeling and nourish national courage. This shall be the fortifying bedrock for our persecuted language; here shall be its home where it shall rest after its long ostracism. Here shall be the centre from which it can finally burgeon forth to take its place, as befits its amazing qualities, among the other languages of Europe.

But what does it mean, Honourable Estates, this, as it were, mocking smile I can see on certain faces? [. . .]

Surely this smile arises because the theatre is not so significant as to be regarded as a public concern. How differently did the nobility of Pest County think, those generous and foresightful patriots whose efforts deserved gratitude, not coldness and mockery! How differently did the banished French think, when on the prairies of America they built theatres before they built themselves homes! Let us laugh at them, if we dare, lest in their presence we blush in embarrassment at our own pettiness! [. . .]

## II BUILDING AND MANAGING A NATIONAL THEATRE, 1832–8

*The formation of a shareholders' company*

With the establishment in 1825 of the Hungarian Academy of Sciences, which supported and actively promoted the cause of the National Theatre, this latter gradually acquired a higher priority as the counties grew impatient at the stagnation of Kultsár's plan. The interest on the mortgage on the not-fully-paid-for lot meant a burden for Pest County throughout the 1820s which was made still heavier as several counties withdrew their initial financial contribution. Overruling Kultsár's protest and his pledge to cover future interest payments out of his own pocket, the county decided in 1828 to sell the lot purchased in 1814 for the site of the National Theatre. The cause was back to point zero.

Although, on the one hand, the increasing number and quality of Hungarian plays and performances actually improved the chances of the National Theatre movement (in fact, there existed a 'National Theatre Company' operating nationwide), on the other hand, the materialization of a single central institution was not in sight as late as 1830. In that year Parliament approved legislation on the institutional cultivation of the Hungarian language by the Academy, assigning it the establishment of a National Theatre as one of its tasks.

Having returned from Parliament, the delegates of Pest County directed their attention to the theatrical cause with renewed enthusiasm. A permanent Theatre Committee was formed under the chairmanship of Deputy County Head Gábor Földváry (1787–1854). Count István Széchenyi, founder of the Academy, was also invited to join the committee – a step which became the source of a major conflict. Determined to realize the dream of the Hungarian National Theatre, the committee of Pest County recommended the establishment of a shareholders' company.

### 187 Pest County recommends a joint stock company, 14 January 1832

Kádár, vol. 2 (1940), pp. 28–31.

In the opinion of the delegation, the most expedient way is a shareholders' company, as proved by the success of those foreign nations which have already made great advances in the process of refinement. Consequently, the delegation recommends that the establishment of the Hungarian theatre take place through shares, so that the revenue acquired in this way be put, in part, towards the construction of the building and the acquisition of all necessary equipment, while the interest on the other part should be used for the salaries of the actors in order that, regardless of the daily financial uncertainties of the institution, they should not have to worry about their fate; instead, they could devote themselves wholly to the perfection of good taste and the theatrical profession.

*Count Széchenyi promotes an elitist theatre*

The driving social forces behind the county's plan were the middle and lower strata of the nobility. Széchenyi represented just a small segment of the upper stratum: those patriotic aristocrats who, familiar with European conditions, recognized but also occasionally overestimated Hungary's economic and cultural limitations. Fearing a failure of some hasty and over-ambitious plan, Széchenyi recommended the establishment of a small but tasteful theatrical venture for an educated and opulent elite. He distrusted the plan of a nationwide theatrical attraction appealing to all social classes.

## 188 Count Széchenyi's aristocratic doubts about a grandiose Hungarian theatre, 1832

István Széchenyi: *Magyar játékszínrül* [*The Hungarian playhouse*] (Pest: Landerer, 1832), pp. 50–3.

I hope, wish and would like to believe that soon there shall be not just in Pest but in every well-known place a magnificent theatre and every other prosperous institution befitting free nations. But is it conceivable, I ask in all honesty, that a luxurious theatre should arise on a sudden out of the hitherto infantile state of our theatrical arts? [. . .]

But even if we had the talent to build the world's most magnificent and greatest theatre, would we be acting with good sense? I believe not, since there must be a harmony in all things. The number of our actors today, the development of artistic standards and other of our theatrical preparations would not suffice for a rather large, magnificent and luminous theatre. Thus, the higher the expectations of the audiences are raised by the superiority of the place, the lower the public's esteem for our inexperienced actors. [. . .]

The actors are beginners, the audience are also beginners; and because of such a strong consonance – which, if anywhere, is surely necessary at the seat of Apollo – the first permanent theatre should not be a dazzling palace of luminosity, but a small, attractive home of subdued light.

The two aforesaid reasons, however, are nothing compared to the philosophical consideration which counsels, even supposing the greatest talent, building not a theatre which is too big and too bright but one which is more suitable. [. . .]

Very large and magnificent theatres usually require either large support in order to survive in luxury and a shared understanding which exudes a festive atmosphere, or else they are uncomfortable and people visit them only on rare occasions or holidays. On the other hand, smaller theatres, where it is warm in the winter, cool in the summer, and, may we say, where everyone feels at home, can become a regular meeting-place. And if we ask not only the big audiences of Paris and London and the honoured public but ourselves as well, can we deny that a small, pretty theatre where we feel at home is more attractive than some vulgar, dirty building where we sit as freely as in a public market, where one cannot really see or hear, where one is chilly or sweating, and where for a slight and fleeting entertainment one often takes home a great and lasting rheumatism.

The selection of plays also deserves much consideration. In the rather large theatres those plays are appropriate which affect our senses rather than our hearts and intellects, plays in which there is more grandeur and noise than witty rhetoric, poetic sublimity and ingenious action. And would not the performance of such plays be too much for our talents? Definitely! Because for these plays a large cast, expensive costumes, costly lighting, etc., would be needed. But even if we had the capability to bear such costs, and the audience also had the money to pay as high an entrance fee as they do at the London or Paris opera, would it still befit our present situation to perform plays which affect our senses and are perhaps a flash in the pan rather than plays which deeply move the heart and soul and awake, develop and refine man's deepest sensibilities?

But if all this were not reason enough for us to build a pretty, suitable and moderate theatre, rather than a luxurious and large one, and even if we could gather together a million forints for the construction of the theatre and another million to maintain its operation, would we not still be making a mistake by wasting so much talent on such an object, even though it *may* be very useful, when more useful things could be done in this country, for instance the perfect controlling of the Danube?

### *A site for the theatre is found*

While Széchenyi disapproved of the shareholders' company and repeatedly mentioned the lack of experience of the Hungarians in theatrical matters, Földváry and his supporters among the county nobility carried on with their project, driven by a fanatical zeal. Rejecting Széchenyi's aspiration for a fancy site along the Danube, the Theatre Committee recommended accepting a lot which lay outside the city walls, along a much-travelled but little developed highway.

## 189 Theatre Committee accepts a site for the playhouse, 11 June 1834

Kádár, vol. 2 (1940), pp. 33–5.

The permanent deputation, formed to deal with the matter of the Hungarian theatre, reports that Prince Antal Grassalkovich, responding to the Deputy County Head's call under decree 4042–1833, donated that part of his farm lot just outside the Hatvani gates which had been used for wood storage, for the building site of the Hungarian theatre, under the following conditions: that it never be sold or used for any other purpose than for building a Hungarian theatre on it. The named Deputy County Head accepted the donation with grateful thanks and in the hope of approval from the county. – Having deliberated next on how to acquire the funds to construct the building, the deputation is of the opinion that a shareholders' company should be established for this purpose, as well as a lottery, which has already received approval from the county. For the planning of these enterprises and of the construction and budget of the theatre, a sub-deputation was formed. [. . .]

Since the deputation is already confident of the outcome, it believes that construction should begin this year with the money already collected for this purpose, so that at last some results can be shown to patriots who would be all the more willing to offer support, having seen the long-awaited work already begun.

### *Földváry goes over the head of the competition*

In 1833 one part of the theatre company of Kolozsvár (Kassa, currently Košice, Czechoslovakia) started offering regular performances in the Palace Theatre of Buda, recently vacated by a German theatre company. This time, the performances were also financially successful: the country appeared to be ready for a national theatre. At the same time, the city of Pest, the county called Pest, Pilis and Solt, and the parliamentary lobby led by Count Széchenyi were at loggerheads. The still predominantly German-speaking city reproached the county for not consulting its City Renewal Commission, while in the Parliament Szćhenyi did not cease to agitate against the county's plan for building the theatre.

The county's representative, Gábor Földváry, was determined to establish a *fait accompli*. For years, he ardently promoted the plan and subsidized it out of his own pocket. Now, he decided to approach the Viceroy of Hungary, thereby appealing to an authority above his challengers. As it happened, however, the Viceroy was, by Hungarian law, also Földváry's immediate superior as *ex officio* head of Pest, Pilis and Solt County in which the royal capital was situated. In his two consecutive letters written to Palatine Joseph in the fall of 1835, Földváry asserted his stand against his two adversaries, the city of Pest and Count Széchenyi, and bluntly informed the Palatine that construction had already begun.

## 190a The theatre in Kolozsvár, built in 1821

Reproduced in *Magyar színháztörténet* (1962), opp. p. 112.

## 190b Gábor Földváry's letters to Palatine Joseph on building the Pest theatre, 1835

Originals in Latin; quoted in Kádár, vol. 2 (1940), p. 42, 44–6.

(a) 26 September 1835: With humble respect, I herewith enclose for Your Excellency the resolution of Pest County accepted at the meeting of 26 August of this year regarding the building of the National Theatre, whose construction has already begun on the lot offered for this purpose by Prince Antal Grassalkovich. The Estates of the Realm of Pest County now wish that the city of Pest also lend some assistance in this construction, instead of raising a new one at great expense in the upper section of the city, on the banks of the Danube which would first have to be made secure. Especially since the National Theatre under construction, though called temporary, may after all be sufficient to last through the middle of the century.

(b) 24 October 1835: [. . .] I herewith enclose for your Imperial and Royal Excellency the plan of the National Theatre. At the same time I humbly report that the building of the aforementioned theatre has reached such a point that hereafter construction cannot be abandoned without severe injury to the budget allotted for the theatre and, doubtless, discredit to the Pest County Estates. Likewise, its construction can be neither obstructed nor suspended, if only because the resolutions of a general session of the county cannot be altered by a lower level assembly, and even less so by a delegated committee.

But there are also other reasons which recommend that this so-called 'temporary' theatre be built on Prince Grassalkovich's land. Of these, suffice it to mention one: that obviously not every public building can be in the same section of the city, if only because the city's more neglected regions must also be beautified. Hatvani Street is precisely such a section, and in a few years will be one of the most beautiful streets in Pest.

At the same time, I must also regretfully report to Your Imperial and Royal Excellency that a certain letter arrived from Pozsony to Pest – it is in my hands – which calls for the suspension of work on the construction of the theatre and also demands that the next general session of the county give out similar instructions to the parliamentary delegates. Presumably, similar letters have gone to others as well, since its contents are spreading throughout the city. Such a letter was also sent by someone who, at the county's general session of 26 August this year, publicly supported the building of this temporary theatre and now takes pains to hinder this construction. He does this because, having now changed his mind, he has gone over to the side of those who want to build a theatre on the banks of the Danube; also, on the other hand, perhaps because he wants to put me in a difficult position, even at the cost of discredit to the Estates. Even if this be his goal – since it can be no other – this less costly and less time-consuming construction of a temporary theatre can still be carried out, as can the other one built on the banks of the Danube, although this latter will require greater costs and more time. If the larger ['final'] theatre is already standing, this temporary building can be used for other purposes. Then the aforesaid objective could be easily realized, and Parliament will surely aid the opponents of this temporary theatre to achieve their goal.

[. . .] I humbly ask Your Imperial and Royal Excellency: be so kind as to direct this matter, using your influence, in such a direction, also securing the collaboration of the city of Pest, that [. . .] the theatre be built as soon as possible, and the Estates of Pest County kept from an awkward predicament. May I also request this so that I may thereby receive a gratification far beyond my hopes and merits for my long and not insubstantial efforts. [. . .]

### *Parliament agrees to support a national theatre*

While the Viceroy originally supported Széchenyi's plan and at one point even ordered a temporary stoppage of construction, he probably recognized the irreversibility of the situation. In his reply of 31 October he permitted the construction of the theatre building with the stipulation that it be regarded as a temporary edifice. If this controversy achieved anything, it made the country conscious of the importance of having a national theatre. Also, the victory of the county asserted the role of the reform-minded middle and lower nobility who constituted the government of the counties, foreshadowing their future importance for national development, such as the War of Independence of 1848–9.

It took two years to finish construction of the theatre. On 2 August 1836 Parliament issued Act XLI in which it finally adopted the programme promoting the cause of the National Theatre while regarding the one under construction as a temporary institution; and preferred public donations to the contribution of the counties.

## 191 Parliamentary Act XLI funding the National Theatre, 2 August 1836

Kádár, vol. 2 (1940), p. 63. [The full text is translated there with insignificant contractions.]

The Estates of the Realm recognize the positive influence of a well-established theatre on the advancement of the nation, the refinement of the language and the resultant heightening of morality; therefore, they bring the following decision regarding the national theatre to be erected in Pest:

The deputation delegated to the matter of the bridge to be constructed between Buda and Pest has been instructed [. . .] to develop plans for a splendid national theatre, work out the necessary budget for this; and call on the patriots by official as well as direct channels for donations. If enough money can be collected, the deputation shall erect the Hungarian theatre on the plot of land selected for this purpose [. . .] by the Imperial Royal Archduke, Steward Palatine of the state. Yet, if it does not achieve the desired success, the deputation should make a recommendation at the next national assembly as to the most effective method of achieving this national desire.

### *Competition for the administration of the theatre*

The Theatre Committee of the county now sat down to face the practicalities of a working theatre. One of these was the management and directorship of the theatre, for which the general assembly of Pest County announced a competition.

## 192 General Assembly of Pest County advertises a competition for running the theatre, 1 April 1837

Kádár, vol. 2 (1940), pp. 64–7.

The deputation which supervises the construction of the theatre and generally sees to theatrical matters reports: that they feel it necessary to decide in advance how and by whom the theatre should be directed in order to serve its intended purpose. After deliberation on the matter by all sides, the deputation announced that the best way to accomplish this would be to announce a competition. [. . .]

As to the nature of the candidate, the deputation decided that only two types of person need be ruled out: those who at present are directors of similar institutions either in Pest or Buda; and for the present, Hungarian actors. The former because, although it is difficult to deny that he who directs a similar institution here has many more resources at his disposal than someone else and might thereby aid our institution as well, it is also certain that if he wants to, he also possesses an equal or even greater weapon for the destruction or at least for the complete paralysis of this institution. This is natural, since in a city where the Hungarian population is much smaller than the German-speaking one, and where for the entertainment of the latter there already exists a long-standing theatre which rivals almost any other institution in Europe, the Hungarian theatre can be maintained only by the most persistent, continuous striving for perfection. It follows that the Hungarian theatre will be competing with the German theatre. However, if the Hungarian theatre gets into the hands of a German proprietor, this competition is not even conceivable, and it is immaterial to him whether one of the theatres – we can guess which one – always stays closed.

As for the Hungarian actors, the deputation believes that their exclusion at this time is not only necessary but also natural since there is not one among them in their present condition who is suited to the greatness of the task, which is to provide dignity to this extensive metropolitan theatre which, even in its opulence, requires preparations incomparable to those of the rural theatres.

On the other hand, whoever the candidate be, the deputation deems it necessary that a permanent theatrical committee be named to maintain constant supervision over the candidate in artistic matters without influencing the directorship of the theatre in any other respect. It should be so because the goal of the Estates of the County in building a Hungarian theatre was not only that the Hungarian residents, who until now had to go to German theatres nightly for the sake of amusement, should now receive the same in Hungarian, but also and especially, that Thalia and our nation's artists should help one another, hand in hand, towards the great goal of perfection. That is why this artistic committee is needed to prevent this important and general interest from falling victim to any specific entrepreneur's individual interest. [. . .]

### *The County Assembly ratifies the joint-stock company*

In agreement with the parliamentary decree, on 14 June 1837 the county assembly approved the formation of a shareholders' company, accepted the constitution of this company and entrusted it with the directorship of the theatre. These decrees yield interesting insights into the way in which politics and cultural necessity converge.

## 193 County Assembly's decrees on the National Theatre, 14 June 1837

Kádár, vol. 2 (1940), pp. 71–3.

That deputation which deals with the matter of the Hungarian theatre of Pest reports that the deadline for the rental of the theatre, which was set for 3 April of this year according to the deputation, and for 1 May, by the decision of the county, was not met, and no candidate has applied. At the same time, the principle has been declared by which the county will not take the directorship of the theatre upon itself. [. . .] The particular conclusion was reached that the enthusiasm of the county's estates for the establishment of this theatre did not set the goal merely that there be a place where the resident and visiting Hungarian-speakers of the two royal cities may be able to get in Hungarian that nightly entertainment which hitherto they have been able to get in German. No doubt, this is a primary goal of any theatrical institution; however, the theatre [of Pest] was also supposed to be a stepping-stone towards the artistic and financial advancement of the performing profession. In consideration of this goal, the deputation found [. . .] the formation of an association the best and most suitable means. For this reason the following have formed a shareholders' company by signing a number of 40 pengő-forint-shares:[1] Deputy County Head, Gábor Földváry – 10; Count Gedeon Ráday – 10; Baron Antal Laffert – 10; Miklós Jankovich – 51; Count Sámuel Teleky – 10; András Fáy – 2½; Sándor Ilkey – 10; Péter Benyovszky – 2; Ferenc Nedetzky – 2; Ferenc Steinbach – 2; and Móric Szentkirályi – 2. [. . .]

The assembled Estates [. . .] have already been assured of the correctness both of the plan and of the means of execution by the enthusiasm of the gentlemen who form the company. Consequently, the Estates released the theatre, with all its stage properties, costumes and library, to the disposal of the shareholders' company, from 1 August of this year [1837] to Easter of 1841. The delegation in charge of the advancement of the Hungarian language was instructed that it should direct its attention to the Hungarian theatre as well and should inform the county about the theatre from time to time. Otherwise, that suggestion of the deputation that the district administrators invite the inhabitants of the county to buy shares, and likewise approach the noble counties and other municipalities, having been approved, it was ordered that subscription forms be sent to the district administrators and also to every noble county and to other municipalities.

[1] Approximately £92 sterling today.

*The National Theatre opens*

From the documents it appears as if the years 1835–7 had been full of victory and progress. Actually the county bore the mounting expenses alone, and construction was repeatedly threatened with cessation. The official contribution of the city of Pest was sequestered by Széchenyi for his planned theatre which eventually failed to materialize; the guilds of the city, however, made direct, supplemental contributions to the theatre. In the spring and summer of 1837, the Hungarian ensemble in the Palace Theatre of Buda had to leave the city as the building's new German lessor did not allow further performances. Yet the country was full of expectation by the time the National Theatre was opened on 22 August 1837, under the unassuming name the Hungarian Theatre of Pest. The prelude was a poetic fantasy by the great Romantic poet Mihály Vörösmarty (1800–55) entitled *Árpád ébredése* (*Árpád's Awakening*, about the renowned conqueror and founder of Hungary). It was followed by *Belizar* (*Belisarius*, 1828), the greatest success of Eduard von Schenk (1788–1841), a notoriously conservative Bavarian politician, whose eclectic and epigonistic poetic works were as classical as they were Romantic. Because of the continued shortage of representative Hungarian dramas, the need to perform insignificant imports like Schenk's drama dominated the theatre for years to come.

## 194a Exterior of the National Theatre, built in 1837

Reproduced in Rédey (1937), opp. p. 97.

## 194b Interior of the National Theatre seen from the stage

Reproduced in Rédey (1937), opp. p. 97.

## 194c Directors' report to the shareholders, 6 June 1838

Kádár, vol. 2 (1940), pp. 84–9.

In two days it will have been a year since the shareholders' company, formed for the maintenance of the Hungarian theatre which they had taken over from the honourable and noble Pest County, elected and entrusted us with the direction of this theatre at their first general meeting held on 8 June of last year. Although the goal set for us was promising, and upon our first burst of enthusiasm also seemed easily attainable since it served the national interest, yet, for the same reason, it was also overly ambitious and the road to this goal went untrodden. We realized the unfamiliarity of our task only when at our first step we ran into unforeseen obstacles.

The task was to transform into an enduring entity the newborn Hungarian theatre which had been struggling with every conceivable difficulty from its inception. In Pest, at that! where the majority of the inhabitants are not Hungarian. In Pest, where a German theatre, advanced in many respects, albeit perhaps not satisfying the higher requirement of dramatic art, has been flourishing for a long time and has been able to choose suitable actors from the whole of Germany where excellent actors abound.

Aware that in our position, without a real knowledge or grasp of our circumstances, it was not advisable to leap ahead unless we meant to miss our target, we considered before all else the date for starting the enterprise and those tools which would be needed. The opening of the theatre was set for 22 August, and therefore between the intellectual conception of the enterprise and its realization there were barely two and a half months. The necessities were: actors, orchestra, a repertoire to meet the expectation of the cultured audience of Pest (who could not have been satisfied with plays performed on smaller rural stages, which were mostly bad translations), scores, instruments, a collection of costumes, scenery, staff and a director to oversee all of these expeditiously.

The start of every theatre's season is Easter. As [. . .] the best Hungarian actors were engaged at the [. . .] theatre of Buda, which, since the theatre has had a German lessor, had been performing at Székesfehérvár, we could not count on any actors, and the pressing need could be filled only by inviting a few better-known actors, already contracted by other theatres, as guests. Assembling the orchestra, obtaining the musical scores and the instruments, all of which were lacking, was even harder. [. . .]

It goes without saying how small a selection of performable plays was available to us: anybody familiar with the state of our dramatic literature – which was at that time much poorer than it is now – knows this well. Under such circumstances, then, to speak metaphorically, Minerva had to be born armed and ready for battle. Nor was it an easy task to procure non-existent requisites and assemble dispersed components [so as to create a functioning theatre]. Therefore, it must be admitted it took more than a little determination for Mr József Bajza,[1] in answer to our request, to assume the exhausting (even for one who has no other occupation) role of director. Because of his familiarity with the field of native literature, he was the one we wished to win for this institution since its goal is to disseminate national language and culture.

Nevertheless, the initial trials and tribulations of the struggle are now forgotten, since, despite all these obstacles, on 22 August the theatre did open with the prologue *Árpád's Awakening*, written for this occasion by Vörösmarty, our poet laureate. Since then, excepting the period 13 March to 16 April, when our theatre was also sorely afflicted by the sorrowful days,[2] we have been holding regular performances.

[. . .] What were the results? Briefly, we can submit the following: at the beginning we could perform only twenty-five shows monthly, and only drama, because the small number of actors and the poverty of the repertoire did not allow an increase in that number. We also believed that the audience would take these circumstances into account; and we hoped that patriotism, the novelty of the institution and better acoustics would, for at least a year until we settled our affairs to some extent, compensate for the lack of that variety of dramas, musicals and dance performances which they had enjoyed at the German theatre. We built this hope on the fact that most of the boxes were soon bought by subscribers. Experience, however, showed us after a few days that our reckoning was groundless, since there were very few same-day ticket buyers and subscribers for the pit stalls (who constitute the largest revenue; nay, the sole source of income, for any theatre); while requests for new plays and musical performances were all the more frequent.

We were daily eye- and ear-witnesses to all of this. If we were not to shut our eyes deliberately, plug our ears and deceive ourselves into a state of pleasant bemusement that the audience, solely out of patriotism, would be willing to pay the price of admission to our theatre to be bored daily for at least two hours, while only a few hundred steps away in the German theatre they might enjoy ever new delights, we had to provide various ways and means of arousing the interest of the audience in our theatre. One of these means, we thought, would be to provide musicals with Hungarian singers comprised partly of our own company and partly invited from elsewhere; and to ask foreign artists to appear on our stage as well – if not in the entire play, at least in a few scenes. [. . .]

[1] József Bajza (1804–58), poet, creator of modern Hungarian theatrical criticism, twice director of the National Theatre (1837–8, 1847–8). Some of his major writings (notably *Szózat a pesti magyar színház ügyében* ['In the matter of the Hungarian theatre of Pest', 1839]) are regarded as pioneering studies on the sociology of theatre.

[2] An allusion to a devastating flood of the Danube in 1838.

### *The ongoing crises of the National Theatre*

While the ambitions of Pest County played an indisputable role in the establishment of the Hungarian Theatre, the inexperience, both theatrical and financial, of the directors actually led to trouble. By 1840, the theatre was deeply in crisis. In that year, Parliament approved Act XLIV which declared the Hungarian Theatre of Pest to be the Hungarian National Theatre (as of 8 August). Even so, years passed before the National Theatre lived up to its name, and decades before the competing German language disappeared from the stages of the united twin cities of Budapest. For almost half a century, the National Theatre also performed musical dramas. The second permanent Hungarian theatre of the capital, the People's Theatre (Népszínház), which opened in 1875, lured away several popular actors and actresses, along with that part of the public which took pleasure mostly in the traditional light and folksy musicals called 'popular plays' (*népszínmű*). With the opening of the Royal Hungarian Opera in 1884, the National Theatre became an entirely dramatic performing institution.

As an epilogue to the history of the Hungarian National Theatre, which is itself full of ironies, one should be aware of the ambivalence that authorities at different levels demonstrated towards this institution also in its later years. The National Theatre was originally intended as a temporary building; by the turn of the century, its structure and technical apparatus deteriorated to unacceptable standards. In 1908, the government ordered the theatre to move into the building of the People's Theatre (which, after its initial success, lost its popularity and was near bankruptcy) – until a final structure, worthy of its name, could be erected. The original building was consequently demolished. The First World War thwarted the plan to accomplish a permanent and respectable edifice, and the National Theatre operated at its 'temporary' and far from ideal location for more than fifty years. In 1965, under the pretext of building the Budapest subway and re-developing a busy intersection nearby, the government decided to tear down the building. The National Theatre moved into the renovated chamber theatre (built in 1897 and operated under the name Hungarian Theatre [Magyar Színház] until the Second World War) – a most unpretentious edifice squeezed between the fork of two side streets, where it has been operating ever since – 'temporarily,' of course.

# *Rumania, 1818–1852*

Edited by BOGDAN MISCHIU

## INTRODUCTION

By 1859, when the Danubian Principalities of Wallachia and Moldavia united to form Rumania, large subsidized theatres had already been established at both Bucharest, the capital of Wallachia, and Jassy (Iaşi), the capital of Moldavia. It was in these two cities that, roughly at the same time, the Rumanian national theatre emerged.

## I EARLY RUMANIAN-LANGUAGE PERFORMANCES IN BUCHAREST, 1818–19

### *Bucharest's first season*

Opened in 1818, when a clubhouse located at Cişmeaua Roşie was converted into a permanent theatre, the city's first theatrical season was recorded by William Wilkinson, the British consul-general at the time.

### 195 An Englishman describes the city's first theatrical season, 1818–19

William Wilkinson: *An account of the principalities of Wallachia and Moldavia* (London: Longman, Hurst, Rees, Orme and Brown, 1820); reprint edn (New York: Arno Press, 1971), pp. 140–1.

Last year [1818] a company of German actors[1] came to Bukorest, and after some performances, were encouraged to establish a regular theatre. They gave German operas, and comedies translated into Wallachian, and the first two or three months they attracted crowds from all the classes, who, without exception, seemed to have taken a true liking to the new sort of amusement; but latterly the charm of novelty had begun to wear off, and the Boyars [the hereditary nobility] of the first order, with some of the principal foreign residents, seemed to be the only persons disposed to support the continuance of the establishment, more with a view of making it a place of general union of the society than from the attractions of the stage.

[1] This company was headed by Johann Gerger of Brasov, a German actor and theatre manager of considerable fame in his native Transylvania, where, in 1815, he gave his first documented performance in Rumanian with Kotzebue's *Die gefährliche Nachbarschaft* on the stage of Brasov's *Theater in dem Redoutensaal*. In Bucharest, where he performed regularly for two seasons (1818–20), he attracted attention with his open-air production of Schiller's *Die Räuber* in a wooded area on the outskirts of the city.

### *The first Rumanian production*

In 1819, the theatre at Cişmeaua Roşie has its first documented Rumanian production: students at St Sava college staged Euripides' *Hecuba*, translated by A. Nănescu, with Ion Heliade Rădulescu (1802–72) in the title role. Poet, translator, essayist and politician, he was one of the most important and controversial figures in nineteenth-century Rumania. Director and treasurer of the Philharmonic Society [see **198**], where he taught literature and mythology, Heliade is generally considered to have been the most effective promoter of the idea of a national Rumanian theatre in Wallachia.

The performance opened with a prologue, the text of a dramatic tableau called *Saturn*, by Ion Văcărescu (1792–1863), which later became known as the artistic credo of the early Rumanian theatrical promoters and practitioners. These are its most famous stanzas.

## 196 Praise to the venture in Văcărescu's prologue to *Hecuba*, 1819

*Curierul românesc* [*Rumanian Courier*] 17 January 1830, quoted in I. Massoff, *Teatrul românesc* (*The Rumanian Theatre*), vol. 1 (Bucharest: Editura pentru literatură, 1961–74), p. 518.

I gave you the theatre, guard it closely,
As a shrine for the muse
You'll be famous for it shortly
With far-reaching news.

The vices it will defy
And the mind it will sharpen,
Your mother tongue 'twill beautify
With words Rumanian.

## 197 Prince Alexandru Şuţu's decree founding an Office of Theatre to exercise censorship, 8 November 1819

D. Ollănescu: *Teatrul la români* [*Theatre in Rumania*], edited by C. Dumitrescu (Bucharest: Eminescu, 1981), p. 115–16.

Our most honourable and highborn boyar and Great Spatar[1] Iacovachi Rizo, Our best beloved! The founding of public theatres has, after much research and political consideration, been determined to be a very useful thing for the nation, for the theatre succeeds in obliterating evil-doing. Dramatic presentation has proved to be a school for good morals, commensurate in its zeal and power with its endeavour to combat wickedness and make virtue triumph, showing us how to distinguish between vice and virtue. Comedy exposes evil through laughter [. . .] while tragedy brings about the good through the miraculous. The pupil in such a school not only hears but sees with his own eyes that which he must say and do, and finally becomes persuaded, or better yet, is forced to admit that it is more seemly to fail with honour, so that one's contemporaries and posterity bewail one's spiritual torments, than to prevail by dishonesty and to laugh.

That is what *Teatrus* is like when the selection of plays is carefully made. Theatre does indeed compensate for the shortcomings of the law, which cannot alone root out all wrongdoing, nor can it achieve one's perfect education. But when the selection of plays is poorly made, they abuse the law, become a school for laxity and bad habits and defile civic custom.

Consequently, since it may happen at one time or another that pernicious doctrines penetrate the theatre of Bucharest, owing to the lack of an official to supervise and censor the selection of plays, We, in accordance with Our princely duty, with good intent, appoint You by this Our decree and order to summon before you the German representative of melodrama, comedy and German tragedy[2] and the head of the Greek dramatic association[3] and, informing them of the establishment of this Office, announce to them that: whichever dramas may be libellous to religion, the state and public morality are to be prohibited from performance in the theatre of Bucharest and at the fairs, while all others are permitted for the use and entertainment of the citizenry.

The respective theatre directorships are responsible for informing this Office in advance which performances they plan to give, so that these can be censored in due time. Do so and may God preserve you in good health.

[1] Head of the police (in Wallachia).

[2] Johann Gerger.

[3] Because of its nationalistic and anti-despotic character, the Greek theatre at Cişmeaua Roşie was particularly influential on early Rumanian theatrical endeavours. In fact, Costache Aristia (1800–80), the leading Greek actor at Cişmeaua Roşie, later became one of the principal founders of the Rumanian theatre. [See **201**]

## II THE PHILHARMONIC SOCIETY OF BUCHAREST, 1834–7

### *The Philharmonic Society is founded*

First enunciated in Article 7 of the Statutes of the Literary Society of 1827, the idea of founding a Rumanian national theatre was quickly embraced by the majority of the city's intelligentsia. Finally, on 20 January 1834, Ion Cîmpineanu and Ion Heliade Rădulescu took positive action and opened Wallachia's first conservatory, the Philharmonic Society. Cîmpineanu (1798–1863), a nationalist politician, was the depository of the Society's statutes, and it was at his residence that the members held their first meetings.

## 198 Goals of the Philharmonic Society, 1834

*Curierul românesc* [*Rumanian Courier*] 7 January 1834, quoted in Ollănescu (1981), p. 127.

Most of the boyars and other citizens, touched by the truth demonstrated over so many centuries that theatre, hand in hand with public education, is the surest and most straightforward way of uprooting bad habits and forming the taste of a nation, all in one breath and with one accord across all classes, have begun to express their great wish that a means be devised to secure a national theatre over the course of time. Thus, it has been deemed appropriate to form a fellowship or Philharmonic Society, each of whose members will make an annual contribution in order to establish a school of literature, declamation and vocal music, the purpose of this school being the training of young men and women in order, on the one hand, to make a theatre possible and, on the other, to establish and disseminate vocal music in the Principality. There were enough of those willing to be called patrons and, owing to their generosity and efforts, a sum of money has already been collected with which to cover all these expenses.

### *The first public performance*

On 29 August 1834, the students at the Philharmonic took their first 'public examination' by producing Voltaire's *Mahomet, ou Le fanatisme* at the newly built Momolo Theatre. This wood and plaster playhouse had been built the previous year by the Italian cook and entrepreneur Ieronim Momolo, who first rented it to the German opera impresario Theodor Müller, on condition that the latter provide all the furnishings. For nearly two decades the Momolo was the only theatre in the city – Cişmeaua Roşie had been destroyed by fire in 1825. It is interesting to note that, perhaps by coincidence, Momolo built his theatre on the same spot on which the Diorama of 1812 had stood, on the property of Iordache Slătineanu (who in 1797 had translated the first play in the Rumanian language, Metastasio's *Achille in Sciro*).

## 199 Heliade-Rădulescu's speech at the first 'examination', 29 August 1834

*Curierul românesc* [*Rumanian Courier*] 39 (1834), quoted in Ollănescu (1981), pp. 135–6.

[. . .] it will be a long time before the world gets a second Talma, if the theatre is not made a career for young people and if the one who decides to defy all prejudice is considered by society as a political pariah, a shameless buffoon, when hoping to obtain his or her sustenance by the good will of audiences.

If, however, a state-endowed directorship is set up as well as an office to collect the income of the theatre so that the actors can be paid as government employees for the formation of the national language and public morality, with all the rights possessed by other employees, then we shall see young men and women of talent and education, fearless of the venomous tongue of blind prejudice, arise on the stage and establish a national theatre that will serve as a model to other peoples as well.

## 200 Statutes of the Philharmonic Society, 27 October 1834

Ollănescu (1981), p. 140.

ARTICLE 6

[. . .] the Society, with the monies collected from the patrons and other sources, shall conduct a school for boys and girls in the following manner:

(i) Appointments shall be made for one teacher of declamation, one of vocal and another of instrumental music, one of dance and fencing, and one of the Rumanian language [. . .]

(ii) Room and board shall be provided for as many girls as is deemed necessary, free of charge, with the food, clothing and tuition paid from the Society's treasury.

(iii) For as long as they remain enrolled, the students shall receive a small monthly cash stipend, and for this, both boys and girls shall certify in writing upon graduation that they will remain and work as actors in Wallachia in conformity with the regulations to be adopted regarding their duties and rights and regarding their salary.

### *Student performances*

From 1835 to 1837, when political suspicion and rowdy personal disputes put an end to the Philharmonic, the students performed regularly at the Momolo. One of their successes was recorded in a local newspaper.

## 201 Review of a student performance, 1835

*Curierul românesc* [*Rumanian Courier*] 73 (1835) in Ollănescu (1981), p. 372.

On Monday, 11 March 1835, the students at the Philharmonic Society staged for the first time Molière's comedy *Le Mariage forcé*, translated into Rumanian by Mr [Costache] Aristia, their teacher of declamation, the translator of Alfieri's immortal tragedies *Brutus*, *Virginia* and *Saul*. The speech of each character and the flavour of the comedy, adapted to the genius of our tongue, were very appropriate. The students, each and every one of them, played their parts rather well, and, despite some justified criticism which, as beginners, they were to expect, the pit was very satisfied and, at the request of many, the performance will be given again next month, for a second time. I wish, however, that the students, in order better to satisfy the zeal of the regulars as well as the innocent taste of the occasional spectators, would, as much as possible, use fewer gestures and not employ their facial muscles for so much caricature, which cannot be natural. The same little piece of advice can be given to the older actors as well: but our dilettantes, because they are still students, should gladly learn a few lessons early on from the audience too, which is the best teacher and appraiser of an actor.

## III ESTABLISHING A STATE THEATRE IN BUCHAREST, 1840–52

*First steps towards a state theatre*

The first legal step towards the establishment of a state-subsidized national theatre was taken in 1840, when, on the initiative of Heliade, Wallachia's General Assembly requested in a petition submitted to Prince Alexandru D. Ghica, ruler of Wallachia 1834–42, (who later assented to it) 'the establishment of a project for the building and operation of a national theatre and for a repertoire for the education of the youth'.[1] The nature of the project made Ghica's successor as Prince, Gheorghe Bibescu (1804–73), overlook cost overruns as becomes apparent from this Resolution.

[1] Quoted in Ollănescu (1981), p. 196.

### 202 The Prince of Wallachia resolves to overlook cost overruns, 15 August 1843

G. Potra: *Din Bucureştii de altădată* [*Out of the Bucharest of Yore*] (Bucharest: Editura ştiinţifică şi enciclopedică, 1981), p. 305.

We would have liked the theatre to be founded with only the 13,000 galbeni[1] which will be allocated for this building until the end of 1845 – and again, for this purpose, we summon up all the zeal and competence of the Commission[2] to economize as much as possible – but, being aware of the progress of the work, of the absolute need to add the sum of 7,000 galbeni which is the deficit of the budget of the theatre until the year 1845, this will undoubtedly be appropriated, either from the City Hall funds if possible or from the extraordinary fund of the treasury. The building of the theatre in the city of Bucharest is a matter which concerns not only the citizens of this city but also of the whole Rumanian nation, through the positive influence it will have on good mores and the perfection of the Rumanian language and the development of Rumanian literature. The Commission shall therefore immediately proceed with the preparatory works so that by next spring the construction of the theatre may begin.

[1] At the time the annual salary of a civil servant was approximately 100 galbeni.
[2] The governmental commission in charge of the national theatre project.

*A resident troupe is organized*

In 1845, Costache Caragiale (1815–77), a former student at the Philharmonic, established at the Momolo the city's first resident troupe to include Rumanian plays in its repertoire. These plays were for the most part farces, vaudevilles and satirical comedies. (Serious drama did not become popular with Rumanian playwrights until after the success of B.P. Haşdeu's historical drama *Răzvan and Vidra* [*Răzvan şi Vidra*, 1867].)

Costache Caragiale, uncle of Rumania's foremost dramatist Ion Luca Caragiale, is one of the principal founders of the Rumanian theatre and the only student of the Philharmonic who, upon its closing in 1837, pursued a theatrical career in Rumania. A rather pathetic actor but an innovative producer, he was also one of the most gifted dramatists of his day; his best remembered work is the satirical comedy *A Soirée in Suburbia* (*O soirée la mahala*, 1847), which is also the first Rumanian play to require multiple settings.

A year after Caragiale founded his troupe, Cezar Bolliac (1813–81), perhaps the foremost dramatic critic of the time, commented on this phenomenon. Bolliac was also the author of the first tragedy in Rumanian, *Matilda* (1835), inspired by a novel by Sophie Cottin. Aristia considered the play lacking in action and declined to produce it, which led Bolliac, in a moment of depression, to destroy the manuscript.

## 203 Cezar Bolliac praises original drama, 1846

*Curierul românesc* [*Rumanian Courier*] 27 (1846), quoted in Simion Alterescu, ed.: *Istoria teatrului în România* [*History of the theatre in Rumania*], vol. 1 (Bucharest: Editura Academiei RSR, 1965–73) p. 230, and Ollănescu (1981), p. 388.

The influence of the national theatre is also making itself felt in our literature; *Mr Iorgu from Sadagura*, *A good education*, and *A sly servant*,[1] are three entirely original plays that we saw on the Rumanian stage in our capital. If we are to judge by the progress dramatic art has made in our country and the improvement shown by these plays, we tend to believe that dramatic art will some day become the most significant part of our literature.

[1] *Cuconu Iorgu de la Sadagura*, 1844, one of Vasile Alecsandri's most successful comedies, contrasts the Westernizer Iorgu with a number of conservative figures [see **210**]. *O bună educaţie*, 1845, a light comedy by Costache Bălăcescu. *Sluga isteaţă*, 1845, one of Costache Caragiale's minor comedies.

*The Great Theatre opens*

Because of the intervening Revolution of 1848, it was only in 1852 that the 1,000-seat Great Theatre (renamed the National Theatre in 1877) opened its doors to the public. The event was given enthusiastic coverage in the press of the day.

## 204 The opening of the Great Theatre, 31 December 1852

*Vestitorul românesc* [*Rumanian Herald*] (January 1853), p. 6; reprinted in Potra (1981), pp. 307–8.

On Wednesday the 31st [of December] at 8 o'clock p.m. the solemn opening of the new theatre took place [. . .] The Inauguration was made with the performance of the play *Zoé, or The Loan of a Lover*[1] by the Rumanian actors, and a number of arias and a trio from various operas sung by the top artists of the Italian troupe under the directorship of Mr Papanicola. [. . .]

At about a quarter to eight, His Exalted Majesty our Prince[2] arrived and was greeted by the entire audience with the most enthusiastic acclaim; at once the orchestra played a national tune which was listened to with true satisfaction by the spectators and which made their Rumanian hearts throb with joy.

Whereupon the curtain rose and the Rumanian actors played their respective parts with an art which did honour to the leader of the company, [Costache] Caragiale.

1 *Zoé ou L'amant prêté* by Scribe and Mélesville (1830).

2 Barbu Dmitrie Ştirbeiu or Ştirbey (1799–1869), brother of Gheorghe Bibescu, was ruler of Wallachia 1849–58, when he worked for Rumanian unity.

## 205a A description of the theatre building, 1853

*Bukarester Deutsche Zeitung* [*Bucharest German Times*] 2 (1853); reprinted in Ollănescu (1981), p. 384, and in Potra (1981), p. 309.

[The theatre] is built in a noble and truly artistic style; its proportions are harmonious and its distinguished simplicity is stately. If the general appearance seems from the outside somewhat sombre, on entering the building one is pleasantly surprised. The elegance, resplendent light and joy which spring from every corner of the playhouse seem to intensify one's pleasure and are a proof not only of the architect's competence and love of beauty, but also those of the committee appointed by the government for the supervision of the construction. As to the acoustics, again the theatre seems to be so well conceived that from any part of the auditorium one can hear admirably both speech and song on the stage.

The new theatre in Bucharest undoubtedly is one of the most beautiful theatres in Europe and a jewel of the capital. It has an orchestra with 338 stalls, divided into two categories, three tiers of boxes beautifully decorated and above them a larger and spacious gallery. The decorations are the work of Muhldorfer,[1] and were built along with the stage machinery, all at Mannheim; and the architect of the monument is Mr Heft of Vienna,[2] who made his honourable debut at this type of construction.

[1] His name also appears as Mülldorfer (according to Massoff) or Michldorger (according to Potra); a German industrialist, whose son supervised the training of stage technicians at the Great Theatre.

[2] Following the excellent reception of his work in Bucharest, he was appointed head of Wallachia's Office of Architecture.

## 205b Contemporary engraving of the Great Theatre of Bucharest as it looked at the time of its completion in 1852

Alterescu (ed.) (1965–73), vol. 2, p. 20.

## IV THE THEATRE IN JASSY, 1832–46

### 206 Opening of the first permanent playhouse, the Théâtre des variétés, 1832

*Albina româneasca* [*Rumanian Bee*], 74 and 97 (1832); in T. Burada: *Istoria teatrului în Moldova* [*History of the theatre in Moldavia*] (edited by I. Chiţimia) (Bucharest: Minerva, 1975), p. 91.

The wish of the nobility and the cultivated public in this capital to have a theatre will be fulfilled. The troupe led by Messrs Fouraux[1] is in charge of this enterprise, and the conversion work proceeds so smoothly at Mr Talpan's houses that the opening of the theatre could take place as soon as mid-October.

Neculai Şuţu,[2] one of the most enlightened and art-loving boyars in Moldavia, is responsible for the inspection and supervision of the theatre as well as for the censorship of the plays to be presented. [. . .]

Among the new and useful public institutions our capital can be proud of is the establishment of a theatre, which is a school where, while amusing itself, the public learns good things that greatly influence mores and character-building.

This theatre is elliptical in shape, with three tiers of boxes and a gallery artfully adorned. The sets and decorations were painted by Mr Livaditi,[3] who drew on the curtain all the muses carrying out their respective activities.

[1] The French brothers Jean and Baptiste Fouraux or Fourreaux established Jassy's first resident troupe, with which they presented, in French, variety shows, vaudevilles and operas.

[2] A member of one of Moldavia's most distinguished families, he occupied various positions in the Moldavian government. For two decades (with interruptions), he was responsible for the administration of the country's theatrical matters.

[3] Niccolò Livaditti (1804–58), painter and scene designer born in Trieste, Italy. A member of the Carbonari and a friend of Giuseppe Mazzini, he came to Rumania as a political refugee following the failure of the Piedmontese revolution of 1821. In 1832, he settled in Jassy, where he became the principal founder of Moldavian scene design.

*Competition from French troupes*

In 1836, a Philharmonic Dramatic Conservatory was established in Jassy on the model of the Bucharest Philharmonic Society [see **198**]; its activities were less intense and more conservative than those of its precursor, and it closed in 1839 owing to financial difficulties.

In a letter addressed to Gheorghe Asachi (1788–1869), director of the Philharmonic Dramatic Conservatory, Costache Negruzzi (1808–68),[1] examined the principal difficulty encountered by the emerging Rumanian theatre.

[1] A classic of Moldavian literature, he wrote one of the most successful comedies of the century, *The muse from Burdujeni* (*Muza de la Burdujeni*, 1851). Between 1840–2 he was joint director of the Jassy Variety Theatre with Alecsandri and Kogălniceanu [see **209**].

## 207 Negruzzi voices the problem of competition from French troupes, 21 July 1838.

Burada (1975), p. 168.

I must tell you, my good sir, that we have a very debauched character. We like to ape foreigners and defame ourselves. Therefore, we have been in turn Turcophiles, Græcophiles or God knows what else; now, by God's mercy, we are Francophiles, but we may soon cross the Channel in a hot-air balloon and then you shall see us become Anglophiles.

When, in 1832, the Fouraux brothers established a theatre here, do you remember how we crowded at its gates? How we laughed when we saw Pierrot eat the candle and how we gasped when Harlequin's dummy was shot from a wooden cannon? You know how the theatre resounded with applause when Mme Baptiste[1] was doing the rope-dance called *Nec plus ultra*! But as soon as the vaudeville *Derlindindin* was presented, we would see neither Harlequin nor Pierrot, nor the dance called *Nec plus ultra* for that matter; we demanded vaudevilles. The poor French actors had to oblige us. Oh, wasn't that wonderful! A few little verses sung to the cadence of a galopade made us happy. The little air 'Te souviens-tu' made us cry. By watching the French grenadier on the stage, we became Bonapartists [. . .]

In such a state of exaltation, we forgot we were in Jassy, and we started craving operas and monstrous melodramas. We killed Scribe as we had killed Harlequin. How could anyone then think that we might like a Rumanian theatre?

[1] Baptiste Fouraux's wife.

### *First Rumanian troupe in Jassy*

The first major inroad into French control of the Jassy stage took place in late 1839 when the Wallachian Costache Caragiale established the city's first Rumanian troupe.

## 208 Kogălniceanu[1] describes the first Rumanian troupe. 1840

*Dacia literară* [*Literary Dacia*], vol. 1 (1840) in I. Berlogea and G. Muntean, eds: *Pagini din istoria gîndirii teatrale românești* [*Pages from the history of Rumanian theatrical thought*] (Bucharest: Meridiane, 1972), pp. 40–1.

Last winter at Jassy a society of Rumanian actors was formed under the directorship of one of its members [Costache Caragiale] in order to give a series of twelve Rumanian-language productions composed of comic pieces, melodramas and regular tragedies. The plan was grand but the execution poor. At the news of such an event, the public applauded and by its numerous presence at all performances showed how much it wanted a Rumanian stage. Various plays translated from the French and the German were presented. We are now at the tenth performance. An audience is never lacking, the applause is immeasurable; but, in our country, applause is not yet proof of the quality of the play or of the talent of the players. The spectators applaud because they are satisfied to have as little as that, without most of them asking themselves whether our theatre could improve further. [. . .] The plays are poorly chosen, cut and assembled; stage illusion is not observed; and since the players – if not all, then certainly most – act poorly, at least the sets and costumes ought to be beautiful and appropriate to the content of the plays; but this is entirely otherwise. Oftentimes one can notice the greatest anachronisms on stage, in all their absurdity; costumes and peoples separated by centuries meet each other in Rumanian productions. For instance, in *Les Fourberies de Scapin* one could see an hussar from the age of Napoleon, an elegant musketeer from the age of Molière and a coquette from our own day and age.

Messrs Caragiale, Pandeli and Jan[2] alone make the duration of the performance tolerable. Thus, it was with the greatest pleasure that we saw Mr Caragiale play *The Madman*.[3] His passionate and truthful acting enchanted us. We would crave only one thing more of him, namely more simplicity and more naturalness. We demand a lot of Mr Caragiale, but his talent gives us good reason to expect even more; therefore we are confident. [. . .]

The fact remains that the National Theatre can flourish; but in order to achieve this goal, all considerations of profit must be put aside. A desire for glory, a will for the good, and a great determination to make important sacrifices are also necessary. Only then will the Rumanian stage produce true art rather than shallow puppetry.

[1] Mihail Kogălniceanu (1817–91), politician and man of letters, the founder of modern literary criticism in Moldavia and the publisher of the country's first literary periodical, *Dacia literară* (*Literary Dacia*, 1840). He was the author of two comedies, *Two Women against One Man* (*Două femei împotriva unui bărbat*) and *The Happy Blind Man* (*Orbul fericit*), (both 1840, when he was appointed joint director of the Jassy Variety Theatre).

[2] Pandeli, a minor Moldavian actor, noted for his Moor Caidam in Caragiale's *Furiosul*. Jan remains obscure.

[3] *Furiosul*, a melodramatic comedy, adapted from Donizetti's *Il Furioso all'isola di San Domingo*, itself based on Cervantes's *Don Quixote*, was the most popular piece in Costache Caragiale's repertoire.

*Unification of French and Rumanian theatres*

In May 1840, the Moldavian government united the city's Rumanian and French theatres under a single subsidized directorship, whose members were Costache Negruzzi, Vasile Alecsandri and Mihail Kogălniceanu, perhaps the three most important cultural personalities of the time.

## 209 Contract of the first Rumanian theatrical directorate, 18 March 1840

Burada (1975), pp. 179–80.

Art. 1. The Government entrusts to Messrs Negruzzi, Alecsandri and Kogălniceanu the directorate of the French and Rumanian theatres for a period of four years beginning 15 May 1840.
Art. 2. The aforesaid entrepreneurs are hereby bound to make provision for a French troupe of dramatic artists. [. . .]
Art. 3. The entrepreneurs are also bound to make provision for a Moldavian troupe, whose size is to be left to their discretion. [. . .]
Art. 5. The theatrical repertory shall be composed of those plays which will have enjoyed the greatest success in the theatres of Paris. The censorship of the plays shall be conducted by the State Secretariat, except in cases when it shall be entrusted to any one of the entrepreneurs, who shall assume all responsibility.
Art. 6. Arrangements for performances shall be conducted in such a manner that those plays that have only one or two acts shall be prohibited from being produced more than once or twice during one subscription season, unless they are specifically requested. Those with more than two acts, as well as operas, shall be exempt from this regulation.
Art. 7. The set pieces and costumes entrusted to the entrepreneurs shall correspond to the subject of each play and shall always be in good condition. [. . .]
Art. 9. The Government shall grant the entrepreneurs an annual subsidy of 600 galbeni[1] for the French troupe and 200 galbeni for the Moldavian troupe. [. . .]
Art. 11. The entrepreneurs shall have the right to the proceeds of two winter subscriptions of 50 performances each, 100 performances altogether, of which 75 shall be French and 25 shall be Moldavian.

[1] See **202**, note 1.

## 210 Public attitudes to Rumanian theatre satirized in 1844

Vasile Alecsandri,[1] *Cuconu Iorgu de la Sadagura, sau Nepotu-i salba dracului* [*Mr Iorgu from Sadagura or A nephew is a limb of Satan*] (Jassy, 1844).

KIULAFOGLU [. . .] Where are you going?
IORGU I'm going to reserve a box for tonight at the National Theatre.
KIULAFOGLU Ha, ha, ha . . . At the Moldavian Theatre! . . . Don't you feel bad about the money you'll be throwing away to see some boys who don't even know how to speak . . . and to listen to some worthless plays?
IORGU If everyone thought as you do, sir, then the national theatre could never be established in this country; but, praise the Lord, there are people who know how to appreciate the vicissitudes of an emerging theatre such as ours; who are not ashamed to go to national plays and who, finally, showing forgiveness for the actors' mistakes, encourage them and provide them with the necessary support . . . Those people are worthy of all praise and the national theatre will always be grateful to them.
KIULAFOGLU All I know is that I haven't the courage to go and yawn for four hours for the sake of patriotism.
IORGU As for you, sir, the national theatre will leave you in peace to do as you please; on one condition though, that you too leave it in peace to pursue its career as best it can and do not criticize it blindly.

[1] Vasile Alecsandri (1821–90), Moldavia's foremost dramatist and a great lyric poet. Born at Bacău to a noble family, in 1840 he was appointed joint director of the Jassy Variety Theatre and came into prominence as the author of the most popular Rumanian play of the season *Farmazonul din Hîrlău* (*The Freemason from Hîrlău*), a comedy he wrote specially for Costache Caragiale. Two modern theatres have been named after him – the National Theatre in Jassy (in Rumania) and the Moldavian Musical-Dramatic Theatre at Bălţi (in Soviet Moldavia).

### *Censorship enforced*

Censorship was strictly enforced by the Prince of Moldavia, Mihail Sturza (1795–1884), who was incensed at the political liberties taken in the production of Alecu Russo's *Corn-factor Bucket or A Provincial goes to the National Theatre* (*Jicnicerul Vadră sau Un provincial la teatrul naţional*). This play, a satire on the popular violent melodramas of the time, is now lost. Russo (1819–59), its author, was confined like the actors, but to a different monastery (Soveja), and was later exiled because of his revolutionary activities.

Sturza issued the following Order to Nicu Ruset, the Governor of Bacău county.

## 211 Prince Mihail Sturza suppresses the play *Corn-factor Bucket*, 26 February 1846

Burada (1975), p. 269.

Because some of the actors at the national theatre, namely: Neculai Teodoru, Teodor Teodorini and Neculai Luchian[1] chose to ignore the duties assigned to their profession by delivering on the stage of the theatre phrases banned by the censor, which led to scandals and disruption of public order, contrary to the purpose of this establishment which pursues entirely moral goals, we could not overlook such impertinent behaviour. Having therefore decided to put them under lock and key at the Caşin monastery in the domain of our county so that they repent and desist, We hereby command that, as soon as the aforesaid individuals arrive at the said place escorted by guards, who shall entrust them to the abbot of the monastery, you shall arrange that they be closely watched and forced to fast and pray for the whole term they shall serve there, making certain at the same time not only that they are prevented from leaving the monastery but also that they are denied correspondence and visits, and after you settle these matters by mutual understanding with the abbot, you engage for the whole term of the detention of the aforesaid individuals at the monastery two capable and intelligent guards, commanding them, upon severe penalty, to keep an unswerving and vigilant eye on them, you yourself taking good care periodically to ensure that these things We ordain are strictly enforced.

[1] Teodoru (d. 1856), Moldavian actor who excelled in parts of overseers and yeomen; his early death was perceived as a great loss to the Moldavian stage.

Teodorini (1823–73), Moldavian actor and theatre manager trained first by Caragiale, then, more thoroughly, by Millo under whom he performed until 1852, when he joined Caragiale's company at the Great Theatre in Bucharest. He died in an insane asylum in Vienna and was buried there in an unmarked grave. Equally good in both comedy and tragedy, he was at his best in melodrama.

Luchian (1821–93), Moldavian comedian, trained at the Philharmonic-Dramatic Conservatory, then in Paris under Frédérick Lemaître; he made his debut in Jassy in 1844 and continued to play there until his death. Between 1856 and 1859 he served as director of the Great Theatre in Jassy. He was at his best in plays of Alecsandri, who, in 1862, wrote 'comic ditties' for him.

### *The Great Theatre opens*

Mihail Sturza, notorious in Rumanian history for his intolerance and corruption, is also remembered for having offered his house at Copou for Jassy's Great Theatre (Teatrul cel Mare).

## 212a The opening of the Great Theatre on 22 December 1846

*Albina românească* [*Rumanian Bee*] 102 (1846) in Burada (1975), p. 288.

The number of public buildings in our capital has been increased due to the establishment of the new theatre, which had to take place considering that the taste for theatrical performances had become a real need in our society.

Thanks to the generosity of the Government and to the measures and sacrifices of the directorship which was entrusted to Prince N. Şuţu and Mr M. Millo,[1] this construction was completed within the short space of six months.

An orchestra pit in the shape of an amphitheatre surrounded by three tiers of boxes and crowned with a gallery and a large stage, provides a beautiful auditorium, which is adorned with white columns, all tastefully gilded with arabesque motifs. All seats and benches are covered with red velvet, while the large chandelier which is of a novel design, sheds an abundance of light which, without hurting the eye, illuminates the whole theatre adequately.

[1] Matei Millo (1814–96), Moldavia's greatest nineteenth-century actor and a successful dramatist. Of a noble family, he made his debut in 1834 in the first Moldavian production at the *Théâtre des variétés*, Gheorghe Asachi's *The Moldavian Shepherds's Festival* (*Serbarea păstorilor moldoveni*), presented in honour of Pavel Kiselëv, the departing Russian Governor of the country; later appointed joint director of the Great Theatre. Short and stocky, he excelled in women's roles and made his greatest triumph as Lady Chiriţa, Alecsandri's most popular character, whom he is said to have interpreted with great naturalness. His most successful was the 'operetta-witchey', *Hîrca the Hag* (*Baba Hîrca*, 1848).

## 212b Contemporary engraving of the exterior view of the Great Theatre at Copou (Jassy) as it appeared before its destruction by fire in 1888

I. Massoff (1975), vol. 1, p. 577.

# *Russia, 1812–1898*

Edited by LAURENCE SENELICK

## INTRODUCTION

How national was the Russian theatre before the nineteenth century? The Russian word *narodny* can be translated as *national* but also means *popular, people's*, and even *folk*, depending on its context. The word was launched in the early nineteenth century by Pushkin's friend Prince Pëtr Vyazemsky, and Pushkin himself in an unfinished essay on *narodnost'*[1] argued that a truly national theatre in Russia should turn its back on the court and draw its inspiration from the public square and the marketplace.

30 August 1756 is the traditional date assigned to commemorate the foundation of a Russian public theatre, for that is when the Empress Elizabeth enjoined the Senate to subsidize a patent theatre in St Petersburg. The company was formed by combining the amateur dramatic society of the Cadet Corps with the semi-professional Yaroslavl' troupe headed by Fëdor Volkov, and placed under the direction of the Cadet dramatist A.P. Sumarokov. Previously, German, then French and Italian players had provided entertainments for a court which, by Petrine edicts, was compelled to attend on the sovereign and serve in the capital. The patent theatre was barely in existence three years when, owing to the financial difficulties that would prove the bane of most private theatrical enterprises in Russia, it was subsumed into the Imperial household. So the national theatre in St Petersburg became in essence a court entertainment, and Elizabeth's successor Catherine the Great lavished on the Imperial Theatre money, buildings and even plays from her own hand, always with an eye to winning herself a European reputation for enlightenment.

In the 'other capital', Moscow, a number of private enterprises sprang up, beginning with the Moscow University company in 1755. These were usually run by foreigners, such as the Italian impresario Giovanni-Battista Locatelli and the English showman Michael Maddox, ungrounded in Russian traditions. And the public was sharply divided between an educated aristocracy whose taste ran from neoclassical tragedy and comedy to sentimental drama in the European mode and a commonalty which sought its amusements in fairs, carnivals and pageants.

When Imperial charters of 1762 and 1785 released the nobility from much of its obligation to serve the State, it returned to its estates with an appetite for the kind of pleasures it had experienced in the capitals. Hence the proliferation of serf theatres, which ranged from the most sumptuous to the most slapdash. Staffed by bondsmen, they were primarily pastimes for the owner and his circle, although some proprietors opened their theatres to the public. Soviet commentators have made a great deal of the importance of the serf theatre to the development of a true public, but a problem that regularly faced provincial and capital troupes alike was the sparsity of spectators.

Catherine's heirs had no personal interest in the theatre, and so its control came into the hands of officialdom. Between 1790 and 1825, a gradual centralization of theatrical activity took place under the aegis of the Administration of the Imperial Theatres which had been founded in 1766, a centralization which was to result in a full-scale monopoly. The Administration held the monopoly on bill-printing and -posting from 1804. In 1806 the bulk of the theatrical talent in Moscow was conflated with the Imperial Theatres: this included the dramatic and operatic company from the 1,500-seat public Petrov theatre (formerly Maddox's, which was renamed when it re-opened in 1780), the ballet troupe from the Foundling Hospital, and the serf actors of the landowner Stolypin. Other serfs were sold by their masters into State service: becoming in essence civil servants, they gradually won manumission into a different kind of bondage. Even the few free-born actors were kept in administrative thrall, although permitted to have G. (Gospodin or Gospozha, Mr or Mrs) before their names on the playbills.[2] In 1807 a State Dramatic School opened in Moscow, and the following year, with the erection in Moscow of a new wooden playhouse, private theatres were forbidden to employ actors of the court theatres, effectively reducing their quality.

In the decade before Borodino the only playhouses in St Petersburg were State-controlled, among them the Kushlëv Theatre rented to a German troupe directed by the playwright Kotzebue (1802); the Bol'shoy Kamenny or Great Stone Theatre, devoted to Italian opera and Russian drama; and the Great Wooden Theatre. In Moscow the dramatic troupe played in a circus arena in the house of Pëtr Pashkov, alternating, after 1808, with a new theatre near the Arbat Gates. The Napoleonic invasion forced these venues to close; but they were reopened in 1814 after the government had united private and public enterprises into a single operation. In 1816, during a wave of patriotic sentiment, foreign and provincial troupes were banned from playing in Moscow or Petersburg, although individual stars like Mlle George continued to appear.

[1] It was written in 1830 to preface a review of Nikolay Pogodin's play *Martha the Seneschal's Wife*. An English translation can be found in Senelick (1981), pp. 8–15.

[2] Not until 1839 were leading actors of the Imperial Theatres who had served no less than twenty years granted 'hereditary honorary citizenship' with civil rights. An attempt to bestow this on them seven years earlier had been thwarted by the argument that actors were called upon to do things that would debase the title of citizen.

## I ESTABLISHMENT OF A POST-NAPOLEONIC RUSSIAN THEATRE, 1812–20

### *The Moscow theatre prepares for Napoleon's invasion*

As Napoleon's armies advanced through Russia, first burning Smolensk and then girding up for the battle of Borodino, A.A. Maykov, administrator of the Moscow Imperial Theatre, tried to get some sort of directive from his superiors in St Petersburg.

## 213 The invasion of Moscow, 1812

N.V. Drizen: 'Sto let nazad (Iz èpokhi Otechestvennoy voyny)' ['A hundred years ago (From the era of the Patriotic War)'] in *Ezhegodnik imperatorskikh teatrov* [*Yearbook of the Imperial Theatres*] 5 (1914), pp. 25–32.

(a) *Maykov to A.L. Naryshkin,*[1] *Director of State Theatres, St Petersburg, 19 August 1812*

Under the present conditions all the gentry and the better part of the merchantry are moving out of Moscow to different towns. As a result there is no one to subscribe to next year's subscription series which begins on 10 September 1812. On account of this exodus of audience the performances themselves cannot, in all likelihood, make the theatre any money. Finally, the disposition of the repertoire is too difficult now that the singers who make up the theatre's chorus and who belong to various gentlemen are, at the latters' behest, being sent out of Moscow to other places; hence none of the operas, tragedies and other plays in which they appear can be put on. For all these reasons, unless the aforesaid circumstances alter, going on with theatrical performances promises nothing but certain loss, especially once the current subscription is over. [. . .] Consequently I feel obliged to ask Your Excellency whether it might not be advantageous [. . .] to direct me to send the office, the school, the theatrical wardrobe, the box-office and the most important remainder of the property along with the performers to St Petersburg or some other town Your Exc. will be good enough to designate, using the funds already available in the theatre for needed travel expenses. To which end allow me to treat with the local authorities and request the same subvention from them that has already been made to other State institutions. [. . .]

[Naryshkin replied in the affirmative, noting only that most of the performers should remain in Moscow to await orders from Petersburg for their evacuation. Meanwhile, the Russians lost Borodino, and General Kutuzov, instead of trying to defend the city, ordered the army into full retreat. The result was panic in Moscow.]

(b) *Maykov to Naryshkin, from the town of Vladimir, 8 September 1812*

On the night of 31 August, having received Your Exc.'s orders for me to transfer the box-office, school, performers and other property of the Imperial Moscow theatre in general to a place which Commander-in-Chief Rostopchin[2] shall assign and which he considers safe, early this morning I hastened to him, requesting the provision of 150 carts for the removal. I was refused the provision, with the sole comment that the best place to relocate myself and the whole theatre would be the county seat of Vladimir. After returning to the office and making all the necessary arrangements there was time for, what with the enemy approaching the walls of the capital, I galloped hell for leather back to him and with all my might demanded that he protect the State's interests, the school and those persons necessary to the

Administration. But even then I barely managed to get nineteen carts. Finding myself in such extremities and the most awful anxiety, at the end of my tether, so to speak, and not otherwise, God Himself helped me to send off the cash, the general double-entry ledgers, some portion of the office records, valuable items from the wardrobe and the entire school without exception. All of which at 3 o'clock a.m., 1 September, I sent off in care of clerks, to wit: an assistant in the administrative sector, a treasurer, a secretary, and a wardrobe supervisor; but since it was impossible to transport all this in the peasant tumbrils I have been granted, I rented an additional 11 carts, supplementing them with my own horses. The upshot was that certain actors and actresses had to supply their own transport, and thus I was compelled to give them (along with musicians and members of various theatrical trades) passes so that they could find their own means of escape. Of their number some have caught up with the string of carts on the road, others are following on foot, I happen to know, at some small distance behind them and I think they will all eventually get here.

As it was suggested that our army will defend Moscow in full force, after I locked up the rooms containing the things that had to be left behind, I gave orders to Warrant-Officer Mel'nikov and his squadron of veterans to guard the theatre as long as they could. [. . .]

[During the burning of Moscow, the wooden Arbat Theatre was the first to be consumed, along with its costumes and properties. Most of the actors, as well as the administrators, had been evacuated to Kostroma, but others were widely dispersed; after Napoleon's retreat, the theatrical administration made efforts to retrieve these strays. Maykov asked Naryshkin for permission to set dates by which returning performers must register. The St Petersburg Director replied:]

(c) *Naryshkin to Maykov, late October 1812*

As to the terms of six and three months which you have set for the performers and other theatrical staff to put in an appearance, I find that many are far removed and may not be able to return from the remotest regions of Russian within those time-limits; but assuming that such persons are in Moscow and its environs, they could come to the authorities much sooner or give notice of their place of residence so that, as required, they might be registered at once; meanwhile, many such have already appeared even as you were drawing up your report. [. . .] to save time and thereby protect the box-office profits, I recommend that you first dismiss any persons presently redundant and then immediately send a trustworthy official [. . .] to seek out the various staff members still under your authority [. . .]

[1] Naryshkin maintained a serf troupe in Moscow in 1805; he sold his choristers to the government in 1807, and another sixteen members in 1826.
[2] Fëdor Vasil'evich Rostopchin (1763–1826), military governor of Moscow, was later suspected of instigating the incendiaries who fired the city.

## (d) A troupe of French actors chased out of Moscow in 1812

Coloured engraving by A.G. Venetsianov, 1812; reproduced in Ettore Lo Gatto: *Storia del teatro russo* [*History of the Russian Theatre*], vol. 1 (Florence: G.C. Sansoni, 1952), p. 264

### *The so-called Znamensky Theatre*

With his letter Naryshkin included a list of absent performers and freed most of the theatrical staff from State service, including one apothecary, two painters, an architect, six ushers, billposters, a chimney-sweep, and some lamplighters. Only as an afterthought did he free the actors: first the French, four of whom were still to be found in Moscow; then nine ballet supers; and finally the Russian dramatic actors, including Stepan Mochalov,[1] 'because they have not put in an appearance nor given any token of their place of residence'. Most of them chose to remain in service.

From August 1814 to 1818, what was left of the Russian dramatic troupe in Moscow performed a regular repertoire at the home of the merchant S.S. Apraksin on Znamenka Street, which became known as the Znamensky Theatre. They were under the direction of Prince S.M. Golitsyn, who received state subvention.

[1] Stepan Fëdorovich Mochalov (1775–1823), a serf actor owned by N.N. Demidov, had been manumitted when he entered the Imperial service in 1806; he was the father of the tragedian Pavel Mochalov (see **220**, **222**).

## 214 Advertisement for performances at the Znamensky Theatre, Moscow, 1815

Advertisement no. 5, *Moskovskie Vedomosti* [*Moscow Gazette*] 15, 20 February 1815; in F. Vitberg: 'Materialy dlya istorii teatral'nykh zrelischch i publichnykh uveseleny v Rossii', ['Materials for the history of theatrical spectacles and public entertainments in Russia'], *Ezhegodnik imperatorskikh teatrov* [*Yearbook of Imperial Theatres*], vol. 3 (1895–6), p. 64.

To offer more possibilities of satisfying the audience with performances, in accordance with many persons' wishes, it is proposed that two a day be given during Shrovetide: an extra subscription matinee series and, at the usual time in the evening, as is normal with the theatre, a subscription series. Ticket sales for boxes and stalls at the matinees will be carried on at the theatre box-office the day before at 5 o'clock p.m., and for the evening performances and masquerades, at the usual time, i.e. 8 o'clock a.m. of the day of the performance. The matinees will begin at 12.30 a.m., and the evening performances, as before, at 6.30.

*St Petersburg audiences*

The twenty-one-year-old poet and man-about-town, Aleksandr Sergeevich Pushkin (1799–1837), began composing an essay entitled 'My remarks on the Russian theatre', sometime between January and May 1820, in hopes of publishing it in *Syn otechestva* (*Son of the Fatherland*), but it was interrupted by his exile from Petersburg and did not appear in print until 1895. This casual record of current performers raises the important critical issue of the audience as inspiration for native art.

## 215a Pushkin describes St Petersburg audiences in 1820

A.S. Pushkin: *Pushkin i teatr. Dramaticheskie proizvedeniya, stat'i, zametki, dnevniki, pis'ma* [*Pushkin and the theatre. Dramatic works, articles, notes, journals, letters*], edited by B.P. Gorodetsky (Moscow: Iskusstvo, 1953), pp. 323–6; English trans. in Laurence Senelick: *Russian dramatic theory from Pushkin to the Symbolists* (Austin: University of Texas Press, 1981), pp. 4–7.

It is the public that shapes dramatic talents. What is our public like?

Before an opera, a tragedy or a ballet begins, some young fellow saunters through all ten rows of stalls, steps on everyone's feet, and chats with both those he knows and those he does not.

'Where have you been?' – 'With Semënova, Sosnitskaya, Kolosova, Istomina.'[1] – 'Aren't you the lucky boy!' – 'She's singing today – she's acting, she's dancing –

let's give her a round of applause – let's call her before the curtain! She's so charming! Such eyes! Such a dainty foot! Such talent! . . .' The curtain goes up. The young fellow and his friends, moving from seat to seat, get carried away and burst into applause. I have no wish to chide perfervid, boisterous youth, I know that it calls for indulgence. But can we rely on the opinion of such judges? [. . .]

A tragic actor starts to rant more loudly or more vehemently than is his wont, the deafened 'gods' go into transports, the theatre rocks with applause.

An actress . . . But suffice it to say that our actors' talent cannot possibly be measured by the clamorous approbation of our audiences.

Another remark. A considerable portion of our parterre (i.e. the stalls) is too concerned with the fate of Europe and the nation, too careworn with work, too sober-minded, too grand, too cautious in expressing emotional reactions, to have anything to do with the quality of dramatic art (least of all the Russian brand). And if at half-past six the same old faces do arrive from the barracks and council chamber to occupy the first rows of subscription seats, they regard this more as conventional etiquette than enjoyable relaxation. No matter what happens, one cannot expect from their chilly abstraction of mind any sensible notions or judgement, let alone the honest expression of any sort of feeling. Consequently, they serve only as a respectable embellishment of the Bol'shoy Kamenny Theatre,[2] but decidedly do not belong either to the crowd of devotees or to the enlightened or partisan judges.

One more remark. The high-and-mighty of our age, who bear on their faces the monotonous stamp of boredom, arrogance, fretfulness and stupidity – qualities inseparable from their type of occupation – these spectators who habitually fill the first rows, who glower at comedies, yawn at tragedies, doze at operas and pay attention only perhaps at ballets, what can they do perforce but cool the acting of the most zealous of our performers and inspire indolence and languor in their souls, if nature has endowed them with a soul?

[1] Ekaterina Semënovna Semënova (1786–1849), with her stately demeanour and rich contralto voice, was Pushkin's favourite actress, her performances a show of disciplined enthusiasm.

Elena Yakovlevna Sosnitskaya (1799–1855), a lesser member of the Bol'shoy company, later created the role of the bride in Gogol''s *Marriage*.

Evgeniya Ivanovna Kolosova (1780–1869), a sprightly dancer as well as an actress, abandoned cumbersome court dress for the chiton in ballet; her home was much frequented by young men of good society, both for her sake and that of her daughter, Aleksandra.

Avdotya Il'inichna Istomina (1799–1848), a ballerina of exceptional grace and skill, was immortalized by Pushkin in chapter 1, stanza xx of *Evgeny Onegin*.

[2] 'The Great Stone Theatre', the first permanent playhouse in Petersburg, was built in 1783 from designs by Ludwig Philipp Tischbein and held 2,000 spectators. It was remodelled 1802–4, and again in 1836.

## 215b The Bol'shoy Theatre in Petersburg in the early nineteenth century.

Engraving by Dubois from a sketch by Courvoisier; reproduced in V.N. Vsevolodsky-Gerngross: *Istoriya russkogo teatra* [*History of the Russian Theatre*], vol. II (Leningrad–Moscow: Tea-Kino-Pechat', 1929), opp. p. 64.

*Maykov heads the Imperial Theatres*

In 1821, Maykov, after many years as administrator of the Moscow Theatre, was appointed manager of all Imperial theatrical spectacles and music, in place of the autocratic Prince P.I. Tyufyakin. On assuming office, he was presented with an accounting of debits and credits for the past year.

## 216 Budget of the Moscow Imperial Theatre, 1821

E.N. Opochinin: *Teatral'naya starina: istoricheskie ocherki i kur'ëzy* [*Bygone Theatre: historical essays and curiosities*] (Moscow: Tovarishchestvo tipografii A.I. Mamontova, 1902), pp. 136–8.

PROFITS

| | |
|---|---|
| From the Moscow State Chamber for the support of the Imperial Moscow Theatre, excepting 36,000 rubles[1] deducted for the French troupe | 140,000r. –k. |
| From the year's performances | 198,534r. 50k. |
| From benefits, shared half-and-half with the government | 4,087r. 75k. |

| | |
|---|---|
| From masquerades | 4,629r. –k. |
| From concerts | 490r. –k. |
| From performances of the German actor Gappmeyer[2] contracted with the box office of the Moscow Theatre | 456r. –7k. |
| From the buffet | 4,500r. –k. |
| From rental of the auditorium for concerts and other shows | 2,214r.82¼k. |
| From printshop operations (by contract) | 500r. –k. |
| Made from sale of masquerade masks | 386r. 31k. |
| Interest from the Chamber of Guardians,[3] fines of actors and profits from invested silver | 6,721r. 9½k. |
| Total receipts for 1821 were | 449,343r 93½k. [*sic*] |

EXPENSES

| | |
|---|---|
| For the office | 21,118r. 4¼k. |
| For the maintenance of the Russian troupe | 47,649r. 22¼k. |
| For the ballet troupe | 32,432r. 40½k. |
| For the orchestra | 34,670r. 43¾k. |
| For the costume-shop | 17,247r. 44k. |
| For scenery | 17,950r. 64½k. |
| For the dramatic school | 34,657r. 29¼k. |
| Hire of buildings for the theatre, schools, servants, payment of lodging subsidies | 67,641r. 79k. |
| Firewood | 12,822r. 80½k. |
| Carriages | 18,531r. 56¼k. |
| Lighting | 20,269r. 80¼k. |
| Miscellaneous expenses | 25,557r. 12½k. |
| Assignment of a tenth part to the Board of Guardians | 20,774r. 12½k. |
| Petty expenses | 4,306r. 87k. |
| Total expenses for 1821 | 375,629r.68½k. [*sic*] |

[1] Throughout the nineteenth century, ten kopeks were worth an English penny and one ruble = 10d, but British travellers found it easiest to reckon 25 rubles to the pound sterling. Because of devaluation, it took 4 paper or copper rubles to equal one silver ruble. To give some notion of the relative value of money: the annual labour of an average family of serfs was considered worth 100 rubles or £4 to their owner, whereas food and lodging at a good hotel in Petersburg came to 8 rubles or 6s 8d a day.

[2] Johann Gappmeyer toured his German-speaking troupe through the Eastern Baltic region with a repertoire of Shakespeare (much adapted), Schiller and Kotzebue.

[3] Chamber or Board of Guardians, a governmental body set up to administer the estates and properties of the under-aged, incompetent or bankrupt. It could also provide mortgages on such collateral as serfs.

*The Committees on Theatrical Literature are formed*

The reign of Nicholas I began badly in 1825 with the quickly checked Decembrist revolt; in reaction, an intense governmental repression set in, with an increase in control and centralization which had repercussions for the theatre. Months before the revolt, on 3 May, the government had already sanctioned a code of rules and regulations formulated by Maykov, which covered every aspect of theatrical life. The theatrical administration was to be assisted by 'Committees on Theatrical Literature', whose function was to select and supervise an appropriate repertoire. The membership of these committees was composed of both men of letters and state officials; although they were often motivated by a sincere love of art, their collective taste tended towards the conservative, not to say the retrograde.

## 217 Minutes of the Chief Theatrical Committee, 1825–6

S.V. Taneev: *Iz proshlogo imperatorskikh teatrov* [*From the past of the Imperial theatres*] (St Petersburg: Universitetskaya tipografiya M. Katkova, 1885–6), pp. 5–7.

(a) *On rehearsals, 13 April 1825*

If the attention of the Chief Committee is directed to selecting plays for public presentation, similar attention should be directed to their rehearsals, on whose good organization so much of the success of the performance depends. But since this depends more on, so to speak, in-house arrangements, it may be left to the office to order things so that similar schedules will be set up for rehearsals, the calendar being left entirely up to the office. These schedules will be [. . .] posted, along with the actors cast. Lists of the rehearsals, with the schedules, will be sent to the home of each member of the Committee of the Administration-in-Chief. In these schedules there should be noted, beneath the titles of the plays, the hour in which the rehearsal of each play named is to begin, in which theatre, whether in the foyer or on the stage; the phase of rehearsal, that is, first, second or third read-through, dress rehearsal and so on. For operas, whether with piano or conductor, accompanied, by quartet or full orchestra, and so on.

(b) *On the repertoire*

| | *At the Bol'shoy Theatre:*[1] | *At the Maly Theatre:*[2] |
|---|---|---|
| | | *are to be given* |
| Sundays: | magic shows | German comedy or drama or tragedy |
| Mondays: | benefit or grand opera | German comedy or vaudeville |
| Tuesdays: | tragedy or high comedy | French performance |
| Wednesdays: | grand ballet | German benefit |

| | | |
|---|---|---|
| Thursdays: | opera and light comedy | German tragedy or French play |
| Fridays: | light comedy, vaudeville and *divertissement* | Tragedy and comedy or vaudeville |
| Saturdays: | German grand opera | French play |

(c) *On plays in verse, 12 March 1826*

On inspecting the work offered by Mr Korsakov,[3] the tragedy *Hedwina and Jagellon or Divine Judgement*, we have concluded: (a) except for some rather good monologues and decent construction, we are compelled by the flatness of the denouement, the weakness of the plot and especially the strangeness of the prosody of this play which is written in unrhymed blank verse, not admitted by classical authors, to reject this tragedy and, in accord with the opinion of the Administrator [of St Petersburg theatres], to return it to its author; (b) to make it a rule henceforth to reject any tragedy written in unrhymed blank verse, for such versification, which wholly resembles metrical prose (*prose cadencée*) and is therefore inferior to real prose, not only fails to correspond to the dignity of tragedy, but cannot be tolerated in any dramatic work.

1 The Moscow Bol'shoy or Great Theatre, which had been burnt in 1812, was rebuilt in 1824 and opened in 1825, to replace the Petrov Theatre.

2 The Moscow Maly or Small Theatre, designed by Osip Ivanovich Bove (1784–1834), was built in 1824 on Petrov square, on the site of the house of the merchant Vargin, where the Petrov troupe had been playing.

3 P.A. Korsakov (1790–1844) wrote verse tragedies about the Maccabees and Spartacus, but later turned to vaudevilles and translations of French comic opera.

## II ACTING, 1810–50

### *Realism vs declamation in the native tradition*

From the first, the best Russian acting had been noted for its 'realism'. Dmitrevsky, who had observed Lekain and Garrick, received such praise; yet Mikhail Shchepkin would say in the 1850s that this acting would not have seemed realistic to a later age. Shchepkin himself learned from observing in an amateur actor, Prince Meshchersky, the power of natural phrasing and non-bombastic emoting. However, the realism of this generation of players should not be confused with 'naturalism' or a detailed psychological construction of character. It had to do, among the best Moscow actors, with emotional authenticity, persuasion by means of generic feeling; among the best Petersburg actors, with a canny manipulation of technique, make-up and outward behavioural mimicry. Romantic and sentimental melodrama and vaudeville which were the most popular dramatic genres until the late 1850s required nothing more.

Another favourite dramatic genre of the early nineteenth century was poetic tragedy which modified the neoclassic model by treating national themes and slipping in political commentary in disguised forms; an acting style had to be cultivated that could express these modes. The Free Society of the Admirers of Russian Literature, Sciences and Arts, whose members styled themselves 'Fanciers of What's Theirs,' promoted a national repertory and a specifically Russian acting style. Unfortunately, the prestige of French declamation was such that it made rapid inroads into Russian techniques of performance. It was only natural that Russian actors, in default of a strong native tradition, should be drawn to foreign models, although the genius of the language was not suitable to French styles of declamation.

## 218a Introduction of declamation to the Russian stage

S.P. Zhikharëv:[1] *Zapiski sovremennika. Vospominaniya starogo teatrala* [*Notes of a contemporary. Memoirs of an old theatre-buff*], edited by B.M. Eykhenbaum, vol. II (Moscow–Leningrad: Iskusstvo, 1955), pp. 370–4.

[. . .] Semënova altered her speech patterns only after 1810, and was the first to *croon* in Russian tragedy, for, before she did it, although verse was not recited on stage in the same way as prose and its metre was to some degree observed, still, no one had exactly *sung* it. Semënova's innovation in drawling the verses and putting a prolonged stress on some words derived from a misunderstanding of the delivery of the actress George[2] and was not approved of by our old and experienced actors, who would have nothing to do with this error, despite the great success Semënova won for her singsong declamation.

However, despite the wrong direction taken by Semënova's talent, the talent itself was excellent, although exclusively imitative. Had it rested with Semënova herself, and had she been deprived of the guidance of either Shakhovskoy or Gnedich,[3] she would have been incapable of conceiving her roles or colouring them properly. God had endowed her, like the actress George, with remarkable qualities: proper stature, a symmetrical figure, exceptional beauty, an expressive physiognomy, a powerful, quite appealing and flexible voice, in short, everything a woman ought to have if she devotes herself to the stage, everything except what George herself lacked, that is, a decent education, the ability to understand, and the gift of tears. In her first youth, when playing a few easy roles like Antigone, Moina and Xenia,[4] which she studied under the guidance of Prince Shakhovskoy with Dmitrevsky[5] standing by, she was splendid, and she remained splendid in her simple and natural acting until the Russian advent of the famous French actress, who turned her head and those of many admirers of her talent, chief among them Gnedich, an intelligent, well-intentioned, talented man, staunchly loyal to his predilections but fanatical in his own opinions and vanity.

Who is without faults? Gnedich had never travelled or seen any of the stage celebrities of the time, had had no chance to compare them with one another, which is necessary to an understanding of any art, but particularly the theatre.

And so, for him, the first actress with indisputable talent on whom he set eyes, even though she herself was imitative and modelled on the illustrious Raucourt,[6] became a pattern to be used to train Semënova. Gnedich always crooned verse, because, as a translator of Homer, he had accustomed his ear to the paestic structure of Greek hexametres, which have a remarkably song-like quality. Furthermore, this song-like quality was remarkably attuned to the peculiarities of his own voice and pronunciation, and therefore, once he heard the actress George, he imagined that he had puzzled out the secret of true stage declamation and proclaimed it an indispensable qualification for success on stage.

So Semënova crooned . . . Unfortunately this type of delivery, which had never before been heard in the Russian theatre, found its devotees, pleased the audience, and Semënova was touted as the world's leading actress.

[1] A member of the light-hearted Arzamas circle, which included Pushkin among its literati, Stepan Petrovich Zhikharëv (1788–1860) later became the chairman of the Theatrical Literary Committee of the St Petersburg Imperial Theatre. His diaries, which run to 1817, are a rich source of information on the theatre of his time.

[2] The temperamental French tragedienne, whose real name was Marguerite-Joséphine Weymer (1787–1867), toured Russia with a French company between 1808 and 1812 in a repertoire similar to Semënova's and was instrumental in propagating French neoclassic delivery. In Tolstoy's *War and Peace*, she is depicted delivering a recitation from *Phèdre* at Hélène Bezukhova's home.

[3] Prince Aleksandr Aleksandrovich Shakhovskoy (1777–1846), a prolific playwright, translator, adaptor and, unofficially, a leading trainer of actors at the Alexandra. Grotesque in appearance and eccentric in manner, he upheld the neoclassic artificial style which was rapidly becoming obsolete.

Nikolay Ivanovich Gnedich (1784–1833), writer and translator of the *Iliad* (1813), Schiller's *Fiesco*, Shakespeare's *King Lear* and Voltaire's *Tancred*.

[4] All colourless *ingénue* roles in the tentatively Romantic but largely neoclassical tragedies of Vladislav Ozerov. Antigone appears in *Oedipus in Athens* (*Édip v Afinakh*, 1804), Moina in *Fingal* (1805), and Xenia in *Dimitry of the Don* (*Dimitry Donskoy*, 1807).

[5] Ivan Afanas'evich Dmitrevsky (D'yakonov-Narykov, 1734–1821), Russia's first 'star' actor, had begun in Fëdor Volkov's first professional Russian troupe. On trips abroad in 1765–6 and 1767–8, he had seen Lekain and Garrick, and his own acting, though not devoid of declamation, was praised for its naturalness.

[6] Françoise-Marie-Antoinette-Joseph Saucerotte, known as Raucourt (1756–1815), excelled as tragedy queen at the Comédie-Française. Celebrated for her Sapphic tastes, she befriended and trained several young actresses.

## 218b Semënova as Clytemnestra and Shusherin as Agamemnon in *Iphigenia in Aulis*[1]

Engraving by Chesky;[2] reproduced in V.N. Vsevolodsky-Gerngross, vol. 1 (1929): opp. p. 472.

[1] M.E. Lobanov's translation of Racine's *Iphigénie en Aulide* was first performed in St Petersburg on 6 May 1815. For Shusherin, see **219**, note 1.
[2] The artist imitated Dubois's sketch, engraved by Vendrami, of Mlles George and Bourgoin in the female roles.

*Aksakov advises actors on acting*

A country squire with a mania for the theatre, Sergey Timofeevich Aksakov (1791–1859) was a close friend of Shchepkin, Mochalov and Gogol'. He began writing theatrical reviews for several newspapers from 1825, and served on the censorship committee in Moscow from 1827 to 1832. Aksakov's writing on the theatre was always intended to emend the practice of actors as well as to enlighten the general public. The following ideas were jotted down at his estate in Nadezhino Village on 15 February 1825.

## 219 Aksakov's ideas on acting, 1825

S.T. Aksakov: *Sobranie sochineny* [*Collected works*], vol. 3 (Moscow: Gos. Izd. Khudozhestvennoy literatury, 1955–6), pp. 399–405.

An actor can act well in powerful dramatic roles in two ways: he must either have a fervent imagination and an inordinately affective sensibility that magnifies everything and takes it directly to heart and is excited by what another might scarcely notice – or else simply be an attentive observer of the ways of human passion, cold-blooded but able to imitate them accurately. The first case is talent, the second, art; their combination will constitute *perfection*.

[. . .] Of great importance to an actor – especially one who is not endowed with outstanding physical abilities by nature – is to know how to pace oneself (without cooling off the performance) in the powerful passages of one's role. – Shusherin[1] used this technique with complete success.

It seldom happens that actors endowed with outstanding abilities, talent and good looks attain great art. The reason is obvious and natural: anyone underendowed by Nature (and who has a bent for art and wit) strives to make up for his deficiencies through knowledge, precision in performance, careful choice of roles, examples, advice; whereas talent, enhanced by all the advantages of good looks which spring to the eyes of a pseudo-connoisseur and seduce even cultivated judges with high expectations, extorts loud praise and, blinding the actor with vanity, halts him on his way to perfection. – A distressing example of this was our Yakovlev![2] . . . Yakovlev, created by nature with the greatest spiritual and physical capacity possible for the achievement of perfection, Yakovlev, preordained to be the glory of the Russian theatre, a gem amid the renowned actors of civilized Europe – did not, I make bold to state, sustain one single role! *Passages* were wonderful, but the *whole* was awful! [. . .]

Actors and actresses, at least the bad ones, have a very bad habit: on stage they try to make their voices unnatural and in the most heated passages of their role stare into the spectator's face; and the worst, at that very moment, often adjust their dress, thereby destroying illusion so that the spectator cannot forget himself. Even celebrated actresses are not immune from this fault: Mlle George was susceptible to it.

It is good if, every time an actor walks off stage, he is dissatisfied with himself, however loud the applause.

Many persons argue over whether or not chanting is necessary in declaiming verse tragedy. – In my opinion, it is *indispensable*, but it must be used in moderation and *not throughout*. In passages where passion is expressed without violent excitement, in triumphal speeches to warriors and to the populace, in descriptive passages, in addressing divinities – there must be chanting. What is the point of the great effort of writing verse if it is to be recited like prose? And will not a harmonious drawling of the verse stamp a more vivid impression on the human heart? – People say that such recitation is *unnatural*; but what is so natural about speaking in verse, and in rhyme into the bargain? In the refined arts nature is conventionalized. Is not tragedy a sublime and unusual spectacle? But I do not intend to condone *crooning* in tragedy, as the French actors in Petersburg and even La George herself do it. This extreme crooning was always a feature of famous actors; their talents, ardour, feeling animated the crooning and made it attractive, but their imitators, as is always the case, assumed that the whole secret to the art lay in the thing itself. However, in French, which is not always euphonious, crooning may be employed to a greater degree than in our language. [. . .]

[1] Yakov Emel'yanovich Shusherin (1753–1813), a keenly analytical actor, of meagre temperament, who carefully rehearsed his roles before a mirror. He excelled in classical tragedy.

[2] Aleksandr Semënovich Yakovlev (1773–1817), a former shop-assistant, became the foremost tragic actor of his day. A romantic Hamlet and Othello, he infused his creations with sentimental passion.

### *Mochalov and Karatygin, rival tragedians*

To Russian minds a sharp distinction existed between the two capitals: St Petersburg was seen as 'German', elegant, bureaucratic, aloof and unsympathetic, Moscow as 'Russian', homely, old-fashioned, warm and welcoming. A similar contrast was soon made between the acting styles of the two cities, Petersburg players noted for their precision and well-rehearsed technique, Moscow players for their spontaneity and emotional power. The *loci classici* of this commonplace were Vasily Andreevich Karatygin (1802–53) and Pavel Stepanovich Mochalov (1800–48), the Kemble and Kean of Russia, respectively.

Both sons of actors, Karatygin, controlled and imposing, Mochalov, impetuous and electrifying, were each a favourite in his own hometown, but never in the other's. They often played the same roles, including Hamlet, Othello, Lear, Romeo, Don Carlos and Karl Moor. Critics loved to compare and contrast them.

## 220 Aksakov compares Mochalov and Karatygin, 1828

S.T. Aksakov, '2-e pis'mo iz Peterburga' ['2nd Letter from Petersburg'], *Moskovsky vestnik* [*Moscow Herald*] 21–2 (1828), repr. in Aksakov (1955–6); English trans. in Bertha Malnick: 'Mochalov and Karatygin', *Slavonic and East European Review*, 36, 87 (June 1958), pp. 275–6.

[To] spectators accustomed to this imposing, graceful (if too thin) figure of Karatygin, to his impressive and noble movements, his sonorous voice, his solemn declamation, his singing intonation . . . what must Mochalov seem? A man of middle height who has not the art of bearing himself well on the stage, with a voice far from powerful and speaking as we all do . . . [. . .]

Karatygin is made for the leading parts of young heroes and emperors; Mochalov for the leading roles of lovers and young princes. If they go from one *emploi* to another they are both unsatisfactory [. . .] Each has admirable means for his own parts, but Karatygin's voice is not powerful, it is enchanting and seductive in all its variations. His features are handsome and noble, he expresses tenderness, love, enthusiasm, better than Karatygin, but horror and despair are more powerfully reflected in Karatygin's face. Karatygin's delivery is always powerful and equally true and it makes you forget his singing intonation; but the declamation (or better still, the conversation) of Mochalov is perfection. [. . .] Karatygin is noble on the stage and equally good in all his parts; his movements are graceful and appropriate to the character he represents. Mochalov is awkward, and his unfortunate habits do not forsake him even when he is playing royalty or noblemen. Whether in ceremonial dress or in uniform, there is always the same clumsy gait, the same displeasing movements; he does not always maintain the character of his part, he always acts unevenly, but for all that he achieves sublime moments, magnificent scenes that go straight to the heart and rouse the spectator in frenzied enthusiasm by something that Karatygin's acting does not possess and which it is unlikely to achieve. Karatygin is in command of himself even during the expression of the most violent passions; this is an important condition of art. He may sometimes act better, sometimes worse, but he will never act badly. No one, not even Mochalov himself, can guarantee that Mochalov will act well. His acting is inspiration. [. . .] Nothing better proves the originality of his talent than the introduction of a simple manner of speaking on the stage and his adherence to such a delivery. No one suggested this approach; he chose it as a result of inner conviction. How many difficulties, how much unpleasantness, how many obstacles had first to be overcome! How many people have already changed their opinion about this, and in time all will agree, but to anticipate one's time is the most difficult of the arts, and boldly to fight reigning prejudices is no mean feat. In conclusion: in talent Mochalov is superior to Karatygin; as an actor the latter is infinitely superior to Mochalov. What has not been given by nature cannot be acquired by any effort. Art can be acquired.

*An official records daily activity at the Alexandra Theatre*

Aleksandr Pavlovich Khrapovitsky (1787–1855) was an amateur actor who served as Inspector of the Repertory of the Russian Dramatic Troupe in St Petersburg from 1827 to 1832. Conservative and anti-Muscovite in his theatrical tastes, with a fondness for singsong declamation, he rejected Gogol' when the writer auditioned for an actor's post in the Alexandra company in 1830–1. Ironically, Khrapovitsky was later assigned the staging of the first production of Gogol''s *Inspector*. His diary, published posthumously, reflects typical St Petersburg taste.

## 221 The Inspector of the Repertoire's journal of the Alexandra Theatre,[1] 1831–3

A.P. Khrapovitsky: 'Iz dnevnika inspektora repertuara rossiyskoy truppy A.I. Khrapovitskogo' ['From the diary of the Inspector of the Repertoire of the Russian Troupe Khrapovitsky'], *Russkaya starina* [*Bygone Russia*], 2 (1879), pp. 343–5.

1831

*26 January* Mr Bryansky's benefit. *Woe from Wit* for the first time. Comedy in four acts and verse. Work of A.S. Griboedov.[2] The play was, contrary to expectation, received coolly.
*3 February Hamlet.* Tragedy in five acts and verse, adapted from Shakespeare by S.I. Viskovatov.[3]
A mishap occurred: in Act 4 Karatygin's breeches split.
*6 May The Magic Marksman.* Magical grand opera in three acts.[4]
Beshentsov was supposed to shoot down an eagle, but his gun-hammer had rusted away and he couldn't fire, so the eagle, at Samoylov's[5] command, fell without a shot being fired, which raised a terrible laugh throughout the audience.
*13 May The Robber of the Bohemian Forests.* Tragedy in five acts and verse, in two parts, based on Byron's works.[6]
Before the play was over a stage-carpenter suddenly 'struck' the castle. The actors

were all in a panic and Bryanskaya,[7] seeing her husband lying there (according to the play, he was lying dead) fell into a dreadful fright and screeched out, 'Yasha! Yasha!' (her husband's name). Thereafter an announcement was made that owing to the improper striking of the scenery the tragedy could not be concluded.
*14 June The Spirit of the Times*. Comedy-vaudeville in five acts.
Today cholera showed up in St Petersburg.[8]
*23 June Woe from Wit*. [. . .]
Small house, because yesterday there was a big riot in the Haymarket, the cholera hospital was destroyed. And the same thing might have recurred today except that the presence of the Sovereign put an end to that sort of thing.
*28 June The Love Child*. Drama in five acts by Kotzebue.[9]
Today at midnight the famous Ryazantsev[10] died of cholera.
*1 July Magnanimity or The Recruitment*. Drama in 3 acts by Il'in.[11]
Today there were seventeen performers ill, almost all the leading actors.
*5 July Love's Post-office*. Comic opera by A.A. Shakhovskoy.[12] On this date at noon, by order from the very top, the theatres were closed until such time as the cholera ends. [. . .]

## 1833

*11 April Thirty Years or A Gambler's Life*.[13] The role of Georges de Germigny will be played for the first time by the actor of the Moscow Imperial Theatres Mr Mochalov.
What's there to say about Mochalov? A nasty, loathsome little sort, quite unsuitable.
*18 April Misanthropy and Repentance*. Drama in five acts.[14]
Mochalov was good, i.e. he created something good, but did not, so to speak, follow through with it to the end; hence the best moments failed and the spectator was thoroughly dissatisfied.
*20 April Woe from Wit*, etc. The role of Chatsky will be played by Mr Mochalov.
Mochalov gave us a kind of inn waiter and when he spoke the last line in his part, 'My carriage, send my carriage here' – violent applause broke out as if the audience were showing it wished his prompt departure.

1 The Alexandra (Aleksandrinsky) Theatre, named after the consort of Nicholas I, opened in Petersburg in 1832, built to designs by Carlo Rossi (1775–1849). The stone playhouse, with its six tiers of boxes, was the hub both of a superb compound of buildings and of officially sponsored dramatic events. It came to be viewed as the counterpart and rival of the Moscow Maly, both houses often producing the same plays.

2 Yakov Grigor'evich Bryansky (Grigor'ev) (1790–1853), a cold and monotonous tragedian, inherited Yakovlev's roles after the latter's death.

Griboedov's brilliant comedy *Gore ot uma* was not produced in its entirety in St Petersburg until 26 January 1831, although individual scenes had previously been mounted; even then, there were a number of lines cut.

3 *Gamlet*, which S.I. Viskovatov claimed to have 'imitated from Shakespeare', had first been seen in St Petersburg on 28 November 1810.

4 A version of Weber's *Der Freischütz* (1821).

5 Beshentsov has not been identified.

Vasily Mikhaylovich Samoylov (1782–1839), founder of a dynasty of performers, was a tenor and then a baritone in the opera company of the Petersburg Bol'shoy from 1803 until his death.

6 R.M. Zotov's *Razboynik bogemskikh lesov*, first produced on 16 May 1830, was loosely based on Byron's *Werner*.

7 Anna Matveevna Bryanskaya (Stepanova) (1798–1878) was an undistinguished utility woman who played noble mothers, comic crones and even *ingénues* on occasion.

8 This translation by A.G. Rotchev and N.P. Mundt of E. Raupach's vaudeville *Der Zeitgeist* was first seen at this performance.

Cholera first broke out in Moscow in 1830, and a quarantine was thrown up around St Petersburg. A report by the Third Section informed the Tsar that the cholera was beneficial in deflecting 'minds from political matters, and has given the sovereign an opportunity to demonstrate his love for his people'.

9 This translation of Kotzebue's *Das Kind der Liebe* by A.F. Malinsky had had its Petersburg premiere on 29 June 1796.

10 Vasily Ivanovich Ryazantsev (1800–31), a promising comic actor, had been a protégé of both Shchepkin and Sosnitsky, and left the Maly to come to the Alexandra.

11 N.I. Il'in's popular comedy *Velikodushie, ili Rekrutskoy nabor* was first seen in Petersburg on 13 November 1803.

12 The comic opera *Lyubovnaya pochta* had music by C.A. Cavos and dates from 1806.

13 The melodrama by Victor Ducange and Dinaux (i.e. J.-Ph. Budaine and P.P. Goubaux), *Trente ans ou La Vie d'un joueur*, had first been performed in St Petersburg on 3 May 1828 in a translation by Zotov. Mochalov probably played it in the Moscow translation by F.F. Kokoshkin.

14 A.F. Malinsky's translation of *Menschenhass und Reue* had been seen in Moscow as early as 1791 and in Petersburg in 1797.

### *Mochalov plays Hamlet*

Although Mochalov had appeared with some success in Viskovatov's pallid adaptation of *Hamlet*, it was not until the dramatist Polevoy prepared a more faithful translation and coached the actor in the role that his brilliance became apparent. The critic Vissarion Grigor'evich Belinsky (1811–48) regularly championed Moscow talents, both out of genuine conviction and out of his liberal sympathies with everything that seemed genuine, true to Russian experience and contributory to the improvement of society. He attended the premiere of *Hamlet* at Moscow's Peter (i.e. Bol'shoy) Theatre on 22 January 1837 and was so impressed that he composed a lengthy analytical article. The first part appeared in *The Northern Bee* which was edited by Polevoy himself, but the editor became so alarmed by its outspokenness that he cancelled further serialization; the rest of the piece was published in the *Moscow Observer*, although the censor struck out such 'blasphemous' words as 'holy' and 'bliss' used in relation to the theatre.

## 222 Belinsky describes Mochalov as Hamlet in 1837

V.G. Belinsky, '"Gamlet", drama Shekspira. Mochalov v roli Gamleta' ['Hamlet by Shakespeare. Mochalov in the role of Hamlet'], *Sever'naya pchëla* [*Northern Bee*], 4 (1838); *Moskovsky nablyudatel'* [*Moscow Observer*], 1, 2 (March 1838), 1 (April 1838); English trans. of excerpts in Malnick (1958), pp. 283–7.

[. . .] You should have seen the face with which [Hamlet] meets Polonius; on it could be seen the imprint of madness, an expression of cunning contempt for Polonius, profound grief and the torment of a tortured soul, alone in its sufferings. And the voice with which he answers Polonius's question 'How does my good lord Hamlet?' 'Well, God-a-mercy' and with which to his other question 'Do you know me, my lord?' answers 'Excellent well.' Such a voice cannot be pinned to paper and cannot be repeated even at the will of him who owns it. [. . .] The scene with Guildenstern and Rosencrantz is even more significant in its hidden concentrated force, and thus Mochalov played it. For the first time we were shown how an actor can completely renounce his own personality, forget himself and live another's life, or, better still, let us say make his own life that of another, and thus for a few hours deceive himself and two thousand spectators . . . marvellous art! Here we are brought to despair, we are still able to describe the pronunciation and gestures which accompanied it, but the face and voice – that is quite impossible, and in them was all. [. . .] . . From the first word to the last, the voice continuously changed, but never for a moment lost its half-mad, cunning and disordered tone. [. . .] The whole of this scene was played with inimitable art, with complete success, although not with ultimate perfection, because Mochalov afterwards demonstrated that he could act even better. But in this scene he is particularly brilliant when he is questioned by the courtiers . . . all the interrogation was carried on in a tone of contemptuous ridicule, and when the embarrassed courtiers looked undecidedly at one another, Mochalov cast a glance of ill-tempered cunning at them and, with an expression of profound hatred and a feeling of his superiority over them, said 'Nay, then, I have an eye of you' and suddenly assumed his former disorder. All these transitions were as sudden and unexpected as a flash of lightning. Then he superbly spoke his 'anticipation,' and his voice, face, and manner changed with every word; he grew in stature and lifted up his frame as he spoke of the beauties of nature and the nobility of man; he was threatening and terrible when he said that the earth seemed to him a sterile promontory and the air a pestilent congregation of vapours; 'man delights not me' he concluded raising his voice, sadly and violently shaking his head, and gracefully thrusting out both hands as if thrusting back from his breast that humanity which formerly he pressed so closely to it. [. . .]

My God! we thought, here is a man walking on the stage without any instrument connecting him with us, there is no electrical conductor between us, yet we feel his impact on us; like a magician he oppresses us, tortures us, or rouses us to enthusiasm at his will, and our souls are powerless to withstand his magnetic charm. [. . .]

### *The greatness of Mikhail Shchepkin*

Foremost of the actors who promoted the Russianness of Russian theatre was Mikhail Semënovich Shchepkin (1788–1864), whose influence on the culture of his time was considerable. Born a Ukrainian serf, he began acting as an amateur, then became a leading provincial actor in such towns as Kursk and Khar'kov, and eventually was able to buy his freedom and his family's. He was invited to join the Moscow Maly company in 1823, and remained there until his death on tour. Touring the provinces, inaugurated by Mochalov, was one of Shchepkin's methods of promoting great artistry, as well as supplementing his income.

Owing to a weak voice and a tubby physique, Shchepkin seemed at first limited to a *buffo* line of business; but his streak of pathos and disciplined work enabled him to succeed in high comedy, sentimental melodrama and tragedy as well. Superb in Molière, Gogol', Pushkin (the first *Covetous Knight*), he also incarnated the 'little men' entering Russian literature in the works of Turgenev and Dostoevsky. He was closely allied with both the liberal circle of Herzen and Belinsky and the conservative circle of Gogol' and Aksakov; his own political sentiments were old-fashioned and loyalist, but he was viewed as a radical by the bureaucracy because of his campaigning for actors' rights and his suspect acquaintances. As a teacher, he formed the talents and ideas of Samarin, Lentovsky and Fedotova, and through the last, Stanislavsky, who carried out many of Shchepkin's ideas.

## 223a Shchepkin excels in sentimental drama, 1843

V.A. D'yachenko,[1] 'Khar'kovsky teatr' [Khar'kov Theatre'], *Repertuar i panteon* [*Repertoire and Pantheon*], 11 (1843): 158–60.

From start to finish of [*A Sailor*],[2] you see him as a seaman who loves his country, his reputation and those dear to his heart. How fine was his entrance, how wonderfully he was able to express his joy at returning home and with it a secret sorrow at the thought that perhaps his wife and daughter no longer exist! But when he learns that his wife is alive, and married! Poor sailor Simon, how your heart is stricken by the fatal news! You speak not a word, utter not a single complaint, but there is so much that is terrible in your situation, unfeigned tears glisten in your wild, demented look; and the spectator realizes what is going on in your soul. Yes, at that awful moment Shchepkin said nothing, but his handsome face expressed everything he felt, and the theatre, in reverence, dared not even applaud; so great is the power of fascination in Shchepkin's talent.

The scene after breakfast is the true triumph of art. Shchepkin entered deeply into the situation of a father, who does not dare reveal his name to his wife and daughter. How agonizingly he was able to manifest the wounds of humiliated ambition in a warrior who cannot talk about his glorious deeds and must not wear his decoration because it was bestowed on Simon and Simon no longer exists for his wife and daughter. And those wonderful outcries, 'Wine! More wine!' that pierced so deeply into the soul of anyone who understood the dreadful feelings with which they were pronounced, and those tears, not an actor's stagey tears, but the scalding tears of one who suffers . . . no, this is beyond all description! But poor actor, poor art: the vulgar gallery did not comprehend this dreadful moment, it did not sense how painfully the words 'Wine! More wine!' issued from the distressed, oppressed bosom of the performer, and they laughed when Shchepkin's burning tears dripped into the drink he was hoping would, as it were, extinguish the flame consuming his soul. It appears the authors merely intended the Sailor to drink wine in distraction and grief; Shchepkin, as a true artist, found a profound dramatic meaning in this scene. His calls for 'Wine! More wine!' express his love for his daughter as it struggles with the noble self-sacrifice he has resolved on. He drinks wine not only to numb his grief, but also so that no one will doubt the sincerity of his feelings and his joy which, through the frailty of human nature, yields inwardly to soulful suffering, but shows outwardly in the firmness of his will-power. The play was over. The curtain came down. The spectators dared neither breathe nor stir; each one was self-absorbed, and tears glistened in many an eye . . . that was the moment when art triumphed, a moment that should make an actor proud!

[1] Viktor Antonovich D'yachenko (1818–76) was a prolific dramatist, who specialized in well-made melodramas of everyday life, full of intrigues, sudden reversals and mawkish climaxes.

[2] This 'comédie' in one act was a translation by D.A. Shepelev of *Un Matelot* by T. Sauvage and J.-J.-G. De Lurieu. It had its premiere at the Maly on 8 February 1835.

## 223b Shchepkin and his daughter Aleksandra as Simon the sailor and *his* daughter, 1838

Pen and sepia drawing by K.A. Danneberg fro the album of A.F. Koni, Bakhrushin State Theatre Museum; reproduced in Laurence Senelick: *Serf actor: the life and art of Mikhail Shchepkin* (Westport, Conn.: Greenwood Press, 1984), p. 90.

## 224 Belinsky[1] anatomizes the qualities of Shchepkin's acting, 1845

V.G. Belinsky: 'Aleksandrinsky teatr' ['Aleksandra Theatre'] in *Fiziologiya Peterburga* [*The Physiology of Petersburg*], 1845; repr. in V.G. Belinsky: *Belinsky o drame i teatre: izbrannye stat'i i vyskazyvaniya* [*On drama and theatre: selected articles and pronouncements*], edited by V.A. Ostrovskaya, M.B. Zagorsky and A.M. Lavretsky (Moscow–Leningrad: Iskusstvo, 1948), pp. 357–9.

There is an actor in Moscow who combines the requisite conditions for greatness – talent and art – in himself. We speak of Shchepkin; he is as original, as without imitators (successful ones, of course) as Karatygin and Mochalov. True, there are other remarkable comic talents on the stages of Petersburg and Moscow (Messrs Martynov and Karatygin II, Messrs Zhivokini and Sadovsky);[2] but Shchepkin's talent is not exclusively comic. No one denies that Shchepkin is wonderful in the roles of Famusov and the Mayor (in *The Inspector*),[3] but these roles do not constitute his true line of business. Anyone who has ever seen Shchepkin in the small role of the sailor in the play of that name (and who has not?) may easily conceive Shchepkin's real line of business: preferably middle-class roles, roles of simple folk, but ones which demand not only a comic but a deeply pathetic element from the actor's talent. Shchepkin was trained in the classical school and cut his teeth on Molière, whom he saw as the high ideal of comic creativity. The old-fashioned repertoire provided him with no one good role which wholly suited his talent; and if the plays of Molière and Kotzebue supplied him with roles to study and ponder, still they restricted his talent wihin a purely comic and one-dimensional range. Despite his background and scanty education, Shchepkin educated himself both as actor and as man. [. . .] He barely knew Shakespeare, except insofar as his plays appeared in Russian, yet joyously and without the prejudice inherent in cultured persons, he followed the progress of Russian literature. But Shakespeare has only recently been presented on our stage and only a few of his plays at that. Shchepkin has appeared only in the role of Shylock and that twice,[4] whereas he has to appear in such roles at least ten times to master them fully and show what an actor with such gifts as his can make of them. Perhaps if Shchepkin had made Shakespeare's acquaintance earlier, he might be in a position to master even the role of Lear, which is no more outside the scope of his talent than is that of the Fool in the same play (a role whose profound meaning some of us understand but which, precisely because Shchepkin had never played it, has always been performed in a remarkably wretched and mindless fashion) or the role of Falstaff. Perhaps many persons would be surprised to learn that an artist like Shchepkin speaks fervently about the small role of the gardener in *Richard II*; but if he were to appear in it, they would realize that there are no insignificant parts in Shakespeare. Shchepkin is excellent as the musician Miller in Schiller's *Love and Intrigue*. Russian literature could not provide him with roles corresponding to the richness of his talent (for the roles of Famusov and the Mayor are purely comic). Translated and adapted vaudevilles could still less supply him with roles; although the part of the Sailor seems written for him and constitutes the triumph of his talent. Generally speaking, Shchepkin's lot as an actor is most unenviable; for a long time he did not know his true calling, but when he did recognize it, could not find a spacious enough scope for it within our repertoire. However, this far from gratifying situation has not made him neglect his roles, be they what they may; he prepares for each one sedulously and plays each one meticulously. If he is assigned one which is totally empty, his acting endows it with those qualities it lacks – meaning and even distinction. Shchepkin's person does not allow him to appear in such roles as young men or anyone of slender build. His chief flaw as an actor consists in a certain monotony, the reason for which is abundantly expressed by his build. His flaws also include an overabundance of passion and emotion which sometimes keeps him from being in complete control of his role – a purely Muscovite flaw! . . . Passion constitutes the overriding characteristic of his acting not only in pathetic but in purely comic roles; just as some actors have terrific difficulty in displaying anger in comedy without silly tricks or internal combustion, so Shchepkin has great difficulty in keeping his comic vivacity within reasonable bounds. The triumph of his art consists not only in knowing how to evoke laughter and tears at the same time, but also in knowing how to interest the spectator in the fate of a common man and make him sob and tremble at the suffering of some sailor, just as Mochalov makes him sob and tremble at the suffering of Prince Hamlet or General Othello. [. . .] He could take fuller advantage of his great success did his artistic conscience not prevent him from going for effects and gratifying the taste of the mob. Therefore, he is, by choice, an actor for a select public capable of appreciating the subtlety and nuances of truly artistic acting.

[1] Belinsky as a student had been a supporter and soon became an intimate of Shchepkin (for a time he was in love with the actor's daughter Fanny); he regularly contrasted the former serf's virtuosity and dedication to art with the sloppiness and affectation of other, especially Petersburg, players. In the last year of his life, Belinsky accompanied Shchepkin on a tour of the Southwestern provinces.

[2] Aleksandr Evstafevich Martynov (1816–60), a comic actor on the Alexandra stage, who moved with ease into more pathetic roles in the newer realistic repertoire.

For Pëtr Karatygin, see **245b**.

Vasily Ignat'evich Zhivokini (1807–74), an actor at the Maly for fifty years, was renowned for his hilarious gagging; his best role was Lensky's old ham, Lëv Gurych Sinichkin [see **249**].

For Prov Sadovsky, see **235**.

[3] Famusov is the pompous old dignitary in Griboedov's *Woe from Wit*. Shchepkin created the role at its Moscow premiere, as he did the Mayor in Gogol''s *Inspector*.

[4] Shchepkin's best Shakespearean role was to be Polonius to Mochalov's Hamlet; eventually he also played, usually for a single benefit performance, Second Murderer in *Richard III*, Old Capulet, Apemantus, Aegeon, Old Gobbo, Brabantio and, in 1859, the Fool in *Lear*.

## III GOGOL' AND THE CALL FOR A NEW REPERTOIRE, 1836–42

### *Gogol''s opinions on the theatre of his time*

Neither Griboedov nor Pushkin had the dubious pleasure of seeing his full-length plays on stage in his lifetime. Only after Griboedov, as emissary to Persia, had been pulled to pieces by a mob of mullahs in Teheran was *Woe from Wit* (1824) staged in a slightly cut version in 1831. Only long after Pushkin had been killed in a duel was *Boris Godunov* (1831) staged in a heavily cut version in 1866. Nikolay Vasil'evich Gogol' (1809–52) was the first Russian dramatist of genius to see his best work produced, and then it was without pleasure. Stage-struck from childhood, an intimate of the Shchepkin–Aksakov circle, Gogol' brought all his acquaintances' influence to bear to get his plays put on, but at the crucial moment he plunged into depression or fled responsibility.

In 1837 Gogol' combined an article on 'The Petersburg Stage' with an earlier piece comparing 'Moscow and Petersburg', and published the composite as 'Petersburg Notes for 1836'. Primarily a plea for a national repertoire that would express a popular ideal, the essay has a hidden agenda: to prepare the way for the kind of drama Gogol' himself hoped to write. A comic writer, he claimed for comedy the role in the modern theatre that tragedy had once filled; he wanted it, to quote Sumarokov's *Epistles*, 'to emend manners by scorn'.

## 225 Gogol' inveighs against vaudeville and melodrama, 1836

N.V. Gogol': 'Peterburgskie zapiski za 1836g.' ['Petersburg notes for 1836'], *Sovremennik* [*The Contemporary*] 6 (1837); repr. in *Gogol'i teatr* [*Gogol' and the theatre*], edited by M.P. Zagorsky and N.L. Stepanova (Moscow: Iskusstvo, 1952), pp. 366–71; English translation from Senelick (1981), pp. 20–1, 24–5.

[. . .] The dramatic stage has been taken over by melodrama and vaudeville, transient guests who were masters of the house in the French theatre, but play a singularly odd role on the Russian stage. It has long been acknowledged that Russian actors are somewhat incongruous when they impersonate marquesses, viscounts and barons, quite as ridiculous as the French would probably be if they ventured to imitate Russian peasants; but those scenes of balls, soirées and fashionable routs that turn up in Russian plays – what are they doing there? And vaudevilles? . . . It's been a while now since vaudevilles first crept on to the Russian stage, amusing folk of middling quality since it is easy to make them laugh. Who would have thought that vaudeville would survive on the Russian stage not only in translation but as original plays? A Russian vaudeville! It's really most peculiar, peculiar because this feather-brained, insipid plaything could have originated only among the French, a nation temperamentally devoid of a profound, staid aspect, but when the still somewhat austere and ponderous Russian temperament forces itself to twirl around like a *petit-maître* . . . it calls to mind one of our corpulent, crafty, broad-bearded merchants, who has never been shod except with a heavy boot and who now dons a tight slipper and open-work stocking while he simply leaves his other foot in its boot, and in this fashion leads the first measure in a French quadrille. [. . .]

Behold the strange monster which, disguised as melodrama, has stolen in among us! Where is our life? Where are we with all our modern passions and quirks? Could we but see some of it reflected in our melodramas! But our melodrama tells lies in the most shameless manner. [. . .]

The bizarre has become the theme of current drama. Its whole concern is to relate some adventure, unquestionably novel and unquestionably bizarre, never seen or heard of before: murders, arson, the most savage passions, not an iota of which exists in modern society! It's as if the sons of torrid Africa had donned our European dress-coats! Hangmen, poisons – stage effects, everlasting stage effects and not a single character to evoke any sympathy! Never yet has a spectator left the theatre affected and in tears; on the contrary, in a rather overwrought state he hurriedly climbs into his carriage and for a long while cannot collect and coordinate his thoughts. Such is the style of show preferred by our refined and cultivated society! [. . .]

The plight of Russian actors is a sorry one. An untried public throbs and seethes all about them, yet they are cast as characters whom they have never seen. What are they to make of these outlandish heroes, who are neither French nor German, but merely hare-brained freaks with absolutely no well-defined passion or clear-cut demeanour? How are they to show themselves off to advantage? How is their talent to be developed? For heaven's sake, give us Russian characters, give us ourselves, our own scoundrels and cranks! On stage with them, subject them to general laughter! Laughter is a wonderful thing: it jeopardizes neither life nor property, but in its presence a guilty party is like a hare caught in a trap . . . We are grown so indifferent from watching insipid French plays that now we are afraid to look at ourselves. If we are confronted with some lifelike character, we start to wonder whether it is based on a specific person, because the character shown us is quite unlike the *paysan*, stage villain, rhymester and such-like worn-out characters whom toothless authors pack into their plays. [. . .]

We have turned the theatre into a plaything, much like those rattles used to attract children, and we have forgotten that it is a rostrum from which a living lesson is read directly to a mass of people [. . .]

### *The premiere of Gogol''s Inspector*

Gogol''s comedy *The Inspector* (*Revizor*) was allegedly licensed for production because the Tsar took a hand, but it was not to the taste of the Petersburg public. No care had been given to the production, the costumes and sets were old and inappropriate, and the acting veered towards the farcical. Gogol' tried hard to make his intentions known through reading the text aloud but the officials and troupe of the Alexandra openly scorned him.

Pavel Vasil'evich Annenkov (1813–87), a distinguished critic and man of letters, an 'idealistic aesthete', became, after Belinsky's death, editor of the influential organ *The Contemporary* (*Sovremennik*). Although published forty years after the event, Annenkov's memories of the opening night of *The Inspector* were based on his journals at the time.

## 226a Gogol''s comedy *The Inspector* opens, 19 April 1836

P.V. Annenkov: *Vospominaniya i kriticheskie ocherki; sobranie statey i zametok. 1849–1860* [*Reminiscences and critical essays; collected articles and notes*], vol. 1 (St Petersburg: M. Stasyulevich, 1877), pp. 192–3.

Gogol' was much more concerned with public opinion than with the opinions of connoisseurs, friends and seasoned judges of literature – a characteristic common to all professionals who aim at social significance, but the Petersburg public regarded Gogol′ if not with complete hostility then, at least, with suspicion and distrust.

The *coup de grâce* was inflicted by the production of *The Inspector*. [. . .] The author's busy involvement with the staging of his play, which seemed a strange departure from the norm and even, people said, from common decency, was, alas, justified by the vaudeville interpretation imparted to the leading character in the comedy[1] and the vulgarly caricatural one reflected in the others. Gogol′ was in agony all that night. I hope that I, a witness of the premiere, may be allowed to say that, for four hours, the auditorium itself presented the most remarkable spectacle that I have ever seen. No sooner was the first act over when incomprehension was written on every face (the audience was elite in the full sense of the word), literally nobody knew what to think about the scene that had just been shown. This incomprehension grew with each subsequent act. As if finding reassurance in the assumption that it was a farce, most of the spectators, jarred out of all their theatrical expectations and habits, latched on to this assumption with unshakeable resolve. And yet this farce was full of traits and scenes revealing such lifelike truth that a couple of times, especially at moments least opposed to the definition of comedy accepted by most of the spectators, general laughter broke out. Something quite different occurred in Act IV: at times laughter would still fly from one end of the hall to the other, but it was a kind of tentative laughter, immediately broken off; there was almost no applause at all, but rather, strained attention, a convulsive and intense following of all the nuances of the play, sometimes a dead silence that showed that the spectator's heart had been passionately gripped by what was going on on stage. By the end of the act the earlier incomprehension had degenerated into almost unanimous displeasure, which was consummated by Act V. Many called for the author because he had written a comedy, others because he had shown talent in certain scenes, the general public because it had laughed, but the common verdict to be heard from all parts of the élite public was: 'This is something inadmissible, a slander and a farce.' After the performance, Gogol′ turned up at N. Ya. Prokopovich's[2] in an irritated mood. The host thought to hand him a copy of *The Inspector* hot off the presses, with the words, 'Take a look at your offspring.' Gogol′ flung the book to the floor, walked over to the table and, leaning on it, murmured pensively, 'Good Lord! why, if only one or two had been insulting then God go with them, but all of them, all of them . . .'

[1] Nikolay Osipovich Dyur (1807–39), a dexterous player in vaudevilles, specializing in the roles of social butterflies, created the role of Khlestakov. Gogol′ said of him, 'Dyur hasn't the foggiest notion what Khlestakov is all about. Khlestakov became something like a whole team of vaudeville addlepates.'

[2] Nikolay Yakovlevich Prokopovich (1810–57), a school-mate of Gogol′'s and his closest friend, a poet who edited the first edition of Gogol′'s works in 1842.

## 226b I.I. Sosnitsky[1] as the Mayor in *The Inspector*

A photograph taken in the late 1850s; reproduced in Senelick (1981), p. 119.

[1] For Sosnitsky, who created the role of the Mayor in St Petersburg, see **230**, note 4. This is the moment in the last act when the Mayor is berating himself for his stupidity at not recognizing the false Inspector.

*Gogol' publishes* A Theatre Lets Out

Gogol''s reaction to the public rejection of *The Inspector* rapidly grew paranoid. Despite the pleas of Shchepkin, who was to play the Mayor at the Moscow Maly, he refused to take any part in that premiere and fled abroad. Over the next few years, he kept penning instructions on how to play his comedy, descriptions of the characters, and eventually an allegorical interpretation that turned the piece into a morality drama. The one-act play *A Theatre Lets Out* is his most extended, most lucid attempt to analyse public reactions to his play and his own morning-after justification.

## 227 Gogol' defends *The Inspector* from its critics, 1842

N.V. Gogol': 'Teatral'nyy raz"ezd posle predstavleniya novoy komedii' ['A theatre lets out after the performance of a new comedy'] (1842); reprinted in *Gogol' i teatr* (1952), pp. 314–44; English trans. from Senelick (1981), pp. 48–9, 56–7.

FIRST [SPECTATOR] Try and explain this to me: Why is it that when you anatomize each action, character and personality separately it all looks true and lifelike, grounded in nature, but taken all together it seems out of proportion, exaggerated, a caricature, so that when you leave the theatre, you can't help but ask, can such people exist? Yet they're certainly not what you'd call villains.

SECOND [SPECTATOR] Certainly not, they're not at all villains. They're as the proverb says, 'His crime's not grave, He's just a knave.'

FIRST And then, too, there's something else: that vast conglomeration, that excess – isn't that a defect in comedy? Tell me, where is there a society that consists entirely of such people, without at least some, if not half, decent folks? If a comedy is supposed to be a portrait and reflection of our social life, it ought to mirror it with total accuracy.

SECOND First, as I see it, this comedy is by no means a portrait, but rather an emblematic frontispiece. You see, both the scene and the locale of the action are idealized. [. . .] In its initial outburst of annoyance, the audience took personally something that pertains not to an individual but more or less to all human personality. The play is a focal point: from all over, from every corner of Russia, perversions of truth, self-delusions and abuses have swarmed here to serve a single idea – to produce in the spectator a clear-cut and noble-minded revulsion from much that is vile. The impression made is all the stronger because none of the characters has lost his human aspect: one can sense the humanity throughout. As a result the heart shudders all the more violently. [. . .] I think the funniest things the author hears must be the reproaches – 'Why aren't his characters and heroes attractive?' – since he used every device he knew to alienate them from us. If even one honourable character were added to the comedy, fully empowered to attract us, all these people would side with the one honourable character and would entirely forget the others who so frighten them at present. [. . .]

THE PLAY'S AUTHOR [. . .] I'm sorry that no one noticed the honourable character in my play. Yes, there was one honourable noble character, who performed throughout from the start to finish. This honourable, noble character was *Laughter*. [. . .] Indeed, laughter is more meaningful and profound than people think. Not the laughter engendered by temporary irritation, by a splenetic and morbid frame of mind, nor the frivolous laughter which serves as a holiday diversion and recreation – but the laughter which issues from man's brighter nature, because at its source lies an ever-gushing fountainhead which sounds a subject deeply and brings out clearly what would otherwise have gone unnoticed, without whose penetrating force the pettiness and vacuity of life would not so terrify man. [. . .]

## IV STAGING AND MANAGEMENT, 1839–50

### *Slipshod staging and haphazard directing*

In contrast to the centralized control exercised over the operation of theatres, the artistic side of things was often neglected. Only when an author was particularly involved in the production of his play or when an official showed special interest were productions mounted with anything approaching unity of style. Still. throughout this period there was a growing importance of the stage-manager's role in *mise-en-scène* which would lead to the primacy of the director by the end of the century.

Most of the thriving private provincial enterprises had folded during the Napoleonic war, when impoverished landowners gave up their serf troupes or sold them to the government. The public provincial theatres patronized by old debauchees and young rakes, bedevilled by temperamental stars and incompetent staff, was accurately satirized in the enduring Russian vaudeville *Lëv Gurych Sinichkin* (1839). This comedy was a masterful adaptation of Théaulon and Bayard's *Le Père de la débutante*, fitted to the manners of the Russian provincial stage by Dmitry Timofeevich Lensky (1805–60), a popular comic actor and expert farceur. In the course of the action, an old barnstormer tries, against increasing obstacles, to arrange a debut for his daughter. In Act II, the impresario Pustoslavtsev (Vainglory) and the stage manager Nalimov (Burbot) are trying to arrange the stage for a rehearsal of a new play *Pizarro and the Spaniards in Peru*, evidently stolen from Kotzebue. The indignant actors have just been made to clear the stage, after waiting hours to rehearse.

## 228 A provincial rehearsal, 1839

D.T. Lensky: *Lëv Gurych Sinichkin ili Provintsial'naya debyutantka* [*Leo Fitzgeorge Tittlebat or An actress's debut in the provinces*] (1839); reprinted in *Russkiy vodevil'* [*Russian vaudevilles*], edited by V.V. Uspensky (Moscow: Iskusstvo, 1959), pp. 182–3.

PUSTOSLAVTSEV Loafers! Pay them a salary, feed them, but don't dare waste a couple of extra hours at rehearsal! Stap me vitals, the devil's own brood!
MIT'KA [the stage carpenter] (*shouts aloft*) Proshka! Why ain't you let down the sea by now?
STAGE HAND (*from above*) Right away! It got caught! . . .
MIT'KA With you everything catches. (*To another stage hand*) Well, quick, you, get the set-pieces! (*To Nalimov*) The waves won't move; have to grease 'em with lard most likely.
NALIMOV (*to Pustoslavtsev*) What should we do?
PUSTOSLAVTSEV Don't bother: there's no storm in the play, so the sea can stand still.
NALIMOV Very good, sir. (*To Mit'ka*) Strike the waves!
MIT'KA And the clouds up yonder got another hole in 'em, a pretty big one.
NALIMOV Patch it with some old canvas and touch it up with paint.
(*The stagehands continue to set up the scenery.*)
PUSTOSLAVTSEV Stap me vitals, what a lot of bother over new plays. Too little of this, not enough of that. Fork out for this, that, the other! . . . Especially ballets . . . it turns out shoes are no good, everyone needs boots. There, the set's in place; are all the musicians in *their* places?
MUSICIAN (*from the orchestra pit*) The kettledrum's at the pub.
PUSTOSLAVTSEV Send for him at once! . . . What a sot! (*To the orchestra*) For pity's sake, gentlemen, play more quietly, especially the double-bass. Stap me vitals, you can't hear a word.
CONDUCTOR No great loss for the audience!
PUSTOSLAVTSEV Shut up, stand still, look sharp! Of course it's not important . . . after all the author's not here yet, so why not tell the truth? But all the same, don't blow too loudly . . . To work, gentlemen, to work! . . . The set's up . . . where's the prompter?
NALIMOV Here he is: crawling out from under the stage into his kennel.
PUSTOSLAVTSEV (*to the prompter*) What's this, my good man? You should be the first one in your place: you're the main attraction, even though no one sees you, you're the leading character in the play, especially since nobody knows it at speed . . . Prompt the comic more loudly: he hasn't got the sense to know a word of it. (*To Nalimov.*) Has the leading man shown up?
NALIMOV Not yet.
PUSTOSLAVTSEV Fine him!
NALIMOV The old ladies aren't here either.

PUSTOSLAVTSEV Fine 'em!
NALIMOV The same for Raisa Min'ishna Surmilova?
PUSTOSLAVTSEV Fine 'er, fine 'er . . . (*Coming to his senses.*) Shut up, stand still, look sharp . . . How can you fine the leading lady, the star actress! Wait and see, she'll probably land me in trouble with Prince Zephyrov again . . . [. . .]

*The rebuilt Maly Theatre in Moscow*

Beginning in 1829, the governing committee of the Moscow Imperial Theatres, whose members often had a real flair for drama, was replaced by a single offical invested with power over both the theatres in that city. The two Imperial playhouses over which he held sway were the Bol'shoy Petrovsky or Great Peter, a sumptuous opera-house rebuilt in 1824 on the site of Apraksin's Petrov Theatre, and the Maly or Small Theatre, opened in October of the same year to house the Russian dramatic company. The Maly became and would remain for some decades the seat of the best in Russian acting and playwriting, dominated by Shchepkin and later Ostrovsky. It came to be known as 'the second Moscow University'.

## 229 Shakespeare and stage design at the Maly Theatre in the 1840s

V.I. Rodislavsky:[1] 'Moskovskie teatry dobrago starago vremeni' ['Moscow theatres in the good old days', *Ezhegodnik imperatorskikh teatrov sezon 1900–1901gg.* [*Yearbook of the Imperial Theatres*], prilozhenie 2, 13–6, 21–2.

The newly rebuilt Maly Theatre opened on 8 November 1840. For the most part they put on French plays, but sometimes Russian ones; very seldom were two performances scheduled in the same day, i.e. one at the Bol'shoy and another at the Maly. Performances were given as part of a subscription series and as extra-subscription shows announced on the posters. Things went on in this way until 1842, when, at the time the Moscow and Petersburg administrations were merged under Administrator A.M. Gedeonov,[2], it was announced that all performances would be given as part of a subscription series. Until that time, Russian subscription performances occurred only twice a week. What kind of dramatic repertory was there in 1840? Three of Shakespeare's plays were put on that year: *Hamlet* (in Polevoy's translation), *The Life and Death of Richard III* (tragic chronicle in five acts by Shakespeare, verse adaptation from a literal translation by Ya. G. Bryansky; this play was first revived in 1840), and *King Lear* (in Karatygin's translation); the leading roles in all three plays were performed by Mochalov.

Their productions were very far from splendid as regards costumes and scenery; even so, there were far fewer cuts made in these plays than in later productions.

True, in 1840 *Hamlet* was still played without Fortinbras and his embassy, which had first appeared on stage in 1837, but on the other hand many scenes left out of later productions, such as that of Polonius and his servant, had not yet been jettisoned in the 1840s.

[. . .] In 1840 the tragic school had not yet outlived its time, and therefore even Shakespeare was more or less understood and performed in terms of classical tragedy. So one can understand why in 1840, after Shakespeare's *Othello* had already been staged in Moscow in Panaev's[3] translation, they revived the monstrous adaptation of this play by Ducis[4] (Ducis's adaptation seemed even more tragical and stageworthy than Shakespeare's drama), why Polevoy in his translation of *Hamlet* considered it necessary to alter and adapt the original,[5] why the clever and talented Orlova[6] turned quiet, meek Ophelia into some kind of tempestuous, melodramatic heroine, why Orlov[7] in the role of Iago played a dreadful tragic villain, why Varlamov[8] wrote music to Ophelia's songs so inconsistent with her character.

[. . .] it must be said that whatever the case, whether or not Moscow audiences and performers at this time understood Shakespeare, whether or not he was well performed on our stage, nevertheless *Hamlet* and *King Lear* belonged to the number of plays beloved by the audience, who attended him with great enthusiasm, and they served as a good school both for the audience itself and for the actors. [. . .]

In 1840 the staging of dramatic performances was very poor; they almost never bothered with new productions and scenery for them. All the scenery for interiors at the Bol'shoy Theatre were wing-and-border pieces, although the first experiment with a box set had been made as early as the early 1830s and had been noted, as a novelty, by the newspaper *The Tatler* [*Molva*]. Only with the opening of the Maly Theatre in 1840 did box sets become standard practice, but all the same they were used only at the Maly, for this innovation was not transferred to the Bol'shoy. [. . .]

At that time there were two talented men connected with the Moscow theatres: the machinist Pinaud and the set-designer Braun,[9] and thanks to them, the machines Pinaud created and the scenery Braun painted were excellent. Let me mention at least the opera *Askol'd's Tomb*.[10] In the third act of this opera the flowing of the Dnieper in the moonlight, organized by Pinaud and Braun by means no longer in use, was excellent, and one cannot help but lament that these techniques are now obsolete. Nowadays they use a most inadequate technique, unproductive of the appropriate effect, both in *Askol'd's Tomb* and in general for the movement of moonlit waves. They use a transparent water-sheet, cut out in a few places; behind it hangs a piece of glazed silk brocade which is constantly in motion. Between the silk brocade and the lamps on the water-sheet, they arrange other lamps, and the flickering of the lamplight reflected on the silk produces the illusion of rocking waves, but nowhere near as beautifully as Pinaud did it in *Askol'd's Tomb*. But the storm on the Dnieper in Act IV of this opera was quite as unsuccessful then as now! Still, it was done with round rollers set in motion that produced an incomparably better effect than the present so-called layering effect.

[1] Vladimir Ivanovich Rodislavsky (1828–85), amateur actor, dramatist and translator, was one of the founders of the Society of Russian Dramatic Writers and Opera Composers, which organized in Moscow in 1874 to protect royalties.

[2] For Gedeonov, see **230**.

[3] Ivan Ivanovich Panaev (1812–62) published his prose version of *Othello* in 1836.

[4] Ducis, who knew no English, had based his French adaptations of Shakespeare on the Italian versions of Leoni. His *Othello* was translated into Russian by I. A. Vel'yaminov, which thus put the play at three removes from its original.

[5] Polevoy had, in fact, injected his own brand of misanthropy into *Hamlet*.

[6] Of the Ophelia of Praskov'ya Ivanovna Orlova (Kulikova, 1815–1900), Belinsky wrote that she was too mannered, except in the mad scene when she had 'soul'.

[7] Il'ya Vasil'evich Orlov (Kopylov, 1806–52), a landowner from Novgorod, became an actor at the Maly in 1828; essentially a utility man with a rich baritone voice, he made his best Shakespearean impression as the gravedigger in *Hamlet*.

[8] Aleksandr Egorovich Varlamov (1801–48) was a composer-of-all-work at the Maly, writing music for vaudevilles, entr'actes, and Zotov's patriotic spectacle *Bulat-Temir*.

[9] Louis-Pierre de Pinaud (1811–55), chief machinist of the Moscow theatres, was occasionally criticized for the eclecticism of his scenery. Karl Iosifovich Braun, from 1824 scene-painter at the Moscow and Petersburg Imperial theatres, was noted for the sumptuousness of his designs.

[10] *Askol'dova mogila*, with music by A.N. Verstovsky and a libretto by M.N. Zagoskin from his novel, was first produced at the Moscow Bol'shoy Theatre in 1835. It is regarded as the *fons et origo* of Russian opera.

## *The management of the Maly Theatre*

The gifted composer Aleksey Nikolaevich Verstovsky (1799–1862) had been right-hand man to M.N. Zagoskin, director of the Moscow theatres, and expected to take over the office when the latter retired. However, he was pre-empted by a new governmental move which put both Moscow and Petersburg under the supervision of a supreme administrator of the Imperial Theatres. This was Aleksandr Mikhaylovich Gedeonov (1790–1867), an astute career official who occupied that powerful position from 1833 to 1858. Verstovsky had to be contented with the post of Manager of the Moscow Office of Russian Theatres, which he held from 1848 to 1862, running things in a high-handed but efficient fashion. Part of his job was to send regular reports on the daily affairs of the theatre to his Petersburg superior. Having no interest in Russian art, Gedeonov promoted Italian opera, French actors and ballet over the native repertoire and performers. Both officials shared a contempt for 'the new drama' and looked askance at Shchepkin, Mochalov, Turgenev and Ostrovsky.

## 230 Weekly report of the Director of the Moscow Theatre to the Administrator of State Theatres, May 1843

'Perepiska A.N. Verstovskago s A.M. Gedeonova (1843–1853g.)' ['Correspondence between Verstovsky and Gedeonov'], *Ezhegodnik imperatorskikh teatrov* [*Yearbook of the Imperial Theatres*] (1912) no. 7, 63–6.

3 May [1843]. Usachëv's[1] benefit performance was a great success! And if the government's takings don't exceed 521 silver rubles, 65 kopeks, it is only because there wasn't enough time to advertise Liszt's playing and many people were put off by the very nasty weather. It rained and snowed the whole day during an excessively cold spell. Still, the beneficiary made nearly 2,000 rubles, which he had never done before and never expected!

The drama *The Merchant Brothers*,[2] in its dramatic aspect, was incomparably stronger than when it had been acted in Petersburg! That Samarin[3] was more forceful than Karatygin came as no surprise, but I was surprised that Mochalov was incomparably inferior to Sosnitsky![4] And all the more because, judging by rehearsals, I expected his role to be a great success. At the very start of the play, his acting dragged and, by the middle of Act III, was exactly like Lear and that's quite the best proof that all these actors who play by inspiration must always take a back seat to technical actors when it comes to the general overall shape of a role! Sosnitsky for all his shortcomings in drama was far superior to Mochalov and all his effects. Kavalerova,[5] who was much inferior to Bormotova,[5] took the role to be a Xantippe or a Praxagora! The rest of the roles were decently done! The play was excellently costumed. Mr Voytot[6] proved thereby what a great master of his craft he is, and deserves unbiassed respect all the more because most of the costumes were remade from old material and yet looked better than the most magnificent costumes had in the war years! He is, with justice, beginning to complain of Chernevsky,[7] who in fact is starting to get out of hand with his negligence and, in addition, a certain pomposity! Curtain calls at the play's end for Samarin and, force of habit, Mochalov.

In the vaudeville *Three Little Stars*, adapted from a story by Balzac,[8] Zhivokini was very funny. The entire audience's expectations were focussed on Liszt,[9] who, though somewhat belated, nevertheless played three pieces which prolonged the performance to about eleven-twenty! Liszt was welcomed rapturously. Before the performance he had been at a gypsy concert, which somewhat affected the performance and, retaining an impression of the gypsy songs, he was inspired in one of his pieces to play an excellent fantasy on their themes, which merits great respect for its arrangement.

The day after Usachëv's benefit all the floors in the dressing-rooms, reception rooms and staircases in the Imperial and Ministerial boxes in the Bol'shoy Theatre were taken up. Work is now in full swing and we await your imminent arrival, so that the construction can be done in your presence, for in your absence it would soon be botched.[10]

The conjurer Rudolph arrived in Moscow, finer at his art than Bosco[11] and all those who preceded him in this skill. I don't know why, but the Moscow aristocrats have shown the liveliest interest in him, especially Mme Senyavina.[12] Maybe because he's a friend of the Sultan or because he has a frightful beard, but they do make much of him. He gave his first performance in Nebol'sin's[13] drawing-room, and everyone extolled it! He wanted to show his tricks on the stage of the Maly Theatre, which at the moment would not be unprofitable for us! He agrees to give half his performances there, sharing 50 per cent of the State's evening expenses, but firmly insists that the seat prices be raised for his performances, and this seems not unprofitable, especially for the earlier ones. Shall I [. . .] try one or two performances as an experiment while Your Honour pleases to decide whether they be continued with this proviso or cut short? Rudolph intends to stay here all summer if his performances meet with success! [. . .]

[1] Fëdor Nikiforovich Usachëv (1797–1882), a wooden character actor who performed at the Maly for forty years; best as a *raisonneur*, he played Horatio to Mochalov's Hamlet.

[2] *Brat'ya-kuptsy, ili Igra schast'ya* was P.G. Obodovsky's verse translation of the five-act drama by K. Toepfer, *Gebrüder Foster, oder Das Glück mit seinen Launen.*

[3] Ivan Vasil'evich Samarin (1817–85), one of Shchepkin's best pupils, was an actor and director at the Maly from 1837 until his death; versatile and subtle, he was an outstanding Khlestakov and Chatsky, and excelled in melodrama.

[4] Ivan Ivanovich Sosnitsky (1794–1871), a polished and brilliant player of high comedy and vaudevilles, and a luminary of the Alexandra. He was a sparkling Figaro, created the Mayor in Gogol''s *Inspector*, and made a masterpiece of the cameo role Repetilov in *Woe from Wit.*

[5] Elena Matveevna Kavalerova (Borisova, 1791–1863), specialized in comic old women at the Maly, and later moved easily into the Ostrovsky repertoire.

Nastas'ya Bormotova (1822–67) was a ballerina who began on the St Petersburg stage in 1838.

[6] Adolphe Voytot and his wife Louise, French costume designers, worked in Russia in 1842 and 1856.

[7] Sergey Antipovich Chernevsky (1838–1901), Voytot's *ad hoc* assistant, later became a leading stage director at the Maly from 1852 until his death.

[8] P.A. Karatygin's translation of *Les Trois étoiles*, a one-act vaudeville by Léon Halévy and E. Gem.

[9] The Hungarian composer Ferenc Liszt (1811–86) was fascinated by gypsy music; see his 'La Musique des Bohémiens'.

[10] The theatre was rebuilt by the architect Tonn, who rendered it sumptuous but Italianate and rather out of the keeping with the characteristic architecture of Moscow. The newly designed theatre reopened with Glinka's opera *A Life for the Tsar.*

[11] Bartolomeo Bosco (1793–1863), an Italian soldier of Napoleon, began his career entertaining his prison guards in Siberia, and conjured his way back to Paris through the courts of Europe on a simple black-draped stage; he is mentioned by both Gogol' and Sukhovo-Kobylin.

[12] Aleksandra Vasil'evna Senyavina, wife of the governor of Moscow, whose home was a hub of social activity.

[13] Grigory Pavlovich Nebol'sin (1811–96), writer and official.

*The censorship shows its teeth*

The Russian theatre was subject to a double censorship: publication of plays was licensed by the Ministry of Public Enlightenment, while authorization for stage production was granted or withheld by the Ministry of Interior. In 1826, when the Third Section of the Imperial Chancellery, a sort of secret police, was set up, it assumed this latter function and instigated stringent regulations. Originally its mandate took in only the Imperial Theatres in the capitals, but by 1842 it had extended its surveillance to provincial playhouses and touring companies, which had hitherto been subject only to local ordinances. Theatrical reviewing in periodicals also had to be submitted to the censor: overmuch praise of works disapproved of by the government and overmuch rebuke of performers favoured by the government were both frowned upon.

The next year, in issue No. 256 of the only daily newspaper in Russia, the St Petersburg *Northern Bee* (*Sever'naya pchëla*), a gossip column featured a brief reference to a performance of Bellini's *Norma*: 'We won't say one little word about this performance, in accord with the Latin proverb: *aut bene aut nihil*. We took much more pleasure in Mr Zam's menagerie,[1] etc.' Prince Volkonsky[2] was outraged by this slur and insisted on a report from the Minister for Public Enlightenment to the Emperor, to say who had written it and who had authorized it for publication. Ironically, the author was the ambitious and unscrupulous Faddey Venediktovich Bulgarin (1789–1859), one of the government's most loyal time-servers. His column had been passed by two censors who protested that they were forbidden by law to proscribe writing simply on grounds of bad taste. However, the Third Section so loathed Bulgarin's toadyism that they often pulled him up on such charges.

[1] V. Zam's menagerie, opened in the capital in the 1840s, served as the basis for the St Petersburg Zoological Gardens.

[2] Prince Pëtr Mikhaylovich Volkonsky (1776–1852), Minister of the Imperial Court and Field-Marshal.

## 231 A critic truckles to the censorship, 1843

N.V. Drizen: *Dramaticheskaya tsenzura dvukh èpokh, 1825–1881* [*Dramatic censorship in two eras*] (Petrograd: Prometey, 1917), pp. 138–41.

### (a) *Bulgarin to Volkonsky*

Most Serene Prince, knowing Your Serenity's sound judgement, I am convinced that you will not condemn a man without first hearing his defence, and therefore I venture to trouble Your Serenity with my letter: ever since the publishers of *The Northern Bee* received an orally communicated order from Count Aleksandr Khristoforovich [Benckendorff][1] to send *theatrical articles* via his chancellery for preliminary inspection by Your Serenity, this order has been religiously observed even at times when Your Serenity was absent from the capital with the Most August Family. The article in No. 256 of *The Northern Bee* entitled 'Journalist's

Salmagundi' was not sent because I did not consider it to be *an article about theatrical matters*, for it did not contain anything about *the performers' acting or singing*. Having witnessed the displeasure of the audience, among them leading persons in the government, *during the first performance of Norma*, I explained in my article that *I did not want to discuss this performance at all*, supposing that to be preferable to a reporter's account of the audience's hissing and catcalls. I wished thereby to *shield*, so to speak, the performers and not to insult them a second time. I am extremely sorry that I was inept at expressing my intention and that my good intentions were taken amiss. My shift from opera to menagerie was not at all intended to insult the performers so much as to indicate a new *meaning* of menagerie, which has nothing to do with theatre or performers. A menagerie is a serious philosophico-political article meant to refute the destructive ideas of so-called liberalism – *without any connection* to the foregoing. As in *a miscellany*, everything is lumped together into a heap, the menagerie coming after the opera is only fortuitous, as I make bold to assure Your Serenity on my personal *word of honour*. The very first sentence in the article about the menagerie is, as the French say, *une transition*, a shift from one matter to another, and without any intention of saying that I would be *better entertained* in a menagerie, I thought how unpleasant I found it to behold the bad behaviour of the audience at the opera. Clearly I dared not upbraid the public nor do I dare now for a newspaper is a public servant! For the first time in the course of my twenty-five years' journalistic career I am subject to the displeasure of the supreme authorities over *an article of my own*, and I swear I was not ill-intentioned. If I expressed myself poorly, I admit that I am, as the folk saying goes, *innocently guilty*, and I ask Your Serenity to be indulgent to the inadvertent slip of one of the oldest of Russian men of letters and journalists and not to interpret *a mistake* as *a premeditated crime* [. . .]

(b) *Prince Volkonsky to the Minister of Public Enlightenment*:

[The sternest of reproofs is to be issued to Bulgarin, and] in addition, His Majesty pleases that publishers of all journals and gazettes in which articles about the Imperial Theatres are allowed to appear print nothing that has not been previously inspected by the Minister of the Court and that such articles be submitted to him via the established channels, through the Third Section of His Imperial Majesty's chancellery, bearing the signatures of their authors not only by first initials but fully spelt out. Thereafter these articles are to be submitted to the inspection of the ordinary censors as a general rule.

[1] Count Aleksandr Khristoforovich Benckendorff (d. 1844), personally a humane and gentle individual, served as Chief of Gendarmes under Nicholas I and tripled the size of the feared Third Section.

*Audiences at the Moscow Maly and the Petersburg Alexandra*

## 232 Belinsky explains the difference between Moscow and Petersburg audiences, 1845

V.G. Belinsky: 'Aleksandrinsky teatr' ['Aleksandra Theatre'] in *Fiziologiya Peterburga* [*Physiology of Petersburg*], 1845; repr. in Belinsky (1948), pp. 359–62.

The difference between the Russian theatres in Moscow and Petersburg derives primarily from the audiences in the capitals. To be frank, there is no audience for the theatre in Moscow. In the Peter Theatre[1] in Moscow persons of various ranks, various levels of education, various tastes and demands intermingle. There you see bearded merchants and beardless merchants and students and persons who live in Moscow because it's the only place where it's fun to live and who have to be where the fun is; there you see fashionable tailcoats with yellow gloves and dashing dolmans and paletots and old-fashioned cloaks with turned-down collars and knee-length winter overcoats and bearskin coats and ladies' bonnets and peaked caps and hats that are virtually nightcaps and hats with ostrich plumes and dainty bonnets lined with rabbit-skin and heads in kerchiefs of brocade, silk and calico. There you find people who think even *Filat'ka and Miroshka*[2] an entertaining and interesting play; and people for whom even the European repertoire holds all too few treasures; people who want to see nothing but Shakespeare; people who regard Gogol''s comedies as no more than vulgar farces, though not devoid of talent; people who regard Mr Kukol'nik's[3] dramas as works of sophistication and people who see nothing in them but tedium. In short, a theatrical audience in Moscow contains almost as many tastes and opinions as it contains individuals, and it is not uncommon to meet the most subtle and cultivated, the most refined taste sitting next to the crudest, most vulgar taste. It is not uncommon to hear from one's neighbour on one side the most intelligent judgements, and on the other side the most absurd. [. . .] In Moscow they are fonder of tragedy or pathetic drama and value it more highly than comedy or vaudeville. This makes sense: you need a better educated audience for comedy than for tragedy, because the latter relates directly to human passion and feeling, even unconsciously, and will powerfully awake even a deeply slumbering soul, whereas the former requires for its appreciation people who have grown up with a background of mature civilization, it demands an Attic subtlety of taste, perspicacity of intelligence capable of grasping every nuance as it flies by, every barely glimpsed detail. In Moscow even the merchants – bearded and beardless – love tragedy [. . .] these are, for the most part, persons who are easily stirred, persons who are open only to the most powerful sensations: give them a fistfight, one on one, or a combat between the celebrated bear Akhan and some mastiffs back of

Rogozh gate; so if they decide to go to the theatre, give them Mochalov, whom they call 'MochaLov' [. . .] Many of them at his benefits pay one or two hundred rubles or more for a box which ordinarily costs under fifty rubles; they love Mochalov and, glancing down at their beards, they love to tell their friends long before the benefit and long after it, 'I paid thus and such for MochaLov's benefit, I did.' A purely Muscovite trait [. . .]

There is no such audience at the Alexandra Theatre in St Petersburg. This is an audience in the real, the true sense of the word: no heterogeneous ranks here, but all persons of a certain rank in the civil and military services; no heterogeneous attitudes, demands and tastes; it demands one thing only, is satisfied by one thing only. It never contradicts itself, is always true to itself. It is a single individual, one person; not a multitude but one man, respectably dressed, substantial, neither too exigent nor too complaisant, a man who fears extremes and regularly keeps to a reasonable mean, in short, a man of great respectability and loyalty of mien. Exactly the same stratum as those most respected in France and Germany: the bourgeoisie and philistines. The audience of the Alexandra Theatre is completely at home in its auditorium; it feels free and easy there; it doesn't like to see 'strangers' in its midst, and there are almost never any strangers there. Persons of exalted circles occasionally drop in at the Alexandra only for the plays of Gogol', who is much disliked and deservedly held in contempt by the subtle, refined taste, infused with decent social tone, of the Alexandra audience which cares not for obscenity and insipidity. [. . .] No playwright or actor, if he is canny, will risk making a fool of himself; he writes or acts without ever taking a chance, knowing how to please his audience. Recognition of merit – a property of noble souls – constitutes one of the most distinguished features of the character of the Alexandra audience; it loves its performers and does not stint on curtain calls or applause. It greets all its favourites with a thunderous ovation, from Karatygin down to Grigor'ev I[4] inclusively. But in so doing, it acts not rashly or without subtle calculation, and knows how to mete out its rewards in proportion to each performer's deserts, as an educated and cultivated audience should. So, for instance, it will call forth no one but Karatygin fifteen times in a single night; some actors will be called forth no more than once at the end of a performance; but the average number of its curtain calls regularly stays between five and fifteen. Even Karatygin himself is seldom called as many as thirty times. They applaud incessantly; but this is not the result of generosity but of the too-evident worth of all the plays presented to them and all the performers who labour to satisfy them. But if, as seldom happens, a performer does not know how to win its favour at once – he will not hear its applause.

[1] That is, the Bol'shoy Theatre.

[2] *Filat'ka and Miroshka, Rivals, or Four Suitors and One Bride* (*Filat'ka i Miroshka, soperniki*, 1831), a

crude one-act farce about kind-hearted gentry and stupid peasants, was the most popular vaudeville of P.G. Grigor'ev, who wrote several sequels with the same characters.

[3] Nestor Vasil'evich Kukol'nik (1809–68) was one of the most popular playwrights of his time for his verbose but effective patriotic dramas: *The Hand of the Supreme Being Hath Saved the Fatherland* (*Ruka Vsevyshniago otechestvo spasla*, 1834) was the favourite play of Tsar Nicholas I.

[4] Pëtr Ivanovich Grigor'ev (1806–71), a utility actor at the Alexandra, who specialized in caricatures of army officers.

### *The function of the stage manager*

The French term *régisseur* first appeared in Russian in Maykov's 1825 rules and regulations, where it designated the administrator formerly known as Inspector of the Troupe; he was to have complete authority over production and cast, rehearsals, discipline and finished production. In practice, the Russian *regissër* was a glorified stage manager, who had to deal with the day-to-day tasks that were beneath the attention of a bureaucratic administrator. Although some authors, among them Gogol', Turgenev and Ostrovsky, took a keen interest in the mounting of their plays, this was generally the task of the *regissër*. As in Central Europe, the term eventually came to be applied to the stage director, so that the two functions, total artistic control and physical *mise-en-scène*, became invested in one individual.

## 233 The stage manager's duties in the 1840s and 1850s

S.P. Solov'ëv:[1] 'Dvadtsat' pyat' let iz zhizni Moskovskogo teatra' ['Twenty-five years in the life of the Moscow theatre'], *Ezhegodnik imperatorskikh teatrov 1902–1903* [*Yearbook of the Imperial Theatres*] prilozhenie 1, 98–100.

For both dramatic and operatic productions [in Moscow] there was only one stage manager. I came in as the stage manager S.L. Krotov was retiring; after him, for a few months this function was carried out by the actor Kozlovsky, and then by the stage manager Aleksey Fëdorovich Akimov,[2] whose assistant I was at first, until they made me separate stage manager for vaudevilles.

[. . .] The stage manager is invisible and inaudible; he is everywhere and nowhere; his place, during the performance, is backstage; he is like an invisible but indispensable cog in a machine, like the steam in a locomotive. Take him away – and the machine stops short! The stage manager is a hidden but main spring, which sets the whole mechanism of theatrical activity in motion. He is, so to speak, the soul of a stage performance. He should be a man of culture and specially versed in all stage conditions; moreover, he should have a lively imagination, ingenuity and a serenely self-assured efficiency in his work, which is often very onerous and requires the greatest expedition. [. . .] The stage manager, once he gets the play, reads it with the most concentrated attention and, going by the details he finds in it, defines the time and place of the action and the social background of the characters. Taking all this into consideration, he composes a complete scene-plot for the play and sends it to the office for an estimate of necessary expenses, then gives detailed notes to the machinist, the set-designer, the costumier, the wigmaker, the lighting man and the property-man (the person concerned with furniture and all the minor items used on stage). After this, he turns over the play to be copied into roles. When the roles are ready, the stage manager, in accord with the performers' lines of business and abilities, writes on each role which performer is to play it. Afterwards his casting is endorsed by the Inspector of the Repertoire, and the roles are distributed to the performers. The read-through begins. The performers, with role and pencil in hand, sit around a table and, if the author is absent, the stage-manager reads the play; the performers listen and check over their roles. In reading, he has to characterize each character and provide the general tone of the whole play. If sometimes he neglects to do this, it may be because of the stage manager's personal education and his private situation within the company of performers. After a few days have elapsed, rehearsals begin, not at first on stage, but in the rehearsal hall. Here the stage manager tells each performer where he is to enter, what position he takes on stage, when and where he crosses during the action. To do this, the stage manager first rereads the play several times and notes the order of the characters in each scene, where they have to be on stage and all their moves. He must guide young inexperienced actors in the very interpretation of their parts. At stage rehearsals, the stage manager's concern is the amicable, rational progress of the play – the ensemble; he organizes with the set-designer and the machinist the whole technical production; he arranges the furniture and all the minor set-pieces that the play requires.

Finally everything is set and the play goes smoothly. A day is named for the first performance and the stage manager appears at the theatre a few hours before the show, inspects to see that everything is ready on-stage and off-, then goes to the dressing-room to see whether the costumes, shoes and so on have been set out for the actors. At six o'clock the first bell rings, by which time the performers must be dressed. That moment initiates the stage manager's dread ordeal: in the dressing-room, from all sides, voices, male and female, ring out: 'Mr Stage Manager! My costume is too tight.' 'These shoes are so big I'm bound to lose them on stage.' 'I was not cast as a washerwoman and I refuse to go on in this disgusting frock. You hear me – I won't go on for the world!' 'The dresser still hasn't been to see me and I'm sitting here in my underwear! If I miss my entrance, don't blame me!' 'Mr Stage Manager, order them to give me gloves!' And so on, always the same story, only delivered in different tones of voice. Finally, the stage manager, intensely tormented in mind and body, sets things to rights, the performers are dressed, they go on stage, everything's ready and, at seven o'clock, he gives the sign to start the overture, at the end of which the curtain will rise.

During the action the stage manager sends the actors on stage, and so he must follow the whole play word for word; he raises and lowers the curtain, gives the signal to make it day or night; everything to be done backstage, such as thunder, knocking, shouts, bells, gunshots, etc. is all the responsibility of the stage manager.

The play is over and if, through its technical shortcomings, it seemed inadequate and the audience responded coldly, the author will blame this failure more on the stage manager than on anyone else, he will complain that he was not properly staged and given too few rehearsals.

To the number of professional responsibilities of a stage manager, one must add having to listen to the authorities privately reprimand the faults and carelessness of others and endure unpleasant clashes with the performers. Besides the obligations I have described, the stage manager also has many clerical and purely official tasks: after the performance he devotes nearly an hour to proof-reading the playbills for the next day. It is appropriate to remark here that during the winter season there are two benefits every week, and new plays for each one. You can imagine the amount of work for the stage manager. [...] His life, both professional and private, is very peculiar and idiosyncratic. He cannot have any friends or acquaintances outside the theatre, because, busy at the theatre from morning to late at night, he has no time to foster such relationships. Yet at the theatre, everyone is familiar with him but no one is friendly, the chief and sole cause of this, in my opinion, being his duties themselves. Through his professional obligations, the stage manager must take note of the performers' imperfections and record fines for them, which, of course, no one can find pleasant; he also transmits to the performers all the authorities' unpleasant remarks and reprimands; and sometimes it happens that an official who has cause to reprimand an actor, but has some special reason not to quarrel with him, delegates the stage manager to do it, as if on his own initiative. Of course, in such cases the stage manager tries with might and main to gild the pill, but the pill is still a pill, and the performers' animosity to the stage-manager grows stronger every day.

[1] Sergey Petrovich Solov'ëv (1817–79), actor, dramatist and translator, served as stage manager at the Maly from 1836 to 1850.

[2] Dates for Krotov have not been found.

Dmitry Fedoseevich Kozlovsky (d. 1842), an actor at the Maly from 1823, noted for his provincial pronunciation and insufferable declamation.

Aleksey Fëdorovich Akimov (1810–55) supplemented his work by translating and adapting vaudevilles.

### *Staging an early Turgenev play*

Ivan Sergeevich Turgenev (1818–83) said of his comedy *The Bachelor* (*Kholostyak*), it 'is written mostly for the sake of a single role (Shchepkin's)', since the earlier play he had composed for Shchepkin, *The Charity Case* (*Nakhlebnik*), was forbidden by the censor. *The Bachelor* had its debut at the Alexandra Theatre on 14 October 1849, and met with considerable success, although audiences were surprised that the leading character, an elderly nonentity, should be allowed to win the girl at the end. Shchepkin revived the play at the Moscow Bol'shoy in January 1850. This staging plot is typical of hundreds provided by the stage manager prior to production. In this case, it is of interest in listing the requisites for a play of contemporary Russian life.

## 234 Staging plot for Turgenev's *The Bachelor*, 1850

Maly Theatre Archives in V.A. Maslikh: 'Montirovki pervykh postanovok p'es I.S. Turgeneva na stsene Malogo teatra' ['Stagings of the first productions of Turgenev's plays at the Maly Theatre'], *Teatral'noe nasledstvo: Soobshcheniya publikatsiya* [*Theatrical Legacy: report of publications*] (edited by A. Ya. Al'tshuller, S.S. Danilov and G.A. Lapkina) (Moscow: Iskusstvo, 1956), unpag.

THE BACHELOR

To the Office of the Imperial Moscow Theatres
Staging-plot for the 3-act comedy *The Bachelor*

[. . .]

ACTORS AND ROLES

Moshkin, collegiate assessor, age 50 – Mr Shchepkin.[1]

Costume: in Act I at start in a surtout, a cross in the buttonhole, then dons a tailcoat and bowtie which are ready on stage behind a screen. Kerchief. In Act II wears a surtout. In Act III wears a Caucasian overcoat. Ready backstage a furcoat and hat.

Vilitsky, collegiate assessor, age 23 – Mr Samarin I.[2]

Costume: in Act I wears a tailcoat, in Act II a surtout or paletot, then dons an undress uniform, put on in the wings. Hat.

Von Fonck, titular councilor, age 29 – Mr Lensky.[3]

Costume: tailcoat, hat.

Shpundik, a landowner of the steppes, age 45 – Mr Zhivokini Sr.[4]

Costume: in Act I wears a long pea-green surtout, then wears an old-fashioned black tailcoat with a very narrow waist and high collar. White, tight stock with buckle, extremely short striped velvet waistcoat with mother-of-pearl buttons and bright pea-green trousers. Handkerchief. At first a warm visored cap, then a beaver hat. In Act III the same pea-green surtout. Visored cap.

Belova – Miss Kositskaya.[5]

Costume: in Act I at first wears a lady's winter coat and bonnet, then in white dress with light-blue ribbon at the neck. In Act II wears a bonnet with the veil down. In Act III in a house dress.

Pryazhkina, age 48 – Mrs Saburova I.[6]

Costume: in Act I at start wears a lady's winter coat and bonnet, then dressed foppishly, with a big bow of yellow ribbons on her cap. In Act III wears a house dress. Bonnet lies on the table.

[. . .]
Stratilat, a house-boy, age 16 – Mr Milyukov[7]

Costume: wears a casaque

[. . .]
Postilion – Mr Zhivokini Jr[8]

Costume: postilion's outfit, shako

Scenery, Act I: a humble drawing-room. At right two windows. Left of centre another door. Two wall lamps are to be hung on the back curtain.
Properties, Act I: On stage, a divan, a round table, a few armchairs. Between the windows a mirror. Beneath the mirror a little table, on it a hairbrush. The right corner of the room is partitioned off by a green screen. A wall clock shows two o'clock. On the round table a book. Behind the screen Mr Shchepkin's tailcoat and tie. To distribute by hand: Mr Shchepkin a package, cross for buttonhole, snuffbox, twenty-five kopek piece, and a phial of eau-de-Cologne wrapped up in paper. To be ready backstage: change of clothes for Mr Zhivokini; for Mr Shchepkin a cone of sugar, a bottle of Madeira and a cardboard lady's hatbox; for Mrs Saburova I a reticule; for Mr Milyukov two lighted wall lamps. Hors d'œuvre on a tray, must include caviare. For the stage manager a little chime to strike the hour and the usual bell.
Scenery, Act II: a rather shabby room. At centre a door, at right another door, with a key in it.
Properties, Act II: On stage, a divan, a table on which lie pipe tobacco and matches. A few chairs. A chest of drawers. Books on a little shelf, chibouks in the corners. To distribute by hand: to Mr Samarin I a book. To be ready backstage: For

Mr Kremnev a written and sealed letter; undress uniform for Mr Samarin I.
Scenery, Act III. Same setting as for Act I.
Properties, Act III. On stage: the same as in Act I, only with the lamps removed from the wall. On the table place a carafe of water and glasses. On the other table lies Mrs Saburova I's bonnet. To be ready backstage: for Mr Milyukov a samovar, a written letter, sealed; for Mr Shchepkin a cap and furcoat.
Action takes place in Petersburg, Winter 1842.

18 January 1850. Regisseur *Akimov*.[9]

[1] For Shchepkin, see **223**.
[2] For Samarin, see **230**, note 3.
[3] For Lensky, see **249**.
[4] For Zhivokini, see **224**, note 2.
[5] Lyubov' Pavlovna Nikulina-Kositskaya (1827–68), a tragic actress who was able successfully to transfer her emotional romanticism into Ostrovskyan drama.
[6] Agrafena Timofeevna Saburova (1795–1867), at the Maly from 1824, a specialist in comic old women.
[7] Nikolay Milyukov, dates unknown.
[8] Dmitry Vasil'evich Zhivokini (1829–90), son of Vasily Zhivokini, acted at the Maly from 1848 until his death, usually in secondary comic roles.
[9] For Akimov, see **233**.

## V THE ADVENT OF OSTROVSKY, 1855–60

### *Sadovsky creates an Ostrovskyan acting style*

The importance of Aleksandr Nikolaevich Ostrovsky (1823–86) to the development of a nationalist stage cannot be overstated, not only for his contribution of forty-eight highly actable plays to the repertory or his dramatization of special areas of Russian life, but also because of his almost exclusive commitment to the theatre as an instrument of enlightenment. Whole segments of Russian life that had hitherto been neglected or cartooned by the drama were suddenly revealed in vivid detail: the Moscow merchantry, the peasants and townsfolk of the Volga, backwater landowners, touring actors, figures from folklore. From the first, Ostrovsky's partisanship was fought for by two contending camps: the Slavophiles saw him as a recorder of Russian folkways, customs and speech, the Westernizers hailed him as an adversary of Russian backwardness.

The first of Ostrovsky's plays to be staged at the Moscow Maly was *Paddle Your Own Canoe* (*Ne v svoi sani ne sadis'*) in 1853. The older generation of actors, including Shchepkin, found Ostrovsky unsympathetic, too veristic for their tastes and abilities. His ideal interpreter turned out to be Prov Mikhaylovich Sadovsky (Ermilov, 1818–72), who had led a hard wandering life as a provincial actor before fetching up at the Maly in 1839. Although he had made a name for himself in comedy, he found his true niche in Ostrovsky's plays, to whose popularity he was a major contributor. One of his earliest successes in this new repertoire was as the drunken ne'er-do-well Lyubim Tortsov in *Poverty's No Crime* (*Bednost' ne porok*, 1854), who proves to be the hero of the piece. Well in the tradition of the humiliated and offended 'little man', he was taken by many to be an emblem of the Russian character: virtuous and courageous beneath an exterior of vice and boorishness.

## 235 Prov Sadovsky plays Lyubim Tortsov in 1855

D.A. Koropchevsky:[1] 'Vospominaniya o moskovskom teatre' ['Memories of the Moscow theatre'], *Ezhegodnik imperatorskikh teatrov* [*Yearbook of the Imperial Theatres*] (1894–5) prilozhenie 2, 24–8.

Even now I can see the ragged, unshaven fellow, shrivelled with the cold, colliding in the doorway with Lyubov' Gordeevna and halting her with a clownish cry of greeting. He steps into the room, his shoulders hunched, his hands tightly clenched and shoved into his pockets, like a man frozen to the bone, and in this pitiful pose he knows how to invest himself with dignity, to evoke simultaneously genuine laughter and deep sympathy and lively interest. He continues to clown it up, uttering his comical saws in sing-song, especially when they rhyme ('He found to his cost His fortune he'd lost'). Affected buffoonery gives way to bitter humour, to the ponderous laugh at himself. This grief over a wasted youth, over money stupidly squandered seemed to emerge in even greater relief from the theatrically tragic tone in which he presented it, with a great variety of nuance, parodying the lofty intonations of the declamatory tragedians of the time. This was a remarkably successful device, whereby certain passages were distinguished by a remarkable naturalness and aptness. [. . .]

The impression made by the first act was wonderfully consummated in the last. [. . .] Sadovsky's exit – a serious one, with head proudly held high – was a worthy finish to this powerful scene. In his last lines all affectation – both tragic and comic – fell from Lyubim Tortsov: he became touchingly simple and this endowed his last lines with affecting strength. The spectator felt that this 'creeping worm, the nonentity of nonentities', as he calls himself, has experienced a moment of true triumph. [. . .] The unwonted excitement has already abated in Lyubim Tortsov when he lends his voice to the pleas of the women and Mitya. Sincerely and tenderly Sadovsky's voice sounded when he said 'Brother, give Lyubushka to Mitya!' Tears sounded in his voice when, skipping before his brother, he showed him 'what a fop he'd become'. And when he got on his knees, pleading 'Pity even Lyubim Tortsov', no one in the theatre could refrain from shedding a few tears on hearing the bitter request of this man, eroded with suffering. There is no way to describe this effect: it all lay in the player's voice, which pierced deeply into the soul, touching its most sensitive chords. 'Brother, give Lyubushka to Mitya – he will grant me a corner. Freezing to death I was, starving to death . . .' – even now I seem to hear the inexpressibly heart-rending sound of those words. Need I add that such a performance made the play's rapid denouement seem entirely natural. [. . .]

Sadovsky's performance revealed the role of Lyubim Tortsov to be a dramatic high-point, and secured it forever a place in the Russian repertoire. This performance entered our theatrical traditions as an ideal. Other interpreters gave other variants, emphasizing this or that aspect of the role, but the stage figure of Lyubim Tortsov and the basic type were provided by Sadovsky. The elevated level of dramatic quality to which he raised this role continues even now and will probably long continue to serve as a touchstone in roles of everyday life.

[1] Dmitry Andreevich Koropchevsky (1842–1903), journalist and translator.

*Ostrovsky is co-opted by the Westernizers*

Modern Soviet criticism of Ostrovsky is founded on the essays of Nikolay Aleksandrovich Dobrolyubov (1836–61), an ex-seminarian who became a journalist on *The Contemporary*, an organ of the Westernizers. His radical political sympathies led him to interpret Ostrovsky as a realist in arms against the social causes of Russia's benighted state, typified by *samodurstvo* or domestic tyranny. In this excerpt, he hints at the constraints of censorship that prevented Russian drama from dealing with a wide range of subjects.

## 236 Dobrolyubov defines Ostrovsky's 'Realm of Darkness', 1859

N.A. Dobrolyubov: 'Tëmnoe tsarstvo' ['The Realm of Darkness'], *Sovremennik* [*The Contemporary*] 7 (1859); Eng. trans. from J. Fineberg in N.A. Dobrolyubov: *Selected Philosophical Essays* (Moscow: Foreign Languages Publishing House, 1948), pp. 243–4, 247–8.

Ostrovsky is able to peer into the depths of a man's soul, he is able to distinguish his *nature* from the deformities and excrescences introduced from outside; hence, outside pressure, the weight of the whole environment that presses down upon a man, is felt in his works far more than in many stories. [. . .]

Ostrovsky's comedies do not show the higher classes of our society; they are confined to the middle classes and therefore cannot provide the clue to many of the ugly scenes that are depicted in them. Nevertheless, they easily suggest numerous analogous thoughts concerning the life with which they do not directly deal. This is due to the fact that the types in Ostrovsky's comedies often possess not only merchant or governmental official features, but also the common national features of the people.

Public activity is scarcely dealt with in Ostrovsky's comedies, and this is undoubtedly due to the fact that our civic life, while abounding in formalities of every kind, provides scarcely any examples of real activity in which the *human being* can freely and broadly express himself. On the other hand, Ostrovsky's comedies bring out with extreme fullness and relief two kinds of relationships to which a man in this country can still devote his soul, namely, *family* relationships and *property* relationships. It is not surprising, therefore, that the subjects and the very titles of Ostrovsky's plays deal with the family, bridegrooms, brides, riches and poverty.

All the dramatic collisions and catastrophes in Ostrovsky's plays take place as a result of the conflict of two parties, namely, *the old and the young, the rich and the poor, the arrogant and the timid*. Clearly, by the very nature of the case, the climax of such conflicts must be fairly abrupt and smack of casualness.

[. . .] Thus, in the realm of darkness that Ostrovsky depicts, external submission and dull, concentrated grief that reaches the stage of downright imbecility and the most deplorable obliteration of personality are interwoven with slavish cunning, with the most despicable deception and the most shameless perfidy. Here nobody can trust another; at any moment you may expect your friend to boast about how skilfully he has cheated or robbed you [. . .] a bridegroom will cheat the matchmaker; the bride will deceive her father and mother, a wife will deceive her husband. Nothing is sacred, nothing is pure, there is no justice in this dark world: the savage, unreasonable and unjust tyranny that reigns over them has driven all sense of honesty and justice from their minds . . . These cannot exist where tyrants have shattered and have arrogantly trampled upon human dignity, the freedom of the individual, faith in love and happiness and the sacredness of honest toil.

And yet right near by, only on the other side of the wall, there is another life, bright, clean and enlightened . . . Both sides in the realm of darkness are aware of the superiority of this life, and they are frightened by it at one moment and attracted to it at another. But the principles of this life, its inherent strength, are totally unintelligible to the wretched creatures who have grown unaccustomed to all reason and truth in their daily relationships. [. . .]

And so, through the whole life of the *tyrants* and through the entire life of suffering of the *oppressed* runs this struggle against the tide of the free new life which, of course, will one day flow over the age-old accumulations of mud and convert the marsh into a bright and magnificent river, but which today as yet only stirs up this mud, becomes itself submerged in it, and with it decays and stinks . . . At present, the new principles of life are only disturbing the minds of all the inhabitants of the realm of darkness like a distant vision, or a nightmare. [. . .]

Such is the general impression that is created by Ostrovsky's comedies as we understand them.

### *The critics clash over Thunderstorm*

Ostrovsky's play *Thunderstorm* (*Groza*, 1860) set the seal on his fame; this gloomy picture of sexual and spiritual repression in a small town is often taken to be the closest Russian drama has come to tragedy. It won its author a prize from the Academy of Sciences, much to the disgust of Shchepkin who was appalled by what he saw as the play's coarseness and cynicism.

The critic Apollon Aleksandrovich Grigor'ev (1822–64) had coined the phrase 'a new word in the theatre' to describe Ostrovsky in his article 'On the comedies of Ostrovsky and their significance to literature and the stage' (*The Muscovite* [*Moskvityanin*] 3, 1855). In 'After *Thunderstorm*', he refashioned that article as a counterblast to Dobrolyubov's 'Dark Realm' interpretation of Ostrovsky. Grigor'ev aimed at 'organic criticism', which was meant to discover the peculiarly national characteristics of any work under examination and avoid tendentious moralizing.

Dobrolyubov's response, 'A Ray of Light in the Realm of Darkness', offered the doomed protagonist of *Thunderstorm*, Katerina Kabanova, as a harbinger of progress. Ignoring her desperate suicide, he lauded her as an heroic type, pointing a way out of the dark kingdom.

## 237a Grigor'ev stresses Ostrovsky's uniqueness, 1860

A.P. Grigor'ev: 'Posle *Grozy* Ostrovskogo: dva otkrytye pis'ma k I.S. Turgenevu' ['After Ostrovsky's *Thunderstorm*: two open letters to Turgenev'], *Russkiy Mir* [*Russian World*] nos. 5, 6, 9, 11 (1860); repr. in A.P. Grigor'ev: *Sobranie sochineny* [*Collected works*], edited by V.F. Sadovnik, vol. 11 (Moscow: I.N. Kushnerëv, 1915–16).

[. . .] Ostrovsky is first of all a dramatist: he does not create his types for Mr –bov, author of articles about 'The Realm of Darkness', or for you, for any one person, but for a mass audience, for whom, if you please, he, as its poet, a people's poet, is also a teacher, but a teacher from that high vantage point accessible to the masses and not to you or me or Mr –bov, a vantage point the masses understand and share. [. . .]

The term *domestic tyranny* is too narrow to express the meaning of all those strange relations in life that somewhere, at some time, got out of joint, as depicted by an artist with profundity and compassion; and the appellations 'satirist', 'negative writer' are not very suitable for a poet who can play all the tunes of popular life in every key, who can create the energetic nature of a Nadya, the passionately tragic dilemma of a personality like Katerina, the sublime character of a Kuligin, a Grusha who radiates life and an ability to live with feminine dignity in the popular drama *Don't Live as You List*, and, in the same play, old Agafon with his unbounded and somewhat pantheistic love which extends to all living things.[1]

The appellation for such a writer, for such a great writer, for all his defects, is not satirist, but poet of the people. The clue to his works is not 'domestic tyranny' (*samodurstvo*) but 'nationality' (*narodnost'*). Only this word can act as a key to understanding his creations. Any other, more or less narrow, more or less theoretical and arbitrary, will cramp his creativity. [. . .]

From 1847 to 1855 (I am still considering only the *first* period of Ostrovsky's writing), Ostrovsky wrote but nine works in all, and only five of them are considerable in size and six in content; only four of them were performed in the theatre; but these four, to put it bluntly, *created* a people's theatre;[2] partly created, partly propelled the performers forward, evoked a general sympathy throughout society, altered many views on Russian life, familiarized us with types whose existence we had not suspected and who, nevertheless, do undoubtedly exist, with extremely novel and dramatic relationships, with the multifarious aspects of the Russian soul, profound and moving and tender aspects which no one had even touched before then. The right of literary citizenship was bestowed on a multitude of clear-cut, well-defined images, new, vivid creations in the world of art, and all this took place without the critics learning anything. [. . .]

1 Grusha and Agafon are characters in *Don't Live As You List* (*Ne tak zhivi, kak khochetsya*, 1854), a one-act play set in eighteenth-century Moscow during the Shrovetide fair. Nadya is the put-upon heroine of *The Ward* (*Vospitannitsa*, 1859). Katerina is the heroine of *Thunderstorm*, in which Kuligin appears as a well-meaning inventor.

2 'people's drama', i.e. *narodnaya drama* can also be translated as 'national drama'. Popular theatre, in the sense of fairbooth entertainments and folk-plays, was usually termed *nizovoy narodny teatr* or lower-class theatre.

## 237b The climactic scene in *Thunderstorm* at the Alexandra Theatre, St Petersburg, 1859[1]

Water-colour sketch by A. Charlemagne, 1859; reproduced in Vsevolodsky-Gerngross, vol. 2 (1929), opp. p. 116.

[1] This is the scene in which the storm brings home to Katerina her adulterous guilt and drives her to suicide. It is worth noting that the style of decor, lighting and acting are all operatic rather than 'realistic'.

## 238 Dobrolyubov perceives *A Ray of Light in the Realm of Darkness*, 1860

N.A. Dobrolyubov: 'Luch sveta v tёmnom tsarstve,' *Sovremennik* [*The Contemporary*] 10 (1860); English trans. by J. Fineberg from Dobrolyubov (1948), pp. 578, 594.

[...] We have already observed in the case of Ostrovsky's previous plays that they are not comedies of intrigue, and not even character comedies in the strict sense of the term, but something new, which we would call 'plays of life' if that term were not too wide, and, therefore, not quite definite. What we want to say is that in the foreground of his plays we always find the general conditions of life which are not dependent upon any of the personages in the play. He punishes neither the villain nor his victim; both look pitiful to you, not infrequently both are comical, but they are the direct objects of the sentiments which the play rouses in you. You see that their conditions dominate over them, and you blame them only for failing to display sufficient energy to extricate themselves from them. The very tyrants who should naturally rouse your indignation turn out, on closer examination, to be deserving of pity rather than anger; they are virtuous and even intelligent in their own way, within the limits prescribed for them by routine and maintained by their position. [. . .]

Thus, the struggle which theory demands from the drama takes place in Ostrovsky's plays not in the monologues of the personages, but in the facts which dominate their actions. Often the personages in the comedies themselves have no clear conception, or conception at all, of the meaning of their position and of their struggle; on the other hand, this struggle takes place very distinctly and consciously in the heart of the spectator who [involuntarily][1] protests against [the conditions] which give rise to such facts. [. . .]

The point is that, as portrayed in *Thunderstorm*, Katerina's character marks a step forward not only in Ostrovsky's dramatic activites, but also in the whole of our literature. It corresponds to the new phase of our [national] life, it has long demanded portrayal in literature, our best writers have toyed with it, but they were only able to appreciate its necessity, they were unable mentally to grasp and to feel its substance. Ostrovsky was able to do that. Not a single critic of *Thunderstorm* has been willing or able to write a correct appreciation of this character, and for that reason we take the liberty to continue our essay a little longer in order to explain rather fully how we understand Katerina's character [and why we think its creation is so important for our literature].

[Russian life has at last reached the stage where virtuous and esteemed, but weak and spineless individuals no longer satisfy the public conscience and are regarded as totally useless. An urgent need is now felt for men who, if less beautiful in character, are more active and energetic. Nor can it be otherwise.] As soon as the consciousness of truth [and right], as soon as common sense awoke in the minds of men, it imperatively demanded not only agreement with it in the abstract [(in which the virtuous heroes of the past were always so brilliant)] but its application to life, to activity. But before it can be applied to life, many obstacles [raised by the Dikoys, Kabanovas and their ilk][2] have to be overcome, and to overcome these obstacles [enterprising,] determined and persevering characters are required. These must personify, merge themselves with the [general] demand for truth [and right] which has [at last] awakened [in men] and is breaking through all the barriers [erected by the Dikoy tyrants]. The great problem now is, how should the character which the new phase of social life [in this country] is calling for be formed and manifest itself? [. . .]

[1] Throughout this excerpt, the words in brackets are those omitted by the tsarist censor before publication was permitted.

[2] The villains in *Thunderstorm*, two repressive members of the merchant class. Dikoy means 'savage', Kabanova 'wild sow'.

## VI ACTOR TRAINING, 1850–90

### *The paucity of dramatic training*

Although a State Dramatic School had been started in Moscow as early as 1809, there was little in the way of formal training for actors. Occasionally a star like Shchepkin might drop into a class and bestow the fruits of his experience on the students, but for the most part the curriculum in both capitals consisted of recitation for expression and enunciation, and deportment taught by dancing-masters. With the emergence of a newly realistic repertory, it became clear that actors would need to learn new methods, particularly as the old *emploi* system of type-casting was irrelevant to the Ostrovsky school.

An early appeal for professional if more traditional training came from Rafail Mikhaylovich Zotov (1796–1871), secretary to the Administrator of the Imperial Theatre Naryshkin before running the Russian Dramatic troupe in St Petersburg for a decade (1826–36). The author and translator of over 100 plays, Zotov believed, with Scribe, that the stage was an independent world which should create its own images rather than imitate reality. The training he recommends would support an old-fashioned and artificial style of performance.

## 239 An artistic conservative declares the need to train actors, 1850

R.M. Zotov: 'O dramaticheskom iskusstve v Rossii i o sredstvakh k obrazovaniyu artistov' ['On dramatic art in Russian and on the way to educate performers'] in P.N. Arapov and Avgust Roppol't: *Dramatichesky al'bom s portretami russkikh artistov i snimkami s rukopisey* [*Dramatic album with portraits of Russian performers and autographed portraits from photographs*] (Moscow: Universitetskaya tipografiya i V. Got'e, 1850), pp. 146–8.

Here in Russia as elsewhere people throw themselves into a theatrical career without any preliminary knowledge of that art. Having memorized some role and played it in an amateur theatrical, they imagine that that is all it takes to make an actor. Future development of talent they leave to suggestion (inspiration) and chance. [. . .] An actor must have some specialized technical training for his art. Here in Russia, unfortunately, there are no suitable textbooks – and even fewer instructors. [. . .]

We might think that the truest and best preceptor of stage art would be an *actor*, but this is wrong. Not one famous performer is the pupil of an actor, and not a single great performer has yet trained a good student. Specialized teachers must come from among cultured men of letters. [. . .] The sole concern of a specialist-teacher will be to explain to the actor the meaning of every line, of his roles and his situations, and to bear in mind only a refined ideal and not an imitation of one actor or another.

[. . .] The first subject of an actor's special education must be *recitation*. [. . .] On stage, when the spectator in the gallery 140 or 150 yards from the fifth or sixth groove must hear every sound, a word must without fail be pronounced in its entirety. Many actors muffle or, as people say, swallow the ends of words, and this is most intolerable to the auditor. Acoustically, sound grows fainter as it drifts into the distance and becomes indistinct. Consequently, the slightest muffling of its ending makes every line indistinct, the spectator fails to understand it and says he cannot hear it. Raising one's voice will not mend matters. Even a whisper must be made distinct. [. . .] The teacher of dramatic recitation must have the the student recite a good deal for a long time, daily increasing the distance and stopping him at every swallowed ending. [. . .]

The second class of the dramatic course must deal with artistic recitation, that is, the students must recite their role with all the intonations required by the lines in their role. [. . .] On stage monotony is intolerable. Variegated sounds are necessary to make sense of the lines spoken and the passions expressed. We knew one passionate theatrical amateur who often performed in domestic theatricals. He had the chance to educate some of our actors and therefore established a kind of musical scale, by which the pupils were to recite their roles. They laughed at him, and he lost his students. And yet there is a substantial basis for this very method; only the teacher must not limit himself to mechanics, and should know how to endow the lines with animation. Obviously, such a teacher must be a man of culture, who knows how to feel and how to communicate his thoughts.

The third phase of learning for the actor is *acting*, that is, the technical devices of movement, gait, posture and facial mimicry. This is to be learned on stage, not when an actor has joined a real troupe, but in practice performances to be arranged as often as necessary. [. . .] In general, inadequacies in performance result from under-rehearsal. One may love art and engage in it fervently and yet not be an actor; to be an actor one must *act* at rehearsals just the same as one does in performance, and even repeat the unsuccessful passages a few times over. [. . .]

Finally, we advise all true actors to attend foreign performances as often as they can. Vanity makes them think they have nothing to learn from each other. No! even another's mistakes serve as a lesson. One must always be learning. The greatest actor, when he is not learning, goes stale. Likewise, we would wish that fully cultured performers seek out criticism and be not offended by it. [. . .]

For the generally successful run of a play it is likewise necessary that not everyone try to be cast in the lead, for first-class actors should also play insignificant parts. They should not find this degrading, for it is beneficial and pleasant for play and audience alike.

*A proposal for a state-sponsored acting class*

Zotov's ideas were more philosophical than practical. The first attempt to organize a curriculum came from Evgeny Ivanovich Voronov, a student of Pëtr Karatygin, who had begun as an actor and then served as stage manager of the Alexandra Theatre from 1852 until his death in 1868. A specialist at crowd scenes, he insisted on discipline, and his proposed curriculum reflects this, along with a more organic approach to creating a role. His project was not realized by the authorities.

## 240 A stage manager offers a project for an acting class at the Imperial theatre in Petersburg, 1867

E.I. Voronov: 'Proèkt dramaticheskogo klassa imperatorskogo S.-Peterburgskogo teatral-'nogo uchilishcha (1867g.)' ['Project for an acting class at the Imperial St Petersburg theatrical school'] in V. Vsevolodsky-Gerngross: *Khrestomatiya po istorii russkogo teatra* [*Chrestomathy for the history of the Russian theatre*] 'Moscow: Khudozhestvennaya literatura, 1936), pp. 393–4.

[. . .] The more talented the student, the sooner and the better will he learn and perform the assignments set by the teacher; the more skilled the teacher, the sooner and the better will he bring out the innate capabilities of the student. It is impossible to prescribe rules. One can only suggest the following means as a beginning:

First of all, deliver a good lecture to the students on the way one should learn or, rather, study a role. Establish the following invariable rules:

1 Read through the play attentively.

2 Read through and con your own role in the play.

3 Find in the play (in speeches of other characters, and sometimes even in your own role) indications of the nature of the person to be portrayed.

4 Trace his relations with other persons and the measure of his participation in the action of the play as a whole and in each separate scene in particular. (To this end, the teacher should instil in the student an awareness, for instance, that if he occupies a secondary place on stage, he should not creep into the foreground and thus spoil the effect; that in every scene there is bound to be one character who presides [the protagonist] and who is to be abetted. So, for instance, if the aim of the scene is to move the spectator, he should not raise laughter by his inopportune comedy, etc.)

5 To present, so to speak, the character one has learned through details and to create it on a foundation of knowledge gained in the preparatory classes.

6 Finally, grounding oneself in this character, to devise a makeup and costume for it.

NOTE The most important failings of Russian performers: *wishy-washiness* and *unevenness* in roles. Wishy-washiness derives from our lack of energy. The cause of unevenness is our native 'lackadaisical', 'not to worry', 'somehow or other' attitude.

Use practical means as an aid: make them act without a prompter – this involuntarily teaches young people to memorize their roles and always be on the alert, because, when acting without a prompter, the slightest inattention and distraction will result in a dead standstill.

*A new curriculum in Moscow makes little difference*

The acting school at the Moscow Maly was closed in 1871, the result of administrative lack of interest; but in 1888 a special curriculum for actors was introduced at the Moscow Theatre School, with famous performers on the faculty. Required courses included history of Russian and foreign literature, dramatic and theatrical history, church history, civil history, one foreign language, diction, fencing, singing, painting, 'drama practicum' and preparation of examination scenes. This was founded on the curriculum of the Comédie française, following the recommendation of the dramatist P.A. Boborykin [see **257(b)**].

That formal instruction still took second place to on-the-job training is made clear in actors' memoirs. Yury Mikhaylovich Yur'ev (1872–1849) studied acting at the Moscow Philharmonic Institute in 1889, and then entered Lensky's class at the Moscow Theatre school. From 1893 to 1917, he was leading man at the Alexandra Theatre, where Meyerhol'd directed him as Molière's Dom Juan and Arbenin in Lermontov's *Maskarad*.

## 241 An actor recollects the lack of training in the 1880s

Yu. M. Yur'ev: *Zapiski* [*Notes*, 1849], vol. 1 (Leningrad–Moscow: Iskusstvo, 1963), pp. 292–3.

In autumn 1888 the newly-organized courses at the Moscow Maly Theatre opened their doors. From now on the Russian dramatic theatre had its first serious school of stage art. Previously, the professional training of dramatic actors in Russia had been purely sporadic. True, a dramatic class did exist at the Moscow Conservatory, which was presided over for a short space by I.V. Samarin.[1] There was also a dramatic class at the Philharmonic which opened a few years before the Imperial courses were established. But at both the Philharmonic and the Conservatory training in dramatic art played second fiddle to musical and vocal instruction which had pride of place. [. . .]

In those days all dramatic theatres were more or less the same. [. . .] Privately-owned theatres in the provinces generally resembled state theatres in the capitals.

It was quite natural that the Imperial Theatres were generally filled by the strongest talents of the provincial stages. Provincial actors always aspired to act in the capitals, and therefore the management of the Imperial Theatres spent little time worrying about creating a school, and was temporarily satisfied with a class in drama which comprised a secondary subject in the ballet school.

And, to tell the truth, not without results. The irresistible interest of some ballet students in drama and the frequent occasions to exercise it (perhaps both these things) gave the Imperial Theatres a chance to swell the ranks of outstanding dramatic artists with those who came out of the ballet school [. . .]

Many [graduates] first went out to the provinces for practice and then, on their return to the capital, were enrolled on the State stage; others were lucky enough to achieve a position *via* that notorious practice, staying in one place. At first they would be cast in a role 'without a thread', then 'with a thread', that is, with lines – and by such a long route the most successful talents would sometimes reach the front rank. That is why practice prevailed and was considered the unique method for creating an actor, to the absolute disparagement of schools.

But opponents of theory and systematic education forgot how much time and energy even the most talented actors had wasted, forced to meander along the path of their development, what powers had been squandered in the struggle with error and delusion. [. . .]

And we know the appalling conditions in which that struggle took place! If a production met with success it was played two, three, four times, with a prompter, without the lines being firmly memorized. Only individual 'sides' were studied, individual monologues, the most effective ones, with the intention of 'gripping' the audience, 'punching' it in its so-called 'guts', extorting applause, without considering that those same 'guts' often had nothing to do with the way the character figured in the play, but simply constituted a professional stimulant, a so-called 'push-button', which Stanislavsky[2] has so accurately characterized as a 'reflex action' or, as they call it in the circus, 'the clincher'. [. . .]

[1] For Samarin see **230, note** 3.
[2] For Stanislavsky see *IX*, pp. 411–18.

## VII IMPERIAL THEATRES, 1855–1900

### *Repertoire and management after the death of Nicholas I*

The European revolutions of 1848 had impelled the autocrat Nicholas I to form a special secret committee, under his personal direction, to oversee the arts and exclude liberal ideas from literature. A law of 1854 promulgated a monopoly of the Imperial Theatres in the capitals; the only exceptions were acrobatic and conjuring shows and foreign-language performances, except for those in Yiddish.

With the Tsar's death in 1855, in part hastened by the reversals of the Crimean War, the secret committee to censor the censors was abolished, but the double censorship of plays – one scrutiny for publication, another for production – continued until 1865 (four years after the emancipation of the serfs). Still, the early reign of Alexander II promised reform, and a number of previously banned plays at last got on the stage, albeit with cuts and rewrites: among them, Pushkin's *Boris Godunov*, Turgenev's *The Charity Case*, and Ostrovsky's *A Lucrative Post* (*Dokhodnoe mesto*, 1854, first performed 1863). Others remained arbitrarily prohibited. The loosening in censorship was unfortuntely accompanied by a laxity in artistic standards under an incompetent administration.

Most actors were recruited from professional dynasties or protégés, friends of friends or outstanding provincials with outrageous styles. A number of remarkable talents – Lensky, Ermolova, Fedotova in Moscow, Varlamov, Savina, Davydov in Petersburg – managed to emerge, although showcased in an increasingly shoddy frame. The same forced-perspective scenery reappeared no matter what the locale of the drama, and actors were expected to supply their own costumes in contemporary plays. Historicity and local color were totally lacking in the physical productions, and *mise-en-scène* was a matter of the star taking centre stage, secondary characters taking the hindmost.

Consequently, a vociferous debate arose on the need for private theatres, liberals insisting on its cultural benefits to society, conservatives deploring the likely proliferation of cheap and meretricious entertainments [see VIII, pp. 395–402]. The debate concluded, surprisingly, in the abolition of the State monopoly on theatre in the capitals. The decree, signed on 24 March 1882 by Alexander III, lumped the dramatic stage together with masquerades and concerts as 'public amusements, performances and celebrations', indicating that the government still ignored and discounted the value of the theatre for society. Within the Imperial playhouses, matters continued much as before, with strict if inconsistent regulations. Actors were still subject to fines, punishments including arrest (this recourse was almost never taken), and the day-to-day insolence of office. Although the playwrights Ostrovsky and Potekhin were invited in as company managers, they took on the coloration of their surroundings, becoming as authoritarian and peremptory as any bureaucrat. Only towards the end of the century, with the success of private theatres like Korsh's, Suvorin's and the Moscow Art, did the Imperial Theatres feel impelled to renovate their repertoires and their methods.

## 242 Repertoire statistics for St Petersburg theatres, 1855–81

A.I. Vol'f: *Khronika peterburgskikh teatrov s kontsa 1855 do nachala 1881 goda* [*Chronicle of Petersburg theatres from late 1855 to early 1881*] (St Petersburg: P. Golike, 1884), pp. 75, 78–80.

WORKS PERFORMED 30 AUGUST 1855 TO 1 MARCH 1881

*Plays from earlier repertoires*

| | | | | | |
|---|---|---|---|---|---|
| Original dramas and comedies | 82 | vaudevilles | 97 | total | 179 |
| Translated " " " | 69 | " | 152 | " | 221 |
| Total " | 151 | " | 249 | total | 400 |

*New plays*

| | | | | | |
|---|---|---|---|---|---|
| Original dramas and comedies | 316 | vaudevilles | 51 | total | 367 |
| Translated " " " | 170 | " | 164 | " | 334 |
| Total " | 486 | " | 215 | " | 701 |

*All plays*

| | | | | | |
|---|---|---|---|---|---|
| Original dramas and comedies | 398 | vaudevilles | 148 | total | 546 |
| Translated " " " | 239 | " | 316 | " | 555 |
| Total " | 637 | " | 464 | " | 1,101 |

*Plays most often performed*

| Original dramas and comedies | No. of performances |
|---|---|
| *The Inspector*, Gogol' | 158 |
| *Woe from Wit*, Griboedov | 105 |
| *Krechinsky's Wedding*, Sukhovo-Kobylin | 100 |
| *Thunderstorm*, Ostrovsky | 96 |
| *Poverty's No Crime*, Ostrovsky | 79 |
| *A Fiancé from Debtor's Prison*, Chernyshev | 79 |
| *The Death of Ivan the Terrible*, Count A. Tolstoy | 65 |
| *Petersburg Clutches*, Khudekov and Zhulev | 65 |
| *The Ward*, Ostrovsky | 63 |
| *Marriage*, Gogol' | 62 |
| *The Tutor*, D'yachenko[1] | 61 |

[. . .]

| *Translated and adapted dramas and comedies* | No. of performances |
|---|---|
| *Uncle Tom's Cabin* | 67 |

| | |
|---|---|
| *Behind the Convent Wall* | 55 |
| *Thirty Years or A Gambler's Life* | 46 |
| *Take It to Court!* | 45 |
| *Hamlet* | 43 |
| *The Two Orphans* | 43 |
| *The Second-storey Window* | 37 |
| *Richelieu*[2] | 36 |

[. . .]

| *Translated* [. . .] *operettas* [. . .] | No. of performances |
|---|---|
| *La Belle Hélène* | 124 |
| *Idle Creature* | 113 |
| [. . .] | |
| *La Périchole* | 79 |
| *Orpheus in the Underworld* | 78 |

[. . .]

*No. of performances of works by famous authors*

Shakespeare: *Hamlet* 43 performances, *King Lear* 28, *Merchant of Venice* 19, *Much Ado about Nothing* 7, *Othello* 6, *The Tempest* 5, *Macbeth* 3, *Timon of Athens* 2. *Total 113 performances*
Molière: *The Miser* 7, *Dom Juan* 7, *The Doctor in spite of Himself* 7, *Tartuffe* 6, *School for Husbands* 6, *School for Wives* 5, *Love's the Best Doctor* 5, *Scapin's Shenanigans* 3, *Georges Dandin* 2, *Marriage on Compulsion* 2. *Total 50 performances*
Beaumarchais: *The Marriage of Figaro*, 13.
Schiller: *The Robbers* 4, *Love and Intrigue* 2, *Don Carlos* 2. *Total 8 performances*
Lessing: *Emilia Galotti* 2.
V. Hugo: *Castilian Honour* 2, *The Actress of Venice* 1.[4] *Total 3 performances*

*No. of performances of Old Russian drama*

Fonvizin: *The Minor* [*Nedorosol'*, 1782] 12; *The Brigadier* [*Brigadir*, 1766] 2. *Total 14 performances*
Ablesimov: *The Miller as Magician, Mountebank and Matchmaker* [*Mel'nik – koldun, obmanshchik i svat*, 1781], *14 performances*
Il'in: *Magnanimity or The Recruitment* [*Velikodushie, ili Rekrutskoy nabor*, 1804]. 2 performances
I.A. Krylov: *The School for Daughters* [*Urok dochkami*, 1807] 3.
*Total 33 performances*

[1] Russian titles and dates of St Petersburg premieres for plays not already cited: *Svad'ba Krechinskogo*, 1856; *Smert' Ioanna Groznogo*, 1866; *Peterburgskie kogti*, 1871; *Vospitannitsa*, 1859; *Zhenit'ba*, 1842; and *Guvernër*, 1864. An oddity in this company, *Zhenikh iz dolgovogo otdeleniya*, 1858, was based on 'A Passage in the Life of Mr Watkins Tottle' in Dickens's *Sketches by Boz*.

[2] Russian titles, original sources, with authors, composers, and dates of Petersburg premiere: *Knizhina dyady Toma* from *La Case de l'oncle Tom* by D'Ennery, trans. M.P. Fëdorov, 1869; *Za monastyrskoy stenoy*, from *Suor Teresa o Elisabeta Soarez* by L. Camoletti, trans. V.S. Kurochkin, 1876; *K mirovomu!* by V.A. Krylov, 1870; *Gamlet, Prints datsky* in Polevoy's translation, 1837; *Dve sirotki*, from *Les Deux orphelines* by D'Ennery and Cormon, trans. P.I. Yurkevich, 1875; *Okno v vtorom ètazhe* from *Okno na pierswzym piętrze* by Józef Korzeniowski, adapt. from *Une Faute* by Scribe, trans. Stadowski, 1850; *Richelieu* by Bulwer-Lytton, trans. M.S. Stepanov, 1866.

[3] *Prekrasnaya Elena*, book by Meilhac and Halévy, trans. V.A. Krylov, music by Offenbach, 1868; *Bezzabotnaya*, from *Flâneuse* by Pitteau-Deforges and Saint-Yves, music by Kazhinsky, 1856; *Ptichki pevchie*, book by Meilhac and Halévy, trans. V.A. Krylov, music by Offenbach, 1869; *Orfey v adu*, from *Orphée aux enfers* by H. Crémieux, trans. V.A. Krylov, music by Offenbach, 1865.

[4] *Hernani*, trans. V.A. Karatygin, 1851, and *Angélo, tyran de Padoue*, trans. M.V. Samoylova, 1835.

## 243 The benighted regime of Administrator Saburov, 1858–62

Vol'f (1884), pp. 4–5.

The post of Administrator was filled by Mr Saburov,[1] heretofore Superintendent of the Court of his Imperial Highness Grand Duke Constantine. He was entirely unacquainted with matters theatrical and in the beginning did not dispose his subordinates in his favour by his rude manner of address, arrogance and hauteur. After four years as administrator, he had accomplished nothing beneficial either for the performers or for art. The ever-to-be-remembered Pavel Stepanovich [Fëdorov][2] continued to lord it over the Russian theatre and school without supervision, while the new official concerned himself only with the Italian opera and the French theatre. Mr Saburov did not keep a close eye on the government's money and squandered it senselessly right and left, to foreign performers, of course, with the aim of being praised to the skies by the foreign press and glorified as a highly enlightened *grand seigneur*. He engaged the farce actor Ravel[3] for three seasons, granting him 60,000 francs a season; Ravel was a complete failure in Russia, seldom played and all the same took 180,000 francs out of Russia. The engagement of the superannuated Ristori[4] and her whole troupe for two seasons was even more devastating; the theatre was almost entirely empty, while the maintenance of the sizeable troupe cost a huge amount. [. . .] [In 1859] He undertook the wholly unnecessary rebuilding of the Michael Theatre,[5] which had been a wonder of perfection, partly for its acoustics and partly for its comfortable accommodations for spectators: one could see and hear splendidly even from the most distant seats in the amphitheatre. The theatre was decorated simply but elegantly and tastefully; the number of seats was quite sufficient for the number of those who attended French and, more especially, German performances. The new administrator, however, thought it necessary to enlarge the dimensions of the auditorium considerably and solicited 400,000 from designated funds to satisfy his whims, promising to repay these sums from increased box office receipts. The receipts, however, did not increase after the reconstruction, whereas the expenses did from year to year, and therefore it is quite likely that the loan remained unrepaid, or was paid back from some outside source. The rebuilt theatre, as everyone knows, is extremely poor acoustically; almost nothing is audible from the farthest rows of stalls or from many boxes, the balcony and the gallery. The interior dimensions of the auditorium and the stage turned out to be disproportionate, as a result of having to enlarge them within the old walls. The height is entirely out of proportion to the width, the large Imperial box is incongruously small; the interior decoration is motley and tasteless. In short, 400,000 down the drain.

1 Andrey Ivanovich Saburov (1797–1866), a former hussar; his cynical attitude to the theatre is summed up in his remark on hearing of the death of the popular actor Martynov: 'Pity! Now ticket-sales will drop off'.

2 Pavel Stepanovich Fëdorov was in charge of the St Petersburg repertoire 1854–79; his chief interest was to insure that amateurs, who paid heavily for the privilege, could use the government stages.

3 Pierre-Alfred Ravel (1814–81), a celebrated Parisian comedian, particularly good in monologues.

4 The only importance to Russia of the Italian star Adelaide Ristori (1822–1906) was her influence on the provincial actress A. Strelkova.

5 The Michael or Mikhaylovsky Theatre, built in 1833 from designs by A.P. Bryullov, housed French and German troupes, and therefore played exclusively to the cream of Petersburg society and to foreigners.

## 244a Management and staging at the Imperial Theatres in the 1880s and 1890s

V.A. Nelidov:[1] *Teatral'naya Moskva (sorok let moskovskikh teatrov* [*Theatrical Moscow (forty years of Moscow theatres)*] (Berlin–Riga: S. Kretschetow, 1921), pp. 101–3, 127–37.

The entire personnel serving the Imperial Theatres of Moscow and Petersburg consisted of 4,011 persons. This included two operatic, two ballet and two dramatic troupes, two orchestras and two choruses, a French troupe, two dramatic schools, three theatres in Moscow and three in Petersburg completely equipped with such things as workmen, costume designers, ushers, carriages, etc., etc., etc.

The budget of the Imperial Theatre came to nearly 4 million a year, and the box-office takings seldom exceeded two. In sum, on an average, there was a veritable deficit of nearly 300,000 for each theatre, but this amount was a trifle in itself, to put it mildly, since the theatres also maintained ballet and dramatic schools, carriages and ushers, whose overall cost was most considerable.

How was the business run and who ran it? The Administrator's passport read Nobleman. Under him were the administrative offices for Petersburg and Moscow. At certain periods, these posts were filled by more or less suitable persons. At other times, they were illiterates. [. . .] The press of the day called the 1880s and 1890s the era of theatrical second lieutenants, for the Minister of the Imperial Court Count Vorontsov-Dashkov[2] favoured the Finland regiment of Life-guards, and when he was appointed minister in 1881 packed the theatre jobs with indigent officers who had served in the Turkish campaign of 1877–9. [. . .]

The offices were divided in turn into four parts: administrative (i.e. chancellery), accounting, managerial, and theatrical, which took care of all the external aspects of all the productions. The administrator was, in addition, assigned an assistant who was the theatre's police superintendant, for the ordinary police could not deal with the Imperial Theatre except by permission from this police superintendant. Then there was a salaried civilian functionary on special assignment, who for some reason ran the box-offices. [. . .] Suffice it to say that the annual budget of the office with all its staff was at the time 28,000 rubles (the administrator got 5,000, the assistant 3,000, the other persons listed 1,800 a head annually). Legends about the infinite number of employees are nothing but legends. [. . .]

The office did not serve the theatre. On the contrary, it was taken for granted that *office* was a dirty word in the ears of the theatre, while for the office, the word *theatre* had an element of revolution about it. For the office, all performers were 'employees'; for the performers, all office workers were 'bureaucrats'. Anyone who tried to reconcile them was looked upon as a traitor by both sides. [. . .]

The office administrator of the time, Pchel'nikov[3] (1882–98), by no means a bad man personally, was born under a lucky star: he inherited from the previous management the Maly Theatre's wonderful troupe, Al'tani and Bartsal[4] built him an opera, in his simplicity he decided this was the best of all possible worlds for what more could one ask: the drama was being acted, the opera was being sung and the ballet danced, and everything was done well. But he gave no thought to developing the form, to the fact that if art is not progressing every second it rapidly rolls backward, for it cannot stand still. Although he himself loved the theatre, he expected total 'loyalty' and was averse to 'rocking the boat'; there were times when, in love with power as well, he could be cruel to the point of idiocy. [. . .]

About sixteen to eighteen plays were staged each year. Four were brought out at benefits, when the performers themselves had the right to choose their plays and, it must be said, all the best and most worthwhile plays appeared at these benefits. Half of the worthless plays had been recommended to [Pchel'nikov] by somebody, and the rest were supplied by hacks, mere hacks, certainly not playwrights, not even play-doctors.

[. . .] The Maly troupe referred to these administrative arrangements as 'gravedigging', when plays were tailored to the troupe. This is what would happen: one of the powers-that-be would favour a play and an enormous amount of money would be spent on it. Such was the case with Shpazhinsky's drama *Princess Kuragina*,[5] which had the luck to suit the taste of the wife of the head of the ministerial chancellery. It was also unthinkable that a new author should work his way up in the theatre. He had to be either Lëv Tolstoy or a flunkey. [. . .]

[Backstage] I would hear the cry, 'Where are those wretched chemists?' At first I failed to understand, but then puzzled it out: chemists was what they called the lighting men, probably because the lighting then was gas (electricity was introduced in 1893), and gas is the product of a chemical conversion and smells too. Hence chemists. And 'wretched' because the lights never worked and everyone went into despair.

There were three effects: white light and then blue or red glass before the footlights. Morning and night arrived as they do at the Equator – blue glass was slipped in all at once, and then red, or else vice versa, and that was that. [. . .]

Once the stage manager was given a play, he cast the roles. You might think that would take some considering, but the company was so rich in talent that any theatre-buff could have done it without going wrong. Furthermore, the stage manager wrote the 'staging', i.e. filled in blanks under the rubrics: 'Cast, setting, furniture, costumes, wigs, properties, scenery, effects' (nine or ten rubrics). Under the rubric Scenery, say, he would write 'prison, forest, drawing-room' and so on, nothing more. Under furniture, the words: poor or rich. Costumes were described as 'civilian' or 'historical.' Wigs: 'bald, grey, red,' etc.

The office saw to it. Often the stage manager and the performers would not set eyes on the physical production until the dress rehearsals and sometimes not even until the performance, for it was considered enough that they be informed of the ground-plan, i.e. that the door would be here and the desk there.

Rehearsals were run quite simply. People came on stage holding scripts, read their roles and were 'distributed positions', i.e. it was agreed that X would stand there and Y sit there. Ten or twelve was the largest number of rehearsals. After the third rehearsal scripts were discarded. The role had to be learned by heart, so one, two or three days were set aside for memorization, depending on the size of the part.

[. . .] New scenery was always an event and that is how they treated it. The standard sets for all plays were: drawing-room, rich and poor, likewise studies, prison, cottage, summer and winter forests, and 'sky', i.e. a light-blue backcloth for the depiction of open space. If a bedroom or an office or something like that was needed, they would try to put it together 'from what's on hand'.

The classic plays of Shakespeare, Schiller and Hugo were served by the two notorious 'Gothic' sets with variations applied. King Lear divided his kingdom,

Hamlet spoke 'To be or not to be', Elizabeth signed Mary's death warrant – all in the same 'Gothic set'.

Things were not better with furniture. First, only the 'essentials', i.e. the things it was impossible to do without, the things the play said the actors needed; second, the same 'garnish': the difference between rich and poor furniture was that they would stuff springs into rich furniture and tack linings underneath (to hold in the springs). And the spectator sitting in the stalls would see the 'garnish' on stage, potbellied bags swagged with bulging stuffing. So backstage the styles were known as 'poor and paunchy'.

The properties were even worse than the furniture, for the chattels of the Bol'shoy and Maly theatres were held in common, which was all right in principle, for why buy duplicates when you could use what was there? However, there were not enough properties, and here's the sort of thing that would happen. Lensky, the pride of the Maly Theatre, was playing Benedick in *Much Ado about Nothing*.[6] Before the third act a dresser came up to him and took away his sword, for it was needed in an opera in which an Italian celebrity was singing. And when Lensky explained that he could not go on without a sword (they had outfitted him with a nineteenth-century spadroon), the poor costumier said, 'How was I to know?', for the authorities, taking into consideration that the Bol'shoy Theatre was bigger than the Maly, gave it preferential treatment.

The stage manager did not argue against such practices, first, because he had no conception that there might be other ways of doing things, and second, because 'argument and protest' were in themselves considered to be 'revolution'. One was allowed, though without success, 'to have the honour to request most humbly'.

[1] Vladimir Aleksandrovich Nelidov (1869–1926) held a minor job in the Maly office when he was appointed to take charge of the repertoire of the dramatic theatre; he filled this post from 1900 to 1907, and for the next two years managed the acting troupe. An astute observer, briefly married to the Maly star Ol'ga Gzovskaya, he failed to be taken seriously by the theatre's staff and troupe who called him 'the racetrack tout', owing to his avocation as treasurer of a jockey club. His memoirs, written while he was an *émigré* in Riga, provide lively descriptions of the Moscow stage of his time.

[2] Count Illarion Ivanovich Vorontsov–Dashkov (1837–1916) proved to be a wise administrator when he served as Viceroy in the Caucasus; his leading virtue in running the theatre was that he showed no personal interest in the actresses.

[3] Pavel Mikhaylovich Pchel'nikov (1851–1931) was a former military man. In 1882, the Moscow theatres lost their autonomous office and were made answerable to a 'Director of the Moscow office of the Imperial Theatres,' sitting in St Petersburg. Pchel'nikov held that post until 1898.

[4] Ippolit Karlovich Al'tani (1846–1919), conductor of the Petersburg Bol'shoy Theatre, and Anton Ivanovich Bartsal (1847–1927), tenor at the Bol'shoy and director of the opera troupe there (1878–1903).

[5] Ippolit Shpazhinsky's five-act drama opened at the Maly on 15 November 1888.

[6] For Lensky, see **249**.

## 244b Caricature of the Maria Theatre gallery

Reproduced in V.A. Telyakovsky: *Vospominaniya* (*Reminiscences*) (Leningrad–Moscow: Iskusstvo, 1965), unpag.

*Reforms in costuming*

As Nelidov attests, at the Imperial Theatres the Russian repertoire was generally clothed in old scenery, often hand-me-downs from operas. Costumes were drawn from stock or, if modern dress, provided by the actors. But increased demands for realism in staging were to be heard. In 1879, a Maly production of *Woe from Wit* was put on in modern dress which caused sophisticated critics like Prince Urusov [see **255**] to rebuke the theatre for its lack of historicity. The rearguard attitude, which deplored modern attempts at authentic costuming, was voiced by conservatives such as Pëtr Andreevich Karatygin (1805–79). Brother of the tragedian, he was a successful comic actor and farce-writer whose memoirs paint a vivid picture of life on the St Petersburg stage in the first half of the nineteenth century.

## 245a *Woe from Wit* in modern dress at the Moscow Maly Theatre in the 1850s: I.V. Samarin as Chatsky, M.S. Shchepkin as Famusov and G.S. Ol'gin as Skalozub

Phototype by Panov; reproduced in Senelick (1981), p. 97.

## 245b Pëtr Karatygin attacks historical costuming in 1879

P.A. Karatygin: *Zapiski (1880)* [*Notes*], vol. 2 (Leningrad: Academia, 1929–30), pp. 167–8.

Now about costuming. Many theatre critics, both in Moscow and Petersburg, have made the demand that the costumes of the characters [in *Woe from Wit*] conform to the period when the comedy was written. I don't want to foist my own opinion on anyone but I declare that for the management to spend its money on old-fashioned costumes is not only unprofitable, but will even damage the play. Everyone knows that a long obsolete fashion is a caricature and raises mirth without meaning to; what's the good of Chatsky appearing in a frockcoat with the widest of collars rising to his occiput, close-fitting sleeves, raised puffs on his shoulders, his waist almost up to his armpits, narrow coat-skirts, an abbreviated waistcoat, a high stock, a collar coming up to his cheeks, topboots with tassels and so on? I am sure that on his first entrance the greater part of the audience could not withhold its laughter and, I'm afraid, its laughter will set the actor himself to laughing. [. . .]

Griboedov wrote his comedy in the last years of the reign of Tsar Alexander I. If the theatrical management were to answer the demand of our critics, there would be great difficulty in selecting which of the fashion plates of that time to prefer – why not the funniest-looking one?

*Scene- and costume-shops*

Despite the shoddiness of the physical productions for the Russian dramatic troupe, the opera and ballet continued to enjoy munificent subsidies and lavish *mises-en-scène*. The 'shops' connected with these theatres comprised veritable industries.

## 246 Organization of workshops at the Imperial Theatres, St Petersburg in 1911

L.M., 'Imperatorskie SPb.Teatry' ['Imperial theatres of St Pbg.'], *Ezhegodnik imperatorskikh teatrov* [*Yearbook of the Imperial theatres*] (1911), vol. 2, 35–52.

[. . .] II Properties workshop. [. . .] This workshop is under the direction of a specialist in artistic sculpture, who has under him the necessary number of workmen in various specialities: locksmiths, joiners, modellers, property-men, upholsterers, housepainters and decorators, chasers and so on, whose average number during a season comes to some twenty or twenty-five persons. The work carried out in the workshop is distinguished by its great variety: period furniture, frames, clocks, vases and other items of decoration, different kinds of weapons both metal and wooden, necklaces and metal ornaments for costumes, heraldic articles – all this is executed in the Administration's own workshop. For this operation the workshop is adequately equipped with all kinds of machines and tools for carpentry and locksmithing, as well as machinery of a specialized nature. This includes a press fitted with different moulds for stamping out various metal tokens in the enormous quantity used in decorating costumes. With the aid of this press one can stamp out 5,000 or more a day. [. . .]

III Dyer's workshop. [. . .] This workshop is headed by an expert artist who employs ten men constantly in his operation on the different processes of dyeing, although during the season this team is amplified with day-labourers as need arises.

The work carried out here, of the most varied kind, can be subsumed into five categories.

(1) Dyeing and redyeing various fabrics of different textures used for costumes, such as: silks, wools, woollen mixtures, hessian, hemp, metallic brocades.

(2) Painting various costume fabrics and materials needed by the properties and set-design departments, such as: tapestries, carpets, tablecloths, upholstery, curtains, etc.

(3) Preparation of imitation brocade and hides.

(4) Cleaning and tinting costumes, boots, shoes, gloves and various knitted articles.

(5) Preparation and mending of knitted articles, such as tights, sweaters, etc. [. . .]

IV Costume workshop. All costumes, headgear and underwear used in operas, ballets and dramatic plays in the Imperial St Petersburg theatres are prepared in their own costume shops by their own workers.

To this end, the Administration has at its disposal three such workshops, located on the first-floor front of the Administration Building on Theatre Street, to wit: (1) the workshop for preparing women's costumes for Russian operas and drama, (2) the workshop for preparing women's costumes for ballet and French drama; and finally, (3) the workshop for preparing men's costumes for Russian opera and Russian and French drama. [. . .]

*Ermolova's goal as a young actress*

Emilia Galotti was the debut role of a prompter's daughter, Mariya Nikolaevna Ermolova (1853–1928), after eight years in the Moscow drama school. She soon came to be regarded not only as the greatest Russian actress but as equal to most European or American tragedians. Cultivated by mentors like the Shakespearean scholar Storozhenko and the theatrical expert Yur'ev, she brought a keen intelligence and a vivid pathos both to modern and classical roles. These excerpts from a youthful diary reveal the conscientiousness that was the hallmark of the best Russian actors.

## 247 The actress Ermolova's diary for 1871–2

M.N. Ermolova, 'Dnevnik i pis'ma' ['Diary and letters'] in N. Abalkin, ed. *Maly Teatr SSSR 1824–1927* [*Maly Theatre of the USSR*], vol. 1 (Moscow: Vserossiyskoe teatral'noe obshchestvo, 1978), pp. 320–2, 328.

10 October Sunday [1871]

I'm so happy now! So satisfied! O blessed day, I've played Emilia Galotti,[1] quite out of the blue, they just cast me in it. Whenever I play this role, I feel a certain something, a kind of fire inside, I'm carried away, I forget everything, but only in this role. Yes, it's my one and only love, my favourite. I played well. I got a splendid reception, yet I thought that, like last time we played on a holiday, we wouldn't be well received. What happened to Samarin?[2] When he and I came out for calls, he said to me, 'As you came off, you were so pretty, so interesting that I started to weep', and later, backstage he kissed my hand. Can I possibly have moved him so? N.M.[3] also praised me. [. . .] Everyone was taken by surprise that *Emilia Galotti* was scheduled. Of course they'd all forgotten their lines.

All in all I'm very happy. Oh, more: Nikolay Timofeevich[4] brought me an *Emilia Galotti*, a present in a special binding – *Emilia Galotti*. [. . .]

28 [January 1872]

[. . .] I performed *Cricket*[5] and . . . it was passable. I'm dissatisfied with myself. My success had turned my head a bit, but now that I'm over it, I see that it doesn't suit.

And I was dreaming of being a great actress. Yet who among us doesn't wish to be someone special when we are still very young. Anyway, it's no disappointment, no, I will work. Indeed, I've been working very indolently . . . Not long ago G[irchich][4] asked me why I loved the stage. Should I admit that it does me good or that my incentives are vanity and applause . . . I couldn't give him an answer, because I haven't ever thought seriously about it, but I'll try to give myself an answer. I would like a poor man to leave the theatre with the notion that there is another life, a good one, or, sympathizing with the actress's sufferings, he'll forget his own suffering and grief, I'd like him to have a hearty laugh and forget that he is in the theatre. That is why I love art. I hope with all my soul that it does me good, but whether or not it does . . . I don't know.

But I know all about vanity. I love it when I get applause, if this applause is really prompted by sincere sympathy for me. Applause expresses sympathy, and I want them to sympathize with me. Earlier I hadn't thought, didn't quite realize that I like it, but G[irchich] made me think about it. But all this is mingled with a feeling of satisfaction when I'm on stage. In some imperceptible way I sometimes experience another person's life.

1 Ermolova had first played Lessing's drama in the translation by A.N. Yakhontov at her debut at the Maly on 30 January 1870.
2 For Samarin, see **230, note 3**.
3 Nadezhda Mikhaylovna Medvedeva (1832–99), character actress who successfully made the transition from melodrama to Ostrovsky's plays, imbuing her creations with the reality of a genre-painting.
4 Unidentified even by Ermolova's biographers.
5 M.D. de Walden's and A. Kaiser's translation of *Die Grille*, a five-act comedy by Charlotte Birch-Pfeiffer, itself a dramatization of George Sand's *La Petite Fadette*. It was first played at the Maly on 20 January 1872, with Ermolova as Fadette.

### *Ermolova as Joan of Arc*

Ermolova was identified with liberal causes and the intelligentsia greeted creations such as Laurencia in *Fuenteovejuna* as declarations of progressivism. In 1878, she planned to appear as Joan of Arc in V.A. Zhukovsky's translation of Schiller's *Jungfrau von Orléans*;[1] but owing to the repressive spirit of the era, she was threatened with suspension and did not play it until 1884. It was hailed as a symbol of the struggle against social and political oppression; she considered it her 'unique service to Russian society'.

This description is by Aleksandr Ivanovich Yuzhin-Sumbatov (1857–1927), a Georgian prince who gained popularity at the Maly as a romantic leading man and author of problem plays.

[1] *Orleanskaya deva*, premiere at the Maly, 29 January 1884.

## 248a Yuzhin describes Ermolova as the Maid of Orléans in 1884

A.I. Yuzhin: 'M.N. Ermolova' in *Sbornik M.N. Ermolova* [*Ermolova Anthology*], edited by A. Brodsky (Leningrad: Academia, 1925), pp. 31–9.

In battle Joan encounters Lionel. The ascetic turns into a woman. It is impossible to convey this turning-point with greater truth to life, greater simplicity than she did. Without taking her eyes off the face of the overthrown Lionel, Ermolova in helmet and coat of mail, sword in hand, loses precisely everything that would justify a woman having a sword and a coat of mail and a helmet. From the lowered, suddenly powerless arms to the eyes, filled both with terror at the new power that has suddenly subdued her spirit and a sort of doubt in the presence of the mighty and unexpected feeling overwhelming her, all of Ermolova's being, her whole body, her face, her utterances became deeply feminine, beautifully helpless. [. . .]

At every one of the more than a hundred performances of this play, when I came on stage after this encounter and supported Joan as she fell into my arms, I could not avoid the impression that I was holding a girl, almost a child, dying from some terrible spiritual upheaval. [. . .] And if you ask me after these more than a hundred performances, *the way* Ermolova acted it, I must, in total candour, reply: no way. There was no acting. Not a single tragic gesture or artful gasp or sound. Not a single excruciated twitch of the face. She simply died, when, at my words, 'But blood is flowing!', she replied in a barely audible voice, 'Let it bear my life with it.'

The curtain came down. There were calls. It was over. Ermolova went to her dressing-room. I followed her on the way to mine. And looking at her shoulders, her bowed neck, I could not refrain from thinking, this is the dying Joan. People met her in passing, chatted, sometimes joked with her, sometimes she would answer with a smile – in short, offstage life went on – but Ermolova still radiated what she had undergone on stage – the moment of dying. And it was beyond her control: she could no longer wrench herself, Ermolova, from what she had turned herself into. [. . .]

## 248b Ermolova as Joan of Arc in armour

Photograph of the 1880s, reproduced in Abalkin, vol. 1 (1978), unpag.

*The actor Lensky*

The most versatile of the actors at the Moscow Maly was Aleksandr Pavlovich Lensky (1847–1908). Illegitimate son of Prince Gagarin and an Italian ballerina whose name Verviziotti he had first adopted, he served an apprenticeship for years in most of the provincial theatres. At the Maly, he made a name for himself in both the Russian classics and the Western repertoire, especially as Benedick, Petruchio, and Famusov in *Woe from Wit*. He also enjoyed a great reputation as a teacher of acting, a director and a theorist. These 'notes on acting' reveal the growing tendency towards an inner life in the Russian actor, although Lensky put great stress on gesture and make-up as well.

## 249 Lensky's notes on acting, 1894

A.P. Lensky: 'Zametki aktëra' ['An actor's notes'], *Artist* [*The Performer*] 36, 43 (April and November 1894), repr. in A.P. Lensky: *Stat'i, pis'ma, zapiski* [*Articles, letters, notes*] (Moscow, 1950), pp. 96–149.

[. . .] As an actor studies his role four phases of his labour may be distinguished: the first consists in the work of his imagination, when the words of the role are not as important as its general subject matter. In his imagination the actor creates an ideal, whose facsimile he will try to achieve in his impersonation and in which there is nothing resembling the actor himself. The second phase consists in applying his techniques of expression to the ideal he has created, i.e. he tries as precisely as possible to imitate intonations, gestures, demeanour, everything that he can descry in it. Only then does he begin to study the words. Approaching the ideal as closely as his talents and outward attributes allow, once he has mastered all this, the actor moves to the third phase, the final synthesis, i.e. the absorption of the text [. . .] Then comes the fourth phase of his work: the application on stage of everything he has mastered privately in his studies; for, even though the actor has achieved all perfection he can in intonations, mimicry and gestures, even though he is complete master of the words of his role, at the first rehearsals *off book* he is master of neither his voice nor even the words of his role. And there must be many rehearsals before the actor can transfer to the stage half of what he has mastered in the study, before he can make temperament help and not hinder him in conveying subtle details of artistic speech. The rate of transition from each phase to the next is, of course, conditional on the quality of the actor's talent. [. . .]

An actor can no more recreate his role at each performance with the same *élan* and passion than a virtuoso can play at every concert with the same inspiration; both of them, when afflatus is absent, have recourse to a cultivated technique; at such moments both of them present only the *results* of their earlier creative work, they, so to speak, seem to imitate themselves. But when an artistic actor is inspired, then, in repeating his earlier work he creates anew, and creates a work of art, if I may use the expression, *semi-consciously*. This is the supreme moment when his whole being starts to be controlled not by his human but some higher will, when his mind suddenly becomes lucid, when the scales seem to fall from the eyes of his spirit, and he begins to understand what he had not understood before, to feel what before he had only intuited and, lovingly absorbing the poet's ideas into his soul, identifying with the poet, he becomes his prophet.

*The actress Fedotova and the bureaucracy*

Glikeriya Nikolaevna Fedotova (1846–1925) had been one of Shchepkin's last students and in the 300 roles she played throughout her long career remained faithful to the principles of realism he had instilled. She was renowned in comedy, where Ermolova could not touch her, and in tragedy, as Ostrovsky's Katerina as well as Lady Macbeth and Schiller's Queen Elizabeth. Young Stanislavsky studied with her, imbibing the Shchepkinian lessons. Much beloved and considered a force for progress in Moscow society, at the height of her fame she was still subject to supercilious neglect on the part of the theatrical bureaucracy.

## 250 The star Fedotova sues the Administration for redress in bureaucratic stalemate, 1897

G.N. Fedotova, 'Vospominaniya yunosti i pis'ma' ['Reminiscences of her youth and letters'] in Abalkin, vol. 1 (1978), pp. 284–5.

To the Administration of the Moscow Maly Theatre, 1897
I have addressed you, Baron,[1] to explain my fate and request your kind intercession. All my life, from childhood on, has been devoted to the Imperial Theatre, where I have worked conscientiously for thirty-five years, bearing the repertoire on my shoulders and invariably enjoying the gracious attention of the sovereign emperor Alexander II, who was always especially gracious to me, ever since my years in school. I need not mention the audience, which has always treated me as its favourite. For twenty years I received such a small salary that it hardly sufficed to meet the expenses of my wardrobe, which at that period cost me a great deal of money, when I had to perform daily in plays that required nearly five new frocks each time. After twenty years I was the first actress in Russia to receive a salary of 12,000 rubles. On the other hand, when in 1894 my son,[2] who already held a stable post in the civil service and had graduated from the University with honours in whatever he did, cast all this away to go on the stage, I, hoping to make it possible for him to receive straightway the salary he requested of the Imperial Theatre, made over to him 2,000 rubles from my own salary and thus received only 10,000 a year.

With the decline of the repertoire, which began a long time ago, I began more and more to feel that having to perform roles of little interest was a burden to me and I began to ask the Administration to grant me a two-years' leave of absence, so I might be able to travel around Russia and somewhat refresh my failing nerves by playing my favourite roles for a new public. P.M. Pchel'nikov[3] entirely concurred with my arguments and very sympathetically acceded to my wishes. [. . .] In my travels I met a heartfelt and kindly welcome everywhere, such as I did not expect. Finally, the term of leave began to come to an end, and at Shrovetide of the present year I made my request to Mr Pchel'nikov to prolong my leave until 1 September, whereupon he replied that he could not do so on his own authority, without permission from his superiors, but said not a word to me about any changes in the conditions of my service on my return from leave. Then, in July of the present year, my son, at the behest of [Pchel'nikov] wrote me that the Administration wished to know on what conditions I desired to continue my service. Unforewarned, as I have said, of the possibility of a change in my conditions, I wrote a private letter to [Pchel'nikov], expressing my desire to receive my former salary, i.e. 10,000 rubles. [. . .] [He] told my son that the Administration could not offer me 10,000 rubles in view of my move to more elderly roles and, so far as he knew, I could count on a salary of 9,000 rubles, equal to that of my schoolmate Mme Nikulina,[4] who is three years older than I. Wholly reconciled to the Administration's decision, I acceded to this. On my return to Moscow on 2 September, I went to [Pchel'nikov] and learned from him that there was no definite answer to my agreement, but seeing that the Administrator of Theatres had given him some kind of *evasive* answer which he could not show me, he advised me to talk personally with Ivan Aleksandrovich Vsevolozhsky,[5] but first to make an appointment with him by telegram. [. . .] That was on 4 September. Since that time there has been neither word nor whisper of my case, and I find myself in a curious position. On the one hand, I find that I am employed, because my leave is terminated, but, on the other, I receive no salary, and must earn my bread; I have already received many offers of engagements, but cannot accept them because the Administration has said neither 'yes' nor 'no' to me. I cannot express how humiliating such strange and offhand behaviour on the part of the Administration is to me both as a woman and as an actress with a high reputation, an Administration for which I have worked my whole life, but such behaviour is leading directly to the direst financial loss for me. [. . .] If the Administration, in contrast with the entire Russian public, considers my involvement in the theatres it runs as useless, then with your Supreme Excellency's permission, I will, as is my civic right, lay at the feet of the monarch my petition that I be released from the service and be granted by His Gracious Majesty an increased pension, since the pension of 1,140 rubles I now receive is too paltry even for a retired existence. Otherwise, if the answer is favourable, I will continue my employment as long as my strength holds out. There is nowhere else for me to turn, because the authorities closest to me drive me from pillar to post, giving no definite answer and placing me in a situation impossible in all respects, and therefore I have resolved to trouble you, Baron. Truly, I have in no way deserved such inhumane and cruel treatment.[6]

[1] Baron Vladimir Borisovich Frederiks (1838–1927), Minister of the Imperial Court from 1897 to 1917.

[2] Aleksandr Aleksandrovich Fedotov (1863–1909) entered the Maly in 1893, and was a conscientious, thoughtful and versatile actor, whose work occasionally went beyond mediocrity.

[3] For Pchel'nikov, see **243, note 3**.

[4] Nadezhda Alekseevna Nikulina (1845–1923) acted at the Maly from 1863 to 1914. Ostrovsky considered her to be the best of *ingénues*, and her comic talents never flagged in old age, although she was not up to the psychological complexity of naturalistic drama. The critic, N. Èfros judged that 'Nikulina was always the slave of her talent, Fedotova the complete mistress of hers'.

[5] Ivan Aleksandrovich Vsevolozhsky (1835–1909), Administrator of the Moscow and Petersburg theatres from 1881 to 1899, a cultured individual more interested in opera and ballet than in drama.

[6] Evidently, Fedotova's plea was answered affirmatively, for she rejoined the Maly troupe, adding Volumnia to her roster of characters in 1902; she retired in 1905.

## VIII PROVINCIAL, PRIVATE AND PEOPLE'S THEATRES, 1870–97

### *Provincial theatre in the late nineteenth century*

Although provincial theatres throve in such populous centres as Kazan, Kiev and Odessa, the artistic level remained low. The impresarios, interested exclusively in profit, maintained overworked, underpaid troupes; the actresses were often chosen for their physical allure and were expected to entertain wealthy merchants after the show. Stages were set up in assembly-halls, adorned with tawdry backdrops and ancient costumes. Guest stars like Shchepkin and Fedotova could not single-handedly improve conditions, particularly since audiences continued to prefer operetta and farce to serious drama. The cancellation of the State monopoly encouraged a new breed of entrepreneurs to attempt higher quality and to direct their efforts at a new public of students and intellectuals. The first permanent provincial theatre was Nikolay Solovtsov's in Kiev, where Russian and European works of literary stature were presented.

Of the earlier provincial entrepreneurs, Pëtr Mikhaylovich Medvedev (1837–1906) had the highest reputation for honesty, conscientiousness and good taste. Even he, however, went bankrupt and joined the Alexandra as an actor in 1889. Among the talents he fostered were Davydov, Strepetova, Varlamov, Lensky, Lentovsky and, not least, Mariya Gavrilovna Savina (née Podramanetsova, 1854–1915). With Medvedev's troupe she toured to Kazan, Saratov and Orlov, before joining the Alexandra in 1874, where she became a leading lady, the first Verochka in Turgenev's *A Month in the Country*.

## 251 Savina remembers Medvedev's troupe in Kazan in 1872–3

M.P. Savina, 'Kak nashël menya P.M. Medvedev' ['How P.M. Medvedev discovered me'], *Teatr i iskusstvo* [*Theatre and art*] 46 (1903), 855–6.

[. . .] A contract was signed for 250 rubles a month (for my husband[1] and me) and two half-benefits. It was enough to turn one's head. [. . .] The repertoire was arranged one month, sometimes two months, in advance, and posted in the office – P.M.'s office. Cases of illness or change of play were rare. Drama and comedies alternated with operettas, which we learned to the accompaniment of the conductor's fiddle and then, after two orchestra rehearsals, sang along, acting the way we now act comedy. [. . .]

In one show I had seven changes of clothes. Now about costumes: nowadays a question has been raised about 'actresses' morals', on account of the luxuriousness of their toilettes. At that time toilettes were necessary and also expensive (relative to salaries), but this was no reflection of morality. Such was my case working for P.M. Medvedev. Cast in the role of Fernande in the play of that name (also known as *A Woman's Revenge*),[2] I decided to dress very modestly in Act I, because I am coming with my mother, 'a poor widow', to seek a place. I had not yet been to the French theatre or even to Moscow. The action takes place in summer, and I put on a cheery little bright-coloured calico-print dress and a straw hat with a sprig of lilac. My God, to hear Pëtr Mikhaylovich bawl me out! – 'What are you playing – a parlour maid or a heroine?! Who would believe that a Marquis would fall in love with you at first sight . . . To play leading roles you've got to have a wardrobe.' I didn't dare excuse myself by saying that on my salary it was impossible to have a 'wardrobe', and that dresses in *ingénue* roles should be 'ingenuous'. After a good cry I fully agreed that 'a Marquis couldn't fall in love with me.' The next day after rehearsal, P.M. escorted me to the best shop and 'vouched' for my charging things; I bought material (nothing but material) at a cost of 125 rubles (that is, my entire monthly salary). P.M. later deducted the money from my benefit. For my enormous labour, diligence and success I was rewarded by P.M.'s scheduling my benefit at the best time: 28 December. He knew both how to demand and how to appreciate.

1 N.N. Savin (né Slavich) met and married her when they were both acting in the Khar'kov troupe of M.P. Lentovsky. He later ran ambitious enterprises in Riga and Kiev, which failed miserably.

2 *Mest' zhenshchiny* (1871) was E.N. Grekova's translation of *Fernande*, a 4-act melodrama by Victorien Sardou (1870), later made popular in the US in an adaptation by David Belasco.

*Fairground theatre*

Although unrecognized by the authorities, one of the most thriving theatres in Russia since the middle of the eighteenth century was the *balagan* or fairground showbooth, which staged folk plays, pantomimes and acrobatic exhibitions. In 1880 a former actor Aleksey Yakovlevich Alekseev-Yakovlev (1850–1939), who managed a showbooth in St Petersburg's Field of Mars during Shrovetide, decided to replace Harlequin, Pierrot and Columbine with a bill of legitimate drama. Despite interference from the police, it was successful for some seasons.

## 252 Alekseev-Yakovlev stages drama in a fairground booth in 1880

A. Ya. Alekseev-Yakovlev: *Russkie narodnye gulyanya, v zapisi i obrabotke E.M. Kuznetsova* [*Russian popular entertainments, recorded and adapted by E.M. Kuznetsov*] (Moscow–Leningrad: Iskusstvo, 1948), pp. 78, 80, 84.

My model pleased Dmitriev[1] [. . .] and he agreed, as a test, to rent a space 'at the foot of the mountains'[2] and build a small wooden theatre. But because the potential results were uncertain, he did not want to run to all sorts of expense. Finally, it was contracted that he, Dmitriev, would supply the wood, the labour and the least possible money to acquire sets and costumes; my contribution would be the staging, and to guarantee the partial cost of the sets and costumes I put in a thousand rubles, and we would see what we would see. [. . .] Within a month and a half, not long before Carnival, Dmitriev suddenly died. His heirs, unsympathetic towards his 'frivolous' interests, refused pointblank to go on with the work begun. [My saviour] was Abram Petrovich Leyfert, who owned a small print-shop and ran a money-lending business which subsidized some of the entrepreneurs of suburban amusements, and in time he became one of the greatest impresarios in Petersburg.

And so, in Shrovetide week of 1880, on the Field of Mars, or, as they then said, on Empress Lake, in its humblest precincts, by the Pavlov barracks, the small showbooth 'Recreation and Profit' opened.

Contrary to the practice of decorating the auditorium pretentiously but in stencilled, painted calico, the walls of 'my theatre' were covered with a grey-green shade of linen, ornamented with portraits of Pushkin, Lermontov, Gogol', Griboedov, Nekrasov and Ostrovsky, painted in oils by the portraitist Bitelev.

The poster on the front read: '"Recreation and Profit" Theatre'. In the course of Shrovetide week there was a daily performance of a scene from Pushkin's *Boris Godunov*: 'An Inn on the Lithuanian Border'. And as a finale tableaux vivants – illustrations to the works of Russian writers, 'with explanations'. The reception was much more modest than we expected, but it could not be otherwise given the conditions of the opening. In Holy Week there were two series of living pictures on themes from fairy tales by Pushkin, Krylov's fables, Nekrasov's poems, with readings of excerpts from these authors' works. The costumes were made from my sketches, and the sets from sketches by the designer of the Maria Theatre I.P. Andreev.[3] [. . .]

The following year we set up in the same place but played only Shrovetide week. The censor forbade our staging of Nekrasov's 'The Market-Gardener' (because of the assassination of Alexander II, a period of mourning was declared and shows were closed).

But the next Shrovetide 'Recreation and Profit' was already in the foremost place, opposite the Summer Garden [. . .]. The hall held a thousand persons – the maximum number of spectators possible. I ought to mention that in building the showbooth the civic authorities provided a strip of land no greater than 106 square metres, this was one of the government restrictions on the scope of temporary theatre buildings for popular amusements. [. . .]

In the first years I staged dramatizations of 'The Sleeping Beauty', 'The Lady Turned Peasant-Girl', 'The Rusalka', and 'The Prisoner of the Caucasus' from Pushkin. The last production was especially successful and 'was the making' of us. We also presented similar dramatizations of Gogol''s works such as 'Vakula the Smith', 'May Night', 'Taras Bulba' and Russian fairy tales like 'The Little Humpbacked Horse' from Ershov, 'The Tale of Ostolop the Merchant' from Pushkin, etc. [. . .] The censor looked on my repertoire with ill-will, fault-finding and indubitable bias. For a second time he forbade the dramatization of Nekrasov's 'Market-Gardener' which I presented in a new version: the censor's verdict was curt: 'The production is deemed unsuitable'. My attempt to argue for authorization with the censor, some Baltic German, led nowhere.

[1] A Moscow contractor and lumber-dealer.

[2] *Pod gorami* ('downhill'), at the base of the giant ice-slides.

[3] Although he lived in Moscow, Ivan Petrovich Andreev (1847–96) was designer at the Maria Theatre in Petersburg and painted the sets for the first productions of the operas *Judith* and *Ruslan and Lyudmila*.

### *Sinel'nikov promotes innovations in staging*

Credited as the leading innovator of the Russian provincial stage, Nikolay Nikolaevich Sinel'nikov (1855–1939) began as an actor and operetta singer, but turned to directing in Kazan in 1882. His work in Rostov-on-Don pioneered many reforms which forecast the programme of the Moscow Art Theatre: long rehearsal periods, a subscription system, ensembles rather than stars and the abolition of intermission music and curtain-calls during acts. He later directed in Novocherkass, Moscow where he brought success to Korsh's Theatre in 1900, and Odessa.

## 253 Sinel'nikov describes his directorial reforms in the provinces in 1882

N.N. Sinel'nikov: *Shest'desyat let na stsene* [*Sixty years on the stage*] (Khar'kov: Izd. Khar'kovskogo gos. teatra russkoy dramy, 1935), pp. 198–9.

What did I want to achieve, what did I want to show in my independent debut as a director? To avoid the clichés that I had found intolerable and that surrounded me on all sides.

I wanted to show off the actor's mastery in gratifying material by Ostrovsky, utilizing individual facets of the performer's talents. *Mise-en-scène* was my particular concern. I set myself the task of eliminating the characters' invariable stampede downstage centre to the prompter's box. I tried to change the traditional ground-plan with its sofa and armchair set downstage right and two armchairs and some little tables downstage left. That was the way every room was furnished in every play. If a garden or a forest had to be depicted on stage, invariably a few pairs of border-pieces were pushed forward to stand like soldiers in serried ranks assembled, while at the back a curtain with trees painted on it was let down. And overhead hung the tormentors – four or five strips of linen with leaves drawn all over them. Stage centre represented an open clearing with a conspicuously wooden floor. Actors habitually came down to the forestage, which is where both intimate and crowd scenes took place. The position by the prompter's box was considered to be the most effective.

My secret dreams: to discard all these clichés, these stereotypes that set one's teeth on edge, and exchange them for a natural, beautiful, truthful arrangement of persons and objects on stage. A realistically furnished room, pictures hanging on the walls, not just an arrangement of characters on the forestage but even whole episodes taking place at the back walls – all this seemed new and unusual. Not a painted tree-stump, but a constructed one, on which one might actually lean, for, firmly nailed down, it would not wobble on contact. Earth and grass beneath one's feet. All this seemed the height of novelty, and to my delight the actors found this 'novelty' comfortable, natural and most acceptable. The first step had been taken.

### *The campaign for a people's theatre*

Attempts to create a low-priced theatre accessible to the common-folk had begun in the 1870s with the Populist or *Narodnik* movement, the first official experiment being A. Fedotov's anti-alcohol theatre at the Moscow Polytechnic Exposition in 1872. It succumbed to governmental repression (its name had to be changed from people's [*narodny*] to publicly-accessible or open-to-all [*obshchedostupny*]), interference from the Maly, and the economic recession resulting from the Russo-Turkish War.

In August 1881, Ostrovsky composed a memorandum on the state of theatrical affairs in hopes of setting up a Commission to investigate the legal statutes governing all aspects of theatrical activity within the bureaucracy; it was submitted to the Minister of Internal Affairs in November, and reworked into an article that appeared in the *Government Bulletin* (*Pravitel'stvenny vestnik*, 9 March 1882). Ostrovsky intended to open a privately run people's theatre, but the cancellation of the government monopoly in May 1882 stopped him, for he did not want to compete with the new commercial managements.

## 254 Ostrovsky pleads for a people's theatre, 1881

A.N. Ostrovsky: 'Zapiska o polozhenii dramaticheskogo iskusstva v Rossii v nastoyashchee vremya (1881)' ['Note on the situation of dramatic art in Russia at the present time'] in A.N. Ostrovsky: *Polnoe sobranie sochineny* [*Complete collected works*], vol. 10 (Moscow: Iskusstvo, 1973–80), pp. 126–42.

It may be said without exaggeration that in Moscow theatre exists *in name* only. The civilizing influence of dramatic art in the capital is not only negligible, but does not exist at all for the vast majority of the public. [. . .]

A people's theatre, even apart from a repertoire, i.e. the building itself, will stir the people's patriotism.

A national theatre is a sign of a nation's maturity, as are academies, universities, museums. Possession of one's own native theatre and pride in it are desiderata for the whole people, the whole tribe, the whole language, significant and insignificant, dependent and independent. [. . .] Moscow must have such a model theatre before full freedom will be granted to theatre as a whole. Commercial speculation will not build a model Russian theatre: it promises no rich profits and, in its early phases, may even be unprofitable and incur losses. If Moscow does not have a model Russian theatre, the freedom of the theatres will cause Russian dramatic art more harm than the monopoly did. An irrational competition will arise, managers will go bankrupt, good work will be compromised, and art of substance will, in the course of time, quite go to seed. [. . .]

Without a model theatre art will be profaned by speculation; without a model repertoire the audience will go astray, with no beacon to indicate where true art resides and what it is. Among the underdeveloped, ill-educated people there are persons with serious ideas and aesthetic instincts if not taste: they must learn to discriminate and understand that one thing is real, eternal art and another is an ephemeral derivation from it, inherited from some advanced but anti-artistic nation. This thing is melodrama with impossible events and inhuman passions, that thing is operetta wherein heathen gods and priests, kings and ministers, troops and common folk, merry or sad, dance the cancan; this thing is the *féerie*, wherein scenery is changed twenty-four times, where over the course of an evening the spectator manages to go all over the world and to the moon and down to the underworld as well, and where the same naked women appear in all twenty-four tableaux. If such a choice is made apparent, it may be hoped that the majority of the common people will desire true, wholesome art; which is highly likely, given the freshness of feeling and serious bent of mind with which a Russian is endowed. [. . .]

It is very easy to put a repertoire down on paper, but very difficult to sustain it on stage, i.e. to mount the plays in this repertoire so that an audience will enjoy watching them. To stabilize the repertoire, to give good plays a firm foothold, to attract the public regularly and have a civilizing effect on it, one needs a full company, expertly chosen, one needs the performers to be prepared in advance to serve art seriously, one needs strict artistic discipline if this is to come to pass. All this should compel entrepreneurs not only to refrain at this time (and for quite some time) from any thought of profit, but to be prepared for considerable sacrifices.

The most proper party to build a Russian theatre in Moscow would be the city, i.e. the Duma,[1] but at the moment it doesn't have funds available for such a purpose; such a theatre can be built by patriots, respected delegates of the rich Moscow merchantry. A Russian theatre in Moscow is needed primarily by merchants, therefore merchants should build it. They will be masters of the house, they know what they need, they will manage its affairs impeccably, guided solely by a patriotic desire to see dramatic art flourish in their fatherland. Aided by specialists in dramatic art and experts at scenic work, the Russian theatre in the hands of an enlightened merchantry will become firmly grounded in Moscow and will gradually arrive at perfection. [. . .]

1 Duma, literally 'deliberation', was the representative assembly of a town.

## 255 Prince Urusov[1] campaigns for privately managed theatres, 1881

A.I. Urusov: 'Teatr. Zametki i vpechatleniya' [Theatre. Notes and Impressions], *Poryadok* [*Order*] (15 January 1881); repr. in A.I. Urusov: *Stat'io o teatre, literature i ob iskusstve. Pis'ma ego. Vospominaniya o nëm* [*Articles on theatre, literature and art. His letters. Remembrances of him*], vol. 1 (Moscow: I.N. Kolchëv i ko., 1907), pp. 241–3.

Returning from Moscow, I was convinced that private theatre is an entity that is currently taking shape in Russia, and one must come to terms with it. It exists and it can be eliminated only by violating justice and the interests of society. The theatre's beneficial effects is a subject exhausted long ago and has now become a 'truism'. All arguments in favour of the theatre's beneficial effects have now become commonplaces. Everyone knows or suspects what an important resource the theatre is when it comes to culture or, if one may use the expression, 'political hygiene'. The growing population in the capitals, the growing number of persons apt for rational amusement has prompted a demand for private initiative in theatrical affairs. The government interest has not suffered thereby: for the State theatres are constantly full. Is it not time to admit what cannot be denied? Is it not time to settle the major issue of theatrical affairs in Russia? Is it not time to give legislative licence to theatrical entrepreneurship? [. . .]

Perhaps the time is not far off when even the *pium desiderium* expressed here for a 'modicum of legitimacy' will be in fact substantiated by way of a compromise. The general rise in political temperature has already had a beneficial reflection even in the theatre. The theatrical censorship committee, which had instigated a persecution of Mr Aleksey Potekhin,[2] drowned its ire in mercy and lifted disgrace from the author of *Mishura* [1858]. In Moscow there are rehearsals under way for a comedy which, if I am not mistaken, has been under a ban for over ten years – *The Vacant Post* [*Vakantnoe mesto*, 1859]. A.A. Potekhin had given his word not to write for the stage until this play was licensed – and he kept his word. Now he has changed his mind, categorically. *The Torn Rag* [*Otrezanny lomot'*, 1865] and *Mishura* were also banned from the State stages! Now, they say, things have got looser: they are permitted again. For how long? 'A modicum of legitimacy' and Russian literature will breathe more freely, as will the theatre in its wake. One should be concerned not with its flourishing but with the very conditions for sustaining life. One must unbind its hands and feet and not wonder why it walks so clumsily with ten-ton weights on its ankles.

1 Prince Aleksandr Ivanovich Urusov (1843–1900), critic for a number of periodicals, was a proponent of naturalistic theatre as prescribed by Zola.

2 Aleksey Antipovich Potekhin (1829–1908) made his reputation as a playwright with works about peasant and middle-class life. In the early 1880s he was running the repertoire committee of the Alexandra, and later took charge of the dramatic troupe of the Imperial Theatres: he proved to be interested only in his own plays and once forbade Ermolova to appear in *Mary Stuart*.

### *Private theatres in the capitals*

Contrary to predictions, ending the State monopoly did not create a wave of fly-by-night enterprises, and few private theatres managed to survive financially. In Moscow, the first such attempt had preceded the end of the monopoly: in 1880, the cultivated, politically liberal actress Anna Alekseevna Brenko (1848?–1934) received permission to expand her public readings into 'A.A. Brenko's Dramatic Theatre in Malkiel House'. Popularly known as the Pushkin Theatre, because it was near the Pushkin monument, it was aimed at the upper-middle-class intelligentsia. Brenko eliminated the star system, paid her actors higher salaries than were available at the State or large provincial houses, insisted on three weeks' rehearsal and new scenery for each production. Despite full houses, the costs outweighed the profits and she was forced to close in 1882, just as the monopoly ended.

Her building and troupe were taken over by Fëdor Abramovich Korsh (1852–1923), a barrister and ticket-broker for Brenko; owing to his shrewd balance of commercialism and experimentation, he put them on a sound financial basis and Korsh's Theatre survived until the Revolution when it was nationalized. Korsh mixed boulevard farces, drawing-room melodrama and Russian classics in his regular repertoire; he employed clever publicity, offered the first matinees at special prices for students, and every Friday staged a new play, allowing contemporary Russian drama to gain a hearing. It was Korsh who commissioned and first staged Chekhov's *Ivanov* (1887).

Mikhail Valentinovich Lentovsky (1843–1906), one of Shchepkin's last students, realized Ostrovsky's worst fears when he opened his Fantasy Theatre in 1882: it specialized in elaborately mounted *féeries* and operettas and enjoyed great popularity. Less successful was Lentovsky's New Theatre (Novy Teatr), founded the same year; devoted to legimitate drama, it soon foundered and was succeeded by his Mountebank (Skomorokh) Theatre in 1886. Meant to be a playhouse for the working class, it was to open with Tolstoy's *The Power of Darkness*; but the Procurator of the Holy Synod interfered, bringing about a double censorship for 'people's theatre'. Lentovsky did manage to stage other works by Tolstoy, Ostrovsky and Pisemsky, but was best known for his spectacular productions of sensational melodrama from the French. He went bankrupt in 1894 and turned the theatre over to others.

In St Petersburg, Chekhov's friend, Aleksey Sergeevich Suvorin (1834–1912), the millionaire editor of the ultra-conservative *Novoe Vremya* (*New Times*), had much greater success with his private Literary-Artistic Society Theatre; owing to his intimacy with government officials, he was enabled not only to stage the first productions of *The Power of Darkness* (1895) and A.K. Tolstoy's *Tsar Fëdor Ioannovich* (1898) but to introduce Russian audiences to Ibsen, Hauptmann, Maeterlinck and Rostand.

The financial problems these theatres faced suggests that the public was too heterogeneous in its tastes to provide a large audience for any one company. The following spectrum of the Moscow theatre scene gives a good picture of the new diversity of entertainments and the stratification of its audiences.

## 256a A journalist catalogues Moscow audiences in the 1880s

Vl. A. Gilyarovsky:[1] *Lyudi teatra. Povest' aktërskoy zhizni* [*Theatre people. A tale of the life of actors*] (Moscow–Leningrad: Iskusstvo, 1941), pp. 133–7.

Every Moscow theatre had its own audience. The most demanding and strait-laced audience was at the Maly theatre. On opening nights there were always the same strict, true lovers of art. People who had seen the best of everything abroad, they were able to pay huge prices to the ticket-scalpers or got box office tickets through the pull of connections and acquaintances.

And the reviewers of the time were strict and self-important. They filled the seats from the second to the fourth rows; each newspaper had its own seat. Pompously and ceremoniously they would enter the auditorium after the rest of the audience was already seated. [. . .] At Maly premieres, along with genuine theatre buffs, there were also the foremost Moscow merchants; their families sparkled with diamonds in the boxes in the dress circle and at stalls level. A cautious audience, commercially wary, anxious not to applaud out of turn. An unpropitious audience for actors and authors.

At the premieres of the Bol'shoy Theatre, the parterre was occupied by lordlings who still recalled the era of serfdom, who missed the bygone days, who grumbled at everything modern and never liked anything.

On the other hand, up above was a noisy, merry lot. The true opera-lovers, failed singers, students, pupils at various music and vocal schools, which had only just begun to appear in Moscow at the time, and who usually got into the theatre on passes and under the protection of the chief ushers. [. . .]

In the upper boxes sat a 'cantankerous' audience. An upper box cost five rubles, and some ten clerks and counter-jumpers would pack one to the rafters 'at two rubles a nose', forming a compact wall as they stood behind their seated ladies who munched apples and sucked acid-drops.

'Why're the actors singing and not talking, you can't make out a word,' the occupants of such boxes would complain.

'It's only a song, there's no words!'

The boxes in the dress circle and at stalls level were occupied throughout by merchantry: an Ostrovskian audience.

Sometimes a muffled shot would ring out in a rear box: but the audience wasn't alarmed; everyone knew that a bridegroom from the Nozhevoy district was treating his bride to lemonade.

Premieres at Korsh's Theatre were usually overcrowded: writers, actors, and fans of writers and actors, sportsmen, provincial tourists come to the races, middle-rank merchants and their ladies – all persons who loved to laugh or shed a tear to their heart's content at 'sensation drama', the best audience for an actor and an author. Applause that turned to foot-stamping and shouts of 'bis, bis' at the curtain-calls time and time again. [. . .]

At Rodon's Theatre,[2] operetta [. . .] had its own audience. A fast-living, jaded audience – old debauchees, scrutinizers of bare torsos, peering through opera-glasses to see if the actresses' tights had split anywhere. An audience trained at night clubs, music halls and theatrical masquerades.

There were two more theatres – 'Nemchinovka' and 'Sekretarevka'. That's where the amateur clubs performed. Many of these clubs produced good actors and the theatres could be hired by the performance. And every club had its own audience. A friend of mine, a reporter, would stand at the door with his eyes closed and guess, strictly by smell, which club was playing: fishmongers or butchers or greengrocers from Huntsman's Row. Whichever tradesman was on, that was his audience as well: it had its peculiar aroma or odour, like Gogol''s Petrushka.[3] Especially the fishmongers. [. . .]

A very special picture might be seen at M.V. Lentovsky's luckless offspring, the 'Mountebank' Theatre. This was called a 'people's' theatre and had been founded on money provided by Moscow merchants. Of course it was not the 'people's' in any real sense of the word. The prices were much too high, although there were seats from five kopeks up, but the abundance of ticket-scalpers made it inaccessible not only for the people but also for the middle-class public.

Nor did it have a suitable repertoire, but the acting company was very fine, and the public came in droves. The audience that attended the 'Mountebank' was the most variegated: long cloth jackets, caftans, sheepskin coats, ladies' cloaks, low-cut gowns of silk, wool, calico, and sarafans. Over the buffet in the lobby hung a cloud of smoke from all sorts of tobacco down to coarse shag inclusively. The audience gave off an aroma of sheepskin coats and greased boots. [. . .]

1 Vladimir Alekseevich Gilyarovsky (1853–1935) acted in the provinces from 1873, and in Andreev-Burlyak's troupe in Moscow. As a journalist he became a minor celebrity, a kind of Slavic G.A. Sala, his rotund figure and walrus moustache fixtures at bohemian gatherings.

2 Viktor Ivanovich Rodon (né Gabel, 1846–92) was a popular operetta singer who, in Lentovsky's employ, managed the New Theatre (1886–8) and the Moscow Paradis (1891–2).

3 In Gogol''s *Dead Souls*, Chichikov's servant Petrushka transfers his own pong to his surroundings, wherever he goes.

## 256b Korsh's Theatre as designed by the architect M.N. Chichagov

Reproduced in *Anton Pavlovich Chekhov v teatre* [*Chekhov in the theatre*] (Moscow: Gos. Izd. Izobrazitel'nogo Iskusstva, 1955), p. 19.

*The First All-Russian Congress of Stage Workers*

Outside the capitals, a rash of theatres of peasants, soldiers and factory-workers flourished, despite police control over repertoires. The earliest of these, established by S. Yur'ev in his summer residence in 1862, had begun as a paternalistic attempt to educate his newly-liberated serfs but turned into a hands-on experiment with peasant participation. In all these cases, the existence of the theatres depended less on the enthusiasm of their public than on the vagaries of the authorities, and whenever a theatre proved to be too popular, it was closed down.

The proliferation of theatrical activity throughout the nation led to questions about professionalism, unions, job security, artistic programmes and educational missions. In 1897 the Russian Theatre Society convened a congress in Moscow of 'stage workers' from all parts of Russia. Their deliberations concluded that sound theatrical education was indispensable if the theatre was to progress.

## 257 Speeches and reports of the First All-Russian Congress of Stage Workers, 9–23 March 1897

*Trudy Pervago Vserossyskago s"ezda stsenicheskikh deyateley, 9.3–23.3 1897* [*Proceedings of the First All-Russian Congress of Stage Workers*], chast' 1 (St Petersburg: Nadezhda, 1898), pp. 8–9, 52–82; chast' 2 (Moscow: A.A. Levenson, 1898), pp. 162, 283–7.

(a) Questions to be deliberated by the Congress:

1 The contemporary situation of theatrical work in Russia, its demands and needs.
2 Establishing set general rules for theatrical undertakings (managers, unions, etc.)
3 Establishing set general rules for performance work, the infringement of which will be considered a performer's deviation from carrying out the professional obligations he has accepted.
4 Establishing set general rules for mutual relations between stage workers and managers, or unions.
5 Making theatres accessible to a general public.
6 Municipal and district theatres and the participation of municipal governments and zemstvos [elected provincial councils] in organizing theatrical matters.
7 The serious repertoire, the educational and artistic tasks of the theatre, the need for excluding from a definition of theatre all institutions that serve inartistic purposes, and for seeking means to develop and maintain an art theatre.
8 Qualifications for stage workers: managers, performers, stage directors, reviewers, etc.
9 The scale of remuneration for stage workers.
10 Material security for stage workers, the betterment of their daily life and securing an education for their children.

(b) Boborykin[1] on the stage proletariat:

Sad though it may be, a stage proletariat exists. Up to now the mass of stage workers has been oppressed by an utter lack of material security. And the contrast in material competency and earnings between the elite of the stage and the masses grows ever greater. However great a source of indignation the acquisitive instincts of the impresarios may be, the situation of the majority would be more tolerable, if, over the past decade or two, the pursuit of gain had not increased or if outstanding talents had been more moderate in their pecuniary demands, if the size of their honoraria did not influence the fate of theatrical undertakings. These sizes seldom relate to reality, for they are much greater than what this or that actor or actress can win from the public via the box-office. The proletariat grows all the more numerous because too often a theatrical career is regarded simply as a craft. [. . .]

(c) Karpov[2] on people's theatre:
Some twenty-five years ago in 1871 on Varvarka in Moscow the first people's theatre at popular prices was opened during the All-Russian Polytechnic Exposition. Having decided to be a serious school of art, accessible to anyone willing to devote his leisure not to cards and drink but to rational recreation, the cultivation of the mind, the uplifting of the soul, a theatre at popular prices opened its doors wide to a public with little money. A throng of 'common' people filled it from top to bottom every day. [. . .]

After existing for three years with the full sympathy of the public, this first people's theatre, after such a brilliant beginning, closed its doors forever 'for reasons outside one's control' [. . .] But the example did not go without imitators. Several more times theatrical entrepreneurs tried to create a people's theatre at popular prices in Moscow. Thanks to many complex causes and mainly the absence of any evidence of artistic purpose in the entrepreneurs, these attempts were not crowned with success. [. . .]

The first theatre for workers appeared in Petersburg, the so-called Basil Island Theatre.[3] In its wake the Nevsky Society, an organization for popular amusements, was organized and opened a summer and winter theatre behind the Nevsky Gate in Petersburg. As many as 10,000 working-class persons gathered for the shows of the Nevsky Society. An enormous crowd attended with bated breath to the plays of Ostrovsky, Gogol', Pisemsky and others. With excitement and gratitude, the working man treated the organizers of the theatrical enterprise and the performers to a surplus that more than covered the expenses incurred in putting on the productions. Following this example, factories in Moscow, Yaroslavl' and Serpukhov quickly arranged performances for workers. Thus the phenomenon spread quickly and remarkably. At the present time theatres for the working man have been set up throughout almost all Russia, in Archangel and Astrakhan, Shuya and Khar'kov, Ufa and Ivanov-Voznesensk, Ekaterinburg and Odessa. [. . .]

The basic repertoire of a people's theatre should consist, in my opinion, of the dramatic works of Russian authors and foreign classics, precisely because this is a *Russian people's theatre*. [. . .] I cannot understand why some fear that the people will not grasp such plays as *Hamlet, King Lear, Othello, The Robbers* and so on. Even if they do not comprehend all the subtleties of Hamlet's spiritual fluctuations, they will undoubtedly grasp the mental anguish of an unhappy son who has seen his beloved mother wed his father's murderer. [. . .]

The production of these plays should be distinguished by assiduous historical accuracy and artistic taste. Led by an incorruptible director, a people's theatre at popular prices in Moscow will probably have an enormous success. It will bring great benefit to all Russia, illuminating it like a guiding star, uniting all who want to work honourably for the glory of Russian art, shedding its light upon the darkest corners of our expansive fatherland. [. . .]

(d) Kremlev[4] on the actor's social significance:

1 The actor by means of his art carries out a high educational mission. Artistically portraying man with all his idiosyncrasies, qualities as well as defects, in both spiritual repose and moments of spiritual turmoil, incarnating in himself now the features of a great victim and martyr, now the image of a mighty hero, now the repulsive soul of a tyrant, the actor is an artist who reveals to us our own moral world, teaches us to recognize our own heart and that of our brother, teaches us to recognize ourselves and our fellowman.
2 Transforming himself into the type sketched by a great artist, the actor becomes an interpreter, a commentator on that type, an intermediary between the artist and the masses, an explicator to the masses of all the profound attributes of the great talent or genius, a consummator of the work the great poet has begun.
3 Precisely because of the power of such tasks, the actor at every step of his work has the obligation to implement the development of artistic taste and understanding in society.

(e) Vekhter[5] on keeping Jews off the stage:

[. . .] to be at the top of their craft, actors should be those persons who, by right of their vocation, talent or dramatic gifts, deserve to be on stage. Unfortunately, this is seldom the case. One of the current evils of the stage seems to be the penetration of the Jewish element into the midst of the acting profession. We do not speak of those talents who are above nationality; it is extremely painful that the Jewish element has grown so strong that for all its lack of talent it threatens to oust our national Russian influence. We do not deny that the Jews are a capable people; with rare patience, they can even overcome their own accent; it is hard to compete with them at keeping their noses to the grindstone, but, as a rule, that's all they have to offer.

The *Jewish influx* happened because, once they receive a diploma from a dramatic school, they are free of military obligations. Consequently, they attend not for the sake of art and vocation, but *to avoid military service*.

People will say that no one is preventing Russians from going to dramatic school. Quite true. But Russians are often poor and, regrettably, not distinguished by the same unity and mutual solidarity as Jews. A poor Jew, with the aid of his fellow paupers, will find the needed funds and get admitted to a dramatic school. [. . .]

(f) Burdzhalov[6] on establishing theatre in a peasant village:
[For three summers, Burdzhalov ran a theatre in the small hamlet of Krivtsov in the Orlov gubernia, playing a repertoire that included Ostrovsky's *Poverty's No Crime*, Gogol''s *Marriage*, Molière's *Georges Dandin*, the medieval farce *Lawyer Pathelin* and nine scenes from Pushkin's *Boris Godunov*.] [. . .] For the illiterate portion of the audience the performance of *Boris Godunov* [. . .] was chiefly liked for its historical trappings. What they particularly appreciated about the costumes and staging as well as the subject matter was the depiction of olden days. In retelling the historical plot they would add with compassion, 'But we didn't learn if he [Dmitry the Pretender] got to be tsar or not.' They said that if it weren't for the theatre, they would never get a chance to see the bygone tsars or learn anything about them, of course these tsars and boyars lived a long time ago and did exactly what was shown on stage – they did not assume that those who played them were the same people – they add with conviction. 'When we get together for a chat now,' said one peasant woman, 'we sit and drink tea and repeat all the speeches like they said 'em in the kee-ayter.' Walking through the village in holiday time, one could hear the speeches of Boris and the Pretender. [. . .]

The fact must be stated that *a village audience grasped the essence of plays, understood the nature of the characters, even when they come from the most alien ways of life and, following the action on stage with the liveliest interest, expressed its sympathy with the characters' plight – in short, the most immediate sensation was produced.* [. . .] Therefore, *the flair for understanding works of art, the conviction that everything depicted on stage is true, the immediacy of sensation* have an impression even on the repertoire which must consist *only of works of art*, both Russian and foreign, with no place for coarse farce or, naturally, operetta, and must be composed with great care. [. . .] It is not superfluous to note that evidently *peasants are very fond of costume plays, remote in subject and accoutrements from their grey village life.*

[1] Pëtr Dmitrievich Boborykin (1836–1921), a boulevard playwright, who believed that the Russian theatre ought to copy European models. Nevertheless, he was staunchly anti-naturalist.

[2] Evtikhy Pavlovich Karpov (1857–1926) had been arrested for his populist activites before he became an actor and playwright. He directed a peasant theatre in the village of Rozhdestvo outside Petersburg (1889–91) and a workers' theatre for the Nevsky Society (1892). He was then a director at the Alexandra from 1896 until his death, staging the much under-valued first production of Chekhov's *Seagull*.

[3] The Basil Island (Vasileostrov) People's Theatre for workers (1887–1907 with interruptions) was originally a private enterprise run by actors; from 1892 it came under the control of the Society for Cheap Eatinghouses, Teahouses and Houses of Industry. It produced mainly melodramas and farces, but in 1902–6 plays by Zola, Chekhov and Gor'ky were staged.

[4] A.N. Kremlev, a lawyer who had projected a St Petersburg people's theatre in 1896, without success, was secretary to the Congress. In his definition, 'public or people's theatre must not be for the common people as it is often mistakenly understood, but *for all the people*'.

[5] N.S. Vekhter (né Vekhtershteyn, which suggests he was a converted Jew) was an actor in Gorin-Goryainov's troupe in Saratov before making unsuccessful attempts at management in provincial towns in the 1890s; his most memorable failure took place in Orël.

[6] Georgy Sergeevich Burdzhalov (né Burdzhalyan, 1869–1924), an actor with the Moscow Art and Literary Society and from 1898 a charter member of the Moscow Art Theatre, where he ran the acting school.

## IX FOUNDATION OF THE MOSCOW ART THEATRE, 1897–8

### *Stanislavsky and Nemirovich-Danchenko meet*

The foundation of the Moscow Art Theatre can be seen as the culmination of reforming tendencies present in the Russian theatre from the beginning of the nineteenth century. Its principles had been enunciated as early as Shchepkin. There was the same emphasis on the stage as a rostrum from which to educate the public; the insistence on discipline, devotion and intelligence in the actor's work; dedication to the high ideals of art and literature, especially Russian art and literature; and unity of ensemble, directing and design in the *mise-en-scène*. The concerns set forth at the Congress of Stage Workers – the view of the actor as a harbinger of progress, the dignity of every member of the team, and the need to make theatre accessible to the poor and disenfranchised – were also contributing factors. The very year, 1898, when the Art Theatre opened its doors, the New (Novy) Theatre, a filial of the Imperial theatres, arose in St Petersburg; it was the brainchild of Lensky, who saw it as an arena for young performers. That same year, Dyagilev and Benois founded the *World of Art* movement. The face of Russian theatre was to change radically.

The milieu out of which the Art Theatre arose was that of the educated merchant class, exemplified by Savva Mamontov the millionaire industrialist who ran his own private opera. Although Soviet historians play down this influence, had it not been for the patronage of such enlightened tycoons, it is unlikely that the Moscow Art Theatre would have had the financial support or the audience to make a go of it.

Konstantin Sergeevich Alekseev (1863–1938) was the son of a wealthy textile manufacturer; from childhood, he had been stage-struck, acted as an amateur under the Polish-sounding name Stanislavsky, took classes with Fedotova, and helped organize the theatricals of the amateur Art and Literary Society. Inspired by the tour of the Meiningers in 1890, he devised richly atmospheric productions of historic drama.

Vladimir Ivanovich Nemirovich-Danchenko (1858–1943), seasoned by acting in the provinces, was a successful playwright, specializing in problem dramas of modern life. In 1890 he headed the acting class at the Moscow Philharmonic and for seven years butted his head against the administration of the Imperial Theatres, trying to implement his ideas for reform.

The decision of these two men to pool their creative resources was epochal. Their eighteen-hour meeting on 22 June 1897 has become a set-piece in theatre history. The attractiveness of the anecdote and the ideals of its protagonists have made one forget how many of the principles they pronounced were not to work out in practice. The autonomy of the literary and artistic vetoes eventually proved a major bone of contention between them, since Nemirovich-Danchenko favoured drama of social purpose and straightforward productions, while Stanislavsky was uninterested in politics and fascinated by innovation in theatrical techniques. Similarly, the best actors at the MAT became to all intents and purposes stars.

## 258 Stanislavsky and Nemirovich-Danchenko enunciate the first principles in 1897

K.S. Stanislavsky: *My life in art* (Boston: Little, Brown, 1924), pp. 294–5, 298–9; trans. by J.J. Robbins, revised by Laurence Senelick.

[. . .] in June 1897, I received a note from Nemirovich-Danchenko, inviting me to come for a talk in the restaurant, 'Slav Bazaar'. We met and he explained to me the purposes of our meeting. They lay in the foundation of a new theatre, which I was to enter with my group of amateurs, and he with his group of pupils. To this nucleus we were to add chosen professional actors from Petersburg, Moscow, and the provinces. The most important questions before us were these: how far the artistic principles of the chief directors of the new theatre agreed with each other, what compromises each of them was willing to make, and whether there were any points in common between us. [. . .] In the minutes I entered:

'The literary veto belongs to Nemirovich-Danchenko, the artistic veto to Stanislavsky.' [. . .]

We also spoke of artistic ethics and entered our decisions in the minutes, at times even using aphorisms.

'There are no small parts, there are only small actors.'

'One must love art, and not one's self in art.'

'Today Hamlet, tomorrow a supernumerary, but even as a supernumerary you must be an artiste.'

'The poet, the actor, the designer, the costumier, the stagehand serve one goal, which was set by the poet at the very basis of his play.'

'Violation of the rules of creative life in the theatre is a crime.'

'Lateness, laziness, caprice, hysterics, bad disposition, ignorance of the role, the necessity of repeating everything twice are all equally harmful to our enterprise and must be rooted out.'

### *The original rationale of the Moscow Art Theatre*

Originally, the proposed theatre was aimed at low-income groups, students, professionals of moderate means, workers with aspirations to culture. The repertoire planned was highly ambitious, ranging from ancient Greek tragedy to the latest Russian problem play. Stanislavsky and Nemirovich-Danchenko requested a subsidy from the Moscow Duma or

City Council, and, to clarify their aims, the latter made this report at a meeting of the Permanent Commission on Technical Education and the sanitary division of the Moscow Department of the Russian Technical Society. It spells out the theatre's rationale and budget.

## 259 Nemirovich-Danchenko sets the basic tasks for the Art Theatre, 15 January 1898

*Otchet o deyatel'nosti Khudozhestvenno-Obschedostupnogo Teatra za 1-y god* [*Account of the activity of the Art and Publicly Accessible Theatre for the 1st year*] (Moscow, 1899), p. 4.; repr. in *Moskovsky Khudozhestvenny teatr v illyustratsiyakh i dokumentakh 1898–1917* [*Moscow Art Theatre in illustrations and documents*] (Moscow: Izd. Moskovskogo ordena Lenina khudozhestvennogo akademicheskogo teatra Soyuza SSR imeni M. Gor'kogo, 1938), pp. 679–80.

First – the comparatively popular accessibility of the theatre, an aspiration to permit the poorer class of persons, especially the class of poor but educated persons, to get decent seats in the theatre at low prices. Second task – an artistic one – consists in the attempt to bring a new spirit to Russian stage art by striving to remove it from the constraints of routine and hokum. Third task – so to speak, the pedagogical one – is to give young talents, who have received a special theatrical education, the possibility to develop. The carrying-out of these three tasks should endow our theatre with a characteristic profile. [. . .]

Of 815 seats in the theatre:

440 or 54% – more expensive than 1 ruble
275 or 34% – from 1 ruble down to 50 kopeks
140 or 12% – from 50 kopeks

[. . .]

New price scale: for special matinees
Of 815 seats:

95 seats or 12% – more expensive than 1 ruble
341 seats or 41% – from 1 ruble down to 50 kopeks
379 seats or 47% – from 50 kopeks

### *The Art Theatre becomes a joint-stock company*

When the Duma failed to respond (the answer when it finally came in 1899 was No), Stanislavsky was extremely reluctant to finance the enterprise himself as a private theatre. Instead, he supported the notion of a share-holders' company as being in key with his philanthropic goals. The two founders re-organized as a joint stock company and approached potential outside investors with their plans. The banker and industrialist Savva Timofeevich Morozov (1862–1905) offered a gift of 10,000 rubles on the understanding that he would always be the sole donor and principal shareholder; despite

Nemirovich's misgivings, his offer was accepted. Morozov was to take an active part in the theatre's decisions. The first shareholders' meeting was held in May 1898.

## 260 Programme and budget for the first year of the Moscow Art Theatre, May 1898

V.I. Nemirovich-Danchenko: 'Tovarishchestvo dlya uchrezdeniya Obshchedostupnogo teatra. 12 maya 1898 goda. Programma i smeta pervogo goda' ['Joint-stock company for the establishment of a Publicly Accessible Theatre. 12 May 1898. Programme and estimates for the first year'], repr. in *Moskovsky Khudozhestvenny teatr* [*Moscow Art Theatre*] (1938), pp. 697–700.

[. . .] In the first year of the theatre's existence, the seats cannot be popularly priced. If they were, the Syndicate would risk a total deficit. The seat prices will be of three categories: (1) ordinary theatrical – from 3 rubles, 50 kopeks a seat; (2) nearly half-price reductions for matinee holiday performances, i.e. normally popularly priced; and (3) higher prices – for benefit performances. But even the ordinary theatrical prices will provide a greater number of cheap seats than in other theatres. [. . .]

The organizers found it to be absolutely necessary to begin rehearsals four months before the opening of the season. Especially since there are many young persons in the company, who require an even greater number of rehearsals than experienced actors do and innumerable instructions from the directors. [. . .] The company will be formed from (1) members of the Society of Art and Literature, who have decided to dedicate themselves to the theatre; (2) the best students from some of the recent graduating classes of the Philharmonic Institute School,[1] and (3) a few actors who have not been to that or any other school.

Contracts with both the lessor of the theatre and the actors are concluded by the year, with the right of renewal for two years. In this respect, the *right* of contract renewal of actors, considering their minimal pay the first year, is stipulated to be a rise in pay scale by nearly one-third annual salary each year. Thus, if an actor who made 900 rubles this year should turn out to be indispensable, the organizers of the Syndicate have the right to retain him at 1,200 rubles a year. He may refuse to take less, but he has not the right to ask for more.

The repertoire is to be selected from the following plays: *Tsar Fëdor Ioannovich*, a tragedy by Count A. Tolstoy, previously banned by the dramatic censor, a most brilliant work of Russian literature. So far this tragedy has been passed only for the Literature and Art Circle's theatre in Petersburg. To the organizer's inquiry, the censor replied that the tragedy will be passed for our theatre as well, if His Highness the Governor General of Moscow supports the application. In His

Highness's absence the organizers turned to his most august spouse and received a most solemn promise to that effect. As another, more important novelty for the Russian stage, Sophocles' *Antigone* has been selected, to be staged with a chorus and a production that will create a complete illusion of the ancient world. The next production proposed is *Hannele*, which also seems to be a virtual novelty. Later to follow are *The Merchant of Venice*, *The Marriage of Figaro*, Ibsen's *Lady from the Sea*, *An Enemy of the People*, *The Sunken Bell*, *Uriel Acosta*, etc. For realistic plays, proposals have been made for two plays by Chekhov, *The Seagull* and *Ivanov*, a few plays by Ostrovsky, Pisemsky and Gogol'.[2]

We propose to give 160 performances before the Great Fast,[3] to be divided into the following groups:

(a) 17 premiere performances, so to speak, on specific days (Wednesdays or Tuesdays);

(b) 20 student artistic 'matinees' for young people (on holidays), with the participation of the best professors and outstanding critics of Moscow and Petersburg, many of whom have already promised their cooperation. They will deliver short lectures, akin to Parisian *conférences*, on the aforesaid plays.

(c) 12 matinee performances at popular prices.

(d) from 20 to 30 benefit performances. These performances will be profitable, first, in being solidly guaranteed, second by training for the theatre an audience that seldom attends an unfamiliar theatre. But because the prices at these performances will be high (otherwise their organizers would make no profit in playing an evening for 700 rubles), the theatre's organizers will suggest a couple of plays, for instance, *Antigone* and *The Marriage of Figaro*, to provide these productions with a long run, if not a whole season.

[. . .] In forming the company the most important attention will, of course, be paid to the directorial aspect, which ought to be the strongest element in the whole affair.

However economical the organization of the company and the estimate of other expenses, it is equally impossible to skimp in estimating expenses of costumes and scenery. The designer Simov[4] has been invited for the scenery. The costumes, i.e. the most characteristic of them, will be made at our own expense and will remain the property of the theatre.

The four and a half month season, following four months of rehearsals, will be very exhausting for the actors. In view of this, it will hardly be possible, in case of a success, to give performances during the Great Fast. But in the Spring season, the whole company ought to travel to one or two big cities (Petersburg, Odessa, Kiev). Material success is more than likely there, because neither a repertoire like this nor such productions have yet been seen in the provinces.

COST ESTIMATES IN ROUND FIGURES

| | |
|---|---|
| Theatre | 15,000 rubles |
| Outlay for its maintenance | 2,000 rub. |
| Theatre in Pushkino | 800 rub. |
| Office and library | 500 rub. |
| Posters and publicity | 4,000 rub. |
| Authors' rights | 2,000 rub. |
| Scenery | 9,000 rub. |
| Properties and stage hands | 3,000 rub. |
| Music where necessary | 3,000 rub. |
| Wigmaker | 1,800 rub. |
| Costumes and toilettes | 4,000 rub. |
| Property insurance | 500 rub. |
| Telephone | 250 rub. |
| Police and fireman's wages | 600 rub. |
| Salaries: (a) administrative and directorial management | 15,800 rub. |
| (b) acting company | 33,000 rub. |
| Unforeseen contingencies | 2,750 rub. |
| Total | 98,000 rub. |

APPROXIMATE ESTIMATE OF RECEIPTS

Box-office:

| | | |
|---|---|---|
| | 17 opening nights at 900 rubles | 15,300 rub. |
| | 14 club appearances | 5,000 rub. |
| | 30 benefits at 500 rubles | 15,000 rub. |
| | 32 holiday evenings at 900 rubles | 28,800 rub. |
| | 20 'matinees' at 350 rubles | 7,000 rub. |
| | 12 popularly-priced matinees at 250 rubles | 3,000 rub. |
| | 33 weekdays at 400 rubles | 13,200 rub. |
| | 3 at Pushkino | 1,000 rub. |
| Total | 161 plus 2 complimentary performances | 88,300 rub. |

This is the second year (Not counting 30–40 performances in the Spring or Lenten season)

[1] These students included Ol'ga Knipper, (later to marry Anton Chekhov), Ivan Moskvin and Vsevolod Meyerhold.

[2] Of the planned repertoire, *Tsar Fëdor* opened the season and was a great success, owing to Stanislavsky's veristic recreation of sixteenth-century Muscovy. *Hannele* was censored by the Holy Synod, and replaced by *The Sunken Bell*. Ibsen was represented by *Hedda Gabler*. *Antigone*, *The*

*Merchant of Venice* and a revival of the Art and Literary Society's *Twelfth Night* were not successes. Only Chekhov's *Seagull* at the first year's end saved the day and made the MAT's reputation and house style. Stanislavsky did not get to direct *Marriage of Figaro* until 1927.

3 The seven Lenten weeks preceding Easter, when balls and theatrical performances were banned at the State theatres.

4 Viktor Andreevich Simov (1858–1935) had designed *The Sunken Bell* for the Art and Literary Society in 1897; he would remain with the MAT until his death, providing the sets for its first productions of *Tsar Fëdor*, Chekhov, Gor'ky, etc.

*Rehearsals begin*

Rehearsals for *Tsar Fëdor* began in Tsarskoe Selo, interrupted by excursions to historic towns and monasteries to collect costume materials, properties, sketch details and architecture [see *Theatre in Europe: A Documentary History – Naturalism and its Alternatives*]. Stanislavsky's opening speech is typical of his flowery idealism.

## 261 Stanislavsky's speech at the opening rehearsal, 14 June 1898

MAT Archives; pub. in K.S. Stanislavsky: *Sobranie sochineny* [*Collected works*], vol. 5 (Moscow: Iskusstvo, 1954–61), pp. 174–5; English trans. by E.R. Hapgood in *Stanislavski's Legacy* (New York: Theatre Arts Books, 1968), pp. 3–4.

[. . .] For me this theatre is a long-hoped-for, long-promised child. It is not for the sake of material gain that we have waited so long for it. No, it is the answer to our prayer for something to bring light and beauty into our humdrum lives. Let us be careful to appreciate what has fallen into our hands lest we shall soon be crying like the child who has broken his favourite toy. If we do not come to this enterprise with clean hands we shall defile it, disgrace ourselves and be scattered to the ends of Russia: some will go back to prosaic duties of everyday life, others, for the sake of keeping the wolf from the door, will profane their art in dirty, ramshackle theatres. Do not forget that if we break up with such a black mark against us we deserve to be laughed to scorn, because here we have undertaken something which is not a simple, private matter, but bears a public character.

Do not forget either that our goal is to bring enlightenment into the lives of the poor, to give them some aesthetic enjoyment amid the gloom in which they have been living. We are attempting to create the first thoughtful, high-minded, popular theatre – and to this great goal we are dedicating our lives.

Be careful not to crush this beautiful flower, else it will wilt and its petals fall. [. . .]

For the sake of such a purpose let us leave trivial matters at home, let us gather here in a common effort and not engage in petty squabbles and the settling of scores. [. . .] Let us be guided by the motto of 'common work, friendly work' [. . .]

*Regulations for the new theatre*

The founders gradually realized that financial constraints would force prices up, which, combined with governmental restrictions, limited their appeal to a popular audience; instead, their first public was and would remain the educated, white-collar middle-class. The Moscow Artistic and Publicly-Accessible Theatre (*Moskovsky khudozhestvenno-obshchedostupny teatr*) opened on 14 October 1898 in the modest Hermitage Theatre in Carriage Row. [For documents of the opening productions, see vol. 13 of *Theatre in Europe: A Documentary History*.] The house rules which Nemirovich-Danchenko posted backstage make an interesting contrast with the codified regulations that had governed the Imperial Theatres: although no actor is required, at risk of a fine, to learn twenty-five lines a day, his duties and latitude are as rigidly defined. The difference is that in the Imperial Theatres the rules were used to stifle dissent and make for the orderly running of a bureaucratic mechanism. At the MAT, where the theatre was regarded as a temple, the rules were intended to serve Art with a capital A, not least by maintaining the moods in rehearsals and performances.

## 262 Rules for the normal running of productions and rehearsals, 1898

*Moskovsky Khudozhestvenny teatr* [*Moscow Art Theatre*] (1938), pp. 702–5.

1 In order to avoid misunderstandings about time, the theatre's clock will be considered the correct one.

2 Rehearsals will begin precisely at the time appointed, as called by the director or his assistant, and every actor will see to his own entrance.

3 The wearing of overcoats, galoshes, etc. may be allowed during rehearsals only in exceptional cases.

4 The end of the rehearsal will be announced by the director. If the actor has concluded his role before the rehearsal is over, he will ask the assistant director whether he may be considered at liberty.

5 Smoking on stage, during either a performance or a rehearsal, is unconditionally forbidden.

6 The actors who take part in the first half of a performance are requested to be at the theatre one hour and a half before the start of the performance; those taking part in the latter acts, half an hour before. Negligence in this regard will be taken as nothing less than an insulting slight on the director, whose concern is the strict and untroubled running of the production.

7 The actors must be ready one quarter hour before the start of the act in which they appear.

8 Before the start of each act, these calls will be given in the dressing-rooms: No. 1 informs one that the stage is set; by No. 2 each participant must come on

stage without delay; No. 3 is given before the curtains part. (Note: Between scenes only the second call will be given.) No other warning will be used.

9 It is requested that during the course of the act the greatest silence be maintained backstage. Persons not taking part in the act under way are absolutely forbidden to be on the stage.

10 Actors may not bring unauthorized persons backstage or into the dressing-rooms without exceptional permission from the company manager in each case. The manager may permit an individual only once in each season.

NOTE Actors' servants may remain in the dressing-room but not backstage, save in exceptional cases when the actor must change clothes quickly.

11 During the intermissions before the second call the stage must be completely vacated, even by those persons involved in the play.

12 Whenever any disrepair or defect is detected in any requisite item, the actors, without entering into any arguments with costumiers, wigmakers and property-men, will address themselves solely to the director or his assistant.

NOTE In the course of the performance the assistant director will be regarded as invested with all the rights and responsibilities of the director.

13 One half-hour after the performance is over, the person in charge of electricity will give a signal that the lighting on stage and in the dressing-rooms will soon be extinguished. In exceptional cases an actor may send a request to keep the lights on to the superintendent of the theatre.

14 All actors, if absent from home, will without fail leave an address at which they may be reached with urgent messages before 6 o'clock p.m.

15 One half-hour before the start of the performance no letters or telegrams will be accepted on stage.

NOTE The ladies and gentlemen of the company are requested to arrange matters at home so that urgent communications are addressed to the play's director or his assistant.

16 If an actor appears in the audience after he has finished his role in the early acts of the play, it will be considered a tactless breach of the artistic integrity of the performance.

17 Actors not involved in the play may occupy vacant seats no closer than the third row of stalls.

NOTE Actors are requested not to join in either applause or, for the most part, ovations initiated by the audience.

18 Persons unconnected with the theatre will under no circumstances be allowed at ordinary rehearsals, and at previews only by permission of the company manager and the play's director.

19 Valuable items – either costume or property – must be treated with special care.

20 An account of each rehearsal and each performance will be entered into a special book by the assistant director, including all the actors' requests.

21 Both the proposed repertoire of performances and schedule of rehearsals will be drawn up daily and a signed copy issued at the theatre office every Saturday. In addition, an announcement of the schedule of the next day's rehearsal and performance will be posted daily on the director's board. Special bulletins will be distributed only to understudies and in cases of a change in the announced repertoire.

22 The administration most earnestly requests all persons connected with the Theatre to pay heed to the notifications posted on the board, because in many cases the administration has no other means of bringing the desired information to the attention of the ladies and gentlemen of the company.

23 Collaborators, students in courses and other participants in the performances and rehearsals of the Theatre will submit to the present rules on the same footing as the actors.

24 Without strict order and respect for the work of one's colleagues and, in general, all persons implementing the success of the affair in one way or another, the Theatre cannot attain the high level worthy of its best artistic endeavour. Therefore everyone who takes part in the Theatre is requested to maintain this discipline personally along with that careful attitude to the cherished work, without which a truly cultured institution is unthinkable.

# Bibliography

SCANDINAVIA

## General


Losnedahl, Kari Gaarder (ed.) *Teatersamlinger i Norden.* (2nd revised edn) (Bergen: Nordic Center for Theatre Documentation, 1986). [Lists museums, libraries and archives in Denmark, Finland, Norway and Sweden].

Marker, Frederick J. and Lise-Lone Marker. *The Scandinavian theatre: a short history.* (Oxford: Basil Blackwell, 1975).


## Denmark


Agerholm, Edvard. *Dr Ryge, et bidrag til belysningen af det Kgl. teaters indre historie i den første halvdel af det forrige aarhundrede.* (Copenhagen and Christiania: Gyldendal, 1913).

Aschengreen, Erik *et al.* (eds.) *Perspektiv på Bournonville.* (Copenhagen: Nyt nordisk forlag, 1980).

Aumont, Arthur and Edgar Collin. *Det danske nationaltheater 1748–1889.* (Copenhagen: J. Jørgensen, 1896–8).

Bech, Viben and Ellen Andersen. *Kostumer og modedragter fra Det kgl. Teaters herregarderobe, Nationalmuseet.* (Copenhagen: Nationalmuseet, 1979).

*Betænkning afgiven af den i Henhold til skrivelse fra Kirke – og Underviisningsministeriet af 7de Juni 1867 sammentraadte Theatercommission.* (Copenhagen, 1868). [**30**]

Bloch, William. 'Nogle bemærkninger om skuespilkunst', *Tilskueren* (1896).

Bojsen, Else. *Fra 'Den Stundesløse' til 'Gorm den Gamle': Maskinmesteroptegnelser fra det Kgl. Teater 1782–1785.* (Copenhagen: Akademisk forlag, 1982).

Bournonville, August. *Danske theaterforhold.* (Copenhagen: C.A. Reitzel, 1866).

*Det Kongelige danske theater, som det er.* (Copenhagen: C.A. Reitzel, 1849).

*Kritiske efterrætninger.* (Copenhagen, 1873).

*Mit theaterliv.* 3 vols. (Copenhagen: Reitzel, 1848–77).

*Et nyt skuespilhuus i Kjøbenhavn: fortsættelse af 'Vort Theatervesen'.* (Copenhagen: C.A. Reitzel, 1852).

*Nytaarsgave for danse-yndere eller anskuelse af dansen som skiøn kunst og behagelig tidsfordriv.* (Copenhagen, 1829).

*Vort theatervesen: randgloser til det nye lov-udkast.* (Copenhagen: C.A. Reitzel, 1851).

Brandes, Edvard. *Dansk skuespilkunst. Portrætstudier.* (Copenhagen: no pub., 1880).

*Holberg og hans scene, opførelser og fremstillere.* (Copenhagen: Gyldendal, 1898).

'Et vendepunkt i dansk theaterhistorie', *Det 19. Aarhundrede* (1875). [**33**]

Brandes, Georg. *Kritiker og portræter* (2nd revised edn). (Copenhagen: no pub., 1885). [**32**]

Campbell, Oscar James. *The comedies of Holberg.* (Cambridge, Mass.: Harvard University Press, 1914).

Christensen, Hjalmar. *Det Kgl. theater i aarene 1852–59.* (Copenhagen, 1890).

Clausen, Julius and Torben Krogh (eds.) *Danmark i fest og glæde.* 6 vols. (Copenhagen: Chr. Erichsen, 1935).

Collin, Edgar (ed.) *Af Jonas Collins papirer: bidrag til det Kgl. Theaters og dets kunstneres historie.* (Copenhagen: L.A. Jørgensen, 1871).

*Corsaren.* (Copenhagen, 1840). [**21a**]

*Danish Journal.* Special issue: *The Royal Danish Ballet and Bournonville* (Copenhagen, 1979).

Ewald, Johannes. *De brutale klappere.* (Copenhagen, 1771). [**9**]

Fabris, Jacopo. *Instruction in der teatralischen Architectur und Mechanique* (edited by Torben Krogh). (Copenhagen: Levin & Munksgaard, 1930).

*Fædrelandet.* (Copenhagen, 1843–48). [**23**]

Fenger, Henning. *The Heibergs* (translated and edited with an introduction by F.J. Marker). (New York: Twayne, 1971).

Fog, Dan. *The Royal Danish Ballet 1760–1958 and August Bournonville.* (Copenhagen: Fog, 1961).

Gjelten, Bente Hatting. *H.C. Andersen som teaterconnaisseur.* (Copenhagen: Selskabet for dansk theaterhistorie, Nyt nordisk forlag, 1982).

Grandjean, Marianne. *Ludvig Holbergs kunstsyn og dramaturgi.* (Copenhagen: Teatervidenskabelige institut, Københavns universitet, 1980).

Hansen, Peter. *Den danske skueplads: illustreret theaterhistorie.* 3 vols. (Copenhagen: Ernst Bojesens Kunstforlag, 1889–96). [**7c, 7d, 8, 21b, 22, 23, 25, 26, 31c**]

Heiberg, J.L. *Om vaudeville, som dramatisk digtart, og om dens betydning paa den danske skueplads.* (Copenhagen: Schultz, 1826). [**17**]

*Prosaiske skrifter.* 11 vols. (Copenhagen: J.H. Schubothe, 1861–2). [**18, 29**]

Heiberg, Johanne Luise. *Et liv genoplevet i erindringen.* 4 vols. (5th revised edn, edited by Niels Birger Wamberg.) (Copenhagen: Gyldendal, 1973–4). [**24a**]

Henriques, Alf, Torben Krogh *et al. Teatret paa Kongens Nytorv 1748–1948.* (Copenhagen: Berlingske forlag, 1948).

Hertz, Henrik. *Et og andet om skuespillerens kunst.* (Copenhagen: Thaning & Appel, 1846).

Holberg, Ludvig. *Epistler* (edited by F.J. Billeskov Jansen). 8 vols. (Copenhagen: H. Hagerup, 1944–54). [**4, 5**]

Jacobsen, Kirsten. Introduction to *William Bloch om skuespilkunst og sceneinstruktion.* (Copenhagen: Opuscula, 1979).

*Et vendepunkt i dansk theaterhistorie? En undersøgelse af Frederik Ludvig Høedts betydning for teaterudviklingen i årene før naturalismens gennembrudd i Danmark.* (Copenhagen: Det teatervidenskabelige institut, Københavns universitet, 1976).

Kragh-Jacobsen, Svend and Torben Krogh. *Den Kongelige danske ballet.* (Copenhagen: Selskabet til udgivelse af kulturskrifter, 1952).

Krogh, Torben. *Danske teaterbilleder fra det 18de aarhundrede: en teaterhistorisk undersøgelse.* (Copenhagen: Levin & Munksgaard, 1932). [An index by Ernst Bræmme and Klaus Neiiendam was published by Det Teatervidenskabelige Institut, Københavns Universitet in 1976.]

*Holberg i det kongelige teaters ældste regieprotokoller.* (Copenhagen: Gyldendal, 1943). [**10a, 10b, 11**]

*Oehlenschlägers indførelse på den danske skueplads. Hakon Jarls opførelse.* (Copenhagen: Branner og Koch, 1954).

*Skuespilleren i det 18de aarhundrede: belyst gennem danske kilder.* (Studier fra Sprog- og Oldtidsforskning 205) (Copenhagen: P. Branner, 1948).

*Studier over de sceniske opførelser af Holbergs komedier i de første aar paa den genoprettede danske skueplads.* (Studier fra Sprog- og Oldtidsforskning 39) (Copenhagen: Jespersen og Pio, 1929).

(ed.) *Komediehuset paa Kongens Nytorv.* (Copenhagen: Thaning & Appel, 1948).

(ed.) *Det kgl. teaters ældste regiejournal (1781–7).* (Copenhagen: Kongelige teater og kapel, 1927). [**13**]

Langberg, Harald. *Kongens teater. Komediehuset på Kongens Nytorv 1748–1774.* (Copenhagen: The author, 1974).

*Love og Anordninger samt andre offentlige kundgjørelser Danmarks Lovgivning vedkommende for aaret 1870.* (Copenhagen: Gyldendal, 1871). [**31a**]

Marker, Frederick J. *Hans Christian Andersen and the romantic theatre.* (Toronto: University of Toronto Press, 1971). [**7b**]

'Negation in the blond kingdom: the theatre criticism of Edvard Brandes', *Educational Theatre Journal* (December 1968), pp. 506–15.

Marker, Lise-Lone and Frederick J. 'Fru Heiberg: a study of the art of the romantic actor', *Theatre Research/Recherches théâtrales*, 13, 1 (1973), pp. 22–37.

Mitchell, P.M., *A history of Danish literature.* (Copenhagen: Gyldendal, 1957; New York: American-Scandinavian Foundation, 1958).

(trans. and ed.) *Selected essays of Ludvig Holberg* (2nd edn) (Westport, Conn.: Greenwood Press, 1976).

Nathansen, Henri. *William Bloch.* (Copenhagen: Busck, 1928).

Neiiendam, Karen. *Skuespillerinden Anna Nielsen: belyst gennem hendes barndoms- og ungdomserindringer, rejsedagbog og enkelte breve.* (Copenhagen: Nyt norsk forlag, 1985).

Neiiendam, Klaus. *Caroline Walter: personlighed og skuespilkunst.* (Copenhagen: Nyt nordisk forlag Arnold Busck, 1983).

'Cramers tegninger fra Hofteatret og Kongens Nytorv' *Robert Neiiendam in memoriam.* (Copenhagen: Teatermuseet, 1967), 55–68. [This volume contains a bibliography of Robert Neiiendam's works compiled by Sven Houmøller, pp. 69–95.]

'Danske teaterdragter fra det 18. århundrede', *Arv og Eje* (1965), 5–25.

*Hofteatret og teatermuseet ved Christiansborg* (revised edn) (Copenhagen: Teatermuseet, 1982).

*Om iscenesætelsen på teatret i Lille Grønnegade.* (Copenhagen: Gad, 1981).

'Scenebilder af Peter Cramer', *Kunstmuseets Årsskrift*, 51–2 (1964–5), 99–116.

(ed.) *Dr Ryges dagbog: Paris 1831.* (Copenhagen: Nyt nordisk forlag, 1979).

Neiiendam, Robert (ed.) *Breve fra danske skuespillere og skuespillerinder.* 2 vols. (Copenhagen: J.L. Lybecker, 1911–12). [vol. 2 includes an autobiographical sketch by Ryge and Mrs Emilie Wiehe's recollections.] [**14**, **16**, **20b**, **27**]

*Det Kgl. teaters dramatiske elevskole 1886–1936.* (Copenhagen: Kongelige teater og kapel, 1936).

*Det Kgl. teaters historie 1874–1922.* 4 vols. (Copenhagen: V. Pio, 1921–30). [**34**, **35**, **37**]

*Michael Wiehe og Frederik Høedt.* (Copenhagen: V. Pio, 1920).

'Omkring H.C. Andersens dramatik', *Anderseniana*, 2, 2 (1953), p. 201–15.

*Rigsdagen og det Kongelige teater.* (Copenhagen, 1953). [Offprint from vol. 5 of *Den danske Rigsdag 1849–1949*, pp. 599–657.]

Normann, J.C. *Holberg paa teatret.* (Copenhagen: no pub., 1919).

Nystrøm, Eiler. *Offentlige forlystelser i Frederik den Sjettes tid: et bidrag til dansk kulturhistorie.* (Copenhagen: Dansk historisk håndbogsforlag, 1986).

Oehlenschläger, Adam. *Breve fra og til Adam Oehlenschläger, Januar 1798–November 1809* (edited by H.A. Paludan *et al.*) (Copenhagen: Gyldendal, 1945). [**15**]

*Erindringer.* 4 vols. (Copenhagen: A.F. Høst, 1850–1).

Overskou, Thomas. *Af mit liv og min tid* (edited by R. Neiiendam). 2 vols. (Copenhagen: A. Busck, 1962).

*Den danske skueplads.* 7 vols. (Copenhagen: Thiele, 1856?–76). [**1**, **2**, **3**, **6**]

*Den danske skueplads og staten.* (Copenhagen, 1867).

*Oplysninger om theaterforhold i 1849–1858.* (Copenhagen: C.W. Stinck, 1858).

*Plakater fra Theatret i Lille Grønnegade*, udg. i facsimile af Selskabet for dansk theaterhistorie. (Med en indledning ved Julius Clausen). (Copenhagen, 1912).

Preisler, J.D. *Journal over en reise igiennem Frankerige og Tydskland.* (Copenhagen, 1789).

Rahbek, K.L. *Bidrag til den danske skuepladses historie i dens første aarhundrede, fra den aabnedes den 23de September 1722 intil dens jubilæum den 23de September 1822.* (Copenhagen: Tryckt i den Schultziske officin, 1822).

*Breve fra en gammel skuespiller til hans søn.* (Copenhagen and Leipzig: Christian Gottlob Frost, 1782).

*Dramaturgiske samlinger.* (Copenhagen, 1789).

*Om Holberg som lystspildigter*. (Copenhagen: Brødrene Thiele, 1816).
*Om skuespilkunsten*. (Copenhagen: 1809).
Rask, Elin. *Trolden med de tre hoveder: Det Kongelige teater siden 1870, bygningshistorisk og kulturpolitisk*. (Copenhagen: Akademisk forlag, 1980).
*Regulativ angaaende de til opførelse paa det Kongelige Theater indsendte og antagne stykker*. (Copenhagen, 1856). [**28**]
Rosenstand-Goiske, Peder. *Den dramatiske journal* (edited by Carl Behrens). 2 vols. (Copenhagen: H.H. Thiel, 1915–19).
*Kritiske efterretninger om den kongelige danske skueplads, dens forandringer efter 1773 og dens tilstand, med bedømmelse over skuespillere og dandsere af begge kiøn, 1778–80* (edited by C. Molbech). (Copenhagen, 1839). [**12**]
Ryge, J.C. *Critisk sammenligning imellem nogle af det Kongelige theaters skuespillere og skuespillerinder*. (Copenhagen, 1832). [**19**]
Schwarz, Frederik. *Lommebog for skuespilyndere for 1785. Teatervidenskabelige Studier*. (Copenhagen: Institute for Theatre Research, University of Copenhagen). [An early source for Thomas Overskou.] [vol. 2, 1972, includes six papers in English on Bournonville; vol. 7, 1979, is on Oehlenschläger; vol. 9, 1984, is on Holberg on the stage.]
Schyberg, Frederik. *Dansk teaterkritik indtil 1914*. (Copenhagen: Gyldendal, 1937).
Waal, Carla. 'William Bloch's *The Wild Duck*', *Educational Theatre Journal* (December 1978), pp. 495–512.
Wiingaard, Jytte. *William Bloch og Holberg*. (Copenhagen: Gad, 1966). [**36**]
Zinck, Otto. *Joachim Ludvig Phister. Et teaterliv*. (Copenhagen: Gyldendal, 1896).
*Oehlenschläger og det kongelige Theater. Et bidrag til den danske skuepladses historie*. (Copenhagen: Samfundet til den danske litteraturs fremme, 1868).

### *Sweden*

Arpe, Verner. *Das schwedische Theater von den Gauklern bis zum Happening*. (Stockholm: Larömedelsförlagen, 1969).
Beijer, Agne. *Slottsteatrarna på Drottningholm och Gripsholm*. (Stockholm: Lindsfors bokförlag, 1937).
Bergman, Bo. 'Minne av Olof Ulrik Torsslow', *Svenska Akademiens Handlingar*, 55 (Stockholm: P.A. Norstedt, 1945), 49–233. [Bound with the proceedings in this volume are the Laws of the Swedish Academy, dated 20 March 1786.]
Bergman, Gösta M. *Regi och spelstil under Gustaf Lagerbjelkes tid vid Kungl. teatern. Studier kring några av hans insceneringar*. (Stockholm: P.A. Norstedt & söner, 1946). [**56**, **58**]
Bergman, Gösta M. and Niklas Brunius (eds.) *Dramaten 175 år. Studier i svensk scenkonst*. (Stockholm: P.A. Norstedt & söner, 1963). [**44**, **45**, **46**, **47**, **48**, **51**, **54**, **72a**, **81**, **82b**, **82c**]
Beskow, Bernhard von. *Lefnadsminnen; tecknade*. (Stockholm: Norstedt, 1870). [**55**]
Bjørnson, Bjørnstjerne. *Bjørnstjerne Bjørnsons Brevekslingmed Svenske 1858–1909* (edited by Ø. Anker, F. Bull and Ö. Lindberger). 2 vols. (Oslo and Stockholm: Gyldendal, 1960). [**71**]
Boberg, Stig. *Gustav III och tryckfriheten 1774–1787*. (Stockholm: Natur och kultur, 1951).
Carlén, Johan Gabriel. *Theatercensuren i Sverge* [*sic*]; *redogörelse för dess uppkomst och andegång*. (Stockholm: C.M. Thimgren, 1859). [**63**]
Dahlgren, F.A. *Förteckning öfver svenska skådespel uppförda på Stockholms theatrar 1737–1863 och Kongl. theatrarnes personal 1773–1863*. (Stockholm: P.A. Norstedt, 1866). [**38**]
Edholm, Erik af. *Mot seklets slut*. (Stockholm: P.A. Norstedt, 1948). [**73**, **74**]
Flodmark, Johan. *Bollhusen och Lejonkulen i Stockholm*. (Stockholm: K.L. Beskman, 1897).
*Kongl. svenska skådeplatsen i Stockholm 1737–83*. (Stockholm: Central-Tryckeriet, 1887). [**39**]
*När dramatiska teatern grundades*. (Stockholm, 1914).
*Stenborgska skådebanorna; bidrag til Stockholms teaterhistoria*. (Stockholm: P.A. Norstedt & söner, 1893). [**40**, **41**]

Fredrikson, Gustaf. *Teaterminnen.* (Stockholm: Albert Bonnier, 1918). [79]

Grandinson, Emil. *Teatern vid Trädgårdsgatan, 1842–1901.* (Stockholm: H.W. Tullberg, 1902).

Hedberg, Frans. *Svenska skådespelare: karateristiker och porträtter.* (Stockholm: C.E. Fritze, 1884). [**65a**, 67, **68**]

Hedberg, Tor. *Ett decennium*, vol. 3, *Teater.* (Stockholm: A. Bonnier, 1913). [**80**, **82a**]

Josephson, Ludvig. *Teater-regie.* (Stockholm, 1892).

*Våra teater-förhållande: betraktelser och uppsatser.* (Stockholm: Samson & Wallin, 1870). [**69**]

Kexél, Olof. 'Inhemske theatre-tidninger och nyheter för 1782', reprinted in *Kongl. teatern 1782 och 1882.* (Stockholm, 1882). [42]

Levertin, Oscar, 'Teater och drama under Gustaf III', *Samlade skrifter*, vol. 17. (2nd edn). (Stockholm: A. Bonnier, 1911). [43]

Lewenhaupt, Eugene. *Bref rörande teatern under Gustaf III, 1788–92.* (Uppsala: Akademisk boktryckeriet, 1894). [**49**, **50**]

Lindberg, Johan August. *De första teaterminnerna.* (Stockholm: A. Bonnier, 1916). [**72b**]

Lindeberg, Anders. *Några upplysningar rörande kungl. theatern.* (Stockholm, 1834). [**62**]

Nordensvan, Georg. *Svensk teater.* 2 vols. (Stockholm: Albert Bonnier, 1917–18). [**52**, **60b**, **61b**, **65b**, **66b**, **66c**, **70b**]

Personne, Nils. *Svenska teatern.* 8 vols. (Stockholm: Wahlström & Widstrand, 1913–27). [**53**, **57**, **60a**, **61a**]

Richardson, Gunnar. *Oscarisk teaterpolitik.* (Stockholm: Scandinavian University Books, 1966). [**76**]

Silfverstolpe, Magdalena. *Memoarer.* 4 vols. (Stockholm: Bonnier, 1908–11).

Stjernström, Edvard. *Några ord om teatern.* (Stockholm, 1870). [**59**]

Stribolt, Barbro. *Stockholms 1800-talsteatrar.* (Stockholms-monografier 45) (Stockholms kommun, 1982). [**66a**, **75**, **77**, **78**]

Strindberg, August. *Tjänstekvinnans son.* 2 vols. (Stockholm: Albert Bonnier, 1886). [**70a**]

Svanberg, Johannes. *Kungl. Teatrarne under ett halft sekel 1860–1910.* 2 vols. (Stockholm: Nordisk familjeboks forlag, 1917–18).

Torsslow, Gustaf L. (ed.) *Handlingar rörande kongl. teatern.* 2 vols. (Stockholm: D.M. Lublin, 1834–37). [64]

Torsslow, Stig. *Dramatenaktörernas republik.* (Stockholm: Dramatiska teatern, 1975).

## *Norway*

*Aftenbladet.* (Christiania, 1865). [114]

Almquist, Olaf. *Johannes Brun. En skildring av hans liv og samtidige. Med kunstnerens dagbog i uddrag.* (Kristiania: Alb. Cammermeyer, 1898).

Anker, Øyvind. *Christiania Theaters Repertoire 1827–99.* (Oslo: Gyldendal, 1956). [Sub-titled in English, 'The Repertoire of Christiania Theatre 1827–99. A complete record of performances, authors, translators and composers. Index to seasons'.]

*Den danske teatermaleren Troels Lund og Christiania theater.* (Oslo: Gyldendal, 1962). [**88a**, **92**]

*Henrik Ibsens Brevveksling med Christiania Theater 1878–1899.* (Oslo: Gyldendal, 1965).

*Johan Peter Strömberg. Mannen bak det første offentlige teater i Norge.* (Oslo: Gundersen, 1958).

*Kristiania norske theaters repertoire 1852–1863.* (Oslo: Gyldendal, 1956).

*Scenekunsten i Norge fra fortid til nutid.* (Oslo: Bokcentralen, 1968).

Ansteinsson, Eli. *Teater i Norge: dansk scenekunst, 1813–1863 Kristiansand-Arendal-Stavanger.* (Oslo: Universitetsforlaget, 1968).

*Bergensposten.* (Bergen, 1882). [115]

*Bergens Stiftstidende.* (Bergen, 6 January 1850). [97]

*Bergens Tidende* (Bergen, 25 October 1926). [121]

Bernhoft, Theodor Christian. *Kristianias theaterforholde 1799–1837.* (Kristiania: I Kommission hos Steensballe, 1855).

Bjørnson, Bjørn. *Det gamle teater: kunsten og menneskene.* (Oslo: H. Aschehoug, 1937). [**124**, **126**]
Bjørnson, Bjørnstjerne. *Artikler og taler* (edited by Chr. Collin and H. Eitrem). 2 vols. (Kristiania and Copenhagen: Gyldendal, 1912–13).
Blanc, Tharald Høyerup. *Christiania theaters historie 1827–1877.* (Christiania: J.W. Cappelen, 1899).
*Henrik Ibsen og Christiania theater 1850–1899: Et bidrag til den Ibsenske digtnings scenehistorie.* (Kristiania: J. Dybwad, 1906). [**122a**]
*Norges første nationale scene. (Bergen, 1850–1863); et bidrag til den norske dramatiske kunstshistorie.* (Kristiania: no pub., 1884). [Contains a list of all productions 1850–63, and the laws adopted for the theatre in 1850.] [**95**]
Blytt, Peter. *Minder fra den første norske Scene i Bergen i 1850-Aarene. Et kulturhistorisk Forsøg.* (2nd edn) (Bergen: Stencilled from author's ms., 1907).
Botten-Hansen, Paul. *Theater-Anliggender – Et Stridsskrift af Nyhedsbladets Redaktør.* (Christiania: The author, 1858).
Brandes, Georg and Edvard. *Brevveksling med Bjørnsen, Ibsen, Kielland, Elster, Garborg, Lie* (edited by Francis Bull with Morten Borup). (Oslo: Gyldendal, 1939–41).
Bull, Francis, *Tradisjoner og minner.* (Oslo: Gyldendal, 1946). [The chapter 'Teaterminner', pp. 274–305]
Bull, Marie, født Midling. *Minder fra Bergens første nationale scene* (edited by H. Wiers-Jenssen). (Bergen: H. Wiers-Jenssen, 1905). [**93**, **94a**, **98**]
Bull, Ole. *Ole Bulls breve i uddrag* (edited by Alexander Bull). (Copenhagen: Gyldendal, 1881). [**96**]
*Christiania Aftenblad*, (Christiania, 1829). [**85**]
*Christiania Intelligentssedler.* (Christiania, 1825). [**83**]
*Christiania-Posten.* (Christiania, 1850). [**109**]
*Constitutionelle, Den.* (Christiania, 1837). [**89**]
Dunker, Bernhard. *Ole Bulls proces med Bergens politi.* (Copenhagen: B. Luno, 1851).
Elster, Kristian, d.y. *Skuespillerinden Johanne Dybwad. Til belysning av realismen i skuespilkunsten.* (Oslo: H. Aschehoug, 1931).
Erbe, Berit. *Bjørn Bjørnsons vej mod realismens teater.* (Oslo: Universitetsforlaget, 1976). [**124**]
Fahlstrøm, Alma. *17 portrettmedaljonger fra det gamle Christiania Theater.* (Oslo: H. Aschehoug, 1944).
Frisvold, Øyvind. *Teatret i norsk kulturpolitik: bakgrunn og tendenser fra 1850 til 1970-årene.* (Oslo: Universitetsforlaget, 1980).
Grieg, Joachim. Historical survey in the special theatre number of *Bergens Tidende* (25 October 1926) marking the 50th anniversary of the Bergen theatre's re-opening in 1876.
Haakonsen, Daniel. *Henrik Ibsen: mennesket og kunstneren.* (Oslo: Aschehoug, 1981). [Richly illustrated and documented critical biography and compendium of international Ibsen productions.]
Hansen, Harald. 'Kristiania Theater 1837–1899', *Folkebladet* (31 May 1899). [Especially valuable for its wealth of portrait photographs.]
Heiberg, Gunnar. *Artikler om teater og dramatikk* (edited by Hans Heiberg). (Oslo: Aschehoug, 1972). [**120**]
*Ibsen og Bjørnson på scenen.* (Kristiania: W. Nygaard, 1918).
*Norsk teater.* (Kristiania: H. Aschehoug, 1920).
Huidtfeldt, H. *Christiania Theaterhistorie.* (Copenhagen, 1876).
Ibsen, Henrik. *Artikler og Taler*, vol. 15 of the centenary edition of Ibsen's *Samlede værker* (edited by Francis Bull, Halvdan Koht and Didrik Arup Seip). (Oslo: Gyldendal, 1930). [**110**]
Jæger, Henrik. *Mixed pickles: feuilletoner og skitser.* (Kristiania: A. Cammermeyer, 1889). [Especially the essays on 'Johannes Brun', pp. 91–109; 'Sigvard Gundersen', 110–20; and 'Møllergaden no. 1', 121–32.]
Johansen, David Monrad. *Edvard Grieg.* (Oslo: Gyldendal, 1934).
Josephson, Ludvig. *Ett och annat om Henrik Ibsen och Kristiania Teater.* (Stockholm, 1898).
Just, Carl. *Litteratur om norsk teater. Bibliografi.* (Oslo: N.W. Damm, 1953).
*Schrøder og Christiania theater: et bidrag til norsk teaterhistorie.* (Oslo: Cammermeyer, 1948). [**123a**]

Krogness, Johan Richard. *Tro og detailleret fremstiling av det berømte theaterslag*. (Christiania: N.F. Axelsen, 1838). [91]

Lorentzen, Bernt. *Det første Norske Teater*. (Oslo, 1949).

Lund, Audhild. *Henrik Ibsen og det norske teater 1857–63*. (Oslo: Det Mallingske bogtrykkeri, 1925). [113]

McFarlane, James Walter (ed.) *The Oxford Ibsen*. 7 vols. (London: Oxford University Press, 1960–70). [Appendices provide rich documentation in English; select bibliography lists much English-language material.]

*Manden*. (Christiania, 1851). [100, 110]

Marum, Reidar A. *Teaterslag og pipekonserter*. (Oslo: Cammermeyer, 1944). [112]

Meyer, Michael. *Henrik Ibsen*. 3 vols. (London: Hart-Davis, 1967–71). Abridged one-volume edition (Harmondsworth: Penguin, 1985).

[Introduction to and stage histories of fifteen Ibsen plays in English accompanying Meyer's translations.] (London, 1960–6).

Monrad, M.J. 'Om theater og nationalitet og om en norsk dramatisk skole', *Norsk Tidsskrift for Videnskab og Litteratur* (1854–5), pp. 1–33. [111]

*Morgenbladet*. (Christiania, 1827–56). [84, 87, 99, 102, 103, 112]

*Nationaltheatret i Kristiania: Festskrift i anledning af Nationaltheatrets aabning 1ste september 1899*. (Kristiania, 1899). [127]

Nygaard, Knut. *Gunnar Heiberg: teatermannen*. (Oslo: Universitetsforlaget, 1975).

*Holbergs teaterarv*. (Bergen: J.W. Eide, 1984).

Paulson, Andreas. *Komediebakken og engen: femti års teatererindringer*. (Oslo: Gyldendal, 1932).

Reimers, Sophie. *Teaterminner fra Kristiania teater*. (Kristiania: A. Cammermeyer, 1917).

Rudler, Roderick. 'Ibsens teatergjerning i Bergen', *Drama och Teater* (1968), pp. 59–68. [Rudler, of the Institute of Theatre Science at the University of Oslo, has written essays and articles too numerous to be listed here on many aspects of early theatre life in Norway, and notably on Ibsen's early experience of theatre and his practice as a director, reviewer, etc.]

Sagen, L. and H. Foss. *Bergens beskrivelse*. (Bergen: C. Dahl, 1824). [Description of Bergen theatre built in 1800 on p. 604]

*St. Hallvard* 3 (1985). [Special theatre number of this periodical devoted to Oslo, including an historical essay by Trine Næss and a chronological survey of all theatre ventures in the capital by Reider Jamvold.]

[Siversen, Ivar]. *Theaterstriden i Bergen 1873 belyst ved akstykkerne. Udgivet som bidrag til den bergenske theatersags historie ved I.S.* (Bergen: Gyldendal, 1894). [116]

Sperati, Octavia. *Fra det gamle komediehus*. (Kristiania: Gyldendal, 1916). [118]

*Theatererindringer*. (Kristiania, 1911). [117]

Steen, Ellisiv. *Det norske nasjonalhistoriske drama 1756–1974*. (Oslo: Gyldendal, 1976). [Descriptive and historical register of Norwegian historical plays.]

Svendsen, Arnljot Strømme. *Den nationale scene. Det norske repertoire 1876–1974*. (Bergen: no pub., 1975).

Svendsen, Arnljot Strømme, Berit Erbe and Kirsten Broch (eds.), for Kjetil Bang-Hansen and Den Nationale Scene. *Ludvig Holberg: en bergenser uten grenser*. (Bergen: Universitetsforlaget, 1984).

*Theatervennen*. (Bergen, 1851). [101]

*Undersøgelses-Commissionens forhandlinger i anledning det forefaldne i Christiania offentlige skuespilhuus den 4de November 1827*. (Christiania: Udgivne af Christiania Byes Formaend, 1828). [86]

Waal, C.R. *Johanne Dybwad, Norwegian actress*. (Oslo: Universitetsforlaget, 1967).

Wergeland, Henrik. *Samlede skrifter, trykt og utrykt* (edited by H. Jæger and D.A. Seip). 6 vols. (Oslo: Steenske forlag, 1918–40). [87]

Wiers-Jenssen, Hans. *Nationalteatret gjennem 25 aar 1899–1924*. (Kristiania: Gyldendal, 1924).

Wiers-Jenssen, Hans and J. Nordahl Olsen. *Den nationale scene: De første 25 aar*. (Bergen: Det Mallingske boktrykkeri, 1926).

Wiesener, A.M. *Henrik Ibsen og 'Det norske teater' i Bergen 1851–1857*. (Bergen: Det Mallingske bogtrykkeri, 1928).

Winter-Hjelm, K.A. *Af Kristiania teaterliv i den seneste tid*. (Kristiania: J.W. Cappelen, 1875). [Includes a list of all theatre personnel in 1875, some biographical sketches, and the repertories for the 1870/71 to 1874/75 seasons.]

Wolf, Lucie. *Fra skuespillerinden Lucie Wolfs livserindringer* (3rd edn). (Kristiania: A. Cammermeyer, 1898). [**106**]

POLAND

Bernacki, Ludwik. *Teatr, dramat i muzyka za Stanisława Augusta; 68 podobiznani*. 2 vols. (Lvov: Zakład narodowy im. Ossolińskich, 1925).

Bogusławski, Wojciech. *Dzieje Teatru Narodowego na trzy czesci podzielone oraz wiadomosci o życiu slawnych artystów* (1820–1). (Warsaw: Wydawnictwa Artystcyzne i Filmowe, 1965). [**128, 133, 134, 142**]

*Mimika* (edited by J. Lipiński and T. Sivert). (Warsaw: Państwowy Instytut Wydawniczy, 1965). [**143**]

Brumer, Wiktor. *Służba narodowa W. Bogusławskiego*. (Warsaw: Nakł. Księgarni F. Hoesicka, 1929).

Coleman, Marion Moore. *The Polish drama and theatre. A bibliography compiled for the American Association of Teachers of Slavonic and East European Languages*. (New York: AATSEEL, 1945).

Czartoryski, Adam Kazimierz. *Myśli o pismach polskich z uwagami nad sposobem pisania w rozmaitych materyach*. (Vilna: Józef Zawadzki, 1810). [**131**]

Estreicher, Karol. 'Historia sceny warszawskiej do roku 1850' in *Pamiętnik literacki*, 4 (1936).

*Teatra w Polsce*. (1873–9) 3 vols. (2nd edn) (Warsaw: Państwowy Instytut Wydawniczy, 1953).

Galle, Leon. *Wojciech Bogusławski i repertuar teatru polskiego w pierwszym okresie jego działalności – do roku 1794*. (Warsaw: M. Arct, 1925).

*Gazeta Korespondenta Warszawskiego*. (Warsaw, 1811–16). [**141, 145, 146**]

*Gazeta Polska*. (Warsaw, 1829). [**150**]

*Gazeta Warszawska*. (Warsaw, 1810–15). [**140, 144**]

Got, Jerzy. *Na wyspie Guaxara – W. Bogusławski i teatr lwowski 1789–1799*. (Cracow: Wydawnictwo Literackie, 1971).

Jabłoński, Zbigniew. *Dzieje teatru w Krakowie w latach 1781–1830*. (Cracow: Wydawnictwo Literackie, 1980).

Karasowski, M. *Rys historyczny opery polskiej*. (Warsaw: M. Glücksberg, 1859).

Klimowicz, Mieczysław. *Początki teatru stanisławowskiego 1765–1773*. (Warsaw: Państwowy Instytut Wydawniczy, 1965).

Korseniewski, Bohdan. *Drama w warszawskim Teatrze Narodowym podczas dyrekcji L. Osińskiego 1814–1831*. (Warsaw: Kasa im. Mianowskiego, 1934).

'Poglądy na gre aktorów za czasów Stanisława Augusta' in *Sprawozdania Towarzystwa Naukowego Warszawskiego* (1939).

Król-Kaczorowska, Barbara. 'Antonio Sacchetti – dekorator romantyczny. Działalność w latach 1829–1895' in *Pamiętnik teatralny*, 1–3 (1959).

*Teatr v dawnej Polsce. Budynki, dekoracje, kostiumy*. (Warsaw: Państwowy Instytut Wydawniczy, 1971).

Łukasik, S. *Le Prince A. Czartoryski et la renaissance national en Pologne au XVIIIe siècle*. (Grenoble: J. Aubert, 1926).

Miller, Antoni. *Teatr Polski i muzyka na Litwe*. (Vilna: Wydawnictwo im. Lopachińskich, 1936).

*Polski słownik biograficzny*. 28 vols. (Cracow: Zakład narodowy im. Ossolińskich, 1935 *et seq*.)

[Raimund, Ferdinand]. *Chlop milionowy czyli i Dziewczyna ze świata czarownego, melodrama alegoryczna w trzech aktach z niemieckiego pana Rajmund przerobiona*. (Warsaw, 1829). [**151**]

Raszewski, Zbigniew. *Bogusławski* (2nd edn). (Warsaw: Państwowy Instytut Wydawniczy, 1982).

*Krótka historia teatru polskiego*. (Warsaw: Państwowy Instytut Wydawniczy, 1977).

*Recenzje teatralne towarzystwa Iksów 1815–1819* (edited by J. Lipiński). (Wrocław: Zakład Narodowy im. Ossolińskich, 1956). [**144**, **145**, **146**]
Recke, Elisa von der. *Mein Journal. Elisas neu aufgefunde Tagebücher aus den Jahren 1791 und 1793–1795*. (Leipzig: Koehler & Ameland, 1928). [**136**]
*Repertuar teatrów warszawskich 1814–1831*, edited by E. Szwankowski. (Warsaw, 1973).
Rulikowski, Mieczysław. *Teatr warszawki od czasów Osińskiego*. (Lvov: Wydawnictwo Szkolnych Ksiazek, 1938).
Schultz, Friedrich. *Reise eines Liefländers von Riga nach Warschau*. (Berlin: bei F. Vieweg dem ältern, 1795–6). [**137a**]
Seume, J.G. *Einige Nachrichten über die Vorfälle in Polen im Jahre 1794*. (Leipzig, 1796). [**138a**]
Simon, L. *Dykcjonarz teatrów polskich czynnych od czasów najdawniejszych do roku 1863*. (Warsaw, 1935).
*Słownik biograficzny teatru polskiego 1765–1965*. (Warsaw: Państwowy Wydawnictwo Naukowe, 1973).
Straus, S. *Bibliografia tytułów czasopism teatralnych*. (Wrocław: Zakład im. Ossolińskich, 1953).
*Bibliografia żródel do historii teatru w Polsce*. (Wrocław: Zakład Narodowy im. Ossolińskich, 1957).
Świerczewski, E. *Wojciech Bogusławski i jego scena*. (Warsaw: Nakł. Związku Artystów scen polskich, 1929).
*Teatr Narodowy 1765–1794* (edited by Jan Kott). [Contributors: J. Jackl, B. Król-Kaczorowska, J. Pawłowiczowa, K. Wierzbicka-Michalska, Z. Wołoszynska, W. Zawadzki] (Warsaw: Państwowy Instytut Wydawniczy, 1967). [**131**, **132**, **135a**, **135b**, **136**, **137a**, **138a**, **145b**]
*Teatr Wojciecha Bogusławskiego w latach 1799–1814*, edited by E. Szwankowski. (Wrocław: Zakład Narodowy im. Osslińskich, 1954). [**139**]
Wierzbicka, Karyna. *Żródła do historii teatru warszawskiego od roku 1762 do roku 1833*. 2 vols. (Wrocław: Zakład narodowy im. Ossolińskich, 1951, 1955.) [**129**, **130**, **147**]
*Życie teatralne w Warszawie za Stanisława Augusta*. (Warsaw: Tow. Milosnikow Historii, 1949).
Wierzbicka-Michalska, Karyna. *Aktorzy cudzoziemscy w Warszawie w XVIII w*. (Wrocław: Zakład Narodowy im. Ossolińskich, 1975).
*Aktorzy cudzoziemscy w Warszawie w latach 1795–1830*. (Wrocław: Wydawnictwo Polskiej Akademii Nauk, 1988).
*Sześć studiów o teatrze stanisławowskim*. (Wrocław: Zakład Narodowy im. Ossolińskich, 1967).
*Teatr narodowy w dobie Oświecenia. Księga pámiątkowa sesji poświęconej 200-leciu teatru narodowego*. (Wrocław: Zakład narodowy im. Ossolińskich, 1967). [**132**, **135a**, **135b**]
*Teatr w Polsce w XVIII wieku*. (Warsaw: Państwowy Wydawnictwo Naukowne, 1977). [Includes a full bibliography] [**132**, **137b**, **137c**, **138b**]
*Teatr warszawski za Sasów*. (Wrocław: Zakład narodowy im. Ossolińskich, 1964).
Wilski, Zbigniew. *Polskie szkolnictwo teatralne 1811–1944*. (Wrocław: Zakład Narodowy im. Ossolińskich, 1978).

### CZECH LANDS

Archiv hlavního města Prahy. *Documenta Pragensia c. III* (*Vydáno na počest 100. výročí otevření Národního divadla*). (Prague: AHMP, 1983.) [**152**]
Bartoš, Jan. *Národní divadlo a jeho budovatelé*. vol. 1 of *Dějiny Národního divadla* (edited by Jaroslav Jelínek). (Prague: Sbor pro zřízení druhého Národního divadla, 1933). [**175b**]
Baťha, F. 'Dva dokumenty k historii počátku českého divadla v Praze', *Divadlo*, 10 (1958), p. 755.
Benda, Jaroslav (ed.) *Založení Národního divadla, 1868: Vydáno na pamět padesátého výroči, 1918*. (Prague: Vyd. Slavnostní výbor pro jubileum Národního divadla, 1918).
Blesík, Jan. *U sv. Kajetána pod Hradem pražským: bývalé divadlo J.K. Tyla*. (Prague: Kolej Redemptoristů, 1947).
*Česká včela*. (Prague, 1834–5). [**160**, **163**]

*České umění dramatické* (edited by F. Götz and F. Tetauer). vol. 1. *Činohra*; vol. 2. *Zpěvohra*. (Prague: Šolc a Šimáček, 1941).

Česnáková-Michalcová, Milena. *Přemeny Divadla (Inonárodné divadla na Slovensku do roku 1918*. (Bratislava: Veda vydavatélstvo Slovenskej akadémie vied, 1981).

Chmelenský, Josef Krasoslav. 'Stav divadla českého od měsíce dubna 1824 až po konec r. 1826' in *Časopis spolenčenství vlastenského musea v Čechách*, (1827) 127–31. [**158**]

Coleman, Arthur P. *Kotzebue and the Czech stage*. (Schenectady, N.Y.: Electric City Press, 1936).

Coleman, Marion Moore. *The Czech drama and theatre*. (New York: American Association of Teachers of Slavonic and East European Languages, 1945.)

*Čtení o Národním divadle. Útržky dějin a osudů*. (Edited by Hana Konečná and collaborative team). (Prague: Odeon, 1983). [**178b**]

*Dějiny českého divadla* (edited by František Černý and Ljuba Klosová). 4 vols. (Prague: Academia, nakladatelství Československé akademie věd Praha, 1968–77). [**153b**, **156b**, **166b**, **172a**, **175a**, **176b**]

*Divadelní periodika v Čechách a na Moravě 1772–1963* (edited by Miroslav Laiske). (Prague: Divadelní ústav, 1967).

*Divadlo v české kultuře 19. století (Sborník sympozia v Plzni 10–12 březnа 1983)* (edited by Milena Freimanová). (Prague: Národní galerie, 1985).

Engelmüller, Karel. *Z letopisů českého divadelnictví*. 2 vols. (Prague: Jos. R. Vilímek, 1946–7). [**162a**, **166a**]

Fischer, Otakar. 'Le théâtre national de Prague', *La Revue française de Prague* (March 1936), 13–34.

Frič, J.V. and J.L. Turnovský. *Almanach matice divadelní k slavnému otevření Národního divadla*. (Prague: J. Otto, 1881). [**154**]

Havlíček, Karel. *Karel Havlíček Borovský. Politické spisy* (edited by Z. Tobolka). vol. 2. (Prague: J. Laichter, 1902). [**170**]

Hof, Karel Vít. *Dějiny velkého národního divadla v Praze, od prvních počátků až do kladení základního kamena*. (Prague: Nakl. Slavostního výboru, 1868).

Honzl, Jindřich (ed.) *The Czechoslovak Theatre*. (Prague: Orbis, 1948).

Hostinský, Otakar. *Otakar Hostinský o divadle; Sborník* (edited by Miloš Jůzl). (Prague: Divadelní ústav, 1981). [**179**]

Kačer, Miroslav. *Václav Thám*. (Prague: Svobodné slovo, 1965). [**153a**]

Kačer, Miroslav and Otruba, Mojmír. *Tvůrčí cesta Josefa Kajetána Tyla*. (Prague: Státní nakl. krásné literatury a umvění, 1961).

Kadlec, Karel. 'František Palacký a české divadlo v Praze', *Památník na oslavu stých narozenin Františka Palackého*. (Prague: Matice česká, 1898).

*Karel Havliček Borovský*. 2 vols. (Prague: Československý spisovatel, 1986).

Kaška-Zbraslavský, Jan. *Kajetánské divadlo*. (Prague, 1937). [**162b**]

Kimball, Stanley Buchholz. *Czech nationalism: a study of the national theatre movement, 1845–83*. (Urbana, Ill.: University of Illinois Press, 1964). [**171**, **173**, **178a**]

Klicpera, Václav Kliment. *Divadlo Klicperovo*. vol. 1. (Hradec Králové, 1920). [**159**]

Klosová, Lyubov. 'Le Méphistophélès tchèque', *Revue d'histoire du théâtre* (April–June 1967), 143–50.

*Květy*. (Prague, 1835–45). [**161**, **164**, **165**, **168**, **176b**]

Ladecký, Jan. *Přispěvky k dějinám českého divadla*. (Prague: Divadelní odbor N.V.Č., 1895).

Laiske, Miroslav. *Pražská dramaturgie (Česká divadelni představení v Praze do otevření Prozatimního divadla)*. vol. 1, 1762(?)–1843; vol. 2, 1844–62. (Prague: Ústav pro českou a světovou literaturu ČSAV, 1974).

Máchal, Jan. *Dějiny českého dramata*. (Prague: F. Topič, 1929).

Matějček, Antonin. *Národni divadlo a jeho výtvarníci*. (Prague: Dějiny Národního divadla, 1934.)

Menčík, Ferdinand. 'Příspěvky k dějinám českého divadla', *Rozpravy české akademie Císaře Fr. Josefa pro vědy, slovesnost a umění*, LV, Trida 2, CL. 1895.

*Národní divadlo a jeho budovatelé, 1850–1881: Katalog výstavy*. (Prague: Dějiny Narodního divadla, 1931).
*Národní listy*. (Prague, 1874). [177]
*Národní noviny*. (Prague, 1848–9). [170, 171]
*Národní slavnost v Praze dne 14. května 1868*. (Prague, 1869).
Nejedlý, Zdeněk. *Opera Národního divadla do roku 1900*. (Prague: Národní divadlo, 1935).
Neruda, Jan. *Sebrané spisy*. vol. 25: *Pro české divadlo/Divadelní táčky*. (Prague: Topič, 1912).
*Spisy*. vol. 17: *České divadlo IV*. (Prague: Československý spisovatel, 1958). [177]
Pařiková, Marie. *České divadlo*. (Prague: Městská knihovna v Praze, 1983).
Píša, A.M. *O smyslu a poslání Národního divadla*. (Prague: Athos, 1948).
*Pokrok*. (Prague, 1881), [179]
Pravda, E.J. 'K otevření Národního divadla', *Slovanský sborník*, 12 (December 1883), 623–6.
*Rodinná kronika* (Prague, 1863–4) [175a]
Rutte, Miroslav. 'Národní divadlo k svému padesátému výročí', *Divadlo a doba*, 11, 6 (October 1932).
Šedivý, Prokop. *Krátké pojednání o užitku, který ustavičně stojící a dobře spořádané divadlo způsobiti může*. (Prague, 1793); (reprinted edition with a postscript by Pavel Eisner) (Prague, 1955). [155]
*Slovan*. (Prague, 1851). [173]
Štěpánek, Jan Nepomuk. 'Osvobození vlasti aneb Korytané v Čechách' in *Divadlo od J.N. Štěpánka*. (Prague, 1822). [156a]
Stloukal, Karel. 'Legenda o budovatelích Národního divadla, I', *Český časopis historický*, 41 (1935), pp. 83–105.
'Legenda o budovatelích Národního divadla, II', *Český časopis historický*, 41 (1935), p. 321–51.
Stöger, J.A. 'Preisausschreibung für böhmische Dramen', *Bohemia* (1 January 1843). [167]
Šubert, František Adolf. *Das Königl. Böhmische Landes- und National-Theater in Prag*. (Prague: Verlag des National-theaterconsortiums, 1892).
*Národní divadlo v Praze: dějiny jeho i stavba dokončená*. (Prague: J. Otto, 1881). [174, 178a, 180]
Teuber, Oscar. *Geschichte des Prager Theaters*. 3 vols. (Prague: N. Haase, 1883–88). [166c]
Titova, L.N. *Cheshky teatr èpokhi natsional'nogo vozrozhdeniya konets XVIII-pervaya polovina XIX v*. (Moscow: Nauka, 1980).
Turnovský, J.L. *Život a doba J.K. Tyla*. (Prague: Hynek, 1892). [169]
Tyl, Josef Kajetán. *Spisy Josefa Kajetána Tyla* (edited by J.L. Turnovský). 15 vols. (Prague: A. Hynek, 1888–92). [See esp. vols. 11–13, *Divadelní hry*, and vol. 14, *Spisy drobné*.] [172b]
Tyrrell, John. *Czech Opera*. (Cambridge University Press, 1988).
*Upomínka na slavnostní položení základního kamena k velikému národnímu divadlu českému v Praze*. (Prague, 1868). [176a]
Vondráček, Jan. *Dějiny českého divadlo, doba obrozenská 1771–1824*. (Prague: Orbis, 1956). [154, 156a, 157, 158]
*Dějiny českého divadlo, doba předbřeznová, 1824–1846*. (Prague: Orbis, 1957). [167]
*Přehledné dějíny českého divadlo*. (Prague: F. Svoboda, 1926–30).

## HUNGARY

*A Nemzeti Színház* (edited by György Székely). (Budapest: Gondolat, 1965).
*A Nemzeti Színház 1837–1887*. (Budapest: Franklin, 1887.) [Reprinted from *Magyar Salon*]
*A százéves Nemzeti Színház: az 1937–38–as centenáris év emlékalbuma*. (Budapest: Pallas, 1938).
Bajza, József. *Szózat a Pesti Magyar Színház ügyében*. (Buda: Egytemi Nyomda, 1839).
Báthory, István. *A Nemzeti Színház építésének és lebontásának története*. (Budapest: Pátria, 1914).
Bayer, József. *A nemzeti játékszín törtenete*. 2 vols. (Budapest: Hornyánszky, 1887).
*Nemzeti játékszín, mint közügy*. (Budapest: *Budapesti Szemle*, 1900).
Benke, József. *A Pesten felállítandó magyar játékszínről*. (Pest: Trattner, 1832).

Bíró, Lajos Pál. *A Nemzeti Színház története, 1837–1841*. (Budapest: Pfeifer, 1931).
Fáy, András, Ferenc Kállay and István Jakab. *Magyar játékszíni feleletek a Magyar Tudós Társaságnak azon kérdésére: miképpen lehetne a magyar játékszínt Budapesten állandóan megalapítani?* (Buda: Egyetemi Nyomda, 1834).
Ferenczi, Zoltán. *A kolozsvári színészet és színház törtenete*. (Kolozsvár: Ajtai K. Albert Magyar Polgár Könyv nyomdáju, 1897).
Fogarasi, János. *Egyetlen egy mód a magyar játékszín célirányos megalapítására*. (Pest: Trattner, 1834).
Gergely, Pál. *Az Akadémia szerepe a Nemzeti Színház létrehozásában*. (Budapest: Magyar Tudományos Akadémia, 1963).
Horvát, András. *A nemes szívű magyarokhoz a pesti nemzeti teátrom ügyében*. (Buda: no pub., 1815).
Kádár, Jolán [Mrs Pukánszky]. *A Nemzeti Színház százéves története*. 2 vols. (Budapest: Magyar Történelmi Társulat, 1938–40). **[181, 182, 183b, 184, 187, 189, 190b, 191, 192, 193, 194c]**
*A Nemzeti Színházunk és a közvélemény a XIX. században*. (Budapest: Franklin, 1937). [Reprinted from *Budapesti Szemle*.]
'La naissance du Théâtre national de Hongrie', *Revue de l'histoire du théâtre* (January–March 1970), 27–31.
Katona, József. 'Mi az oka, hogy Magyarországon a jatékszíni költőmesterség lábra nem tud kapni?', *Tudományos Gyűjtemény* (April 1821). **[185]**
Kerényi, Ferenc. *A régi magyar színpadon 1790–1849*. (Budapest: Magvető, 1981).
Kölcsey, Ferenc. *Magyar játéksin*. (Pest, 1827). **[186]**
Kujáni, János. *Adalékok a magyar színjátszás és színpadi szavalat történetéhez: a Nemzeti Színház első évtizede*. (Pécs: Dunántúl, 1928).
Lugosi, Döme. *Kelemen László és az első* 'Magyar Játszó Színi Társaság'. (Makó: Csanádvármegyei Könyvtár, 1927).
Magyar, Bálint. *A Nemzeti Színház előtti magyar színészet történetének vázlata*. (Budapest: Athenæum, 1948).
*A százéves Nemzeti Színház*. (Budapest: *Magyar Szemle* Társaság, 1937).
*Magyar játékszín: Nagy elődeink harca a nemzeti színjátszásért* (edited by Anikó Laszló). (Budapest: Művelt Nép, 1954).
*Magyar színháztörténet* (edited by Ferenc Hont). (Budapest: Gondolat, 1962). **[183a, 190a]**
Mályusz, Edit. 'Les débuts du théâtre professionel hongrois', *Revue d'histoire du théâtre* (January–March 1970), 23–7.
Nagy, Artur. *Olasz színművek és színészek a Nemzeti Színházban 1837-től 1884-ig*. (Budapest: Pázmány Péter Tudományegyetem Olasz Intézete, 1940).
Németh, Antal (ed.) *Színészeti Lexikon*. 2 vols. (Budapest: Györ, 1930).
Pataki, József. *A magyar színészet története, 1790–1890*. (Budapest: Táltos, 1922).
Pekhata, Károly. *A Budapesten felállítandó játékszínről*. (Buda: Egyetemi Nyomda, 1834.)
Rédey, Tivadar. *A Nemzeti Színház története: az első félszázad*. (Budapest: Királyi Magyar Egyetemi Nyomda, 1937). **[194a & b]**
Rexa, Dezső. *A Nemzeti Színház megnyitásának története*. (Budapest: Pest-Pilis-Solt-Kiskun Vármegye Kiadása, 1927).
Schöpflin, Aladár (ed.) *Magyar színművészeti lexikon*. 4 vols. (Budapest, 1930).
Staud, Géza. *Kelemen László naplója és feljegyzései*. (Budapest: Színháztudományi Intézet, 1961).
*Magyar színészeti szakkönyvek bibliográfiája, 1945–60*. (Budapest: Színháztudomány i Intézet & Országos Színháztörténeti Múzeum, 1961).
Szabolcs, Ferenc. *A nemzeti játékszín eszméje a magyar és német irodalomban*. (Budapest: Királyi Magyar Egyetemi Nyomda, 1938).
Széchenyi, István. *Magyar játékszínrül*. (Pest: Landerer, 1832). **[188]**
Székely, József. *Magyar játékszín: a Nemzeti Színház félszázados ünnepélye*. (Budapest: Légrády, 1887).
Szinovátz, György. *Rövid értekezés a magyar játékszínnek Budapesten állandóan leendő megalapításáról, s a színész tagoknak jelenlegi állapotjokról*. (Pozsony: Schmid, 1835).

RUMANIA

*Albina româneasca*. (Jassy, 1832–46). [206, 212a]
Alecsandri, Vasile. *Cuconu Iorgu de la Sadagura sau Nepotu-i salba dracului*. (Jassy, 1844). [210]
Alterescu, Simion. *Actorul şi vîrstele teatrului românesc*. (Bucharest: Meridiane, 1982).
(ed.) *An abridged history of Romanian theatre*. (Bucharest: Editura Academiei RSR, 1983).
(ed.) *Istoria teatrului în România*. 3 vols. (Bucharest: Editura Academiei RSR, 1965–73). [203, 205b]
Baiculescu, G. and I. Massoff. *Teatrul românesc acum 100 de ani*. (Bucharest: Vremea, 1935).
Belador, M. *Istoria teatrului român*. (Craiova: Ralian şi Ignat Samitca, 1895).
Berlogea, I. and G. Muntean (eds.) *Pagini din istoria gîndirii teatrale româneşti*. (Bucharest: Meridiane, 1972). [208]
Bogdan, N. *Oraşul Iaşi*. (Jassy: no pub., 1913).
*Bukarester Deutsche Zeitung*. (Bucharest, 1853). [205a]
Burada, T. *Istoria teatrului în Moldova* (new edition revised by I. Chiţimia). (Bucharest: Minerva, 1975). [206, 207, 209, 211]
*Curierul românesc*. (Bucharest, 1830–43). [196, 198, 199, 201, 203]
*Dacia literară*. (Jassy, 1840). [208]
Diacu-Xenofon, I. *Viaţa şi opera unui nedreptăţit: Costache Caragiale*. (Bucharest: Biblioteca Teatrului National, 1940).
Florea, M. *Matei Millo*. (Bucharest: Meridiane, 1966).
*Scurtă istorie a teatrului românesc*. (Bucharest: Meridiane, 1955).
Ghica, I. *Scrisori către V. Alecsandri*. 3 vols. (Bucharest: Editura Cultura Româneasca, 1940).
Gorovei, A. 'Teodor Teodorini. Documente şi informaţii despre el şi familia lui', *Arhivele Olteniei* (1928), p. 185.
Ionescu, Medeea. *A concise history of theatre in Romania* (translated by D.S. Lecca). Bucharest: Editura Ştiinţifica şi enciclopedică, 1981.
Ionescu-Gion, I. *Istoria Bucureştilor*. (Bucharest: Socec, 1898).
Kogălniceanu, M. *Scrisori. 1834–1849*. (Bucharest: Minerva, 1913).
Manoliu, E. *O privire retrospectivă asupra teatrului moldovenesc*. (Jassy: no pub., 1925).
Massoff, I. *Teatrul românesc*. 5 vols. (Bucharest: Editura pentru literatură, 1961–74). [196, 212b]
Mititelu, A. *Teatro romeno*. (Milan: Nuova Accademia, 1960).
Niculescu, A. (ed.) *Primii noştri dramaturgi*. (Bucharest: ESPLA, 1956)
Ollănescu, D. *Teatrul la români* (new revised edition by C. Dumitrescu). (Bucharest: Eminescu, 1981). [197, 199, 200, 201, 203, 205a]
Potra, G. *Din Bucureştii de altădată*. (Bucharest: Editura ştiinţifică şi enciclopedică, 1981). [202, 204, 205a]
Rădulescu, I.H. *Contribuţiuni la istoria teatrului din Muntenia (1833–1853)*. (Bucharest: Institutul de istorie literară şi folclor, 1935).
Tornea, F. *Un artist cetăţean: Costache Caragiale*. (Bucharest: ESPLA, 1954).
Trifu, C. *Cronica dramatică şi începuturile teatrului românesc*. (Bucharest: Minerva, 1970).
Vasiliu, M. *Istoria teatrului românesc*. (Jassy: Albatros, 1972).
*Vestitorul românesc*. (Bucharest, 1853). [204]
Wilkinson, William. *An account of the principalities of Wallachia and Moldavia*. (London: Longman, Hurst, Rees, Orme and Brown, 1820); reprint edn (New York: Arno Press, 1971). [195]

RUSSIA

### 1 *Bibliographies and study guides*

Adaryukov, V. Ya. *Bibliografichesky ukazatel' knig, broshyur, zhurnalnykh statey i zametok po istorii russkogo teatra*. (St Petersburg: É. Arngol'd, 1904).

Aganbekyan, A. *Moskovsky Khudozhestvenny teatr, 1898–1938. Bibliografichesky ukazatel'* (edited by S.N. Durylin). (Moscow–Leningrad: Vserossiyskoe teatral'noe obshchestvo, 1939).

Fridenberg, A.F. 'Rukopisnye materialy, khranyashchiyasya v Gos. tsentral'nom teatral'nom muzeye' in *Trudy Gos. tsentral'nogo teatral'nogo muzeya.* (Moscow–Leningrad: Iskusstvo, 1941).

Lisovsky, N.M. *Obozrenie literatury po teatru i muzyke za 1889–1891.* (St Petersburg: Tip, imp. spb. teatrov, 1893).

Martínek, Karel. *Ruská předrevoluční divadelní kultura. Přehled základních pramenů ke studiu předrevoluční ruské divadelní kultury od počátků do roku 1917.* (Prague: Vydal Scénografický ústav, 1973).

*Materialy k istorii russkogo teatra v Gosudarstvennykh archiv SSSR, XVII vek – 1917. Obzory dokumentov XVII vek-1917 g.* (edited by I.F. Petrovskaya). (Moscow: Glavnoe arkhivnoe upravlenie pri Soveta Ministrov SSSR, 1966).

Petrovskaya, I.F. *Istochnikovedenie istorii russkogo dorevolyutsionnogo dramaticheskogo teatra.* (Leningrad: Iskusstvo, 1971).

(ed.) *Materialy k istoriii russkogo teatra v gosudarstvennykh arkhivakh SSSR. Obzory dokumentakh XVII vek.-1917g.* (Moscow: Glavnoe arkhivnoe upravlenii pri Sovete ministrov SSSR, 1966).

*Teatr i muzyka. Dokumenty i materialy.* (Moscow–Leningrad: Izd. Akademii Nauk, 1963).

Vishnevsky, V. *Teatral'naya periodika (1774–1940).* 2 vols. (Moscow: Iskusstvo, 1949).

## *2 General histories and collections*

Ashukin, N.S., V.N. Vsevolodsky-Gerngross, Yu. V. Sobol'ëv. *Khrestomatiya po istorii russkogo teatra XVIII i XIX vekov* (edited by G.I. Goyan). (Leningrad–Moscow: Iskusstvo, 1940).

Bozheryanov, I.N. *Illyustrirovannaya istoriya russkogo teatra XIX v.* 2 vols. (St Petersburg: no pub., 1903).

Danilov, S.S. (ed.) *O teatre; sbornik statey.* (Leningrad: Iskusstvo, 1929).

*Ocherki po istorii russkogo dramaticheskogo teatra.* (Leningrad–Moscow: Iskusstvo, 1948).

Danilov, S.S. and S.S. Portugalova. *Russky dramatichesky teatr XIX veka.* 2 vols. (Leningrad: Iskusstvo, 1974).

Drizen, N.V. *Materialy k istorii russkogo teatra.* (Moscow: A.A. Levenson, 1905; Moscow: no pub., 1913).

*Ezhegodnik imperatorskikh teatrov.* (St Petersburg: Tipografiya Imp. Spb. Teatrov, 1892–1915.) [**213, 214, 229, 230, 233, 235, 246**]

Institut istorii iskusstv Ministerstva kul'tury SSSR. *Istoriya russkogo dramaticheskogo teatra* (edited by E.G. Kholodov). 7 vols. (Moscow: Iskusstvo, 1977–87).

Khaychenko, G.A. (ed.) *Istoriya teatro-vedeniya narodov SSSR.* (Moscow: Nauka, 1985).

Lo Gatto, Ettore. *Storia del teatro russo.* 2 vols. (Florence: G.C. Sansoni, 1952). [**213d**]

L'vov, N.I. and I. Maksimov (eds.) *Masterstvo aktëra: khrestomatiya* (edited by B. Alpers and P. Novitsky). (Moscow: Khudozhestvennaya literatura, 1935).

Senelick, Laurence (ed. and trans.) *Russian dramatic theory from Pushkin to the Symbolists: an anthology.* (Austin, Texas: University of Texas Press, 1981). [**215a, 225, 227**]

Taneev, S.V. *Iz proshlogo imperatorskikh teatrov.* 3 vols. (St Petersburg: Universitetskaya tipografiya M. Katkova, 1885–6). [**217**]

*Teatral'naya entsiklopediya* (edited by S.S. Mokul'skiy and P.A. Markov). 5 vols and supplement. (Moscow: Sovetskaya Entsiklopediya, 1961–7).

Varneke, B.V. *Istoriya russkogo teatra.* (Kazan, 1908; 3rd edn, Moscow–Leningrad: Iskusstvo, 1939). [The English translation by B. Brasol, *History of the Russian theatre* (New York: Macmillan, 1951) lacks the notes and bibliographic material.]

Vsevolodsky-Gerngross, V.N. *Istoriya russkogo teatra.* 2 vols. (Leningrad–Moscow: Tea-Kino-Pechat', 1929). [**215b, 218b, 237b**]

*Khrestomatiya po istorii russkogo teatra.* (Moscow: Khudozhestvennaya literatura, 1936). [**240**]

*Teatr v Rossii v èpokhu Otechestvennoy voyny.* (St Petersburg: no pub., 1912).

### 3 *Studies of specific persons, theatres and phenomena*

*A.N. Ostrovsky. Novye materialy i issledovaniya. Literaturnoe nasledstvo* 88. 2 vols. (Moscow: Nauka, 1980).

*A.N. Ostrovsky v vospominaniyakh sovremennikov* (edited by A.I. Revyakin). (Moscow: Khudozhestvennya literatura, 1966).

Abalkin, N. (ed.) *Maly Teatr SSSR 1824–1917*. vol. 1. (Moscow: Vserossiyskoe teatral'noe obshchestvo, 1978). **[247, 248b, 250]**

*Akademichesky teatr dramy imeni A.S. Pushkina* (edited by E.K. Norkute). (Leningrad: Iskusstvo, 1983).

Aksakov, S.T. *Sobranie sochineny*. vols. 2 and 3. (Moscow: Gos. Izd. Khudozhestvennoy literatury, 1955–6). **[219, 220]**

Alekseev-Yakovlev, A. Ya. *Russkie narodnye gulyanya, v zapisi i obrabotke E.M. Kuznetsova*. (Moscow–Leningrad: Iskusstvo, 1948). **[252]**

Alpers, Boris. *Aktërskoe iskusstvo v Rossii*. (Moscow: Iskusstvo, 1945).

Amiard-Chevrel, Claudine. *Le Théâtre artistique de Moscou (1898–1917)*. (Paris: Éditions du Centre national de la recherche scientifique, 1979).

Anikst, A. *Teoriya dramy v Rossii ot Pushkina do Chekhova*. (Moscow: Nauka, 1972).

Annenkov, P.V. *Vospominaniya i kriticheskie ocherki; sobranie statey i zametok. 1849–1860gg*. 3 vols. (St Petersburg: M. Stasyulevich, 1877–81). **[226a]**

*Anton Pavlovich Chekhov v teatre*. (Moscow: Gos. Izd. Izobrazitel'nogo Iskusstva, 1955). **[256b]**

Arapov, P.N. *Letopis' russkogo teatra*. (St Petersburg: N. Tiblen, 1861).

Arapov, P.N. and Avgust Roppol't. *Dramatichesky al'bom s portretami russkikh artistov i snimkami s rukopisey*. (Moscow: Universitetskaya tipografiya i V. Got'e, 1850). **[239]**

*Arkhiv direktsii imperatorskikh teatrov*, vols. 1–4, 1746–1901. (St Petersburg: Tip, imp. spb. teatrov, 1892–1902).

Belinsky, V.G. *Belinsky o drame i teatre: izbrannye stat'i i vyskazyvaniya* (edited by V.A. Ostrovskaya, M.B. Zagorsky and A.M. Lavretsky). (Moscow–Leningrad: Iskusstvo, 1948). **[222, 224, 232]**

*O drame i teatre*. 2 vols. (Moscow: Iskusstvo, 1983).

Benedetti, Jean Norman. *Stanislavski. A biography*. (London: Methuen, 1988).

Benyash, P.M. *Katerina Semënova*. (Leningrad: Iskusstvo, 1987).

Boborykin, P.D. *Teatral'noe iskusstvo*. (St Petersburg: no pub., 1872).

*Vospominaniya*. 2 vols. (Moscow: Khudozhestvennaya literatura, 1965).

Brenko, A.A. 'Avtobiografiya' in *Trudy gosudarstvennogo tsentral'nogo teatral'nogo muzeya im. A.A. Bakhrushina*. (Moscow–Leningrad, 1941).

Brodsky, A. (ed.) *Sbornik M.N. Ermolova*. (Leningrad: Academia, 1925). **[248a]**

Bryansky, A.M. 'K istoriografii russkogo provintsialnogo teatra' in *O teatre*. (Leningrad–Moscow: Iskusstvo, 1940).

Bulgarin, F.V. *Vospominaniya. Otryvki iz videnogo, slyshannogo i ispytannogo v zhizni*. 6 vols. (St Petersburg: M.D. Ol'shin, 1846–9).

Burgess, Malcolm. 'Russian Public Theatre Audiences of the 18th and Early 19th Centuries', *Slavonic and East European Review*, 36 (December 1958).

Danilov, S.S. *'Revizor.' Stsenicheskaya istoriya v illyustrativnykh materialakh*. (Moscow–Leningrad: Gos. Izd. izobrazitel'nykh iskusstv, 1936).

Davydov, V.N. *Iz proshlogo*. 2 vols. (Moscow, 1914–17).

*Rasskaz o proshlom*. (Moscow–Leningrad: Academia, 1931; Leningrad–Moscow: Iskusstvo, 1962).

Davydova, M.B. *Ocherki po istorii russkogo teatral'nogo iskusstva XVIII-nachala XX v*. (Moscow: Nauka, 1974).

Dmitriev, Yu. A. 'Iz istorii russkoy rezhissury 1880–1890-kh godov' in *Teatr i dramaturgiya* (Leningrad: Iskusstvo, 1967), 237–52.

*Mikhail Lentovsky*. (Moscow: Iskusstvo, 1978).

Dobrolyubov, N.A. *Polnoe sobranie sochineny* (edited by P.I. Lebedev-Polyansky). 6 vols. (Moscow–Leningrad: Gos. Izd. Khudozhestvennoy literatury, 1934–41). **[236, 238]**

*Selected Philosophical Essays* (translated by J. Fineberg). (Moscow: Foreign Languages Publishing House, 1948). [**236, 238**]
Doroshevich, V.M. *Staraya teatral'naya Moskva.* (Petrograd: Izd-vo Petrograd, 1923).
Drizen, N.V. *Dramaticheskaya tsenzura dvukh èpokh, 1825–1881.* (Petrograd: Prometey, 1917). [**231**]
*Sorok let teatra, Vospominaniya, 1875–1915.* (Petrograd: no pub., 1916?).
'Sto let nazad (Iz èpokhi Otechestvennoy voyny)' in *Ezhegodnik imperatorskikh teatrov*, 5 (1914). [**213**]
Durylin, S.N. *Mariya Nikolaevna Ermolova 1853–1928. Ocherk zhizni i tvorchestva.* (Moscow: Izd. Akademii Nauk SSR, 1953).
D'yachenko, V.A. 'Khar'kovsky teatr', *Repertuar i panteon*, 11 (1843), 158–60. [**223a**]
Dynnik, Tat'yana. *Krepostnoy teatr.* (Moscow: Academia, 1933).
Éfros, N.E. *Moskovsky Khudozhestvenny teatr, 1898–1905*, vol. 1. (Moscow: no pub., 1924).
Ermolova, M.N. *Pis'ma, iz literaturnogo naslediya, vospominaniya sovremennikov* (edited by S.N. Durylin). (Moscow: Vserossiyskoe teatral'noe obshchestvo, 1955).
*Pis'ma M.N. Ermolovoy.* (Moscow–Leningrad: Iv. Fëdorov, 1939).
Fel'dman, O.M. (ed.) *'Gore ot uma' na russkom i sovetskom stsene.* (Moscow: Iskusstvo, 1987).
Filippov, V.A. 'Materialy k stsenicheskoy istorii "Revizora"', *Teatr* 8 (1954).
*Zadachi narodnogo teatra i ego proshloe v Rossii.* (Moscow: no pub., 1918).
Gilyarovsky, Vl. A. *Lyudi teatra. Povest' aktërskoy zhizni.* (Moscow–Leningrad: Iskusstvo, 1941). [**256a**]
Gnedich, P.P. 'Khronika russikh dramaticheskikh spektakley na imperatorskoy peterburgskoy stsene, 1881–1890' in *Sbornik istoriko-teatral'noy sekstsii*, vol. 1. (Petrograd, 1918).
*Kniga zhizni, vospominaniya, 1855–1918.* (Moscow: Priboy, 1929).
Gogol', N.V. *Gogol' i teatr* (edited by M.B. Zagorsky and N.L. Stepanova). (Moscow: Iskusstvo, 1952). [**225, 227**]
*Gogol' v vospominaniyakh sovremennikov.* (Moscow: Goslitizdat, 1952).
Goyan, Georg. *Glikeriya Fedotova: zhizn' i tvorchestvo velikoy russkoy artistki, monografiya.* (Moscow–Leningrad: Iskusstvo, 1940).
Grigor'ev, A.A. *Sobranie sochineny* (edited by V.F. Sadovnik). 14 vols. (Moscow: I.N. Kushnerëv, 1915–16). [**237a**]
Grits, T.S. *M.S. Shchepkin, Letopis' zhizni i tvorchestva* (edited by A.P. Klinchin). (Moscow: Nauka, 1966).
Grossman, L.P. *Pushkin v teatral'nykh kreslakh. Kartiny russkoy stseny 1817–1820 godov.* (Leningrad: Brokgauz-Éfron, 1926).
Grover, S.R. *Savva Mamontov and the Mamontov Circle: 1870–1905. Art patronage and the rise of nationalism in Russian art.* Ph.D. dissertation, University of Wisconsin, 1971.
Gurevich, L. Ya. *Istoriya russkogo teatral'nogo byta*, vol. 1. (Moscow–Leningrad: Iskusstvo, 1939).
Ignatov, I.N. *Teatr i zriteli, tom 1, Pervaya polovina XIX veka.* (Moscow: Zadruga, 1916).
Ivanov, I.I. 'Vospominaniya antreprenëra', *Istorichesky vestnik*, 10 (1891).
Karatygin, P.A. *Zapiski.* 2 vols. (Leningrad: Academia 1929–30); 1 vol. (edited by N.V. Koroleva). (Leningrad: Iskusstvo, 1970). [**245b**]
Karpov, E.P. and N.N. Okulov. *Organizatsiya narodnogo teatra i poleznykh razvlecheny dlya naroda.* (St Petersburg: A. Leyfert, 1899).
Khaychenko, G.A. *Russky narodny teatr kontsa XIX-nachala XX veka.* (Moscow: Iskusstvo, 1975).
Khrapovitsky, A.P. 'Iz dnevnika inspektora repertuara rossiyskoy truppy A.I. Khrapovitskogo', *Russkaya starina*, 2 (1879). [**221**]
Khripunov, Yu. D. *Arkhitektura Bol'shogo Teatra* (edited by V.E. Bykov). (Moscow: Gos. izd. lit-ry po stroitel'stvu i arkhitekture, 1955).
*Khudozhestvenno-obshchedostupny teatr. Ochet o deyatel'nosti za pervy god, 14.7.1898–20.2.1899.* (Moscow, 1899).
Kogan, A.P. *Letopis' zhizni i tvorchestva A.N. Ostrovskogo.* 2 vols. (n.p.: Izd. Kul'turno-Presvetitel'noy literatury, 1953).

Koropchevsky, D.A. 'Vospominaniya o moskovskom teatre', *Ezhegodnik imperatorskikh teatrov (1894–95)*, Prilozhenie 2 (St Petersburg, 1895). [235]
Korovkin, N.A. 'Tayny russkikh provintsialnykh teatrov', *Repertuar i Panteon*, 8 (1845).
Lensky, A.P. *Stat'i, pisma, zapiski*. (Moscow, 1950). [249]
Lentovsky, M.A. '45 let v teatre' in *Yubileyny sbornik*. (Moscow, 1930).
Lirondelle, André. *Shakespeare en Russie, 1748–1840. Étude de littérature comparée*. (Paris: Hachette, 1912).
Lotman, L.M. *A.N. Ostrovsky i russkaya dramaturgiya ego vremeni*. (Leningrad: Akademiya Nauk SSSR, 1961).
Malnick, Bertha. 'A.A.Shakhovskoy', *Slavonic and East European Review*, 32, 78 (December 1953).
'The actors Shchepkin and Sosnitsky', *Slavonic and East European Review*, 38, 91 (June 1960).
'Mochalov and Karatygin', *Slavonic and East European Review*, 36, 87 (June 1958). [220, 222]
'The theory and practice of Russian drama in the early 19th century', *Slavonic and East European Review*, 34, 82 (December 1955).
Maslikh, V.A. 'Montirovki pervykh postanovok p'es I.S. Turgeneva na stsene Malogo teatra', *Teatral'noe nasledstvo: soobshcheniya publikatsiya* (edited by A. Ya. Al'tshuller, S.S. Danilov and G.A. Lapkina). (Moscow: Iskusstvo, 1956). [234]
Mikhaylova, R.F. 'Vopros o teatral'noy monopolii, 1856–1858', *Nauchnye doklady vysshey shkoly, Istoricheskie nauki*, 3 (1960).
'K voprosu o sozdanii narodnogo teatra v Rossii v kontse 60-kh, nachale 70-kh godov XIX veka', *Vestnik Leningradskogo gos. universiteta*, 8 (1961).
Mochalov, P.S. *Pavel Stepanovich Mochalov. Zametki o teatre, pis'ma, stikhi, p'esy* (edited by Yu. Dmitriev and A.P. Klinchin. (Moscow: Iskusstvo, 1953).
*Moskovsky Khudozhestvenny teatr v illyustratsiyakh i dokumentakh 1898–1938*. (Moscow: Izd. Moskovskogo ordena Lenina khudozhestvennogo akademicheskogo teatra Soyuza SSR imeni M. Gor-'kogo, 1938). [259, 260, 262]
*Moskovsky Khudozhestvenny teatr, tom 1, 1898–1917*. (Moscow: Gos. izd. izobrazitel'nykh iskusstv, 1955).
*Narodny teatr, sbornik* (edited by E.V. Lavrov and N.A. Popov). (Moscow, 1896).
Nekrylova, A.F. *Russkie narodnye gorodskie prazdniki, uveseleniya i zrelishcha konets XVIII-nachalo XX veka*. (Leningrad: Iskusstvo, 1988).
Nelidov, V.A. *Teatral'naya Moskva (sorok let moskovskikh teatrov)*. (Berlin–Riga: S. Kretschetow, 1921). [244a]
Nemirovich-Danchenko, Vl. I. *Iz proshlogo*. (Moscow: Academia, 1936).
*Teatral'noe nasledie*. 2 vols. (Moscow, 1952–4).
Nikulina-Kositskaya, L.P. 'Zapiski', *Russkaya starina*, 1, 2, 4 (1878).
Nosov, Ivan. *Khronika russkago teatra*. (Moscow: Izd. imp. Ob-va istorii i drevnostey rossiyskikh pri Moskovskom universitete, 1883).
Oksman, Yu. G. 'K istorii stsen i komedii' in *I.S. Turgenev. Issledovaniya i materialy*, vypusk 1, 75–98. (Odessa: Vseukrainskoe gos. izd., 1921).
Opochinin, E.N. *Teatral'naya starina: istoricheskie ocherki i kur'ëzy*. (Moscow: Tovarishchestvo tipografii: A.I. Mamontova, 1902). [216]
'Za kulisami starogo teatra', *Istorichesky vestnik*, 4, 5, 6 (1889).
Ostrovsky, A.N. *Polnoe sobranie sochineny*. 12 vols. (Moscow: Iskusstvo, 1973–80). [254]
Ozarovsky, Yu. A. *P'esy khudozhestvennogo repertuara i postanovka ikh na stsene*. 2 vols. (St Petersburg: D.M. Musina, 1911).
Panaeva, A. *Vospominaniya*. (Leningrad: Academia, 1929).
Pavlova, T. '"Davydovskie sezony" u Korsha (1886–1888 gody),' *Vosprosy teatra 72. Sbornik statey i materialov*. Moscow: Vserossiyskoe teatral'noe obshchestvo, 1973.
'Teatr F.A. Korsha i zritel'' in *Problemy sotsiologii teatra: sbornik statey* (edited by N. Khrenov). (Moscow: Vserossiyskoe teatral'noe obshchestvo/Ministerstvo kultury SSSR, 1974).

'Perepiska A.N. Verstovskago s A.M. Gedeonovym (1843–1859g.)' in *Ezhegodnik imperatorskikh teatrov*, 7 (1912), pp. 51–66; 1 (1913), pp. 98–125; 2 (1913), pp. 33–55; 3 (1913), pp. 62–80; 1 (1914), pp. 34–56; 2 (1914), pp. 37–65; 4 (1914), pp. 50–70. **[230]**

Petrovskaya, I. *Teatr i zritel' provintsial'noy Rossii vtoraya polovina XIX veka.* (Leningrad: Iskusstvo, 1979).

Pogozhev, V.O. *Proèkt zakonopolozheniy ob imperatorskikh teatrakh.* 3 vols. (St Petersburg: Tip, Glav, upr, udelov, 1900).

*Stoletie organizatsii imperatorskikh moskovskikh teatrov.* 2 vols. (St Petersburg: Izd. Direktsii Imp. teatrov, 1906–8).

Polyakova, M. (ed.) *Russkaya teatral'naya parodiya kontsa XIX-nachala XX veka.* (Moscow: Iskusstvo, 1976).

Pushkin, A.S. *Pushkin i teatr. Dramaticheskie proizvedeniya, stat'i, zametki, dnevniki, pis'ma* (edited by B.P. Gorodetsky). (Moscow: Iskusstvo, 1953). **[215a]**

Rodina, T.M. *Russkoe teatral'noe iskusstvo v nachale XIX v.* (Moscow: Akademiya Nauk SSSR, 1961).

Rodislavsky, V.I. 'Moskovskie teatry dobrago starago vremeni', *Ezhegodnik imperatorskikh teatrov sezon 1900–1901gg.* (St Petersburg, 1901). **[229]**

Rossieva, Pavla. 'Iz zapisok teatrala 40–60kh godov', *Ezhegodnik imperatorskikh teatrov*, 7. (St Petersburg, 1910).

*Russkiy provintsialny teatr; vospominaniya* (edited by B.A. Babochkin). (Leningrad: Iskusstvo, 1937).

*Russkiy vodevil'* (edited by V.V. Uspensky). (Moscow: Iskusstvo, 1959). **[228]**

Sankt-Peterburgsky Komitet gramotnosti. *Komissiya po voprosy o narodynykh teatrakh.* (St Petersburg, 1870).

Savina, M.P. 'Kak nashël menya P.N. Medvedev', *Teatr i iskusstvo*, 46 (1903). **[251]**

Senelick, Laurence. 'Rachel in Russia: The Shchepkin-Annenkov Correspondence', *Theatre Research International*, 3, 2 (February 1978), 93–114.

*Serf actor: the life and art of Mikhail Shchepkin.* (Westport, Conn.: Greenwood Press, 1984). **[223b, 226b, 245a]**

Shcheglov, I. *O narodnom teatre.* (Moscow: D. Sytin, 1895).

*Narod i teatr. Ocherki i izsledovaniya sovremennago narodnago teatra v 6 chastyakh.* (Petrograd: P.P. Soykin, 1912).

Shchepkin, M.S. *Mikhail Semënovich Shchepkin zhizn' i tvorchestvo* (edited by T.M. El'nitskaya and O.M. Fel'dman). 2 vols. (Moscow: Iskusstvo, 1984).

Shubert, A.I. *Moya zhizn'. Vospominaniya artistki 1827–1883* (edited by A. Derman). (Leningrad: Academia, 1929).

Sinel'nikov, N.N. *Shest'desyat let na stsene.* (Khar'kov: Izd. Khar'kovskogo gos. teatra russkoy dramy, 1935). **[253]**

Sirotinin, A.A. 'Ocherki razvitiya russkogo stsenicheskogo iskusstva', *Artist*, 6. 17, 26 (1891).

Sleptsov, Vasily. 'Neizvestnye stranitsy' in *Literaturnoe nasledstvo* (Moscow: Izd. Akademii Nauk SSSR, 1963).

Solov'ëv, S.P. 'Dvadtsat' pyat' let iz zhizni moskovskogo teatra', *Ezhegodnik imperatorskikh teatrov 1902–1903*, prilozhenie 1. (St Petersburg, 1903). **[233]**

'Iz vospominany starogo rezhissëra moskovskogo teatra', *Russky arkhiv*, 10 (1873).

'Otryvki iz pamyatnoy knizhki otstavnogo rezhissëra', *Ezhegodnik imperatorskikh teatrov 1895–1896*, 1. (St Petersburg, 1896).

Stakhovich, A. *Klochki vospominaniya.* (Moscow, 1904).

Stanislavsky, K.S. *My life in art* (translated by J.J. Robbins). (Boston: Little Brown, 1924). **[258]**

*Sobranie sochineny.* 8 vols. (Moscow: Iskusstvo, 1954–61). **[261]**

*Sobranie sochineny* (edited by V. Ya. Vilenkin and A.M. Smelyansky), 9 vols. (Moscow: Iskusstvo, 1988, in progress).

*Stanislavski's Legacy* (edited and translated by E.R. Hapgood). (New York: Theatre Arts Books, 1968) **[261]**

Stepanov, V. *Vzglyad na ideal'ny narodny teatr i ego zadachi v nashe vremya*. (Moscow, 1897).

Strepetova, P.A. *Vospominaniya i pis'ma*. (Moscow–Leningrad, 1934).

Syrkina, F. Ya. *Russkoe teatral'no-dekoratsionnoe iskusstvo vtoroy poloviny XIX veka; ocherki*. (Moscow: Iskusstvo, 1956).

Tal'nikov, D.L. *Sistema Shchepkina*. (Moscow–Leningrad: Iskusstvo, 1939).

Taneev, S.V. *Teatral'nye tipy*. (St Petersburg, 1889).

Taranovskaya, M. *Arkhitektor K. Rossi. Zdanie Akademicheskogo Teatra Dramy imeni A.S. Pushkina (Aleksandrinsky) v Leningrade*. (Leningrad: Gos. izd. lit-ry po stroitel'stvu i arkhitekture, 1956).

Telyakovsky, V.A. *Vospominaniya*. (Leningrad–Moscow: Iskusstvo, 1965). **[244b]**

Thurston, Gary. 'The impact of Russian popular theatre, 1886–1915', *Journal of Modern History*, 55 (June, 1983).

'Theatre and acculturation in Russia from peasant emancipation to the First World War', *Journal of Popular Culture*, 18, 2 (Fall 1984).

*Trudy Pervago Vserossiyskago s"ezda stsenicheskikh deyateley, 9.3–23.3 1897g. v Moskve. Chast' pervaya*. (St Petersburg: Nadezhda, 1898). **[257, b, c, d]**

*Trudy Pervago Vserossiyskago s"ezda stsenicheskikh deyateley. Chast' vtoraya*. (Moscow: A.A. Levenson, 1898). **[257e, f]**

Turgenev, I.S. *Turgenev i teatr* (edited by G.P. Berdnikov) (Moscow: Iskusstvo, 1953).

Urusov, A.I. *Stat'i o teatre, literature i ob iskusstve. Pis'ma ego. Vospominaniya o nëm*. 3 vols. (Moscow: I.N. Kolchëv, 1907). **[255]**

Vinogradskaya, I. *Zhizn' i tvorchestvo K.S. Stanislavskogo*. vol. 1. (Moscow: Iskusstvo, 1971).

Vitberg, F. 'Materialy dlya istorii teatral'nykh zrelishch i publichnykh uveseleny v Rossii', *Ezhegodnik imperatorskikh teatrov*, vol. 3 (1895–6). **[214]**

Vitenzon, R.A. *Anna Brenko*. (Leningrad: Iskusstvo, 1985).

Vladybin, G.I. (ed.) *A.N. Ostrovsky v russkoy kritike: sbornik statey*. (Moscow: Gos. Izd. Khudozhestvennoy literatury, 1953).

Vol'f, A.I. *Khronika peterburgskikh teatrov s kontsa 1826 do nachala 1855 goda*. 2 vols. (St Petersburg: P. Golike, 1877).

*Khronika peterburgskikh teatrov s kontsa 1855 do nachala 1881 goda*. (St Petersburg: P. Golike, 1884). **[242, 243]**

Yur'ev, Yu. M. *Zapiski*. (Moscow–Leningrad: Iskusstvo, 1948); 2 vols. (Leningrad–Moscow: Iskusstvo, 1963). **[241]**

Yuzhin-Sumbatov, A.I. *Vospominaniya, zapisi, stat'i, pisma* (edited by V. Filippov). (Moscow–Leningrad: Iskusstvo, 1941).

Zhikharëv, S.P. *Zapiski sovremennika. Vospominaniya starogo teatrala*. (Moscow–Leningrad: Academia, 1934); (edited by B.M. Eykhenbaum, Moscow–Leningrad: Iskusstvo, 1955). **[218a]**

Zograf, N.G. *Maly teatr vtoroy poloviny XIX veka*. (Moscow: Akad. Nauk, 1960).

Zotov, R.M. *Teatral'nye vospominaniya*. (St Petersburg, 1859).

# Index